The Landscape *of* Qualitative Research

College of Nursing
Department of Undergraduate
Box 2275, SDSU
Brookings, SD 57007-0296

The Landscape *of* Qualitative Research

Theories and Issues

Norman K. Denzin
Yvonna S. Lincoln

Editors

SAGE Publications
International Educational and Professional Publisher
Thousand Oaks London New Delhi

For information:

SAGE Publications, Inc.
2455 Teller Road
Thousand Oaks, California 91320
E-mail@sagepub.com

SAGE Publications Ltd.
6 Bonhill Street
London EC2A 4PU
United Kingdom

SAGE Publications India Pvt. Ltd.
M-32 Market
Greater Kailash I
New Delhi 110048 India

Printed in the United States of America

Library of Congress Cataloging-in-Publication Data

Main entry under title:

The landscape of qualitative research: Theories and issues / edited
    by Norman K. Denzin and Yvonna S. Lincoln.
       p. cm.
     Includes bibliographical references and index.
     ISBN 0-7619-1433-1 (pbk. : acid-free paper)
      1. Social sciences—Research. 2. Qualitative reasoning.
    I. Denzin, Norman K. II. Lincoln, Yvonna S.
    H62.L274 1998
    300'.7'2—dc21   98-8869

98 99 00 01 02 03 04 8 7 6 5 4 3 2 1

Acquiring Editor:	Peter Labella
Production Editor:	Astrid Virding
Production Assistant:	Karen Wiley
Typesetter/Designer:	Danielle Dillahunt
Indexer:	Juniee Oneida
Cover Designer:	Ravi Balasuriya
Print Buyer:	Anna Chin

Contents

Preface vii

1. Introduction: Entering the Field
   of Qualitative Research 1
   Norman K. Denzin and Yvonna S. Lincoln

PART I. Locating the Field 35

2. Qualitative Methods: Their History
   in Sociology and Anthropology 41
   Arthur J. Vidich and Stanford M. Lyman

3. Traditions, Preferences, and Postures
   in Applied Qualitative Research 111
   David Hamilton

4. Working the Hyphens: Reinventing Self
   and Other in Qualitative Research 130
   Michelle Fine

5. Politics and Ethics in Qualitative Research 156
   Maurice Punch

PART II. Major Paradigms and Perspectives   185

6. Competing Paradigms
   in Qualitative Research   195
   Egon G. Guba and Yvonna S. Lincoln

7. Constructivist, Interpretivist
   Approaches to Human Inquiry   221
   Thomas A. Schwandt

8. Rethinking Critical Theory
   and Qualitative Research   260
   Joe L. Kincheloe and Peter L. McLaren

9. Feminisms and Models
   of Qualitative Research   300
   Virginia Olesen

10. Ethnic Modeling in Qualitative Research   333
    John H. Stanfield II

11. Audiencing: Cultural Practice
    and Cultural Studies   359
    John Fiske

PART III. The Future of Qualitative Research   379

12. What Comes (Just) After "Post"?
    The Case of Ethnography   383
    George E. Marcus

13. The Fifth Moment   407
    Yvonna S. Lincoln and Norman K. Denzin

Suggested Readings   431

Name Index   437

Subject Index   449

About the Authors   465

Preface

◆ For more than two decades, a quiet methodological revolution has been taking place in the social sciences. A blurring of disciplinary boundaries has occurred. The social sciences and humanities have drawn closer together in a mutual focus on an interpretive, qualitative approach to research and theory. Although these trends are not new, the extent to which the "qualitative revolution" has overtaken the social sciences and related professional fields has been nothing short of amazing.

Reflecting this revolution, a host of textbooks, journals, research monographs, and readers have been published in recent years. In 1994, we published the *Handbook of Qualitative Research* in an attempt to represent the field in its entirety, to take stock of how far it had come and how far it might yet go. Although it became abundantly clear that the "field" of qualitative research is defined primarily by tensions, contradictions, and hesitations—and that they exist in a less-than-unified arena—we believed that the handbook could be valuable for solidifying, interpreting, and organizing the field in spite of the essential differences that characterize it.

Putting together the *Handbook* was a massive undertaking that was carried out over several years, the full story of which can be found in the preface to the *Handbook* (which can also be found on the Web site for the *Handbook*: http://www.sagepub.com/sagepage/denzin_lincoln.htm).

We have been enormously gratified and heartened by the response to the *Handbook* since its publication. Especially gratifying has been that it has been used and adapted by such a wide variety of scholars and graduate students in precisely the way we had hoped: as a starting point, a springboard for new thought and new work.

◆ The Paperback Project

There was one constituency we did not focus on centrally as we developed the plan for the *Handbook*: students in the classroom. The sheer size of the *Handbook,* with its corresponding expense, seemed to make the book a difficult one to assign in courses. Yet within a year of publication, it became clear that the material contained in the *Handbook* was deemed sufficiently valuable to override some considerations of size and expense.

Despite the reception the *Handbook* received in the classroom, students and teachers alike have urged us to publish the book in a less expensive, paperback iteration. We and our publisher, Sage Publications, decided to devise a plan to do this.

Peter Labella, our editor at Sage, canvassed more than 50 scholars and students about the way the *Handbook* works in the classroom setting. Through a series of phone interviews and e-mail surveys—which themselves led to an ongoing conversation—a plan to do the book as a series of paperbacks began to emerge. The three-volume plan was codified at a series of meetings in the spring of 1997.

It was decided that the part structure of the *Handbook* could serve as a useful point of departure for the organization of the paperbacks. Thus Volume 1, titled *The Landscape of Qualitative Research: Theories and Issues,* takes a look at the field from a broadly theoretical perspective, and is composed of the *Handbook*'s Parts I ("Locating the Field"), II ("Major Paradigms and Perspectives"), and VI ("The Future of Qualitative Research." Volume 2, titled *Strategies of Qualitative Inquiry,* focuses on just that, and consists of Part III of the *Handbook.* Volume 3, titled *Collecting and Interpreting Qualitative Materials,* considers the tasks of collecting, analyzing, and interpreting empirical materials, and comprises the *Handbook*'s Parts IV ("Methods of Collecting and Analyzing Empirical Materials") and V ("The Art of Interpretation, Evaluation, and Presentation").

We decided that nothing should be cut from the original *Handbook.* Nearly everyone we spoke to who used the *Handbook* had his or her own way of using it, leaning heavily on certain chapters and skipping others altogether. But there was consensus that this reorganization made a great deal of sense both pedagogically and economically. We and Sage are committed to making this iteration of the *Handbook* accessible for class-room use. This commitment is reflected in the size, organization, and price of the paperbacks, as well as in the addition of end-of-book bibliographies.

It also became clear in our conversations with colleagues who used the *Handbook* that the single-volume, hard-cover version has a distinct place and value, and Sage will keep the original version available until a revised edition is published.

◆ Organization of This Volume

The Landscape of Qualitative Research attempts to put the field of qualitative research into context. Part I locates the field, starting with history, then applied qualitative research traditions, studying the "other," and the politics and ethics of field research. Part II isolates what we regard as the major historical and contemporary paradigms now structuring and influencing qualitative research in the human disciplines. The chapters move from competing paradigms (positivist, postpositivist, constructivist, critical theory) to specific interpretive perspectives. Part III considers the future of qualitative research.

◆ Acknowledgments

Of course, this book would not exist without its authors or the editorial board members for the *Handbook* on which it is based. These individuals were able to offer both long-term, sustained commitments to the project and short-term emergency assistance.

In addition, we would like to thank the following individuals and institutions for their assistance, support, insights, and patience: our respective universities and departments, as well as Jack Bratich and Rob Leffel, our respective graduate students. Without them, we could never have kept this project on course. There are also several people to thank at Sage Publications. We thank Peter Labella, our new editor; this three-volume version of the *Handbook* would not have been possible without Peter's wisdom, support, humor, and grasp of the field in all its current diversity. Peter had the vision to understand how a three-volume set could be better suited to the classroom and to the needs of students than the original format of the *Handbook*.

As always, we appreciate the efforts of Lenny Friedman, the director of marketing at Sage, along with his staff, for their indefatigable efforts in getting the word out about the *Handbook* to teachers, researchers, and methodologists around the world. Astrid Virding was essential in moving this project through production; we are also grateful to the copy editor, Judy Selhorst, and to those whose proofreading and indexing skills were so central to the publication of the *Handbook* on which these volumes are based. Finally, as ever, we thank our spouses, Katherine Ryan and Egon Guba, for their forbearance and constant support.

The idea for this three-volume paperback version of the *Handbook* did not arise in a vacuum, and we are grateful for the feedback we received from countless teachers and students, both informally and in response to our formal survey. We wish especially to thank the following individuals: Jim Barott, University of Utah; Joanne Cooper, University of Hawaii; Fran Crawford, Curtin University; Morten Ender, University of North Dakota; Rich Hoffman, Miami University of Ohio; Patti Lather, Ohio State University; Michael Lissack, Henley-on-Thames; Martha MacLeod, University of Northern British Columbia; Suzanne Miller, University of Buffalo; Peggy Rios, University of Miami; Cynthia Russell, University of Tennessee, Memphis; Diane Schnelker, University of Northern Colorado; Coleen Shannon, University of Texas at Arlington; Barry Shealy, University of Buffalo; Ewart Skinner, Bowling Green State University; Jack Spencer, Purdue University; and Carol Tishelman, Karolinska Institute.

NORMAN K. DENZIN
University of Illinois at Urbana-Champaign

YVONNA S. LINCOLN
Texas A&M University

1

Introduction

Entering the Field
of Qualitative Research

Norman K. Denzin & Yvonna S. Lincoln

◆ Qualitative research has a long and distinguished history in the human disciplines. In sociology the work of the "Chicago school" in the 1920s and 1930s established the importance of qualitative research for the study of human group life. In anthropology, during the same period, the pathbreaking studies of Boas, Mead, Benedict, Bateson, Evans-Pritchard, Radcliffe-Brown, and Malinowski charted the outlines of the fieldwork method, wherein the observer went to a foreign setting to study the customs and habits of another society and culture (for a critique of this tradition, see Rosaldo, 1989, pp. 25-45). Soon qualitative research would be employed in other social science disciplines, including education, social work, and communications. The opening chapter in Part I, Volume 1, by Vidich and Lyman, charts key features of this history.

In this introductory chapter we will briefly define the field of qualitative research, then review the history of qualitative research in the human disciplines, so that this volume and its contents may be located in their proper historical moment. A conceptual framework for reading the qualitative

AUTHORS' NOTE: We are grateful to the many people who have helped with this chapter, including Mitch Allen, Katherine E. Ryan, and Harry Wolcott.

1

research act as a multicultural, gendered process will be presented. We will then provide a brief introduction to the chapters that follow.

◆ Definitional Issues

Qualitative research is a field of inquiry in its own right. It crosscuts disciplines, fields, and subject matter.[1] A complex, interconnected family of terms, concepts, and assumptions surround the term *qualitative research*. These include the traditions associated with positivism, poststructuralism, and the many qualitative research perspectives, or methods, connected to cultural and interpretive studies (the chapters in Part II of Volume 1 take up these paradigms). There are separate and detailed literatures on the many methods and approaches that fall under the category of qualitative research, such as interviewing, participant observation, and visual methods.

Qualitative research operates in a complex historical field that crosscuts five historical moments (we discuss these in detail below). These five moments simultaneously operate in the present. We describe them as the traditional (1900-1950), the modernist or golden age (1950-1970), blurred genres (1970-1986), the crisis of representation (1986-1990), and postmodern or present moments (1990-present). The present moment is defined, Laurel Richardson (1991) argues, by a new sensibility, the core of which "is doubt that any discourse has a privileged place, any method or theory a universal and general claim to authoritative knowledge" (p. 173).

Successive waves of epistemological theorizing move across these five moments. The traditional period is associated with the positivist paradigm. The modernist or golden age and blurred genres moments are connected to the appearance of postpositivist arguments. At the same time, a variety of new interpretive, qualitative perspectives made their presence felt, including hermeneutics, structuralism, semiotics, phenomenology, cultural studies, and feminism.[2] In the blurred genres phase the humanities became central resources for critical, interpretive theory, and the qualitative research project was broadly conceived. The blurred genres phase produced the next stage, the crisis of representation, where researchers struggled with how to locate themselves and their subjects in reflexive texts. The postmodern moment is characterized by a new sensibility that doubts all previous paradigms.

2

Any description of what constitutes qualitative research must work within this complex historical field. *Qualitative research* means different things in each of these moments. Nonetheless, an initial, generic definition can be offered: Qualitative research is multimethod in focus, involving an interpretive, naturalistic approach to its subject matter. This means that qualitative researchers study things in their natural settings, attempting to make sense of, or interpret, phenomena in terms of the meanings people bring to them. Qualitative research involves the studied use and collection of a variety of empirical materials—case study, personal experience, introspective, life story, interview, observational, historical, interactional, and visual texts—that describe routine and problematic moments and meanings in individuals' lives. Accordingly, qualitative researchers deploy a wide range of interconnected methods, hoping always to get a better fix on the subject matter at hand.

The Qualitative Researcher as *Bricoleur*

The multiple methodologies of qualitative research may be viewed as a bricolage, and the researcher as *bricoleur*. Nelson, Treichler, and Grossberg (1992, p. 2), Lévi-Strauss (1966, p. 17), and Weinstein and Weinstein (1991, p. 161) clarify the meaning of these two terms.[3] A *bricoleur* is a "Jack of all trades or a kind of professional do-it-yourself person" (Lévi-Strauss, 1966, p. 17). The *bricoleur* produces a bricolage, that is, a pieced-together, close-knit set of practices that provide solutions to a problem in a concrete situation. "The solution (bricolage) which is the result of the *bricoleur's* method is an [emergent] construction" (Weinstein & Weinstein, 1991, p. 161) that changes and takes new forms as different tools, methods, and techniques are added to the puzzle. Nelson et al. (1992) describe the methodology of cultural studies "as a bricolage. Its choice of practice, that is, is pragmatic, strategic and self-reflexive" (p. 2). This understanding can be applied equally to qualitative research.

The qualitative researcher-as-*bricoleur* uses the tools of his or her methodological trade, deploying whatever strategies, methods, or empirical materials as are at hand (Becker, 1989). If new tools have to be invented, or pieced together, then the researcher will do this. The choice of which tools to use, which research practices to employ, is not set in advance. The "choice of research practices depends upon the questions that are asked, and the questions depend on their context" (Nelson et al., 1992, p. 2),

3

what is available in the context, and what the researcher can do in that setting.

Qualitative research is inherently multimethod in focus (Brewer & Hunter, 1989). However, the use of multiple methods, or triangulation, reflects an attempt to secure an in-depth understanding of the phenomenon in question. Objective reality can never be captured. Triangulation is not a tool or a strategy of validation, but an alternative to validation (Denzin, 1989a, 1989b, p. 244; Fielding & Fielding, 1986, p. 33; Flick, 1992, p. 194). The combination of multiple methods, empirical materials, perspectives and observers in a single study is best understood, then, as a strategy that adds rigor, breadth, and depth to any investigation (see Flick, 1992, p. 194).

The *bricoleur* is adept at performing a large number of diverse tasks, ranging from interviewing to observing, to interpreting personal and historical documents, to intensive self-reflection and introspection. The *bricoleur* reads widely and is knowledgeable about the many interpretive paradigms (feminism, Marxism, cultural studies, constructivism) that can be brought to any particular problem. He or she may not, however, feel that paradigms can be mingled, or synthesized. That is, paradigms as overarching philosophical systems denoting particular ontologies, epistemologies, and methodologies cannot be easily moved between. They represent belief systems that attach the user to a particular worldview. Perspectives, in contrast, are less well developed systems, and can be more easily moved between. The researcher-as-*bricoleur*-theorist works between and within competing and overlapping perspectives and paradigms.

The *bricoleur* understands that research is an interactive process shaped by his or her personal history, biography, gender, social class, race, and ethnicity, and those of the people in the setting. The *bricoleur* knows that science is power, for all research findings have political implications. There is no value-free science. The *bricoleur* also knows that researchers all tell stories about the worlds they have studied. Thus the narratives, or stories, scientists tell are accounts couched and framed within specific storytelling traditions, often defined as paradigms (e.g., positivism, postpositivism, constructivism).

The product of the *bricoleur*'s labor is a bricolage, a complex, dense, reflexive, collagelike creation that represents the researcher's images, understandings, and interpretations of the world or phenomenon under analysis. This bricolage will, as in the case of a social theorist such as Simmel, connect the parts to the whole, stressing the meaningful relation-

4

ships that operate in the situations and social worlds studied (Weinstein & Weinstein, 1991, p. 164).

Qualitative Research as a Site of
Multiple Methodologies and Research Practices

Qualitative research, as a set of interpretive practices, privileges no single methodology over any other. As a site of discussion, or discourse, qualitative research is difficult to define clearly. It has no theory, or paradigm, that is distinctly its own. As Part II of this volume reveals, multiple theoretical paradigms claim use of qualitative research methods and strategies, from constructivism to cultural studies, feminism, Marxism, and ethnic models of study. Qualitative research is used in many separate disciplines, as we will discuss below. It does not belong to a single discipline.

Nor does qualitative research have a distinct set of methods that are entirely its own. Qualitative researchers use semiotics, narrative, content, discourse, archival, and phonemic analysis, even statistics. They also draw upon and utilize the approaches, methods, and techniques of ethnomethodology, phenomenology, hermeneutics, feminism, rhizomatics, deconstructionism, ethnographies, interviews, psychoanalysis, cultural studies, survey research, and participant observation, among others (see Nelson et al., 1992, p. 2).[4] All of these research practices "can provide important insights and knowledge" (Nelson et al., 1992, p. 2). No specific method or practice can be privileged over any other, and none can be "eliminated out of hand" (p. 2).

Many of these methods, or research practices, are also used in other contexts in the human disciplines. Each bears the traces of its own disciplinary history. Thus there is an extensive history of the uses and meanings of ethnography and ethnology in education (Hymes, 1980; LeCompte & Preissle, 1992); participant observation and ethnography in anthropology (Marcus, Volume 1, Chapter 12), sociology (Atkinson & Hammersley, Volume 2, Chapter 5), and cultural studies (Fiske, Volume 1, Chapter 11); textual, hermeneutic, feminist, psychoanalytic, semiotic, and narrative analysis in cinema and literary studies (Lentricchia & McLaughlin, 1990; Nichols, 1985; see also Manning & Cullum-Swan, Volume 3, Chapter 9); archival, material culture, historical, and document analysis in history, biography, and archaeology (Hodder, Volume 3, Chapter 4; Smith, Volume 2, Chapter 8; Tuchman, Volume 2, Chapter 9); and discourse and

qualitative researchers who are attached to poststructural, postmodern sensibilities (see below; see also Vidich & Lyman, Volume 1, Chapter 2, and Richardson, Volume 3, Chapter 12). These researchers argue that positivist methods are but one way of telling a story about society or the social world. They may be no better or no worse than any other method; they just tell a different kind of story.

This tolerant view is not shared by everyone. Many members of the critical theory, constructivist, poststructural, and postmodern schools of thought reject positivist and postpositivist criteria when evaluating their own work. They see these criteria as irrelevant to their work, and contend that these criteria reproduce only a certain kind of science, a science that silences too many voices. These researchers seek alternative methods for evaluating their work, including verisimilitude, emotionality, personal responsibility, an ethic of caring, political praxis, multivoiced texts, and dialogues with subjects. In response, positivists and postpositivists argue that what they do is good science, free of individual bias and subjectivity; as noted above, they see postmodernism as an attack on reason and truth.

Capturing the individual's point of view. Both qualitative and quantitative researchers are concerned about the individual's point of view. However, qualitative investigators think they can get closer to the actor's perspective through detailed interviewing and observation. They argue that quantitative researchers seldom are able to capture the subject's perspective because they have to rely on more remote, inferential empirical materials. The empirical materials produced by the softer, interpretive methods are regarded by many quantitative researchers as unreliable, impressionistic, and not objective.

Examining the constraints of everyday life. Qualitative researchers are more likely than quantitative researchers to confront the constraints of the everyday social world. They see this world in action and embed their findings in it. Quantitative researchers abstract from this world and seldom study it directly. They seek a nomothetic or etic science based on probabilities derived from the study of large numbers of randomly selected cases. These kinds of statements stand above and outside the constraints of everyday life. Qualitative researchers are committed to an emic, idiographic, case-based position, which directs their attention to the specifics of particular cases.

Securing rich descriptions. Qualitative researchers believe that rich descriptions of the social world are valuable, whereas quantitative researchers, with their etic, nomothetic commitments, are less concerned with such detail.

The five points of difference described above (uses of positivism, acceptance of postmodern sensibilities, capturing the individual's point of view, examining the constraints of everyday life, and securing rich descriptions) reflect commitments to different styles of research, different epistemologies, and different forms of representation. Each work tradition is governed by a different set of genres; each has its own classics, its own preferred forms of representation, interpretation, and textual evaluation (see Becker, 1986, pp. 134-135). Qualitative researchers use ethnographic prose, historical narratives, first-person accounts, still photographs, life histories, fictionalized facts, and biographical and autobiographical materials, among others. Quantitative researchers use mathematical models, statistical tables, and graphs, and often write about their research in impersonal, third-person prose.

With the differences between these two traditions understood, we will now offer a brief discussion of the history of qualitative research. We can break this into four historical moments, mindful that any history is always somewhat arbitrary.

◆ The History of Qualitative Research

The history of qualitative research reveals, as Vidich and Lyman remind us in Chapter 2 of Volume 1, that the modern social science disciplines have taken as their mission "the analysis and understanding of the patterned conduct and social processes of society." The notion that this task could be carried out presupposed that social scientists had the ability to observe this world objectively. Qualitative methods were a major tool of such observations.[6]

Throughout the history of qualitative research, investigators have always defined their work in terms of hopes and values, "religious faiths, occupational and professional ideologies" (Vidich & Lyman, Volume 1, Chapter 2). Qualitative research (like all research) has always been judged on the "standard of whether the work communicates or 'says' something to us" (Vidich & Lyman, Volume 1, Chapter 2), based on how we conceptualize our reality and our images of the world. *Epistemology* is the word that has historically defined these standards of evaluation. In the contemporary period, as argued above, many received discourses on epistemology have been "disprivileged," or cast into doubt.

The history presented by Vidich and Lyman covers the following (somewhat) overlapping stages: early ethnography (to the seventeenth century); colonial ethnography (seventeenth-, eighteenth-, and nineteenth-century explorers); the ethnography of the American Indian as "other" (late nineteenth- and early twentieth-century anthropology); the ethnography of the "civic other," or community studies, and ethnographies of American immigrants (early twentieth century through the 1960s); studies of ethnicity and assimilation (mid-century through the 1980s); and the present, which we call the *fifth moment.*

In each of these eras researchers were and have been influenced by their political hopes and ideologies, discovering findings in their research that confirmed prior theories or beliefs. Early ethnographers confirmed the racial and cultural diversity of peoples throughout the globe and attempted to fit this diversity into a theory about the origin of history, the races, and civilizations. Colonial ethnographers, before the professionalization of ethnography in the twentieth century, fostered a colonial pluralism that left natives on their own as long as their leaders could be co-opted by the colonial administration.

European ethnographers studied Africans and other Third World peoples of color. Early American ethnographers studied the American Indian from the perspective of the conqueror, who saw the life world of the primitive as a window to the prehistoric past. The Calvinist mission to save the Indian was soon transferred to the mission of saving the "hordes" of immigrants who entered the United States with the beginnings of industrialization. Qualitative community studies of the ethnic other proliferated from the early 1900s to the 1960s, and included the work of E. Franklin Frazier, Robert Park, and Robert Redfield and their students, as well as William Foote Whyte, the Lynds, August Hollingshead, Herbert Gans, Stanford Lyman, Arthur Vidich, and Joseph Bensman. The post-1960s' ethnicity studies challenged the "melting pot" hypothesis of Park and his followers and corresponded to the emergence of ethnic studies programs that saw Native Americans, Latinos, Asian Americans, and African Americans attempting to take control over the study of their own peoples.

The postmodern challenge emerged in the mid-1980s. It questioned the assumptions that had organized this earlier history, in each of its colonial-izing moments. Qualitative research that crosses the "postmodern divide" requires one, Vidich and Lyman argue, to "abandon all established and preconceived values, theories, perspectives, . . . and prejudices as resources for ethnographic study." In this new era the qualitative researcher does more than observe history; he or she plays a part in it. New tales of the field will now be written, and they will reflect the researcher's direct and personal engagement with this historical period.

Vidich and Lyman's analysis covers the full sweep of ethnographic history. Ours, presented below, is confined to the twentieth century and complements many of their divisions. We begin with the early foundational work of the British and French, as well the Chicago, Columbia, Harvard, and Berkeley schools of sociology and anthropology. This early founda-tional period established the norms of classical qualitative and ethno-graphic research.

◆ The Five Moments of Qualitative Research

As noted above, we divide our history of qualitative research in this century into five phases, each of which is described in turn below.

The Traditional Period

We call the first moment the traditional period (this covers Vidich and Lyman's second and third phases). It begins in the early 1900s and continues until World War II. In this period, qualitative researchers wrote "objective," colonializing accounts of field experiences that were reflective of the positivist scientist paradigm. They were concerned with offering valid, reliable, and objective interpretations in their writings. The "other" who was studied was alien, foreign, and strange.

Here is Malinowski (1967) discussing his field experiences in New Guinea and the Trobriand Islands in the years 1914-1915 and 1917-1918:

> Nothing whatever draws me to ethnographic studies. . . . On the whole the
> village struck me rather unfavorably. There is a certain disorganization . . .

the rowdiness and persistence of the people who laugh and stare and lie discouraged me somewhat. . . . Went to the village hoping to photograph a few stages of the *bara* dance. I handed out half-sticks of tobacco, then watched a few dances; then took pictures—but results were poor. . . . they would not pose long enough for time exposures. At moments I was furious at them, particularly because after I gave them their portions of tobacco they all went away. (quoted in Geertz, 1988, pp. 73-74)

In another work, this lonely, frustrated, isolated field-worker describes his methods in the following words:

In the field one has to face a chaos of facts. . . . in this crude form they are not scientific facts at all; they are absolutely elusive, and can only be fixed by interpretation. . . . Only laws and generalizations are scientific facts, and field work consists only and exclusively in the interpretation of the chaotic social reality, in subordinating it to general rules. (Malinowski, 1916/1948, p. 328; quoted in Geertz, 1988, p. 81)

Malinowski's remarks are provocative. On the one hand they disparage fieldwork, but on the other they speak of it within the glorified language of science, with laws and generalizations fashioned out of this selfsame experience.

The field-worker, during this period, was lionized, made into a larger-than-life figure who went into and then returned from the field with stories about strange people. Rosaldo (1989) describes this as the period of the Lone Ethnographer, the story of the man-scientist who went off in search of his native in a distant land. There this figure "encountered the object of his quest . . . [and] underwent his rite of passage by enduring the ultimate ordeal of 'fieldwork' " (p. 30). Returning home with his data, the Lone Ethnographer wrote up an objective account of the culture he studied. These accounts were structured by the norms of classical ethnography. This sacred bundle of terms (Rosaldo, 1989, p. 31) organized ethnographic texts in terms of four beliefs and commitments: a commitment to objectivism, a complicity with imperialism, a belief in monumentalism (the ethnography would create a museumlike picture of the culture studied), and a belief in timelessness (what was studied never changed). This model of the researcher, who could also write complex, dense theories about what was studied, holds to the present day.

14

The myth of the Lone Ethnographer depicts the birth of classic ethnography. The texts of Malinowski, Radcliffe-Brown, Margaret Mead, and Gregory Bateson are still carefully studied for what they can tell the novice about fieldwork, taking field notes, and writing theory (see the discussion of Bateson and Mead in Harper, Volume 3, Chapter 5). Today this image has been shattered. The works of the classic ethnographers are seen by many as relics of the colonial past (Rosaldo, 1989, p. 44). Although many feel nostalgic about this image, others celebrate its passing. Rosaldo (1989) quotes Cora Du Bois, a retired Harvard anthropology professor, who lamented this passing at a conference in 1980, reflecting on the crisis in anthropology: "[I feel a distance] from the complexity and disarray of what I once found a justifiable and challenging discipline. . . . It has been like moving from a distinguished art museum into a garage sale" (p. 44).

Du Bois regards the classic ethnographies as pieces of timeless artwork, such as those contained in a museum. She detests the chaos of the garage sale, which Rosaldo values: "It [the garage sale] provides a precise image of the postcolonial situation where cultural artifacts flow between unlikely places, and nothing is sacred, permanent, or sealed off. The image of anthropology as a garage sale depicts our present global situation" (p. 44). Old standards no longer hold. Ethnographies do not produce timeless truths. The commitment to objectivism is now in doubt. The complicity with imperialism is openly challenged today, and the belief in monumentalism is a thing of the past.

The legacies of this first period begin at the end of the nineteenth century, when the novel and the social sciences had become distinguished as separate systems of discourse (Clough, 1992, pp. 21-22). However, the Chicago school, with its emphasis on the life story and the "slice-of-life" approach to ethnographic materials, sought to develop an interpretive methodology that maintained the centrality of the narrated life history approach. This led to the production of the texts that gave the researcher-as-author the power to represent the subject's story. Written under the mantle of straightforward, sentiment-free social realism, these texts used the language of ordinary people. They articulated a social science version of literary naturalism, which often produced the sympathetic illusion that a solution to a social problem had been found. Like films about the Depression-era juvenile delinquent and other social problems (Roffman & Purdy, 1981), these accounts romanticized the subject. They turned the deviant into the sociological version of a screen hero. These sociological stories, like their film counterparts, usually had happy endings, as they followed individuals through the three stages of the classic morality tale: existence in a state of grace, seduction by evil and the fall, and finally redemption through suffering.

The Modernist Phase

The modernist phase, or second moment, builds on the canonical works of the traditional period. Social realism, naturalism, and slice-of-life ethnographies are still valued. This phase extended through the postwar years to the 1970s; it is still present in the work of many (see Wolcott, 1992, for a review). In this period many texts attempted to formalize qualitative methods (see, for example, Bogdan & Taylor, 1975; Cicourel, 1964; Filstead, 1970; Glaser & Strauss, 1967; J. Lofland, 1971; Lofland & Lofland, 1984).[7] The modernist ethnographer and sociological participant observer attempted rigorous, qualitative studies of important social processes, including deviance and social control in the classroom and society. This was a moment of creative ferment.

A new generation of graduate students, across the human disciplines, encountered new interpretive theories (ethnomethodology, phenomenology, critical theory, feminism). They were drawn to qualitative research practices that would let them give a voice to society's underclass. Postpositivism functioned as a powerful epistemological paradigm in this moment. Researchers attempted to fit the arguments of Campbell and Stanley (1963) about internal and external validity to constructionist and interactionist models of the research act. They returned to the texts of the Chicago school as sources of inspiration (see Denzin, 1970, 1978).

A canonical text from this moment remains *Boys in White* (Becker et al., 1961). Firmly entrenched in mid-century methodological discourse, this work attempted to make qualitative research as rigorous as its quantitative counterpart. Causal narratives were central to this project. This multimethod work combined open-ended and quasi-structured interviewing with participant observation and the careful analysis of such materials in standardized, statistical form. In a classic article, "Problems of Inference and Proof in Participant Observation," Howard S. Becker (1958/1970) describes the use of quasi-statistics:

> Participant observations have occasionally been gathered in standardized form capable of being transformed into legitimate statistical data. But the exigencies of the field usually prevent the collection of data in such a form

to meet the assumptions of statistical tests, so that the observer deals in what have been called "quasi-statistics." His conclusions, while implicitly numerical, do not require precise quantification. (p. 31)

In the analysis of data, Becker notes, the qualitative researcher takes a cue from statistical colleagues. The researcher looks for probabilities or support for arguments concerning the likelihood that, or frequency with which, a conclusion in fact applies in a specific situation. Thus did work in the modernist period clothe itself in the language and rhetoric of positivist and postpositivist discourse.

This was the golden age of rigorous qualitative analysis, bracketed in sociology by *Boys in White* (Becker et al., 1961) at one end and *The Discovery of Grounded Theory* (Glaser & Strauss, 1967) at the other. In education, qualitative research in this period was defined by George and Louise Spindler, Jules Henry, Harry Wolcott, and John Singleton. This form of qualitative research is still present in the work of such persons as Strauss and Corbin (1990) and Miles and Huberman (1993), and is represented in their chapters in this three-volume set.

The "golden age" reinforced a picture of qualitative researchers as cultural romantics. Imbued with Promethean human powers, they valorized villains and outsiders as heroes to mainstream society. They embodied a belief in the contingency of self and society, and held to emancipatory ideals for which "one lives and dies." They put in place a tragic and often ironic view of society and self, and joined a long line of leftist cultural romantics that included Emerson, Marx, James, Dewey, Gramsci, and Martin Luther King, Jr. (West, 1989, chap. 6).

As this moment came to an end, the Vietnam War was everywhere present in American society. In 1969, alongside these political currents, Herbert Blumer and Everett Hughes met with a group of young sociologists called the "Chicago Irregulars" at the American Sociological Association meetings held in San Francisco and shared their memories of the "Chicago years." Lyn Lofland (1980) describes the 1969 meetings as a

moment of creative ferment—scholarly and political. The San Francisco meetings witnessed not simply the Blumer-Hughes event but a "counter-revolution." . . . a group first came to . . . talk about the problems of being a sociologist and a female. . . . the discipline seemed literally to be bursting with new . . . ideas: labelling theory, ethnomethodology, conflict theory, phenomenology, dramaturgical analysis. (p. 253)

17

Thus did the modernist phase come to an end.

Blurred Genres

By the beginning of the third stage (1970-1986), which we call the moment of blurred genres, qualitative researchers had a full complement of paradigms, methods, and strategies to employ in their research. Theories ranged from symbolic interactionism to constructivism, naturalistic inquiry, positivism and postpositivism, phenomenology, ethnomethodology, critical (Marxist), semiotics, structuralism, feminism, and various ethnic paradigms. Applied qualitative research was gaining in stature, and the politics and ethics of qualitative research were topics of considerable concern. Research strategies ranged from grounded theory to the case study, to methods of historical, biographical, ethnographic action and clinical research. Diverse ways of collecting and analyzing empirical materials were also available, including qualitative interviewing (open-ended and quasi-structured) and observational, visual, personal experience, and documentary methods. Computers were entering the situation, to be fully developed in the next decade, along with narrative, content, and semiotic methods of reading interviews and cultural texts.

Two books by Geertz, *The Interpretation of Cultures* (1973) and *Local Knowledge* (1983), defined the beginning and end of this moment. In these two works, Geertz argued that the old functional, positivist, behavioral, totalizing approaches to the human disciplines were giving way to a more pluralistic, interpretive, open-ended perspective. This new perspective took cultural representations and their meanings as its point of departure. Calling for "thick description" of particular events, rituals, and customs, Geertz suggested that all anthropological writings were interpretations of interpretations. The observer had no privileged voice in the interpretations that were written. The central task of theory was to make sense out of a local situation.

Geertz went on to propose that the boundaries between the social sciences and the humanities had become blurred. Social scientists were now turning to the humanities for models, theories, and methods of analysis (semiotics, hermeneutics). A form of genre dispersion was occurring: documentaries that read like fiction (Mailer), parables posing as ethnographies (Castañeda), theoretical treatises that look like travelogues (Lévi-Strauss). At the same time, many new approaches were emerging: post-structuralism (Barthes), neopositivism (Philips), neo-Marxism (Althusser),

18

micro-macro descriptivism (Geertz), ritual theories of drama and culture (V. Turner), deconstructionism (Derrida), ethnomethodology (Garfinkel). The golden age of the social sciences was over, and a new age of blurred, interpretive genres was upon us. The essay as an art form was replacing the scientific article. At issue now is the author's presence in the interpretive text, or how the researcher can speak with authority in an age when there are no longer any firm rules concerning the text, its standards of evaluation, and its subject matter (Geertz, 1988).

The naturalistic, postpositivist, and constructionist paradigms gained power in this period, especially in education in the works of Harry Wolcott, Egon Guba, Yvonna Lincoln, Robert Stake, and Elliot Eisner. By the end of the 1970s several qualitative journals were in place, from *Urban Life* (now *Journal of Contemporary Ethnography*) to *Qualitative Sociology, Symbolic Interaction,* and *Studies in Symbolic Interaction.*

Crisis of Representation

A profound rupture occurred in the mid-1980s. What we call the fourth moment, or the crisis of representation, appeared with *Anthropology as Cultural Critique* (Marcus & Fischer, 1986), *The Anthropology of Experience* (Turner & Bruner, 1986), *Writing Culture* (Clifford & Marcus, 1986), *Works and Lives* (Geertz, 1988), and *The Predicament of Culture* (Clifford, 1988). These works made research and writing more reflexive, and called into question the issues of gender, class, and race. They articulated the consequences of Geertz's "blurred genres" interpretation of the field in the early 1980s.

New models of truth and method were sought (Rosaldo, 1989). The erosion of classic norms in anthropology (objectivism, complicity with colonialism, social life structured by fixed rituals and customs, ethnographies as monuments to a culture) was complete (Rosaldo, 1989, pp. 44-45). Critical and feminist epistemologies and epistemologies of color now compete for attention in this arena. Issues such as validity, reliability, and objectivity, which had been settled in earlier phases, are once more problematic. Interpretive theories, as opposed to grounded theories, are now more common, as writers continue to challenge older models of truth and meaning (Rosaldo, 1989).

Stoller and Olkes (1987) describe how the crisis of representation was felt in their fieldwork among the Songhay of Niger. Stoller observes: "When I began to write anthropological texts, I followed the conventions of my training. I 'gathered data,' and once the 'data' were arranged in neat piles, I 'wrote them up.' In one case I reduced Songhay insults to a series of neat logical formulas" (p. 227). Stoller became dissatisfied with this form of writing, in part because he learned "everyone had lied to me and . . . the data I had so painstakingly collected were worthless. I learned a lesson: Informants routinely lie to their anthropologists" (Stoller & Olkes, 1987, p. 229). This discovery led to a second, that he had, in following the conventions of ethnographic realism, edited himself out of his text. This led Stoller to produce a different type of text, a memoir, in which he became a central character in the story he told. This story, an account of his experiences in the Songhay world, became an analysis of the clash between his world and the world of Songhay sorcery. Thus did Stoller's journey represent an attempt to confront the crisis of representation in the fourth moment.

Clough (1992) elaborates this crisis and criticizes those who would argue that new forms of writing represent a way out of it:

> While many sociologists now commenting on the criticism of ethnography view writing as "downright central to the ethnographic enterprise" [Van Maanen, 1988, p. xi], the problems of writing are still viewed as different from the problems of method or fieldwork itself. Thus the solution usually offered is experiments in writing, that is, a self-consciousness about writing. (p. 136)

However, it is this insistence on the difference between writing and fieldwork that must be analyzed.

In writing, the field-worker makes a claim to moral and scientific authority. These claims allow the realist and the experimental ethnographic text to function as sources of validation for an empirical science. They show, that is, that the world of real lived experience can still be captured, if only in the writer's memoirs, fictional experimentations, or dramatic readings. These works have the danger of directing attention away from the ways in which the text constructs sexually situated individuals in a field of social difference. They also perpetuate "empirical science's hegemony" (Clough, 1992, p. 8), for these new writing technologies of the subject become the site "for the production of knowledge/power . . . [aligned] with . . . the capital/state axis" (Aronowitz, 1988, p. 300, quoted in Clough, 1992, p. 8). Such experiments come up against, and then back away from, the difference between empirical science and social criticism. Too often they fail to engage fully a new politics of textuality that would "refuse the identity of empirical science" (Clough, 1992, p. 135). This new social criticism "would intervene in the relationship of information economics, nation-state politics, and technologies of mass communication, especially in terms of the empirical sciences" (Clough, 1992, p. 16). This, of course, is the terrain occupied by cultural studies.

Richardson, in Volume 3, Chapter 12, and Clandinin and Connelly, Volume 3, Chapter 6, develop the above arguments, viewing writing as a method of inquiry that moves through successive stages of self-reflection. As a series of writings, the field-worker's texts flow from the field experience, through intermediate works, to later work, and finally to the research text that is the public presentation of the ethnographic and narrative experience. Thus do fieldwork and writing blur into one another. There is, in the final analysis, no difference between writing and fieldwork. These two perspectives inform each other throughout every chapter in this volume. In these ways the crisis of representation moves qualitative research in new, critical directions.

A Double Crisis

The ethnographer's authority remains under assault today. A double crisis of representation and legitimation confronts qualitative researchers in the social sciences. Embedded in the discourses of poststructuralism and postmodernism (Vidich & Lyman, Volume 1, Chapter 2; Richardson, Volume 3, Chapter 12), these two crises are coded in multiple terms, variously called and associated with the *interpretive, linguistic,* and *rhetorical* turns in social theory. This linguistic turn makes problematic two key assumptions of qualitative research. The first is that qualitative researchers can directly capture lived experience. Such experience, it is now argued, is created in the social text written by the researcher. This is the representational crisis. It confronts the inescapable problem of representation, but does so within a framework that makes the direct link between experience and text problematic.

The second assumption makes the traditional criteria for evaluating and interpreting qualitative research problematic. This is the legitimation crisis. It involves a serious rethinking of such terms as *validity, generalizability,* and *reliability,* terms already retheorized in postpositivist, constructionist-naturalistic (Lincoln & Guba, 1985, p. 36), feminist (Fonow & Cook, 1991, pp. 1-13; Smith, 1992), and interpretive (Atkinson, 1990; Hammersley, 1992; Lather, 1993) discourses. This crisis asks, How are qualitative studies to be evaluated in the poststructural moment? Clearly these two crises blur together, for any representation must now legitimate itself in terms of some set of criteria that allows the author (and the reader) to make connections between the text and the world written about.

The Fifth Moment

The fifth moment is the present, defined and shaped by the dual crises described above. Theories are now read in narrative terms, as "tales of the field" (Van Maanen, 1988). Preoccupations with the representation of the "other" remain. New epistemologies from previously silenced groups emerge to offer solutions to this problem. The concept of the aloof researcher has been abandoned. More action-, activist-oriented research is on the horizon, as are more social criticism and social critique. The search for grand narratives will be replaced by more local, small-scale theories fitted to specific problems and specific situations (Lincoln, 1993).

Reading History

We draw four conclusions from this brief history, noting that it is, like all histories, somewhat arbitrary. First, each of the earlier historical moments is still operating in the present, either as legacy or as a set of practices that researchers still follow or argue against. The multiple, and fractured, histories of qualitative research now make it possible for any given researcher to attach a project to a canonical text from any of the above-described historical moments. Multiple criteria of evaluation now compete for attention in this field. Second, an embarrassment of choices now characterizes the field of qualitative research. There have never been so many paradigms, strategies of inquiry, or methods of analysis to draw upon and utilize. Third, we are in a moment of discovery and rediscovery, as new ways of looking, interpreting, arguing, and writing are debated and discussed. Fourth, the qualitative research act can no longer be viewed from within a neutral, or objective, positivist perspective. Class, race, gender, and ethnicity shape the process of inquiry, making research a multicultural process. It is to this topic that we next turn.

◆ Qualitative Research as Process

Three interconnected, generic activities define the qualitative research process. They go by a variety of different labels, including *theory, method* and *analysis,* and *ontology, epistemology,* and *methodology.* Behind these terms stands the personal biography of the gendered researcher, who speaks from a particular class, racial, cultural, and ethnic community perspective. The gendered, multiculturally situated researcher approaches the world with a set of ideas, a framework (theory, ontology) that specifies a set of questions (epistemology) that are then examined (methodology, analysis) in specific ways. That is, empirical materials bearing on the question are collected and then analyzed and written about. Every re-searcher speaks from within a distinct interpretive community, which configures, in its special way, the multicultural, gendered components of the research act.

Behind all of these phases of interpretive work stands the biographically situated researcher. This individual enters the research process from inside an interpretive community that incorporates its own historical research traditions into a distinct point of view. This perspective leads the researcher to adopt particular views of the "other" who is studied. At the same time, the politics and the ethics of research must also be considered, for these concerns permeate every phase of the research process.

◆ The Other as Research Subject

From its turn-of-the-century birth in modern, interpretive form, qualitative research has been haunted by a double-faced ghost. On the one hand, qualitative researchers have assumed that qualified, competent observers can with objectivity, clarity, and precision report on their own observations of the social world, including the experiences of others. Second, re-searchers have held to a belief in a real subject, or real individual, who is present in the world and able, in some form, to report on his or her experiences. So armed, researchers could blend their observations with the observations provided by subjects through interviews and life story, per-sonal experience, case study, and other documents.

These two beliefs have led qualitative researchers across disciplines to seek a method that would allow them to record their own observations

23

accurately while still uncovering the meanings their subjects bring to their life experiences. This method would rely upon the subjective verbal and written expressions of meaning given by the individuals studied, these expressions being windows into the inner life of the person. Since Dilthey (1900/1976), this search for a method has led to a perennial focus in the human disciplines on qualitative, interpretive methods.

Recently, this position and its beliefs have come under attack. Poststructuralists and postmodernists have contributed to the understanding that there is no clear window into the inner life of an individual. Any gaze is always filtered through the lenses of language, gender, social class, race, and ethnicity. There are no objective observations, only observations socially situated in the worlds of the observer and the observed. Subjects, or individuals, are seldom able to give full explanations of their actions or intentions; all they can offer are accounts, or stories, about what they did and why. No single method can grasp the subtle variations in ongoing human experience. As a consequence, as argued above, qualitative researchers deploy a wide range of interconnected interpretive methods, always seeking better ways to make more understandable the worlds of experience that have been studied.

Table 1.1 depicts the relationships we see among the five phases that define the research process. Behind all but one of these phases stands the biographically situated researcher. These five levels of activity, or practice, work their way through the biography of the researcher.

Phase 1: The Researcher

Our remarks above indicate the depth and complexity of the traditional and applied qualitative research perspectives into which a socially situated researcher enters. These traditions locate the researcher in history, both guiding and constraining work that will be done in any specific study. This field has been characterized constantly by diversity and conflict, and these, David Hamilton argues in Volume 1, Chapter 3, are its most enduring traditions. As a carrier of this complex and contradictory history, the researcher must also confront the ethics and politics of research. The age of value-free inquiry for the human disciplines is over, and researchers now struggle to develop situational and transsituational ethics that apply to any given research act.

TABLE 1.1 The Research Process

Phase 1: The Researcher as a Multicultural Subject
        history and research traditions
        conceptions of self and the other
        ethics and politics of research
Phase 2: Theoretical Paradigms and Perspectives
        positivism, postpositivism
        constructivism
        feminism(s)
        ethnic models
        Marxist models
        cultural studies models
Phase 3: Research Strategies
        study design
        case study
        ethnography, participant observation
        phenomenology, ethnomethodology
        grounded theory
        biographical method
        historical method
        action and applied research
        clinical research
Phase 4: Methods of Collection and Analysis
        interviewing
        observing
        artifacts, documents, and records
        visual methods
        personal experience methods
        data management methods
        computer-assisted analysis
        textual analysis
Phase 5: The Art of Interpretation and Presentation
        criteria for judging adequacy
        the art and politics of interpretation
        writing as interpretation
        policy analysis
        evaluation traditions
        applied research

Phase 2: Interpretive Paradigms

All qualitative researchers are philosophers in that "universal sense in which all human beings . . . are guided by highly abstract principles" (Bateson, 1972, p. 320). These principles combine beliefs about ontology (What kind of being is the human being? What is the nature of reality?), epistemology (What is the relationship between the inquirer and the known?), and methodology (How do we know the world, or gain knowledge of it?) (see Guba, 1990, p. 18; Lincoln & Guba, 1985, pp. 14-15; see also Guba & Lincoln, Volume 1, Chapter 6). These beliefs shape how the qualitative researcher sees the world and acts in it. The researcher is "bound within a net of epistemological and ontological premises which—regardless of ultimate truth or falsity—become partially self-validating" (Bateson, 1972, p. 314).

This net that contains the researcher's epistemological, ontological, and methodological premises may be termed a *paradigm* (Guba, 1990, p. 17), or interpretive framework, a "basic set of beliefs that guides action" (Guba, 1990, p. 17). All research is interpretive, guided by a set of beliefs and feelings about the world and how it should be understood and studied. Some of these beliefs may be taken for granted, only assumed; others are highly problematic and controversial. However, each interpretive paradigm makes particular demands on the researcher, including the questions that are asked and the interpretations that are brought to them.

At the most general level, four major interpretive paradigms structure qualitative research: positivist and postpositivist, constructivist-interpretive, critical (Marxist, emancipatory), and feminist-poststructural. These four abstract paradigms become more complicated at the level of concrete specific interpretive communities. At this level it is possible to identify not only the constructivist, but also multiple versions of feminist (Afrocentric and poststructural)[8] as well as specific ethnic, Marxist, and cultural studies paradigms. These perspectives, or paradigms, are examined in Part II of Volume 1.

The paradigms examined in Volume 1, Part II, work against and alongside (and some within) the positivist and postpositivist models. They all work within relativist ontologies (multiple constructed realities), interpretive epistemologies (the knower and known interact and shape one another), and interpretive, naturalistic methods.

Table 1.2 presents these paradigms and their assumptions, including their criteria for evaluating research, and the typical form that an interpre-

TABLE 1.2 Interpretive Paradigms

Paradigm/Theory	Criteria	Form of Theory	Type of Narration
Positivist/ postpositivist	internal, external validity	logical-deductive, scientific, grounded	scientific report
Constructivist	trustworthiness, credibility, transferability, confirmability	substantive-formal	interpretive case studies, ethnographic fiction
Feminist	Afrocentric, lived experience, dialogue, caring, accountability, race, class, gender, reflexivity, praxis, emotion, concrete grounding	critical, standpoint	essays, stories, experimental writing
Ethnic	Afrocentric, lived experience, dialogue, caring, accountability, race, class, gender	standpoint, critical, historical	essays, fables, dramas
Marxist	emancipatory theory, falsifiable, dialogical, race, class, gender	critical, historical, economic	historical, economic, sociocultural analysis
Cultural studies	cultural practices, praxis, social texts, subjectivities	social criticism	cultural theory as criticism

tive or theoretical statement assumes in the paradigm.[9] Each paradigm is explored in considerable detail in Volume 1, Part II, by Guba and Lincoln (Chapter 6), Schwandt (Chapter 7), Kincheloe and McLaren (Chapter 8), Olesen (Chapter 9), Stanfield (Chapter 10), and Fiske (Chapter 11). The positivist and postpositivist paradigms have been discussed above. They work from within a realist and critical realist ontology and objective epistemologies, and rely upon experimental, quasi-experimental, survey, and rigorously defined qualitative methodologies. In Volume 3, Chapter 7, Huberman and Miles develop elements of this paradigm.

The constructivist paradigm assumes a relativist ontology (there are multiple realities), a subjectivist epistemology (knower and subject create understandings), and a naturalistic (in the natural world) set of methodological procedures. Findings are usually presented in terms of the criteria of grounded theory (see Strauss & Corbin, Volume 2, Chapter 7). Terms such as *credibility, transferability, dependability,* and *confirmability* replace the usual positivist criteria of *internal* and *external validity, reliability,* and *objectivity.*

Feminist, ethnic, Marxist, and cultural studies models privilege a materialist-realist ontology; that is, the real world makes a material difference in terms of race, class, and gender. Subjectivist epistemologies and naturalistic methodologies (usually ethnographies) are also employed. Empirical materials and theoretical arguments are evaluated in terms of their emancipatory implications. Criteria from gender and racial communities (e.g., African American) may be applied (emotionality and feeling, caring, personal accountability, dialogue).

Poststructural feminist theories emphasize problems with the social text, its logic, and its inability ever to represent fully the world of lived experience. Positivist and postpositivist criteria of evaluation are replaced by others, including the reflexive, multivoiced text that is grounded in the experiences of oppressed peoples.

The cultural studies paradigm is multifocused, with many different strands drawing from Marxism, feminism, and the postmodern sensibility. There is a tension between humanistic cultural studies stressing lived experiences and more structural cultural studies projects stressing the structural and material determinants (race, class, gender) of experience. The cultural studies paradigm uses methods strategically, that is, as resources for understanding and for producing resistances to local structures of domination. Cultural studies scholars may do close textual readings and discourse analysis of cultural texts as well as local ethnographies, open-ended interviewing, and participant observation. The focus is on how race, class, and gender are produced and enacted in historically specific situations.

Paradigm and history in hand, focused on a concrete empirical problem to examine, the researcher now moves to the next stage of the research process, namely, working with a specific strategy of inquiry.

Phase 3: Strategies of Inquiry and Interpretive Paradigms

Table 1.1 presents some of the major strategies of inquiry a researcher may use. Phase 3 begins with research design, which, broadly conceived, involves a clear focus on the research question, the purposes of the study, "what information most appropriately will answer specific research questions, and which strategies are most effective for obtaining it" (LeCompte & Preissle, 1993, p. 30). A research design describes a flexible set of guidelines that connects theoretical paradigms to strategies of inquiry and methods for collecting empirical material. A research design situates researchers in the empirical world and connects them to specific sites, persons, groups, institutions, and bodies of relevant interpretive material, including documents and archives. A research design also specifies how the investigator will address the two critical issues of representation and legitimation.

A strategy of inquiry comprises a bundle of skills, assumptions, and practices that researchers employ as they move from their paradigm to the empirical world. Strategies of inquiry put paradigms of interpretation into motion. At the same time, strategies of inquiry connect the researcher to specific methods of collecting and analyzing empirical materials. For example, the case study method relies on interviewing, observing, and document analysis. Research strategies implement and anchor paradigms in specific empirical sites, or in specific methodological practices, such as making a case an object of study. These strategies include the case study, phenomenological and ethnomethodological techniques, as well as the use of grounded theory, the biographical, historical, action, and clinical methods. Each of these strategies is connected to a complex literature; each has a separate history, exemplary works, and preferred ways for putting the strategy into motion.

Phase 4: Methods of Collecting and Analyzing Empirical Materials

The researcher has several methods for collecting empirical materials,[10] ranging from the interview to direct observation, to the analysis of artifacts, documents, and cultural records, to the use of visual materials or personal experience. The researcher may also use a variety of different methods of reading and analyzing interviews or cultural texts, including content, narrative, and semiotic strategies. Faced with large amounts of qualitative materials, the investigator seeks ways of managing and interpreting these documents, and here data management methods and computer-assisted models of analysis may be of use.

Phase 5: The Art of Interpretation

Qualitative research is endlessly creative and interpretive. The researcher does not just leave the field with mountains of empirical materials and then easily write up his or her findings. Qualitative interpretations are constructed. The researcher first creates a field text consisting of field notes and documents from the field, what Roger Sanjek (1990, p. 386) calls "indexing" and David Plath (1990, p. 374) calls "filework." The writer-as-interpreter moves from this text to a research text: notes and interpretations based on the field text. This text is then re-created as a working interpretive document that contains the writer's initial attempts to make sense out of what he or she has learned. Finally, the writer produces the public text that comes to the reader. This final tale of the field may assume several forms: confessional, realist, impressionistic, critical, formal, literary, analytic, grounded theory, and so on (see Van Maanen, 1988).

The interpretive practice of making sense of one's findings is both artful and political. Multiple criteria for evaluating qualitative research now exist, and those we emphasize stress the situated, relational, and textual structures of the ethnographic experience. There is no single interpretive truth. As we argued earlier, there are multiple interpretive communities, each having its own criteria for evaluating an interpretation.

Program evaluation is a major site of qualitative research, and qualitative researchers can influence social policy in important ways. David Hamilton, in Volume 1, Chapter 3, traces the rich history of applied qualitative research in the social sciences. This is the critical site where theory, method, praxis, or action, and policy all come together. Qualitative researchers can isolate target populations, show the immediate effects of certain programs on such groups, and isolate the constraints that operate against policy changes in such settings. Action-oriented and clinically oriented qualitative researchers can also create spaces for those who are studied (the other) to speak. The evaluator becomes the conduit for making such voices heard. Greene, in Volume 3, Chapter 13, and Rist, in Volume 3, Chapter 14, develop these topics.

◆ The Fifth Moment: What Comes Next?

Marcus, in Volume 1, Chapter 12, argues that we are already in the post "post" period—post-poststructuralism, post-postmodernism. What this means for interpretive, ethnographic practices is still not clear, but it is certain that things will never be the same. We are in a new age where messy, uncertain, multivoiced texts, cultural criticism, and new experimental works will become more common, as will more reflexive forms of fieldwork, analysis, and intertextual representation. The subject of our final essay in this volume is this "fifth moment." It is true that, as the poet said, the center cannot hold. We can reflect on what should be at a new center.

Thus we come full circle. The chapters in these volumes take the researcher through every phase of the research act. The contributors examine the relevant histories, controversies, and current practices associated with each paradigm, strategy, and method. They also offer projections for the future—where specific paradigms, strategies, or methods will be 10 years from now.

In reading the chapters that follow, it is important to remember that the field of qualitative research is defined by a series of tensions, contradictions, and hesitations. This tension works back and forth between the broad, doubting postmodern sensibility and the more certain, more traditional positivist, postpositivist, and naturalistic conceptions of this project. All of the chapters that follow are caught in and articulate this tension.

Notes

1. Qualitative research has separate and distinguished histories in education, social work, communications, psychology, history, organizational studies, medical science, anthropology, and sociology.

2. Definitions of some of these terms are in order here. *Positivism* asserts that objective accounts of the world can be given. *Postpositivism* holds that only partially objective accounts of the world can be produced, because all methods are flawed. *Structuralism* asserts that any system is made up of a set of oppositional categories embedded in language. *Semiotics* is the science of signs or sign systems—a structuralist project. According to *poststructuralism*, language is an unstable system of referents, thus it is impossible ever to capture completely the meaning of an action, text, or intention. *Postmodernism* is a contemporary sensibility, developing since World War II, that privileges no single authority, method, or paradigm. *Hermeneutics* is an approach to the analysis of texts that stresses how prior understandings and prejudices shape the interpretive process. *Phenomenology* is a complex system of ideas associated with the works of Husserl, Heidegger, Sartre, Merleau-Ponty, and Alfred Schutz. *Cultural studies* is a complex, interdisciplinary field that merges critical theory, feminism, and poststructuralism.

3. According to Weinstein and Weinstein (1991), "The meaning of *bricoleur* in French popular speech is 'someone who works with his (or her) hands and uses devious means compared to those of the craftsman.' . . . the *bricoleur* is practical and gets the job done" (p. 161). These authors provide a history of this term, connecting it to the works of the German sociologist and social theorist Georg Simmel and, by implication, Baudelaire.

4. Here it is relevant to make a distinction between techniques that are used across disciplines and methods that are used within disciplines. Ethnomethodologists, for example, employ their approach as a method, whereas others selectively borrow that method as a technique for their own applications. Harry Wolcott (personal communication, 1993) suggests this distinction. It is also relevant to make distinctions among topic, method, and resource. Methods can be studied as topics of inquiry—for instance, how a case study gets

done. In this ironic, ethnomethodological sense, method is both a resource and a topic of inquiry.

5. Indeed, any attempt to give an essential definition of qualitative research requires a qualitative analysis of the circumstances that produce such a definition.

6. In this sense all research is qualitative, because "the observer is at the center of the research process" (Vidich & Lyman, Volume 1, Chapter 2).

7. See Lincoln and Guba (1985) for an extension and elaboration of this tradition in the mid-1980s.

8. Olesen (Volume 1, Chapter 9) identifies three strands of feminist research: mainstream empirical, standpoint and cultural studies, and poststructural, postmodern, placing Afrocentric and other models of color under the cultural studies and postmodern categories.

9. These, of course, are our interpretations of these paradigms and interpretive styles.

10. *Empirical materials* is the preferred term for what are traditionally described as data.

◆ References

Aronowitz, S. (1988). *Science as power: Discourse and ideology in modern society*. Minneapolis: University of Minnesota Press.

Atkinson, P. A. (1990). *The ethnographic imagination: Textual constructions of reality*. London: Routledge.

Bateson, G. (1972). *Steps to an ecology of mind*. New York: Ballantine.

Becker, H. S. (1970). Problems of inference and proof in participant observation. In H. S. Becker, *Sociological work*. Chicago: Aldine. (Reprinted from *American Sociological Review, 1958, 23, 652-660*)

Becker, H. S. (1986). *Doing things together*. Evanston, IL: Northwestern University Press.

Becker, H. S. (1989). Tricks of the trade. *Studies in Symbolic Interaction, 10,* 481-490.

Becker, H. S. (1993, June 9). *The epistemology of qualitative research*. Paper presented at the MacArthur Foundation Conference on Ethnographic Approaches to the Study of Human Behavior, Oakland, CA.

Becker, H. S., Geer, B., Hughes, E. C., & Strauss, A. L. (1961). *Boys in white: Student culture in medical school*. Chicago: University of Chicago Press.

Bogdan, R., & Taylor, S. J. (1975). *Introduction to qualitative research methods: A phenomenological approach to the social sciences*. New York: John Wiley.

Brewer, J., & Hunter, A. (1989). *Multimethod research: A synthesis of styles*. Newbury Park, CA: Sage.

Campbell, D. T., & Stanley, J. C. (1963). *Experimental and quasi-experimental designs for research*. Chicago: Rand McNally.

Carey, J. W. (1989). *Communication as culture: Essays on media and society*. Boston: Unwin Hyman.

Cicourel, A. V. (1964). *Method and measurement in sociology*. New York: Free Press.

Clifford, J. (1988). *The predicament of culture: Twentieth-century ethnography, literature, and art*. Cambridge, MA: Harvard University Press.

Clifford, J., & Marcus, G. E. (Eds.). (1986). *Writing culture: The poetics and politics of ethnography*. Berkeley: University of California Press.

Clough, P. T. (1992). *The end(s) of ethnography: From realism to social criticism.* Newbury Park, CA: Sage.

Denzin, N. K. (1970). *The research act.* Chicago: Aldine.

Denzin, N. K. (1978). *The research act* (2nd ed.). New York: McGraw-Hill.

Denzin, N. K. (1989a). *Interpretive interactionism.* Newbury Park, CA: Sage.

Denzin, N. K. (1989b). *The research act* (3rd ed.). Englewood Cliffs, NJ: Prentice Hall.

Dilthey, W. L. (1976). *Selected writings.* Cambridge: Cambridge University Press. (Original work published 1900)

Fielding, N. G., & Fielding, J. L. (1986). *Linking data.* Beverly Hills, CA: Sage.

Filstead, W. J. (Ed.). (1970). *Qualitative methodology.* Chicago: Markham.

Flick, U. (1992). Triangulation revisited: Strategy of validation or alternative? *Journal for the Theory of Social Behaviour, 22,* 175-198.

Fonow, M. M., & Cook, J. A. (1991). Back to the future: A look at the second wave of feminist epistemology and methodology. In M. M. Fonow & J. A. Cook (Eds.), *Beyond methodology: Feminist scholarship as lived research* (pp. 1-15). Bloomington: Indiana University Press.

Geertz, C. (1973). *The interpretation of cultures: Selected essays.* New York: Basic Books.

Geertz, C. (1983). *Local knowledge: Further essays in interpretive anthropology.* New York: Basic Books.

Geertz, C. (1988). *Works and lives: The anthropologist as author.* Stanford, CA: Stanford University Press.

Glaser, B. G. (1992). *Emergence vs. forcing: Basics of grounded theory.* Mill Valley, CA: Sociology Press.

Glaser, B. G., & Strauss, A. L. (1967). *The discovery of grounded theory: Strategies for qualitative research.* Chicago: Aldine.

Guba, E. G. (1990). The alternative paradigm dialog. In E. G. Guba (Ed.), *The paradigm dialog* (pp. 17-30). Newbury Park, CA: Sage.

Hammersley, M. (1992). *What's wrong with ethnography? Methodological explorations.* London: Routledge.

Hymes, D. (1980). Educational ethnology. *Anthropology and Education Quarterly, 11,* 3-8.

Lather, P. (1993). Fertile obsession: Validity after poststructuralism. *Sociological Quarterly, 34,* 673-693.

LeCompte, M. D., & Preissle, J. (1992). Toward an ethnology of student life in schools and classrooms: Synthesizing the qualitative research tradition. In M. D. LeCompte, W. L. Millroy, & J. Preissle (Eds.), *The handbook of qualitative research in education* (pp. 815-859). New York: Academic Press.

LeCompte, M. D., & Preissle, J., with Tesch, R. (1993). *Ethnography and qualitative design in educational research* (2nd ed.). New York: Academic Press.

Lentricchia, F., & McLaughlin, T. (Eds.). (1990). *Critical terms for literary study.* Chicago: University of Chicago Press.

Lévi-Strauss, C. (1966). *The savage mind* (2nd ed.). Chicago: University of Chicago Press.

Lincoln, Y. S. (1993, January 27-28). *Notes toward a fifth generation of evaluation: Lessons from the voiceless, or, Toward a postmodern politics of evaluation.* Paper presented at the Fifth Annual Meeting of the Southeast Evaluation Association, Tallahassee, FL.

Lincoln, Y. S., & Guba, E. G. (1985). *Naturalistic inquiry.* Beverly Hills, CA: Sage.

Lofland, J. (1971). *Analyzing social settings: A guide to qualitative observation and analysis.* Belmont, CA: Wadsworth.

Lofland, J., & Lofland, L. H. (1984). *Analyzing social settings: A guide to qualitative observation and analysis* (2nd ed.). Belmont, CA: Wadsworth.

Lofland, L. (1980). The 1969 Blumer-Hughes talk. *Urban Life, 8,* 248-260.

Malinowski, B. (1948). *Magic, science and religion, and other essays.* New York: Natural History Press. (Original work published 1916)

Malinowski, B. (1967). *A diary in the strict sense of the term.* New York: Harcourt Brace.

Marcus, G., & Fischer, M. (1986). *Anthropology as cultural critique: An experimental moment in the human sciences.* Chicago: University of Chicago Press.

Miles, M. B., & Huberman, A. M. (1993). *Qualitative data analysis: A sourcebook of new methods* (2nd ed.). Newbury Park, CA: Sage.

Nelson, C., Treichler, P. A., & Grossberg, L. (1992). Cultural studies. In L. Grossberg, C. Nelson, & P. A. Treichler (Eds.), *Cultural studies* (pp. 1-16). New York: Routledge.

Nichols, B. (Ed.). (1985). *Movies and methods* (Vol. 2). Berkeley: University of California Press.

Plath, D. (1990). Fieldnotes, filed notes, and the conferring of note. In R. Sanjek (Ed.), *Fieldnotes: The makings of anthropology* (pp. 371-384). Albany: State University of New York Press.

Richardson, L. (1991). Postmodern social theory. *Sociological Theory, 9,* 173-179.

Roffman, P., & Purdy, J. (1981). *The Hollywood social problem film.* Bloomington: Indiana University Press.

Rosaldo, R. (1989). *Culture and truth: The remaking of social analysis.* Boston: Beacon.

Sanjek, R. (Ed.). (1990). *Fieldnotes: The makings of anthropology.* Albany: State University of New York Press.

Smith, D. (1992). Sociology from women's perspective: A reaffirmation. *Sociological Theory, 10,* 88-97.

Spindler, G., & Spindler, L. (1992). Cultural process and ethnography: An anthropological perspective. In M. D. LeCompte, W. L. Millroy, & J. Preissle (Eds.), *The handbook of qualitative research in education* (pp. 53-92). New York: Academic Press.

Stoller, P., & Olkes, C. (1987). *In sorcery's shadow: A memoir of apprenticeship among the Songhay of Niger.* Chicago: University of Chicago Press.

Strauss, A. L., & Corbin, J. (1990). *Basics of qualitative research: Grounded theory procedures and techniques.* Newbury Park, CA: Sage.

Turner, V., & Bruner, E. (Eds.). (1986). *The anthropology of experience.* Urbana: University of Illinois Press.

Van Maanen, J. (1988). *Tales of the field: On writing ethnography.* Chicago: University of Chicago Press.

West, C. (1989). *The American evasion of philosophy.* Madison: University of Wisconsin Press.

Weinstein, D., & Weinstein, M. A. (1991). Georg Simmel: Sociological flaneur bricoleur. *Theory, Culture & Society, 8,* 151-168.

Wolcott, H. F. (1992). Posturing in qualitative research. In M. D. LeCompte, W. L. Millroy, & J. Preissle (Eds.), *The handbook of qualitative research in education* (pp. 3-52). New York: Academic Press.

PART I

◆ Locating the Field

This part begins with history and the socially situated observer, and then turns to the ethics and politics of qualitative research.

◆ History and Tradition

Chapter 2, by Arthur Vidich and Stanford Lyman, and Chapter 3, by David Hamilton, reveal the depth and complexity of the traditional and applied qualitative research perspectives that are consciously and unconsciously inherited by the researcher-as-*bricoleur*.[1] These traditions locate the investigator in history, both guiding and constraining work that will be done in any specific study. They are part of his or her tool kit.

Vidich and Lyman show how the ethnographic tradition extends from the Greeks through the fifteenth- and sixteenth-century interests of Westerners in the origins of primitive cultures, to colonial ethnology connected to the empires of Spain, England, France, and Holland, to several twentieth-century transformations in the United States and Europe. Throughout this history the users of qualitative research have displayed commitments to a small set of beliefs,

35

including objectivism, the desire to contextualize experience, and a willingness to interpret theoretically what has been observed. These beliefs supplement the positivist tradition of complicity with colonialism, commitment to monumentalism, and production of timeless texts discussed in Chapter 1. Recently, of course, as we noted, these beliefs have come under attack.

Hamilton complicates this situation in his examination of applied qualitative research traditions. He begins with Evelyn Jacob's important, but contested, fivefold division of qualitative research traditions (ecological psychology, holistic ethnography, ethnography of communication, cognitive anthropology, symbolic interaction), noting that the history of this approach is several centuries old. The desire to chart and change the course of human history extends back to the ancient Greeks. Hamilton then offers a history of applied research traditions extending from Descartes to the work of Kant, Engels, Dilthey, Booth, and Webb to the Chicago school, and finally to Habermas. This history is not linear and straightforward. It is more like a diaspora, a story of the dispersion and migration of ideas from one spot to another, one thinker to another. Hamilton suggests that this area of inquiry has constantly been characterized by diversity and conflict, and that these are its most enduring traditions.

However, Hamilton notes that in the contemporary period at least three propositions organize applied research: Late twentieth-century democracies should empower all citizens; liberal social practice can never be morally neutral; and research cannot be separated from action and practice. These propositions organize much of action research as well as participatory, cooperative, and collaborative research. It is no longer the case that researchers can choose which side they are on, for sides have already been taken (Becker, 1967).

◆ Situating the Other and the Ethics of Inquiry

The contributions of Michelle Fine (Chapter 4) and Maurice Punch (Chapter 5) can be easily fitted to this discussion. Fine argues that a great deal of qualitative research has reproduced a colonizing discourse of the "Other"; that is, the Other is interpreted through

36

the eyes and cultural standards of the researcher. Fine reviews the traditions that have led researchers to speak on behalf of the Other, especially those connected to the belief systems identified by Lyman, Vidich, and Rosaldo. She then examines a set of postmodern texts that interrupt this process.

Punch examines the problems of betrayal, deception, and harm in qualitative research. These are problems directly connected to a deception model of ethical practice (see below). Punch argues for a commonsense, collaborative social science research model that makes the researcher responsible to those studied. This perspective supplements recent critical, action, and feminist traditions that forcefully align the ethics of research with a politics of the oppressed. Punch can be easily located within the contextualized-consequentialist model outlined below.

◆ Five Ethical Positions

Clearly, all researchers, as Punch and Fine argue, must immediately confront the ethics and politics of empirical inquiry. Qualitative researchers continue to struggle with the establishment of a set of ethical standards that will guide their research (see Deyhle, Hess, & LeCompte, 1992). Historically, and most recently, one of five ethical stances (absolutist, consequentialist, feminist, relativist, deceptive) has been followed; often these stances merge with one another.

The *absolutist stance* argues that social scientists have no right to invade the privacy of others. Thus disguised research is unethical. However, social scientists have a responsibility to contribute to a society's self-understanding. Any method that contributes to this understanding is thereby justified. However, because invasions of privacy can cause harm, social scientists should study only those behaviors and experiences that occur in the public sphere.

The absolutist model stands in sharp contrast to the *deception model,* which endorses investigative voyeurism in the name of science, truth, and understanding (see Douglas, 1976, chap. 8; see also Mitchell, 1993).[2] In this model the researcher uses any method necessary to obtain greater and deeper understanding in a situation. This may involve telling lies, deliberately misrepresenting oneself, duping others, setting people up, using adversarial interviewing techniques, building friendly trust, and infiltrating settings. These techniques are justified, proponents of this position argue, because frequently people in power, like those out of power, will attempt to hide the truth from the researcher.

The *relativist stance* assumes that researchers have absolute freedom to study what they see fit, but they should study only those problems that flow directly from their own experiences. Agenda setting is determined by personal biography, not by some larger scientific community. The only reasonable ethical standard, accordingly, is the one dictated by the individual's conscience. The relativist stance argues that no single set of ethical standards can be developed, because each situation encountered requires a different ethical stance (see Denzin, 1989, pp. 261-264). However, the researcher is directed to build open, sharing relationships with those investigated, and thus this framework is connected to the feminist and consequentialist models.

Guba and Lincoln (1989, pp. 120-141) review the traditional arguments supporting the absolutist position. Professional scholarly societies and federal law mandate four areas of ethical concern, involving the protection of subjects from harm (physical and psychological), deception, and loss of privacy. Informed consent is presumed to protect the researcher from charges that harm, deception, and invasion of privacy have occurred. Guba and Lincoln analyze the weaknesses of each of these claims, challenging the warrant of science to create conditions that invade private spaces, dupe subjects, and challenge subjects' sense of moral worth and dignity.

Lincoln and Guba (1989) call for an empowering, educative ethic that joins researchers and subjects together in an open, collegial relationship. In such a model deception is removed, and threats of harm and loss of privacy operate as barriers that cannot be crossed.

The *contextualized-consequentialist model* (House, 1990; Smith, 1990) builds on four principles (principles compatible with those espoused by Lincoln and Guba): mutual respect, noncoercion and nonmanipulation, the support of democratic values and institutions, and the belief that every research act implies moral and ethical decisions that are contextual. Every ethical decision, that is, affects others, with immediate and long-range consequences. These conse-

38

quences involve personal values held by the researcher and those studied. The consequentialist model requires the researcher to build relationships of respect and trust that are noncoercive and that are not based on deception.

The consequentialist model elaborates a feminist ethic that calls for collaborative, trusting, nonoppressive relationships between researchers and those studied (Fonow & Cook, 1991, pp. 8-9). Such a model presumes that investigators are committed to an ethic that stresses personal accountability, caring, the value of individual expressiveness, the capacity for empathy, and the sharing of emotionality (Collins, 1990, p. 216). This is the position we endorse.

◆ Notes

1. Any distinction between applied and nonapplied qualitative research traditions is somewhat arbitrary. Both traditions are scholarly; both have long traditions and long histories, and both carry basic implications for theory and social change. Good nonapplied research should also have applied relevance and implications. On occasion, it is argued that applied research is nontheoretical, but even this conclusion can be disputed.

2. Mitchell does not endorse deception as a research practice, but points to its inevitability in human (especially research) interactions.

◆ References

Becker, H. S. (1967). Whose side are we on? *Social Problems, 14,* 239-248.

Collins, P. H. (1990). *Black feminist thought: Knowledge, consciousness and the politics of empowerment.* New York: Routledge.

Denzin, N. K. (1989). *The research act* (3rd ed.). Englewood Cliffs, NJ: Prentice Hall.

Deyhle, D. L., Hess, G. A., Jr., & LeCompte, M. D. (1992). Approaching ethical issues for qualitative researchers in education. In M. D. LeCompte, W. L. Millroy, & J. Preissle (Eds.), *The handbook of qualitative research in education* (pp. 597-641). New York: Academic Press.

Douglas, J. D. (1976). *Investigative social research.* Beverly Hills, CA: Sage.

Fonow, M. M., & Cook, J. A. (1991). Back to the future: A look at the second wave of feminist epistemology and methodology. In M. M. Fonow & J. A. Cook (Eds.), *Beyond methodology: Feminist scholarship as lived research* (pp. 1-15). Bloomington: Indiana University Press.

Guba, E. G., & Lincoln, Y. S. (1989). *Fourth generation evaluation.* Newbury Park, CA: Sage.

House, E. R. (1990). An ethics of qualitative field studies. In E. G. Guba (Ed.), *The paradigm dialog* (pp. 158-164). Newbury Park, CA: Sage.

Lincoln, Y. S., & Guba, E. G. (1989). Ethics: The failure of positivist science. *Review of Higher Education, 12,* 221-241.

Mitchell, R. J., Jr. (1993). *Secrecy and fieldwork.* Newbury Park, CA: Sage.

Smith, L. M. (1990). Ethics, field studies, and the paradigm crisis. In E. G. Guba (Ed.), *The paradigm dialog* (pp. 139-157). Newbury Park, CA: Sage.

2

Qualitative Methods

Their History in Sociology

and Anthropology

Arthur J. Vidich & Stanford M. Lyman

◆ Modern sociology has taken as its mission the analysis and understanding of the patterned conduct and social processes of society, and of the bases in values and attitudes on which individual and collective participation in social life rests. It is presupposed that, to carry out the tasks associated with this mission, the sociologist has the following:

1. The ability to perceive and contextualize the world of his or her own experience as well as the capacity to project a metaempirical conceptualization onto those contexts of life and social institutions with which he or she has not had direct experience. The sociologist requires a sensitivity to and a curiosity about both what is visible and what is not visible to immediate perception—and sufficient self-understanding to make possible an empathy with the roles and values of others.

2. The ability to detach him- or herself from the particular values and special interests of organized groups in order that he or she may gain a level of understanding that does not rest on a priori commitments. For every individual and group, ideologies and faiths define the distinction between good and evil and lead to such nonsociological but conventional orientations

as are involved in everyday judging and decision making. The sociologist's task in ethnography is not only to be a part of such thoughts and actions but also to understand them at a higher level of conceptualization.

3. A sufficient degree of social and personal distance from prevailing norms and values to be able to analyze them objectively. Usually, the ability to engage in self-objectification is sufficient to produce the quality of orientation necessary for an individual to be an ethnographic sociologist or anthropologist.

Qualitative ethnographic social research, then, entails an attitude of detachment toward society that permits the sociologist to observe the conduct of self and others, to understand the mechanisms of social processes, and to comprehend and explain why both actors and processes are as they are. The existence of this sociological attitude is presupposed in any meaningful discussion of methods appropriate to ethnographic investigation (see Adler, Adler, & Fontana, 1991; Hammersley, 1992).

Sociology and anthropology are disciplines that, born out of concern to understand the "other," are nevertheless also committed to an understanding of the self. If, following the tenets of symbolic interactionism, we grant that the other can be understood only as part of a relationship with the self, we may suggest a different approach to ethnography and the use of qualitative methods, one that conceives the observer as possessing a self-identity that by definition is re-created in its relationship with the observed—the other, whether in another culture or that of the observer.

In its entirety, the research task requires both the act of observation and the act of communicating the analysis of these observations to others (for works describing how this is accomplished, see Johnson, 1975; Schatzman & Strauss, 1973; see also Pratt, 1986). The relationships that arise between these processes are not only the determinants of the character of the final research product, but also the arena of sociological methods least tractable to conventionalized understanding. The data gathering process can never be described in its totality because these "tales of the field" are themselves part of an ongoing social process that in its minute-by-minute and day-to-day experience defies recapitulation. To take as one's objective the making of a total description of the method of gathering data would shift the frame of ethnological reference, in effect substituting the means for the end. Such a substitution occurs when exactitude in reporting research methods takes priority over the solution to substantive sociological problems.

In fact, a description of a particular method of research usually takes place as a retrospective account, that is, a report written after the research has been completed. This all-too-often unacknowledged fact illustrates the part of the research process wherein the acts of observation are temporally separated from the description of how they were accomplished. Such essays in methodology are reconstructions of ethnographic reality; they take what was experienced originally and shrink it into a set of images that, although purporting to be a description of the actual method of research, exemplify a textbook ideal.

The point may be clarified through a comparison of the world of a supposedly "scientific" sociologist with that of such artists as painters, novelists, composers, poets, dancers, or chess masters. Viewing a painting, listening to music, reading a novel, reciting a poem, watching a chess game, or attending to the performance of a ballerina, one experiences a finished production, the "front region," as Goffman (1959, p. 107) puts it. The method seems to be inherent in the finished form (Goffman, 1949, pp. 48-77). More appropriately, we might say that the method—of composing, writing, painting, performing, or whatever—is an intrinsic part of the creator's craftsmanship, without which the creation could not be made. If the artist were to be asked, "How did you do it? Tell me your method," his or her answer would require an act of ex post facto reconstruction: the method of describing the method. However, the original production would still retain its primordial integrity; that cannot be changed, whatever conclusions are to be drawn from later discussions about how it was accomplished. Speaking of sociological methods, Robert Nisbet (1977) recalls:

> While I was engaged in exploration of some of the sources of modern sociology [it occurred to me] that none of the great themes which have provided continuing challenge and also theoretical foundation for sociologists during the last century was ever reached through anything resembling what we are to-day fond of identifying as "scientific method." I mean the kind of method, replete with appeals to statistical analysis, problem design, hypothesis, verification, replication, and theory construction, that we find described in textbooks and courses on methodology. (p. 3)

From Nisbet's pointed observation we may conclude that the method-in-use for the production of a finished sociological study is unique to that study and can be neither described nor replicated as it actually occurred. That societal investigators may choose to use different kinds of material as their data—documents for the historian, quantified reports for the demographer, or direct perception of a portion of society for the ethnographer—does not alter the fact that social scientists are observers. As observers of the world they also participate in it; therefore, they make their observations within a mediated framework, that is, a framework of symbols and cultural meanings given to them by those aspects of their life histories that they bring to the observational setting. Lurking behind each method of research is the personal equation supplied to the setting by the individual observer (Clifford, 1986). In this fundamental sense all research methods are at bottom qualitative and are, for that matter, equally objective; the use of quantitative data or mathematical procedures does not eliminate the intersubjective element that underlies social research. Objectivity resides not in a method, per se, but in the framing of the research problem and the willingness of the researchers to pursue that problem wherever the data and their hunches may lead (Vidich, 1955; see also Fontana, 1980; Goffman, 1974).[1] If, in this sense, all research is qualitative—because the observer is at the center of the research process—does this mean that the findings produced by the method are no more than the peculiar reality of each observer (Atkinson, 1990)?

One simple answer is that we judge for ourselves on the standard of whether the work communicates or "says" something to us—that is, does it connect with our reality?[2] Does it provide us with insights that help to organize our own observations? Does it resonate with our image of the world? Or does it provide such a powerful incursion on the latter that we feel compelled to reexamine what we have long supposed to be true about our life world?

Or, put another way, if the method used is not the issue, by what standards are we able to judge the worth of sociological research (Gellner, 1979)? Each is free to judge the work of others and to accept it or reject it if it does not communicate something meaningful about the world; and what is meaningful for one person is not necessarily meaningful for another.

In the present and for the foreseeable future, the virtually worldwide disintegration of common values and a deconstruction of consensus-based societies evoke recognition of the fact that there exist many competing realities, and this fact poses problems not previously encountered by sociology. In effect, this situation sets up a condition wherein the number of possible theoretical perspectives from which the world, or any part of it, may be viewed sociologically is conditioned only by the number of extant scientific worldviews. As for the potential subjects of investigation, their outlooks are limited only by the many religious faiths, occupational and professional ideologies, and other *Weltanschauungen* that arise to guide or upset their lives. At the time of this writing, a new outlook on epistemology has come to the fore. It disprivileges all received discourses and makes discourse itself a topic of the sociology of knowledge.[3]

The history of qualitative research suggests that this has not always been the case (Douglas, 1974). In the past, the research problems for many investigators were given to them by their commitment to or against a religious faith or an ethnic creed, or by their identification with or opposition to specific national goals or socioeconomic programs. In the historical account of the use of qualitative methods that follows, we shall show that their use has been occasioned by more than the perspective of the individual observer, but also that the domain assumptions that once guided qualitative research have lost much of their force. However, the faiths, creeds, and hopes that had given focus to the work of our predecessors have not disappeared altogether from the sociologist's mental maps (Luhmann, 1986). Rather, they remain as a less-than-conscious background, the all-too-familiar furniture of the sociological mind. Milan Kundera (1988) has pointed to a central issue in our present dilemma in *The Art of the Novel*: "But if God is gone and man is no longer the master, then who is the master? The planet is moving through the void without any master. There it is, the unbearable lightness of being" (p. 41).

Throughout all of the eras during which social science made use of observational methods, researchers have entered into their studies with problems implicitly and, in some cases, explicitly defined by hopes and faiths. Focusing on the substance of these problems and their ideational adumbrations, we shall confine our discussion of this history to the qualitative methods used by anthropologists and sociologists in ethnographic research, that is, the direct observation of the social realities by the individual observer. Our history proceeds along a continuum that begins with the first encounters of early ethnographers with the New World and ends with the practical and theoretical problems facing the work of our contemporaries.

45

◆ Early Ethnography:
The Discovery of the Other

Ethnos, a Greek term, denotes a people, a race or cultural group (A. D. Smith, 1989, pp. 13-18). When *ethno* as a prefix is combined with *graphic* to form the term *ethnographic,* the reference is to the subdiscipline known as descriptive anthropology—in its broadest sense, the science devoted to describing ways of life of humankind. *Ethnography,* then, refers to a social scientific description of a people and the cultural basis of their peoplehood (Peacock, 1986). Both descriptive anthropology and ethnography are thought to be atheoretical, to be concerned solely with description. However, the observations of the ethnographer are always guided by world images that determine which data are salient and which are not: An act of attention to one rather than another object reveals one dimension of the observer's value commitment, as well as his or her value-laden interests.

Early ethnography grew out of the interests of Westerners in the origins of culture and civilization and in the assumption that contemporary "primitive" peoples, those thought by Westerners to be less civilized than themselves, were, in effect, living replicas of the "great chain of being" that linked the Occident to its prehistoric beginnings (Hodgen, 1964, pp. 386-432). Such a mode of ethnography arose in the fifteenth and sixteenth centuries as a result of fundamental problems that had grown out of Columbus's and later explorers' voyages to the Western hemisphere, the so-called New World, and to the island cultures of the South Seas.

The discovery of human beings living in non-Occidental environments evoked previously unimagined cosmological difficulties for European intellectuals, who felt it necessary to integrate the new fact into the canon of received knowledge and understanding.[4] Because the Bible, especially the book of Genesis, was taken to be the only valid source on which to rely for an understanding of the history of geography and processes of creation, and because it placed the origin of humankind in the Garden of Eden—located somewhere in what is today called the Middle East—all human beings were held to be descended from the first pair, and, later, in accordance with flood ethnography (Numbers, 1992) from the descendants of Noah and his family, the only survivors of a worldwide deluge. Linking Columbus's encounter with what we now know as the Taino, Arawak, and Carib (Keegan, 1992; Rouse, 1992) peoples in the New World to the biblical account proved to be difficult. Specifically, the existence of others outside the Christian brotherhood revealed by his "discovery" posed this question: How had the ancestors of these beings reached the Americas in pre-Columbian times? Any thesis that they had not migrated from Eurasia or Africa was held to be heresy and a claim that humankind might have arisen from more than one creative act by God.

In general, the racial and cultural diversity of peoples throughout the globe presented post-Renaissance Europeans with the problem of how to account for the origins, histories, and development of a multiplicity of races, cultures, and civilizations (see Baker, 1974; Barkan, 1992; Trinkhaus & Shipman, 1993). Not only was it necessary for the cosmologist to account for the disconcerting existence of the "other," [5] but such a scholar was obliged to explain how and why such differences in the moral values of Europeans and these "others" had arisen. In effect, such a profusion of values, cultures, and ways of life challenged the monopolistic claim on legitimacy and truth of the doctrines of Christianity. Such practices as infanticide, cannibalism, human sacrifice, and what at first appeared as promiscuity reopened the problem of contradictions among cultural values and the inquiry into how these contradictions might be both explained and resolved (Oakes, 1938).

These issues of value conflicts were conflated with practical questions about the recruitment, organization, and justification for the division of labor in the Spanish settlements in the Americas, and these confusions are to be found in the debates of Bartolome de Las Casas with Juan Gines de Sepulveda at the Council of Valladolid. Sepulveda, "who used Aristotle's doctrine of natural slavery in order to legitimize Spanish behavior against the Indians" (Hosle, 1992, p. 238) in effect won the day against Las Casas, who insisted that the peoples we now call Native Americans were "full fellow human beings, possessing valid traditions, dignity and rights" (Marty, 1992, p. xiii). Today, despite or perhaps because of the new recognition of cultural diversity, the tension between universalistic and relativistic values remains an unresolved conundrum for the Western ethnographer (Hosle, 1992).[6] In practice, it becomes this question: By which values are observations to be guided? The choices seem to be either the values of the ethnographer or the values of the observed—that is, in modern parlance, either the *etic* or the *emic* (Pike, 1967; for an excellent discussion, see Harré, 1980, pp. 135-137). Herein lies a deeper and more fundamental problem: How is it possible to understand the other when the other's values are not one's own? This problem arises to plague ethnography at a time when Western Christian values are no longer a surety of truth and, hence, no longer the benchmark from which self-confidently valid observations can be made.

◆ Colonial Mentalities and the Persistence of the Other

Before the professionalization of ethnography, descriptions and evaluations of the races and cultures of the world were provided by Western missionaries, explorers, buccaneers, and colonial administrators. Their reports, found in church, national, and local archives throughout the world and, for the most part, not known to contemporary ethnologists, were written from the perspective of, or by the representatives of, a conquering civilization, confident in its mission to civilize the world (for pertinent discussion of this issue, see Ginsburg, 1991, 1993). Some of the seventeenth-, eighteenth-, and nineteenth-century explorers, missionaries, and administrators have provided thick descriptions of those practices of the "primitives" made salient to the observer by his Christian value perspective.[7] For societies studied by these observers (see, for example, Degerando, 1800/ 1969), the author's ethnographic report is a reversed mirror image of his own ethnocultural ideal. That these early ethnographies reveal as much about the West as about their objects of study may explain why they have not been recovered and reanalyzed by contemporary anthropologists: Present-day ethnographers hope to separate themselves from the history of Western conquest and reject the earlier ethnographies as hopelessly biased (see "Symposium on Qualitative Methods," 1993). Recently they have begun to take seriously the accounts the natives have given of their Western "discoverers" and to "decenter" or "disprivilege" the reports presented by the latter (Abeyesekere, 1992; Salmond, 1991; Todorov, 1984).

A rich resource, through which one can discern the effects that this early ethnographic literature had on the subjugation of these peoples, is to be found in the works of latter-day colonial administrators (e.g., Olivier, 1911/1970). Ethnology arose out of the reports written by administrators of the long-maintained seaborne empires of the Spanish, English, French, and Dutch (Maunier, 1949). These empires provided opportunities for amateur and, later, professional ethnologists not only to examine hosts of "native" cultures,[8] but also to administer the conditions of life affecting the "cultural advancement" of peoples over whom their metropole exercised domination (Gray, 1911/1970, pp. 79-85). In respect to the seaborne empires, European interest was often confined to exploiting the labor power of the natives, utilizing their territory for extractive industry and/or establishing it in terms of the strategic military advantage it provided them in their struggles against imperialist rivals (for some representative examples, see Aldrich, 1990; Boxer, 1965; Duffy, 1968; Gullick, 1956; Suret-Canale, 1988a, 1988b). Hence the anthropology that developed under colonial administrators tended toward disinterest in the acculturation of the natives and encouragement for the culturally preservative effects of indirect rule. Their approach came to be called pluralistic development (M. G. Smith, 1965). Colonial pluralism left the natives more or less under the authority of their own indigenous leaders so long as these leaders could be co-opted in support of the limited interests of the colonial administration (Lugard, 1922/1965). This tendency led to the creation of a market economy at the center of colonial society (Boeke, 1946; Furnivall, 1956) surrounded by a variety of local culture groups (Boeke, 1948), some of whose members were drawn willy-nilly into the market economy and suffered the effects of marginalized identity (Sachs, 1947).

Ethnographers who conducted their field studies in colonialized areas were divided with respect to their attitudes toward cultural and/or political nationalism and self-determination. A few became champions of ethnocultural liberation and anticolonial revolt. Some respected the autonomy of the traditional culture and opposed any tendency among natives in revolt against colonialism to seek further modernization of their lifestyles. The latter, some of whom were Marxists, admired the anticolonial movement but were concerned to see that the natives remained precapitalist. Some of these might have imagined that precapitalist natives would practice some form of primitive communism (see Diamond, 1963, 1972) as described by Friedrich Engels (1884) in *The Origins of the Family, Private Property and the State*. Engels, in fact, had derived his idea of primitive communism from Lewis Henry Morgan's (1877/1964) *Ancient Society*, an original study in the Comtean ethnohistorical tradition of American aborigines that conceived of the latter as "ancestors" to the ancient Greeks (for a recent critique, see Kuper, 1988). Others, no longer concerned to prove that "mother-right" preceded "father-right" by presenting ethnographic accounts of Melanesians, Tasmanians, Bantus, or Dayaks (for a fine example, see Hartland, 1921/1969), turned their attention to acculturation, and, unsure of how long the process might take and how well the formerly colonized subjects would take to Occidental norms, reinvoked "the doctrine of survivals" (Hodgen, 1936) to account for elements of the natives' culture that persisted (see, e.g., Herskovitz, 1958, 1966), or marveled at how well some native peoples had traded "new lives for old" (Mead, 1956/1975). These diverse value and ideological orientations are pervasive in the work of early professional ethnologists and provided anthropology the grounding for most of its theoretical debates.

◆ **The "Evolution" of Culture and Society: Comte and the Comparative Method**

Even before the professionalization of anthropology engulfed the discipline, the enlightened ethnographer had abandoned any attitude that might be associated with that of a merciless conqueror and replaced it with that of an avatar of beneficent evolutionary progress. Value conflicts arising within anthropology from the history of colonialism, and with the moral relativism associated with them were, in part, replaced by theories of social evolution. The application of Darwinian and Spencerian principles to the understanding of how societies and cultures of the world have developed over eons freed the ethnographer from the problems presented by moral relativism; it permitted the assertion that there existed a spatiotemporal hierarchy of values. These values were represented synchronically in the varieties of cultures to be found in the world, but might be classified diachronically according to the theory of developmental advance.

This new approach to comprehending how the lifeways of the Occident related to those of the others had first been formally proposed by Auguste Comte and was soon designated the "comparative method" (Bock, 1948, pp. 11-36). According to Comte and his followers (see Lenzer, 1975), the study of the evolution of culture and civilization would postulate three stages of culture and would hold fast to the idea that the peoples and cultures of the world are arrangeable diachronically, forming "a great chain of being" (Lovejoy, 1936/1960). Moreover, these stages are interpretable as orderly links in that chain, marking the epochs that occurred as human societies moved from conditions of primitive culture to those of modern civilization.[9] By using technological as well as social indicators, ethnographers could discover where a particular people belonged on the "chain" and thus give that people a definite place in the evolution of culture. (For a recent discussion and critique of Comte as a theorist of history and

50

evolution, see R. Brown, 1984, pp. 187-212.) The seemingly inconvenient fact that all of these different cultures coexisted in time—that is, the time in which the ethnographer conducted his or her field study—was disposed of by applying the theory of "uneven evolution," that is, the assertion, in the guise of an epistemological assumption, that all cultures except that of Western Europe had suffered some form of arrested development (Sanderson, 1990; Sarana, 1975). In this way, and in the absence of documentary historical materials, ethnographers could utilize their on-the-spot field studies to contribute to the construction of the prehistory of civilization and at the same time put forth a genealogy of morals. Following Comte, this diachrony of civilizational development was usually characterized as having three progressive and irreversible stages: savagery, barbarism, and civilization. The peoples assigned to each of these stages corresponded to a color-culture hierarchical diachrony and fitted the ethnocentric bias of the Occident (Nisbet, 1972).

In the nineteenth century, Comte had formalized this mode of thinking for both anthropologists and sociologists by designating as epochs of moral growth (Comte's terms) three stages that, he averred, occurred in the development of religion. The ethnologists' adaptation of Comte's comparative method to their own efforts provided them with a set of a priori assumptions on the cultures of "primitives"—assumptions that vitiated the need to grant respect to these cultures in their own terms—that is, from the perspective of those who are its participants (for a countervailing perspective, see Hill-Lubin, 1992). The imposition of a preconceived Eurocentric developmental framework made the work of the ethnographer much simpler;[10] the task became that of a classifier of cultural traits in transition, or in arrest. Ultimately, this approach was institutionalized in the Human Relations Area Files (HRAF) housed at Yale University, which became the depository for an anthropological data bank and the resource for a vast project dedicated to the classification and cross-classification of virtually all the extant ethnographic literature—in the drawers of the HRAF any and all items of culture found a secure classificatory niche (Murdock, 1949/1965). A Yale-produced handbook of categories provided the ethnographer with guidelines to direct his or her observations and provided the basis for the classification of these and other collections of cultural traits.[11] The trait data in the Yale cross-cultural files represent ethnography in a form disembodied from that of a lived social world in which actors still exist. They are a voluminous collection of disparate cultural items that represent the antithesis of the ethnographic method.

◆ **Twentieth-Century Ethnography:**
   Comteanism and the Cold War

Two twentieth-century developments have undermined both the various "colonial" anthropological perspectives and evolutionary schemes. Within 30 years of the termination of World War II, the several decolonization movements in Africa and Asia succeeded in ending the direct forms of Western global colonialism. As part of the same movements, an anticolonial assault on Western ethnocentrism led to a critical attack on the idea of "the primitive" and on the entire train of ethnological thought that went with it (Montagu, 1968). In effect, by the 1960s anthropologists had begun not only to run out of "primitive" societies to study but also to abandon the evolutionary epistemology that had justified their very existence in the first place.

A new term, *underdeveloped,* tended to replace *primitive.* The colonial powers and their supporters became defendants in an academic prosecution of those who were responsible for the underdevelopment of the newly designated "Third World" and who had neglected to recognize the integrity of "black culture" and that of other peoples of color in the United States (see Willis, 1972).[12] Ethnologists discovered that their basic orientation was under attack. Insofar as that orientation had led them or their much-respected predecessors to cooperate with imperial governments in the suppression and exploitation of natives, or with the American military and its "pacification" programs in Vietnam, anthropologists began to suffer from the effects of a collective and intradisciplinary guilt complex (see Nader, 1972).[13]

Changes in what appeared to be the direction of world history led anthropologists to retool their approach to ethnography. Because, by definition, there were few, if any, primitives available for study, and because the spokespersons for the newly designated Third World of "underdeveloped" countries often held anthropologists to have contributed to the latter condition, access to tribal societies became more difficult than it had been. As opportunities for fieldwork shrank, recourse was had to the study of linguistics, to the data banks of the Yale files, or to the discovery of the ethnographic possibilities for anthropological examinations of American society. Anthropology had come full circle, having moved back to a study of its own society, the point of departure—as well as the benchmark—for its investigation of more "primitive" cultures. Linguistics and data banks lend themselves to the study of texts, as does the study of Western society, with its rich literary and historical archives. These tendencies opened ethnography to the modernist and, later, the postmodernist approaches to the study of exotic peoples and to the investigation of alien culture bearers residing within industrial societies of the Occident.

However, even as anthropology was convulsed by decolonization movements and constrained by restricted access to its traditional fieldwork sites, the Cold War gave to sociology an opportunity to revive Comte's and Spencer's variants of evolutionary doctrine in modernist form and to combine them with a secular theodicy harking back to America's Puritan beginnings.

Talcott Parsons's (1966, 1971) two-volume study of the development of society restored the Calvinist-Puritan imagery, applying the latter to those "others" not yet included in the Christian brotherhood of the Occident. Written during the decades of the U.S. global contest with the Soviet Union, it arranged selected nations and societies in a schema according to which the United States was said to have arrived at the highest stage of societal development; other peoples, cultures, and civilizations were presumed to be moving in the direction plotted by America, "the first new nation" (Lipset, 1979; for a critique, see Lyman, 1975), or to be suffering from an arrest of advancement that prevented them from doing so. That developmental scheme held to the idea that economic progress was inherent in industrialization and that nation building coincided with capitalism, the gradual extension of democratization, and the orderly provision of individual rights. Despite the pointed criticisms of the comparative method that would continue to be offered by the school of sociohistorical thought associated with Frederick J. Teggart (1941) and his followers (Bock, 1952, 1956, 1963, 1974; Hodgen, 1974; Nisbet, 1969, 1986; for a critical discussion of this school, see Lyman, 1978; see also Kuper, 1988), a Comtean outlook survived within sociology in the work of Talcott Parsons and his macrosociological epigoni.

Social scientific literature during the Cold War included such titles as Robert Heilbroner's *The Great Ascent,* A. F. K. Organski's *The Stages of Political Development,* and W. W. Rostow's *The Stages of Economic Growth.* The American political economy and a democratic social order replaced earlier images of the ultimate stage of cultural evolution. Changes in the rest of the nations of the world that seemed to herald movement toward adoption of an American social, political, and economic institutional structure became the standard by which social scientists could measure the "advance" of humankind. This standard provided the analyst-ethnographer with a new measure for evaluating the "progress" of the "other" (which, after 1947, included the peoples and cultures of the Soviet Union as well as those of the "underdeveloped" world). The matter reached epiphany in the early 1990s, when students and scholars of the cosmological, moral, economic, and military problems faced by claimants of the right to spread a benevolent variant of Christianized Western civilization throughout the world began to rejoice over the collapse of communism, the disintegration of the Soviet Union, and the decomposition of its allies and alliances in Eastern Europe (Gwertzman & Kaufman, 1992). But for some there arose a new apprehension: worry over whether these events signaled the very end of history itself (see Fukuyama, 1992).[14]

The end of the Cold War and the deconstruction of the Soviet Union revived nationalist and ethnic claims in almost every part of the world. In such a newly decentered world, cultural pluralism has become a new watchword, especially for all those who hope to distinguish themselves from ethnonational "others." The dilemmas once posed by cultural relativism have been replaced by the issues arising out of the supposed certainties of primordial descent. Ethnographers now find themselves caught in the cross fire of incommensurable but competing values.

◆ The Ethnography of the American Indian: An Indigenous "Other"

In the United States, the Calvinist variant of the Protestant errand into the wilderness began with the arrival of the Puritans in New England. Convinced of their own righteousness and of their this-worldly mission to bring to fruition God's kingdom on the "new continent," the Puritans initially set out to include the so-called Indians in their covenant of faith. But, having misjudged both the Indians' pliability and their resistance to an alien worldview, the Puritans did not succeed in their attempt (Calloway, 1991, pp. 57-90; A. T. Vaughan, 1965). Nevertheless, they continued their missionary endeavors throughout the nineteenth and twentieth centuries (Coleman, 1985; Keller, 1983; Milner & O'Neil, 1985). American political and jurisprudential policy toward the Indian, as well as the ethnographic work on the cultures of Native Americans, derive from this failure and shape its results. As one consequence, the several tribes of North American aborigines would remain outside the ethnographic, moral, and cultural pale of both European immigrant enclaves and settled white American communities.

From the seventeenth through the nineteenth centuries—that is, during the period of westward expansion across the American continent—ethnographic reports on Indian cultures were written from the perspective of the Euro-American conqueror and his missionary allies (Bowden, 1981). Even more than the once-enslaved Africans and their American-born descendants, the Indians have remained in a special kind of "otherness." One salient social indicator of this fact is their confinement to reservations of the mind as well as the body. In the conventional academic curriculum, the study of Native Americans is a part of the cultural anthropology of "primitive" peoples, whereas that of European and Asian immigrants and American blacks is an institutionalized feature of sociology courses on "minorities" and "race and ethnic relations."

In the United States a shift in ethnographic perspective from that written by missionaries and military conquerors to that composed exclusively by anthropologists arose with the establishment of the ethnology section of the Smithsonian Institution (Hinsley, 1981). However, ethnographies of various Indian "tribes" had been written earlier by ethnologists in service to the Bureau of Indian Affairs (BIA) (Bieder, 1989; two representative examples of pre-Smithsonian Amerindian ethnography are found in McKenney & Hall, 1836/1972; Schoolcraft, 1851/1975). In addition to being "problem peoples" for those theorists who wished to explain Indian origins in America and to construct their ancestry in terms consistent with the creation and flood myths of the Bible, the presence of the Indians within the borders of the United States posed still another problem: their anomalous status in law (R. A. Williams, 1990). Politically, the Indian "tribes" regarded themselves as separate sovereign nations and, for a period, were dealt with as such by the colonial powers and the U.S. government. However, in 1831, their legal status was redesignated in a Supreme Court case, *Cherokee Nation v. Georgia* (1831). In his decision, Chief Justice Marshall declared the Indians to occupy a unique status in law. They form, he said, "a domestic dependent nation." As such, he went on, they fell into a special "ward" relationship to the federal government. The latter had already established the Bureau of Indian Affairs to deal with them. Within the confines and constraints of this decision, the BIA administered the affairs of the Indian. From the special brand of anthropology that it fostered, American ethnography developed its peculiar outlook on Native Americans.[15]

The BIA and later the Smithsonian Institution employed ethnographers to staff the various reservation agencies and to study the ways of the

Indians. The focus of study for this contingent of observers was not the possible conversion of Indians, but rather the depiction of their cultures—ceremonies recorded, kinship systems mapped, technology described, artifacts collected—all carried out from a secular and administrative point of view.[16] The theoretical underpinning of the BIA's perspective was the civilized/primitive dichotomy that had already designated Indians as preliterates. In effect, the tribal lands and reservation habitats of these "domestic, dependent nationals" became a living anthropological museum from which ethnologists could glean descriptions of the early stages of primitive life. In those parts of the country where Indians lived in large numbers—especially the Southwest[17]—and where archaeological artifacts were numerous, the Comtean evolutionary perspective was used to trace the ancestry of existing tribes back to an origin that might be found by paleontological efforts. From the beginning, however, the Southwest would also be the setting where debates—over how ethnography was to be carried out, and what purpose it ought to serve—would break out and divide anthropologists not only from missionaries and from federal agents, but from one another (Dale, 1949/1984; Dockstader, 1985).

The life world of "the primitive" was thought to be a window through which the prehistoric past could be seen, described, and understood. At its most global representation, this attitude had been given the imprimatur of ethnological science at the St. Louis World's Fair in 1904, when a scientifically minded missionary, Samuel Phillips Verner, allowed Ota Benga, a pygmy from the Belgian Congo, to be put on display as a living specimen of primitivism. A year later, Ota Benga was exhibited at the Monkey House of the Bronx Zoo (Bradford & Blume, 1992). In 1911, the American anthropologist Alfred Kroeber took possession of Ishi, the last surviving member of the Yahi tribe, and placed him in the Museum of Anthropology at the University of California. In the two years before his death, Ishi dwelled in the museum and, like Ota Benga before him, became, in effect, a living artifact, a primitive on display, one to be viewed by the civilized in a manner comparable to their perspective on the presentation of Indians in American museum dioramas (see Kroeber, 1962, 1965; for contemporary accounts in newspapers and other media, see Heizer & Kroeber, 1979).

Although U.S. Indian policy established both the programs and the perspectives under which most ethnographers worked, its orthodoxy was not accepted by all of the early field-workers. Among these heterodoxical ethnologists, perhaps the most important was Frank Hamilton Cushing

56

(1857-1900), who became a Zuni shaman and a war chief while working as an ethnologist for the Smithsonian Institution (see Cushing, 1920/1974, 1979, 1901/1988, 1990; see also Culin, 1922/1967).[18] Cushing's case stands out because, though he was an active participant in Zuni life, he continued to be a professional ethnographer who tried to describe both Zuni culture and the Zuni worldview from an indigenous perspective. Moreover, Cushing joined with R. S. Culin in proposing the heterodoxical thesis that America was the cradle of Asia, that is, that in pre-Columbian times the ancestors of the Zuni had migrated to Asia and contributed significantly to the development of Chinese, Japanese, Korean, and other Asiatic civilizations that in turn had been diffused over the centuries into Africa and Europe (Lyman, 1979, 1982a, 1982b).

Without attempting to become a native himself, Paul Radin (1883-1959) devoted a lifetime to the ethnographic study of the Winnebago Indians (see Radin, 1927, 1927/1957a, 1937/1957b, 1920/1963, 1933/1966, 1953/ 1971b, 1923/1973, 1956/1976).[19] Maintaining that an inner view of an alien culture could be accomplished only through a deep learning of its language and symbol system, Radin documented the myths, rituals, and poetry in Winnebago and, in his reports, provided English translations of these materials. Taking Cushing's and Radin's works as a standard for Amerindian ethnography, their perspective could be used to reinterpret the works of earlier ethnographers; they might enable future field investigators to comprehend the cultural boundedness of American Indian ethnography and at the same time provide the point of departure for a critical sociology of ethnological knowledge (Vidich, 1966). But, in addition, their work recognizes both the historicity of preliterate cultures and the problems attendant upon understanding the world of the other from the other's point of view. In this, as in the work of Thucydides and in the Weberian conception of a sociology of understanding (*verstehende* sociology), Cushing and Radin transcended the problem of value incommensurability.

◆ The Ethnography of the Civic Other: The Ghetto, the Natural Area, and the Small Town

The Calvinist mission to save and/or include the Indian found its later counterpart in a mission to bring to the urban ghetto communities of blacks and Asian and European immigrants the moral and communitarian values of Protestantism. That these immigrants had carried their Catholic, Judaic, or Buddhist religious cultures to the United States and that the lifestyles of the recently emancipated blacks did not accord with those of the white citizens of the United States were causes for concern among representatives of the older settled groups, who feared for the future integrity of America's Protestant civilization (Contosta, 1980, pp. 121-144; Hartmann, 1948/1967; Jones, 1992, pp. 49-166). Initially, efforts to include these groups focused on Protestant efforts to preach and practice a "social gospel" that found its institutionalization in the settlement houses that came to dot the urban landscape of immigrant and ghetto enclaves (Holden, 1922/1970; Woods & Kennedy, 1922/1990).

About three decades after the Civil War, when it became clear that the sheer number and cultural variety of the new urban inhabitants had become too great to be treated by individual efforts, recourse was had to the statistical survey. It would provide a way to determine how many inhabitants from each denomination, nationality, and race there were in any one place, and to describe each group's respective problems of adjustment (C. A. Chambers, 1971; Cohen, 1981; McClymer, 1980). In this manner, the "other" was transformed into a statistical aggregate and reported in a tabular census of exotic lifestyles. These quantified reports, sponsored in the first years by various churches in eastern cities of the United States, were the forerunners of the corporate-sponsored surveys of immigrants and Negroes and of the massive government-sponsored surveys of European, Asian, Mexican, and other immigrant laborers in 1911 (Immigration Commission, 1911/1970). The church surveys and their corporate and sociological successors were designed to facilitate the "moral reform" and social adjustment of newcomer and ghetto populations. What is now known as qualitative research in sociology had its origins in this Christian mission (see Greek, 1978, 1992).

It was out of such a movement to incorporate the alien elements within the consensual community that the first qualitative community study was carried out. W. E. B. Du Bois's (1899/1967) *The Philadelphia Negro,* a survey of that city's seventh ward, was supported by Susan B. Wharton, a leader of the University of Pennsylvania's college settlement. To Wharton, Du Bois, and their colleagues, the "collection and analysis of social facts were as much a religious as a scientific activity offered as a form of prayer for the redemption of dark-skinned people" (Vidich & Lyman, 1985, p. 128). This study, which included 5,000 interviews conducted by Du Bois, aimed not only at description, but also at the uplift of Philadelphia's Negro population by the Quaker community that surrounded it. The tone of noblesse oblige that inspires the final pages of Du Bois's book are a stark reminder of the paternalistic benevolence underlying this first ethnographic study of a community.

Church- and corporate-sponsored survey methods continued to dominate social research until the early 1920s (see Burgess, 1916), when Helen and Robert Lynd began their study of Middletown. Robert Lynd, a newly ordained Protestant minister, was selected by the Council of Churches, then concerned about the moral state of Christian communities in industrial America, to examine the lifeways of what was thought to be a typical American community. Rather suddenly catapulted into the position of a two-person research team, the Lynds consulted the anthropologist Clark Wissler (1870-1947), then on the staff of the American Museum of Natural History,[20] for advice on how to conduct such a survey and how to report it once the data had been gathered. Wissler provided them with what was then known as the cultural inventory, a list of standard categories used by anthropologists to organize field data (see Wissler, 1923, chaps. 5, 7). Those categories—getting a living, making a home, training the young, using leisure, engaging in religious practices, engaging in community activities—became the organizing principle of Lynd and Lynd's (1929/1956) book and provided them with a set of cues for their investigation. Although the Middletown study was designed to provide its church sponsors with information that might be used to set church policy, the Lynds approached the Middletown community in the manner of social anthropologists. As Wissler (1929/1956) states in his foreword to the published volume of the study, "To most people anthropology is a mass of curious information about savages, and this is so far true, in that most of its observations are on the less civilized. . . . The authors of this volume have approached an American community as an anthropologist does a primitive tribe" (p. vi). In Middletown, the "other" of the anthropologist found its way into American sociological practice and purpose. Moreover, from the point of view of the policy makers in the central church bureaucracy, he who had once been assumed to be the civic "brother" had to all intents and purposes become the "other," an ordinary inhabitant of Muncie, Indiana.

Shortly after the publication of *Middletown* in 1929, the Great Depression set in. Soon, the Lynds were commissioned to do a restudy of Muncie. Published in 1937 as *Middletown in Transition: A Study in Cultural Conflicts,* this investigation reflected not only changes in the town, but also a transformation in the outlook of its two ethnographers. During the early years of the Depression, Robert Lynd, a church progressive, had begun to look to the Soviet Union for answers to the glaring contradictions of capitalism that seemed to have manifested themselves so alarmingly in Depression-ridden America. This new political orientation was reflected in both what the Lynds observed and how they reported it. Where the first volume had made no mention of the Ball family's domination of what was a virtual "company town," or of the family's philanthropic sponsorship of Ball State University and the local library and hospital, or its control over the banks, *Middletown in Transition* included a chapter titled "The X Family: A Pattern of Business-Class Control," and an appendix titled "Middletown's Banking Institutions in Boom and Depression." Responding to what they believed to be the utter failure of America's laissez-faire, free market economy, the Lynds abandoned the ethnographic categories they had used in *Middletown.* Choosing instead to employ categories and conceptualizations derived from their own recently acquired Marxist outlook, they shifted the sociological focus from religious to political values.

Middletown in Transition would become a standard and much-praised work of sociological ethnography for the next half century. At Columbia University, where Robert Lynd taught generations of students, explicit Christian values and rhetoric were replaced by those of an ethically inclined political radicalism. With the radicalization of many Columbia-trained youths (as well as of their fellow students at City College, many of whom would later become prominent sociologists), variants of Marxism would provide a counterperspective to that of the anthropologically oriented ethnographic observer of American communities. Ironically, however, Middletown's second restudy, conducted by a team of non-Marxist sociologists nearly 50 years after *Middletown in Transition* was published, returned the focus to the significance of kinship and family that had characterized the early anthropological perspective, combining it with the kind of concern for Protestant religiosity that had been the stock-in-trade of the earlier American sociological orientation (Caplow, Bahr, Chadwick, Hill, & Williamson, 1982, 1983).

Even before the Lynds' original study, ethnography as a method of research had become identified with the University of Chicago's Department of Sociology. The first generation of Chicago sociologists, led by Albion W. Small, supposed that the discipline they professed had pledged itself to reassert America's destiny—the nation that would be "the city upon a hill." America would become a unified Christian brotherhood, committed to a covenant through which the right and proper values would be shared by all (Vidich & Lyman, 1985, p. 179). Small sought a sociological means to impress the values and morals of Protestantism upon the inhabitants of the newer ethnic, racial, and religious ghettos then forming in Chicago. However, this explicitly Christian attitude—in service to which the University of Chicago had been brought into existence by John D. Rockefeller in 1892—did not survive at Chicago. It was discarded after Robert E. Park, Ernest W. Burgess, W. I. Thomas, and Louis Wirth had become the guiding professoriat of Chicago's sociology, and after Park's son-in-law, Robert Redfield, had become an important figure in that university's anthropology program. Park's secular conceptualization of the "natural area" replaced the Christian locus of the unchurched in the city, while, at the same time, and in contradistinction to Park's point of view, Redfield's formulation of the morally uplifting "little community" introduced a counterimage to that of the metropolis then emerging in Chicago.

Park (1925/1967) conceived the city to be a social laboratory containing a diversity and heterogeneity of peoples, lifestyles, and competing and contrasting worldviews. To Park, for a city to be composed of others, ghettoized or otherwise, was intrinsic to its nature. Under his and Ernest W. Burgess's direction or inspiration, a set of ethnographic studies emerged focusing on singular descriptions of one or another aspect of human life that was to be found in the city. Frequently, these studies examined urban groups whose ways of life were below or outside the purview of the respectable middle classes. In addition to providing descriptions of the myriad and frequently incompatible values by which these groups lived, these ethnographies moved away from the missionary endeavor that had characterized earlier studies. Instead, Park and his colleagues occupied themselves with documenting the various forms of civil otherhood that they perceived to be emerging in the city (see Burgess & Bogue, 1967).

Central to Park's vision of the city was its architectonic as a municipal circumscription of a number of "natural areas," forming a mosaic of minor communities, each strikingly different from the other, but each more or less typical of its kind. Park (1952a) observed, "Every American city has its slums; its ghettos; its immigrant colonies, regions which maintain more or less alien and exotic cultures. Nearly every large city has its bohemias and hobohemias, where life is freer, more adventurous and lonely than it is elsewhere. These are called natural areas of the city" (p. 196). For more than three decades, urban ethnography in Chicago's sociology department focused on describing such "natural areas" as the Jewish ghetto (Wirth,

1928/1956), Little Italy (Nelli, 1970), Polonia (Lopata, 1967; Thomas & Znaniecki, 1958, pp. 1511-1646), Little Germany (Park, 1922/1971), Chinatown (Lee, 1978; Siu, 1987; Wu, 1926), Bronzeville and Harlem (Drake & Cayton, 1962; Frazier, 1931, 1937a, 1937b), the gold coast and the slum (Zorbaugh, 1929), hobo jungles (N. Anderson, 1923/1961), single-room occupants of furnished rooms (Zorbaugh, 1968), enclaves of cultural and social dissidents (Ware, 1935/1965),[21] the urban ecology of gangdom (Thrasher, 1927/1963), and the urban areas that housed the suicidal (Cavan, 1928/1965), the drug addicted (Dai, 1937/1970), and the mentally disturbed (Faris & Dunham, 1939/1965), and on the social and economic dynamics of real estate transactions and the human and metro-political effects arising out of the occupational interests of realtors as they interfaced with the state of the economy (Hughes, 1928; McCluer, 1928; Schietinger, 1967). Park's (1952b, 1952c) orientation was that of Montes-quieu; he emphasized the freedom that the city afforded to those who would partake of the "romance" and "magic" of its sociocultural mul-tiverse.

Some of Park's students, on the other hand, following up an idea developed by Louis Wirth (1938), all too often took to contrasting its forms of liberty in thought and action—that is, its encouragement of "segmented" personalities and role-specific conduct and its fostering of impersonality, secondary relationships, and a blasé attitude (see Roper, 1935, abstracted in Burgess & Bogue, 1967, pp. 231-244)—with what they alleged was the sense of personal security—that is, the gratification that came from con-formity to custom, the comfort that arose out of familiar face-to-face contacts, the wholesomeness of whole personalities, and the companion-ability of primary relationships—to be found among the people who dwelt in rural, ethnoracially homogeneous small towns (see Bender, 1978, pp. 3-27; Redfield & Singer, 1973; see also M. P. Smith, 1979). For those who idealized the "folk society," and who conflated it with concomitant ideali-zations of the "little community," "primitive" primordialism, pastoral peace, and the small town, the impending urbanization of the country-side—heralded by the building of highways (Dansereau, 1961; McKenzie, 1968), the well-documented trend of young people departing to the city (for early documentation of this phenomenon, see Weber, 1899/1967), and the intrusion of the automobile (Bailey, 1988; Rae, 1965), the telephone (Ball, 1968; de Sola Poole, 1981), and the radio (Gist & Halbert, 1947, pp. 128, 505-507) on rural folkways—was a portent not merely of change but of irredeemable tragedy (see Blake, 1990; Gusfield, 1975; Lingeman,

1980; Tinder, 1980). On the other hand, for those ethnographers who concluded on the basis of their own field experiences that the processes as well as the anomalies of America's inequitable class structure had already found their way into and become deeply embedded within the language and customs of the nation's small towns, there was an equally portentous observation: America's Jeffersonian ideals were professed but not practiced in the very communities that had been alleged to be their secure repository. As August B. Hollingshead (1949/1961) would point out on the basis of his ethnographic study of "Elmtown's youth": "The . . . American class system is extra-legal . . . [but] society has other dimensions than those recognized in law. . . . It is the culture which makes men face toward the facts of the class system and away from the ideals of the American creed" (pp. 448, 453).

Ethnographic studies that followed in this tradition were guided by a nostalgia for nineteenth-century small-town values, an American past that no longer existed, but during the heyday of which—so it was supposed—there had existed a society in which all had been brothers and sisters.

However, neither the civil otherhood conceived by Park nor the classless brotherhood sought by Hollingshead could account for American society's resistance to the incorporation of blacks. It was to address this point that E. Franklin Frazier (1894-1962) would stress the "otherhood" of the American Negro. Building on the teachings of both Park and Du Bois, Frazier began his sociological studies in Chicago with an analysis of the various lifeways within the black ghetto. In the process, he discovered both the ghetto's separateness and its isolation from the larger social and political economy. In his later evaluation of the rise of the "black bourgeoisie" (1957a) he saw it as a tragic, although perhaps inevitable, outcome of the limited economic and social mobility available to the black middle classes. Based on his observations of largely university-based black middle classes, Frazier presented their lifestyle as an emulation of the lifestyle of the white middle classes: as such, his monograph on the subject should be regarded as much as a study of the white bourgeoisie as of the black. Frazier's ethnographic studies were based on almost a lifetime of observation, not only of this specific class, but also of African American ghetto dwellers in Harlem and Chicago, of black families in the rural South and the urban North, and of Negro youths caught up in the problems of their socioeconomic situation (see Frazier, 1925, 1957b, 1963, 1939/1966, 1940/1967, 1968). Frazier's work stands apart, not only because it points to the exclusion of blacks from both the American ideal of brotherhood and the then-emerging civic otherhood, but also because its research orientation drew on the life histories of his subjects and on his own experience.

The importance of personal experience in ethnographic description and interpretation is implicit in all of Frazier's work. His methodology and chosen research sites are comparable to those employed by a very different kind of ethnographer—Thorstein Veblen. In such studies of American university ghettos as *The Higher Learning in America: A Memorandum on the Conduct of Universities by Businessmen,* Veblen (1918/1965) drew on his own experiences at the University of Chicago, Stanford University, and the University of Missouri, three sites that provided the raw materials for his highly organized and prescient examination of the bureaucratic transformations then occurring in American universities.[22] Frazier's and Veblen's oeuvres are, in effect, examples of qualitative research based on data acquired over the course of rich and varied life experiences. In these studies it is impossible to disentangle the method of study from either the theory employed or the person employing it. Such a method would appear to be the ultimate desideratum of ethnographic research.

The ethnographic orientation at the University of Chicago was given a new twist by William Foote Whyte. Whyte made what was designed to be formal research into part of his life experience and called it "participant observation." The Chicago Sociology Department provided Whyte with an opportunity to report, in *Street Corner Society* (1943a, 1955, 1981), his findings about Italian Americans residing in the North End of Boston. That work, initially motivated by a sense of moral responsibility to uplift the slum-dwelling masses, has become the exemplar of the techniques appropriate to participant observation research: Whyte lived in the Italian neighborhood and in many but not all ways became one of the "Cornerville" boys.[23] Although he presents his findings about Cornerville descriptively, Whyte's theoretical stance remains implicit. The book has an enigmatic quality, because Whyte presents his data from the perspective of his relationships with his subjects. That is, Whyte is as much a researcher as he is a subject in his own book; the other had become the brother of Italian ghetto dwellers.

Anthropology at the University of Chicago was also informed by a qualitative orientation. Until 1929, anthropology and ethnology at that university had been subsumed under "historical sociology" in a department called the Department of Social Science and Anthropology. Anthropological and ethnological studies were at first directed by Frederick A. Starr, formerly head of ethnology at the American Museum of Natural History (Diner, 1975). Starr became a Japanophile after his first trip to Japan, while he was on assignment to bring a few of the Ainu people to be displayed, like Ota Benga, at the St. Louis World's Fair in 1904 (Statler, 1983, pp. 237-255). A separate Department of Anthropology was established in 1929, but, unlike Starr's, it reflected the orientation developed by the sociologists W. I. Thomas and Ellsworth Faris (see Faris, 1970, p. 16). One year before the advent of the new department, Robert Redfield presented his dissertation, *A Plan for the Study of Tepoztlan, Mexico* (1928). Borrowing from Tonnies's (1887/1957) dichotomous paradigm, gemeinschaft-gesellschaft, and drawing upon Von Wiese's and Becker's (1950/1962, 1932/ 1974) sacred-secular continuum, Redfield asserted the virtues of "the folk culture" and what he would later call "the little community" (Redfield, 1962, pp. 143-144; see also Redfield, 1930, 1941, 1960, 1950/ 1962b; Redfield & Rojas, 1934/1962a).

Regarding the metropolis as a congeries of unhappy and unfulfilled others, Redfield stood opposed to the values associated with urban life and industrial civilization. He extolled the lifestyles of those nonindustrial peoples and small communities that had resisted incorporation into the globally emerging metropolitan world. In his final essay, written in 1958, the year of his death, describing an imaginary conversation with a man from outer space, Redfield (1963) abjured the condition of mutually assured destruction that characterized the Cold War, despaired of halting the march of technocentric progress, conflated the pastoral with the premodern, and concluded by lamenting the rise of noncommunal life in the metropolitan city. Redfield's orientation, Rousseauean in its ethos, would provide a generation of anthropologists with a rustic outlook—a postmissionary attitude that sought to preserve and protect the lifeways of the primitive. His was the antiurban variant of Puritanism, a point of view that held small-scale, face-to-face communities to be superior to all others. To those ethnologists who followed in the ideological footsteps of Redfield, these communal values seemed representative of primordial humanity.[24]

A counterimage to that of ethnography's romance with small-town, communitarian and primordial values of primitivism was offered in 1958 when Arthur J. Vidich and Joseph Bensman published their ethnographic account of "Springdale," a rural community in Upstate New York.[25] As their title forewarned, this was a "small town in mass society." [26] Its situation, moreover, was typical of other American towns. Springdale's much-vaunted localism, its claims to societal, economic, and political autonomy, were illusions of a bygone era. Their "central concern," the authors observed in their introduction to a revised edition released 10 years after the original publication of their monograph, "was with the processes by which the small town (and indirectly all segments of American society) are continuously and increasingly drawn into the central machinery, processes and dynamics of the total society" (Vidich & Bensman, 1968, p. xi).

In so presenting their findings, Vidich and Bensman reversed the direction and exploded what was left of the mythology attendant upon the gemeinschaft-gesellschaft (Parsons, 1937/1949, 1973) and folk-urban continua in American sociological thought (Duncan, 1957; Firey, Loomis, & Beegle, 1950; Miner, 1952). Although the theoretical significance of their study was often neglected in the wake of the controversy that arose over its publication and the charge that they had not done enough to conceal the identities of the town's leading citizens (Vidich & Bensman, 1968, pp. 397-476), their concluding observations—namely, that there had occurred a middle-class revolution in America, that the rise and predominance of the new middle classes had altered the character and culture of both the cities and towns of America, and that "governmental, business, religious and educational super-bureaucracies far distant from the rural town formulate policies to which the rural world can respond only with resentment" (p. 323; see also Bensman & Vidich, 1987)—challenged the older paradigms guiding field research on community life.

By 1963, Roland L. Warren would take note of what he called "the 'great change' in American communities" and point out how a developing division of labor, the increasing differentiation of interests and associations, the growing systemic relations to the larger society, a transfer of local functions to profit enterprises and to state and federal governments, urbanization and suburbanization, and the shifts in values that were both cause and consequences of these changes had been accompanied by a "corresponding decline in community cohesion and autonomy" (see Warren, 1972, pp. 53-94). In effect, community ethnography would not only have to adjust to the encroachment of the city and the suburb on the town, but also enlarge its outlook to embrace the effects of the state and the national political economy on the towns and villages of the Third World as well as of the United States (see, e.g., the ethnographies collected in Toland, 1993; see also Marcus, 1986). ("The point is," Maurice Stein [1964] observed in his reflection on nearly six decades of American community studies, "that both the student of the slum and of the suburb [and, he might have added, the small town] require some sort of total picture of the evolution of

66

American communities and of emerging constellations and converging problems"; p. 230. Had the practitioners of American community studies taken their point of departure from Otto von Gierke's, 1868/1990, or Friedrich Ratzel's, 1876/1988, orientations, they might have been more critical of the "Rousseauean" variant of Tonnies's outlook from the beginning of their research. See McKinney, 1957.)[27]

◆ The Ethnography of Assimilation: The Other Remains an Other

A breakdown in another fundamental paradigm affected the ethnographic study of ethnic and racial minorities. Until the 1960s, much of the sociological outlook on race and ethnic relations had focused on the processes and progress of assimilation, acculturation, and amalgamation among America's multiverse of peoples. Guided by the cluster of ideas and notions surrounding the ideology of the "melting pot," as well as by the prediction of the eventual assimilation of everyone that accompanied the widely held understanding of Robert E. Park's theory of the racial cycle, ethnographers of America's many minority groups at first sought to chart each people's location on a continuum that began with "contact," passed consecutively through stages of "competition and conflict" and "accommodation," and eventually culminated in "assimilation" (for critical evaluations of Park's cycle, see Lyman, 1972, 1990b, 1992b). Although by 1937 Park had come to despair of his earlier assertion that the cycle was progressive and irreversible (see Park, 1937/1969b), his students and followers would not give up their quest for a pattern and process that promised to bring an ultimate and beneficent end to interracial relations and their attendant problems.

When the ethnic histories of particular peoples in the United States seemed to defy the unidirectional movement entailed in Park's projected sequence—for example, when Etzioni's (1959) restudy of the Jewish ghetto showed little evidence that either religion or custom would be obliterated, even after many years of settlement in America; when Lee's (1960) discovery that Chinatowns and their old world-centered institutions persisted despite a decline in Sinophobic prejudices; when Woods's (1972) careful depiction of how 10 generations of settlement in America had failed to erode either the traditions or the ethnoracial identity of a marginalized people, the Letoyant Creoles of Louisiana (see also Woods, 1956); and,

67

more generally, when Kramer (1970) had documented the many variations in minority community adaptation in America—there arose a cacophony of voices lamenting the failure of assimilation and calling for a resurgence of WASP hegemony (Brookhiser, 1991, 1993), or expressing grave apprehension about America's ethnocultural future (Christopher, 1989; Schlesinger, 1991; Schrag, 1973).

Even before popularizers and publicists announced the coming of an era in which there would be a "decline of the WASP" (Schrag, 1970) and a rise of the "unmeltable ethnics" (Novak, 1972), some sociologists had begun to reexamine their assumptions about ethnicity in America and to rethink their own and their predecessors' findings on the matter. In 1952, Nathan Glazer caused Marcus Lee Hansen's (1938/1952) hitherto overlooked work on the "law of third generation return" to be republished,[28] sparking a renewed interest in documenting whether, how, and to what extent the grandchildren of immigrants retained, reintroduced, rediscovered, or invented the customs of their old-world forebears in modern America (Kivisto & Blanck, 1990). Stanford M. Lyman (1974, 1986) combined participant observation with documentary and historical analyses to show that the solidarity and persistence over time of territorially based Chinatowns was related in great measure to persistent intracommunity conflict and to the web of traditional group affiliations that engendered both loyalty and altercation. Kramer and Leventman (1961) provided a picture of conflict resolution among three generations of American Jews who had retained many but not all aspects of their ethnoreligious traditions despite, or perhaps because of, the fact that the third generation had become "children of the gilded ghetto." Richard Alba (1985, 1989, 1990) reopened the questions of whether and how European ethnic survival had occurred in the United States, pointing to the several dimensions of its presentation, representation, and disintegration, and carrying out, once more, a study of Italian Americans, a group often chosen by sociologists for ethnographic studies seeking to support, oppose, modify, or reformulate the original assimilation thesis (see, e.g., Covello, 1967; Gans, 1962; Garbaccia, 1984; Landesco, 1968; Lopreato, 1970; Tricarico, 1984; Whyte, 1943a, 1943b).

The reconsideration of assimilation theory in general and Park's race relations cycle in particular produced a methodological critique so telling that it cast doubt on the substance of that hypothesis. In 1950, Seymour Martin Lipset observed that "by their very nature, hypotheses about the inevitability of cycles, whether they be cycles of race relations or the rise and fall of civilization, are not testable at all" (p. 479). Earlier, some ethnographers of racial minority groups in America had attempted to construct lengthier or alternative cycles that would be able to accommodate the findings of their field investigations. Bogardus's (1930, 1940; Ross & Bogardus, 1940) three distinctive cycles for California's diversified Japanese communities and Masuoka's (1946) warning that three generations would be required for the acculturation of Japanese in America and that the third generation would still be victims of "a genuine race problem" evidence the growing disappointment with assimilation's promise. Others, including W. O. Brown (1934), Clarence E. Glick (1955), Stanley Lieberson (1961), and Graham C. Kinloch (1974, pp. 205-209) came to conclusions similar to that of Park's 1937 reformulation—namely, that assimilation was but one possible outcome of sustained interracial contact, and that isolation, subordination, nationalist or nativist movements, and secession ought also to be considered.

Those seeking to rescue the discredited determinism of Park's original cycle from its empirically minded critics turned to policy proposals or hortatory appeals in its behalf. Wirth (1945) urged the adoption of programs that would alleviate the frustration experienced by members of minority groups who had been repeatedly rebuffed in their attempts to be incorporated within a democratic America; Lee (1960, pp. 429-430) converted her uncritical adherence to Park's prophecy into a plaintive plea that Chinese ghetto dwellers live up to it—that is, that they assimilate themselves as rapidly as possible (see also Lyman, 1961-1962, 1963). Still others resolved the ontological and epistemological problems in Park's cycle by treating it as a "logical" rather than "empirical" perspective. Frazier (1953) suggested that, rather than occurring chronologically, the stages in the theory might be spatiotemporally coexistent: "They represent logical steps in a systematic sociological analysis of the subject." Shibutani and Kwan (1965), after examining the many studies of integrative and disintegrative social processes in racial and ethnic communities, concurred, holding that although there were many exceptions to its validity as a descriptive theory, Park's stages provided a "useful way of ordering data on the manner in which immigrants become incorporated into an already-established society" (see pp. 116-135). Geschwender (1978) went further, holding that Park's race relations cycle was "an abstract model of an 'ideal type' sequence which might develop" (p. 25).

In 1918, Edward Byron Reuter had defined America's race issue as "the problem of arriving at and maintaining mutually satisfactory working relations between members of two nonassimilable groups which occupy

69

the same territory" (Reuter, 1918/1969, p. 18). After a half century of sociological studies had seemed to demonstrate that virtually none of the racial or ethnic groups had traversed the cyclical pathway to complete assimilation, America's race problem seemed not only to be immense, but also to have defied as well as defined the basic problematic of sociological theory. Such, at any rate, was the position taken by the ethnological anthropologist Brewton Berry (1963), whose field investigations would eventually include studies of various peoples in Latin America as well as several communities of previously unabsorbed racial hybrids in the United States (see also Lyman, 1964). Having shown that none of the proposed cycles of race relations could claim universal validity on the basis of available evidence, Berry and Tischler (1978) observed, "Some scholars . . . question the existence of any universal pattern, and incline rather to the belief that so numerous and so various are the components that enter into race relations that each situation is unique, and [that] the making of generalizations is a hazardous procedure" (p. 156). Berry's thesis, though not necessarily intended in this direction, set the tone for the subsequent plethora of ethnographies that offered little in the way of theoretical advancements but much more of the detail of everyday life among minorities and other human groups.

During the two decades after 1970, ethnological studies of African American, Amerindian, Mexican American, and Asian peoples also cast considerable doubt on whether, when, and to whose benefit the much-vaunted process of ethnocultural meltdown in America would occur. Ethnographies and linguistic studies of black enclaves, North and South, slave and free, suggested that the tools employed in earlier community analyses had not been honed sufficiently for sociologists to be able to discern the cultural styles and social practices that set African American life apart from that of other segments of the society (see, e.g., Abrahams, 1964, 1970, 1992; E. Anderson, 1978; Bigham, 1987; Blassingame, 1979; Duneier, 1992; Evans & Lee, 1990; Joyner, 1984; Liebow, 1967; for an overview, see Blackwell, 1991). Other critics observed that sociological studies of the "American dilemma" had paid insufficient attention to politics, civil rights, and history (Boxhill, 1992; Button, 1989; Jackson, 1991; Lyman, 1972; V. J. Williams, 1989). Anthropological studies of the culture-preserving and supposedly isolated Native American nations and tribes had to give way in the face of a rising ethnoracial consciousness (Cornell, 1988; Martin, 1987; Sando, 1992), selective demands for the return of Amerindian museum holdings (Berlo, 1992; Clifford, 1990;

Messenger, 1991; Milson, 1991-1992; "A Museum Is Set," 1993), Indian recourse to American courts in quest of redress and treaty rights (see T. L. Anderson, 1992; Jaimes, 1992), and political alliances and the tracing of ethnohistorical descent that would connect Amerindians with Hispanics, African Americans, and Jews (Forbes, 1973, 1988; Gutierrez, 1991; Tobias, 1990; Vigil, 1980). Mexican American studies moved from early historical institutional studies through ethnographies of farmworkers, and in the 1980s became part of the new postmodernist revolution.[29] To the Amerasian peoples conventionally treated by ethnographic sociologists— namely, the Chinese and Japanese—were added more recent arrivals, including Koreans, Thais, Vietnamese, Cambodians, Laotians, and the Hmong (see, e.g., Chan, 1991; Hune et al., 1991; Knoll, 1982; Nomura et al., 1989; Okihiro et al., 1988; Takaki, 1989). And, as in the instance of Mexican American ethnographers, a shift in issues and methods is beginning to emerge—moving away from debates about whether and how to measure assimilation and acculturation and toward such postmodern topics as the character, content, and implications of racial discourse about Asians in America (e.g., K. J. Anderson, 1991; Okihiro, 1988). As East Indians, Burmese, Oceanians, Malaysians, and other peoples of what used to be called "the Orient" began to claim common cause with the earlier-established Asian groups (Espiritu, 1992; Ignacio, 1976; Mangiafico, 1988), but insisted on each people's sociocultural and historical integrity, as well as the right of each to choose its own path within U.S. society, it became clear that the trend toward ethnographic postmodernism would continue (see, e.g., Hune et al., 1991; Leonard, 1992).

In 1980, Harvard University Press issued its mammoth *Harvard Encyclopedia of American Ethnic Groups* (Thernstrom, 1980), a work that includes not only separate entries for "Africans" and "Afro-Americans" but also individual essays devoted to each of 173 different tribes of American Indians and reports on each of the Asian peoples coming to the United States from virtually all the lands east of Suez. Harold J. Abrahamson's entry, "Assimilation and Pluralism," in effect announces American sociology's awakening not only from its dream of the eventual assimilation of every people in the country, but also from its conflation of assimilation with Americanization: "American society . . . is revealed as a composite not only of many ethnic backgrounds but also of many different ethnic responses. . . . There is no one single response or adaptation. The variety of styles in pluralism and assimilation suggest that ethnicity is as complex as life itself" (p. 160; see also Gleason, 1980; Novak, 1980; Walzer, 1980).

71

For the moment, pluralism had won its way onto paradigmatic center stage.[30] But even that orientation did not exhaust the possibilities or dispose of the problems arising out of the presence of diverse races and peoples in America. In 1993, together with Rita Jalali, Seymour Martin Lipset, who had criticized Park's formulation of an inevitable cycle leading to assimilation four decades earlier, observed that "race and ethnicity provide the most striking example of a general failure among experts to anticipate social developments in varying types of societies" (Jalali & Lipset, 1992-1993, p. 585). Moreover, the celebration of pluralism that now prevails in social thought obscures recognition of a fundamental problem: the self-restraint to be placed upon the competitive claims put forward by each ethnic and racial group.

◆ Ethnography Now: The Postmodern Challenge

Historically, the ethnographic method has been used by both anthropologists and sociologists. The guiding frameworks for those who have used this method in the past have all but been abandoned by contemporary ethnographers. The social-historical transformations of society and consciousness in the modern world have undermined the theoretical and value foundations of the older ethnography.

With the present abandonment of virtually every facet of what might now be recognized as the interlocked, secular, eschatological legacies of Comte, Tönnies, Wissler, Redfield, Park, and Parsons—that is, the recognition that the "comparative method" and the anthropology of primitivism is inherently flawed by both its Eurocentric bias and its methodological inadequacies; the determination that the gemeinschaft of the little community has been subverted by the overwhelming force of the national political economy of the gesellschaft; the discovery that assimilation is not inevitable; and the realization that ethnic sodalities and the ghettos persist over long periods of time (sometimes combining deeply embedded internal disharmonies with an outward display of sociocultural solidarity, other times existing as "ghost nations," or as hollow shells of claimed ethnocultural distinctiveness masking an acculturation that has already eroded whatever elementary forms of existence gave primordial validity to that claim, or, finally, as semiarticulated assertions of a peoplehood that has moved through and "beyond the melting pot" without having been fully dissolved in its fiery cauldron)—ethnography and ethnology could emerge on their own terms.[31]

No longer would ethnography have to serve the interests of a theory of progress that pointed toward the breakup of every ethnos. No longer would ethnology have to describe the pastoral peacefulness, proclaim the moral superiority, or document the psychic security supposed to be found in the villages of the nonliterate, the folk societies of non-Western peoples, the little communities of the woods and forests, the small towns of America, or the urban ethnic enclaves of U.S. or world metropolises. No longer would ethnography have to chart the exact position of each traditional and ascriptively based status group as it moved down the socioculturally determined pathway that would eventually take it into a mass, class, or civil society, and recompose it in the process.

Liberated from these conceptual and theoretical constraints, ethnography and ethnology are, for the first time as it were, in a position to act out their own versions of the revolution of "life" against "the forms of life"—a cultural revolution of the twentieth century that Simmel (1968) foresaw as both imminent and tragic. Just as Simmel predicted that the cultural revolutionaries that he saw emerging in pre-World War I Europe would oppose both marriage and prostitution on the grounds that each was a form of the erotic and that they wished to emancipate the erotic from all forms of itself, so the new ethnographers proclaim themselves to be self-liberated from the weight of historical consciousness, relieved of the anxiety of influence (see Bloom, 1979),[32] and, in effect, content to become witnesses to and reporters of the myriad scenes in the quixotic world that has emerged out of the ruins of both religion and secular social theory (see Kundera, 1988).

The proclamation of ethnography as a self-defining orientation and practice in sociology and anthropology and the importation of the postmodernist outlook into it took place recently, irregularly, and in somewhat disorderly moves. Aleksandr Solzhenitsyn (1993) once pointed out that "no new work of art comes into existence (whether consciously or unconsciously) without an organic link to what was created earlier" (p. 3). Such also remains the case in social science, as will be shown with the new developments in sociological and anthropological ethnography.

One beginning of the emancipatory movement in ethnographic methodology is to be found in Peter Manning's seminal essay, "Analytic Induction" (1982/1991). Seeking to set ethnography on an even firmer foundation of the symbolic interactionist perspective and hoping to reinforce its connections to the classical period of the "Chicago school," Manning sought first to warn any practitioners of the sociological enterprise against employing any "concepts and theories developed to deal with the problems of such other disciplines as behavioristic psychology, economics, medicine, or the natural or physical sciences." He identified analytic induction as a procedure derivable from George Herbert Mead's and Florian Znaniecki's writings on scientific method, and he observed that it had been employed with greater or lesser precision by such classical Chicago ethnographers as Thomas and Znaniecki, and, later, by Robert Cooley Angell, Alfred Lindesmith, and Donald Cressey. Distinguishable from deductive, historical-documentary, and statistical approaches, analytic induction was "a nonexperimental qualitative sociological method that employs an exhaustive examination of cases in order to prove universal, causal generalizations." The case method was to be the critical foundation of a revitalized qualitative sociology.

The claim to universality of the causal generalizations is—in the example offered by Manning as exemplary of the method[33]—the weakest, for it is derived from the examination of a single case studied in light of a preformulated hypothesis that might be reformulated if the hypothesis does not fit the facts. And "practical certainty" of the (reformulated) hypothesis is obtained "after a small number of cases has been examined." Discovery of a single negative case is held to disprove the hypothesis and to require its reformulation. After "certainty" has been attained, "for purposes of proof, cases outside the area circumscribed by the definition are examined to determine whether or not the final hypothesis applies to them." If it does, it is implied, there is something wrong with the hypothesis, for "scientific generalizations consist of descriptions of conditions which are always present when the phenomenon is present but which are never present when the phenomenon is absent." The two keys to the entire procedure, Manning points out, are the definition of the phenomenon under investigation and the formulation of the tentative hypothesis. Ultimately, however, as Manning concedes, despite its aim, analytic induction does not live up to the scientific demand that its theories "understand, predict, and control events." After a careful and thoroughgoing critique of the procedure he has chosen over its methodological competitors, Manning asserts, "Analytic induction is not a means of prediction; it does not clearly establish causality; and it probably cannot endure a principled examination of its claims to [be] making universal statements." Indeed, Manning goes further, pointing out that, "according to the most demanding ideal standards of the discipline, analytic induction as a distinctive, philosophical, methodological perspective is less powerful than either enumerative induction or axiomatic-modelling methods." Manning's essay seems about to eject a method intrinsic to ethnography from the scientific community.

Manning's frank appraisal of the weaknesses of analytic induction is "drawn from a positivistic, deductive model of the scientific endeavor, a model seizing on a selected group of concerns." The proponents of that model seek to set the terms and limits of the social sciences according to its criteria. In fact, though few American scholars seem to know much about either the long history or the irresolution of debates over epistemological matters in the social sciences, the very issues of those debates are central to the questions the positivists are raising (see, in this regard, Rorty, 1982, pp. 191-210).

In his defense of analytic induction, Manning invokes an unacknowledged earlier critique by Sorokin (1965), namely, "that what is taken to be [appropriate] methodology at a given time is subject to fads, fashions, and foibles." Manning goes on to credit analytic induction with being a "viable source of data and concepts" and with helping investigators to sort out "the particulars of a given event [and to distinguish them from] those things that are general and theoretical." Erving Goffman, surely a sociological practitioner whose methodological orientation is akin to but not the same as analytic induction, goes even further, however. Opposing, in a defense of his own brand of ethnographic sociology, both system building and enumerative induction, in 1961 he wrote, "At present, if sociological concepts are to be treated with affection, each must be traced back to where it best applies, followed from there wherever it seems to lead, and pressed to disclose the rest of its family. Better, perhaps, different coats to clothe the children well than a single splendid tent in which they all shiver" (p. xiv). A decade later, Goffman (1971) dismissed the scientific claims of positivistic sociologists altogether: "A sort of sympathetic magic seems to be involved, the assumption being that if you go through the motions attributable to science then science will result. But it hasn't" (p. xvi).

With the waning of interest in, support for, or faith in the older purposes for doing ethnology, by the 1970s there had also arisen a concomitant discontent with the epistemological claims as well as the latent or secretive political usages—(see Diamond, 1992; Horowitz, 1967)—of the mainstream perspectives of both sociology—(see Vidich, Lyman, & Goldfarb, 1981)—and anthropology—(e.g., Clifford & Marcus, 1986; Fox, 1991; Manganaro, 1990). An outlook that could be used to carry out research projects and at the same time to treat the very resources of each discipline as a topic to be investigated critically was needed. Postmodernism appeared and seemed to fill that need.

Toward the end of his essay, Manning hints at the issue that would explode on the pages of almost every effort to come to terms with postwar and post-Cold War America: "In an age of existentialism, self-construction is as much a part of sociological method as theory construction." What he would later perceive as a reason for developing a formalistic and semiotic approach to doing fieldwork (Manning, 1987, pp. 7-24, 66-72) was that each construction would come to be seen as inextricably bound up with the other and that each would be said to provide a distorted mirror image of both the body (Cornwell, 1992; Featherstone, Hepworth, & Turner, 1991; Feher, 1989; Sheets-Johnstone, 1990, pp. 112-133; 1992) and the self (Kotarba & Fontana, 1987; Krieger, 1991; Zaner, 1981), of both one's *Umwelt* and the world of the other (the concept of *Umwelt* is developed by Gurwitsch, 1966). But for those who accepted the critique but rejected neoformalism as a technique for ethnography, there opened up a new field of investigation—representation. Hence some of the best postmodern ethnography has focused on the media that give imagery to real life (Bhabha, 1990b; Early, 1993; Gilman, 1991; Trinh, 1991). Justification for turning from the fields of lived experience to what is represented as such is the assumption that the former is itself perceived holographically, calling for the thematization of representation as a problem in the construction of "persuasive fictions" (Baudrillard, 1988a, pp. 27-106; Norris, 1990).

The postmodern ethnographer takes Simmel's tragedy of culture to be a fait accompli: It is not possible at the present time to emancipate free-floating life from all of its constraining forms (Strathern, 1990). The postmodern sociologist-ethnographer and his or her subjects are situated in a world suspended between illusory memories of a lost innocence and millennial dreams of a utopia unlikely to be realized. From such a position, not only is the standpoint of the investigator problematic (Lemert, 1992; Weinstein & Weinstein, 1991), but also that of the people to be investigated. Each person has in effect been "touched by the mass media, by alienation, by the economy, by the new family and child-care systems, by the unceasing technologizing of the social world, and by the threat of nuclear annihilation" (Denzin, 1989, p. 139). And, if the anthropologist-ethnographer is to proceed in accordance with the postmodern perspective, he or she must, on the one hand, become less fearful about "going primitive" (Torgovnick, 1990) and, on the other, contend with the claim that Eurocentric imagery has attended virtually all previous reports from the "primitive" world (Beverly, 1992; Bhabha, 1990a; Dirlik, 1987; Turner, 1992; West, 1992). For these ethnographers, Helmut Kuzmics (1988) observes, "The claim that the 'evolutionary gradualism' of the theory of civilization renders it incapable of explaining the simultaneous appearance of civilization (in a narrower sense than is presupposed by the highest values of the Enlightenment) and 'barbarism' still needs to be confronted more thoroughly" (p. 161).

As analytic induction advocates propose, let us begin with a definition of the new outlook—the postmodern. Charlene Spretnak (1991), a critic of much of the postmodernism she surveys, provides one that is comprehensive and useful:

A sense of detachment, displacement, and shallow engagement dominates deconstructive-postmodern aesthetics because groundlessness is the only constant recognized by this sensibility. The world is considered to be a repressive labyrinth of "social production," a construction of pseudoselves who are pushed and pulled by cultural dynamics and subtly diffused "regimes of power." Values and ethics are deemed arbitrary, as is "history," which is viewed by deconstructive postmodernists as one group or another's self-serving selection of facts. Rejecting all "metanarratives," or supposedly universal representations of reality, deconstructive postmodernists insist that the making of every aspect of human existence is culturally created and determined in particular, localized circumstances about which no generalizations can be made. Even particularized meaning, however, is regarded as relative and temporary. (pp. 13-14)

Spretnak's definition permits us to see how the postmodern ethnographer proceeds. The postmodernist ethnographer enters into a world from which he or she is methodologically required to have become detached and displaced. Such an ethnographer is in effect reconstituted as Simmel's (1950) "stranger" (see also Frisby, 1992) and Park's (1929/1969a) and Stonequist's (1937/1961) "marginalized" person (see also Wood, 1934/1969, pp. 245-284). Like those ideal-typical ethnographers-in-spite-of-themselves, this social scientist begins work as a self-defined newcomer to the habitat and life world of his or her subjects (see Agar, 1980; Georges & Jones, 1980; D. Rose, 1989). He or she is a citizen-scholar (Saxton, 1993) as well as a participant observer (Vidich, 1955). Older traditions and aims of ethnography, including especially the quest for valid generalizations and substantive conclusions, are temporarily set aside in behalf of securing "thick descriptions" (Geertz, 1973) that will in turn make possible "thick interpretations"—joining ethnography to both biography and lived experience (Denzin, 1989, pp. 32-34). History is banished from the ethnographic enterprise except when and to the effect that local folk histories enter into the vocabularies of motive and conduct employed by the subjects.[34] Because crossing the postmodern divide (Borgmann, 1992; I. Chambers, 1990) requires one to abandon all established and preconceived values, theories, perspectives, preferences, and prejudices as resources for ethnographic study, the ethnographer must bracket these, treating them as if they are arbitrary and contingent rather then hegemonic and guiding (Rosenau, 1992, pp. 25-76). Hence the postmodernist ethnographer takes seriously the aim of such deconstructionists as Derrida (e.g., 1976, 1981), Lyotard (e.g., 1989), and Baudrillard (e.g., 1981, 1983, 1988b), namely, to disprivilege all received texts and established discourses in behalf of an all-encompassing critical skepticism about knowledge. In so doing, the ethnographer displaces and deconstructs his or her own place on the hierarchy of statuses that all too often disguise their invidious character as dichotomies (see Bendix & Berger, 1959; for a postmodern analysis of a dichotomy, see Lyman, 1992a). To all of these, instead, is given contingency—the contingencies of language, of selfhood, and of community (Rorty, 1989; C. Taylor, 1989).

For anthropologists, the new forms for ethnography begin with a recognition of their irreducible limitation: the very presentation of ethnographic information in a monograph is a "text" and therefore subject to the entire critical apparatus that the postmodern perspective brings to bear on any text.[35] The ethnographic enterprise is to be conceived as a task undertaken all too often by an unacculturated stranger who is guided by whatever the uneasy mix of poetry and politics gives to his or her efforts to comprehend an alien culture. Above all, an ethnography is now to be regarded as a piece of writing—as such, it cannot be said either to present or to represent what the older and newly discredited ideology of former ethnography claimed for itself: an unmodified and unfiltered record of immediate experience and an accurate portrait of the culture of the "other."

The postmodern critique has engendered something of a crisis among present-day anthropologists. As in the response to other crises, a new self-and-other consciousness has come to the fore, and the imperatives of reflexivity have shifted attention onto the literary, political, and historical features of ethnography as well as onto career imperatives, all of which have hitherto been overlooked. Engaging themselves with these issues, such disciplinary leaders as Clifford Geertz, Mary Douglas, Claude Lévi-Strauss, and the late Victor Turner have blurred the old distinction between art and science and challenged the very basis of the claim to exacting rigor, unblinking truth telling, and unbiased reporting that marked the boundary separating one from the other.

Rereading the works in the classical ethnographic canon has now become a critical task of the highest importance. A new form of structuralist method must be devised if we are to dig beneath the works and uncover both their hidden truths and their limiting blinders. That canon is now to be seen as a product of the age of Occidental colonialism and to have been methodologically constrained by the metropole ideologies and literary conventions that gave voice and quality to them. Yet these ethnographies are not to be relegated to the historical dustbin of a rejectable epoch of disciplinary childhood by today's and tomorrow's anthropologists. Rather, in consideration of the fact that few of the latter will follow career trajectories like those of Malinowski or Powdermaker—that is, either spending decades of their lives in residence with a nonliterate Oceanic people or moving from the ethnographic task of observing at close range a group of South Africans to another, living among blacks in a segregated Mississippi town, and then to still another, closely examining how the Hollywood film industry became a "dream factory"—the ethnologist of the present age and the immediate future is likely to do but one ethnography—a dissertation that stakes his or her claim to the title of ethnologist and to the perquisites of an academic life spent largely away from the field. Moreover, career considerations are not the only element affecting ethnology. The "field" itself has become constricted by the march of decolonization and the modernization that has overtaken once "primitive" peoples. For these reasons, rereading old ethnographies becomes a vicarious way to experience the original ways of the discipline, whereas criticizing them provides the ethnologist with a way to distance him- or herself from modernist foibles. Except for the dissertation ethnography and for those anthropologists who choose to move in on the turf of the equally postmodern sociological ethnographers of urban and industrial settings, the ethnographic task of anthropology may become one devoted to reading texts and writing critiques. The "field" may be located in one's library or one's study.

Given the postmodern ethnographers' epistemological stance and disprivileged social status, two fundamental problems for the sociological version of the new ethnography are its relationship to social change and social action, and the applicable scope of its representations of reality.

The first problem has been posed as well as answered by Michael Burawoy et al. (1992) in their conception of "ethnography unbound" and the role of the "extended case method." They direct the ethnographer toward the macropolitical, economic, and historical contexts in which directly observed events occur, and perceive in the latter fundamental issues of domination and resistance (see also Feagin, Orum, & Sjoberg, 1991). Norman Denzin (1989), a leader of postmodern approaches to ethnography, approaches the generality issue in two distinct though related ways. His advice to ethnographers is that they first immerse themselves in the lives of their subjects and, after achieving a deep understanding of these through rigorous effort, produce a contextualized reproduction and interpretation of the stories told by the subjects. Ultimately, an ethnographic report will present an integrated synthesis of experience and theory. The "final interpretive theory is multivoiced and dialogical. It builds on native interpretations and in fact simply articulates what is implicit in those interpretations" (p. 120). Denzin's strategic move out of the epistemological cul-de-sac presented by such daunting observations as Berry's specific skepticism about the possibility of making valid generalizations in an ethnoracially pluralist society, or by the growing skepticism about the kind and quality of results that sociologists' adherence to positivistic and natural science models will engender (T. R. Vaughan, 1993, p. 120), is to take the onset of the postmodern condition as the very occasion for presenting a new kind of ethnography. He encourages, in effect, an ethnographic attitude of engagement with a world that is ontologically absurd but always meaningful to those who live in it (see Lyman & Scott, 1989). Thus he concludes his methodological treatise by claiming that the world has now entered its Fourth Epoch (following Antiquity, the Middle Ages, and the Modern Age), and that this latest epoch is in fact the "postmodern period" (Denzin, 1989, p. 138). The ethnographic method appropriate to this period, Denzin goes on, is one that is dedicated "to understanding how this historical moment universalizes itself in the lives of interesting individuals" (p. 189). Method and substance are joined in the common recognition that everyone shares in the same world and responds to it somehow. The study of the common condition and the uncovering of the uncommon response become the warp and woof of the fragile but not threadbare sociological skein of the postmodern era.

The postmodern is a cultural form as well as an era of history. As the former, like all the forms noted by Simmel, it invites and evokes its counteracting and rebellious tendencies. It too, then, is likely to suffer the penultimate tragedy of culture—the inability to emancipate life from all of its forms (Weinstein & Weinstein, 1990). However, in this era, the sociologist-ethnographer will not merely observe that history; he or she will participate in its everlasting quest for freedom, and be a partner in and a reporter on "the pains, the agonies, the emotional experiences, the small and large victories, the traumas, the fears, the anxieties, the dreams, fantasies and the hopes" of the lives of the peoples. These constitute this era's ethnographies—true tales of the field (Van Maanen, 1988).

The methods of ethnography have become highly refined and diverse, and the reasons for doing ethnography have multiplied. No longer linked to the values that had guided and focused the work of earlier ethnographers, the new ethnography ranges over a vastly expanded subject matter, limited only by the varieties of experience in modern life; the points of view from which ethnographic observations may be made are as great as the choices of lifestyles available in modern society. It is our hope that the technological refinement of the ethnographic method will find its vindication in the discovery of new sets of problems that lead to a greater understanding of the modern world.

Although it is true that at some level all research is a uniquely individual enterprise—not part of a sacrosanct body of accumulating knowledge—it is also true that it is always guided by values that are not unique to the investigator: We are all creatures of our own social and cultural pasts. However, in order to be meaningful to others, the uniqueness of our own research experience gains significance when it is related to the theories of our predecessors and the research of our contemporaries. Social and cultural understanding can be found by ethnographers only if they are aware of the sources of the ideas that motivate them and are willing to confront them—with all that such a confrontation entails.

Notes

1. For a discussion of the fundamental similarities between so-called quantitative and qualitative methods, see Vidich and Bensman (1968, chap. 13).

2. Here we merely gloss a serious problem in the philosophy and epistemology of the social sciences and present one possible approach to it. Some of the issues are discussed and debated in such recent works as those by C. W. Smith (1979), Rabinow and Sullivan (1979), G. Morgan (1983), Fiske and Schweder (1986), Hare and Blumberg (1988), Ashmore (1989), Minnich (1990), Bohman (1991), Sadri (1992, pp. 3-32, 105-142), and Harré (1984).

3. Many of the issues raised by this new outlook are treated in the essays collected in A. Rose (1988).

4. The following draws on Lyman (1990a).

5. This orientation differs from that used by Thucydides (1972) in *History of the Peloponnesian War*. His observations were made from the perspective of a participant who detached himself from the norms of both warring sides while never making explicit his own values. His book has confounded legions of scholars who have attempted to find his underlying themes, not understanding that the work is replete with ambiguities that do not lend themselves to a single viewpoint. For various perspectives on Thucydides' work, see Kitto (1991, pp. 136-152), Kluckhohn (1961, pp. 4, 34-35, 55, 64-66), Humphreys (1978, pp. 94, 131, 143, 227-232, 300-307), and Grant (1992, pp. 5, 45, 148-149).

6. When discussing the crimes committed by the Spaniards against the Indians, Hosle (1992) states: "It is certainly not easy to answer the following question: Were the priests who accompanied the conquistadors also responsible, even if they condemned the violence committed, insofar as their presence in a certain sense legitimized the enterprise? It is impossible to deny that by their mere presence they contributed to Christianity appearing as an extremely hypocritical religion, which spoke of universal love and nevertheless was the religion of brutal criminals. Yet it is clear that without the missionaries' presence even more cruelties would have been committed. Hypocrisy at least acknowledges in theory certain norms, and by so doing gives the oppressed the possibility to claim certain rights. Open brutality may be more sincere, but sincerity is not the only value. Sincere brutality generates nothing positive; hypocrisy, on the other side, bears in itself the force which can overcome it" (p. 236). If it does anything, Hosle's defense of Christianity reveals the difficulty still remaining in debates over universalistic as opposed to relativistic values and leaves wide open any resolution of the problem. See also Lippy, Choquette, and Poole (1992). For further history and discussion of the de Las Casas-Sepulveda dispute and its implications for ethnohistory and ethnology of the Americas, see Hanke (1949/1965, 1959/1970, 1974).

7. A fine example is the ethnographic study by Bishop Robert Henry Codrington (1891) titled *The Melanesians*. Codrington's study provided the sole source for Yale University anthropologist Loomis Havemeyer's (1929) chapter on the Melanesians (pp. 141-160). See Codrington (1974) for an excerpt from *The Melanesians* titled "Mana." See also the critical discussion in Kuper (1988, pp. 152-170).

8. A good example that also illustrates the anthropologists' despair over the disastrous effects of missionary endeavor on native life and culture is to be found in the last published work of William Hale R. Rivers (1922/1974).

9. Thus if the reader wishes to peruse one well-known exposition of "primitive" culture, George Peter Murdock's (1934) *Our Primitive Contemporaries,* as an example of one aspect of the "comparative method," he or she will discover therein ethnographies of 18 peoples who occupy time and space coincident to that of the author, arranged in terms

of geography, but—with the term *primitive* as the descriptive adjective in use throughout—making the title of the book historically (that is, diachronically) oxymoronic. For a thoughtful critique, see Bock (1966).

10. Two exceptions to this mode of ethnocentric expression are worthy of note: William Graham Sumner (1840-1910), who coined the term *ethnocentrism,* seemed also to suggest that the failure of either Congress or the courts to do anything to halt the lynching of Negroes in the South signaled something less than that nation's rise to perfected civilization that other ethnologists were willing to credit to America and to other republics of the Occident: "It is unseemly that anyone should be burned at the stake in a modern civilized state" (Sumner, 1906/1940, p. 471; see also Sumner, 1905/1969). Thorstein Veblen (1857-1929) used such categories as "savagery" and "barbarism" tongue-in-cheek, often treating the moral codes and pecuniary values of the peoples so labeled as superior to those of the peoples adhering to the Protestant ethic or the spirit of capitalism, and disputing the claims of Aryan superiority so much in vogue in his day (see Veblen, 1899/1959, 1914/1990, 1919/1961a, 1919/1961b; see also A. K. Davis, 1980; Diggins, 1978; Tilman, 1991).

11. The Human Relations Area Files were reproduced, marketed, and distributed to anthropology departments in other universities. This not only added an element of standardization and uniformity to culture studies, but also made it possible for the analyst of ethnography to forgo a trip to the field. That this approach is still in vogue is illustrated by two researches by the Harvard sociologist Orlando Patterson (1982). Patterson relies on Murdock's "World Sample" of 61 slaveholding societies (out of a total of 186 societies), which are arranged geographically, but rearranges them temporally to make them serve a developmentalist thesis that seeks to uncover the variations in as well as the functional origins of slavery. On the basis of this method, it is not surprising to find that in the sequel to his study Patterson (1991) believes he can show that "the Tupinamba, the ancient Greeks and Romans, and the southerners of the United States, *so markedly different in time, place, and levels of sociocultural development,* nonetheless reveal the remarkable tenacity of this culture-character complex" (p. 15; emphasis added).

12. For the conceptualization of a sector of the world's peoples as belonging to the Third World, as well as for the conceptualization of "developed" and "undeveloped" or "underdeveloped" societies, see Worsley (1964, 1984).

13. That capitalism had contributed to underdevelopment in both the European overseas empires and America's homegrown "ghetto colonialism" became an assumption and even an article of faith that could shape the perspective of posttraditional ethnography (see Blauner, 1972; Marable, 1983; see also Hechter, 1975).

14. For a historical view on eschatological, millennial, sacred, and secular "end-times" theories, as well as other modes of chronologizing events, see Paolo Rossi (1987).

15. It should be noted that American ethnography up to the beginnings of World War II focused almost exclusively on American Indians and the aboriginal inhabitants of American colonies. Anthropologists' interests in the high cultures of Central and South America were archaeologically oriented and were designed both to fill in the "prehistoric record" and to fill museums. Some ethnographic work was carried out in the U.S.-controlled Pacific Islands (in association with the Bernice P. Bishop Museum in Hawaii). Margaret Mead worked on American Samoa and is one of the earliest of the nonmissionaries to ethnograph a Pacific Island. Her work, aimed in part at criticizing the Puritanical sexual mores of America, overstated the actual situation in Oceania and eventually led to a counterstatement

(see Freeman, 1983; Holmes, 1987; Mead, 1928/1960a, 1930/1960b, 1949/1960c, 1935/1960d).

16. This was the same perspective used by anthropologists who administered the Japanese relocation centers during World War II and who had had some of their training on the reservation. For accounts by those anthropologists who moved from Amerindian to Japanese American incarceration ethnography and administration, see Leighton (1945), Wax (1971), Spicer, Hansen, Luomala, and Opler (1969), and Myer (1971). For a spirited critique, see Drinnon (1987).

17. For some representative ethnographies of the southwestern Amerindian peoples, see Schwatka (1893/1977), Nordenskiold (1893/1979), McGee (1899/1971), Goddard (1913/1976), White (1933/1974), Spier (1933/1978), and Kluckhohn (1944). See also Eggan (1966, pp. 112-141).

18. A recent ethnography of the Zuni by Tedlock (1992) both reflects upon and critically appraises Cushing's work among that tribe.

19. Radin (1935/1970, 1936/1971a) also did fieldwork among the Italians and Chinese of San Francisco.

20. Clark Wissler (1940/1966a, 1938/1966b) established his credentials on the basis of a lifetime in service to ethnohistorical and ethnographic study of the United States.

21. Although not carried out at the University of Chicago, this study bears the stamp of that school's approach.

22. In that report, he was the first to see the new role of the university president as an administrative "Captain of Erudition," the beginnings of university public relations designed to protect the image of learning, and the business foundations in real estate and fund-raising (endowments) of the university system in the United States.

23. In 1992, when new questions were raised about the ethnocultural and ethical aspects of Whyte's study of "Cornerville," a symposium reviewed the matter extensively (see "*Street Corner Society* Revisited," 1992).

24. A social variant of Redfield's perspective found its way into some of the urban community, ethnic enclave, and small-town studies of America that were conducted or supervised by anthropologists or Chicago sociologists (see Hannerz, 1980; Lyon, 1987; Suttles, 1972, pp. 3-20). (A revival of ecological studies rooted in the idea that the uses of space are socially constructed was begun with the publication of Lyman & Scott, 1967; see also Ericksen, 1980.) As early as 1914, M. C. Elmer, a promising graduate student at the University of Chicago, had written a Ph.D. dissertation on social surveys in urban communities that reflected the shift from the church to the "scientific" survey tradition in both the social gospel movement and the discipline of sociology; seven years later, Raleigh Webster Stone (1921) in effect signaled that the transition to a newer orientation was well under way when he offered *The Origin of the Survey Movement* as his Ph.D. dissertation at Chicago. In 1933, Albert Bailie Blumenthal submitted *A Sociological Study of a Small Town* as his doctoral dissertation at the same university (Faris, 1970, pp. 135-140). However, the central thrust of ethnological studies in Chicago's sociology department after Robert E. Park had joined its faculty concerned community and subcommunity organization within the city (see, e.g., N. Anderson, 1959), and, for some, how the gemeinschaft could be reconstituted in the metropolis (see Fishman, 1977; Quandt, 1970).

25. That ethnographies of small towns and large cities adopted an approach more or less consistent with the macropolitical-economic orientation emphasized by Vidich and

Bensman is evidenced in works by P. Davis (1982), Wallace (1987), Arsenault (1988), Campbell (1992), Moorhouse (1988), and Reid (1992).

26. Earlier, Vidich (1952, 1980) had contributed to the reconsideration of anthropological approaches to so-called primitive societies, reconceiving such studies as requiring an orientation that focused on the effects of global colonialism and its rivalries on the structure and process of colonialized societies. For the connections between his anthropological study of Palau under various colonial administrations and the study of "Springdale," see Vidich (1986).

27. British approaches to the historical sociology of small towns did not adopt Tönnies's theoretical stance (see, e.g., Abrams & Wrigley, 1979).

28. See also Glazer (1954). "Hansen's law" was the basis for work by Kennedy (1944) and Herberg (1960).

29. For monographs illustrating the stages in the evolution of these studies, see Blackman (1891/1976), P. S. Taylor (1930/1970, 1983), Gamio (1930/1969, 1931/1971), Bogardus (1934/1970), and Galarza (1964, 1970, 1977). For community studies in New Mexico, see Gonzalez (1967), Sanchez (1967), and Forrest (1989). For Arizona, see Sheridan (1986); for Texas, see Rubel (1971); for Indiana, see Lane and Escobar (1987); for Chicago, see Padilla (1985). For general and historical studies, see Burma (1985), Officer (1987), and D. J. Weber (1992). For the shift from eth-class to postmodern analysis, see Barrera (1979, 1988).

30. Subsequent works (e.g., Fuchs, 1990; Keyes, 1982; Kivisto, 1984, 1989; Lieberson, 1980; Lieberson & Waters, 1988; Royce, 1982; Steinberg, 1981; Waters, 1990) emphasized pluralism, contingency, and the voluntary and social constructionist aspects of race and ethnicity.

31. In anthropology, the shift toward a new outlook included a critical reevaluation and commentary on virtually every aspect of ethnology and ethnography in what has thus far produced seven volumes of essays edited by George W. Stocking, Jr. (1983, 1984, 1985, 1986, 1988, 1989, 1991). A turn toward the classics of antiquity and their relation to modern and postmodern anthropology was appraised by Redfield's son (see J. Redfield, 1991).

32. One element of intellectual and moral influence has given rise to anxiety, recriminations, and rhetorical attempts to excuse, justify, or escape from the burden it lays on those who believe that postmodernism is a countercultural orientation of the Left, namely, the accusation that its preeminent philosophical founders—Heidegger and de Man—were sympathetic to and supporters of the Hitler regime and Nazism. For debates on this far-from-resolved issue, see Habermas (1983), Farias (1989), Neske and Kettering (1990), Ferry and Renaut (1990), Lyotard (1990), Rockmore (1992), Derrida (1992), Hamacher, Hertz, and Keenan (1989), and Lehman (1992). Another important contributor to postmodernism, Michel Foucault, has aroused apprehension over the extent to which his sexual preferences and promiscuous lifestyle affected his philosophical perspective. For various opinions on the matter, see Poster (1987-1988), Foucault (1992), Eribon (1991), Miller (1993); and Nikolinakos (1990). See also Paglia (1991).

33. The procedural example used by Manning is from Cressey (1953, p. 16).

34. For a discussion of the several issues involved in the relationship of history to ethnography, see Comaroff and Comaroff (1992); compare Natanson (1962).

35. The following draws on the essays and commentaries in Clifford and Marcus (1986).

◆ References

Abeyesekere, G. (1992). *The apotheosis of Captain Cook: European mythmaking in the Pacific.* Princeton, NJ: Princeton University Press.

Abrahams, R. D. (1964). *Deep down in the jungle: Negro narrative folklore from the streets of Philadelphia.* Hatboro, PA: Folklore Associates.

Abrahams, R. D. (1970). *Positively black.* Englewood Cliffs, NJ: Prentice Hall.

Abrahams, R. D. (1992). *Singing the master: The emergence of African American culture in the plantation South.* New York: Pantheon.

Abrahamson, H. J. (1980). Assimilation and pluralism. In S. Thernstrom (Ed.), *Harvard encyclopedia of American ethnic groups.* Cambridge, MA: Harvard University Press.

Abrams, P., & Wrigley, E. A. (Eds.). (1979). *Towns and societies: Essays in economic history and historical sociology.* Cambridge: Cambridge University Press.

Adler, P. A., Adler, P., & Fontana, A. (1987). Everyday life sociology. In K. Plummer (Ed.), *Symbolic interactionism: Vol. 1. Foundations and history* (pp. 436-454). Brookfield, VT: Edward Elgar.

Agar, M. H. (1980). *The professional stranger: An informal introduction to ethnography.* New York: Academic Press.

Alba, R. (1985). *Italian Americans: Into the twilight of ethnicity.* Englewood Cliffs, NJ: Prentice Hall.

Alba, R. (Ed.). (1989). *Ethnicity and race in the U.S.A.: Toward the twenty-first century.* New York: Routledge, Chapman Hall.

Alba, R. (1990). *Ethnic identity: The transformation of white America.* New Haven, CT: Yale University Press.

Aldrich, R. (1990). *The French presence in the South Pacific, 1842-1940.* Honolulu: University of Hawaii Press.

Anderson, E. (1978). *A place on the corner.* Chicago: University of Chicago Press.

Anderson, K. J. (1991). *Vancouver's Chinatown: Racial discourse in Canada, 1875-1980.* Montreal: McGill-Queen's University Press.

Anderson, N. (1959). *The urban community: A world perspective.* New York: Henry Holt.

Anderson, N. (1961). *The hobo: The sociology of the homeless man.* Chicago: University of Chicago Press. (Original work published 1923)

Anderson, T. L. (Ed.). (1992). *Property rights and Indian economics.* Lanham, MD: Rowman & Littlefield.

Arsenault, R. (1988). *St. Petersburg and the Florida dream, 1888-1950.* Norfolk, VA: Donning.

Ashmore, M. (1989). *The reflexive thesis: Writing sociology of scientific knowledge.* Chicago: University of Chicago Press.

Atkinson, P. A. (1990). *The ethnographic imagination: Textual constructions of reality.* London: Routledge.

Bailey, B. L. (1988). *From front porch to back seat: Courtship in twentieth century America.* Baltimore: Johns Hopkins University Press.

Baker, J. R. (1974). *Race.* New York: Oxford University Press.

Ball, D. W. (1968). Toward a sociology of telephones and telephoners. In M. Truzzi (Ed.), *Sociology and everyday life* (pp. 59-75). Englewood Cliffs, NJ: Prentice Hall.

Barkan, E. (1992). *The retreat of scientific racism: Changing concepts of race in Britain and the United States*. Cambridge: Cambridge University Press.

Barrera, M. (1979). *Race and class in the Southwest: A theory of racial inequality*. Notre Dame, IN: University of Notre Dame Press.

Barrera, M. (1988). *Beyond Aztlan: Ethnic autonomy in comparative perspective*. Notre Dame, IN: University of Notre Dame Press.

Baudrillard, J. (1981). *For a critique of the political economy of the sign* (C. Levin, Trans.). St. Louis, MO: Telos.

Baudrillard, J. (1983). *In the shadow of the silent majorities, or, the end of the social and other essays* (P. Foss, J. Johnston, & P. Patton, Trans.). New York: Semiotext(e).

Baudrillard, J. (1988a). *America* (C. Turner, Trans.). London: Verso.

Baudrillard, J. (1988b). *The ecstasy of communication* (S. Lotringer, Ed.; B. Schutze & C. Schutze, Trans.). New York: Semiotext(e).

Becker, H. (1962). *Through values to social interpretation: Essays on social contexts, actions, types, and prospects*. New York: Greenwood. (Original work published 1950)

Becker, H. (1974). *Systematic sociology: On the basis of the Beziehungslehre and Begildlehre of Leopold von Wiese*. New York: Arno. (Original work published 1932)

Bender, T. (1978). *Community and social change in America*. New Brunswick, NJ: Rutgers University Press.

Bendix, R., & Berger, B. (1959). Images of society and problems of concept formation in sociology. In L. Gross (Ed.), *Symposium on sociological theory* (pp. 92-118). Evanston, IL: Row, Peterson.

Bensman, J., & Vidich, A. J. (1987). *American society: The welfare state and beyond* (2nd ed.). Amherst, MA: Bergin & Garvey.

Berlo, J. C. (Ed.). (1992). *The early years of Native American art history: The politics of scholarship and collecting*. Seattle: University of Washington Press.

Berry, B. (1963). *Almost white*. New York: Macmillan.

Berry, B., & Tischler, H. (1978). *Race and ethnic relations* (4th ed.). Boston: Houghton Mifflin.

Beverly, J. (1992). The margin at the center: On *testimonio* (testimonial narrative). In S. Smith & J. Watson (Eds.), *De/colonizing the subject: The politics of gender in women's autobiography*. Minneapolis: University of Minnesota Press.

Bhabha, H. K. (Ed.). (1990a). *Nation and narration*. London: Routledge.

Bhabha, H. K. (1990b). The other question: Differences, discrimination and the discourse of colonialism. In R. Ferguson et al. (Eds.), *Out there: Marginalization and contemporary cultures* (pp. 71-88). Cambridge: MIT Press.

Bieder, R. E. (1989). *Science encounters the Indian, 1820-1880: The early years of American ethnology*. Norman: University of Oklahoma Press.

Bigham, D. E. (1987). *We ask only a fair trial: A history of the black community of Evansville, Indiana*. Bloomington: Indiana University Press/University of Southern Indiana.

Blackman, F. M. (1976). *Spanish institutions of the Southwest*. Glorieta, NM: Rio Grande. (Original work published 1891)

Blackwell, J. E. (1991). *The black community: Diversity and unity* (3rd ed.). New York: HarperCollins.

Blake, C. N. (1990). *Beloved community: The cultural criticism of Randolph Bourne, Van Wyck Brooks, Waldo Frank, and Lewis Mumford.* Chapel Hill: University of North Carolina Press.

Blassingame, J. W. (1979). *The slave community: Plantation life in the antebellum South* (rev. ed.). New York: Oxford University Press.

Blauner, R. (1972). *Racial oppression in America.* New York: Harper & Row.

Bloom, H. (1979). *The anxiety of influence: A theory of poetry.* London: Oxford University Press.

Blumenthal, A. B. (1933). *A sociological study of a small town.* Unpublished doctoral dissertation, University of Chicago.

Bock, K. E. (1948). *The comparative method.* Unpublished doctoral dissertation, University of California, Berkeley.

Bock, K. E. (1952). Evolution and historical process. *American Anthropologist, 54,* 486-496.

Bock, K. E. (1956). *The acceptance of histories: Toward a perspective for social science.* Berkeley: University of California Press.

Bock, K. E. (1963). Evolution, function and change. *American Sociological Review, 27,* 229-237.

Bock, K. E. (1966). The comparative method of anthropology. *Comparative Studies in Society and History, 8,* 269-280.

Bock, K. E. (1974). Comparison of histories: The contribution of Henry Maine. *Comparative Studies in Society and History, 16,* 232-262.

Boeke, J. H. (1946). *The evolution of the Netherlands Indies economy.* New York: Institute of Pacific Relations.

Boeke, J. H. (1948). *The interests of the voiceless Far East: Introduction to Oriental economics.* Leiden, Netherlands: Universitaire Pers Leiden.

Bogardus, E. S. (1930). A race relations cycle. *American Journal of Sociology, 35,* 612-617.

Bogardus, E. S. (1940). Current problems of Japanese Americans. *Sociology and Social Research, 25,* 63-66.

Bogardus, E. S. (1970). *The Mexican in the United States.* New York: Arno/New York Times. (Original work published 1934)

Bohman, J. (1991). *New philosophy of social science.* Cambridge: MIT Press.

Borgmann, A. (1992). *Crossing the postmodern divide.* Chicago: University of Chicago Press.

Boxer, C. R. (1965). *Portuguese society in the tropics: The municipal councils of Goa, Macao, Bahia, and Luanda.* Madison: University of Wisconsin Press.

Boxhill, B. R. (1992). *Blacks and social justice* (rev. ed.). Lanham, MD: Rowman & Littlefield.

Bradford, P. V., & Blume, H. (1992). *Ota Benga: The Pygmy in the zoo.* New York: St. Martin's.

Brookhiser, R. (1991). *The way of the WASP: How it made America, and how it can save it, so to speak.* New York: Free Press.

Brookhiser, R. (1993, March 1). The melting pot is still simmering. *Time,* p. 72.

Brown, R. (1984). *The nature of social laws: Machiavelli to Mill.* Cambridge: Cambridge University Press.

Brown, W. O. (1934). Culture contact and race conflict. In E. B. Reuter (Ed.), *Race and culture contacts* (pp. 34-47). New York: McGraw-Hill.

Bowden, H. W. (1981). *American Indians and Christian missions: Studies in cultural conflict.* Chicago: University of Chicago Press.

Burawoy, M., Burton, A., Ferguson, A. A., Fox, K. J., Gamson, J., Gartrell, N., Hurst, L., Kurzman, C., Salzinger, L., Schiffman, J., & Ui, S. (Eds.) (1992). *Ethnography unbound: Power and resistance in the modern metropolis.* Berkeley: University of California Press.

Burgess, E. W. (1916). The social survey: A field for constructive service by departments of sociology. *American Journal of Sociology, 21,* 492-500.

Burgess, E. W., & Bogue, D. J. (Eds.). (1967). *Contributions to urban sociology.* Chicago: University of Chicago Press.

Burma, J. H. (Ed.). (1985). *Mexican-Americans in comparative perspective.* Washington, DC: Urban Institute.

Button, J. W. (1989). *Blacks and social change: Impact of the civil rights movement in southern communities.* Princeton, NJ: Princeton University Press.

Calloway, C. G. (Ed.). (1991). *Dawnland encounters: Indians and Europeans in northern New England.* Hanover, NH: University Press of New England.

Campbell, W. D. (1992). *Providence.* Atlanta, GA: Longstreet.

Caplow, T., Bahr, H. M., Chadwick, B. A., Hill, R., & Williamson, M. H. (1982). *Middletown families: Fifty years of change and continuity.* Minneapolis: University of Minnesota Press.

Caplow, T., Bahr, H. M., Chadwick, B. A., Hill, R., & Williamson, M. H. (1983). *All faithful people: Change and continuity in Middletown's religion.* Minneapolis: University of Minnesota Press.

Cavan, R. S. (1965). *Suicide.* New York: Russell & Russell. (Original work published 1928)

Chambers, C. A. (1971). *Paul U. Kellogg and the survey: Voices for social welfare and social justice.* Minneapolis: University of Minnesota Press.

Chambers, I. (1990). *Border dialogues: Journeys into postmodernity.* London: Routledge.

Chan, S. (1991). *Asian Americans: An interpretive history.* Boston: Twayne.

Cherokee Nation v. Georgia, 30 U.S. (5 Pet.) 1 (1831).

Christopher, R. C. (1989). *Crashing the gates: The de-WASPing of America's power elite.* New York: Simon & Schuster.

Clifford, J. (1986). On ethnographic self-fashioning: Conrad and Malinowski. In T. C. Heller, M. Sosna, & D. E. Wellbery (Eds.), *Reconstructing individualism: Autonomy, individuality, and the self in Western thought* (pp. 140-162). Stanford, CA: Stanford University Press.

Clifford, J. (1990). On collecting art and culture. In R. Ferguson et al. (Eds.). *Out there: Marginalization and contemporary cultures* (pp. 1-169). Cambridge: MIT Press.

Codrington, R. H. (1891). *The Melanesians.* Oxford: Clarendon.

Codrington, R. H. (1974). Mana. In A. Montagu (Ed.), *Frontiers of anthropology* (pp. 255-259). New York: G. P. Putnam's Sons. (Reprinted from *The Melanesians,* Oxford: Clarendon, 1891)

Cohen, S. R. (1981). *Reconciling industrial conflict and democracy: The Pittsburgh survey and the growth of social research in the United States.* Unpublished doctoral dissertation, Columbia University.

Coleman, M. C. (1985). *Presbyterian missionary attitudes toward American Indians, 1837-1893.* Jackson: University Press of Mississippi.

Comaroff, J., & Comaroff, J. (1992). *Ethnography and the historical imagination.* Boulder, CO: Westview.

Contosta, D. R. (1980). *Henry Adams and the American experiment.* Boston: Little, Brown.

Cornell, S. (1988). The transformation of tribe: Organization and self-concept in Native American ethnicities. *Ethnic and Racial Studies, 11,* 27-47.

Cornwell, R. (1992). Interactive art: Touching the "body in the mind." *Discourse: Journal for Theoretical Studies in Media and Culture, 14,* 203-221.

Covello, L. (1967). The social background of the Italo-American school child: A study of the southern Italian family mores and their effect on the school situation in Italy and America (F. Cordesco, Ed.). Leiden, Netherlands: E. J. Brill.

Cressey, D. (1953). *Other people's money.* New York: Free Press.

Culin, S. (1967). Zuni pictures. In E. C. Parsons (Ed.), *American Indian life* (pp. 175-178). Lincoln: University of Nebraska Press. (Original work published 1922)

Cushing, F. H. (1974). *Zuni breadstuff.* New York: Museum of the American Indian, Keye Foundation. (Original work published 1920)

Cushing, F. H. (1979). *Zuni: Selected writings of Frank Hamilton Cushing* (J. Green, Ed.). Lincoln: University of Nebraska Press.

Cushing, F. H. (1988). *Zuni folk tales.* Tucson: University of Arizona Press. (Original work published 1901)

Cushing, F. H. (1990). *Cushing at Zuni: The correspondence and journals of Frank Hamilton Cushing, 1878-1884* (J. Green, Ed.). Albuquerque: University of New Mexico Press.

Dai, B. (1970). *Opium addiction in Chicago.* Montclair, NJ: Patterson Smith. (Original work published 1937)

Dale, E. E. (1984). *The Indians of the Southwest: A century of development under the United States.* Norman: University of Oklahoma Press. (Original work published 1949)

Dansereau, H. K. (1961). Some implications of modern highways for community ecology. In G. A. Theodorsen (Ed.), *Studies in human ecology* (pp. 175-187). Evanston, IL: Row, Peterson.

Davis, A. K. (1980). *Thorstein Veblen's social theory.* New York: Arno.

Davis, P. (1982). *Hometown: A contemporary American chronicle.* New York: Simon & Schuster.

de Sola Poole, I. (Ed.). (1981). *The social impact of the telephone.* Cambridge: MIT Press.

Degerando, J.-M. (1969). *The observation of savage peoples* (F. C. T. Moore, Trans.). London: Routledge & Kegan Paul. (Original work published 1800)

Denzin, N. (1989). *Interpretive interactionism.* Newbury Park, CA: Sage.

Derrida, J. (1976). *Of grammatology* (G. C. Spivak, Trans.). Baltimore: Johns Hopkins University Press.

Derrida, J. (1981). *Positions* (A. Bass, Trans.). Chicago: University of Chicago Press.

Derrida, J. (1992). *The other heading: Reflections on today's Europe* (P.-A. Brault & M. B. Naas, Trans.). Bloomington: Indiana University Press.

Diamond, S. (1963). The search for the primitive. In I. Goldston (Ed.), *Man's image in medicine and anthropology* (pp. 62-115). New York: International University Press.

Diamond, S. (1972). Anthropology in question. In D. Hymes (Ed.), *Reinventing anthropology* (pp. 401-429). New York: Pantheon.

Diamond, S. (1992). *Compromised campus: The collaboration of universities with the intelligence community, 1945-1955*. New York: Oxford University Press.

Diggins, J. P. (1978). *The bard of savagery: Thorstein Veblen and modern social theory*. New York: Seabury.

Diner, S. J. (1975). Department and discipline: The Department of Sociology at the University of Chicago, 1892-1920. *Minerva, 13,* 518-519, 538.

Dirlik, A. (1987). Culturalism as hegemonic ideology and liberating practice. *Cultural Critique, 6,* 13-50.

Dockstader, F. J. (1985). *The Kachina and the white man: The influences of white culture on the Hopi Kachina religion* (rev. ed.). Albuquerque: University of New Mexico Press.

Douglas, J. (1974). A brief history of sociologists of everyday life. In J. Douglas et al. (Eds.), *Introduction to the sociologies of everyday life* (pp. 182-210). Boston: Allyn & Bacon.

Drake, S. C., & Cayton, H. R. (1962). *Black metropolis: A study of Negro life in a northern city* (rev. ed., Vols. 1-2). New York: Harper Torchbooks.

Drinnon, R. (1987). *Keeper of concentration camps: Dillon S. Myer and American racism*. Berkeley: University of California Press.

Du Bois, W. E. B. (1967). *The Philadelphia Negro: A social study*. New York: Benjamin Blom. (Original work published 1899)

Duffy, J. (1959). *Portuguese Africa*. Cambridge, MA: Harvard University Press.

Duncan, O. D. (1957). Community size and the rural-urban continuum. In P. K. Hatt & A. J. Reiss, Jr. (Eds.), *Cities and society: The revised reader in urban sociology* (pp. 35-45). Glencoe, IL: Free Press.

Duneier, M. (1992). *Slim's table: Race, respectability, and masculinity*. Chicago: University of Chicago Press.

Early, G. (Ed.). (1993). *Lure and loathing: Essays on race, identity, and the ambivalence of assimilation*. New York: Allen Lane/Penguin.

Eggan, F. (1966). *The American Indian: Perspectives for the study of social change* (The Lewis Henry Morgan Lectures). Cambridge: Cambridge University Press.

Elmer, M. C. (1914). *Social surveys of urban communities*. Unpublished doctoral dissertation, University of Chicago.

Engels, F. (1884). *The origins of the family, private property and the state*. Moscow: Foreign Languages.

Eribon, D. (1991). *Michel Foucault* (B. Wing, Trans.). Cambridge, MA: Harvard University Press.

Ericksen, E. G. (1980). *The territorial experience: Human ecology as symbolic interaction*. Austin: University of Texas Press.

Espiritu, Y. L. (1992). *Asian American panethnicity: Bridging institutions and identities*. Philadelphia: Temple University Press.

Etzioni, A. (1959). The ghetto: A re-evaluation. *Social Forces, 37,* 255-262.

Evans, A. S., & Lee, D. (1990). *Pearl City, Florida: A black community remembers*. Boca Raton: Florida Atlantic University Press.

Farias, V. (1989). *Heidegger and Nazism* (J. Margolis & T. Rickmore, Eds.; P. Burrell & G. Ricci, Trans.). Philadelphia: Temple University Press.

Faris, R. E. L. (1970). *Chicago sociology, 1920-1932*. Chicago: University of Chicago Press.

Faris, R. E. L., & Dunham, H. W. (1965). *Mental disorders in urban areas: An ecological study of schizophrenia and other psychoses*. Chicago: University of Chicago Press. (Original work published 1939)

Feagin, J. R., Orum, A., & Sjoberg, G. (1991). The present crisis in U.S. sociology. In J. R. Feagin, A. M. Orum, & G. Sjoberg, *A case for the case study* (pp. 269-278). Chapel Hill: University of North Carolina Press.

Featherstone, M., Hepworth, M., & Turner, B. S. (Eds.). (1991). *The body: Social process and cultural theory*. London: Sage.

Feher, M. (Ed.). (1989). *Fragments for a history of the human body* (Vols. 1-3). Cambridge: MIT Press/Zone.

Ferry, L., & Renaut, A. (1990). *Heidegger and modernity* (F. Philip, Trans.). Chicago: University of Chicago Press.

Firey, W., Loomis, C. P., & Beegle, J. A. (1950). The fusion of urban and rural. In J. Labatut & W. J. Lane (Eds.), *Highways in our national life: A symposium* (pp. 154-163). Princeton, NJ: Princeton University Press.

Fishman, R. (1977). *Urban utopias in the twentieth century: Ebenezer Howard, Frank Lloyd Wright, and Le Corbusier*. New York: Basic Books.

Fiske, D. W., & Schweder, R. A. (Eds.). (1986). *Metatheory in social science: Pluralism and subjectivities*. Chicago: University of Chicago Press.

Fontana, A. (1974). Toward a complex universe: Existential sociology. In J. Douglas et al. (Eds.), *Introduction to the sociologies of everyday life* (pp. 155-181). Boston: Allyn & Bacon.

Forbes, J. D. (1973). *Aztecs del norte: The Chicanos of Aztlan*. Greenwich, CT: Fawcett.

Forbes, J. D. (1988). *Black Africans and Native Americans: Color, race and caste in the evolution of red-black peoples*. New York: Basil Blackwell.

Forrest, S. (1989). *The preservation of the village: New Mexico's Hispanics and the New Deal*. Albuquerque: University of New Mexico Press.

Foucault, M. (1992). *Michel Foucault, philosopher* (T. J. Armstrong, Ed. & Trans.). New York: Routledge, Chapman & Hall.

Fox, R. G. (Ed.). (1991). *Recapturing anthropology: Working in the present*. Santa Fe, NM: School of American Research Press.

Frazier, E. F. (1925). Durham: Capital of the black middle class. In A. Locke (Ed.), *The new Negro* (pp. 333-340). New York: Albert & Charles Boni.

Frazier, E. F. (1931). *The Negro family in Chicago*. Unpublished doctoral dissertation, University of Chicago.

Frazier, E. F. (1937a). The impact of urban civilization upon Negro family life. *American Sociological Review, 2*, 609-618.

Frazier, E. F. (1937b). Negro Harlem: An ecological study. *American Journal of Sociology, 43*, 72-88.

Frazier, E. F. (1953). The theoretical structure of sociology and sociological research. *British Journal of Sociology, 4*, 292-311.

Frazier, E. F. (1957a). *Black bourgeoisie: The rise of a new middle class in the United States*. Glencoe, IL: Free Press/Falcon's Wing.

Frazier, E. F. (1957b). *The Negro in the United States* (rev. ed.). New York: Macmillan.

Frazier, E. F. (1963). *The Negro church in America*. New York: Schocken.

Frazier, E. F. (1966). *The Negro family in the United States* (rev. ed.). Chicago: University of Chicago Press/Phoenix. (Original work published 1939)

Frazier, E. F. (1967). *Negro youth at the crossways: Their personality development in the middle states.* New York: Schocken. (Original work published 1940)

Frazier, E. F. (1968). *E. Franklin Frazier on race relations: Selected papers* (G. F. Edwards, Ed.). Chicago: University of Chicago Press.

Freeman, D. (1983). *Margaret Mead and Samoa: The making and unmaking of an anthropological myth.* Cambridge, MA: Harvard University Press.

Frisby, D. (1992). *Simmel and since: Essays on Georg Simmel's social theory.* London: Routledge.

Fuchs, L. H. (1990). *The American kaleidoscope: Race, ethnicity, and the civic culture.* Hanover, NH: University Press of New England.

Fukuyama, F. (1992). *The end of history and the last man.* New York: Free Press.

Furnivall, J. S. (1948). *Colonial policy and practice: A comparative study of Burma and Netherlands India.* New York: New York University Press.

Galarza, E. (1964). *Merchants of labor: The Mexican bracero story—an account of the managed migration of Mexican farm workers in California, 1942-1960.* San Jose, CA: Rosicrucian.

Galarza, E. (1970). *Spiders in the house and workers in the field.* Notre Dame, IN: University of Notre Dame Press.

Galarza, E. (1977). *Farm workers and agri-business in California, 1947-1960.* Notre Dame, IN: University of Notre Dame Press.

Gamio, M. (1969). *Mexican immigration to the United States: A study of human migration and adjustment.* New York: Arno/New York Times. (Original work published 1930)

Gamio, M. (1971). *The life story of the Mexican immigrant: Autobiographic documents.* New York: Dover. (Original work published 1931)

Gans, H. J. (1962). *The urban villagers: Group and class in the life of Italian-Americans.* New York: Free Press.

Garbaccia, D. R. (1984). *From Sicily to Elizabeth Street: Housing and social change among Italian immigrants, 1880-1930.* Albany: State University of New York Press.

Geertz, C. (1973). Thick description: Toward an interpretive theory of culture. In C. Geertz, *The interpretation of cultures: Selected essays* (pp. 3-32). New York: Basic Books.

Gellner, E. (1979). Beyond truth and falsehood, or no method in my madness. In E. Gellner, *Spectacles and predicaments: Essays in social theory* (pp. 182-198). Cambridge: Cambridge University Press.

Georges, R. A., & Jones, M. O. (1980). *People studying people: The human element in fieldwork.* Berkeley: University of California Press.

Geschwender, J. A. (1978). *Racial stratification in America.* Dubuque, IA: William C. Brown.

Gilman, S. L. (1991). *Inscribing the other.* Lincoln: University of Nebraska Press.

Ginsburg, C. (1991). *Ecstasies: Deciphering the witches' sabbath* (R. Rosenthal, Trans.). New York: Pantheon.

Ginsburg, C. (1993). The European (re)discovery of the shamans. *London Review of Books, 15,* 2.

Gist, N. P., & Halbert, L. A. (1947). *Urban society* (2nd ed.). New York: Thomas Y. Crowell.

Glazer, G. (1954). Ethnic groups in America: From national culture to ideology. In M. Berger, T. Able, & C. H. Page (Eds.), *Freedom and control in modern society* (pp. 158-173). New York: D. Van Nostrand.

Gleason, P. (1980). American identity and Americanization. In S. Thernstrom (Ed.), *Harvard encyclopedia of American ethnic groups* (pp. 31-58). Cambridge, MA: Harvard University Press.

Glick, C. E. (1955). Social roles and social types in race relations. In W. A. Lind (Ed.), *Race relations in world perspective* (pp. 239-262). Honolulu: University of Hawaii Press.

Goddard, P. E. (1976). *Indians of the Southwest*. Glorieta, NM: Rio Grande. (Original work published 1913)

Goffman, E. (1949). *Some characteristics of response to depicted experience*. Master's thesis, University of Chicago.

Goffman, E. (1959). *The presentation of self in everyday life*. Garden City, NY: Doubleday.

Goffman, E. (1961). *Asylums: Essays on the social situation of mental patients and other inmates*. Garden City, NY: Doubleday.

Goffman, E. (1971). *Relations in public: Microstudies of the public order*. New York: Basic Books.

Goffman, E. (1974). Frame analysis: An essay on the organization of experience. New York: Harper Colophon.

Gonzalez, N. L. (1967). *The Spanish Americans of New Mexico: A heritage of pride*. Albuquerque: University of New Mexico Press.

Grant, M. (1992). *A social history of Greece and Rome*. New York: Charles Scribner's Sons.

Gray, J. (1970). The intellectual standing of different races and their respective opportunities for culture. In G. Spiller (Ed.), *Papers on inter-racial problems communicated to the First Universal Race Congress, University of London, July 26-29, 1911* (pp. 79-85). New York: Citadel. (Original work published 1911)

Greek, C. E. (1978). The social gospel movement and early American sociology, 1870-1915. *Graduate Faculty Journal of Sociology, 3*(1), 30-42.

Greek, C. E. (1992). *The religious roots of American sociology*. New York: Garland.

Gullick, J. M. (1956). *The story of early Kuala Lumpur*. Singapore: Donald Moore.

Gurwitsch, A. (1966). The last work of Edmund Husserl. In A. Gurwitsch, *Studies in phenomenology and psychology*. Evanston, IL: Northwestern University Press.

Gusfield, J. R. (1975). *Community: A critical response*. New York: Harper Colophon.

Gutierrez, R. A. (1991). *When Jesus came the corn mothers went away: Marriage, sexuality and power in New Mexico, 1500-1846*. Stanford, CA: Stanford University Press.

Gwertzman, B., & Kaufman, M. T. (Eds.). (1992). *The decline and fall of the Soviet empire*. New York: New York Times.

Habermas, J. (1983). Martin Heidegger: The great influence (1959). In J. Habermas, *Philosophical-political profiles* (F. G. Lawrence, Trans.) (pp. 53-60). Cambridge: MIT Press.

Hamacher, W., Hertz, N., & Keenan, T. (Eds.). (1989). *On Paul de Man's wartime journalism*. Lincoln: University of Nebraska Press.

Hammersley, M. (1992). *What's wrong with ethnography? Methodological explorations*. London: Routledge.

Hanke, L. (1965). *The Spanish struggle for justice in the conquest of America*. Boston: Little, Brown. (Original work published 1949)

Hanke, L. (1970). *Aristotle and the American Indians: A study in race prejudice in the modern world.* Bloomington: Indiana University Press. (Original work published 1959)

Hanke, L. (1974). *All mankind is one: A study of the disputation between Bartolome de Las Casas and Juan Gines de Sepulveda on the religious and intellectual capacity of the American Indians.* De Kalb: Northern Illinois University Press.

Hannerz, U. (1980). *Exploring the city: Inquiries toward an urban anthropology.* New York: Columbia University Press.

Hansen, M. L. (1952). The problem of the third generation immigrant. *Commentary, 14,* 492-500. (Original work published 1938)

Hare, A. P., & Blumberg, H. H. (1988). *Dramaturgical analysis of social interaction.* New York: Praeger.

Harré, R. (1980). *Social being: A theory for social psychology.* Totowa, NJ: Rowan & Littlefield.

Harré, R. (1984). *Personal being: A theory for individual psychology.* Cambridge, MA: Harvard University Press.

Hartland, E. S. (1969). *Primitive society: The beginnings of the family and the reckoning of descent.* New York: Harper & Row. (Original work published 1921)

Hartmann, E. G. (1967). *The movement to Americanize the immigrant.* New York: AMS. (Original work published 1948)

Havemeyer, L. (1929). *Ethnography.* Boston: Ginn.

Hechter, M. (1975). *Internal colonialism: The Celtic fringe in British national development, 1536-1966.* London: Routledge & Kegan Paul.

Heizer, R. F., & Kroeber, T. (Eds.). (1979). *Ishi the last Yahi: A documentary history.* Berkeley: University of California Press.

Herberg, W. (1960). *Protestant-Catholic-Jew: An essay in American religious sociology.* Garden City, NY: Doubleday.

Herskovitz, M. (1958). *The myth of the Negro past.* Boston: Beacon. (Original work published 1941)

Herskovitz, M. (1966). *The new world Negro: Selected papers in Afroamerican studies* (F. S. Herskovitz, Ed.). Bloomington: Indiana University Press.

Hill-Lubin, M. A. (1992). "Presence Africaine": A voice in the wilderness, a record of black kinship. In V. Y. Mudimbe (Ed.), *The surreptitious speech: Presence Africaine and the politics of otherness, 1947-1987* (pp. 157-173). Chicago: University of Chicago Press.

Hinsley, C. M., Jr. (1981). *Savages and scientists: The Smithsonian Institution and the development of American anthropology, 1846-1910.* Washington, DC: Smithsonian Institution Press.

Hodgen, M. T. (1936). *The doctrine of survivals: A chapter in the history of scientific method in the study of man.* London: Allenson.

Hodgen, M. T. (1964). *Early anthropology in the sixteenth and seventeenth centuries.* Philadelphia: University of Pennsylvania.

Hodgen, M. T. (1974). *Anthropology, history and cultural change.* Tucson: University of Arizona Press/Wenner-Gren Foundation for Anthropological Research.

Holden, A. C. (1970). *The settlement idea: A vision of social justice.* New York: Arno/New York Times. (Original work published 1922)

Hollingshead, A. B. (1961). *Elmtown's youth: The impact of social classes on adolescents.* New York: Science Editions. (Original work published 1949)

Holmes, L. D. (1987). *Quest for the real Samoa: The Mead/Freeman controversy and beyond.* South Hadley, MA: Bergin & Garvey.

Horowitz, I. L. (Ed.). (1967). *The rise and fall of Project Camelot: Studies in the relationship between social science and practical politics.* Cambridge: MIT Press.

Hosle, V. (1992). The Third World as a philosophical problem. *Social Research, 59,* 230-262.

Hughes, E. C. (1928). *A study of a secular institution: The Chicago Real Estate Board.* Unpublished doctoral dissertation, University of Chicago.

Humphreys, S. C. (1978). *Anthropology and the Greeks.* London: Routledge & Kegan Paul.

Hune, S., et al. (Eds.). (1991). *Asian Americans: Comparative and global perspectives.* Pullman: Washington State University Press.

Ignacio, L. F. (1976). *Asian Americans and Pacific Islanders (Is there such an ethnic group?).* San Jose, CA: Pilipino Development Associates.

Immigration Commission (W. P. Dillingham, Chair). (1970). *Immigrants in industry* (25 parts). New York: Arno/New York Times. (Original work published 1911)

Jackson, J. S. (Ed.). (1991). *Life in black America.* Newbury Park, CA: Sage.

Jaimes, M. E. (Ed.). (1992). *The state of Native America: Genocide, colonization and resistance.* Boston: South End.

Jalali, R., & Lipset, S. M. (1992-1993). Racial and ethnic conflicts: A global perspective. *Political Science Quarterly, 107*(4), 585-606.

Johnson, J. M. (1975). *Doing field research.* New York: Free Press.

Jones, J. (1992). *Soldiers of light and love: Northern teachers and Georgia blacks, 1865-1873.* Athens: University of Georgia Press.

Joyner, C. (1984). *Down by the riverside: A South Carolina slave community.* Urbana: University of Illinois Press.

Keegan, W. F. (1992). *The people who discovered Columbus: The prehistory of the Bahamas.* Gainesville: University Press of Florida.

Keller, R. W., Jr. (1983). *American Protestantism and United States Indian policy, 1869-1882.* Lincoln: University of Nebraska Press.

Kennedy, R. J. R. (1944). Single or triple melting pot: Intermarriage trends in New Haven, 1870-1940. *American Journal of Sociology, 44,* 331-339.

Keyes, C. F. (Ed.). (1982). *Ethnic change.* Seattle: University of Washington Press.

Kinloch, G. C. (1974). *The dynamics of race relations.* New York: McGraw-Hill.

Kitto, H. D. F. (1951). *The Greeks.* London: Penguin.

Kivisto, P. (1984). *Immigrant socialists in the United States: The case of Finns and the Left.* Cranbury, NJ: Associates University Presses.

Kivisto, P. (Ed.). (1989). *The ethnic enigma: The salience of ethnicity for European-origin groups.* Philadelphia: Balch Institute Press.

Kivisto, P., & Blanck, D. (Eds.). (1990). *American immigrants and their generations: Studies and commentaries on the Hansen thesis after fifty years.* Urbana: University of Illinois Press.

Kluckhohn, C. (1944). *Navajo witchcraft.* Boston: Beacon.

Kluckhohn, C. (1961). *Anthropology and the classics: The Colver Lectures in Brown University, 1960.* Providence, RI: Brown University Press.

Knoll, T. (1982). *Becoming Americans: Asian sojourners, immigrants and refugees in the western United States.* Portland, OR: Coast to Coast.

Kotarba, J. A., & Fontana, A. (Eds.). (1987). *The existential self in society.* Chicago: University of Chicago Press.

Kramer, J. R. (1970). *The American minority community.* New York: Thomas Y. Crowell.

Kramer, J. R., & Leventman, S. (1961). *Children of the gilded ghetto: Conflict resolutions of three generations of American Jews.* New Haven, CT: Yale University Press.

Krieger, S. (1991). *Social science and the self: Personal essays as an art form.* New Brunswick, NJ: Rutgers University Press.

Kroeber, T. (1962). *Ishi in two worlds: A biography of the last wild Indian in North America.* Berkeley: University of California Press.

Kroeber, T. (1965). *Ishi: Last of his tribe.* New York: Bantam.

Kundera, M. (1988). *The art of the novel* (L. Ascher, Trans.). New York: Grove.

Kuper, A. (1988). *The invention of primitive society: Transformations of an illusion.* London: Routledge.

Kuzmics, H. (1988). The civilizing process (H. G. Zilian, Trans.). In J. Keane (Ed.), *Civil society and the state: New European perspectives.* London: Verso.

Landesco, J. (1968). *Organized crime in Chicago* (Part 3 of the Illinois Crime Survey, 1929). Chicago: University of Chicago Press.

Lane, J. B., & Escobar, E. J. (Eds.). (1987). *Forging a community: The Latino experience in Northwest Indiana, 1919-1975.* Chicago: Cattails.

Lee, R. H. (1960). *The Chinese in the United States of America.* Hong Kong: Hong Kong University Press.

Lee, R. H. (1978). *The growth and decline of Chinese communities in the Rocky Mountain region.* New York: Arno.

Lehman, D. (1992). Signs of the times: Deconstruction and the fall of Paul de Man. *Contention: Debates in Society, Culture and Science, 1*(2), 23-38.

Leighton, A. H. (1945). *The governing of men: General principles and recommendations based on experience at a Japanese relocation camp.* Princeton, NJ: Princeton University Press.

Lemert, C. (1992). Subjectivity's limit: The unsolved riddle of the standpoint. *Sociological Theory, 10,* 63-72.

Lenzer, G. (Ed.). (1975). *Auguste Comte and positivism: The essential writings.* New York: Harper Torchbooks.

Leonard, K. I. (1992). *Making ethnic choices: California's Punjabi Mexican Americans.* Philadelphia: Temple University Press.

Lieberson, S. (1961). A societal theory of race and ethnic relations. *American Sociological Review, 26,* 902-910.

Lieberson, S. (1980). *A piece of the pie: Blacks and white immigrants since 1880.* Berkeley: University of California Press.

Lieberson, S., & Waters, M. C. (1988). *From many strands: Ethnic and racial groups in contemporary America.* New York: Russell Sage Foundation.

Liebow, E. (1967). *Tally's corner: A study of Negro street corner men.* Boston: Little, Brown.

Lingeman, R. (1980). *Small town America: A narrative history, 1620-the present.* New York: G. P. Putnam's Sons.

Lippy, C. H., Choquette, R., & Poole, S. (1992). *Christianity comes to the Americas, 1492-1776.* New York: Paragon.

Lipset, S. M. (1950, May). Changing social status and prejudice: The race theories of a pioneering American sociologist. *Commentary, 9,* 475-479.

Lipset, S. M. (1963). *The first new nation: The United States in historical and comparative perspective.* New York: Basic Books.

Lipset, S. M. (1979). *The first new nation: The United States in historical and comparative perspective* (rev. ed.). New York: W. W. Norton.

Lopata, H. Z. (1967). The function of voluntary associations in an ethnic community: "Polonia." In E. W. Burgess & D. J. Bogue (Eds.), *Contributions to urban sociology* (pp. 203-223). Chicago: University of Chicago Press.

Lopreato, J. (1970). *Italian Americans.* New York: Random House.

Lovejoy, A. O. (1960). *The great chain of being: A study of the history of an idea.* New York: Harper Torchbooks.

Lugard, L. (1965). *The dual mandate in British tropical Africa.* Hamden, CT: Archon/Shoe String. (Original work published 1922)

Luhmann, N. (1986). The individuality of the individual: Historical meanings and contemporary problems. In T. C. Heller, M. Sosna, & D. E. Wellbery (Eds.), *Reconstructing individualism: Autonomy, individuality, and the self in Western thought* (pp. 313-328). Stanford, CA: Stanford University Press.

Lyman, S. M. (1961-1962). Overseas Chinese in America and Indonesia: A review article. *Pacific Affairs, 34,* 380-389.

Lyman, S. M. (1963). Up from the "hatchet man." *Pacific Affairs, 36,* 160-171.

Lyman, S. M. (1964). The spectrum of color. *Social Research, 31,* 364-373.

Lyman, S. M. (1972). *The black American in sociological thought: A failure of perspective.* New York: G. P. Putnam's Sons.

Lyman, S. M. (1974). Conflict and the web of group affiliation in San Francisco's Chinatown, 1850-1910. *Pacific Historical Review, 43,* 473-499.

Lyman, S. M. (1975). Legitimacy and consensus in Lipset's America: From Washington to Watergate. *Social Research, 42,* 729-759.

Lyman, S. M. (1978). The acceptance, rejection, and reconstruction of histories. In R. H. Brown & S. M. Lyman (Eds.), *Structure, consciousness and history* (pp. 53-105). New York: Cambridge University Press.

Lyman, S. M. (1979). Stuart Culin and the debate over trans-Pacific migration. *Journal for the Theory of Social Behaviour, 9,* 91-115.

Lyman, S. M. (1982a). Stewart Culin: The earliest American Chinatown studies and a hypothesis about pre-Columbian migration. *Annual Bulletin of the Research Institute for Social Science* (Ryukoku University, Kyoto, Japan), 12, 142-162.

Lyman, S. M. (1982b). Two neglected pioneers of civilizational analysis: The cultural perspectives of R. Stewart Culin and Frank Hamilton Cushing. *Social Research, 44,* 690-729.

Lyman, S. M. (1986). *Chinatown and Little Tokyo: Power, conflict and community among Chinese and Japanese immigrants in America.* Millwood, NJ: Associated Faculty.

Lyman, S. M. (1990a). Asian American contacts before Columbus: Alternative understandings for civilization, acculturation, and ethnic minority status in America. In S. M. Lyman, *Civilization: Contents, discontents, malcontents and other essays in social theory.* Fayetteville: University of Arkansas Press.

Lyman, S. M. (1990b). *Civilization: Contents, discontents, malcontents and other essays in social theory.* Fayetteville: University of Arkansas Press.

Lyman, S. M. (1992a). The assimilation-pluralism debate: Toward a postmodern resolution of the American ethnoracial dilemma. *International Journal of Politics, Culture and Society, 6,* 181-210.

Lyman, S. M. (1992b). *Militarism, imperialism and racial accommodation: An analysis and interpretation of the early writings of Robert E. Park.* Fayetteville: University of Arkansas Press.

Lyman, S. M., & Scott, M. B. (1967). Territoriality: A neglected sociological dimension. *Social Problems, 15,* 236-248.

Lyman, S. M., & Scott, M. B. (1989). *A sociology of the absurd* (2nd ed.). Dix Hills, NY: General Hall.

Lynd, R. S., & Lynd, H. M. (1937). *Middletown in transition: A study in cultural conflicts.* New York: Harcourt, Brace.

Lynd, R. S., & Lynd, H. M. (1956). *Middletown: A study in modern American culture.* New York: Harcourt, Brace. (Original work published 1929)

Lyon, L. (1987). *The community in urban society.* Chicago: Dorsey.

Lyotard, J.-F. (1989). The sign of history. In A. Benjamin (Ed.), *The Lyotard reader* (pp. 393-411). Cambridge, MA: Basil Blackwell.

Lyotard, J.-F. (1990). *Heidegger and "the jews"* (A. Michel & M. Roberts, Trans.). Minneapolis: University of Minnesota Press.

Manganaro, M. (1990). Textual play, power, and cultural critique: An orientation to modernist anthropology. In M. Manganaro (Ed.), *Modern anthropology: From fieldwork to text* (pp. 3-47). Princeton, NJ: Princeton University Press.

Mangiafico, L. (1988). *Contemporary American immigrants: Patterns of Filipino, Korean, and Chinese settlement in the United States.* New York: Praeger.

Manning, P. K. (1987). *Semiotics and fieldwork.* Newbury Park, CA: Sage.

Manning, P. K. (1991). Analytic induction. In K. Plummer (Ed.), *Symbolic interactionism: Vol. 2. Contemporary issues* (pp. 401-430). Brookfield, VT: Edward Elgar. (Reprinted from R. Smith & P. K. Manning, Eds., *Qualitative methods,* Cambridge, MA: Ballinger, 1982)

Marable, M. (1983). *How capitalism underdeveloped black America: Problems in race, political economy, and society.* Boston: South End.

Marcus, G. E. (1986). Contemporary problems of ethnography in the modern world system. In J. Clifford & G. E. Marcus (Eds.), *Writing culture: The poetics and politics of ethnography* (pp. 165-193). Berkeley: University of California Press.

Martin, C. (Ed.). (1987). *The American Indian and the problem of history.* New York: Oxford University Press.

Marty, M. E. (1992). Foreword. In Bartolome de Las Casas, *In defense of the Indians: The defense of the most reverend Lord, Don Fray Bartolome de Las Casas, of the Order of Preachers, late Bishop of Chiapa, against the persecutors and slanderers of the peoples of the New World discovered across the seas* (C. M. S. Poole, Ed. & Trans.) (original work published 1552). De Kalb: Northern Illinois University Press.

Masuoka, J. (1946). Race relations and Nisei problems. *Sociology and Social Research, 30,* 452-459.

Maunier, R. (1949). *The sociology of colonies: An introduction to the study of race contact* (Vols. 1-2) (E. O. Lorimer, Ed. & Trans.). London: Routledge & Kegan Paul.

McCluer, F. L. (1928). *Living conditions among wage-earning families in forty-one blocks in Chicago.* Unpublished doctoral dissertation, University of Chicago.

McClymer, J. F. (1980). *War and welfare: Social engineering in America, 1890-1925.* Westport, CT: Greenwood.

McGee, W. J. (1971). *The Seri Indians of Bahia Kino and Sonora, Mexico* (Seventeenth Annual Report of the Bureau of American Ethnology to the Secretary of the Smithsonian Institution, 1895-1896, part 1). Glorieta, NM: Rio Grande. (Original work published 1899)

McKenney, T. L., & Hall, J. (1972). *The Indian Tribes of North America—with biographical sketches and anecdotes of the principal chiefs* (Vols. 1-3). Totowa, NJ: Rowman & Littlefield. (Original work published 1836)

McKenzie, R. D. (1968). *On human ecology: Selected writings* (A. H. Hawley, Ed.). Chicago: University of Chicago Press.

McKinney, J. C., in collaboration with Loomis, C. P. (1957). The application of *Gemeinschaft* and *Gesellschaft* as related to other typologies. In F. Tonnies, *Community and society (Gemeinschaft und Gesellschaft)* (C. P. Loomis, Ed. & Trans.) (pp. 12-29). East Lansing: Michigan State University Press.

Mead, M. (1960a). *Coming of age in Samoa: A psychological study of primitive youth for Western civilization.* New York: Mentor. (Original work published 1928)

Mead, M. (1960b). *Growing up in New Guinea: A comparative study of primitive education.* New York: Mentor. (Original work published 1930)

Mead, M. (1960c). *Male and female: A study of the sexes in a changing world.* New York: Mentor. (Original work published 1949)

Mead, M. (1960d). *Sex and temperament in three primitive societies.* New York: Mentor. (Original work published 1935)

Mead, M. (1975). *New lives for old: Cultural transformation—Manau, 1928-1953.* New York: William Morrow. (Original work published 1956)

Messenger, P. M. (Ed.). (1991). *The ethics of collecting cultural property: Whose culture? Whose property?* Albuquerque: University of New Mexico Press.

Miller, J. (1993). *The passion of Michel Foucault.* New York: Simon & Schuster.

Milner, C. A., II, & O'Neil, F. A. (Eds.). (1985). *Churchmen and the Western Indians, 1820-1920.* Norman: University of Oklahoma Press.

Milson, K. (1991-1992). (En)countering imperialist nostalgia: The Indian reburial issue. *Discourse: Journal for Theoretical Studies in Media and Culture, 14,* 58-74.

Miner, H. (1952). The folk-urban continuum. *American Sociological Review, 17,* 529-537.

Minnich, E. K. (1990). *Transforming knowledge.* Philadelphia: Temple University Press.

Montagu, A. (Ed.). (1968). The concept of the primitive. New York: Free Press.

Morgan, G. (Ed.). (1983). *Beyond method: Strategies for social research.* Beverly Hills, CA: Sage.

Morgan, L. H. (1964). *Ancient society* (L. White, Ed.). Cambridge, MA: Belknap.

Moorhouse, G. (1988). *Imperial city: New York.* New York: Henry Holt.

Murdock, G. P. (1965). *Social structure.* New York: Free Press. (Original work published 1949)

Murdock, G. P. (1934). *Our primitive contemporaries.* New York: Macmillan.

A museum is set to part with its Indian treasures. (1993, February 19). *New York Times,* p. A12.

Myer, D. S. (1971). *Uprooted Americans: The Japanese Americans and the War Relocation Authority during World War II.* Tucson: University of Arizona Press.

Nader, L. (1972). Up the anthropologist: Perspectives gained from studying up. In D. Hymes (Ed.), *Reinventing anthropology* (pp. 284-311). New York: Pantheon.

Natanson, M. (1962). History as a finite province of meaning. In H. Natanson, *Literature, philosophy and the social sciences: Essays in existentialism and phenomenology* (pp. 172-178). The Hague: Martinus Nijhoff.

Nelli, H. S. (1970). *The Italians in Chicago, 1880-1930.* New York: Oxford University Press.

Neske, G., & Kettering, E. (1990). *Martin Heidegger and National Socialism: Questions and answers* (L. Harries & J. Neugroschel, Trans.). New York: Paragon House.

Nikolinakos, D. D. (1990). Foucault's ethical quandary. *Telos, 23,* 123-140.

Nisbet, R. A. (1969). *Social change and history: Aspects of the Western theory of development.* New York: Oxford University Press.

Nisbet, R. A. (1972). Ethnocentrism and the comparative method. In A. R. Desai (Ed.), *Essays on modernization of underdeveloped societies* (Vol. 1, pp. 95-114). New York: Humanities Press.

Nisbet, R. A. (1977). *Sociology as an art form.* New York: Oxford University Press.

Nisbet, R. A. (1986). Developmentalism: A critical analysis. In R. A. Nisbet, *The making of modern society* (pp. 33-69). New York: New York University Press.

Nomura, G. M., et al. (Eds.). (1989). *Frontiers of Asian American studies: Writing, research and commentary.* Pullman: Washington State University Press.

Nordenskiold, G. (1979). *The cliff dwellers of the Mesa Verde* (O. L. Morgan, Trans.). Glorieta, NM: Rio Grande. (Original work published 1893)

Norris, C. (1990). Lost in the funhouse: Baudrillard and the politics of postmodernism. In R. Boyne & A. Rattansi (Eds.), *Postmodernism and society* (pp. 119-153). New York: St. Martin's.

Novak, M. (1972). *The rise of the unmeltable ethnics: Politics and culture in the seventies.* New York: Macmillan.

Novak, M. (1980). Pluralism: A humanistic perspective. In S. Thernstrom (Ed.), *Harvard encyclopedia of American ethnic groups* (pp. 772-781). Cambridge, MA: Harvard University Press.

Numbers, R. (1992). *The creationists: The evolution of scientific creationism.* New York: Alfred A. Knopf.

Oakes, K. B. (1938). *Social theory in the early literature of voyage and exploration in Africa.* Unpublished doctoral dissertation, University of California, Berkeley.

Officer, J. E. (1987). *Hispanic Arizona, 1536-1856.* Tucson: University of Arizona Press.

Okihiro, G. Y. (1988). The idea of community and a "particular type of history." In G. Y. Okihiro et al. (Eds.), *Reflections on shattered windows: Promises and prospects for Asian American studies* (pp. 175-183). Pullman: Washington State University Press.

Okihiro, G. Y., et al. (Eds.). (1988). *Reflections on shattered windows: Promises and prospects for Asian American studies.* Pullman: Washington State University Press.

Olivier, S. (1970). The government of colonies and dependencies. In G. Spiller (Ed.), *Papers on inter-racial problems communicated to the First Universal Race Congress, University of London, July 26-29, 1911* (pp. 293-312). New York: Citadel. (Original work published 1911)

Padilla, F. M. (1985). *Latino ethnic consciousness: The case of Mexican Americans and Puerto Ricans in Chicago.* Notre Dame, IN: University of Notre Dame Press.

Paglia, C. (1991). Junk bonds and corporate raiders: Academe in the hour of the wolf. *Arion: A Journal of Humanities and the Classics* (third series), *1*(2), 139-212.

Park, R. E. (1952a). *The collected papers of Robert Ezra Park: Vol. 2. Human communities: The city and human ecology* (E. C. Hughes et al., Eds.). Glencoe, IL: Free Press.

Park, R. E. (1952b). Community organization and the romantic temper. In R. E. Park, *The collected papers of Robert Ezra Park: Vol. 2. Human communities: The city and human ecology* (E. C. Hughes et al., Eds.) (pp. 64-72). Glencoe, IL: Free Press.

Park, R. E. (1952c). Magic, mentality and city life. In R. E. Park, *The collected papers of Robert Ezra Park: Vol. 2. Human communities: The city and human ecology* (E. C. Hughes et al., Eds.) (pp. 102-117). Glencoe, IL: Free Press.

Park, R. E. (1967). The city: Suggestions for the investigation of human behavior in the urban environment. In R. E. Park, E. W. Burgess, & R. D. McKenzie (Eds.), *The city* (pp. 1-46). Chicago: University of Chicago Press. (Original work published 1925)

Park, R. E. (1969a). Human migration and the marginal man. In E. W. Burgess (Ed.), *Personality and the social group* (pp. 64-77). Freeport, NY: Books for Libraries Press. (Original work published 1929)

Park, R. E. (1969b). Introduction. In R. Adams, *Interracial marriage in Hawaii: A study of mutually conditioned responses to acculturation and amalgamation* (pp. xiii-xiv). Montclair, NJ: Patterson Smith. (Original work published 1937)

Park, R. E. (1971). *The immigrant press and its control: The acculturation of immigrant groups into American society.* Montclair, NJ: Patterson Smith. (Original work published 1922)

Parsons, T. (1949). *The structure of social action: A study on social theory with special reference to a group of recent European writers.* Glencoe, IL: Free Press. (Original work published 1937)

Parsons, T. (1966). *Societies: Evolutionary and comparative perspectives.* Englewood Cliffs, NJ: Prentice Hall.

Parsons, T. (1971). *The system of modern societies.* Englewood Cliffs, NJ: Prentice Hall.

Parsons, T. (1973). Some afterthoughts on *Gemeinschaft* and *Gesellschaft.* In W. J. Cahnman (Ed.), *Ferdinand Tonnies: A new evaluation* (pp. 140-150). Leiden, Netherlands: E. J. Brill.

Patterson, O. (1982). *Slavery and social death: A comparative study.* Cambridge, MA: Harvard University Press.

Patterson, O. (1991). *Freedom: Vol. 1. Freedom in the making of Western culture.* New York: Basic Books.

Peacock, J. L. (1986). *The anthropological lens: Harsh lights, soft focus.* Cambridge: Cambridge University Press.

Pike, K. (1967). *Language in relation to a unified theory of the structure of human behaviour.* The Hague: Mouton.

Poster, M. (1987-1988). Foucault, the present and history. *Cultural Critique, 8,* 105-121.

Pratt, M. L. (1986). Fieldwork in common places. In J. Clifford & G. E. Marcus (Eds.), *Writing culture: The poetics and politics of ethnography*. Berkeley: University of California Press.

Quandt, J. B. (1970). *From the small town to the great community: The social thought of the progressive intellectuals*. New Brunswick, NJ: Rutgers University Press.

Rabinow, P., & Sullivan, W. M. (Eds.). (1979). *Interpretive social science: A reader*. Berkeley: University of California Press.

Radin, P. (1927). *The story of the American Indian*. New York: Boni & Liveright.

Radin, P. (1957a). *Primitive man as philosopher*. New York: Dover. (Original work published 1927)

Radin, P. (1957b). *Primitive religion: Its nature and origin*. New York: Dover. (Original work published 1937)

Radin, P. (1963). *The autobiography of a Winnebago Indian: Life, ways, acculturation, and the peyote cult*. New York: Dover. (Original work published 1920)

Radin, P. (1966). *The method and theory of ethnology: An essay in criticism*. New York: Basic Books. (Original work published 1933)

Radin, P. (1970). *The Italians of San Francisco: Their adjustment and acculturation*. San Francisco: R & E Research Associates. (Original work published 1935)

Radin, P. (Ed.). (1971a). *The golden mountain: Chinese tales told in California, collected by Jon Lee*. Taipei: Caves. (Original work published 1936)

Radin, P. (1971b). *The world of primitive man*. New York: Dutton. (Original work published 1953)

Radin, P. (1973). *The Winnebago tribe*. Lincoln: University of Nebraska Press. (Original work published 1923)

Radin, P. (1976). *The trickster: A study in American Indian mythology*. New York: Schocken. (Original work published 1956)

Rae, J. B. (1965). *The American automobile: A brief history*. Chicago: University of Chicago Press.

Ratzel, F. (1988). *Sketches of urban and cultural life in North America* (S. A. Stehlin, Ed. & Trans.). New Brunswick, NJ: Rutgers University Press. (Original work published 1876)

Redfield, J. (1991). Classics and anthropology. *Arion: A Journal of Humanities and the Classics* (third series), *1*(2), 5-23.

Redfield, R. (1928). *A plan for the study of Tepoztlan, Mexico*. Unpublished doctoral dissertation, University of Chicago.

Redfield, R. (1930). *Tepoztlan—A Mexican village: A study of folk life*. Chicago: University of Chicago Press.

Redfield, R. (1941). *The folk culture of Yucatan*. Chicago: University of Chicago Press.

Redfield, R. (1960). *The little community and peasant society and culture*. Chicago: University of Chicago Press.

Redfield, R. (1962a). The folk society and civilization. In M. P. Redfield (Ed.), *The papers of Robert Redfield: Vol. 1. Human nature and the study of society*. Chicago: University of Chicago Press.

Redfield, R. (1962b). *A village that chose progress: Chan Kom revisited*. Chicago: University of Chicago Press. (Original work published 1950)

Redfield, R. (1963). Talk with a stranger. In M. P. Redfield (Ed.), *The papers of Robert Redfield: Vol. 2. The social uses of social science* (pp. 270-284). Chicago: University of Chicago Press.

Redfield, R. & Rojas, A. V. (1962). *Chan Kom: A Maya village*. Chicago: University of Chicago Press. (Original work published 1934)

Redfield, R., & Singer, M. B. (1973). The cultural role of the cities: Orthogenetic and heterogenetic change. In G. Germani (Ed.), *Modernization, urbanization, and the urban crisis* (pp. 61-71). Boston: Little, Brown.

Reid, D. (Ed.). (1992). *Sex, death and God in L.A.* New York: Pantheon.

Reuter, E. B. (1969). *The mulatto in the United States: Including a study of the role of mixed-blood races throughout the world*. New York: Negro Universities Press. (Original work published 1918)

Rivers, W. H. R. (1974). The psychological factor. In A. Montagu (Ed.), *Frontiers of anthropology* (pp. 391-409). New York: G. P. Putnam's Sons. (Reprinted from W. H. R. Rivers, Ed., *Essays on the depopulation of Melanesia,* Cambridge: Cambridge University Press, 1922)

Rockmore, T. (1992). *On Heidegger's Nazism and philosophy*. Berkeley: University of California Press.

Roper, M. W. (1935). *The city and the primary group*. Unpublished doctoral dissertation, University of Chicago.

Rorty, R. (1982). *Consequences of pragmatism: Essays, 1972-1980*. Minneapolis: University of Minnesota Press.

Rorty, R. (1989). *Contingency, irony and solidarity*. Cambridge: Cambridge University Press.

Rose, A. (Ed.). (1988). *Universal abandon? The politics of postmodernism*. Minneapolis, MN: University of Minnesota.

Rose, D. (1989). *Patterns of American culture: Ethnography and estrangement*. Philadelphia: University of Pennsylvania Press.

Rosenau, P. M. (1992). *Post-modernism and the social sciences: Insights, inroads, and intrusions*. Princeton, NJ: Princeton University Press.

Ross, R. H., & Bogardus, E. S. (1940). The third generation race relations cycle: A study in Issei-Nisei relationships. *Sociology and Social Research, 24,* 357-363.

Rossi, P. (1987). *The dark abyss of time: The history of the earth and the history of nations from Hooke to Vico* (L. G. Cochrane, Trans.). Chicago: University of Chicago Press.

Rouse, I. (1992). *The Tainos: Rise and decline of the people who greeted Columbus*. New Haven, CT: Yale University Press.

Royce, P. (1982). *Ethnic identity: Strategies of diversity*. Bloomington: Indiana University Press.

Rubel, A. J. (1971). *Across the tracks: Mexican Americans in a Texas city*. Austin: University of Texas Press.

Sachs, W. (1947). *Black anger*. New York: Grove.

Sadri, A. (1992). *Max Weber's sociology of intellectuals*. New York: Oxford University Press.

Salmond, A. (1991). *Two worlds: First meetings between Maori and Europeans, 1642-1772.* Honolulu: University of Hawaii Press.

Sanchez, G. S. (1967). *Forgotten people: A study of New Mexicans*. Albuquerque: Calvin Horn.

Sanderson, S. K. (1990). *Social evolutionism: A critical history.* Cambridge: Basil Blackwell.

Sando, J. S. (1992). *Pueblo nations: Eight centuries of Pueblo Indian history.* Santa Fe, NM: Clear Light.

Sarana, G. (1975). *The methodology of anthropological comparison: An analysis of comparative methods in social and cultural anthropology.* Tucson: University of Arizona Press.

Saxton, S. L. (1993). Sociologist as citizen-scholar: A symbolic interactionist alternative to normal sociology. In T. R. Vaughan, G. Sjoberg, & L. J. Reynolds (Eds.). *A critique of contemporary American sociology* (pp. 232-251). Dix Hills, NY: General Hall.

Schatzman, L., & Strauss, A. L. (1973). *Field research: Strategies for a natural sociology.* Englewood Cliffs, NJ: Prentice Hall.

Schietinger, E. F. (1967). Racial succession and changing property values in residential Chicago. In E. W. Burgess & D. J. Bogue (Eds.), *Contributions to urban sociology* (pp. 86-99). Chicago: University of Chicago Press.

Schlesinger, A. M., Jr. (1991). *The disuniting of America: Reflections on a multicultural society.* Knoxville, TN: Whittle.

Schoolcraft, H. R. (1975). *Personal memoirs of a residence of thirty years with the Indian tribes of the American frontiers, with brief notices of passing events, facts and opinions, A.D. 1812 to A.D. 1842.* New York: Arno. (Original work published 1851)

Schrag, P. (1970). *The decline of the WASP.* New York: Simon & Schuster.

Schrag, P. (1973). *The end of the American future.* New York: Simon & Schuster.

Schwatka, F. (1977). *In the land of cave and cliff dwellers.* Glorieta, NM: Rio Grande. (Original work published 1893)

Sheets-Johnstone, M. (1990). *The roots of thinking.* Philadelphia: Temple University Press.

Sheets-Johnstone, M. (Ed.). (1992). *Giving the body its due.* Albany: State University of New York Press.

Sheridan, T. E. (1986). *Los Tucsonenses: The Mexican community in Tucson, 1854-1941.* Tucson: University of Arizona Press.

Shibutani, T., & Kwan, K. M.(1965). *Ethnic stratification: A comparative approach.* New York: Macmillan.

Simmel, G. (1950). The stranger. In G. Simmel, *The sociology of Georg Simmel* (K. H. Wolff, Ed. & Trans.) (pp. 402-408). Glencoe, IL: Free Press.

Simmel, G. (1968). *The conflict in modern culture and other essays* (K. P. Etzkorn, Ed. & Trans.). New York: Teachers College Press.

Siu, P. C. P. (1987). *The Chinese laundrymen: A study of social isolation* (J. K. W. Tchen, Ed.). New York: New York University Press.

Smith, A. D. (1989). *The ethnic origin of nations.* New York: Basil Blackwell.

Smith, C. W. (1979). *A critique of sociological reasoning: An essay in philosophical sociology.* Oxford: Basil Blackwell.

Smith, M. G. (1965). *The plural society in the British West Indies.* Berkeley: University of California.

Smith, M. P. (1979). *The city and social theory.* New York: St. Martin's.

Solzhenitsyn, A. (1993, February 7). The relentless cult of novelty and how it wrecked the century. *New York Times Book Review,* p. 3.

Sorokin, P. (1965). *Fads and foibles in modern sociology and related sciences.* Chicago: Henry Regnery-Gateway.

Spicer, E. A., Hansen, A. T., Luomala, K., & Opler, M. K. (1969). *Impounded people: Japanese-Americans in the relocation centers.* Tucson: University of Arizona Press.

Spier, L. (1978). *Yuman tribes of the Gila River.* New York: Dover. (Original work published 1933)

Spretnak, C. (1991). *States of grace: The recovery of meaning in the postmodern age.* New York: HarperCollins.

Statler, O. (1983). *Japanese pilgrimage.* New York: William Morrow.

Stein, M. R. (1964). The eclipse of community: Some glances at the education of a sociologist. In A. J. Vidich, J. Bensman, & M. R. Stein (Eds.), *Reflections on community studies.* New York: John Wiley.

Steinberg, S. (1981). *The ethnic myth: Race, ethnicity, and class in America.* New York: Atheneum.

Stocking, G. W., Jr. (Ed.). (1983). *Observers observed: Essays on ethnographic field work.* Madison: University of Wisconsin Press.

Stocking, G. W., Jr. (Ed.). (1984). *Functionalism historicized: Essays on British social anthropology.* Madison: University of Wisconsin Press.

Stocking, G. W., Jr. (Ed.). (1985). *Objects and others: Essays on museums and material culture.* Madison: University of Wisconsin Press.

Stocking, G. W., Jr. (Ed.). (1986). *Malinowski, Rivers, Benedict and others: Essays on culture and personality.* Madison: University of Wisconsin Press.

Stocking, G. W., Jr. (Ed.). (1988). *Bones, bodies, behavior: Essays on biological anthropology.* Madison: University of Wisconsin Press.

Stocking, G. W., Jr. (Ed.). (1989). *Romantic motives: Essays on anthropological sensibility.* Madison: University of Wisconsin Press.

Stocking, G. W., Jr. (Ed.). (1991). *Colonial situations: Essays on the contextualization of ethnographic knowledge.* Madison: University of Wisconsin Press.

Stone, R. W. (1921). *The origin of the survey movement.* Unpublished doctoral dissertation, University of Chicago.

Stonequist, E. V. (1961). *The marginal man: A study in personality and culture conflict.* New York: Russell & Russell. (Original work published 1937)

Strathern, M. (1990). Out of context: The persuasive fictions of anthropology, with comments by I. C. Jarvie, Stephen A. Tyler and George E. Marcus. In M. Manganaro (Ed.), *Modern anthropology: From fieldwork to text* (pp. 80-130). Princeton, NJ: Princeton University Press.

Street corner society revisited [Special issue]. (1992). *Journal of Contemporary Ethnography, 21*(1), 3-132.

Sumner, W. G. (1940). *Folkways: A study of the sociological importance of usages, manners, customs, mores, and morals.* Boston: Ginn. (Original work published 1906)

Sumner, W. G. (1969). Foreword. In J. E. Cutler, *Lynch-law: An investigation into the history of lynching in the United States* (p. v). Montclair, NJ: Patterson Smith. (Original work published 1905)

Suret-Canale, J. (1988a). The end of chieftancy in Guinea. In J. Suret-Canale, *Essays on African history: From the slave trade to neocolonialism* (C. Hurst, Trans.). Trenton, NJ: Africa World.

Suret-Canale, J. (1988b). Guinea in the colonial system. In J. Suret-Canale, *Essays on African history: From the slave trade to neocolonialism* (C. Hurst, Trans.). Trenton, NJ: Africa World.

Suttles, G. D. (1972). *The social construction of communities*. Chicago: University of Chicago Press.

Symposium on qualitative methods. (1993, January). *Contemporary Sociology, 22*(1), 1-15.

Takaki, R. (1989). *Strangers from a different shore: A history of Asian Americans*. New York: Penguin.

Taylor, C. (1989). *Sources of the self: The making of modern identity*. Cambridge, MA: Harvard University Press.

Taylor, P. S. (1970). *Mexican labor in the United States* (Vols. 1-2). New York: Arno/New York Times. (Original work published 1930)

Taylor, P. S. (1983). *On the ground in the thirties*. Salt Lake City: Peregrine Smith.

Tedlock, B. (1992). *The beautiful and the dangerous: Encounters with the Zuni Indians*. New York: Viking.

Teggart, F. J. (1941). *The theory and processes of history*. Berkeley: University of California Press.

Thernstrom, S. (Ed.). (1980). *Harvard encyclopedia of American ethnic groups*. Cambridge, MA: Harvard University Press.

Thomas, W. I., & Znaniecki, F. (1958). *The Polish peasant in Europe and America*. New York: Dover.

Thrasher, F. M. (1963). *The gang: A study of 1,313 gangs in Chicago*. Chicago: University of Chicago Press. (Original work published 1927)

Thucydides. (1972). *History of the Peloponnesian War* (R. Warner, Trans.). Harmondsworth: Penguin.

Tilman, R. (1991). *Thorstein Veblen and his critics, 1891-1963*. Princeton, NJ: Princeton University Press.

Tinder, G. (1980). *Community: Reflections on a tragic ideal*. Baton Rouge: Louisiana State University Press.

Tobias, H. J. (1990). *A history of the Jews in New Mexico*. Albuquerque: University of New Mexico Press.

Todorov, T. (1984). *The conquest of America* (R. Howard, Trans.). New York: Harper & Row.

Toland, J. D. (Ed.). (1993). *Ethnicity and the state*. New Brunswick, NJ: Transaction.

Tönnies, F. (1957). *Community and society (Gemeinschaft und Gesellschaft)* (C. P. Loomis, Ed. & Trans.). East Lansing: Michigan State University Press. (Original work published 1887)

Torgovnick, M. (1990). *Gone primitive: Savage intellects, modern lives*. Chicago: University of Chicago Press.

Tricarico, D. (1984). *The Italians of Greenwich Village: The social structure and transformation of an ethnic community*. Staten Island, NY: Center for Migration Studies of New York.

Trinh T. M.-H. (1991). *When the moon waxes red: Representation, gender and cultural politics*. New York: Routledge.

Trinkhouse, E., & Shipman, P. (1993). *The Neanderthals: Changing the image of mankind*. New York: Alfred A. Knopf.

Turner, V. (1992). African ritual and Western literature: Is a comparative symbology possible? In V. Turner, *Blazing the trail: Way marks in the exploration of symbols* (E. Turner, Ed.) (pp. 66-88). Tucson: University of Arizona Press.

Van Maanen, J. (1988). *Tales of the field: On writing ethnography.* Chicago: University of Chicago Press.

Vaughan, A. T. (1965). *New England frontier: Puritans and Indians, 1620-1675.* Boston: Little, Brown.

Vaughan, T. R. (1993). The crisis in contemporary American sociology: A critique of the discipline's dominant paradigm. In T. R. Vaughan, G. Sjoberg, & L. J. Reynolds (Eds.), *A critique of contemporary American sociology.* Dix Hills, NY: General Hall.

Veblen, T. (1959). *The theory of the leisure class.* New York: Mentor. (Original work published 1899)

Veblen, T. (1961a). The blond race and the Aryan culture. In T. Veblen, *The place of science in modern civilization and other essays.* New York: Russell & Russell. (Original work published 1919)

Veblen, T. (1961b). The mutation theory and the blond race. In T. Veblen, *The place of science in modern civilization and other essays.* New York: Russell & Russell. (Original work published 1919)

Veblen, T. (1965). *The higher learning in America: A memorandum on the conduct of universities by businessmen.* New York: Augustus M. Kelley. (Original work published 1918)

Veblen, T. (1990). *The instinct of workmanship and the state of the industrial arts.* New Brunswick, NJ: Transaction. (Original work published 1914)

Vidich, A. J. (1952). *The political impact of colonial administration.* Unpublished doctoral dissertation, Harvard University, Boston.

Vidich, A. J. (1955). Participant observation and the collection and interpretation of data. *American Journal of Sociology, 60,* 335-360.

Vidich, A. J. (1966). Introduction. In P. Radin, *The method and theory of ethnology: An essay in criticism* (pp. vii-cxv). New York: Basic Books.

Vidich, A. J. (1980). *The political impact of colonial administration.* New York: Arno.

Vidich, A. J. (1986). *Anthropology and truth: Some old problems.* Paper presented at the annual meeting of the American Anthropological Society, Philadelphia.

Vidich, A. J., & Bensman, J. (1968). *Small town in mass society: Class, power and religion in a rural community* (2nd ed.). Princeton, NJ: Princeton University Press.

Vidich, A. J., & Lyman, S. M. (1985). *American sociology: Worldly rejections of religion and their directions.* New Haven, CT: Yale University Press.

Vidich, A. J., Lyman, S. M., & Goldfarb, J. C. (1981). Sociology and society: Disciplinary tensions and professional compromises. *Social Research, 48,* 322-361.

Vigil, J. D. (1980). *From Indians to Chicanos: The dynamics of Mexican American culture.* Prospect Heights, IL: Waveland.

von Gierke, O. (1990). *Community in historical perspective: A translation of selections from Das Deutsche Genossenschaftsrecht (the German law of fellowship)* (A. Black, Ed.; M. Fischer, Trans.). Cambridge: Cambridge University Press. (Original work published 1868)

Wallace, A. F. C. (1987). *St. Clair: A nineteenth-century coal town's experience with a disaster-prone industry.* New York: Alfred A. Knopf.

Walzer, M. (1980). Pluralism: A political perspective. In S. Thernstrom (Ed.), *Harvard encyclopedia of American ethnic groups* (pp. 781-787). Cambridge, MA: Harvard University Press.

Ware, C. (1965). *Greenwich Village, 1920-1930: A comment on American civilization in the post-war years.* New York: Harper Colophon. (Original work published 1935)

Warren, R. L. (1963). *The community in America.* Chicago: Rand McNally.

Warren, R. L. (1972). *The community in America* (2nd ed.). Chicago: Rand McNally.

Waters, M. C. (1990). *Ethnic options: Choosing identities in America.* Berkeley: University of California Press.

Wax, R. H. (1971). *Doing fieldwork: Warnings and advice.* Chicago: University of Chicago Press.

Weber, A. F. (1967). *The growth of cities in the nineteenth century: A study in statistics.* Ithaca, NY: Cornell University Press. (Original work published 1899)

Weber, D. J. (1992). *The Spanish frontier in North America.* New Haven, CT: Yale University Press.

Weinstein, D., & Weinstein, M. A. (1990). Dimensions of conflict: Georg Simmel on modern life. In M. Kaern, B. H. Phillips, & R. S. Cohen (Eds.), *Georg Simmel and contemporary sociology* (pp. 341-356). Dordrecht, Netherlands: Kluwer.

Weinstein, D., & Weinstein, M. A. (1991). Simmel and the theory of postmodern society. In B. S. Turner (Ed.), *Theories of modernity and postmodernity* (pp. 75-87). London: Sage.

West, C. (1992). Diverse new world. In P. Berman (Ed.), *Debating P.C.: The controversy over political correctness on college campuses* (pp. 326-332). New York: Dell.

White, L. A. (1974). *The A'Coma Indians: People of the sky city* (Forty-Seventh Annual Report of the Bureau of American Ethnology to the secretary of the Smithsonian Institution, 1929-1930). Glorieta, NM: Rio Grande. (Original work published 1933)

Williams, R. A., Jr. (1990). *The American Indian in Western legal thought: The discourses of conquest.* New York: Oxford University Press.

Williams, V. J., Jr. (1989). *From a caste to a minority: Changing attitudes of American sociologists toward Afro-Americans, 1896-1945.* Westport, CT: Greenwood.

Willis, W. S., Jr. (1972). Skeletons in the anthropological closet. In D. Hymes (Ed.), *Reinventing anthropology* (pp. 121-152). New York: Pantheon.

Wirth, L. (1938). Urbanism as a way of life. *American Journal of Sociology, 44,* 1-24.

Wirth, L. (1945). The problem of minority groups. In R. Linton (Ed.), *The science of man in the world crisis* (pp. 347-372). New York: Columbia University Press.

Wirth, L. (1956). *The ghetto.* Chicago: University of Chicago Press. (Original work published 1928)

Wissler, C. (1923). *Man and culture.* New York: Thomas Y. Crowell.

Wissler, C. (1956). Foreword. In R. S. Lynd & H. M. Lynd, *Middletown: A study in modern American culture.* New York: Harcourt, Brace. (Original work published 1929)

Wissler, C. (1966a). *Indians of the United States* (rev. ed.). Garden City, NY: Doubleday. (Original work published 1940)

Wissler, C. (1966b). *Red man reservations.* New York: Collier. (Original work published 1938)

Wood, M. M. (1969). *The stranger: A study in social relationships.* New York: AMS. (Original work published 1934)

Woods, F. J. (1956). *Cultural values of American ethnic groups.* New York: Harper & Brothers.

Woods, F. J. (1972). *Marginality and identity: A colored creole family through ten generations*. Baton Rouge: Louisiana State University Press.

Woods, R. A., & Kennedy, A. J. (1990). *The settlement horizon*. New Brunswick, NJ: Transaction. (Original work published 1922)

Wu, C. C. (1926). *Chinese immigration in the Pacific area*. Unpublished doctoral dissertation, University of Chicago.

Whyte, W. F. (1943a). *Street corner society: The social structure of an Italian slum*. Chicago: University of Chicago Press.

Whyte, W. F. (1943b). A slum sex code. *American Journal of Sociology, 49,* 24-31.

Whyte, W. F. (1955). *Street corner society: The social structure of an Italian slum* (2nd ed.). Chicago: University of Chicago Press.

Whyte, W. F. (1981). *Street corner society: The social structure of an Italian slum* (3rd ed.). Chicago: University of Chicago Press.

Zaner, R. M. (1981). *The context of self: A phenomenological inquiry using medicine as a clue*. Athens: Ohio University Press.

Zorbaugh, H. W. (1929). *The Gold Coast and the slum*. Chicago: University of Chicago Press.

Zorbaugh, H. W. (1968). The dweller in furnished rooms: An urban type. In E. W. Burgess (Ed.), *The urban community: Selected papers from the Proceedings of the American Sociological Society, 1925* (pp. 98-105). Westport, CT: Greenwood.

3

Traditions, Preferences, and Postures in Applied Qualitative Research

David Hamilton

◆ Across the Tuscan hills, Florence is less than 200 kilometers from the seaport of Genoa. Two fifteenth-century contemporaries—Niccolò Machiavelli (1469-1527) and Christopher Columbus (c. 1450-1506)— were born in those respective cities. Their work is widely remembered and, on occasion, even deservedly celebrated. Machiavelli identified a terrain for positive human action; Columbus began the exploitation of such terrain. Together, they set off a chain of political, economic, and intellectual reverberations the impacts of which can still be registered in the late twentieth century. Such was the dawn of Western applied science.

Machiavelli's supreme contribution was to identify a third force in the shaping of the postmedieval world. Conventionally, earlier thinkers had attributed the shaping of nature to two force fields: the hand of God and the hand of Fortuna (Lady Luck). Machiavelli acknowledged these causal constraints, but added a third. In the twenty-fifth chapter of *The Prince* (1513/1988) he suggested, "I am disposed to hold that fortune is the arbiter of half our actions but that it lets us control roughly the other half" (p. 85). Henceforth, Machiavelli implied, the world could be steered according to navigational plans drawn up by human beings, albeit within the confines of God's Grand Design. It is no accident, therefore, that the Renaissance world of Columbus and Machiavelli is also remembered as the age of humanism.

The work of Machiavelli and Columbus engendered immense optimism, itself recorded in the architecture and other expressive arts of the late Renaissance. But how was this optimism to be translated into other humanist ideals? In short, where was humanism going?

Within a century of Columbus's death, answers to this question became available. In the meantime, the world of knowledge had been mapped (see, for example, Strauss, 1966) and new methods of science had been established. As Francis Bacon wrote in the final paragraph of his *Novum Organum* (1620), these innovations would lead to an "improvement in man's estates" and an "enlargement of his power over nature." Bacon's vision, however, portrayed a false dawn. Later seventeenth-century scientists suggested the world was more complicated than it appeared. Alternative maps, encyclopedias, and taxonomies of knowledge were proposed (see, for instance, Slaughter, 1982).

The substance, form, significance, and application of knowledge became a contested domain. The optimism of the Renaissance was tempered by the skepticism of human inquiry. Different maps of knowledge prefigured many different futures. Indeed, the cartographic and taxonomic problems raised by 200 years of Baconian science were eventually satirized in Borges's description of a "certain Chinese encyclopedia," where

> animals are divided into: (a) belonging to the Emperor, (b) embalmed, (c) tame, (d) sucking pigs, (e) sirens, (f) fabulous, (g) stray dogs, (h) included in the present classification, (i) frenzied, (j) innumerable, (k) drawn with a fine camelhair brush, (l) *et cetera,* (m) having just broken the water pitcher, (n) that from a long way off look like flies. (quoted in Foucault, 1973, p. xv)

◆ Structure or Diaspora?

Much the same turbulent history could be written of recent efforts to map the terrain of qualitative research. In 1987, for instance, Evelyn Jacob wrote of a fivefold division of "qualitative research traditions" (ecological psychology, holistic ethnography, ethnography of communication, cognitive anthropology, symbolic interaction). Subsequently, however, she also registered the claim that these were "not the only alternative traditions"

(p. 39). By this disclaimer, of course, Jacob left her argument wide open to counterclaims.

Already, in fact, the uncertainty of her original portrayal had provoked a critical response. Three British researchers, Atkinson, Delamont, and Hammersley (1989), problematized Jacob's 1987 model and, in turn, drew rejoinders from U.S. researchers (Buchmann & Floden, 1989; Lincoln, 1989). In fact, Atkinson et al. did not engage in taxonomic revisionism. Rather, they took a skeptical view of the whole enterprise. They underlined the difficulty of producing unambiguous or noncontroversial intellectual maps. Attempts to compile taxonomies of tradition, they felt, may even be counterproductive—generating emotional heat rather than intellectual light. They could foreshadow an atavistic return to the disputatious scholasticism that Machiavelli and his contemporaries sought to overthrow.

More recently, Harry Wolcott (1992) has offered a resolution of the navigational and taxonomic problems surrounding the Jacob debate. In "Posturing in Qualitative Inquiry" he seeks to aid "researchers new to qualitative inquiry." His efforts hinge upon the fact that the verb *to posture* can be used in two senses, positive or negative. *Posturing* in a negative sense refers to the adoption of an affected or artificial pose, whereas in the positive sense (and with reference to the *Random House Dictionary*), to posture is to "position, especially strategically"; "to develop a policy or stance," for oneself or one's group; or "to adopt an attitude or take an official position" (Wolcott, 1992, p. 4).

Within this conceptual framework, Wolcott's novitiate researchers are encouraged to take up "strategic position[s]" vis-à-vis the "many alternatives" presented by qualitative inquiry. Thereafter, Wolcott claims, beginners are better able to "find their [own] way" in the prosecution of their inquiries (p. 4). In effect, Wolcott offers an eclectic, pluralist, and syncretic prescription. Researchers, he suggests, assemble their theoretical assumptions and working practices from a "marketplace of ideas" (p. 5). Traditions, therefore, serve as preferences. They are not so much inherited as compiled or "invented" (see Hobsbawm & Ranger, 1984).

This last distinction, I feel, captures the separation of the ideas of Atkinson and his colleagues from those advanced by Jacob. Atkinson et al.'s argument accepts an evolutionary or historical view of tradition. A tradition is deemed to be a messy social movement, one that is structured as much by recombination of different activities as by their differentiation, divergence, and continuity.

Jacob, on the other hand, uses a more static image. Nevertheless, her argument has an impressive pedigree. It draws upon the work of Thomas Kuhn, reported in *The Structure of Scientific Revolutions* (1962, 1970). Kuhn suggests that every scientific movement (e.g., Newtonian physics, Lamarckian biology, Freudian psychology) has characteristic ways of achieving the advancement of knowledge. Further, these serve as the building blocks that make up the frameworks, scaffolding, traditions, and paradigms of research. They furnish the preferred modes of working.

Jacob's position, therefore, is comparable to the Kuhnian stance taken by Larry Laudan (1977). A "tradition," according to Laudan, is "a set of general assumptions about the entities and processes in a domain of study, and about the appropriate methods to be used for investigating the problems and constructing the theories in that domain" (p. 81). From the standpoint adopted by Laudan and Jacob, traditions are bounded rather than evolving phenomena. They constitute a "disciplinary matrix" (Kuhn, 1970, p. 182) of interrelating constituent elements. Indeed, Jacob (1989, p. 229) quotes directly from Kuhn (1970, p. 175) to the effect that a disciplinary matrix is "the entire constellation of beliefs, values, techniques and so on shared by members of a given community." Moreover, Jacob explicitly conflates tradition and paradigm: "I use the concept [of paradigm] in the sense of disciplinary matrix as a heuristic framework for examining the social sciences. To signal this modification I use the term tradition rather than paradigm" (p. 229). If the sciences operate with paradigms, the social sciences are steered by traditions.

As with all structural analyses, however, this view of knowledge is problematic. The constituent elements of a tradition or paradigm may be clearly defined. They occupy different positions in conceptual space, and they coexist in harmony. But how does one paradigm become replaced by another—as geocentric cosmologies were replaced by heliocentric worldviews? Certainly, Kuhn addresses this problem as central to the history of science. But can the same argument be applied to the social sciences? Or is it the case that traditions do not replace each other but, rather, emerge spontaneously and coexist alongside each other?

Jacob's efforts pose this problem. They are an innovative, if provocative, attempt to map the qualitative research field without reference to its origins. The outcome is a tidy, easily reproduced map of knowledge. Traditions are represented as separate subfields, each sustained by its own matrix of normative assumptions. Portrayed in such terms, traditions appear as placid archetypes. Unfortunately, however, such formulations are conceptually and practically remote from the swirling currents and posturings of applied science.

This backwater image of tradition is discussed by Ed Shils in *Tradition* (1981). Appeals to tradition have, Shils believes, fallen into "disrepute" among social scientists. That is, the normative—or steering—potential of past research practice has "become very faint," almost "extinguished as an intellectual argument" (p. 1). To explain this atrophy, Shils suggests that the concept of tradition lost its formative value in the eighteenth-century Enlightenment. Knowledge accepted "on the authority of elders" was replaced by "scientific procedure based on the experience of the senses and its rational criticism" (p. 4). "Rational social scientists," Shils wryly observes, "do not mention tradition" (p. 7).

Shils has not been alone in his worries. Alastair MacIntyre (1988) has also suggested that "the standpoint of traditions is necessarily at odds" with the Enlightenment assumptions about the transparency of all knowledge (p. 327). MacIntyre, however, does not let the matter rest at this point. He turns Shils's argument upside down. He resurrects the notion of tradition and reconciles it with the problem identified by Shils:

> Liberalism, beginning as a repudiation of tradition in the name of abstract, universal principles of reason, turned itself into a politically embodied power, whose inability to bring its debates on the nature and context of these universal principles to a conclusion has had the unintended effect of transforming liberalism into a tradition. (p. 349)

If MacIntyre's assertion is accepted, post-Enlightenment traditions share a common feature. They survive because their debates are inconclusive and their disciplinary matrices feature discord rather than harmony. Indeed, a similar conclusion can be reached from a modern reading of the etymology of the term *tradition*.

Like the word *trading*, *tradition* comes from the Latin root *tradere*—to hand over, deliver. According to the *Oxford English Dictionary*, *tradition* connotes the handing over of ecclesiastical artifacts and practices from officebearer to officebearer. Conventionally, it was expected that the sacred practices and artifacts would fall into the right hands. But ecclesiastical courts recognized that this might not always be the case. Hence, if the artifacts (e.g., canonical texts) fell into the wrong hands, the courts could deem that a sin had been committed. Indeed, it was by reference to these normative assumptions that the word *surrender* also came to mean hand over, or relinquish.

From this etymological perspective, traditions have three elements: practitioner-guardians, practices, and artifacts. Equally, etymological precedent—affinities between *trading* and *surrendering*—allows rejection of conservative interpretations of tradition. Just like medieval churches, traditions can be invented, established, ransacked, corrupted, and eliminated. The elements of a tradition are just as easily scattered as they are preserved intact. The history of traditions, therefore, is as much a narrative of diaspora as it is a chronicle of successful parallel cohabitation.

The remainder of this chapter adopts a diasporic view of tradition. It recounts the history of qualitative social science as the genesis and dispersal of a constellation of ideas against which social scientists have positioned themselves (compare Wolcott's "posturing"). Further, this chapter assumes that traditions did not emerge spontaneously, but, instead, from the intellectual heritage of Western thought.

◆ Quantity or Quality?

Qualitative research can be traced back to an eighteenth-century disruption that occurred in the fortunes of quantitative research. For the sake of this account, the most notable innovators were René Descartes (1596-1650) and Immanuel Kant (1724-1804).

Descartes's work, notably *Discourse on Method* (1637), founded the quantitative research field. Descartes (1968) argued that natural philosophy should be refocused around the "certainty and self-evidence" of mathematics (p. 31) and that, in the search for truth, investigators should stand back from those elements of the world that might otherwise corrupt their analytic powers. At the risk of oversimplification, Descartes proclaimed the importance of mathematics and objectivity in the search for truth.

Not all philosophical arguments, however, supported Descartes's stance. The seventeenth and eighteenth centuries were as much an epoch of high controversy as they were an era for the dissemination of Cartesian absolutism. Probably the most significant post-Cartesian intervention came from Immanuel Kant, a philosopher who self-consciously sought to resolve the tensions that had arisen among the Cartesians and the skeptics. Stimulated late in life by the writings of Hume, Kant reworked earlier thought and published his observations in the *Critique of Pure Reason* (1781). By these means, Kant unpacked a range of fundamental ideas—the ultimate source of qualitative thinking—that have proved pivotal in the history of Western thought.

Kant proposed, in effect, that perception is more than seeing. Human perception derives not only from the evidence of the senses but also from the mental apparatus that serves to organize the incoming sense impressions. Kant, therefore, broke sharply with Cartesian objectivism. Human knowledge is ultimately based on understanding, an intellectual state that is more than just a consequence of experience. Thus, for Kant, human claims about nature cannot be independent of inside-the-head processes of the knowing subject.

Kant's model of human rationality, therefore, built the process of knowing and the emergence of knowledge upon an epistemology that transcended the limits of empirical inquiry. In turn, this transcendental perspective (see, for instance, Roberts, 1990) opened the door to epistemologies that allowed, if not celebrated, inside-the-head processes. Such epistemologies are totally at variance with Cartesian objectivism. They include versions of subjectivism, idealism, perspectivism, and relativism (see, e.g., Buchdahl, 1969, p. 481; Ermath, 1978, pp. 38-44; Scruton, 1983).

A Kantian perspective on the creation of knowledge, therefore, must take full cognizance of the investigator. It must concede the significance of interpretation and understanding. But there is another side to Kantian thought that is also central to the social sciences. Given his attention to cognitive processing, Kant was able to posit a distinction between "scientific reason" and "practical reason" (Ermath, 1978, p. 42). The world of nature known by science is a world of strict causal determinism, whereas the world of moral freedom (e.g., applied social research) is "governed by autonomous principles which man prescribes to himself" (p. 42). Knowing the truth about the workings of the world is one thing; knowing what to do about it is something else.

Kant revived a distinction, found in Aristotle, between theoretical and practical knowledge. *Theoretical knowledge* refers to states of affairs whose existence can be checked, tested, and accepted. *Practical knowledge,* on the other hand, refers to decision making. Can humans ever know what to do, with the same kind of certainty that they know the truth? Or does human action merely derive from inclination, passion, or desire? Is there a rationality applicable to the establishment of decisions as there is to the establishment of truths?

At this point, Kantian thought harks back to Machiavelli. The capacity of human beings to make decisions suggests they can play a part in their own self-determination. Further, from a Kantian perspective, decision making presumes human freedom. Likewise, every situation that requires practical action has an empirical status and a moral status. Practical reasoning—or applied social science—relates, therefore, to the application of moral judgments in the realm of human action. What to do relates not only to what is, but also to inseparable notions of what ought to be. It is perhaps no accident that the French word *morale* means both "social" and "ethical," and that, over much of Europe, the social sciences are intimately linked with the moral and political sciences.

Having been inducted into the terms of the debate, Kant's heirs branched off in two opposing new-Kantian directions. Dialecticians, inspired by notions of freedom and practical reasoning, explored the links among the social sciences, social change, and social emancipation, whereas members of the other stream—romantic existentialists such as Kierkegaard (1813-1855) and Nietzsche (1844-1900)—were highly skeptical of claims about the association of planned social change with the unfolding of history and the inevitability of human progress (Roberts, 1990, pp. 283-284).

◆ Explanation or Understanding?

The epistemology of qualitative research, therefore, had its origins in an epistemological crisis of the late eighteenth century (see also Erickson, 1986, p. 122). Kant's arguments may have ushered in the possibility of qualitative inquiry, but other factors eventually brought it into being. In fact, it emerged from the attention given to the collection of data on the human condition. It was assumed that important political lessons could be learned from such descriptive information—typically described as "statistical" (see, for instance, Hacking, 1990).

During the 1830s, statistical inquiry became embroiled in fieldwork. Descriptive data were repeatedly used to illustrate the social and economic disruptions caused by the switch to steam-powered production in urban areas. Investigators from statistical societies served as field-workers for these portrayals. Their portraits of social dislocation had a rhetorical intent: to provoke new government policies with respect, for instance, to poverty and schooling.

One of the classic accounts of British urban life was written, in German, by an intellectual—and dialectical—descendant of Kant, Friedrich Engels. *The Condition of the Working Class in England* (1845/1969) was compiled by Engels from "personal observations and authentic sources" relating to Manchester, a notable center of statistical inquiry. Note the neo-Kantian doubts expressed by Engels in the opening sentences of his dedication (written in English):

> Working Men! To you I dedicate a work, in which I have tried to lay before my German Countrymen a faithful picture of your conditions, of your sufferings and struggles, of your hopes and prospects. I have lived long enough amidst you to know something about your circumstances; I have devoted to their knowledge my most serious attention. I have studied the various official and non-official documents as far as I was able to get hold of them—I have not been satisfied with this, I wanted more than a mere *abstract* knowledge of my subject. I wanted to see you in your own homes, to observe you in your every-day life, to chat with you on your conditions and grievances, to witness your struggles against the social and political power of your oppressors. (p. 323)

Engels's work, therefore, fell within a naturalistic, interpretive, and field study framework. His close-up narrative style was part of a nineteenth-century journalistic literary genre whose boundaries stretched at least from Charles Dickens (1812-1870) to Emile Zola (1840-1902).

In a wider sense, the penetration of Kantian ideas in modern scientific thought can also be demonstrated by two further publications of the 1830s and 1840s: Auguste Comte's *Cours de Philosophie Positiviste* (6 volumes, 1830-1842) and John Stuart Mill's *A System of Logic* (1843). Comte argued that the history of the human mind and human society had passed through three stages—the theological, the metaphysical, and the positive. He believed that human action—Comte coined the term *sociology*—would undergo a similar transformation in the not-too-distant future.

A System of Logic was also seminal. Like Comte's proposals, it also responded to the demand that the practice of all sciences—natural or moral/social—should be dedicated to the identification of lawlike patterns. Yet Mill did not entirely follow Comte's reductionism. For Mill, then, analyses of human activity required reference to psychological facts as well as material truths. The dualism implicit in Mill's analysis had a double consequence that still remains controversial. Some social investigators sought to bring the moral/social sciences within the sphere of the physical sciences, whereas others deepened Mill's dualism.

Wilhelm Dilthey (1833-1911) was a notable member of the latter school of thought. He believed that the sciences had emancipated themselves from Comtean metaphysics, yet that they were still struggling to identify themselves with reference to the natural sciences. Accordingly, Dilthey felt that Mill was too much in the thrall of Comtean scientific thinking. In turn, he trenchantly criticized the reductionist and objectivist positions espoused by positivists and empiricists. They were, Dilthey felt, corrupted by the Cartesian belief that "the connection of all phenomena according to the principle of causality" is a "precondition for a knowledge of the laws of thought and society." Dilthey's rejection of empiricism stemmed directly from Kantian theory. Positivists, he suggested, believed that "the self-active 'I' " is "an illusion" (quoted in Ermath, 1978, pp. 72-73).

Dilthey took this opportunity to distinguish sharply between two kinds of knowledge or science: *Naturwissenschaft* and *Geisteswissenschaft*. Following Kant, Dilthey argued that the thing-in-itself—nature apart from human consciousness—is unknowable in the realm of the natural sciences. The same argument, however, could not be applied to the *Geisteswissenschaften*. The data of the human sciences—historical social realities— include the data of consciousness, which, again following Kant, can be known directly.

Against this background of controversy in the social sciences, German neo-Kantianism rose strongly in the 1860s and 1870s. It stressed the uniquely transcendental dimensions of mind. Dilthey, for instance, emphasized the role of understanding (*Verstehen*), contrasting it with the pre-Kantian, Cartesian practices of explanation (*Erklärung*).

More important, however, was Dilthey's attention to the concept of *Erlebnis*. Roughly translated as "lived experience," *Erlebnis* was "central to Dilthey's project" (Ermath, 1978, p. 219). Every lived experience, Dilthey believed, occurs within historical social reality. It also lies beyond the immediate awareness of mind but, nonetheless, can be brought to consciousness. Thus *Erlebnis* relates to the intimate relationship between the inner and outer states and consequences of human existence.

Further, Dilthey's appreciation of lived experience included a notable stance with respect to human freedom. He accepted that all humans have a will of their own, yet he did not reduce human freedom to voluntarism, nor to determinism. Dilthey stipulated that the human will is not so much free "from" conditions as free "to" respond to a multiplicity of circumstances. Human freedom, therefore, was defined by Dilthey in terms of "a range of possible responses and choices within a concrete situation" (Ermath, 1978, p. 121).

Finally, Dilthey viewed *Erlebnis* as an empirical rather than a metaphysical concept. The relationships between individuals and the social, historical, and cultural matrix of their lives were phenomena that could be explored by the social (or human) sciences.

Dilthey's interest in *Erlebnis* was primarily historical—to comprehend the changes in the human condition and human spirit that had been brought about by the upheavals of the Enlightenment. Dilthey's successors, however, gradually relocated the relationship between lived experience and human existence from the field of history to the field of sociology (see Antoni, 1962).

During the latter part of the nineteenth century, neo-Kantian thought spread widely in the United States and the United Kingdom. One illustration of this influence, for instance, was Charles Booth's "passion to understand" the continuing social and economic disruptions wrought by late nineteenth-century industrialization (Simey, 1969, p. 99). Although Booth is sometimes recalled as a mere fact gatherer, his studies of the London urban poor between 1887 and 1902 were closely linked to the ideas of one of his assistants, Beatrice Webb (1856-1943). Webb grew up in a household frequented by the social Darwinian theorist Herbert Spencer. "He taught me," she reports in her autobiographical account of the craft of the social investigator, "to look on all social institutions exactly as if they were plants or animals—things that could be observed, classified and explained, and the action of which could to some extent be foretold if one knew enough about them" (Webb, 1979, p. 38). Subsequently, Webb adopted a different outlook, one that suggests the influence of German thought:

> From my diary entries [which followed a visit to mainland Europe in 1882] I infer that I should have become, not a worker in the field of sociology, but a descriptive psychologist; either in the novel, to which I was from time to time tempted; or (if I had been born thirty years later) in a scientific analysis of the mental make-up of individual men and women, and their behaviour under particular conditions. (p. 109)

◆ America or Germany?

By the end of the nineteenth century, the kind of census taking pioneered in Europe began to come to terms with a new set of historical circumstances in the United States. Anglo-Saxon social Darwinism jostled with neo-Kantian ideas brought back to the United States by students who had studied in Germany. Furthermore, both currents of thought had to come to terms with homegrown Progressive ideals. Together, the interaction of these currents in intellectual thought did much to induce the "Americanization of social science" (Manicas, 1987, p. 11).

Social Darwinists in the United States transposed the theories of Charles Darwin to the realm of civil society. They believed that the evolution of society should be left to the free play of market forces. As in nature, that is, social evolution should be left to the survival of the fittest. On the other hand, the Progressives took a contrary stance. They argued that, unlike other animals, human beings had the capacity, akin to Kant's "freedom of practical reason," to define and achieve their own futures.

Accordingly, the social Darwinists and the Progressives differed on the responsibilities they allocated to government. The social Darwinists felt that government should intervene only to remove barriers that limited laissez-faire economic practices, whereas the Progressives regarded government as an agency that should sponsor—ideologically, legally, and financially—the pursuit of social progress.

In the end, the Progressive current in social thought achieved dominance. Progressive politicians promoted policies that had major repercussions for all research. First, they endorsed the value of social research—encouraging nongovernment agencies to fund social research. Second, they raised the intellectual status of social science in the universities—rendering them the policy think tanks of Progressivism. And third, they created a new social stratum—welfare professionals who serviced the organs of the Progressive state.

Professionals and academics struggled with the think-tank mission of the universities. The promissory notes issued by Descartes, Newton, and Comte were repeatedly invoked in attempts to create free-floating technologies of social progress. Henceforth, social life was to be rational and rule governed, with the rules to be derived from scientific inquiry. A slogan used to publicize the 1933 Chicago World's Fair neatly captures this technocratic aspiration: "Science Explores: Technology Executes: Mankind Conforms."

But the diversity of higher education in the United States also allowed other standpoints to survive. Besides looking to Descartes, Newton, and Comte, Progressivism had another side. Its belief in the capacity of human beings to define and achieve their own futures also found common cause with Kantian ideals about human freedom and the deployment of practical reason. Verstehen inquiry, therefore, had a legitimate place in the Progressive pantheon. Typically, such work reached back to the anthropological research of Franz Boas in the 1890s, or to work in the Sociology Department of the University of Chicago, which also came into being in the 1890s. Indeed, higher education in the United States has retained long-standing links with Germany—through student sojourns at German universities (see Manicas, 1987, p. 213), through sanctuary offered to German refugees from Nazism (e.g., Theodore Adorno, Herbert Marcuse), and through the co-authoring and translation of theoretical texts in the 1960s and 1970s (e.g., Berger & Luckmann's *The Social Construction of Reality,* 1966; Habermas's *Knowledge and Human Interests,* 1972).

As noted, however, neo-Kantianism has always been a very broad church. Throughout, its adherents and sympathizers in the United States have duly diversified, forming their own intellectual subcultures, specialist terminologies, and social boundaries. Indeed, as suggested above, their fissiparous and hybridization proclivities (or posturings) have provided endless source material for taxonomically inclined commentators.

Indeed, it is at this juncture that Evelyn Jacob (1987) composed her original exploration of the "assumptions about human nature and society" that underpin qualitative research traditions (p. 3). Note, for instance, that each of the selected traditions stems from an *Erlebnis* rationale. Ecological psychology has "psychological habitat" as one of its foci (p. 5), holistic ethnography concerns the "culture shared by particular bounded groups of individuals" (p. 11), ethnography of communication focuses on "patterns of social interaction among members of a cultural group or among members of different cultural groups" (p. 18), cognitive anthropology assumes that "each bounded group in individuals has a unique system for perceiving and organizing the world about them" (p. 23), and symbolic interactionists are interested in understanding how "interpretations [of individuals' experiences] are developed and used by individuals in specific situations of interaction" (p. 27).

Equally, all qualitative research traditions give as much attention to the inner as well as the outer states of human activity. Jacob (1987, table 1), for instance, notes the "subjective perceptions," "emotions," "reflective

123

interpretations," and "mental standards" that can be included within the "characteristics" of qualitative research (see also Bogdan & Biklen, 1982; Sanday, 1983; Wolcott, 1992).

Another way to comprehend the traditions of qualitative inquiry is to note its convergence with Dilthey's interest in ethnographic research. In the United States, anthropological and sociological practitioners gradually annexed a shared territory that they labeled *ethnography*, a term that comes from a Greek root meaning writing about others (Erickson, 1986, p. 123). In the North American case, such "others" had arisen both within and beyond the mainstream culture.

One important consequence of the ethnographic synthesis has been substantial cross-fertilization between the domains of anthropology and sociology. The study of schooling provides a good example. Schooling is a feature of so-called modern societies, whereas anthropology has its roots in the investigation of premodern societies. The examination of schooling through anthropology (see, for instance, Spindler & Spindler, 1992) might, therefore, appear contradictory. Nevertheless, it has done much to remind educationists that there is more to education than schooling. This broader view of education is demonstrated in Margaret Mead's *Coming of Age in Samoa* (1928), and in subsequent institutional studies such as Howard Becker, Blanche Geer, Everett Hughes, and Anselm Strauss's *Boys in White: Student Culture in Medical School* (1961), Jules Henry's *Culture Against Man* (1963), Philip Jackson's *Life in Classrooms* (1968), Harry Wolcott's *The Man in the Principal's Office* (1973), and Hugh Mehan's *Learning Lessons* (1979).

In an important sense, too, recent ethnographies have also resonated with another feature of Dilthey's presumption that *Erlebnis* is an empirical concept. The "how it actually was" of the 1820s (which Leopold Ranke proclaimed as the task of history; see Kreiger, 1977, p. 4) resurfaced in the 1960s as "telling it like it is"; just as the "new" journalism of the 1960s (e.g., Wolfe & Johnson, 1975) had much in common with the magazine-format, muckraking, narrative journalism of the 1890s and earlier.

But the 1960s and 1970s were not the 1890s or even the 1820s. Qualitative research was reactivated by a new intellectual interest. The Cartesian/Newtonian paradigm had begun to lose its intellectual luster. It slipped off the academy's gold standard. Its devaluation not only followed external criticism (see Kuhn, 1962, 1970), it also arose from internalist critiques of science, themselves reminiscent of Beatrice Webb's revaluation of Herbert Spencer's prescriptions.

Two crucial internalist interventions were Donald Campbell and Julian Stanley's "Experimental and Quasi-Experimental Designs for Research on Teaching" (1963) and Lee J. Cronbach's "Beyond the Two Disciplines of Scientific Psychology" (1975). Campbell and Stanley reviewed earlier Cartesian/Newtonian attempts to devise experimental designs that would yield unambiguous results. Their conclusion, prefigured in the title of their paper, was that social research is an impure art. At best, it can only aspire to the organization of quasi-experiments conducted via the imprecision of quasi-control.

Cronbach offered similar reflections on the received paradigm. In 1957 he had written, "Our job is to invent constructs and to form a network of laws which permits prediction" (p. 681). By 1975, however, he confessed that the "line of investigation I advocated in 1957 no longer seems sufficient" (p. 116). "The goal of our work," he concluded in 1975, is "not to amass generalizations atop which a theoretical tower can someday be erected. The special task of the social scientist in each generation is to pin down the contemporary facts" (p. 126).

In an important sense, then, the boundaries between qualitative and quantitative research became blurred in the 1970s. The inherent uncertainty surrounding neo-Kantian research was joined by similar anxieties about the Cartesian paradigm—and both have been forcefully reviewed, for instance, in David Bloor's *Knowledge and Social Imagery* (1976).

◆ Observer or Observed?

Perhaps the most noteworthy outcome of the epistemological disarray of the 1970s has been a return to Kant's concern with human freedom and social emancipation. There has been a significant reexamination of the observer-observed dyad erected by Descartes and redefined by Kant. Both the observer-observed dualism favored by Cartesians and the observer-observed dialectic activated by neo-Kantians have been questioned. In extreme cases, critics have sought to reduce the observer-observed dyad to a unity.

The freedom of thought and action of the privileged observer is transferred to the less privileged subject of the observation. Similarly, the assumed disinterest of the observer is rejected, along with the passivity of the practitioner (or operative). There is a distinct emancipatory sentiment, for instance, in such works as *Action and Knowledge: Breaking the*

Monopoly With Participatory Action-Research (Fals-Borda & Rahman, 1992), *The Reflective Practitioner* (Schön, 1983), *Authority, Education and Emancipation* (Stenhouse, 1983), *Participatory Action Research* (Whyte, 1991), and *Becoming Critical: Education, Knowledge and Action* (Carr & Kemmis, 1986).

At least three propositions seem to have been adopted by this movement. First, late twentieth-century democracies should empower all citizens, not just privileged elites. Second, liberal social practice can never be morally or politically disinterested. And third, the managerial separation of conception (research) from execution (practice) is psychologically, socially, and economically inefficient.

Sophisticated rationales for action or participatory research are beginning to emerge from this theoretical conjuncture. One popular source, also with Kantian roots, has been the work of Jürgen Habermas (see, especially, his 1965 Inaugural Lecture, "Knowledge and Human Interests: A General Perspective," reprinted in Habermas, 1972). Like many recent reviewers of social theory, Habermas (1972) points to the "objectivist illusion" of pure theory. Instead, he espouses the Kantian posture that there are indissoluble links among knowledge, methodology, and human interests (p. 309). Not surprisingly, therefore, Habermas explicitly eschews the objectivism of Cartesian science, with its attempts to describe the "universe theoretically in its law-like order, just as it is" (p. 303).

As a representative of the dialectical strand of neo-Kantian thought, Habermas holds that "unreflected consciousness" could, through "self-reflection," serve "emancipatory" cognitive interests such that "knowledge and interest are one" (pp. 310, 314). Habermas has repeatedly returned to the "unmasking of the human sciences" (1987, p. 295). He has suggested, in Kantian terms for instance, that the "objectifying attitude in which the knowing subject regards itself as it would entities in the external world is no longer *privileged,*" and that the Cartesian "paradigm of the philosophy of consciousness" be replaced with the "paradigm of mutual understanding" (1987, p. 296).

From Habermas's perspective, social research is an interactive rather than a controlling process. Participants aim for mutual understanding over the coordination of their subsequent actions (see, for instance, Brand, 1990; Kemmis, 1995). Applied research, therefore, is not about social conformity but about social justice.

By these considerations, the Renaissance project of Machiavelli and Columbus is joined to the Enlightenment project of Kant and to the

Progressive project espoused by Webb and Adorno. Applied research, action research, qualitative research, humanist research, and their consociates become the pursuit of democratic forms of communication that, in their turn, prefigure planned social change.

◆ One Tradition or Many?

This chapter has outlined the diversity of intellectual movements and social practices that have activated applied research since the Enlightenment. From a basis laid down in the Renaissance, Western science has embraced the application of rationality to the furtherance of human endeavor. By the Enlightenment, however, Western rationality began to prove less assured than its founders had imagined. It was reactivated and replenished by a range of new ideas.

Each new generation has drawn from this well, has become the practitioner-guardian of its own postures and traditions, and has replenished the well with its own sweet water of fresh ideas. If nothing else, the dynamism of this intellectual community assures its own future. Indeed, its commitment to participate rationally in the prosecution of worthwhile, even emancipatory, social change is probably the most enduring tradition of qualitative research.

◆ References

Antoni, C. (1962). *From history to sociology: The transition in German historical thinking* (H. V. White, Trans.). London: Merlin.

Atkinson, P., Delamont, S., & Hammersley, M. (1989). Qualitative research traditions: A British response to Jacob. *Review of Educational Research, 58,* 231-250.

Becker, H. S., Geer, B., Hughes, E., & Strauss, A. (1961). *Boys in white: Student culture in medical school.* Chicago: University of Chicago Press.

Berger, P., & Luckmann, T. (1966). *The social construction of reality.* Garden City, NY: Doubleday.

Bloor, D. (1976). *Knowledge and social imagery.* Chicago: University of Chicago Press.

Bogdan, R. C., & Biklen, S. K. (1982). *Qualitative research for education: An introduction to theory and methods.* Boston: Allyn & Bacon.

Brand, A. (1990). *The force of reason: An introduction to Habermas' theory of communicative action.* Sydney: Allen & Unwin.

Buchdahl, G. (1969). *Metaphysics and the philosophy of science.* Cambridge: MIT Press.

Buchmann, M., & Floden, R. E. (1989). Research traditions, diversity and progress. *Review of Educational Research, 59,* 241-248.

Campbell, D., & Stanley, J. (1963). Experimental and quasi-experimental designs for research on teaching. In N. Gage (Ed.), *Handbook for research on teaching* (pp. 171-246). Chicago: Rand McNally.

Carr, W., & Kemmis, S. (1986). *Becoming critical: Education, knowledge and action.* London: Falmer.

Cronbach, L. J. (1957). The two disciplines of scientific psychology. *American Psychologist, 12,* 671-684.

Cronbach, L. J. (1975). Beyond the two disciplines of scientific psychology. *American Psychologist, 30,* 116-126.

Descartes, R. (1968). *Discourse on method and the meditations.* Harmondsworth: Penguin.

Engels, F. (1969). *The condition of the working class in England.* London: Panther. (Original work published 1845)

Erickson, F. (1986). Qualitative methods in research on teaching. In M. C. Wittrock (Ed.), *Handbook of research on teaching* (3rd ed., pp. 119-161). New York: Macmillan.

Ermath, M. (1978). *Wilhelm Dilthey: The critique of historical reason.* Chicago: University of Chicago Press.

Fals-Borda, O., & Rahman, M. A. (1991). *Action and knowledge: Breaking the monopoly with participatory action-research.* New York: Apex.

Foucault, M. (1973). *The order of things: An archaeology of the human sciences.* New York: Vintage.

Habermas, J. (1972). *Knowledge and human interests* (J. J. Shapiro, Trans.). London: Heinemann.

Habermas, J. (1987). *The philosophical discourse of modernity: Twelve lectures* (F. Lawrence, Trans.). Cambridge: Polity.

Hacking, I. (1990). *The taming of chance.* Cambridge: Cambridge University Press.

Henry, J. (1963). *Culture against man.* New York: Random House.

Hobsbawm, E., & Ranger, T. (Eds.). (1984). *The invention of tradition.* Cambridge: Cambridge University Press.

Jackson, P. (1968). *Life in classrooms.* New York: Holt, Rinehart & Winston.

Jacob, E. (1987). Qualitative research traditions: A review. *Review of Educational Research, 57,* 1-50.

Jacob, E. (1989). Qualitative research: A defense of traditions. *Review of Educational Research, 59,* 229-235.

Kemmis, S. (1995). Emancipatory aspiration in a postmodern era. *Curriculum Studies, 3*(2), 133-167.

Kreiger, L. (1977). *Ranke: The meaning of history.* Chicago: University of Chicago Press.

Kuhn, T. S. (1962). *The structure of scientific revolutions.* Chicago: University of Chicago Press.

Kuhn, T. S. (1970). *The structure of scientific revolutions* (2nd ed.). Chicago: University of Chicago Press.

Laudan, L. (1977). *Progress and its problems: Toward a theory of scientific growth.* Berkeley: University of California Press.

Lincoln, Y. (1989). Qualitative research: A response to Atkinson, Delamont and Hammersley. *Review of Educational Research, 59,* 237-239.

Machiavelli, N. (1988). *The prince* (Q. Skinner & R. Price, Eds.). Cambridge: Cambridge University Press.

MacIntyre, A. (1988). *Whose justice? Which rationality?* London: Duckworth.

Manicas, P. T. (1987). *A history and philosophy of the social sciences.* New York: Basil Blackwell.

Mead, M., (1928). *Coming of age in Samoa: A psychological study of primitive youth for Western civilization.* New York: William Morrow.

Mehan, H. (1979). *Learning lessons: Social organization in the classroom.* Cambridge, MA: Harvard University Press.

Roberts, J. (1990). *German philosophy: An introduction.* Cambridge: Polity.

Sanday, P. R. (1983). The ethnographic paradigm(s). In J. Van Maanen (Ed.), *Qualitative methodology.* Beverly Hills, CA: Sage.

Schön, D. (1983). *The reflective practitioner: How professionals think in action.* New York: Basic Books.

Scruton, R. (1983). *Kant.* Oxford: Oxford University Press.

Shils, E. (1981). *Tradition.* Boston: Faber & Faber.

Simey, T. S. (1969). Charles Booth. In T. Raison (Ed.), *The founding fathers of social science* (pp. 92-99). Harmondsworth: Penguin.

Slaughter, M. (1982). *Universal languages and scientific taxonomy in the seventeenth century.* Cambridge: Cambridge University Press.

Spindler, G., & Spindler, L. (1992). Cultural process and ethnography: An anthropological perspective. In M. D. LeCompte, W. L. Millroy, & J. Preissle (Eds.), *The handbook of qualitative research in education* (pp. 53-92). New York: Academic Press.

Stenhouse, L. (1983). *Authority, education and emancipation.* London: Heinemann.

Strauss, G. (1966). A sixteenth-century encyclopedia. Sebastian Munster's *Cosmography* and its editions. In C. H. Cater (Ed.), *From the Renaissance to the Counter-Reformation: Essays in honour of Garrett Mattingly* (pp. 145-163). London: Cape.

Webb, B. (1979). *My apprenticeship.* Cambridge: Cambridge University Press.

Whyte, W. F. (1991). *Participatory action research.* London: Sage.

Wolcott, H. F. (1973). *The man in the principal's office: An ethnography.* New York: Holt, Rinehart & Winston.

Wolcott, H. F. (1992). Posturing in qualitative inquiry. In M. D. LeCompte, W. L. Millroy, & J. Preissle (Eds.), *The handbook of qualitative research in education* (pp. 3-52). New York: Academic Press.

Wolfe, T., & Johnson, E. W. (Eds.). (1975). *The new journalism.* London: Pan.

4

Working the Hyphens

Reinventing Self and Other
in Qualitative Research

Michelle Fine

I am waiting for them to stop talking about the "Other," to stop even describing how important it is to be able to speak about difference. It is not just important what we speak about, but how and why we speak. Often this speech about the "Other" is also a mask, an oppressive talk hiding gaps, absences, that space where our words would be if we were speaking, if there were silence, if we were there. This "we" is that "us" in the margins, that "we" who inhabit marginal space that is not a site of domination but a place of resistance. Enter that space. Often this speech about the "Other" annihilates, erases: "no need to hear your voice when I can talk about you better than you can speak about yourself. No need to hear your voice. Only tell me about your pain. I want to know your story. And then I will tell it back to you in a new way. Tell it back to you in such a way that it has become mine, my own. Re-writing you, I write myself anew. I am still author, authority. I am still the colonizer, the speak subject, and you are now at the center of my talk." Stop. (hooks, 1990, pp. 151-152)

 Much of qualitative research has reproduced, if contradiction-filled, a colonizing discourse of the "Other." This essay is an attempt to

AUTHOR'S NOTE: My appreciation to Julie Blackman, Norman Denzin, and Yvonna Lincoln for careful reading and comments. Credit is also owed to L. Mun Wong, Cindy Kublik, Sarah Ingersoll, Judi Addelston, and Kim Mizrahi for helping me develop these notions.

review how qualitative research projects have *Othered* and to examine an emergent set of activist and/or postmodern texts that interrupt *Othering*. First, I examine the hyphen at which Self-Other join in the politics of everyday life, that is, the hyphen that both separates and merges personal identities with our inventions of Others. I then take up how qualitative researchers work this hyphen. Here I gather a growing set of works on "inscribing the Other," viewing arguments that critical, feminist, and/or Third World scholars have posed about social science as a tool of domination. This section collects a messy series of questions about methods, ethics, and epistemologies as we rethink how researchers have spoken "of" and "for" Others while occluding ourselves and our own investments, burying the contradictions that percolate at the Self-Other hyphen.

A renewed sense of possibility breathes in the next section, in which I present discussion of qualitative research projects designed for social change. Here readers engage narratives written against Othering, analyzing not just the decontextualized voices of Others, but the very structures, ideologies, contexts, and practices that constitute Othering (Bhavnani, 1992). Qualitative researchers interested in self-consciously working the hyphen—that is, unpacking notions of scientific neutrality, universal truths, and researcher dispassion—will be invited to imagine how we can braid critical and contextual struggle back into our texts (Burawoy et al., 1992; Fine & Vanderslice, 1992).

This essay is designed to rupture the textual laminations within which Others have been sealed by social scientists, to review the complicity of researchers in the construction and distancing of Others, and to identify transgressive possibilities inside qualitative texts.

◆ Selves-Others: Co-constructions at the Hyphen

In September 1989, my niece was sexually assaulted by a department store security officer. He caught her shoplifting and then spent two hours threatening her with prison, legal repercussions, and likely abuse at the hands of other women in prison. She had just turned 16, and half believed him. Filled with terror, she listened for 90 minutes of what would later be determined "unlawful detainment." He offered her a deal, "Give me what women give men and I'll let you go." Surprised, shocked, understanding but not fully, she asked, "What do you mean?" She refused. For another 30 minutes he persisted. Tears, threats, and terror were exchanged. She agreed, ultimately, after he showed her a photo album of "girls who did it." Sheepishly, and brilliantly, she requested that he "get a condom."

March 5, 1992. We won the criminal case for sexual assault, and we are pursuing a civil suit against the department store. Tomorrow my niece is going to be deposed by the store's lawyers. She is, by now, 19, a new mother, living with her longtime boyfriend/father of the baby. She is Latina, and was adopted from Colombia into our middle-class Jewish family 12 years ago.

Writing this essay, I find myself ever conscious about how I participate in constructing Others. Tonight I listen to myself collude in the splitting of Jackie, my niece—the dissection of her adolescent, Latina, female body/consciousness. Family, friends, lawyers, and unsolicited advisers subtly, persistently, and uncomfortably work to present her as white/Jewish (not Latina), sexually innocent (not mother), victim (not shoplifter), the object of male aggression. Stories of her new baby, sexuality, reproductive history, desires, and pains, we all nod across cities, should probably be avoided in her testimony.

At some point in the phone call I realize our collusion in her Othering, and I realize that Jackie has long since grown accustomed to this dynamic. Her life has been punctuated by negotiations at the zippered borders of her gendered, raced, and classed Otherhood. As the good (adopted) granddaughter, daughter, and niece, she always has, and does again, split for us. In a flash I remember that when she was picked up for shoplifting she gave her Spanish name to the police, not the English name she had used for nine years.

Sitting within and across alienating borders, Jackie is now being asked to draw her self-as-good-middle-class-white-woman and to silence her Other-as-bad-Latina-unwed-mother. Valerie Smith (1991) would call these "split affinities." Jackie the Latina street girl had to stay out of court because Jackie the white middle-class young lady was escorted in. That night on the phone we were all circling to find a comfortable (for whom?) space for representation. We struggled with what bell hooks (1990) would call a *politics of location*:

Within a complex and ever shifting realities of power relations, do we position ourselves on the side of colonizing mentality? Or do we continue to stand in political resistance with the oppressed, ready to offer our ways of seeing and theorizing, of making culture, toward that revolutionary effort which seeks to create space where there is unlimited access to pleasure and power of knowing, where transformation is possible? (p. 145)

No surprise, Jackie danced through the deposition shining with integrity, style, and passion. She told all as proud mother, lover, daughter, niece, and survivor. With a smile and a tear, she resisted their, and she resisted our, Othering.

Jackie mingled her autobiography with our surveilled borders on her Self and the raced and gendered legal interpretations of her Other by which she was surrounded. She braided them into her story, her deposition, which moved among "hot spots" and "safe spots." She slid from victim to survivor, from naive to coy, from deeply experienced young woman to child. In her deposition she dismantled the very categories I so worried we had constructed as sedimented pillars around her, and she wandered among them, pivoting her identity, her self-representations, and, therefore, her audiences. She became neither the Other nor the Same. Not even zippered. Her mobile positioning of contradictions could too easily be written off to the inconsistencies of adolescence. Maybe that's why she ultimately won the settlement for damages. But she would better be viewed as an honest narrator of multiple poststructural selves speaking among themselves, in front of an audience searching relentlessly for pigeonholes.

I think again about Jackie as I read a recent essay on ethnicity, identity, and difference written by Stuart Hall. Hall (1991) takes up this conversation by reviewing the representations that have seasoned his autobiography:

> History changes your conception of yourself. Thus, another critical thing about identity is that it is partly the relationship between you and the Other. Only when there is an Other can you know who you are. To discover the fact is to discover and unlock the whole enormous history of nationalism and of racism. Racism is a structure of discourse and representation that tried to expel the Other symbolically—blot it out, put it over there in the Third World, at the margin. (p. 16)

Hall traces the strands of his "self" through his raced and classed body. Recognizing that representations of his selves are always politically situated, he sees them also as personally negotiated. For Hall, the Self constructs as the Other is invented. In this passage, however, Hall appears to slide between two positions. In one, he sees Self and Other as fluid. The other requires the fixing of an Other in order for Self to be constituted.

133

Ironically, by stipulating the binary opposition, Hall reproduces the separation and detours away from investigating what is "between." Unearthing the blurred boundaries "between," as Jackie understood, constitutes a critical task for qualitative researchers.

Biddy Martin and Chandra Talpade Mohanty (1986) extend this conversation when they take up an analysis of *home* as a site for constituting Self and for expelling Others. They write:

> The tension between the desire for home, for synchrony, for sameness and the realization of the repressions and violence that make home, harmony, sameness imaginable, and that enforce it, is made clear in the movement of the narrative by very careful and effective reversals which do not erase the positive desire for unit, for Oneness, but destabilize and undercut it. . . .
>
> The relationship between the loss of community and the loss of self is crucial. To the extent that identity is collapsed with home and community and based on homogeneity and comfort, on skin, blood and heart, the giving up of home will necessarily mean the giving up of self and vice versa. (pp. 208-209)

These writers acknowledge that Self and Other reside on opposite sides of the same door. Home and the "real world" are successfully split. The former codes comfort, whereas the latter flags danger. Othering helps us deny the dangers that loiter inside our homes. Othering keeps us from seeing the comforts that linger outside.

As I write this essay, the *New York Times* lands on the front porch. Another perverse splitting of Identity and Othering explodes on the front page. Lesbian women and gay men in New York City have been informed that they will not be allowed to march in this year's St. Patrick's Day parade. One parade marshal explained, "To be Irish is to know the difference between men and women's characteristics." Ethnic community is being consolidated, whitewashed, through sexual exclusion. At a time when white working-class men and women are struggling to define themselves as whole, to locate their terror outside, and hold some Other responsible for their plight at the hands of late capitalism, we witness public rituals of race purification. A fragile collective identity is secured through promiscuous assaults on Others (African Americans? Asian Americans? women? lesbian women? gay men?) (see Weis, 1990). The exploitations endured today are protected/projected onto Others of varied colors, classes, sexualities, and bodies.

134

Self and Other are knottily entangled. This relationship, as lived between researchers and informants, is typically obscured in social science texts, protecting privilege, securing distance, and laminating the contradictions. Despite denials, qualitative researchers are always implicated at the hyphen. When we opt, as has been the tradition, simply to write *about* those who have been Othered, we deny the hyphen. Slipping into a contradictory discourse of individualism, personalogic theorizing, and decontextualization, we inscribe the Other, strain to white out Self, and refuse to engage the contradictions that litter our texts.

When we opt, instead, to engage in social struggles *with* those who have been exploited and subjugated, we work the hyphen, revealing far more about ourselves, and far more about the structures of Othering. Eroding the fixedness of categories, we and they enter and play with the blurred boundaries that proliferate.

By *working the hyphen,* I mean to suggest that researchers probe how we are in relation with the contexts we study and with our informants, understanding that we are all multiple in those relations. I mean to invite researchers to see how these "relations between" get us "better" data, limit what we feel free to say, expand our minds and constrict our mouths, engage us in intimacy and seduce us into complicity, make us quick to interpret and hesitant to write. Working the hyphen means creating occasions for researchers and informants to discuss what is, and is not, "happening between," within the negotiated relations of whose story is being told, why, to whom, with what interpretation, and whose story is being shadowed, why, for whom, and with what consequence.

◆ Inscribing the Other

Studies which have as their focal point the alleged deviant attitudes and behaviors of Blacks are grounded within the racist assumptions and principles that only render Blacks open to further exploitation. The challenge to social scientists for a redefinition of the basic problem has been raised in terms of the "colonial analogy." It has been argued that the relationship between the researcher and his subjects, by definition, resembles that of the oppressor and the oppressed, because it is the oppressor who defines the problem, the nature of the research, and, to some extent, the quality of interaction between him and his subjects. This inability to understand and research the fundamental problem, neo-colonialism, prevents most social researchers from being able accurately to observe and analyze Black life and culture and the impact racism and oppression have upon Blacks. Their inability to understand the nature and effects of neo-colonialism in the same manner as Black people is rooted in the inherent bias of the social sciences. (Ladner, 1971, p. vii)

Joyce Ladner warned us more than 20 years ago about the racism, bred and obscured, at the Self-Other hyphen of qualitative research. Ladner knew then that texts that sought the coherence of Master Narratives needed, and so created, Others. The clean edges of those narratives were secured by the frayed borders of the Other. The articulate professional voice sounded legitimate against the noisy dialect of the Other. The rationality of the researcher/writer domesticated the outrage of the Other. These texts sought to close contradictions, and by so doing they tranquil-ized the hyphen, ousting the Other.

Master Narratives seek to preserve the social order while obscuring the privileged stances/investments of writers:

Within the discourse of modernity, the Other not only sometimes ceases to be a historical agent, but is often defined within totalizing and universalistic theories that create a transcendental rational White, male Eurocentric subject that both occupies the centers of power while simultaneously appearing to exist outside of time and space. Read against this Eurocentric transcendental subject, the Other is shown to lack any redeeming commu-nity traditions collective voice of historical weight—and is reduced to the imagery of the colonizer. (Giroux, 1991, p. 7)

The imperialism of such scholarship is evident in terms of whose lives get displayed and whose lives get protected by social science. Put another way, why don't we know much about how the rich live? Why don't we study whiteness? How do "their" and "our" lives get investigated (and not)? Whose stories are presented as if "naturally" self-revealing and whose stories are surrounded by "compensatory" theory? Whose "dirty linen," as Yvonna Lincoln would put it, gets protected by such work?

Two years ago, a student of mine, Nancy Porter, asked me if she could design a dissertation around the gendered and classed lives of elite white women. I was embarrassed that I had somehow set up an expectation among students that poverty was "in." Could I really have conveyed that wealth was a bore? Nonetheless, with my blessings and to her delight, she, a professional golfer with lots of access, proceeded to conduct deep qualitative interviews with rich, "registered" Main Line women of Philadelphia, only to learn that the very discourse of wealthy women constricts and betrays few wrinkles, problems, or any outstanding features. These women describe themselves as if they were "typical," don't talk about money, and rarely reveal any domestic or interpersonal difficulties. Only if divorced will they discuss heterosexuality and gender relations critically. Nancy and I soon began to understand that there had been a collusion between social researchers committed to sanitizing/neglecting the elite through scholarly omission *and* an elite discourse of comfort and simplicity which conveys a relatively bump-free story of their lives. Protected then, twice, by the absence of social surveillance—in welfare offices, from public agencies, through social researchers—and the absence of a scholarly discourse on their dysfunctionality, the elite, with their "new class" academic colleagues, retain a corpus of social science material that fingers Them while it powders the faces of Us.

The social sciences have been, and still are, long on texts that inscribe some Others, preserve other Others from scrutiny, and seek to hide the researcher/writer under a veil of neutrality or objectivity. With the publication of Clifford and Marcus's *Writing Culture* (1986) came an explosion of attention to the domination encoded in such texts, and to the troubling transparency of ethnographers and writers. Although it is most problematic that Clifford and Marcus exclude the work of feminists, the essays in their volume confirm the costs in theory and praxis that devolve from the insistence that ethnographic distance be preferred over authentic engagement. By so doing, *Writing Culture* marks a significant moment in the biography of studying Others, documenting the complicity of ethnographic projects in the narration of colonialism.

A close look at these tensions is offered in Mary Louise Pratt's (1985) analysis of early travel journals. Pratt argues that within these texts, "natives" were portrayed through multiple discourses, typically as if they were "amenable to domination" and had great "potential as a labor pool" (p. 139). Written to "capture" the essence of "natives," these journals allowed little interruption and less evidence of leakage, sweat, pleasure, oppression, rude or polite exchanges in the creation of the manuscripts. These journals were written as if there were no constructing narrators. Disinterested translators simply photographed local practices and customs. Pratt (1985) reproduces John Mandeville's *Travels* (circa 1350):

Men and women of that isle have heads like hounds; and they are called Cynocephales. This folk, thereof all they be of such shape, yet they are fully reasonable and subtle of wit. . . . And they gang all naked but a little cloth before their privy members. They are large of stature and good warriors, and they bear a great target, with which they cover all their body, and a long spear in their hand. (p. 139)

Pratt comments:

Any reader recognizes here a familiar, widespread, and stable form of "othering." The people to be othered are homogenized into a collective "they," which is distilled even further into an iconic "he" (the standardized adult male specimen). This abstracted "he"/"they" is the subject of verbs in a timeless present tense, which characterizes anything "he" is or does not as a particular historical event but as an instance of pregiven custom or trait. (p. 139)

Qualitative researchers then, and most now, produce texts through Donna Haraway's (1988) "god trick," presuming to paint the Other from "nowhere." Researchers/writers self-consciously carry no voice, body, race, class, or gender and no interests into their texts. Narrators seek to shelter themselves in the text, as if they were transparent (Spivak, 1988). They recognize no hyphen.

Analogous to Pratt's project on travel journals, sociologist Herb Gans has written and worried about the more recent dense body of work produced on "the underclass." This flourishing area of research has legitimated the category, even amidst multiple slippery frames. Poor adults and children have been codified as Others, as the broader culture is being prepared for a permanent caste of children and adults beyond redemption. Social science has been the intellectual handmaiden for this project, serving to anesthetize the culture with cognitive distinctions that help split the species. These same constructions may, of course, be producing their own subversions, resistances, and transgressions, but, for the moment, "we" don't have to see, smell, hear, feel, or respond to "them." The material and discursive hyphens, again, are being denied.

Michael Katz (1993) narrates a similar story about the historic encoding, within social scientific debates, of the "(un)deserving poor." Katz traces representations of the poor across social science debates and public policies. He argues that social scientists have insinuated moral boundaries of deservingness that thread research and policy, enabling researchers, policy makers, and the public to believe that we can distinguish (and serve) those who are "deserving" and neglect honorably those who are "undeserving" and poor.

We confront, then, one legacy of social research that constructs, legitimates, and distances Others, banishing them to the margins of the culture. Sometimes these texts are used to deprive Them of services; always to rob Them of whole, complex, humanity. Although these portraits of subjugation may be internally slippery, they cohere momentarily around deficiencies, around who they are not. These Others are represented as unworthy, dangerous, and immoral, or as pitiable, victimized, and damaged.

There is, too, a growing postcolonial critique of Othering directed at those literatures written presumably "for" Others. Homi Bhabha (1990), for instance, unravels "nation-centered" discourses that weave ideologies of "common culture." To assure their hermetic seals, he argues these cultures are written in ways that essentialize and silence women's bodies and stories. Like Cornel West (1988) and Kimberle Crenshaw (1992), Bhabha takes affront at "common culture" discourses made coherent by "the subsumption or sublation of social antagonism, . . . the repression of social divisions, . . . the power to authorize an 'impersonal' holistic or universal discourse on the representation of the social that naturalizes cultural difference and turns it into a 'second' nature argument" (p. 242). Thus even "for" Others there are growing, stifling discourses that essentialize to map culture.

At the root of this argument, whether Othering is produced "on" or "for," qualitative researchers need to recognize that our work stands in some relation to Othering. We may self-consciously or not decide *how* to work the hyphen of Self and Other, how to gloss the boundaries between, and within, slippery constructions of Others. But when we look, get involved, demur, analyze, interpret, probe, speak, remain silent, walk away, organize for outrage, or sanitize our stories, and when we construct our texts in or on their words, we decide how to nuance our relations with/for/despite those who have been deemed Others. When we write essays about subjugated Others as if *they* were a homogeneous mass (of vice or virtue), free-floating and severed from contexts of oppression, and as if we were neutral transmitters of voices and stories, we tilt toward a narrative strategy that reproduces Othering on, despite, or even "for." When we construct texts collaboratively, self-consciously examining our relations with/for/despite those who have been contained as Others, we move against, we enable resistance to, Othering.

This is no simple binary opposition of Self and Other, nor of texts that inscribe and texts that resist. There is no easy narrative litmus for Othering. Contradictions litter all narrative forms. And all narratives about Others both inscribe and resist othering. Yet in becoming self-conscious of work at the hyphen, researchers can see a history of qualitative research that has been deeply colonial, surveilling, and exotic (Clifford & Marcus, 1986; Pratt, 1985, 1992; Rosaldo, 1989). Now that the subjects of U.S. ethnography have come home, qualitative accounts of urban and rural, poverty-stricken and working-class, white and of color America flourish. Through these texts, the Other survives next door. But the privileges, interests, biographies, fetishes, and investments of researchers typically remain subtext, buried, protected (Harding, 1987; Haraway, 1988).

Renato Rosaldo (1989) contends that there are no "innocent" ethnographers. When innocence is sought, Rosaldo writes, the "eye of ethnography [often connects with] the I of imperialism" (p. 41). The project at hand is to unravel, critically, the blurred boundaries in our relation, and in our texts; to understand the political work of our narratives; to decipher how the traditions of social science serve to inscribe; and to imagine how our practice can be transformed to resist, self-consciously, acts of othering. As these scenes of translation vividly convey, qualitative researchers are chronically and uncomfortably engaged in ethical decisions about how deeply to work with/for/despite those cast as Others, and how seamlessly to represent the hyphen. Our work will never "arrive" but must always struggle "between."

◆ Writing Against Othering

> I too think the intellectual should constantly disturb, should bear witness to the misery of the world, should be provocative by being independent, should rebel against all hidden and open pressures and manipulations, should be the chief doubter of systems, of power and its incantations, should be the witness to their mendacity. . . . An intellectual is always at odds with hard and fast categories, because these tend to be instruments used by the victors. (Havel, 1990, p. 167)

In contrast to "hard and fast" texts that inscribe and commodify Others, we move now to a set of texts that self-consciously interrupt Othering, that force a radical rethinking of the ethical and political relations of qualitative researchers to the objects/subjects of our work. In this section I review three chunks of work that write against Othering. First, I present those texts that insert "uppity" voices, stances, and critiques to interrupt Master Narratives (see Austin, 1989; Fanon, 1965; Fine, 1992; hooks, 1989; Rollins, 1985). Often, but not always, these are essays written about and by women of color, situated at the intersection of race and gender oppression (Crenshaw, 1992).

Second, I examine texts in which qualitative researchers dissect elites' constructions of Self and Other. Listening to elites as they manicure them-Selves through Othering, we hear the voices of white fraternity brothers interviewed by Peggy Sanday (1990), white high school boys in Lois Weis's (1990) analysis of "working class without work," and nondis-abled researchers' analysis of persons with disabilities, projecting their existential and aesthetic anxieties onto the bodies of disabled Others (Hahn, 1983). In each instance, the words of elites are analyzed by researchers as they evince a discourse of Othering. This work enables us to eavesdrop on privileged consciousness as it seeks to peel Self off of Other.

The third chunk of writing against Othering comprises those texts that press social research for social activism. Engaged with struggles of social transformation, these researchers raise questions about the ethics of in-volvement and the ethics of detachment, the illusions of objectivity and the borders of subjectivity, and the possibilities of collaborative work and the dilemmas of collusion (Burawoy et al., 1992; Fine & Vanderslice, 1992; Kitzinger, 1991; Lykes, 1989).

From the qualitative works discussed here surfaces the next generation of ethical and epistemological questions for qualitative researchers com-mitted to projects of social justice. These writers/researchers mark a space of analysis in which the motives, consciousness, politics, and stances of informants and researchers/writers are rendered contradictory, problem-atic, and filled with transgressive possibilities.

Scene 1: Rupturing Texts With Uppity Voices

Gayatri Chakravorty Spivak (1988) contends that academics/researchers can do little to correct the "material wrongs of colonialism." She argues that "in the face of the possibility that the intellectual is complicit in the persistent constitution of Other as the Self's shadow, a possibility of political practice for the intellectual would be to put the economic 'under erasure' " (p. 280). Like bell hooks and Joan Scott, Spivak asks that researchers stop trying to *know* the Other or *give voice to* the Other (Scott, 1991) and listen, instead, to the plural voices of those Othered, as constructors and agents of knowledge.

Although I would quibble with Spivak's sense of the diminished capacity of researchers to participate in the interruption/transformation of social conditions, central to Spivak's and Scott's project is the notion that researchers/writers need to listen and also reveal. As researchers, we need to position ourselves as no longer transparent, but as classed, gendered, raced, and sexual subjects who construct our own locations, narrate these locations, and negotiate our stances with relations of domination (Giroux, 1991). But toward what end?

Chantal Mouffe (1988) would implore activist academics to "determine what conditions are necessary for specific forms of subordination to produce struggles that seek their abolishment and to fuse these as links in a 'chain of equivalence' " (p. 99). Like Mouffe, Cornel West (1988) details a liberatory agenda for social research in which we undertake inquiry into the supremacist logics of domination, into the micropractices of daily subjugation, and into the macrostructural dynamics of class and political exploitation. Urging us to document evidence of struggle, resistance, and counterhegemony (p. 22), West presses for a research agenda steeped in movements for social justice.

How engaged researchers become with, for, against, despite Othering constitutes a political decision that is never resolved simply "in the neutral" by "not getting involved" and "doing science" instead. As Stanley Aronowitz (1988) has written, "Science purports to separate the domination of nature from human domination and regards itself as ideologically neutral" (p. 527).

The decision to retreat from scenes of domination in the name of science is oxymoronic witnessing injustice without outrage. The Other is constituted. The Self is shadowed. Science is preserved. Prevailing politics prospers. Objectivity is assumed. As Spivak (1988) warns, the benevolent "construc[tion of] a homogeneous Other" only reassures "our own place in the seat of the Same or the Self" (p. 288). Although most qualitative work has refused to engage intentionally with the politics of justice, a few texts have imported Others to crack the binary oppositional discourses within social science and the law. Much of this work comes from African American women writing at the *intersection,* as Kimberle Crenshaw (1992) explains:

> The particular experience of Black women in the dominant culture ideology of American society can be conceptualized as *intersectional.* Intersectional-

ity captures the way in which the particular location of Black women in dominant American social relations is unique and in some sense unassimilable to the discursive paradigms of gender and race domination. (p. 2)

Using the Anita Hill/Clarence Thomas hearings as the ground for her analysis of intersectionality, Crenshaw maintains that although Anita Hill sat at the nexus of race/gender oppression, she was presented "as if" she were the prototype white woman harassment victim pitted against the prototype black man accused of rape. Crenshaw uses these images to explode, as both theoretically inadequate and strategically problematic, the narrow cultural frames that have contained *race* as black and male and *gender* as white and female. Contending that black women's experiences are not binary but profoundly intersectional, and therefore radically threatening to existing frames, Crenshaw sees Anita Hill's status as "situated within two fundamental hierarchies of social power (gender and race)," and says that "the central disadvantage that Hill faced was the lack of available and widely comprehended narratives to communicate the reality of her experience as a Black woman to the world" (p. 2). Crenshaw argues that the double marginality of black women, suppressed within both gender and race narratives, is exacerbated by the silencing of black women within the pact of race solidarity between black women and men. Hill had to be deraced to be recognized as a survivor of sexual harassment, and, Crenshaw contends, this is why so many women of color rejected her story as authentic.

Repositioning Hill as the renegade survivor resisting at the intersection of race and gender codes, unwilling to be silenced, Crenshaw slits open white feminism and black solidarity as cultural narratives that fundamentally marginalize the experience, complexity, and critique of black women. Crenshaw concludes, "The vilification of Anita Hill and the embracing of Clarence Thomas reveals that a Black woman breaking ranks to complain of sexual harassment is a much greater threat than a Black man who breaks ranks over race policy" (p. 32).

In *Sapphire Bound!*, a text authored some three years earlier, Regina Austin (1989) makes visible those ideologies surrounding black women's bodies and minds as they are buried in seemingly coherent legal texts. Austin first inserts autobiographic outrage:

When was the last time someone told you that your way of approaching problems . . . was all wrong? You are too angry, too emotional, too subjective, too pessimistic, too political, too anecdotal and too instinctive? I never know how to respond to such accusations. How can I legitimate my way of thinking? I know that I am not used to flying off the handle, seeing imaginary insults and problems where there are none. I am not a witch solely by nature, but by circumstance and choice as well. I suspect that what my critics really want to say is that I am being too self consciously black (brown, yellow, red) and/or female to suit their tastes and should "lighten up" because I am making them feel very uncomfortable, and that is not nice. And I want them to think that I am nice, don't I or "womanish"? . . . The chief sources of our theory should be black women's critiques of a society that is dominated by and structured to favor white men of wealth and power. We should also find inspiration in the modes of resistance black women mount, individually and collectively. (p. 540)

Austin then details the legal case in which Crystal Chambers, an African American adult woman, single and pregnant, was fired from Omaha Girls' Club because, as the justices argued, "while a single pregnant woman may indeed provide a good example of hard work and independence, the same person may be a negative role model with respect to the girls' club objective of diminishing the number of teenage pregnancies" (p. 551). Austin writes:

A black feminist jurisprudential analysis of Chambers must seriously con-sider the possibility that young, single, sexually active, fertile and nurturing black women are being viewed ominously because they have the temerity to attempt to break out of the rigid, economic, social and political categories that a racist, sexist and less stratified society would impose upon them. . . . Like a treasonous recruit, Crystal turns up unmarried and pregnant. As such, she embodied the enemy . . . to the cause of black cultural containment. (p. 551)

With the body of Crystal Chambers, Austin levers a critical analysis of African American women as they collectively embody the Other in the law. Austin writes against Othering through autobiography, and through the embodied story of Crystal Chambers. In an extension of this stance, Austin (1992) argues in a more recent paper, titled *"The Black Commu-nity," Its Lawbreakers and a Politics of Identification,* for what she calls a "politics of identification," in which there is critical engagement of lawbreakers by the black middle class, in an effort to invent and resusci-tate, discursively and materially, "the [black] community" (p. 1815).

Mari Matsuda (1989), another critical feminist legal scholar of color, self-consciously writes against Othering by reimagining a legal canon

144

written out of the experience of Others. By analyzing how the law buries victims' voices and how it protects an abusive elite, Matsuda invents legal text that would privilege the experiences of victims. She not only legitimates voices of subjugation, but presumes them to be the most substantive wellspring for critical legal knowledge:

> There is an outsider's jurisprudence growing and thriving alongside mainstream jurisprudence in American law schools. The new feminist jurisprudence is a lively example of this. A related, and less celebrated outsider jurisprudence is that belonging to people of color. What is it that characterizes the new jurisprudence of people of color? First is a methodology grounded in the particulars of their social reality and experience. This method is consciously both historical and revisionist, attempting to know history from the bottom. From the fear and namelessness of the slave, from the broken treaties of the indigenous Americans, the desire to know history from the bottom has forced these scholars to sources often ignored: journals, poems, oral histories and stories from their own experiences of life in a hierarchically arranged world. . . .
>
> Outsiders thus search for what Anne Scales has called the ratchet—legal tools that have progressive effect, defying the habit of neutral principals to entrench exiting power. (p. 11)

Crenshaw, Austin, and Matsuda force readers to hear subjugated voices not as Others but as primary informants on Othering and as the source for radical rethinking of the law. Like these legal theorists, sociologist Judith Rollins (1985) studies domination enacted by elite white women on the women of color who work for them as domestics. Committed to the theoretical inversion of Othering, Rollins interrupts what a white reader would recognize as the traditional equipment of narrative legitimacy. Rollins delivers her analysis from the vantage of the women employed as domestics. Reversing who would typically be relied upon to tell the "real" story and who would be portrayed as Other, Rollins allows readers to hear how much subjugated women know about them-Selves and about Others. At the same time, she analyzes how privileged women lack knowledge of Self and knowledge of those who work for them:

> Thus, domestics' stronger consciousness of the Other functions not only to help them survive in the occupation but also to maintain their self response. The worker in the home has a level of knowledge about familial and personal problems that few outsiders do. It is not surprising that domestic

workers do not take the insulting attitudes and judgments of employers seriously; they are in a position to make scathing judgments of their own. (p. 215)

Jean Baker Miller, in her book *Toward a New Psychology of Women* (1976), argues a point similar to that made by Rollins. In colonizing relations, what Miller calls "dominant-subordinate relations," subordinates spend much time studying the Other. They carry, therefore, substantial knowledge about Self and dominants. Given their need to anticipate and survive, they contain this knowledge and remain silent about the extent to which dominants depend on them. Rarely do they display/flaunt their knowledge of the Other. At the same time, the dominant Other suffers for lack of knowledge of self or others.

Patricia Hill Collins (1990) develops standpoint theory (see also Dorothy Smith, 1987, 1992) through African American women, who have been positioned as "outsiders within" the academy and thereby enjoy a "peculiar marginality." She urges women to venture into this marginality and unearth a "collective self defined Black feminist consciousness" by listening to black women's stories as they confront and resist images of themselves as Other. Collins recognizes that dominant groups have a "vested interest in suppressing such thought," and for that reason she encourages women to engage in just such subversive work—in contexts where we're wanted and not, in communities that feel comforting, and in those we know to be strange and dangerous.

Rupturing narratives allow us to hear the uppity voices of informants and researchers who speak against structures, representations, and practices of domination. In these texts, researchers are working the hyphen, reconciling the slippery constructions of Self and Other and the contexts of oppression in which both are invented.

Scene 2: Probing the Consciousness of Dominant Others

This second slice of scholarship written self-consciously against Othering probes how individuals inhabiting a space of dominance construct their sense of Self through the denigration of Others. These social researchers unpack how dominants manufacture and conceptualize their relations with subordinated Others through violence, denigration, and exploitation.

For instance, Peggy Sanday (1990) has studied how white fraternity brothers create a collective sense of brotherhood through acts of homophobia, racism, and sexism, which enables them to deny their homoeroticism. By studying these young men as elites who abuse power over women and over men of color, Sanday articulates the psychodynamics of collective homophobia as it breeds "out-group" violence, allows "in-group" homoeroticism, and hyperconfirms "the brothers' " public heterosexuality.

In parallel intellectual form, disability scholar Harlan Hahn (1983) has reviewed the works of nondisabled researchers of disability, only to conclude that by reading their work we learn more about these researchers' terror of disability than we do about the persons with disabilities about whom they presumably have written. Hahn theorizes that nondisabled researchers carry existential and aesthetic anxieties about bodily dis-integrity that they project onto the bodies of persons with disabilities. Their narratives are laced with anxieties as if they were simply in the bodies of "them" rather than (un)settled within the (un)consciousness of the researchers.

As a last example, I draw upon the work of ethnographer Lois Weis, who has spent much time interviewing white working-class adolescent males in a town whose economy has been ravaged by deindustrialization. Weis (1990) argues that these young men, who would have generated social identities through the trade union movement in previous decades, now develop identities instead along the lines of race and gender antagonism. Having "lost" identities that were once available to their fathers and grandfathers, they narrate white, working-class, male identities saturated with "virulent racism and sexism." In an effort to solidify Self, the young men in Sanday's and Weis's texts, like the researchers in Hahn's work, rehearse publicly their ownership and degradation of Others—women, men of color, and persons with disabilities, respectively.

These researchers study the perversions of Othering that constitute a consciousness of domination. This genre of work seeks to understand how individuals carve out contradictory social identities that sculpt, harass, and repel Others within and outside themselves. Deploying what might be called *technologies of Othering* (borrowing from deLauretis, 1987), those studied seem to narrate collective, homogeneous identities by constructing collective, homogeneous identities for Others. Less well understood, or narrated, are the incoherent threads of these men as individuals struggling to construct Self.

In this cavern of critical, qualitative work, social researchers excavate voices of privilege to understand how Othering works as contradictory identity formation. When we read Sanday or Weis, we hear researchers listening to relatively high-power informants seeking desperately a Self, by constructing and expelling Others. In these works, and my own analysis in *Framing Dropouts* (Fine, 1991) could be included here, qualitative researchers practice what might be called *doubled splitting*. We split ourselves from elite informants as though they and we are contained, stable, and separable. We then study the splitting that they produce with/against subjugated Others. We stabilize, essentialize, and render our elite informants' Other. Norman Denzin (personal communication, February 1992) has written to me, concerned that in the study of power elites there remains a tendency to

> create self (colonizer) and other (colonized) as dichotomous categories, oppositions defined out of clearly defined cultural, ethnic, racial, and gendered differences. Such treatments (after Derrida and Bakhtin) fail to treat the complexities and contradictions that define membership in each category. Fixed immutable ethnic (gendered, etc.) identities are thereby inscribed. A picture of a homogeneous culturally dominant group is pitted against a picture of an equally homogeneous group of outsiders on the periphery. The internal oppositional nature of ethnic and cultural life is thereby minimized. A fixed stereotypical picture of an isolated minority group is pitted against a "coherent white-American, male power structure," etc. The image of overlapping, conflicting, de-centered circles of ethnic (gendered, etc.) identities is never considered.

By creating flat caricatures we may indeed be undermining an opportunity for ourselves as social researchers to "come clean" about the contradictory stances, politics, perspectives, and histories we import to our work. Rendering fluid, and not fixed, our constructions of Selves and Others, and the narratives produced as qualitative research, can reveal our partialities and pluralities.

◆ Endings: Social Research for Social Change

Rereading Malinowski's *Argonauts of the Western Pacific* (1922), I can hear an ethnographer searching for a text superior to "mere journalism," a method of science designed to "capture" native life, and a narrative style able to re-present "savagery" through the eyes of an intelligent member, "whereas in a native society there are none of them." Malinowski invites readers to imagine him, a white man unwilling to retreat to the company of other white men, drinking, reading, lonely, and ultimately enjoying the company of "savagery." His portraits are painted entirely of Them, introducing "order" into the "chaos" of their lives.

Malinowski details the recipe for qualitative Othering. Early in the century, 'twas noble to write of the Other for the purposes of creating what was considered knowledge. Perhaps it still is. But now, much qualitative research is undertaken for what may be an even more terrifying aim—to "help" Them. In both contexts the effect may be Othering: muted voices; "structure" imported to local "chaos"; Others represented as extracted from their scenes of exploitation, social relationships, and meaningful communities. If they survive the decontextualization, they appear socially bereft, isolated, and deficient, with insidious distinctions drawn among the good and the bad Thems (Austin, 1992). Distinctions from Us are understood.

From such texts we often learn little about Others, except their invented shapes and texts, and less about the writers/researchers, except their projections. Domination and distance get sanitized inside science. Portraits of disdain, pity, need, strength, or all of the above are delivered for public consumption. New programs may, or may not, be spawned to "remedy" them—the problem. Either way, Others have been yanked out of the contexts of late capitalism, racism, sexism, and economic decline. The public is left with embodied stories of Them, who, in their own words, can't seem to get better.

More recently, however, and more interestingly, qualitative researchers have begun to interrupt Othering by forcing subjugated voices in context to the front of our texts and by exploiting privileged voices to scrutinize the technologies of Othering. Emerging in some spaces is this cadre of qualitative researchers who see their work with those who have been cut out as Others, on struggles of social injustice, in ways that disrupt Othering and provoke a sense of possibility (Bhavnani, 1992).

Ethnographies produced by Michael Burawoy and colleagues in *Ethnography Unbound* (1992) represent such a collection designed for social theory and action. The chapters in Bookman and Morgan's *Women and the Politics of Empowerment* (1990) were written for and about the struggles pursued by everyday activist women in the politics of housing, education, and health care organizing. Rhoda Linton and Michelle Whitman (1982) have written through qualitative research to further feminist peace movements. Brinton Lykes (1989), writing for and with Guatemalan "indigenous" women, seeks to create an archive of political resistance of a culture in exile. All of these texts are instances of writing on/with/for political change. But lest writing/researching for change appears too facile, I'll end with one specific, self-conscious, and yet imperial instance of research for social change that embodies many of the contradictions addressed thus far. Profoundly a moment of Inscribing the Other, this work cracks open a space for our critical gaze and invites the next round of conversations about ethics, praxis, and qualitative work. Here I refer to those qualitative research projects in which researchers self-consciously translate "for" Others in order to promote social justice.

Sometimes explicitly trading on race/class privilege, in these instances researchers understand the hyphen all too well. Bartering privilege for justice, we re-present stories told by subjugated Others, stories that would otherwise be discarded. And we get a hearing. My own work with high school dropouts exemplifies this politically tense form of ethnography (Fine, 1991).

Here, at the Self-Other border, it is not that researchers are absented and Others fronted. Instead, the class politics of translation demands that a researcher is doused quite evidently in status and privilege as the Other sits domesticated. I (white, academic, elite woman) represent the words and voices of African American and Latino, working-class and poor adolescents who have dropped out of high school, in texts, in court, and in public policy debates (Fine, 1991), and it becomes scholarship. Some even find it compelling. My raced and classed translation grants authority to their "native" and "underarticulated" narratives. My race and class are coded as "good science" (Kitzinger, 1991). The power of my translation comes far more from my whiteness, middle-classness, and education than from the stories I tell.

But my translation also colludes in structures of domination. I know that when dropouts speak, few listen. When African American, Latino, Asian, or Native American scholars do the same kinds of work as I, they are more likely to be heard as biased, self-interested, or without distanced perspective (see Cook & Fine, 1995). Edward Said (1978) has written to this point:

> Since the Orientals cannot represent themselves, they must therefore be represented by others who know more about Islam than Islam knows about itself. Now it is often the case that you can be known by others in different ways than you know yourself, and that valuable insights might be generated accordingly. But that it is quite different than pronouncing it as immutable law that outsiders *ipso facto* have a better sense of you as an insider than

you do yourself. Note that there is no question of an *exchange* between Islam's views and an outsider's: no dialogue, no discussion, no mutual recognition. There is a flat assertion of quality, which the Western policy-maker, or his faithful servant, possesses by virtue of his being Western, Shite, non-Muslim. (p. 97)

The stakes are even higher when we move qualitative translation out of academic journals and into the courts. Consider a most complicated instance of scholarly translation located precisely at the hyphen of Othering— the brilliant work of Julie Blackman. A white social psychologist who works as an expert witness for battered women—white, Latina, and/or African American—who have killed their abusers, Blackman enters courtrooms and retells the stories these women have told her, this time in Standard English. She psychologizes and explains away the contradictions. She makes them acceptable. Blackman's project is to get these women a hearing from a jury of their peers. She has an impressive success rate for keeping these women out of jail (Blackman, 1993).

Draped in white colonizing science, Julie and I, and many others, cut a deal: *Listen to the story as long as the teller is not the Other.* Cut with the knives of racism and classism. Should we refuse? Do we merely reproduce power by playing to power? Do we regenerate the Other as we try to keep her from going to jail? Do we erase and silence as we trade on white/elite privilege?

Herein lie the very profound contradictions that face researchers who step out, who presume to want to make a difference, who are so bold or arrogant as to assume we might. Once out beyond the picket fence of illusory objectivity, we trespass all over the classed, raced, and otherwise stratified lines that have demarcated our social legitimacy for publicly telling their stories. And it is then that ethical questions boil.

I would not argue that only those "in the experience" can tell a story of injustice. Indeed, privileging raw (?) experience over analysis, as if they are separate, is simply a sign of (understandable) political desperation (see Scott, 1991). At some point, people decide, I'm tired of hearing you speak for me. Only I can speak for myself. I'll speak for my people, and these issues. As a white, nondisabled, academic woman, I have been on both sides of this tension. Sometimes I'm telling men to stop speaking for me. Sometimes I'm being told to stop speaking "for"—for adolescents, women of color, women with disabilities, and so on. And yet we all have genders and races, classes, sexualities, dis-abilities, and politics. If poststructuralism has taught us anything, it is to beware the frozen identities and the presumption that the hyphen is real, to suspect the binary, to worry the clear distinctions. If these "virtues" are assumed floating and political signifiers (Omi & Winant, 1986), then it is surely essentialist to presume that only women can/should "do" gender; only people of color can/should do race work; only lesbians and gays can/should "do" sexuality; only women in violence can tell the stories of violence.

Yet the risk for qualitative researchers has been and continues to be imperial translation. Doing the work of social change, as Blackman does, within a context committed to discrediting all women's voices means that social researchers have to be negotiating how, when, and why to situate and privilege whose voices. Those of us who do this work need to invent communities of friendly critical informants who can help us think through whose voices and analyses to front, and whose to foreground.

At the same time, another risk surfaces. This risk lies in the romanticizing of narratives and the concomitant retreat from analysis. In the name of ethical, democratic, sometimes feminist methods, there is a subtle, growing withdrawal from interpretation. Nancie Caraway (1991) writes to this point when she describes "some of the assumptions hidden in standpoint/margin/center claims: beliefs that people act rationally in their own interest, that the oppressed are not in fundamental ways damaged by their marginality, and that they themselves are somehow removed from a will to power" (p. 181).

Caraway is a white woman who worries about the stance of some scholars who claim that no one may speak for Others. She struggles in *Segregated Sisterhood* (1991) to produce a text through and about race among/between women. Relying primarily on the theoretical works of women of color, she, like Blackman and others, argues the responsibility of white women to be engaged in "crossover tracks," in critical, democratic conversations about race and racism. If we recognize race, class, gender, and sexuality to be socially and historically contingent (Hall, 1991), then silence, retreat, and engagement all pose ethical dilemmas. All are tangled with ethics of knowing, writing, and acting (see Richardson, Chapter 12, Volume 3, this series).

In the early 1990s, the whispers of a collective of activist researchers can be heard struggling with these tensions. Seeking to work with, but not romanticize, subjugated voices, searching for moments of social justice, they are inventing strategies of qualitative analysis and writing against Othering. As this corpus of work ages, it too will become a contested site.

Residues of domination linger heavily within these qualitative texts. But today these works constitute the next set of critical conversations among qualitative social researchers, eroding fixed categories and provoking possibilities for qualitative research that is designed *against* Othering, *for* social justice, and pivoting identities of Self and Other *at* the hyphen.

◆ References

Aronowitz, S. (1988). The production of scientific knowledge. In C. Nelson & L. Grossberg (Eds.), *Marxism and the interpretation of culture* (pp. 519-538). Urbana: University of Illinois Press.

Austin, R. (1989). Sapphire bound! *Wisconsin Law Review, 3,* 539-578.

Austin, R. (1992). *"The black community," its lawbreakers and a politics of identification.* Unpublished manuscript.

Bhabha, H. (1990). *Nation and narration.* New York: Routledge.

Bhavnani, K. (1992). Talking racism and editing women's studies. In D. Richardson & V. Robinson (Eds.), *Thinking feminist* (pp. 27-48). New York: Guilford.

Blackman, J. (1993). [Master lecture on legal issues affecting women]. Lecture presented at the annual meeting of the American Psychological Association, Toronto.

Bookman, A., & Morgan, S. (Eds.). (1990). *Women and the politics of empowerment.* Philadelphia: Temple University Press.

Burawoy, M., Burton, A., Ferguson, A. A., Fox, K. J., Gamson, J., Gartrell, N., Hurst, L., Kurzman, C., Salzinger, L., Schiffman, J., & Ui, S. (Eds.). (1992). *Ethnography unbound: Power and resistance in the modern metropolis.* Berkeley: University of California Press.

Caraway, N. (1991). *Segregated sisterhood.* Knoxville: University of Tennessee Press.

Clifford, J., & Marcus, G. E. (Eds.). (1986). *Writing culture: The poetics and politics of ethnography.* Berkeley: University of California Press.

Collins, P. H. (1990). *Black feminist thought: Knowledge, consciousness and the politics of empowerment.* New York: Routledge.

Cook, D., & Fine, M. (1995). Motherwit. In B. B. Swadener & S. Lubeck (Eds.), *Children and families at promise: Deconstructing the discourse of risk.* Albany: State University of New York Press.

Crenshaw, K. (1992). *Intersectionality of race and sex.* Unpublished manuscript.

deLauretis, T. (1987). *Technologies of gender: Essays on theory, film, and fiction.* Bloomington: Indiana University Press.

Fanon, F. (1965). *A dying colonialism.* New York: Grove.

Fine, M. (1991). *Framing dropouts.* Albany: State University of New York Press.

Fine, M. (1992). *Disruptive voices.* Ann Arbor: University of Michigan Press.

Fine, M., & Vanderslice, V. (1992). Reflections on qualitative research. In E. Posavac (Ed.), *Methodological issues in applied social psychology.* New York: Plenum.

Giroux, H. (1991). Postmodernism as border pedagogy. In H. Giroux (Ed.), *Postmodernism, feminism, and cultural politics.* Albany: State University of New York Press.

Hahn, H. (1983, March-April). Paternalism and public policy. *Society*, pp. 36-44.

Hall, S. (1991). Ethnicity, identity and difference. *Radical America, 3*, 9-22.

Haraway, D. J. (1988). Situated knowledges: The science question in feminism and the privilege of partial perspective. *Feminist Studies, 14*, 575-599.

Harding, S. (Ed.). (1987). *Feminism and methodology: Social science issues.* Bloomington: Indiana University Press.

Havel, V. (1990). *Disturbing the peace.* New York: Vintage.

hooks, b. (1989). *Talking back: Thinking feminist, thinking black.* Boston: South End.

hooks, b. (1990). *Yearning: Race, gender, and cultural politics.* Boston: South End.

Katz, M. (Ed.). (1993). *The underclass debate.* Princeton, NJ: Princeton University Press.

Kitzinger, C. (1991). Feminism, psychology and the paradox of power. *Feminism and Psychology, 1,* 111-130.

Ladner, J. (1971). *Tomorrow's tomorrow.* Garden City, NY: Doubleday.

Linton, R., & Whitman, M. (1982). With mourning, rage, empowerment, and defiance: The 1981 Women's Pentagon Action. *Socialist Review, 12*(3-4), 11-36.

Lykes, B. (1989). Dialogue with Guatemalan women. In R. Unger (Ed.), *Representations: Social constructions of gender* (pp. 167-184). Amityville, NY: Baywood.

Malinowski, B. (1922). *Argonauts of the western Pacific.* London: Routledge & Kegan Paul.

Martin, B., & Mohanty, C. T. (1986). Feminist politics: What's home got to do with it? In T. deLauretis (Ed.), *Feminist studies/critical studies.* Bloomington: Indiana University Press.

Matsuda, M. (1993). Public response to racist speech: Considering the victim's story. In M. Matsuda, C. Lawrence, R. Delgado, K. Crenshaug (Eds.), *Words that wound* (pp. 17-52). Boulder, CO: Westview.

Miller, J. B. (1976). *Toward a new psychology of women.* Boston: Beacon.

Mouffe, C. (1988). Hegemony and new political subjects: Toward a new concept of democracy. In C. Nelson & L. Grossberg (Eds.), *Marxism and the interpretation of culture.* Urbana: University of Illinois Press.

Omi, M., & Winant, H. (1986). *Racial formation in the United States: From the 1960s to the 1980s.* New York: Routledge.

Pratt, M. (1985). Scratches on the face of the country. In H. Gates (Ed.), *"Race," writing, and difference* (pp. 138-162). Chicago: University of Chicago Press.

Pratt, M. (1992). *Imperial eyes.* New York: Routledge.

Rollins, J. (1985). *Between women: Domestics and their employers.* Philadelphia: Temple University Press.

Rosaldo, R. (1989). *Culture and truth: The remaking of social analysis.* Boston: Beacon.

Said, E. (1978). *Orientalism.* New York: Pantheon.

Sanday, P. (1990). *Fraternity gang rape: Sex, brotherhood and privilege on campus.* New York: New York University Press.

Scott, J. (1991). Deconstructing equality versus difference. In M. Hirsch & E. Keller (Eds.), *Conflicts in feminism.* New York: Routledge.

Smith, D. E. (1987). *The everyday world as problematic.* Boston: Northeastern University Press.

Smith, D. E. (1992). Sociology from women's experience: A reaffirmation. *Sociological Theory, 10,* 88-98.

Smith, V. (1991). Split affinities. In M. Hirsch & E. Keller (Eds.), *Conflicts in feminism* (pp. 271-287). New York: Routledge.

Spivak, G. C. (1988). Can the subaltern speak? In C. Nelson & L. Grossberg (Eds.), *Marxism and the interpretation of culture* (pp. 280-316). Urbana: University of Illinois Press.

Weis, L. (1990). *Working class without work*. New York: Routledge.

West, C. (1988). Marxist theory and the specificity of Afro-American oppression. In C. Nelson & L. Grossberg (Eds.), *Marxism and the interpretation of culture* (pp. 17-29). Urbana: University of Illinois Press.

5

Politics and Ethics in Qualitative Research

Maurice Punch

◆ "Just Do It!"

Fieldwork is fun; it is easy; anyone can do it; it is salutary for young academics to flee the nest; and they should be able to take any moral or political dilemmas encountered in their stride. There has always been a somewhat pragmatic, if not reductionist, tradition in qualitative research that was exemplified by Everett Hughes's "fly on your own" strategy for students at Chicago (Gans, 1967, p. 301). Of course, the classical anthropologists engaged in long and lonely involvement in distant settings and had to solve their problems individually and on site (Clarke, 1975, p. 105), and something of this tradition—geared to the solo researcher, absent for a considerable period of time, and cut off from the university—was conveyed by the precepts of the Chicago school. This style of qualitative research holds that it is healthy and wholesome for students and aspiring social scientists to get "the seats of their pants dirty by *real* research" (Park, quoted in Burgess, 1982, p. 6; emphasis in original). They should abandon the classroom in order to knock on doors, troop the streets, and join

AUTHOR'S NOTE: I would like to thank the editors of this volume, and the two readers for this chapter, for their valuable comments on my first draft. I also wish to extend my gratitude to Derek Phillips, Peter K. Manning, Hans Werdmolder, and John Van Maanen for their critical advice while I was preparing this chapter.

groups; they should just "get in there and see what is going on" (as Howard Becker advised a bemused British student asking what "paradigm" he should employ in the field; Atkinson, 1977, p. 32).

In contrast, there are voices that alert us to the inherent moral pitfalls of participant observation and that warn us of the essentially "political" nature of all field research. In this model, qualitative research is seen as potentially volatile, even hazardous, requiring careful consideration and preparation before someone should be *allowed* to enter the field. Without adequate training and supervision, the neophyte researcher can unwittingly become an unguided projectile bringing turbulence to the field, fostering personal traumas (for researcher and researched), and even causing damage to the discipline. This position was powerfully argued by John Lofland at an ASA seminar on participant observation, where he virtually demanded a certification of competence before the researcher be let loose in the field. During the past decade, moreover, these two divergent stances have been challenged by the impact of feminist, racial, and ethnic discourse that has not only made visible new research areas but also has raised critical issues related to a politically engaged research dialectic (Welch, 1991). These have profound implications for the ethics and politics of research (Fonow & Cook, 1991; Grossberg, Nelson, & Treichler, 1992; Reinharz, 1992).

My position in this chapter will be to argue forcibly for the "get out and do it" perspective. Understandably, no one in his or her right mind would support a carefree, amateuristic, and unduly naive approach to qualitative research. But, at the same time, I would warn against leaning too far toward a highly restrictive model for research that serves to prevent academics from exploring complex social realities that are not always amenable to more formal methods. My sympathies for this view have been powerfully shaped by my own background as a sociologist who engaged in research that painfully raised a whole range of largely unexpected political and ethical issues (Punch, 1986, 1989), related to stress in the field situation, research fatigue, confidentiality, harm, privacy and identification, and spoiling the field. In two projects that commenced with supportive sponsors, I encountered an accumulation of unanticipated difficulties, such as varying interpretations of the research bargain over time, disputes about contractual obligations, restrictions on secondary access, intimidation via the law, disagreement on publication, and even an (in my view unethical) appeal to professional ethics in an attempt to limit my research. Those issues are not exclusive to projects employing observation, but perhaps they are most likely to occur in an acute way there than in other styles of work.

Furthermore, I trust that many of the views presented in this chapter are also applicable to other styles of qualitative research. Qualitative research covers a spectrum of techniques—but central are observation, interviewing, and documentary analysis—and these may be used in a broad range of disciplines. Indeed, contemporary researchers are to be found within an extensive spectrum of groups and institutions involving differing time spans and types of personal engagement (Burgess, 1982; Hammersley & Atkinson, 1983; Shaffir & Stebbins, 1991). It is probably the case, however, that in Anglo-American universities (with an "apprenticeship" model of graduate education unlike that in most continental European institutes), most researchers will first encounter fieldwork while engaged on a dissertation that is mostly a solo enterprise with relatively unstructured observation, deep involvement in the setting, and a strong identification with the researched. This can mean that the researcher is unavoidably vulnerable and that there is a considerably larger element of risk and uncertainty than with more formal methods.

There is here too an absolutely central point that much field research is dependent on one person's perception of the field situation at a given point in time, that that perception is shaped both by personality and by the nature of the interaction with the researched, and that this makes the researcher his or her own "research instrument." This is fundamentally different from more formal models of research, and it also bedevils our evaluation of what "really" happened because we are almost totally reliant on one person's portrayal of events. This is amplified if we further accept that there are a number of potentially distorting filters at work that militate against full authenticity on methods, and that censor material on the relationships with the human "subjects" concerned.

Here I am assuming that qualitative fieldwork employs participant observation as its central technique and that this involves the researcher in prolonged immersion in the life of a group, community, or organization in order to discern people's habits and thoughts as well as to decipher the social structure that binds them together (McCall & Simmons, 1969; Van Maanen, 1979). Far more than with other styles of social research, then, this implies that the investigator engages in a close, if not intimate, relationship with those he or she observes. Crucial to that relationship is access and acceptance, and elsewhere I have spoken of "infiltration" as a key technique in fieldwork (Punch, 1986, p. 11) even though the concept is negatively associated with spying and deception (Erikson, quoted in Bulmer, 1982, p. 150). Entry and departure, distrust and confidence,

elation and despondency, commitment and betrayal, friendship and abandonment—all are as fundamental here as are dry discussions on the
techniques of observation, taking field notes, analyzing the data, and
writing the report. Furthermore, acute moral and ethical dilemmas may be
encountered while a semiconscious political process of negotiation per-
vades all fieldwork. And both elements, political and ethical, often have to
be resolved *situationally,* and even spontaneously, without the luxury of
being able to turn first to consult a more experienced colleague. The
dynamics and dilemmas associated with this area of fieldwork can be
summarized crudely in terms of getting in and getting out, and of one's
social and moral conduct in relation to the political constraints of the field.

◆ On the Politics of Fieldwork

To a greater or lesser extent, politics suffuses all social scientific research
(Guba & Lincoln, 1989, p. 125). By *politics* I mean everything from the
micropolitics of personal relations to the cultures and resources of research
units and universities, the powers and policies of government research
departments, and ultimately even the hand (heavy or otherwise) of the
central state itself (Bell & Newby, 1977; Hammond, 1964). All of these
contexts and constraints crucially influence the design, implementation,
and outcomes of research (Gubrium & Silverman, 1989). This is important
to convey to fledgling researchers, who may imbibe a false view of the
research process as smooth and unproblematic ("The unchanging researcher makes a unilinear journey through a static setting"; Hunt, 1984,
p. 285), whereas we should be drawing their attention to the political perils
and ethical pitfalls of actually carrying out research. An additional motive
for doing this is to espouse the view that fieldwork is definitely not a soft
option, but, rather, represents a *demanding* craft that involves both coping
with multiple negotiations and continually dealing with ethical dilemmas.

But perhaps collectively we are ourselves largely responsible for the
"conspiracy" in selling the neat, packaged, unilinear view of research.
Successful studies attract the limelight; failures are often neglected. Dilemmas in the field are glossed over in an anodyne appendix, and it may even
be deemed inappropriate for the "scientist" to abandon objectivity and
detachment in recounting descriptions of personal involvement and political battles in the field setting. This can be reinforced by the strictures of
publishers, who may find personal accounts anecdotal, trivial, and scarcely

159

worthy of space (Punch, 1989, p. 203). As Clarke (1975) observes, "A large area of knowledge is systematically suppressed as 'non-scientific' by the limitations of prevailing research methodologies" (p. 96).

In contrast, some accounts of field research touch on the stress, the deep personal involvement, the role conflicts, the physical and mental effort, the drudgery and discomfort—and even the danger—of observational studies for the researcher. Yablonsky (1968) was threatened with violence in a commune, and Thompson (1967) was beaten up by Hell's Angels; Schwartz (1964) was attacked verbally and physically during his study in a mental hospital, where he was seen as a "spy" by both patients and staff; and Vidich and Bensman (1968) were caricatured, in a Fourth of July procession in the town they had studied, by an effigy bending over a manure spreader. Wax (1971) was involved in dangerous and stressful situations in Japanese relocation camps, and she was denounced as a "communist agitator" during research on Native American reservations. Burns (1977) was refused publication for his study of the BBC; Wallis (1977) was tailed and harassed by members of the Scientology movement; and, in a project within a police department, a researcher "literally had to block a file-cabinet with his body to keep two armed internal affairs officers from taking observers' records. Meanwhile the principal investigator was frantically contacting the chief of police to get internal affairs called off " (Florez & Kelling, 1979, p. 17).

These examples could be multiplied by horror stories gleaned from the academic circuit, where "tales of the field" (Van Maanen, 1988) abound of obstructionist gatekeepers, vacillating sponsors, factionalism in the field setting that forces the researcher to choose sides, organizational resistance, respondents subverting the research role, sexual shenanigans, and disputes about publication and the veracity of findings. Such pitfalls and predicaments can rarely be anticipated, yet they may fundamentally alter the whole nature and purpose of the research.

These personal and anecdotal accounts form an oral culture of moral and practical warnings; they are not widely written of, according to John Van Maanen (personal communication, 1993), largely because we have failed to develop a "genre or narrative convention within our standard works" that would shape a taken-for-granted imperative that field-workers own up to the manner in which they solved such issues during their research (but see Sanjek, 1990, on "fieldnotes"). In contrast, there is a stream of thought that does make exposure of affectivity and of the research process central and that is represented by feminist research (Roberts, 1981). This not only attacks traditional methodology as an instrument of repression but also, in some cases, argues for "total immersion" in the field; this new "epistemology of insiderness" (Reinharz, 1992, p. 259) has led feminist scholars to an attempt "to rescue emotion from its discarded role in the creation of knowledge" (Fonow & Cook, 1991, p. 11). This powerful and significant contribution to the recent debate on the politics of research is in reaction to the patriarchal nature of academic life and the "research infrastructure" allied to an effort to construct a feminist epistemology and methodology. Fonow and Cook (1991) focus on a number of themes in the literature on feminist methods: "reflexivity; an action orientation; attention to the affective components of research; and use of the situation-in-hand" (pp. 1-5).

In essence, much research is informed by the experience of oppression owing to sexism, and the research process may well contain an element of "consciousness-raising," of emotional catharsis, and of increased politicization and activism. As the aim of certain strands of feminist research is praxis leading to liberation (Mies, 1991), this has profound implications for "the statement of purpose, topic selection, theoretical orientation, choice of method, view of human nature, and definitions of the researcher's role" (Fonow & Cook, 1991, p. 5). This action component is shared with black studies, Marxism, and gay and lesbian studies and permeates research with an explicitly *political* agenda. Research by women on women to assist women has undoubtedly opened up fresh new arenas largely inaccessible to males, and this enrichment has frequently been embedded within qualitative research precisely because this is held to be more compatible than formal, quantitative methods with feminist scholarship (Hammersley, 1993; Jayaratne & Stewart, 1991; Reinharz, 1992). Feminist research has, for instance, fostered studies of obscene telephone calls, violence against women (shelters for battered females), single-gender college residences, sexual harassment, pornography, AIDS clinics, abortion, and discrimination in the workplace. In effect, the impact of feminist research has been to awaken the whole issue of gender in research activities and to politicize the debate on the conduct of research; similar arguments have been raised about race and ethnicity.

In some cases there is an openness to "complete transformation" through total participation and a belief that consciousness-raising will become the "ground work for friendship, shared struggle and identity change" (Reinharz 1992, p. 68). This has aided in bringing affectivity into

161

accounts of research and has also exposed the reality that much qualitative, observational work was conducted by privileged white males. There are profound epistemological and methodological issues here that I cannot possibly tackle within the confines of this chapter, but I suspect that many traditional ethnographers, brought up in a scholarly convention of "openness" to the field setting and "objectivity" with regard to data, would be concerned that explicitly ideological and political research would overly predetermine the material gleaned in observational studies. This, in turn, would doubtless lead to a riposte about the disingenuousness of believing in objectivity through the eyes of white male academics. My point is that the traditionalists tended to eschew "politics," to avoid "total immersion," and to be wary of "going native," all of which, in contrast, are elements of feminist methods. This debate has illuminated certain research dilemmas in an acute and fresh way that needs to be taken into account in all that follows below. Rather than enter that debate, which poses issues at the ideological and institutional levels, I shall focus here on those practical and mundane elements that continually influence the "politics" of fieldwork in many research projects.

Hence I wish simply to focus on certain features that are not always clearly articulated in accounts but that have a material impact on qualitative research in general and fieldwork in particular and that shape the politics of research.

Researcher personality. The personality of the researcher helps to determine his or her selection of topics, his or her intellectual approach, and his or her ability in the field (Clarke, 1975, p. 104). But often we are left in the dark as to the personal and intellectual path that led researchers to drop one line of inquiry or to pursue another topic. We require more intellectual autobiographies to clarify why academics end up studying what they do (Okely & Callaway, 1992). Family circumstances can be important in terms of absences and travel, and spouse's support, or lack of it, can prove crucial to the continuation of a field project.

Geographic proximity. One simple factor that is often glossed over in terms of selecting topics and field settings is geographic proximity. There may be something romantic about Evans-Pritchard, Malinowski, and Boas setting off stoically into the bush, where they lived in relative isolation and virtuous celibacy, but some researchers just travel conveniently down the road to the nearest morgue, mental hospital, or action group.

Nature of the research object. The nature of the research object—be it a community, a formal organization, or an informal group—is of significance for access, research bargains, funding, and the likelihood of polarity and conflict in the research setting (Punch, 1989; Spencer, 1973).

Researcher's institutional background. The reputation of the researcher's institutional background can be of considerable importance in opening or closing doors. The backing of prestigious academic institutions and figure-heads may be vital to access in some settings but irrelevant, or even harmful, in others. For instance, Platt (1976, p. 45) records a case in which re-searchers in Britain were able to get a member of Parliament to organize a speech in the House of Commons that led to certain doors being opened for them.

Gatekeepers. Gatekeepers can be crucial in terms of access and funding (Argyris, 1969). The determination of some watchdogs to protect their institutions may ironically be almost inversely related to the willingness of members to accept research. Klein (1976) remarks, "Social science is not engaged by 'industry' or organizations, but by individuals in gatekeeping or sponsorship or client roles. The outcome, therefore, is always mediated through the needs, resources, and roles of such individuals" (p. 225). Researchers may suffer by being continually seen as extensions of their political sponsors within the setting despite their denials to the contrary. Furthermore, gatekeepers need not be construed only in terms of govern-ment agencies and corporate representatives, but can also be found in scientific funding bodies, among publishers, and within academia. The intellectual development of the discipline, academic imperialism, the insti-tutional division of labor, the selection and availability of specific supervi-sors, backstage bargaining, precontract lobbying, departmental distribu-tion of perks (research assistance, travel money, typing support), and patronage can all play roles in determining the status of, and resources for, field research, and in specifying why some projects are launched and others buried (Dingwall, Payne, & Payne, 1980; Sharrock & Anderson, 1980; Shils, 1982). It is somewhat encouraging to read that even Whyte had difficulty in publishing his now-classic 1943 book *Street Corner Society,* in having it reviewed and taken seriously, and fluctuating sales have reflected the fads and fashions of postwar sociology. The acceptance of his research for a Ph.D. at Chicago was also contingent on Hughes's championing of him against a critical Wirth (Whyte, 1981, p. 356).

163

Status of field-workers. The impact that the presence of researchers has on the setting is related to the status and visibility of the field-workers. The "lone wolf" often requires no funding, gains easy access, and melts away into the field. The "hired hand," in contrast, may come with a team of people, be highly visible, be tied to contractual obligations, and be expected to deliver the goods within a specified period of time (Wycoff & Kelling, 1978).

Expectations in team research. A feature of research that has rarely been examined is the variety of expectations and roles in *team* research that can hinder behavior in the field and lead to conflict about outcomes. In team research, leadership, supervision, discipline, morale, status, salaries, career prospects, and the intellectual division of labor can promote unexpected tensions in the field and lead to disputes about publication. Junior assistants may fear that a senior researcher will prematurely publish to increase his or her academic status while cynically exploiting their data, spoiling the field, and ruining their chances of collecting separate data for a dissertation. A love affair breaking up between team members can also spell disaster and undermine timetables and deadlines. Workloads, ownership of data, rights of publication, and career and status issues are all affected by the constraints of team research. Al Reiss, Jr., in operating a team investigating police behavior, had to make it clear that serious "deviance" by a team member might threaten the whole project, and that he also had an employer-employee relationship with them that meant he was prepared to dismiss people if necessary (statements made at an ASA seminar on field research). Bell (1977) presents a graphic portrait of the problems that beset the restudy of the community of Banbury in Britain. The project leader was rarely present, the team never really jelled as a unit, the field supervisor left early to take up an academic appointment, and the two research assistants wanted to collect data for their dissertations as well as for the project; further, data were withheld from the supervisor because the others were worried that he "would in some way run off with the data and publish separately" (p. 55).

The structural and status frustrations of the hired hand (particularly the temporary research assistant virtually abandoned to the field) may mean that he or she suffers from poor morale, becomes estranged from the parent organization, is strongly tempted toward co-optation, becomes secretive toward supervisors, and is a "bother" requiring "unusually intense and patient supervision" (Florez & Kelling, 1979, p. 12). He or she is particularly in danger of "going native."

Other factors affecting research in the field. The actual conduct of research and success in the field can be affected by myriad factors, including age, gender, status, ethnic background, overidentification, rejection, factionalism, bureaucratic obstacles, accidents, and good fortune. But, again, we rarely hear of failures, although Diamond (1964) recounts how he was ejected from the field in Nigeria, and Clarke (1975) speaks of field-workers who nearly went insane, panicked, or got cold feet and never actually got to the field, "but we are systematically denied public information on what happens" (p. 106). Observational studies are often associated with young people (graduate students, research assistants), and some settings may require a youthful appearance and even physical stamina (as in Reimer's 1979 study of construction workers).

Gender, and race, close some avenues of inquiry but clearly open up others. Martin (1980), in her study of women in policing, could not penetrate the world of the policemen's locker room or out-of-work socializing. In masculine worlds the female researcher may have to adopt various ploys to deal with prejudice, sexual innuendo, and unwelcome advances. Hunt (1984) realized that she was operating in a culture where several features of her identity—white, female, educated outsider—were impediments to developing rapport and trust with different categories within the police and had to engage in a transformation from "untrustworthy feminine spy" to "street woman researcher" whereby she renegotiated gender to combine elements of masculinity and femininity. The compromises this involved would doubtless enrage many contemporary feminists, but they force the female field-worker to get out or else accept a measure of "interactional shitwork" (Reinharz, 1992). The limitations associated with views on race and gender mean that it is impossible in many police forces for a white female to patrol alone with a black male officer. Women often have to cope too with the conflict between their desire and need to continue research (e.g., for career purposes) and their encountering "sexual harassment, physical danger, and sexual stereotyping"; furthermore, in a society that is "ageist, sexist, and hetero-sexist, the young, female researcher may be defined as a sexual object to be seduced by heterosexual males" (Reinharz, 1992, p. 58).

A young student, however, may be perceived as nonthreatening and may even elicit a considerable measure of sympathy from respondents. But rather than concluding that fieldwork is not for the "over 40s," one could also argue that advancing age and increased status can open doors to fruitful areas of inquiry, such as senior management in business. Personality, appearance, and luck may all play roles in exploiting unexpected avenues or overcoming unanticipated obstacles in the field.

Publishing. A harmonious relationship in the field may come unstuck at the moment of writing an impending publication where the researcher's material appears in cold print. The subjects of research suddenly see themselves summarized and interpreted in ways that may not match up with their own partial perspectives on the natural setting. Where the research bargain includes an implicit or explicit obligation to consult the group or institution on publication, severe differences of opinion can arise. These may be almost completely unanticipated by the researcher, in the sense that it is difficult to predict what organizational representatives will find objectionable (Burns, 1977). Vidich and Bensman's (1968) study of "Springdale" provoked a scandalized reaction that raised fundamental issues related to invasion of privacy, the ethics of research (on identity, harm, ownership of data, and so on), and responsibilities to Cornell University, which had sponsored the research (and which proved unduly sensitive to the outcry from the community). There were also protests from other *academics*. Progressive and radical institutions, highly critical of the establishment and ideologically committed to openness and publication, may themselves be highly sensitive to criticism because of their marginality, susceptibility to discrediting, and desire for legitimacy (Punch, 1986, pp. 49-70).

Social and moral obligations. Finally, what social and moral obligations are generated by fieldwork? This issue forms a major part of what follows in this chapter and can be viewed as having two central parts. On the one hand, there is the nature of the researcher's personal relationships with people he or she encounters in the field. On the other hand, there are the moral and ethical aspects related to the purpose and conduct of research itself. In effect, how far can you go?

◆ Ethical Features of Qualitative Research

Issues

The view that science is intrinsically neutral and essentially beneficial disappeared with the revelations at the Nuremberg trials (recounting the

Nazis' "medical experiments" on concentration camp inmates) and with the role of leading scientists in the Manhattan Project, which led to the dropping of atomic bombs on Japan in 1945. Controlling science, however, raises resilient practical, ethical, and legal issues that are a matter of constant debate. The questions involved confront us with fundamental dilemmas, such as the protection of the subjects versus the freedoms to conduct research and to publish research findings. An understanding of this area needs to be rooted in knowledge of a number of studies that have given rise to moral and ethical questions.

In medical research, for instance, actual physical harm can be done to subjects, as in the Tuskegee Syphilis Study and in the Willowbrook Hepatitis Experiment, and patients' rights can be violated, as when live cancer cells were injected beneath the skin of nonconsenting geriatrics (Barber, 1976; Brandt, 1978; Katz, 1972). This background is important because, for a number of reasons, the attempt to control *biomedical* research, and to protect its subjects, has also become the model for the social sciences (Reiss, 1979). In social science, frequent reference is made to a number of studies that have raised blood pressures on ethical aspects of research. The revelations of Vidich and Bensman (1968) about the community of "Springdale" caused a furor among the townspeople and also fellow academics in relation to identification, harm, sponsorship, and professional ethics. Festinger, Riecken, and Schachter's (1956) work on membership in a sect involved a measure of deception and also implicit if not explicit affirmation for the group that could scarcely be described as nondirective. In the 1960s, American academics were shocked on discovering CIA involvement in the source of funding for "Project Camelot" (Horowitz, 1970). The CIA was also responsible for secretly distributing LSD to visitors to a brothel and then filming the results using a hidden camera; one person committed suicide while under the influence of the LSD (Sieber, 1992, p. 68).

In the Wichita Jury Study, microphones were hidden to record juries' deliberations. Milgram's (1963) renowned psychological experiment on authority required unwitting subjects to think that they were causing "pain" to others in a laboratory situation. Disguise and deception were used in La Pierre's (1934) pioneering study of prejudice, when he entered restaurants and hotels accompanied by a Chinese couple, and also in Lofland and Lejeune's (1960) study of reactions of aspiring members of Alcoholics Anonymous, in which students posed as alcoholics. There is also the well-known, if not now notorious, research of Laud Humphreys (1970, 1972) on homosexuals, whom he observed in a public toilet and later questioned in their homes under the guise of a different project. (He recorded their car license plate numbers on first encounter and traced them to their homes; he then changed his hairstyle, clothes, and car and claimed he was conducting a "social health survey.") On the one hand, he received the coveted C. Wright Mills Award from the SSSP, but on the other hand there were efforts undertaken to revoke his Ph.D. (and an irate Alvin Gouldner socked him on the jaw!). For more details and further debate on these studies, the reader is referred to Klockars and O'Connor (1979) and Bulmer (1982), and also to texts dealing with ethical issues in research, such as Sjoberg (1968), Barnes (1979), Diener and Crandall (1978), Boruch and Cecil (1983), Rynkiewich and Spradley (1976), and special issues of *American Sociologist* (1978) and *Social Problems* (1973, 1980).

In essence, most concern revolves around issues of harm, consent, deception, privacy, and confidentiality of data. And, in a sense, we are all still suffering for the sins of Milgram. His controversial research methods in laboratory experiments, allied to the negative reactions to revelations about medical tests on captive, vulnerable, and nonconsenting populations, led to the construction of various restrictions on social research. Academic associations have formulated codes of professional conduct and of ethics, and some research funding is dependent on researchers' ascribing to ethical guidelines. This codification presents a number of dilemmas, particularly for researchers who engage in fieldwork. For instance, the concept of consent would seem to rule out covert research, but how "honest" do you actually have to be about your research purpose? And the conflict orientation of some scholars—in terms of Becker's (1967) call to take sides or Douglas's (1979) demand that we deceive the establishment in order to expose it—seems to force moral choices upon us. There is a further dimension related to research on "deviants" who may engage in criminal and violent behavior: Does conscience allow us to witness this? Would we be prepared to protect people engaged in illegality from the authorities? The generality of codes often does not help us to make the fine distinctions that arise at the *interactional* level in participant observation studies, where the reality of the field setting may feel far removed from the refinements of scholarly debate and ethical niceties.

These issues have raised fundamental debate about the very nature of the academic enterprise and about the relationships among social science and research ethics, bureaucratic protection and secrecy, political control and individual rights and obligations (Wilkins, 1979, p. 113). Does the end of seeking knowledge justify the scientific means (Homan & Bulmer, 1982,

p. 114)? What is public and what is private? When can research be said to be "harming" people? Does the researcher enjoy any immunity from the law when he or she refuses to disclose information? In what way can one institutionalize ethical norms—such as respect, beneficence, and justice (Reiss, 1979)—to ensure accountability and responsibility in the use and control of information on human subjects? And to what extent do betrayal of trust, deception, and invasion of privacy damage field relationships, make the researcher cynical and devious, enrage the "participants" in research, harm the reputation of social scientific research, and lead to malpractice in the wider society? All of these points generate ethical, moral, legal, professional, and practical problems and positions that continue to reverberate at conferences, during discussions, and in print. Here I intend to examine these issues in terms of a number of practical problems encountered, particularly in fieldwork situations that generate an ethical component. Again, I wish to clarify that my focus is predominantly sociological and anthropological and that I have in mind largely the lone researcher engaged in an observational study, where a personal involvement with the "subjects" in the field continually poses moral and ethical dilemmas.

At a more ideological, methodological, and institutional level, however, I wish first to touch on three developments that have materially affected the ethical dimension in research. First, the women's movement has brought forth a scholarship that emphasizes identification, trust, empathy, and nonexploitive relationships. Feminist research by women on women implies a "standpoint epistemology" that not only colors the ethical and moral component of research related to the power imbalances in a sexist and racist environment, but also inhibits deception of the research "subjects." Indeed, the gender and ethnic solidarity between researcher and researched welds that relationship into one of cooperation and collaboration that represents a personal commitment and also a contribution to the interests of women in general (e.g., in giving voice to "hidden women," in generating the "emancipatory praxis," and in seeing the field settings as "sites of resistance"). In this sense the personal is related to the ethical, the moral, and the political standpoint. And you do not rip off your sisters.

Second, the stream of evolutionist and interventionist work, or "action" research, has developed to a phase where "subjects" are seen as partners in the research process. To dupe them in any way would be to undermine the very processes one wants to examine. Rather, they are seen as "respondents, participants, stakeholders" in a constructivist paradigm that is based on avoidance of harm, fully informed consent, and the need for privacy and confidentiality. If "action research" actually seeks to empower participants, then one must be open and honest with them; as two leading proponents of "fourth-generation evaluation" research put it:

> If evaluators cannot be clear, direct, and undeceptive regarding their wish to know how stakeholders make sense of their contexts, then stakeholders will be unclear, indirect, and probably misleading regarding how they do engage in sense-making and what their basic values are. Thus deception is not only counter to the posture of a constructivist evaluator, in that it destroys dignity, respect, and agency, but it also is counterproductive to the major goals of a fourth generation evaluation. Deception is worse than useless to a nonconventional evaluator; it is destructive of the effort's ultimate intent. (Guba & Lincoln, 1989, p. 122)

Third, and last, the concern with harm, consent, confidentiality, and so on has led some government agencies to insist that financing of research be contingent upon an ethical statement in the research proposal and that academic departments set up review and monitoring bodies to oversee the ethical component in funded research (Kimmel, 1988; Sieber, 1992). In brief, these three forces have had a powerful impact on consciousness about ethics in research and have, in particular, argued against deception and for taking the interests of the research "subjects" into account.

Codes and Consent

One significant element in such codes is the concept of "informed consent," by which the subjects of research have the right to be informed that they are being researched and also about the nature of the research. Federal agencies in the United States follow the rule for sponsored research "that the potential research subject understand the intention of the research and sign an 'informed consent' form, which incidentally must specify that the subject may withdraw from the research project at any time" (Weppner, 1977, p. 41). The key question here is, To what extent is this appropriate to much participant observation research? As Weppner (1977) observes, this threatens the continued existence of much "street-style" ethnography. When Powdermaker (1966), for instance, came face-to-face with a lynch mob in the Deep South, was she supposed to flash an academic identity card at the crowd and coolly outline her presence? In these and comparable circumstances, gaining consent is quite inappropriate, because activity is taking place that cannot be interrupted. In much fieldwork there seems to be no way around the predicament that informed consent—divulging one's identity and research purpose to all and sundry—will kill many a project stone dead.

And there are simply no easy answers provided by general codes to these situational ethics in fieldwork. For instance, researchers often confess to professional "misdemeanors" while in the field (Wax, 1971, p. 168). Malinowski (1967) socked a recalcitrant informant on the jaw; Powder-maker (1966) ceased to concern herself with the ethics of recording events in Hollywood unknown to the participants; Dalton (1964) fed information on salaries to a secretary in exchange for information on her male friend that was necessary for his research; and Bowen (1964) deliberately ma-nipulated the research situation when it became impossible for her to maintain personal objectivity. The doyen of qualitative researchers, Whyte (1955, pp. 333-336), broke the law by "repeating" at elections, engaged in "retrospective falsification," and admits to having violated professional ethics (see also Whyte, 1984). What sanctions should we impose for these breaches of "professional" standards? Should we ignominiously drum these miscreants out of the profession? That seems a rather severe punishment for coming clean on their predicaments in the field.

My position is that a professional code of ethics is beneficial as a *guideline* that alerts researchers to the ethical dimensions of their work, particularly *prior* to entry. I am not arguing that the field-worker should abandon all ethical considerations once he of she has gotten in, but rather that informed consent is unworkable in some sorts of observational research. Further-more, Reiss (1979, pp. 72, 77) notes that consent often serves to *reduce* participation and, although "definitive evidence is lacking," refusals seem more frequent from high-status, powerful people than from low-status, less powerful individuals. The ethicist might rail at my placing practical handi-caps above ethical ideals, but I am seriously concerned that a strict application of codes will restrain and restrict a great deal of informal, innocuous research in which students and others study groups and activities that are unproblematic but where explicitly enforcing rules concerning informed consent will make the research role simply untenable.

Deception

What is plain is that codes and consent are opposed to deception. In contrast, the proponents of conflict methodology, which sometimes closely resembles investigative journalism (Wallraff, 1979), would argue that it is perfectly legitimate to expose nefarious institutions by using a measure of deceit. However, a number of studies that were not inspired by conflict methodology have employed some element of deception. In a neglected classic titled *Men Who Manage,* Dalton (1959) recounts how he investigated management in a number of firms by working covertly as a manager over a period of years. He used secretaries to gain information, employed out-of-work socializing to observe the significance of club membership for managers, utilized malcontents for their grievances against the organization, and manipulated intimates as "catalytic agents" to gain data (Dalton, 1964). In other projects, a researcher has joined a Pentecostal sect as if a novitiate; used plastic surgery, lost weight, lied about age, and adopted a "new personality" in order to study Air Force recruits (Sullivan, Queen, & Patrick, 1958); and entered a mental hospital as if a patient (Caudill, 1958). In other words, researchers have been prepared to use disguise, deception, and dissimulation in order to conduct research.

And perhaps *some* measure of deception is acceptable in *some* areas where the benefits of knowledge outweigh the harms that have been minimized by following convention on confidentiality and identity (and I fully acknowledge the sort of rationalizations this could lead to). One need not always be brutally honest, direct, and explicit about one's research purpose, but one should not normally engage in disguise. One should not steal documents. One should not directly lie to people. And, although one may disguise identity to a certain extent, one should not break promises made to people. Academics, in weighing up the balancing edge between overt-covert, and between openness-less than open, should take into account the consequences for the subjects, the profession, and, not least, for themselves.

I base this position on the view that subjects should not be harmed but also the pragmatic perspective that some dissimulation is intrinsic to social life and, therefore, also to fieldwork. Gans (1962) expresses this latter view neatly: "If the researcher is completely honest with people about his activities, they will try to hide actions and attitudes they consider undesirable, and so will be dishonest. Consequently, the researcher must be dishonest to get honest data" (p. 46). The crux of the matter is that some deception, passive or active, enables you to get at data not obtainable by other means. There are frequent references in the literature to field-workers as "spies" or "voyeurs," and an experienced researcher advises us to enter the field with a nebulous explanation of our purpose, to be careful that our deception is not found out until after we have left, and states that it is not "ethically necessary, nor methodologically sound, to make known specific hypotheses, background assumptions, or particular areas of interest" (Van Maanen, 1978, p. 334). So much for informed consent! Or, as a senior American academic at an ASA seminar on field methods put it bluntly, "You do lie through your teeth."

This is an extremely knotty area, because some academics argue precisely that researchers should be concerned with documenting abuses in public and business life. This is because they feel that convention on privacy, harm, and confidentiality should be waived when an institution is seen to be evading its public accountability (Holdaway, 1980, p. 324). Marx (1980) echoes this view when he suggests that perhaps different standards apply with respect to deception, privacy, informed consent, and avoiding harm to the researched against organizations that themselves engage in "deceitful, coercive and illegal activities" and are publicly accountable (p. 41). Can we salve our academic conscience by arguing that certain institutions deserve what they get? There seems to be no answer to this issue because it is impossible to establish a priori which institutions are "pernicious." One could visualize endless and fruitless debate as to which organizations should be included, particularly as many public bureaucracies of a relatively mundane sort are secretive and protective. The argument that they are also accountable is a telling one. But using covert research methods against them is likely only to close doors rather than to open them. The balance on this matter is ultimately a question for the individual researcher and his or her conscience in relation to feelings of responsibility to the profession and to "subjects." And it seems to be somewhat specious that academics can employ deception with high moral purpose against those they accuse of deception.

It is interesting, and even ironic, that social scientists espouse some of the techniques normally associated with morally polluted professions, such as policing and spying, and enjoy some of the moral ambivalence surrounding those occupations. The ironies and ambivalences are magnified when researchers study "deviants" and run the danger of what Klockars (1979) calls getting "dirty hands" (p. 269). In getting at the dirt, one may get dirty oneself (Marx, 1980, p. 27). Klockars (1979) is clear on this; in research on deviants the academic promises *not* to blow the whistle and maintains "the immediate, morally unquestionable, and compelling good end of keeping one's promise to one's subjects" (p. 275; see also Polsky, 1969). His argument is that researchers *must* be prepared to get their hands dirty, but also that they protect themselves by approaching subjects as "decent human beings," and by engaging in *talk*. By discussing moral dilemmas openly, researchers can avoid the danger of concealing dirty means for "good" ends. Here I would fully support Klockars's (1979) standpoint:

> The implication for field-work is to be most wary of any and all attempts to fashion rules and regulations, general guidelines, codes of ethics, or standards of professional conduct which would allow well-meaning bureaucrats and concerned colleagues to mobilize punishments for morally dubious behavior. Doing so will, I think, only have the effect of forcing decent fieldworkers to lie, deceive, wear masks, misrepresent themselves, hide the methods of their work, and otherwise dirty their hands more than their vocation now makes morally necessary. (p. 279)

In short, my position is to reject "conflict methodology" as a generally inappropriate model for social science. At the same time, I would accept some moderate measure of field-related deception providing the interests of the subjects are protected. A number of academics, however, take a very strong line on this area. Douglas's claim that basically "anything goes" is firmly opposed by Kai Erikson (cited in Bulmer, 1982). Among others, Erikson argues that it is unethical to misrepresent one's identity deliberately to gain entry into private domains one would otherwise be denied. It is also unethical to misrepresent deliberately the character of one's research. Bulmer (1982) supports the contention that the use of covert observation as a method is "neither ethically justified, nor practically necessary, nor in the best interest of sociology as an academic pursuit" (p. 217). This does not mean that it is *never* justified, but "its use requires most careful consideration in the light of ethical and practical considerations."

Bulmer (1982) then goes on to summarize his position in this debate usefully by arguing that the rights of subjects override the rights of science; that anonymity and confidentiality are necessary but not sufficient for subjects of research (we cannot predict the consequences of publication); and that covert observation is harmful to subjects, researchers, and the discipline. He adds that the need for covert research is exaggerated and that more attention should be paid to access as "overt insider." Also, for Bulmer, the role of "covert outsider" is less reprehensible than that of "covert insider and masquerading as a true participant." And, finally, social scientists should look outside their own profession for ethical guidance and should consider carefully the ethical implications of research before em-

174

barking on it. Much of this is sound advice, but it does mean closing avenues to certain types of research. And who is to perform the moral calculus that tells us what to research and what to leave alone?

Privacy, Harm, Identification, and Confidentiality

Conventional practice and ethical codes espouse the view that various safeguards should protect the privacy and identity of research subjects. As Bulmer (1982) puts it, "Identities, locations of individuals and places are concealed in published results, data collected are held in anonymized form, and all data kept securely confidential" (p. 225). The last of these may require considerable ingenuity in these days of computer hackers. In general, there is a strong feeling among field-workers that settings and respondents should not be identifiable in print and that they should not suffer harm or embarrassment as a consequence of research. There are powerful arguments for respecting persons (see the "Belmont Report" on ethical principles governing research, discussed in O'Connor, 1979) and their dignity, and also for not invading their privacy. Exposing people's private domains to academics raises imagery of "Peeping Toms" and "Big Brother" (Mead, 1961). It does seem to be going a bit far to lie under beds in order to eavesdrop on conversations (Bulmer, 1982, p. 116). But what about attending meetings of Alcoholics Anonymous? Can we assume that alcoholics are too distressed to worry about someone observing their predicament (or that their appearance at A.A. meetings signals their willingness to be open about their problem in the company of others)? To a large extent, I feel that we can become too sensitive on this issue. There is no simple distinction between "public" and "private" while observation in many public and semipublic places is tolerable even when the subjects are not aware of being observed. Some areas are nonproblematic, such as observing the work of flight attendants while one is traveling, and others may be related to serious social problems, where some benefit may emerge from focusing on the issue (Weppner, 1977).

The major safeguard to place against the invasion of privacy is the assurance of confidentiality. But even such assurances are not watertight, and "sociologists themselves have often flagrantly betrayed confidence, undoing all the work of covers, pseudonyms, and deletions" (Rock, 1979). I mentioned earlier the tendency to choose sites close to one's university; pseudonyms can often be punctured by looking up the researcher's institutional affiliation at the time of the project. Everyone now knows that

"Middletown" was Muncie, Indiana; that "Rainfall West" was Seattle; and that "Westville" was Oakland, California. Holdaway (1982) painstakingly uses a pseudonym for his research police station, but then refers in his bibliography to publications that make it plain that he studied the Metropolitan Police of London. And how do you disguise research conducted in readily identifiable cities such as London, New York, or Amsterdam? In addition, the cloak of anonymity for characters may not work with insiders who can easily locate the individuals concerned or, what is even worse, *claim* that they can recognize them when they are, in fact, wrong. Many institutions and public figures are almost impossible to disguise, and, if they cooperate in research, may have to accept a considerable measure of exposure, particularly if the popular media pick up on the research.

This makes it sometimes precarious to assert that no harm or embarrassment will come to the researched (Reiss, 1979, p. 70). In the Cambridge-Somerville Youth Study there were apparently long-term negative consequences that emerged only when an evaluation study was conducted *30 years* after the original project (Kimmel, 1988, pp. 18-20). It is extremely difficult to predict to what uses one's research will be put; Wallis (1977) states that we must not cause "undeserved harm," but who is to define "deserved" and "undeserved" harm? Even people who have cooperated in research may feel hurt or embarrassed when the findings appear in print (e.g., the reactions in "Cornerville"—i.e., the North Side of Boston—to the publication of *Street Corner Society*; Whyte, 1955, p. 346). Indeed, Whyte has recently faced more controversy about his research, some 50 years after the fieldwork; he has been accused, among other things, of misleading respondents about publication (Boelen, 1992). Whyte (1992) has convincingly defended himself and has been supported by some of the original participants in the research (see Orlandella, 1992; Orlandella was "Sam Franco" in *Street Corner Society*). If there has been some element of betrayal on reading or learning of the publication, then the respondents will feel that "they have been cheated and misled by someone in whom they reposed trust and confidence" (Bulmer, 1982, p. 15). Respondents may not be fully aware at the time of the research that its findings may be published. Graduate students who speak vaguely of a dissertation may not make it clear that this is also a public document lodged in a library and open to all (Wallis, 1977, p. 159). The more "deviant" and secretive the activity, the more likely it is that subjects will fear consequences, and "the single most likely source of harm in social science inquiry is that the disclosure of private knowledge can be damaging" (Reiss, 1979, p. 73).

176

Trust and Betrayal

One major theme running through the ethical debate on research is that academics should not spoil the field for others. This is reflected among field-workers, where there are strong norms not to "foul the nest." But given that replications are rare in social science, that field-workers continually seek new and more esoteric settings, and that institutions frequently find one piece of research enough, there is a general tendency to hop from topic to topic. This makes spoiling the field less problematic for prospective researchers who look elsewhere rather than follow in someone's footsteps. It may well be problematic, however, for the researched. They may be left seething with rage and determined to skin alive the next aspiring ethnographer who seeks access. In fact, I would be curious to know how many of us have actually made it *easier* for colleagues to gain access to institutions or groups. It is already the case that anthropologists are not welcome in some Third World countries because they are associated with espionage, which is why some have turned to urban anthropology as opportunities abroad diminish. Indeed, one of the most fundamental objections to conflict methodology is that it will effectively close doors to further research.

This is particularly the case in qualitative research, compared with more formal and socially distant methods, because the academic enters into a relatively close relationship with the researched. First, in order to conduct research the field-worker has to break through to some form of social acceptance with a group. Second, full or near full involvement in the setting may bring an almost total identification with the group. This may be reinforced in deviant subcultures, where the illegal nature of the group's activities necessarily cements a close relationship, both as a necessary mechanism of entry and as a continued guarantee of collusion and of silence to outsiders. In a number of studies use was made of involvement in the role as a full participant (during employment, on vacations, as a student, or in early career employment, e.g., Becker as a jazz musician, Ditton as a bread salesman, and Van Maanen at Disneyland). Indeed, the actual or pretended full commitment to the role may be essential to gaining legitimacy and acceptance from the researched. But, third, and crucially, the researcher is essentially a transient who at some stage will abandon the field and will reenter an alternative social reality that is generally far more comforting and supportive. Anderson "became" a hobo, but he did not *remain* one; in fact, he posed as one and, like many researchers, acted out a role. In the end, we leave the researched behind in the field setting, and this can lead to acute feelings of abandonment and betrayal.

For instance, I conducted research with the Amsterdam police, and over a period of six years I became increasingly conscious of the social processes involved that gradually began to contain a covert element. Elsewhere, I wrote of my growing unease as I began to see through the pretense that I shared a common experience with ordinary policemen while I became uncomfortably aware of the manipulative element in the relationships built in the field. This brought me to the notion of *mutual deceit* as virtually inherent to the deeply engaged fieldwork role:

> If a latent aim of field-work is to create trust in the researcher then what was the aim of that trust? And did not the relationship involve a double betrayal: first by them of me but then by me of them? In short, I felt that in field-work the subjects are conning you until you can gain their trust and then, once you have their confidence, you begin conning them. In other words, I could not escape the realization that deceit and dissemblance were part of the research role and I did not feel ethically comfortable with that insight. Lies, deceit, concealment, and bending the truth are mentioned in many reports of field-work. Indeed, Berreman (1964:18) states that "participant observation, as a form of social interaction, always involves impression management. Therefore, as a research technique, it inevitably entails some secrecy and some dissimulation." At the time I found this all genuinely distressing and confusing. (Punch, 1979, p. 189)

My experiences and views on the mutual conning in the field are perhaps more generally true of research involving deep and long commitment to the setting and close, if not intimate, relationships with the research subjects. And it is precisely in such research that the departure of the researcher, and the subsequent publications of his or her findings, may lead to painful feelings of abandonment and betrayal. There may also be an emotional rejection of the published portrait of the research setting and interaction. In using one's personality to enter the field situation, and in acting out a transient role, one has to face the personal and emotionally charged accusations that not infrequently accompany this style of work. This can, for instance, prove an especially painful dilemma for feminists when they feel caught between solidarity in the field and the professional need to depart and start writing up their experiences for academic consumption (see Fonow & Cook, 1991, p. 9).

◆ Conclusion

I have endeavored here to sketch an overview of those elements that researchers need to consider in pondering the ethics and politics of qualitative research. I recognize, however, that this area is a swamp and that I have provided no map. Each individual will have to trace his or her own path. This is because there is no consensus or unanimity on what is public and private, what constitutes harm, and what the benefits of knowledge are. Also, at the individual level there is no effective control to prevent a new Laud Humphreys from employing devious methods to conduct research. Indeed, the conflict methodologists would actually encourage us to use murky means in order to expose powerful institutions (while arguing that professional ethics are "scientific suicide"; Douglas, 1979, p. 32); feminists would condemn with passion and with anger certain offensive practices *prior* to researching them (or probably not researching them at all); and frequently we have been enjoined to "take sides" (with such spokespersons as Becker and Goffman, when the latter was president of the American Sociological Association, arguing for an engaged and committed profession that unmasks the forces of power and oppression); for where you stand will doubtless help to determine not only what you will research but also how you will research it.

In the past, particularly in medical research and psychological experimentation, there was a considerable amount of deception and, in some cases, a demonstrable element of harm. Attempts to control this have also had an impact on social science in general. Some federally funded research in the United States, for instance, must conform to ethical standards and to auditing by review boards, and professional associations have espoused codes of conduct. A number of disparate forces, including feminism and action research, have emphasized that deceptive and/or exploitive research is inimical to treating "subjects" as partners, collaborators, and stakeholders. Feminists express solidarity with the researched, reach a highly emotive empathy with them, and are committed to emancipating the oppressed; deception and exploitation would be diametrically opposed to their ideology and methods. Here the personal is both political and ethical. In other styles of research, such as interventionist or community-based research, any attempt to dupe or mislead the researched would prove counterproductive because it would undermine the very purpose of the project. In essence, there is a strong argument, reinforced from disparate but powerful forces, that "sound ethics and sound methodology go hand in hand" (Sieber, 1992, p. 4).

Finally, it is possible to examine these issues at the societal, institutional, and professional levels. I have preferred to focus more on how certain aspects of politics and ethics impinge on the individual researcher approaching fieldwork as a relative newcomer. But that does not occur in a vacuum and, fortunately, there are available experienced and wise mentors, academic debates on moral and ethical dilemmas in the field, and professional publications and guidelines on good research practice. In general, serious academics in a sound academic community will espouse trust, reject deception, and abhor harm. They will be wary of spoiling the field, of closing doors to research, and of damaging the reputation of their profession—both as a matter of principle and out of self-interest. In practice, however, professional codes and sound advice may not be all that clear and unambiguous in the field setting, in all its complexity and fluidity. This is because participant observation, as Ditton (1977) notes, is *inevitably* unethical "by virtue of being interactionally deceitful" (p. 10). At the situational and interactional level, then, it may be unavoidable that there is a degree of impression management, manipulation, concealment, economy with the truth, and even deception. I would maintain that we have to accept much of this as being in good faith, providing the researchers come clean about their "muddy boots" (Fielding, 1982, p. 96) and "grubby hands" (Marx, 1980, p. 27). Not to do so would unduly restrict observational and qualitative studies. In essence, I echo Hughes's and Becker's summons to "simply go out and do it." But I would add that before you go you should stop and reflect on the political and ethical dimensions of what you are about to experience. Just do it by all means, but think a bit first.

◆ References

American Sociologist. (1978). [Special issue on regulation of research]. Vol. *13*(3).

Argyris, C. (1969). Diagnosing defenses against the outsider. In G. J. McCall & J. L. Simmons (Eds.), *Issues in participant observation* (pp. 115-127). Reading, MA: Addison-Wesley.

Atkinson, M. (1977). Coroners and the categorisation of deaths as suicides: Changes in perspective as features of the research process. In C. Bell & H. Newby (Eds.), *Doing sociological research* (pp. 31-46). London: Allen & Unwin.

Barber, B. (1976). The ethics of experimentation with human subjects. *Scientific American, 234*(2), 25-31.

Barnes, J. A. (1979). *Who should know what? Social science, privacy and ethics.* Harmondsworth: Penguin.

Becker, H. S. (1967). Whose side are we on? *Social Problems, 14,* 239-247.

Bell, C. (1977). Reflections on the Banbury restudy. In C. Bell & H. Newby (Eds.), *Doing sociological research* (pp. 47-66). London: Allen & Unwin.

Bell, C., & Newby, H. (Eds.). (1977). *Doing sociological research.* London: Allen & Unwin.

Boelen, W. A. M. (1992). *Street corner society*: Cornerville revisited. In *Street corner society* revisited [Special issue]. *Journal of Contemporary Ethnography, 21,* 11-51.

Boruch, R. F., & Cecil, J. S. (1983). *Solutions to ethical and legal problems in social research.* New York: Academic Press.

Bowen, E. S. (1964). *Return to laughter.* New York: Random House. (Published under pseudonym L. Bohannon)

Brandt, A. M. (1978). *Racism, research and the Tuskegee Syphilis Study* (Report No. 8). New York: Hastings Center.

Bulmer, M. (Ed.). (1982). *Social research ethics.* London: Macmillan.

Burgess, R. G. (Ed.). (1982). *Field research: A source book and field manual.* London: Allen & Unwin.

Burns, T. (1977). *The B.B.C.* London: Macmillan.

Caudill, W. (1958). *The psychiatric hospital as a small society.* Cambridge, MA: Harvard University Press.

Clarke, M. (1975). Survival in the field: Implications of personal experience in field-work. *Theory and Society, 2,* 95-123.

Dalton, M. (1959). *Men who manage.* New York: John Wiley.

Dalton, M. (1964). Preconceptions and methods in *Men who manage.* In P. Hammond (Ed.), *Sociologists at work* (pp. 50-95). New York: Basic Books.

Diamond, S. (1964). Nigerian discovery: The politics of field-work. In A. J. Vidich, J. Bensman, & M. R. Stein (Eds.), *Reflections on community studies* (pp. 119-154). New York: Harper & Row.

Diener, E., & Crandall, R. (1978). *Ethics in social and behavioral research.* Chicago: University of Chicago Press.

Dingwall, R., Payne, G., & Payne, J. (1980). *The development of ethnography in Britain.* Mimeo, Centre for Socio-Legal Studies, Oxford.

Ditton, J. (1977). *Part-time crime.* London: Macmillan.

Douglas, J. D. (1979). Living morality versus bureaucratic fiat. In C. B. Klockars & F. W. O'Connor (Eds.), *Deviance and decency: The ethics of research with human subjects* (pp. 13-33). Beverly Hills, CA: Sage.

Festinger, L., Riecken, H. W., & Schachter, S. (1956). *When prophecy fails.* New York: Harper & Row.

Fielding, N. (1982). Observational research on the national front. In M. Bulmer (Ed.), *Social research ethics* (pp. 80-104). London: Macmillan.

Florez, C. P., & Kelling, G. L. (1979). *Issues in the use of observers in large scale program evaluation: The hired hand and the lone wolf.* Unpublished manuscript, Harvard University, Kennedy School of Government.

Fonow, M. M., & Cook, J. A. (Eds.). (1991). *Beyond methodology: Feminist scholarship as lived research.* Bloomington: Indiana University Press.

181

Gans, H. J. (1962). *The urban villagers: Group and class in the life of Italian-Americans.* New York: Free Press.

Gans, H. J. (1967). *The Levittowners: Ways of life and politics in a new suburban community.* London: Allen Lane.

Grossberg, L., Nelson, C., & Treichler, P. A. (Eds.). (1992). *Cultural studies.* New York: Routledge.

Guba, E. G., & Lincoln, Y. S. (1989). *Fourth generation evaluation.* Newbury Park, CA: Sage.

Gubrium, J. F., & Silverman, D. (Eds.). (1989). *The politics of field research: Beyond enlightenment.* Newbury Park, CA: Sage.

Hammersley, M. (Ed.). (1993). *Social research: Philosophy, politics and practice.* London: Sage.

Hammersley, M., & Atkinson, P. (1983). *Ethnography: Principles in practice.* London: Tavistock.

Hammond, P. (Ed.). (1964). *Sociologists at work.* New York: Basic Books.

Holdaway, S. (1980). *The occupational culture of urban policing: An ethnographic study.* Unpublished doctoral dissertation, University of Sheffield.

Holdaway, S. (1982). "An inside job": A case study of covert research on the police. In M. Bulmer (Ed.), *Social research ethics* (pp. 59-79). London: Macmillan.

Homan, R., & Bulmer, M. (1982). On the merits of covert methods: A dialogue. In M. Bulmer (Ed.), *Social research ethics* (pp. 105-124). London: Macmillan.

Horowitz, I. L. (1970). Sociological snoopers and journalistic moralizers. *Transaction, 7,* 4-8.

Humphreys, L. (1970). *Tearoom trade: Impersonal sex in public places.* Chicago: Aldine.

Humphreys, L. (1972). *Out of the closet.* Englewood Cliffs, NJ: Prentice Hall.

Hunt, J. (1984). The development of rapport through the negotiation of gender in field work among police. *Human Organization, 43,* 283-296.

Jayaratne, T. E., & Stewart, A. J. (1991). Quantitative and qualitative methods in the social sciences: Current feminist issues and practical strategies. In M. M. Fonow & J. A. Cook (Eds.), *Beyond methodology: Feminist scholarship as lived research* (pp. 85-106). Bloomington: Indiana University Press.

Katz, J. (1972). *Experimentation with human beings.* New York: Russell Sage.

Kimmel, A. J. (1988). *Ethics and values in applied social research.* Newbury Park, CA: Sage.

Klein, L. (1976). *A social scientist in industry.* London: Gower.

Klockars, C. B. (1979). Dirty hands and deviant subjects. In C. B. Klockars & F. W. O'Connor (Eds.), *Deviance and decency: The ethics of research with human subjects* (pp. 261-282). Beverly Hills, CA: Sage.

Klockars, C. B., & O'Connor, F. W. (Eds.). (1979). *Deviance and decency: The ethics of research with human subjects.* Beverly Hills, CA: Sage.

La Pierre, R. T. (1934). Attitudes vs. actions. *Social Forces, 13,* 230-237.

Lofland, J. F., & Lejeune, R. A. (1960). Initial interaction of newcomers in Alcoholics Anonymous. *Social Problems, 8,* 102-111.

Malinowski, B. (1967). *A diary in the strict sense of the term.* New York: Harcourt Brace.

Martin, S. E. (1980). *Breaking and entering: Policewomen on patrol.* Berkeley: University of California Press.

Marx, G. (1980). *Notes on the discovery, collection and assessment of hidden and dirty data.* Paper presented at the annual meeting of the Society for the Study of Social Problems, New York.

McCall, G. J., & Simmons, J. L. (Eds.). (1969). *Issues in participant observation.* Reading, MA: Addison-Wesley.

Mead, M. (1961). The human study of human beings. *Science, 133,* 163-165.

Mies, M. (1991). Women's research or feminist research: The debate surrounding feminist science and methodology. In M. M. Fonow & J. A. Cook (Eds.), *Beyond methodology: Feminist scholarship as lived research* (pp. 60-84). Bloomington: Indiana University Press.

Milgram, S. (1963). Behavioral study of obedience. *Journal of Abnormal and Social Psychology, 67,* 371-378.

O'Connor, F. W. (1979). The ethical demands of the Belmont Report. In C. B. Klockars & F. W. O'Connor (Eds.), *Deviance and decency: The ethics of research with human subjects* (pp. 225-258). Beverly Hills, CA: Sage.

Okely, J., & Callaway, H. (Eds.). (1992). *Anthropology and autobiography.* New York: Routledge.

Orlandella, A. R. (1992). Boelen may know Holland, Boelen may know Barzini, but Boelen "doesn't know diddle about the North End!" In *Street corner society* revisited [Special issue]. *Journal of Contemporary Ethnography, 21,* 69-79.

Platt, J. (1976). *The realities of social research.* London: University of Sussex Press.

Polsky, N. (1969). *Hustlers, beats and others.* Chicago: Aldine.

Powdermaker, H. (1966). *Stranger and friend: The way of an anthropologist.* New York: W. W. Norton.

Punch, M. (1986). *The politics and ethics of fieldwork.* Beverly Hills, CA: Sage.

Punch, M. (1989). Researching police deviance: A personal encounter with the limitations and liabilities of field-work. *British Journal of Sociology, 40,* 177-204.

Reimer, J. W. (1979). *Hard hats.* Beverly Hills, CA: Sage.

Reinharz, S. (1992). *Feminist methods in social research.* New York: Oxford University Press.

Reiss, A. J., Jr. (1979). Governmental regulation of scientific inquiry: Some paradoxical consequences. In C. B. Klockars & F. W. O'Connor (Eds.), *Deviance and decency: The ethics of research with human subjects* (pp. 61-95). Beverly Hills, CA: Sage.

Roberts, H. (Ed.). (1981). *Doing feminist research.* London: Routledge.

Rock, P. (1979). *The making of symbolic interactionism.* London: Macmillan.

Rynkiewich, M. A., & Spradley, J. (Eds.). (1976). *Ethics and anthropology: Dilemmas in fieldwork.* New York: John Wiley.

Sanjek, R. (Ed.). (1990). *Fieldnotes: The makings of anthropology.* Albany: State University of New York Press.

Schwartz, M. (1964). The mental hospital: The researched person in the disturbed world. In A. J. Vidich, J. Bensman, & M. R. Stein (Eds.), *Reflections on community studies* (pp. 85-117). New York: Harper & Row.

Shaffir, W. B., & Stebbins, R. A. (Eds.). (1991). *Experiencing fieldwork: An inside view of qualitative research.* Newbury Park, CA: Sage.

Sharrock, W., & Anderson, R. (1980). *Ethnomethodology and British sociology: Some problems of incorporation.* Paper presented at the annual meeting of the British Sociological Association, University of Lancaster.

Shils, E. (1982). Social enquiry and the autonomy of the individual. In M. Bulmer (Ed.), *Social research ethics* (pp. 125-141). London: Macmillan.

Sieber, J. E. (1992). *Planning ethically responsible research.* Newbury Park, CA: Sage.

Sjoberg, G. (Ed.). (1968). *Ethics, politics, and social research.* Cambridge, MA: Schenkman.

Social Problems. (1973). [Special issue on the social control of social research]. Vol. *21*(1).

Social Problems. (1980). [Special issue on ethical problems of fieldwork]. Vol. *27*(3).

Spencer, G. (1973). Methodological issues in the study of bureaucratic elites: A case of West Point. *Social Problems, 21,* 90-102.

Sullivan, M. A., Queen, S. A., & Patrick, R. C. (1958). Participant observation as employed in the study of a military training program. *American Sociological Review, 23,* 610-667.

Thompson, H. (1967). *Hell's Angels.* Harmondsworth: Penguin.

Van Maanen, J. (1978). On watching the watchers. In P. K. Manning & J. Van Maanen (Eds.), *Policing: A view from the street* (pp. 309-349). Santa Monica, CA: Goodyear.

Van Maanen, J. (Ed.). (1979). Qualitative methodology [Special issue]. *Administrative Science Quarterly, 24,* 519-680.

Van Maanen, J. (1988). *Tales of the field: On writing ethnography.* Chicago: University of Chicago Press.

Vidich, A. J., & Bensman, J. (1968). *Small town in mass society: Class, power and religion in a rural community* (2nd ed.). Princeton, NJ: Princeton University Press.

Wallis, R. (1977). The moral career of a research sociologist. In C. Bell & H. Newby (Eds.), *Doing sociological research* (pp. 149-169). London: Allen & Unwin.

Wallraff, G. (1979). *Beeld van bild.* Amsterdam: Van Gennep.

Wax, R.H. (1971). *Doing fieldwork: Warnings and advice.* Chicago: University of Chicago Press.

Welch, S. (1991). An ethic of solidarity. In H. Giroux (Ed.), *Postmodernism, feminism, and cultural politics* (pp. 83-99). Albany: State University of New York Press.

Weppner, R. S. (1977). *Street ethnography.* Beverly Hills, CA: Sage.

Whyte, W. F. (1943). *Street corner society: The social structure of an Italian slum.* Chicago: University of Chicago Press.

Whyte, W. F. (1955). *Street corner society: The social structure of an Italian slum* (2nd ed.). Chicago: University of Chicago Press.

Whyte, W. F. (1981). *Street corner society: The social structure of an Italian slum* (3rd ed.). Chicago: University of Chicago Press.

Whyte, W. F. (1984). *Learning from the field: A guide from experience.* Beverly Hills, CA: Sage.

Whyte, W. F. (1992). In defense of *Street corner society.* In *Street corner society* revisited [Special issue]. *Journal of Contemporary Ethnography, 21,* 52-68.

Wilkins, L. T. (1979). Human subjects—whose subjects? In C. B. Klockars & F. W. O'Connor (Eds.), *Deviance and decency: The ethics of research with human subjects* (pp. 99-123). Beverly Hills, CA: Sage.

Wycoff, M. A., & Kelling, G. L. (1978). *The Dallas experience: Organizational reform.* Washington, DC: Police Foundation.

Yablonsky, L. (1968). *The hippy trip.* Harmondsworth: Penguin.

PART II

◆ Major Paradigms and Perspectives

In our introductory chapter, following Guba (1990, p. 17), we defined a paradigm as a basic set of beliefs that guide action. Paradigms deal with first principles, or ultimates. They are human constructions. They define the worldview of the researcher-as-*bricoleur*. These beliefs can never be established in terms of their ultimate truthfulness. Perspectives, in contrast, are not as solidified, or as well unified, as paradigms, although a perspective may share many elements with a paradigm, such as a common set of methodological commitments.

A paradigm encompasses three elements: epistemology, ontology, and methodology. *Epistemology* asks, How do we know the world? What is the relationship between the inquirer and the known? *Ontology* raises basic questions about the nature of reality. *Methodology* focuses on how we gain knowledge about the world. Part II of this volume examines the major paradigms and perspectives that now structure and organize qualitative research: positivism, postpositivism, constructivism, and critical theory and related positions.

Alongside these paradigms are the perspectives of feminism, ethnic models of inquiry, and cultural studies. Each of these perspectives adopts its own criteria, assumptions, and methodological practices that are applied to disciplined inquiry within that framework. We have provided a brief discussion of each paradigm and perspective in Chapter 1; here we elaborate them in considerably more detail.

◆ The Positivist Legacy: Epistemology, Ontology, Methodology

Of course, the positivist and postpositivist paradigms provide the backdrop against which other paradigms and perspectives operate. In this volume, these two traditions are analyzed in considerable detail. Conventional positivist social science applies four criteria to disciplined inquiry: *internal validity,* the degree to which findings correctly map the phenomenon in question; *external validity,* the degree to which findings can be generalized to other settings similar to the one in which the study occurred; *reliability,* the extent to which findings can be replicated, or reproduced, by another inquirer; and *objectivity,* the extent to which findings are free from bias.

The received positivist and postpositivist views have recently come under considerable attack. Guba and Lincoln review these criticisms, including the arguments that these paradigms are unable to deal adequately with the issues surrounding the etic, emic, nomothetic, and idiographic dimensions of inquiry. Too many local (emic), case-based (idiographic) meanings are excluded by the generalizing (etic) nomothetic, positivist position. At the same time, the nomothetic, etic approaches fail to address satisfactorily the theory- and value-laden nature of facts, the interactive nature of inquiry, and the fact that the same set of "facts" can support more than one theory.

◆ Constructivism and Critical Theory

Constructivism, as presented by Guba and Lincoln, adopts a relativist (relativism) ontology, a transactional epistemology, and a

186

hermeneutic, dialectical methodology. The inquiry aims of this paradigm are oriented to the production of reconstructed understandings, wherein the traditional positivist criteria of internal and external validity are replaced by the terms *trustworthiness* and *authenticity*.

Thomas Schwandt's subtle analysis in Chapter 7 of constructivist, interpretivist approaches identifies major differences and strands of thought within these approaches, which are unified by their opposition to positivism and their commitment to the study of the world from the point of view of the interacting individual. Yet these perspectives, as Schwandt argues, are distinguished more by their commitment to questions of knowing and being than by their specific methodologies, which basically enact an emic, idiographic approach to inquiry. Schwandt traces out the theoretical and philosophical foundations of constructivist, interpretivist traditions, connecting them back to the works of Schutz, Weber, Mead, Blumer, Winch, Heidegger, Gadamer, Geertz, Ricoeur, Gergen, Goodman, Guba, and Lincoln. The constructivist tradition, as Schwandt notes, is rich, deep, and complex.

A similarly complicated field describes the multiple critical theory, Marxist models that now circulate within the discourses of qualitative research (see Kincheloe & McLaren, Chapter 8, this volume; see also Nelson & Grossberg, 1988). In Guba and Lincoln's framework this paradigm, in its many forms, articulates an ontology based on historical realism, an epistemology that is transactional, and a methodology that is dialogic and dialectical. In their chapter, Joe Kincheloe and Peter McLaren trace the history of critical research (and Marxist theory) from the Frankfurt school through their most recent transformations in poststructural, postmodern, feminist, and cultural studies theory. They develop a "resistance" version of postmodernism that is joined with critical theory and critical ethnography. An added bonus is their treatment of the Birmingham school of cultural studies and the recent critical work of Cornel West and others on women, the Third World, and race. They outline several ways that critical theory-based research can lead to worker empowerment. Critical theorists seek to produce transformations in the social order, producing knowledge that is historical and structural, judged by its degree of historical situatedness and its ability to produce praxis, or action.

There are, however, some critical theorists (see, e.g., Carspecken & Apple, 1992, pp. 547-548) who work to build testable, falsifiable social theory. Others—for example, materialist ethnographers such as Roman (1992)—reject the postpositivist features of these arguments, as do Dorothy Smith (1992, 1993) and Henry Giroux (1992). Other critical theorists and Marxists work more closely from within a traditional, qualitative, grounded theory approach to validity and theory construction (Burawoy, 1992), stressing the extended case study as the focus of analysis.

◆ Interpretive Perspectives

Each of the three feminisms identified by Virginia Olesen in Chapter 9 (standpoint epistemology, empiricist, and postmodernism-cultural studies), takes a different stance toward the postpositivist tradition. Standpoint epistemologists reject "standard good social scientific methodologies [because they] produce people as objects . . . if [sociologists] work with standard methods of thinking and inquiry, they import the relations of ruling into the texts they produce. . . . this is not an issue of quantitative versus qualitative method" (Smith, 1992, p. 91). Using case studies, participant observation, interviewing, and the critical analysis of social texts, Smith deploys a critical, poststructural epistemology and methodology that continually explores the connections between texts and relations of ruling (but see Clough, 1993a, 1993b). Standpoint epistemologists are, then, close to the critical paradigm while sharing certain features with the constructivist paradigm (hermeneutical, dialogic inquiry).

In contrast, empiricist feminisms are aligned with a postpositivist language of validity, reliability, credibility, multimethod research strategies, and so on (see Reinharz, 1992). There is an emphasis on some version of realism, a modified objectivist epistemology, a concern for hypothesis testing, explanation, prediction, cause-effect linkages, and conventional benchmarks of rigor, including internal and external validity. Here the intent is to apply the full range of qualitative methodologies to feminist issues.

Postmodern, cultural studies feminists merge their work with the postmodern, ethnographic turn in anthropology (see Morris, 1988) while exploring autoethnography and other new writing forms (see Franklin, Lury, & Stacey, 1991, p. 181; Wolf, 1992). This tradition draws on the critical and constructivist paradigms, especially in a commitment to relativism and historical realism, transactional epistemologies, dialogic methodologies, and social critique, as well as historically situated and trustworthy empirical materials. However, cultural studies feminists both supplement and at times challenge the more explicit standpoint epistemology projects (Clough, 1993a, 1993b).

Feminist theory and thought is restructuring qualitative research practices. This is especially the case for those approaches shaped by the standpoint epistemology and cultural studies models. From them are coming new ethical and epistemological criteria for evaluating research. At the same time, these perspectives are making lived experience central to qualitative inquiry and developing criteria of evaluation based on ethics of caring, personal responsibility, and open dialogue.

These criteria, as articulated by scholars such as Patricia Hill Collins (1990, p. 219), embody a standpoint epistemology that is fully compatible with the cultural studies paradigm. This is especially the case when these criteria are joined with an emphasis on reflexive textuality and an understanding that there is no dividing line between empirical research activity and the process of theorizing. Theory is interpretation, just as it is also criticism and critique.

Ethnic models of inquiry also move in at least three different directions at the same time. Traditional ethnic empiricists utilize participant observation, interviewing, and case study methods to examine the lived experiences of specific ethnic minorities. They assess their findings in terms quite compatible with the postpositivist project. Marxist ethnic models (Collins, 1990) build upon the standpoint epistemologies of Smith and others to examine explicitly how local cultures and "local knowledges can counteract the hegemonic tendencies of objectified knowledge" (Collins, 1992, p. 74). Postmodern ethnic models (West, 1989) elaborate a variety of different cultural studies models (see below) to examine the ways in which race and ethnicity are repressively inscribed in daily social life. It is possible, then, as with feminism, to map the ethnic models into the postpositivist, critical, and constructivist paradigms.

The three models mentioned in the foregoing paragraph confront a common set of problems, involving the normalization of ethnicity as a way of life in the United States, the hegemonic character of American social science, and the white middle-class origins of this enterprise. Historically, critical ethnic models of qualitative inquiry have been excluded from social science discourse, for example, the work of Carter G. Woodson, William E. B. Du Bois, Horace Mann Bond, and, until recently, Zora Neale Hurston. This has made it more difficult for minority scholars to develop their own paradigms, free of the biases and prejudices of race, positivism, and postpositivism.

Stanfield outlines one version of this project, drawing attention to the neglected historical and participant observation research traditions in the Afro-American scholarly community. He anticipates future debates over the insider-outsider issue in social research, noting that minority scholars have traditionally been treated as outsiders, forced to study their own ethnic communities from the Eurocentric perspective. He also reviews feminist research approaches to race and ethnicity. Stanfield discusses much of the revisionist work in this area that has been shaped by Eurocentric biases and outlines a new ethnic paradigm grounded in the global experiences of people of color. This paradigm is holistic, relational, qualitative, and sensitive to gender, kinship, spirituality, and the oral communicative traditions so central to the experiences of Afro-Americans and other people of color in the United States and elsewhere. A great deal is at issue in this area. Historically, racial and ethnic minorities have lacked the power "to represent themselves to themselves and others as complex human beings" (West, 1990, p. 27). Stanfield shows how this situation can be changed radically. Indeed, all of the chapters address this problem, in one way or another.

Cultural studies cannot be contained within a single framework. There are multiple cultural studies projects, including those connected to the Birmingham school and to the work of Stuart Hall and his associates (see, e.g., Grossberg, 1989, 1992; Hall, 1992). The generic focus of each version involves an examination of how the history people live is produced by structures that have been handed down from the past. Each version is joined by a threefold concern with cultural texts, lived experience, and the articulated relationship between texts and everyday life. Within the cultural text tradition, some scholars examine the mass media and popular culture as sites where history, ideology, and subjective experiences come together, as John Fiske does in Chapter 11. These scholars produce critical ethnographies of the audience in relation to particular historical moments. Other scholars read texts as sites where hegemonic meanings are produced, distributed, and consumed (Giroux, 1992). Within the ethnographic tradition, there is a postmodern concern for the social text and its production.

The open-ended nature of the cultural studies project leads to a perpetual resistance against attempts to impose a single paradigm over the entire project. There are critical-Marxist, constructionist, and postpositivist paradigmatic strands within the formation, as well as emergent feminist and ethnic models. Scholars within the cultural studies project are drawn to historical realism and relativism as their ontology, and to transactional epistemologies and dialogic methodologies, while remaining committed to a historical and structural framework that is praxis and action based.

Fiske's chapter is an example of the text-based, ethnographic, and audience research tradition in cultural studies. He notes that he does not speak for cultural studies in his text. He offers, instead, a review of recent studies of television audiences, showing how these qualitative, ethnographic investigations contribute to the cultural studies project. He argues that his work is not "scientific." It is interpretive, based on discourse analysis, and is not systematic in its model of validation. The data Fiske uses are empirical because they derive from material experience. They are not empiricist; that is, he makes no claim that "the material plane has an objective existence that provides the terms of its own significance." Fiske's work has elements that align it with the critical and constructionist paradigms discussed by Guba and Lincoln in Chapter 6.

◆ In Conclusion

The researcher-as-*bricoleur* cannot afford to be a stranger to any of the paradigms discussed. He or she must understand the basic ontological, epistemological, and methodological assumptions of each, and be able to engage them in dialogue (Guba, 1990). The differences between paradigms have significant and important implications at the practical, everyday, empirical level. A resolution of paradigm differences, Guba and Lincoln cogently note in Chapter 6, is most likely to occur "if and when proponents of these several [paradigms] come together to discuss their differences, not to argue the sanctity of their views."

◆ References

Burawoy, M. (1992). The extended case method. In M. Burawoy, A. Burton, A. A. Ferguson, K. J. Fox, J. Gamson, N. Gartrell, L. Hurst, C. Kurzman, L. Salzinger, J. Schiffman, & S. Ui (Eds.), *Ethnography unbound: Power and resistance in the modern metropolis* (pp. 271-290). Berkeley: University of California Press.

Carspecken, P. F., & Apple, M. (1992). Critical research: Theory, methodology, and practice. In M. D. LeCompte, W. L. Millroy, & J. Preissle (Eds.), *The handbook of qualitative research in education* (pp. 507-554). New York: Academic Press.

Clough, P. T. (1993a). On the brink of deconstructing sociology: A critical reading of Dorothy Smith's standpoint epistemology. *Sociological Quarterly, 34,* 169-182.

Clough, P. T. (1993b). Response to Smith. *Sociological Quarterly, 34,* 193-194.

Collins, P. H. (1990). *Black feminist thought: Knowledge, consciousness and the politics of empowerment.* New York: Routledge.

Collins, P. H. (1992). Transforming the inner circle: Dorothy Smith's challenge to sociological theory. *Sociological Theory, 10,* 73-80.

Franklin, S., Lury, C., & Stacey, J. (1991). Feminism and cultural studies: Pasts, presents, and futures. *Media, Culture & Society, 13,* 171-192.

Giroux, H. (1992). *Border crossings: Cultural workers and the politics of education.* New York: Routledge.

Grossberg, L. (1989). The formations of cultural studies: An American in Birmingham. *Strategies, 2,* 114-149.

Grossberg, L. (1992). *We gotta get out of this place: Popular conservatism and postmodern culture.* New York: Routledge.

Guba, E. G. (1990). The alternative paradigm dialog. In E. G. Guba (Ed.), *The paradigm dialog* (pp. 17-30). Newbury Park, CA: Sage.

Hall, S. (1992). Cultural studies and its theoretical legacies. In L. Grossberg, C. Nelson, & P. A. Treichler (Eds.), *Cultural studies* (pp. 277-294). New York: Routledge.

Morris, M. (1988). Henry Parkes Motel. *Cultural Studies, 2,* 10-47.

Nelson, C., & Grossberg, L. (Eds.). (1988). *Marxism and the interpretation of culture.* Urbana: University of Illinois Press.

Reinharz, S. (1992). *Feminist methods in social research.* New York: Oxford University Press.

Roman, L. G. (1992). The political significance of other ways of narrating ethnography: A feminist materialist approach. In M. D. LeCompte, W. L. Millroy, & J. Preissle (Eds.),

The handbook of qualitative research in education (pp. 555-594). New York: Academic Press.

Smith, D. E. (1992). Sociology from women's experience: A reaffirmation. *Sociological Theory, 10,* 88-98.

Smith, D. E. (1993). High noon in Textland: A critique of Clough. *Sociological Quarterly, 34,* 183-192.

West, C. (1989). *The American evasion of philosophy.* Madison: University of Wisconsin Press.

West, C. (1990). The new cultural politics of difference. In R. Ferguson, M. Geverr, Trinh T. M.-H., & C. West (Eds.), *Out there: Marginalization and contemporary cultures* (pp. 19-36). Cambridge: MIT Press.

Wolf, M. (1992). *A thrice-told tale: Feminism, postmodernism, and ethnographic responsibility.* Stanford, CA: Stanford University Press.

6

Competing Paradigms in Qualitative Research

Egon G. Guba & Yvonna S. Lincoln

◆ In this chapter we analyze four paradigms that currently are competing, or have until recently competed, for acceptance as the paradigm of choice in informing and guiding inquiry, especially qualitative inquiry: positivism, postpositivism, critical theory and related ideological positions, and constructivism. We acknowledge at once our own commitment to constructivism (which we earlier called "naturalistic inquiry"; Lincoln & Guba, 1985); the reader may wish to take that fact into account in judging the appropriateness and usefulness of our analysis.

Although the title of this volume, *Handbook of Qualitative Research,* implies that the term *qualitative* is an umbrella term superior to the term *paradigm* (and, indeed, that usage is not uncommon), it is our position that it is a term that ought to be reserved for a description of types of methods. From our perspective, both qualitative and quantitative methods may be used appropriately with any research paradigm. Questions of method are secondary to questions of paradigm, which we define as the basic belief system or worldview that guides the investigator, not only in choices of method but in ontologically and epistemologically fundamental ways.

AUTHORS' NOTE: We are grateful to Henry Giroux and Robert Stake for their very helpful critiques of an earlier draft of this chapter.

It is certainly the case that interest in alternative paradigms has been stimulated by a growing dissatisfaction with the patent overemphasis on quantitative methods. But as efforts were made to build a case for a renewed interest in qualitative approaches, it became clear that the metaphysical assumptions undergirding the conventional paradigm (the "received view") must be seriously questioned. Thus the emphasis of this chapter is on paradigms, their assumptions, and the implications of those assumptions for a variety of research issues, not on the relative utility of qualitative versus quantitative methods. Nevertheless, as discussions of paradigms/ methods over the past decade have often begun with a consideration of problems associated with overquantification, we will also begin there, shifting only later to our predominant interest.

◆ The Quantitative/Qualitative Distinction

Historically, there has been a heavy emphasis on quantification in science. Mathematics is often termed the "queen of sciences," and those sciences, such as physics and chemistry, that lend themselves especially well to quantification are generally known as "hard." Less quantifiable arenas, such as biology (although that is rapidly changing) and particularly the social sciences, are referred to as "soft," less with pejorative intent than to signal their (putative) imprecision and lack of dependability. Scientific maturity is commonly believed to emerge as the degree of quantification found within a given field increases.

That this is the case is hardly surprising. The "received view" of science (positivism, transformed over the course of this century into postpositivism; see below) focuses on efforts to verify (positivism) or falsify (postpositivism) a priori hypotheses, most usefully stated as mathematical (quantitative) propositions or propositions that can be easily converted into precise mathematical formulas expressing functional relationships. Formulaic precision has enormous utility when the aim of science is the prediction and control of natural phenomena. Further, there is already available a powerful array of statistical and mathematical models. Finally, there exists a widespread conviction that only quantitative data are ultimately valid, or of high quality (Sechrest, 1992).

John Stuart Mill (1843/1906) is said to have been the first to urge social scientists to emulate their older, "harder" cousins, promising that if his advice were followed, rapid maturation of these fields, as well as their emancipation from the philosophical and theological strictures that limited them, would follow. Social scientists took this counsel to heart (probably to a degree that would greatly surprise Mill if he were alive today) for other reasons as well. They were the "new kids on the block"; if quantification could lead to the fulfillment of Mill's promise, status and political leverage would accrue that would enormously profit the new practitioners. Imitation might thus lead both to greater acceptance and to more valid knowledge.

◆ Critiques of the Received View

In recent years, however, strong counterpressures against quantification have emerged. Two critiques, one internal to the conventional paradigm (that is, in terms of those metaphysical assumptions that define the nature of positivist inquiry) and one external to it (that is, in terms of those assumptions defining alternative paradigms), have been mounted that seem not only to warrant a reconsideration of the utility of qualitative data but to question the very assumptions on which the putative superiority of quantification has been based.

Internal (Intraparadigm) Critiques

A variety of implicit problems have surfaced to challenge conventional wisdom; several of these are described below.

Context stripping. Precise quantitative approaches that focus on selected subsets of variables necessarily "strip" from consideration, through appropriate controls or randomization, other variables that exist in the context that might, if allowed to exert their effects, greatly alter findings. Further, such exclusionary designs, while increasing the theoretical rigor of a study, detract from its *relevance,* that is, its applicability or generalizability, because their outcomes can be properly applied only in other similarly truncated or contextually stripped situations (another laboratory, for example). Qualitative data, it is argued, can redress that imbalance by providing contextual information.

Exclusion of meaning and purpose. Human behavior, unlike that of physical objects, cannot be understood without reference to the meanings and purposes attached by human actors to their activities. Qualitative data, it is asserted, can provide rich insight into human behavior.

Disjunction of grand theories with local contexts: The etic/emic dilemma. The etic (outsider) theory brought to bear on an inquiry by an investigator (or the hypotheses proposed to be tested) may have little or no meaning within the emic (insider) view of studied individuals, groups, societies, or cultures. Qualitative data, it is affirmed, are useful for uncovering emic views; theories, to be valid, should be qualitatively grounded (Glaser & Strauss, 1967; Strauss & Corbin, 1990). Such grounding is particularly crucial in view of the mounting criticism of social science as failing to provide adequate accounts of nonmainstream lives (the "other") or to provide the material for a criticism of our own Western culture (Marcus & Fischer, 1986).

Inapplicability of general data to individual cases. This problem is some-times described as the nomothetic/idiographic disjunction. Generaliza-tions, although perhaps statistically meaningful, have no applicability in the individual case (the fact, say, that 80% of individuals presenting given symptoms have lung cancer is at best incomplete evidence that a particular patient presenting with such symptoms has lung cancer). Qualitative data, it is held, can help to avoid such ambiguities.

Exclusion of the discovery dimension in inquiry. Conventional emphasis on the verification of specific, a priori hypotheses glosses over the source of those hypotheses, usually arrived at by what is commonly termed the discovery process. In the received view only empirical inquiry deserves to be called "science." Quantitative normative methodology is thus privileged over the insights of creative and divergent thinkers. The call for qualitative inputs is expected to redress this imbalance.

External (Extraparadigm) Critiques

The intraparadigm problems noted above offer a weighty challenge to conventional methodology, but could be eliminated, or at least amelio-rated, by greater use of qualitative data. Many critics of the received view are content to stop at that point; hence many of the calls for more qualitative inputs have been limited to this methods-level accommodation.

But an even weightier challenge has been mounted by critics who have proposed *alternative paradigms* that involve not only qualification of approaches but fundamental adjustments in the basic assumptions that guide inquiry altogether. Their rejection of the received view can be justified on a number of grounds (Bernstein, 1988; Guba, 1990; Hesse, 1980; Lincoln & Guba, 1985; Reason & Rowan, 1981), but chief among them are the following.[1]

The theory-ladenness of facts. Conventional approaches to research involving the verification or falsification of hypotheses assume the independence of theoretical and observational languages. If an inquiry is to be objective, hypotheses must be stated in ways that are independent of the way in which the facts needed to test them are collected. But it now seems established beyond objection that theories and facts are quite *interdependent*—that is, that facts are facts only within some theoretical framework. Thus a fundamental assumption of the received view is exposed as dubious. If hypotheses and observations are not independent, "facts" can be viewed only through a theoretical "window" and objectivity is undermined.

The underdetermination of theory. This problem is also known as the problem of induction. Not only are facts determined by the theory window through which one looks for them, but different theory windows might be equally well supported by the same set of "facts." Although it may be possible, given a coherent theory, to derive by deduction what facts ought to exist, it is never possible, given a coherent set of facts, to arrive by *induction* at a single, ineluctable theory. Indeed, it is this difficulty that led philosophers such as Popper (1968) to reject the notion of theory *verification* in favor of the notion of theory *falsification*. Whereas a million white swans can never establish, with complete confidence, the proposition that all swans are white, one black swan can completely falsify it. The historical position of science that it can, by its methods, ultimately converge on the "real" truth is thus brought sharply into question.

The value-ladenness of facts. Just as theories and facts are not independent, neither are values and facts. Indeed, it can be argued that theories are themselves value statements. Thus putative "facts" are viewed not only through a theory window but through a value window as well. The value-free posture of the received view is compromised.

The interactive nature of the inquirer-inquired into dyad. The received view of science pictures the inquirer as standing behind a one-way mirror, viewing natural phenomena as they happen and recording them objectively. The inquirer (when using proper methodology) does not influence the phenomena or vice versa. But evidence such as the Heisenberg uncertainty principle and the Bohr complementarity principle have shattered that ideal in the hard sciences (Lincoln & Guba, 1985); even greater skepticism must exist for the social sciences. Indeed, the notion that findings are created through the interaction of inquirer and phenomenon (which, in the social sciences, is usually people) is often a more plausible description of the inquiry process than is the notion that findings are discovered through objective observation "as they *really* are, and as they *really* work."

The intraparadigm critiques, although exposing many inherent problems in the received view and, indeed, proposing some useful responses to them, are nevertheless of much less interest—or weight—than the extraparadigm critiques, which raise problems of such consequence that the received view is being widely questioned. Several alternative paradigms have been proposed, some of which rest on quite unconventional assumptions. It is useful, therefore, to inquire about the nature of paradigms and what it is that distinguishes one inquiry paradigm from another.

◆ The Nature of Paradigms

Paradigms as Basic Belief Systems Based on Ontological, Epistemological, and Methodological Assumptions

A paradigm may be viewed as a set of *basic beliefs* (or metaphysics) that deals with ultimates or first principles. It represents a *worldview* that defines, for its holder, the nature of the "world," the individual's place in it, and the range of possible relationships to that world and its parts, as, for example, cosmologies and theologies do.[2] The beliefs are basic in the sense that they must be accepted simply on faith (however well argued); there is no way to establish their ultimate truthfulness. If there were, the philosophical debates reflected in these pages would have been resolved millennia ago.

Inquiry paradigms define for *inquirers* what it is they are about, and what falls within and outside the limits of legitimate inquiry. The basic beliefs that define inquiry paradigms can be summarized by the responses given by proponents of any given paradigm to three fundamental questions, which are interconnected in such a way that the answer given to any one question, taken in any order, constrains how the others may be answered. We have selected an order that we believe reflects a logical (if not necessary) primacy:

1. *The ontological question.* What is the form and nature of reality and, therefore, what is there that can be known about it? For example, if a "real" world is assumed, then what can be known about it is "how things really are" and "how things really work." Then only those questions that relate to matters of "real" existence and "real" action are admissible; other questions, such as those concerning matters of aesthetic or moral significance, fall outside the realm of legitimate scientific inquiry.

2. *The epistemological question.* What is the nature of the relationship between the knower or would-be knower and what can be known? The answer that can be given to this question is constrained by the answer already given to the ontological question; that is, not just *any* relationship can now be postulated. So if, for example, a "real" reality is assumed, then the posture of the knower must be one of objective detachment or value freedom in order to be able to discover "how things really are" and "how things really work." (Conversely, assumption of an objectivist posture implies the existence of a "real" world to be objective about.)

3. *The methodological question.* How can the inquirer (would-be knower) go about finding out whatever he or she believes can be known? Again, the answer that can be given to this question is constrained by answers already given to the first two questions; that is, not just *any* methodology is appropriate. For example, a "real" reality pursued by an "objective" inquirer mandates control of possible confounding factors, whether the methods are qualitative (say, observational) or quantitative (say, analysis of covariance). (Conversely, selection of a manipulative methodology—the experiment, say—implies the ability to be objective and a real world to be objective about.) The methodological question cannot be reduced to a question of methods; methods must be fitted to a predetermined methodology.

These three questions serve as the major foci around which we will analyze each of the four paradigms to be considered.

Paradigms as Human Constructions

We have already noted that paradigms, as sets of basic beliefs, are not open to proof in any conventional sense; there is no way to elevate one over another on the basis of ultimate, foundational criteria. (We should note, however, that that state of affairs does not doom us to a radical relativist posture; see Guba, 1992.) In our opinion, any given paradigm represents simply the most informed and sophisticated view that its proponents have been able to devise, given the way they have chosen to respond to the three defining questions. And, we argue, the sets of answers given are in *all* cases *human constructions*; that is, they are all inventions of the human mind and hence subject to human error. No construction is or can be incontrovertibly right; advocates of any particular construction must rely on *persuasiveness* and *utility* rather than *proof* in arguing their position.

What is true of paradigms is true of our analyses as well. Everything that we shall say subsequently is *also* a human construction: ours. The reader cannot be compelled to accept our analyses, or our arguments, on the basis of incontestable logic or indisputable evidence; we can only hope to be persuasive and to demonstrate the utility of our position for, say, the public policy arena (Guba & Lincoln, 1989; House, 1977). We do ask the reader to suspend his or her disbelief until our argument is complete and can be judged as a whole.

◆ The Basic Beliefs of Received and Alternative Inquiry Paradigms

We begin our analysis with descriptions of the responses that we believe proponents of each paradigm would make to the three questions outlined above. These responses (as constructed by us) are displayed in Table 6.1, which consists of three rows corresponding to the ontological, epistemological, and methodological questions, and four columns corresponding to the four paradigms to be discussed. The term *positivism* denotes the "received view" that has dominated the formal discourse in the physical and social sciences for some 400 years, whereas *postpositivism* represents efforts of the past few decades to respond in a limited way (that is, while remaining within essentially the same set of basic beliefs) to the most problematic criticisms of positivism. The term *critical theory* is (for us) a blanket term denoting a set of several alternative paradigms, including additionally (but not limited to) neo-Marxism, feminism, materialism, and participatory inquiry. Indeed, critical theory may itself usefully be divided into three substrands: poststructuralism, postmodernism, and a blending

TABLE 6.1 Basic Beliefs (Metaphysics) of Alternative Inquiry Paradigms

Item	Positivism	Postpositivism	Critical Theory et al.	Constructivism
Ontology	naive realism—"real" reality but apprehendable	critical realism—"real" reality but only imperfectly and probabilistically apprehendable	historical realism—virtual reality shaped by social, political, cultural, economic, ethnic, and gender values; crystallized over time	relativism—local and specific constructed realities
Epistemology	dualist/objectivist; findings true	modified dualist/objectivist; critical tradition/ community; findings probably true	transactional/ subjectivist; value-mediated findings	transactional/ subjectivist; created findings
Methodology	experimental/ manipulative; verification of hypotheses; chiefly quantitative methods	modified experimental/ manipulative; critical multiplism; falsification of hypotheses; may include qualitative methods	dialogic/dialectical	hermeneutical/ dialectical

of these two. Whatever their differences, the common breakaway assumption of all these variants is that of the value-determined nature of inquiry—an epistemological difference. Our grouping of these positions into a single category is a judgment call; we will not try to do justice to the individual points of view. The term *constructivism* denotes an alternative paradigm whose breakaway assumption is the move from ontological realism to ontological relativism. These positions will become clear in the subsequent exposition.

Two important caveats need to be mentioned. First, although we are inclined to believe that the paradigms we are about to describe can have meaning even in the realm of the physical sciences, we will not defend that belief here. Accordingly, our subsequent comments should be understood to be limited to the *social sciences* only. Second, we note that except for positivism, the paradigms discussed are all still in formative stages; no final agreements have been reached even among their proponents about their definitions, meanings, or implications. Thus our discussion should be considered tentative and subject to further revision and reformulation.

We will first look down the columns of Table 6.1 to illustrate the positions of each paradigm with respect to the three questions, following with a look across rows to compare and contrast the positions of the paradigms.[3] Limitations of space make it impossible for us to develop our assertions in any depth. The reader will be able to find other evidence, pro and con, in other chapters of this volume, particularly in Chapters 7-11.

◆ Intraparadigm Analyses (Columns of Table 6.1)

Column 1: Positivism

Ontology: realism (commonly called "naive realism"). An apprehendable reality is assumed to exist, driven by immutable natural laws and mechanisms. Knowledge of the "way things are" is conventionally summarized in the form of time- and context-free generalizations, some of which take the form of cause-effect laws. Research can, in principle, converge on the "true" state of affairs. The basic posture of the paradigm is argued to be both reductionist and deterministic (Hesse, 1980).

Epistemology: Dualist and objectivist. The investigator and the investigated "object" are assumed to be independent entities, and the investigator to be capable of studying the object without influencing it or being influenced by it. When influence in either direction (threats to validity) is recognized, or even suspected, various strategies are followed to reduce or eliminate it. Inquiry takes place as through a one-way mirror. Values and biases are prevented from influencing outcomes, so long as the prescribed procedures are rigorously followed. Replicable findings are, in fact, "true."

Methodology: Experimental and manipulative. Questions and/or hypotheses are stated in propositional form and subjected to empirical test to verify them; possible confounding conditions must be carefully controlled (manipulated) to prevent outcomes from being improperly influenced.

Column 2: Postpositivism

Ontology: Critical realism. Reality is assumed to exist but to be only imperfectly apprehendable because of basically flawed human intellectual mechanisms and the fundamentally intractable nature of phenomena. The ontology is labeled as critical realism (Cook & Campbell, 1979) because of the posture of proponents that claims about reality must be subjected to the widest possible critical examination to facilitate apprehending reality as closely as possible (but never perfectly).

Epistemology: Modified dualist/objectivist. Dualism is largely abandoned as not possible to maintain, but objectivity remains a "regulatory ideal"; special emphasis is placed on external "guardians" of objectivity such as critical traditions (Do the findings "fit" with preexisting knowledge?) and the critical community (such as editors, referees, and professional peers). Replicated findings are *probably* true (but always subject to falsification).

Methodology: Modified experimental/manipulative. Emphasis is placed on "critical multiplism" (a refurbished version of triangulation) as a way of falsifying (rather than verifying) hypotheses. The methodology aims to redress some of the problems noted above (intraparadigm critiques) by doing inquiry in more natural settings, collecting more situational information, and reintroducing discovery as an element in inquiry, and, in the social sciences particularly, soliciting emic viewpoints to assist in determining the meanings and purposes that people ascribe to their actions, as well as to contribute to "grounded theory" (Glaser & Strauss, 1967; Strauss & Corbin, 1990). All these aims are accomplished largely through the increased utilization of qualitative techniques.

Column 3: Critical Theory and Related Ideological Positions

Ontology: Historical realism. A reality is assumed to be apprehendable that was once plastic, but that was, over time, shaped by a congeries of social, political, cultural, economic, ethnic, and gender factors, and then crystallized (reified) into a series of structures that are now (inappropriately) taken as "real," that is, natural and immutable. For all practical purposes the structures *are* "real," a virtual or historical reality.

205

Epistemology: Transactional and subjectivist. The investigator and the investigated object are assumed to be interactively linked, with the values of the investigator (and of situated "others") inevitably influencing the inquiry. Findings are therefore *value mediated.* Note that this posture effectively challenges the traditional distinction between ontology and epistemology; what can be known is inextricably intertwined with the interaction between a *particular* investigator and a *particular* object or group. The dashed line separating the ontological and epistemological rows of Table 6.1 is intended to reflect this fusion.

Methodology: Dialogic and dialectical. The transactional nature of inquiry requires a dialogue between the investigator and the subjects of the inquiry; that dialogue must be dialectical in nature to transform ignorance and misapprehensions (accepting historically mediated structures as immutable) into more informed consciousness (seeing how the structures might be changed and comprehending the actions required to effect change), or, as Giroux (1988) puts it, "as transformative intellectuals, . . . to uncover and excavate those forms of historical and subjugated knowledges that point to experiences of suffering, conflict, and collective struggle; . . . to link the notion of historical understanding to elements of critique and hope" (p. 213). Transformational inquirers demonstrate "transformational leadership" (Burns, 1978).

(For more discussion of critical theory, see the contributions in this volume by Olesen, Chapter 9; Stanfield, Chapter 10; and Kincheloe & McLaren, Chapter 8.)

Column 4: Constructivism

Ontology: Relativist. Realities are apprehendable in the form of multiple, intangible mental constructions, socially and experientially based, local and specific in nature (although elements are often shared among many individuals and even across cultures), and dependent for their form and content on the individual persons or groups holding the constructions. Constructions are not more or less "true," in any absolute sense, but simply more or less informed and/or sophisticated. Constructions are alterable, as are their associated "realities." This position should be distinguished from both nominalism and idealism (see Reese, 1980, for an explication of these several ideas).

Epistemology: Transactional and subjectivist. The investigator and the object of investigation are assumed to be interactively linked so that the "findings" are *literally created* as the investigation proceeds. The conventional distinction between ontology and epistemology disappears, as in the case of critical theory. Again, the dashed line of Table 6.1 reflects this fact.

Methodology: Hermeneutical and dialectical. The variable and personal (intramental) nature of social constructions suggests that individual constructions can be elicited and refined only through interaction *between and among* investigator and respondents. These varying constructions are interpreted using conventional hermeneutical techniques, and are compared and contrasted through a dialectical interchange. The final aim is to distill a consensus construction that is more informed and sophisticated than any of the predecessor constructions (including, of course, the etic construction of the investigator).

(For more about constructivism, see also Schwandt, Chapter 7, this volume.)

◆ Cross-Paradigm Analyses (Rows of Table 6.1)

Having noted briefly the positions that proponents of each paradigm might take with respect to the three paradigm-defining questions, it is useful to look across rows to compare and contrast those positions among the several paradigms.

Ontology

Moving from left to right across Table 6.1, we note the move from

1. positivism's position of naive realism, assuming an objective external reality upon which inquiry can converge; to

2. postpositivism's critical realism, which still assumes an objective reality but grants that it can be apprehended only imperfectly and probabilistically; to

3. critical theory's historical realism, which assumes an apprehendable reality consisting of historically situated structures that are, in the absence of insight, as limiting and confining as if they were real; to

4. constructivism's relativism, which assumes multiple, apprehendable, and sometimes conflicting social realities that are the products of human intellects, but that may change as their constructors become more informed and sophisticated.

It is the ontological position that most differentiates constructivism from the other three paradigms.

Epistemology

We note the move from

1. positivism's dualist, objectivist assumption that enables the investigator to determine "how things really are" and "how things really work"; to

2. postpositivism's modified dualist/objectivist assumption that it is possible to approximate (but never fully know) reality; to

3. critical theory's transactional/subjectivist assumption that knowledge is value mediated and hence value dependent; to

4. constructivism's somewhat similar but broader transactional/subjectivist assumption that sees knowledge as created in interaction among investigator and respondents.

It is their epistemological positions that most differentiate critical theory and constructivism from the other two paradigms.

Methodology

We note the move from

1. positivism's experimental/manipulative methodology that focuses on verification of hypotheses; to

2. postpositivism's modified experimental/ manipulative methodology invested in critical multiplism focusing on falsification of hypotheses; to

3. critical theory's *dialogic/dialectical* methodology aimed at the reconstruction of previously held constructions; to

4. constructivism's hermeneutic/dialectic methodology aimed at the reconstruction of previously held constructions.

◆ Implications of Each Paradigm's Position on Selected Practical Issues (Rows of Table 6.2)

Differences in paradigm assumptions cannot be dismissed as mere "philosophical" differences; implicitly or explicitly, these positions have important consequences for the practical conduct of inquiry, as well as for the interpretation of findings and policy choices. We have elected to discuss these consequences for ten salient issues.

The entries in Table 6.2, which consists of four columns corresponding to the four paradigms and ten rows corresponding to the ten issues, summarize our interpretation of the major implications. The reader will note that the first four issues (inquiry aim, nature of knowledge, knowledge accumulation, and quality criteria) are among those deemed especially important by positivists and postpositivists; they are therefore the issues on which alternative paradigms are most frequently attacked. The fifth and sixth (values and ethics) are issues taken seriously by all paradigms, although conventional and emergent responses are quite different. Finally, the last four issues (voice, training, accommodation, and hegemony) are those deemed especially important by alternative proponents; they represent areas on which the received view is considered particularly vulnerable. The entries in the table are based only in part on public positions, given that not all issues have been addressed by all paradigms' proponents. In some cases, therefore, we have supplied entries that we believe follow logically from the basic metaphysical (ontological, epistemological, and methodological) postures of the paradigms. To take one example, the issue of voice is rarely addressed directly by positivists or postpositivists, but we believe the entry "disinterested scientist" is one that would be given by those proponents were they to be challenged on this matter.

An immediately apparent difference between Table 6.1 and Table 6.2 is that whereas in the former case it was possible to make a distinct entry for every cell, in the case of Table 6.2 there is considerable overlap within rows,

TABLE 6.2 Paradigm Positions on Selected Practical Issues

Issue	Positivism	Postpositivism	Critical Theory et al.	Constructivism
Inquiry aim	explanation: prediction and control		critique and transformation; restitution and emancipation	understanding; reconstruction
Nature of knowledge	verified hypotheses established as facts or laws	nonfalsified hypotheses that are probable facts or laws	structural/historical insights	individual reconstructions coalescing around consensus
Knowledge accumulation	accretion—"building blocks" adding to "edifice of knowledge"; generalizations and cause-effect linkages		historical revisionism; generalization by similarity	more informed and sophisticated reconstructions; vicarious experience
Goodness or quality criteria	conventional benchmarks of "rigor": internal and external validity, reliability, and objectivity		historical situatedness; erosion of ignorance and misapprehension; action stimulus	trustworthiness and authenticity
Values	excluded—influence denied		included—formative	
Ethics	extrinsic; tilt toward deception		intrinsic; moral tilt toward revelation	intrinsic; process tilt toward revelation; special problems
Voice	"disinterested scientist" as informer of decision makers, policy makers, and change agents		"transformative intellectual" as advocate and activist	"passionate participant" as facilitator of multivoice reconstruction
Training	technical and quantitative; substantive theories	technical; quantitative and qualitative; substantive theories	resocialization; qualitative and quantitative; history; values of altruism and empowerment	
Accommodation	commensurable		incommensurable	
Hegemony	in control of publication, funding, promotion, and tenure		seeking recognition and input	

particularly for the positivist and postpositivist columns. Indeed, even for those issues in which the entries in those two columns are different, the differences appear to be minor. In contrast, one may note the major

210

differences found between these two paradigms and the critical theory and constructivist paradigms, which tend also to differ among themselves.

We have formulated the issues as questions, which follow.

Row 1: What is the aim or purpose of inquiry?

Positivism and postpositivism. For both these paradigms the aim of inquiry is *explanation* (von Wright, 1971), ultimately enabling the *prediction and control* of phenomena, whether physical or human. As Hesse (1980) has suggested, the ultimate criterion for progress in these paradigms is that the capability of "scientists" to predict and control should improve over time. The reductionism and determinism implied by this position should be noted. The inquirer is cast in the role of "expert," a situation that seems to award special, perhaps even unmerited, privilege to the investigator.

Critical theory. The aim of inquiry is the *critique and transformation* of the social, political, cultural, economic, ethnic, and gender structures that constrain and exploit humankind, by engagement in confrontation, even conflict. The criterion for progress is that over time, restitution and emancipation should occur and persist. Advocacy and activism are key concepts. The inquirer is cast in the role of instigator and facilitator, implying that the inquirer understands a priori what transformations are needed. But we should note that some of the more radical stances in the criticalist camp hold that judgment about needed transformations should be reserved to those whose lives are most affected by transformations: the inquiry participants themselves (Lincoln, 1993).

Constructivism. The aim of inquiry is *understanding and reconstruction* of the constructions that people (including the inquirer) initially hold, aiming toward consensus but still open to new interpretations as information and sophistication improve. The criterion for progress is that over time, everyone formulates more informed and sophisticated constructions and becomes more aware of the content and meaning of competing construc-tions. Advocacy and activism are also key concepts is this view. The inquirer is cast in the role of participant and facilitator in this process, a position that some critics have faulted on the grounds that it expands the inquirer's role beyond reasonable expectations of expertise and competence (Carr & Kemmis, 1986).

211

Row 2: What is the nature of knowledge?

Positivism. Knowledge consists of verified hypotheses that can be accepted as facts or laws.

Postpositivism. Knowledge consists of nonfalsified hypotheses that can be regarded as probable facts or laws.

Critical theory. Knowledge consists of a series of structural/historical insights that will be transformed as time passes. Transformations occur when ignorance and misapprehensions give way to more informed insights by means of a dialectical interaction.

Constructivism. Knowledge consists of those constructions about which there is relative consensus (or at least some movement toward consensus) among those competent (and, in the case of more arcane material, trusted) to interpret the substance of the construction. Multiple "knowledges" can coexist when equally competent (or trusted) interpreters disagree, and/or depending on social, political, cultural, economic, ethnic, and gender factors that differentiate the interpreters. These constructions are subject to continuous revision, with changes most likely to occur when relatively different constructions are brought into juxtaposition in a dialectical context.

Row 3: How does knowledge accumulate?

Positivism and postpositivism. Knowledge accumulates by a process of accretion, with each fact (or probable fact) serving as a kind of building block that, when placed into its proper niche, adds to the growing "edifice of knowledge." When the facts take the form of generalizations or cause-effect linkages, they may be used most efficiently for prediction and control. Generalizations may then be made, with predictable confidence, to a population of settings.

Critical theory. Knowledge does not accumulate in an absolute sense; rather, it grows and changes through a dialectical process of historical revision that continuously erodes ignorance and misapprehensions and enlarges more informed insights. Generalization can occur when the mix

212

of social, political, cultural, economic, ethnic, and gender circumstances and values is similar across settings.

Constructivism. Knowledge accumulates only in a relative sense through the formation of ever more informed and sophisticated constructions via the hermeneutical/dialectical process, as varying constructions are brought into juxtaposition. One important mechanism for transfer of knowledge from one setting to another is the provision of vicarious experience, often supplied by case study reports (see Stake, Chapter 4, Volume 2, this series).

Row 4: What criteria are appropriate for judging the goodness or quality of an inquiry?

Positivism and postpositivism. The appropriate criteria are the conventional benchmarks of "rigor": internal validity (isomorphism of findings with reality), external validity (generalizability), reliability (in the sense of stability), and objectivity (distanced and neutral observer). These criteria depend on the realist ontological position; without the assumption, isomorphism of findings with reality can have no meaning, strict generalizability to a parent population is impossible, stability cannot be assessed for inquiry into a phenomenon if the phenomenon itself can change, and objectivity cannot be achieved because there is nothing from which one can be "distant."

Critical theory. The appropriate criteria are historical situatedness of the inquiry (i.e., that it takes account of the social, political, cultural, economic, ethnic, and gender antecedents of the studied situation), the extent to which the inquiry acts to erode ignorance and misapprehensions, and the extent to which it provides a stimulus to action, that is, to the transformation of the existing structure.

Constructivism. Two sets of criteria have been proposed: the *trustworthiness* criteria of credibility (paralleling internal validity), transferability (paralleling external validity), dependability (paralleling reliability), and confirmability (paralleling objectivity) (Guba, 1981; Lincoln & Guba, 1985); and the *authenticity* criteria of fairness, ontological authenticity (enlarges personal constructions), educative authenticity (leads to improved understanding of constructions of others), catalytic authenticity (stimulates to action), and tactical authenticity (empowers action) (Guba

& Lincoln, 1989). The former set represents an early effort to resolve the quality issue for constructivism; although these criteria have been well received, their parallelism to positivist criteria makes them suspect. The latter set overlaps to some extent those of critical theory but goes beyond them, particularly the two of ontological authenticity and educative authenticity. The issue of quality criteria in constructivism is nevertheless not well resolved, and further critique is needed.

Row 5: What is the role of values in inquiry?

Positivism and postpositivism. In both these paradigms values are specifically excluded; indeed, the paradigm is claimed to be "value free" by virtue of its epistemological posture. Values are seen as confounding variables that cannot be allowed a role in a putatively objective inquiry (even when objectivity is, in the case of postpositivism, but a regulatory ideal).

Critical theory and constructivism. In both these paradigms values have pride of place; they are seen as ineluctable in shaping (in the case of constructivism, creating) inquiry outcomes. Furthermore, even if it were possible, excluding values would not be countenanced. To do so would be inimical to the interests of the powerless and of "at-risk" audiences, whose original (emic) constructions deserve equal consideration with those of other, more powerful audiences and of the inquirer (etic). Constructivism, which sees the inquirer as orchestrator and facilitator of the inquiry process, is more likely to stress this point than is critical theory, which tends to cast the inquirer in a more authoritative role.

Row 6: What is the place of ethics in inquiry?

Positivism and postpositivism. In both these paradigms ethics is an important consideration, and it is taken very seriously by inquirers, but it is *extrinsic* to the inquiry process itself. Hence ethical behavior is formally policed by *external* mechanisms, such as professional codes of conduct and human subjects committees. Further, the realist ontology undergirding these paradigms provides a tilt toward the use of deception, which, it is argued in certain cases, is warranted to determine how "things *really* are and work" or for the sake of some "higher social good" or some "clearer truth" (Bok, 1978, 1982; Diener & Crandall, 1978).

214

Critical theory. Ethics is more nearly *intrinsic* to this paradigm, as implied by the intent to erode ignorance and misapprehensions, and to take full account of values and historical situatedness in the inquiry process. Thus there is a moral tilt that the inquirer be revelatory (in the rigorous meaning of "fully informed consent") rather than deceptive. Of course, these considerations do not *prevent* unethical behavior, but they do provide some process barriers that make it more difficult.

Constructivism. Ethics is *intrinsic* to this paradigm also because of the inclusion of participant values in the inquiry (starting with respondents' existing constructions and working toward increased information and sophistication in their constructions as well as in the inquirer's construction). There is an incentive—a *process tilt*—for revelation; hiding the inquirer's intent is destructive of the aim of uncovering and improving constructions. In addition, the hermeneutical/dialectical methodology itself provides a strong but not infallible safeguard against deception. However, the close personal interactions required by the methodology may produce special and often sticky problems of confidentiality and anonymity, as well as other interpersonal difficulties (Guba & Lincoln, 1989).

Row 7: What "voice" is mirrored in the inquirer's activities, especially those directed at change?

Positivism and postpositivism. The inquirer's voice is that of the "disinterested scientist" informing decision makers, policy makers, and change agents, who independently use this scientific information, at least in part, to form, explain, and justify actions, policies, and change proposals.

Critical theory. The inquirer's voice is that of the "transformative intellectual" (Giroux, 1988) who has expanded consciousness and so is in a position to confront ignorance and misapprehensions. Change is facilitated as individuals develop greater insight into the existing state of affairs (the nature and extent of their exploitation) and are stimulated to act on it.

Constructivism. The inquirer's voice is that of the "passionate participant" (Lincoln, 1991) actively engaged in facilitating the "multivoice" reconstruction of his or her own construction as well as those of all other participants. Change is facilitated as reconstructions are formed and individuals are stimulated to act on them.

Row 8: What are the implications of each paradigm for the training of novice inquirers?

Positivism. Novices are trained primarily in technical knowledge about measurement, design, and quantitative methods, with less but substantial emphasis on formal theories of the phenomena in their substantive specialties.

Postpositivism. Novices are trained in ways paralleling the positivist mode, but with the addition of qualitative methods, often for the purpose of ameliorating the problems noted in the opening paragraphs of this chapter.

Critical theory and constructivism. Novices must first be resocialized from their early and usually intense exposure to the received view of science. That resocialization cannot be accomplished without thorough schooling in the postures and techniques of positivism and postpositivism. Students must come to appreciate paradigm differences (summarized in Table 6.1) and, in that context, to master both qualitative and quantitative methods. The former are essential because of their role in carrying out the dialogic/dialectical or hermeneutical/dialectical methodologies; the latter because they can play a useful informational role in all paradigms. They must also be helped to understand the social, political, cultural, economic, ethnic, and gender history and structure that serve as the surround for their inquiries, and to incorporate the values of altruism and empowerment in their work.

Row 9: Are these paradigms necessarily in conflict? Is it possible to accommodate these several views within a single conceptual framework?

Positivism and postpositivism. Proponents of these two paradigms, given their foundational orientation, take the position that all paradigms can be accommodated—that is, that there exists, or will be found to exist, some common rational structure to which all questions of difference can be referred for resolution. The posture is reductionist and assumes the possibility of point-by-point comparisons (commensurability), an issue about which there continues to be a great deal of disagreement.

Critical theory and constructivism. Proponents of these two paradigms join in affirming the basic incommensurability of the paradigms (although they

216

would agree that positivism and postpositivism are commensurable, and would probably agree that critical theory and constructivism are commensurable). The basic beliefs of the paradigms are believed to be essentially contradictory. For constructivists, either there is a "real" reality or there is not (although one might wish to resolve this problem differently in considering the physical versus the human realms), and thus constructivism and positivism/postpositivism cannot be logically accommodated anymore than, say, the ideas of flat versus round earth can be logically accommodated. For critical theorists and constructivists, inquiry is either value free or it is not; again, logical accommodation seems impossible. Realism and relativism, value freedom and value boundedness, cannot coexist in any internally consistent metaphysical system, which condition of consistency, it is stipulated, is essentially met by each of the candidate paradigms. Resolution of this dilemma will necessarily await the emergence of a metaparadigm that renders the older, accommodated paradigms not less true, but simply irrelevant.

Row 10: Which of the paradigms exercises hegemony over the others? That is, which is predominantly influential?

Positivism and postpositivism. Proponents of positivism gained hegemony over the past several centuries as earlier Aristotelian and theological paradigms were abandoned. But the mantle of hegemony has in recent decades gradually fallen on the shoulders of the postpositivists, the "natural" heirs of positivism. Postpositivists (and indeed many residual positivists) tend to control publication outlets, funding sources, promotion and tenure mechanisms, dissertation committees, and other sources of power and influence. They were, at least until about 1980, the "in" group, and continue to represent the strongest voice in professional decision making.

Critical theory and constructivism. Proponents of critical theory and constructivism are still seeking recognition and avenues for input. Over the past decade, it has become more and more possible for them to achieve acceptance, as attested by increasing inclusion of relevant papers in journals and professional meetings, the development of new journal outlets, the growing acceptability of "qualitative" dissertations, the inclusion of "qualitative" guidelines by some funding agencies and programs, and the like. But in all likelihood, critical theory and constructivism will continue to play secondary, although important and progressively more influential, roles in the near future.

◆ Conclusion

The metaphor of the "paradigm wars" described by Gage (1989) is undoubtedly overdrawn. Describing the discussions and altercations of the past decade or two as wars paints the matter as more confrontational than necessary. A resolution of paradigm differences can occur only when a new paradigm emerges that is more informed and sophisticated than any existing one. That is most likely to occur if and when proponents of these several points of view come together to discuss their differences, not to argue the sanctity of their views. Continuing dialogue among paradigm proponents of all stripes will afford the best avenue for moving toward a responsive and congenial relationship.

We hope that in this chapter we have illustrated the need for such a discussion by clearly delineating the differences that currently exist, and by showing that those differences have significant implications at the practical level. Paradigm issues are crucial; no inquirer, we maintain, ought to go about the business of inquiry without being clear about just what paradigm informs and guides his or her approach.

Notes

1. Many of the objections listed here were first enunciated by positivists themselves; indeed, we might argue that the postpositivist position represents an attempt to transform positivism in ways that take account of these same objections. The naive positivist position of the sixteenth through the nineteenth centuries is no longer held by anyone even casually acquainted with these problems. Although we would concede that the postpositivist position, as enunciated, for example, by Denis Phillips (1987, 1990a, 1990b), represents a considerable improvement over classic positivism, it fails to make a clean break. It represents a kind of "damage control" rather than a reformulation of basic principles. The notion that these problems required a paradigm shift was poorly recognized until the publication of Thomas Kuhn's landmark work, *The Structure of Scientific Revolutions* (1962, 1970), and even then proceeded but slowly. Nevertheless, the contributions of pre-Kuhnian critics should be recognized and applauded.

2. We are reminded by Robert Stake (personal communication, 1993) that the view of paradigms that we present here should not "exclude a belief that there are worlds within worlds, unending, each with its own paradigms. Infinitesimals have their own cosmologies."

3. It is unlikely that a practitioner of any paradigm would agree that our summaries closely describe what he or she thinks or does. Workaday scientists rarely have either the time or the inclination to assess what they do in philosophical terms. We do contend, however, that these descriptions are apt as broad brush strokes, if not always at the individual level.

◆ References

Bernstein, R. (1988). *Beyond objectivism and relativism*. Philadelphia: University of Pennsylvania Press.

Bok, S. (1978). *Lies: Moral choice in public and private life*. New York: Random House.

Bok, S. (1982). *Secrets: On the ethics of concealment and revelation*. New York: Pantheon.

Burns, J. (1978). *Leadership*. New York: Harper.

Carr, W., & Kemmis, S. (1986). *Becoming critical: Education, knowledge and action research*. London: Falmer.

Cook, T., & Campbell, D. T. (1979). *Quasi-experimentation: Design and analysis issues for field settings*. Chicago: Rand McNally.

Diener, E., & Crandall, R. (1978). *Ethics in social and behavioral research*. Chicago: University of Chicago Press.

Gage, N. (1989). The paradigm wars and their aftermath: A "historical" sketch of research and teaching since 1989. *Educational Research, 18,* 4-10.

Giroux, H. (1988). *Schooling and the struggle for public life: Critical pedagogy in the modern age*. Minneapolis: University of Minnesota Press.

Glaser, B. G., & Strauss, A. L. (1967). *The discovery of grounded theory: Strategies for qualitative research*. Chicago: Aldine.

Guba, E. G. (1981). Criteria for assessing the trustworthiness of naturalistic inquiries. *Educational Communication and Technology Journal, 29,* 75-92.

Guba, E. G. (Ed.). (1990). *The paradigm dialog*. Newbury Park, CA: Sage.

Guba, E. G. (1992). Relativism. *Curriculum Inquiry, 22,* 17-24.

Guba, E. G., & Lincoln, Y. S. (1989). *Fourth generation evaluation*. Newbury Park, CA: Sage.

Hesse, E. (1980). *Revolutions and reconstructions in the philosophy of science*. Bloomington: Indiana University Press.

House, E. (1977). *The logic of evaluative argument*. Los Angeles: University of California, Center for the Study of Evaluation.

Kuhn, T. S. (1962). *The structure of scientific revolutions*. Chicago: University of Chicago Press.

Kuhn, T. S. (1970). *The structure of scientific revolutions* (2nd ed.). Chicago: University of Chicago Press.

Lincoln, Y. S. (1991). *The detached observer and the passionate participant: Discourses in inquiry and science*. Paper presented at the annual meeting of the American Educational Research Association, Chicago.

Lincoln, Y. S. (1993). I and thou: Method and voice in research with the silenced. In D. McLaughlin & W. G. Tierney (Eds.), *Naming silenced lives: Personal narratives and the process of educational change.* New York: Routledge.

Lincoln, Y. S., & Guba, E. G. (1985). *Naturalistic inquiry.* Beverly Hills, CA: Sage.

Marcus, G., & Fischer, M. (1986). *Anthropology as cultural critique: An experimental moment in the human sciences.* Chicago: University of Chicago Press.

Mill, J. S. (1906). *A system of logic.* London: Longmans Green. (Original work published 1843)

Phillips, D. C. (1987). *Philosophy, science, and social inquiry.* Oxford: Pergamon.

Phillips, D. C. (1990a). Postpositivistic science: Myths and realities. In E. G. Guba (Ed.), *The paradigm dialog* (pp. 31-45). Newbury Park, CA: Sage.

Phillips, D. C. (1990b). Subjectivity and objectivity: An objective inquiry. In E. Eisner & A. Peshkin (Eds.), *Qualitative inquiry in education* (pp. 19-37). New York: Teachers College Press.

Popper, K. (1968). *Conjectures and refutations.* New York: Harper & Row.

Reason, P., & Rowan, J. (1981). *Human inquiry.* New York: John Wiley.

Reese, W. (1980). *Dictionary of philosophy and religion.* Atlantic Highlands, NJ: Humanities Press.

Sechrest, L. (1992). Roots: Back to our first generations. *Evaluation Practice, 13,* 1-8.

Strauss, A. L., & Corbin, J. (1990). *Basics of qualitative research: Grounded theory procedures and techniques.* Newbury Park, CA: Sage.

von Wright, G. (1971). *Explanation and understanding.* London: Routledge & Kegan Paul.

7

Constructivist, Interpretivist Approaches to Human Inquiry

Thomas A. Schwandt

◆ *Constructivist, constructivism, interpretivist, and interpretivism* are terms that routinely appear in the lexicon of social science methodologists and philosophers. Yet, their particular meanings are shaped by the intent of their users. As general descriptors for a loosely coupled family of methodological and philosophical persuasions, these terms are best regarded as sensitizing concepts (Blumer, 1954). They steer the interested reader in the general direction of where instances of a particular kind of inquiry can be found. However, they "merely suggest directions along which to look" rather than "provide descriptions of what to see" (p. 7).[1]

Proponents of these persuasions share the goal of understanding the complex world of lived experience from the point of view of those who live it. This goal is variously spoken of as an abiding concern for the life world, for the emic point of view, for understanding meaning, for grasping the actor's definition of a situation, for *Verstehen*. The world of lived reality and situation-specific meanings that constitute the general object of investigation is thought to be constructed by social actors. That is, particular

AUTHOR'S NOTE: Thanks to Colleen Larson, John K. Smith, Harry Wolcott, Norman Denzin, and Yvonna Lincoln for their comments on an earlier draft of this chapter.

actors, in particular places, at particular times, fashion meaning out of events and phenomena through prolonged, complex processes of social interaction involving history, language, and action.

The constructivist or interpretivist believes that to understand this world of meaning one must interpret it. The inquirer must elucidate the process of meaning construction and clarify what and how meanings are embodied in the language and actions of social actors. To prepare an interpretation is itself to construct a reading of these meanings; it is to offer the inquirer's construction of the constructions of the actors one studies.

Although they share this general framework for human inquiry, constructivist and interpretivist persuasions are unique in the manner in which each answers these questions: What is the purpose and aim of human inquiry (as distinct from inquiry into the physical world)? How can we know about the world of human action? Each particular persuasion offers a somewhat different conceptualization of what we are about when we inquire into the world of social agents and historical actors.

Furthermore, what is unusual about these approaches cannot be explained through an examination of their methods.[2] They are principally concerned with matters of knowing and being, not method per se. As Harry Wolcott (1988, 1992) and Frederick Erickson (1986) have noted, not only are methods the most unremarkable aspect of interpretive work, but a focus on methods (techniques for gathering and analyzing data) often masks a full understanding of the relationship between method and inquiry purpose. The aim of attending carefully to the details, complexity, and situated meanings of the everyday life world can be achieved through a variety of methods. Although we may feel professionally compelled to use a special language for these procedures (e.g., participant observation, informant interviewing, archival research), at base, all interpretive inquirers watch, listen, ask, record, and examine. How those activities might best be defined and employed depends on the inquirer's purpose for doing the inquiry. Purpose, in turn, is shaped by epistemological and methodological commitments.[3]

Mindful of the risk of drawing too fine a distinction between interpretivist and constructivist perspectives that share a common intellectual heritage, I have nonetheless chosen to discuss the two separately. In the first section of this chapter I examine interpretivism, beginning with a general sketch of some critical issues in social science epistemology that shape this family of persuasions. I then single out several particular interpretivist approaches for a closer look at how each defines the purpose of human inquiry. These include Clifford Geertz's view of interpretive anthropology, the Herbert Blumer-G. H. Mead version of symbolic interactionism, and Norman Denzin's reformulation of interpretive interactionism.

In the second section, I introduce constructivist thinking through the work of Nelson Goodman. I then discuss Ernst von Glasersfeld's radical constructivism, Kenneth Gergen's social constructionism, feminist standpoint epistemologies, Egon Guba and Yvonna Lincoln's constructivist paradigm, and Elliot Eisner's aesthetic approach to educational inquiry as illustrations of constructivist thinking.[4] I conclude the chapter with an overview of several kinds of criticisms often made of both constructivist and interpretivist approaches.

◆ Interpretivist Thinking

Overview

Painted in broad strokes, the canvas of interpretivism is layered with ideas stemming from the German intellectual tradition of hermeneutics and the *Verstehen* tradition in sociology, the phenomenology of Alfred Schutz, and critiques of scientism and positivism in the social sciences influenced by the writings of ordinary language philosophers critical of logical empiricism (e.g., Peter Winch, A. R. Louch, Isaiah Berlin).[5] Historically, at least, interpretivists argued for the uniqueness of human inquiry. They crafted various refutations of the naturalistic interpretation of the social sciences (roughly the view that the aims and methods of the social sciences are identical to those of the natural sciences). They held that the mental sciences (*Geisteswissenschaften*) or cultural sciences (*Kulturwissenschaften*) were different in kind than the natural sciences (*Naturwissenschaften*): The goal of the latter is scientific explanation (*Erklären*), whereas the goal of the former is the grasping or understanding (*Verstehen*) of the "meaning" of social phenomena.[6]

Owing in part to unresolved tensions between their rationalist and romanticist roots, interpretivists wrestle with maintaining the opposition of subjectivity and objectivity, engagement and objectification (Denzin, 1992; Hammersley, 1989). They celebrate the permanence and priority of the real world of first-person, subjective experience. Yet, in true Cartesian fashion, they seek to disengage from that experience and objectify it.[7] They struggle with drawing a line between the object of investigation and the investigator. The paradox of how to develop an objective interpretive science of subjective human experience thus arises. This grappling with a synthesis of phenomenological subjectivity and scientific objectivity is evident in Wilhelm Dilthey's bid to find a basis for the *scientific* investigation of meaning, in Max Weber's struggles with the relationship between the interpretation of meaning and causal explanations and the separation of facts and values in social inquiry, and in Alfred Schutz's analysis of the operation of *Verstehen*.

Contemporary theoretical descendants of these interpretivist founders have addressed this paradox in several ways. Hammersley (1992a, 1992b) is representative of interpretivists who pursue a synthesis between social realism and constructivism. LeCompte and Preissle (1993) and Kirk and Miller (1986) seek refuge in methods as error-elimination strategies. John K. Smith (1989, p. 158) calls this the "middle ground" of methodology: It rejects certain negative characteristics of empiricist thinking but simultaneously holds that inquirers must avoid the subjectivity and error of naive inquiry through the judicious use of method.[8]

A third response is to deny the opposition of subjectivity and objectivity and overcome it by fully accepting the hermeneutical character of existence. Paul Rabinow and William Sullivan (1987) endorse this view, following a line of argument advanced by Martin Heidegger, Hans-Georg Gadamer, and Charles Taylor. They claim that the activity of interpretation is not simply a methodological option open to the social scientist, but rather the very condition of human inquiry itself: "The interpretive turn is not simply a new methodology, but rather a challenge to the very idea that inquiry into the social world and the value of the understanding that results is to be determined by methodology" (p. 20).

This third interpretivist position assumes that the defining characteristic of an *ontological* hermeneutics is that linguisticality (*Sprachlichkeit*) and historicality (*Geschichtlichkeit*) are constitutive of being human (Wachterhauser, 1986). In other words, we do not simply live out our lives *in* time and *through* language; rather, we *are* our history. The fact that language and history are both the condition and the limit of understanding is what makes the process of meaning construction hermeneutical.

Philosophical Anthropology

Viewed from the perspective of philosophical anthropology (the study of the basic categories in which humans and human behavior are to be

224

described and explained) interpretivism holds that human behavior is purposive (Bruner, 1990; Magoon, 1977). Interpretivists repudiate mechanistic, neobehaviorist, associationist (i.e., acquisition of associated connections between stimuli and responses) explanations of behavior in favor of teleological explanations. Social agents are considered autonomous, intentional, active, goal directed; they construe, construct, and interpret their own behavior and that of their fellow agents.[9]

Not surprisingly, given that they reject the unity of the sciences argument, interpretivists, in general, disavow much of the empiricist epistemology and methodology that is intimately associated with a neobehaviorist psychology and philosophical anthropology. For example, they reject the notions of a theory-neutral data language, operationism, and the covering law model of explanation.

Because they focus on meaning as primary, interpretivists construe the nature of social reality quite differently from those who support empiricist social science frameworks. As Taylor (1971/1987) explains, for the empiricist, social reality comprises a set of social facts that include the overt acts (behaviors) of individuals that can be defined physically or institutionally and the beliefs, affective states, and so forth that describe the motivations for behavior. Both of these kinds of facts are thought to be brute data—data that are identifiable and verifiable in such a way so as not to be subject to further interpretation. In this way, the empiricist accounts for both human behaviors and the meanings of those behaviors for the agents involved.

Interpretivist persuasions are predicated on the assumption that the empiricist's picture of social reality omits something most important, namely, intersubjective, common meanings—"ways of experiencing action in society which are expressed in the language and descriptions constitutive of institutions and practices" (Taylor, 1971/1987, p. 75). Accordingly, constructivists and interpretivists in general focus on the processes by which these meanings are created, negotiated, sustained, and modified within a specific context of human action. The means or process by which the inquirer arrives at this kind of interpretation of human action (as well as the ends or aim of the process) is called *Verstehen* (understanding).[10]

Phenomenological Interpretation of *Verstehen*

Although Weber is credited with elevating the importance of *Verstehen* as a process of sociological interpretation, his (and Dilthey's) conceptualization of *Verstehen* as a subjective process led to much confusion.

Neopositivists (e.g., Abel, 1948; Rudner, 1966) seized on the subjective nature of *Verstehen*. They argued that it must mean an act of sympathetic imagination or empathic identification on the part of inquirers that allowed them to grasp the psychological state (i.e., motivation, belief, intention, or the like) of an individual actor. By getting inside the head of another, so to speak, the inquirer could hazard a guess as to the meaning of the actor's behavior; this hypothesis could then be subject to a more rigorous empirical test. In this way, the neopositivists identified *Verstehen* as (at best) a prescientific, heuristic device useful in the context of discovery but without value in the context of justification.

Defenders of the process of *Verstehen* as the key to understanding what is unique about the human sciences countered the latent psychologism of this neopositivist understanding. They claimed that *Verstehen* is less like a process of getting inside the actor's head than it is a matter of grasping intersubjective meanings and symbolizing activities that are constitutive of social life.[11] For example, Schutz (1967) sought to clear up confusion surrounding Weber's notion of *Verstehen* by distinguishing among three senses of the term. In the first sense, *Verstehen* refers to "the experiential form of common-sense knowledge of human affairs" (p. 57). It has nothing to do with introspection or pointing to the subjective states of actors; rather, it refers to the intersubjective character of the world and the complex process by which we come to recognize our own actions and those of our fellow actors as meaningful.

According to Schutz, *Verstehen* could also be explored as an epistemological problem. The central issue here is how *Verstehen* is possible. Schutz's analysis drew on Husserl's notion of the *Lebenswelt* (life world) as ontologically prior or as the grounds from which all inquiry starts and from within which it can only be carried out. Finally, *Verstehen* could be viewed as a method peculiar to the human sciences. Here, Schutz distinguished between two senses of the term. A first-order sense refers to *Verstehen* as the process by which we make sense of or interpret our everyday world. Schutz (1967) argued that, unlike the world of nature, which does not "mean" anything to molecules, electrons, and atoms that inhabit it, "the observational field of the social scientist—social reality—has a specific meaning and relevance structure for the human beings living, acting, and thinking within it. . . . It is these thought objects of theirs which determine their behavior by motivating it" (p. 59). A second-order sense refers to the process by which the social scientist attempts to make sense of the first:

226

The thought objects constructed by the social scientist, in order to grasp this social reality, have to be founded upon the thought objects constructed by the common-sense thinking of men, living their daily life within their social world. Thus the constructs of the social sciences are constructs of the second degree . . . constructs of the constructs made by actors on the social scene. (p. 59)

Hermeneutical Interpretation of *Verstehen*

These efforts to give a phenomenological interpretation to *Verstehen* must be sharply distinguished from the hermeneutical position noted earlier. Taylor (1971/1987), for example, defined the activity of interpretation (and the human sciences more generally) as a hermeneutical undertaking analogous to the interpretation of a text. He argued that interpretive inquirers attempt to establish a certain reading or interpretation of the meaning of social action, and that what they appeal to as the warrant for this interpretation can only be other interpretations. Stated somewhat differently, inquirers not only have no "transcendental ground from which to contemplate the process of which [they are] irretrievably a part" (Bauman, 1978, p. 17), but they participate in the very production of meaning via participation in the circle of readings or interpretations (Gadamer, 1989; Taylor, 1971/1987).

This hermeneutical understanding of *Verstehen* in some interpretivist persuasions draws on a distinction between two kinds of hermeneutics (Bauman, 1978; Bleicher, 1980; Madison, 1988). The objective, validation hermeneutics of (the early) Dilthey, Betti, and Hirsch is an epistemology or methodology (with realist pretensions) for understanding the objectifications (e.g., arts, language, institutions, religions) of the human mind. It assumes that meaning is a determinate, objectlike entity waiting to be discovered in a text, a culture, or the mind of a social actor. In this view, hermeneutics is a particular exegetical method for identifying and explicating these objective meanings. The hermeneutical circle is a *methodological* device (in which one considers the whole in relation to its parts and vice versa) that provides a means for inquiry in the human sciences.

In contrast, the philosophical hermeneutics of Heidegger, Gadamer, and Taylor is concerned with ontology (being). The hermeneutical condition is a fact of human existence, and philosophical hermeneutics is concerned with a phenomenological (i.e., existential) explication of *Dasein* (condition

227

of existence or being-in-the-world). The hermeneutical circle here is an "*ontological* condition of understanding; [it] proceeds from a communality that binds us to tradition in general and that of our object of interpretation in particular; [it] provides the link between finality and universality, and between theory and praxis" (Bleicher, 1980, p. 267; emphasis added).

Interpretivist persuasions aligned with ontological hermeneutics transcend the phenomenologist's concern with "capturing" the actors' point of view, with verification, with discriminating between emic and etic perspectives. Taylor (1971/1987) points to the bid to go beyond dualisms of this kind: He claims that if our interpretations seem implausible or if they are not understood by our interlocutors, "there is no verification procedure we can fall back on. We can only continue to offer interpretations; we are in an interpretative circle" (p. 75).[12]

Method Redefined

But what then of method and procedure in interpretivist persuasions of this kind? Although ontological hermeneutics is not a methodology per se, it does suggest an understanding of method that is at odds with the conception of scientific method associated with logical empiricist social science. G. B. Madison (1988, pp. 28-29) explains that *scientific* method is best characterized as an abstract, formal sense of method. In this sense, method is predicated on the elimination of personal, subjective judgment. As Madison explains "one has only to learn the method itself, in and for itself; it is an intellectual technique. Having done so, one has only to apply it to whatever subject matter one chooses; the only criterion in applying the method is *correctness* of application. . . . one's guide is the method itself, not the subject matter to which it is applied" (p. 28). This sense of method supports a belief in the power of demonstrative reasoning and the value of instrumental rationality and aims at achieving exactitude.

In sharp contrast, ontological hermeneutics supports a *normative* sense of method. This conceptualization reflects a belief in persuasive or practical reasoning (where *practical* is understood in the classic sense of involving both contemplation of the good and means of achieving same). A normative sense of method, according to Madison "far from supplanting personal, subjective judgment, or eliminating the need for it, is meant as an aid to good judgment" (1988, p. 28).

Madison argues that the understanding of method here is less like the application of rules and more like the casuistic activity of using ethical principles to guide the making of an ethical decision (interpretation) in a concrete situation (Jonsen & Toulmin, 1988). One seeks to make a responsible decision and to give good reasons for one's action, but the application of ethical principles does not permit the elimination of judgment on the part of the decision maker. In fact, to be rational in this situation demands or *requires* the exercise of judgment (not the following of procedures or rules) and the making of an interpretation. The interpretation or decision one makes cannot properly be said to be verifiable or testable. Rather, at best, we can appraise the interpretation by applying norms or criteria that are compatible with the very condition that demands we interpret in the first place. Hence to judge an interpretation we might use criteria such as thoroughness, coherence, comprehensiveness, and so forth, and ask whether the interpretation is useful, worthy of adoption, and so on.[13]

Conceiving of the activity of interpretation in terms of an ontological condition (i.e., as a fundamental grounds of our being-in-the-world) rather than as a methodological device is what puts the inquirer on the same plane of understanding, so to speak, as those he or she inquires into. To understand through interpretation is to accept a particular model of being or way of life (Shapiro, 1981). That way of being-in-the-world requires a redefinition of method along the lines suggested by Madison. In this way, the earlier comment by Rabinow and Sullivan (1987) about the significance of interpretive work comes into full relief: "For the human sciences both the object of investigation—the web of language, symbol, and institutions that constitutes signification—and the tools by which the investigation is carried out share inescapably the same pervasive context that is the human world" (p. 6).

◆ Two Examples of Interpretivist Persuasions

Interpretivist alternatives to logical empiricist epistemology abound. Three in particular are described here. Geertz's version of interpretive anthropology blends both phenomenological and hermeneutical perspectives on interpretivism. The form of *Verstehende Soziologie* known as symbolic interactionism as represented by Blumer and Mead reflects a tough-minded respect for the reality of the world of experience. Denzin's reconceptualization of interpretive interactionism draws on insights from both critical hermeneutics and poststructuralism to repudiate what he regards as a soft positivism inherent in the Blumer-Mead version of symbolic interactionism.

Interpretive Anthropology

Clifford Geertz's interpretive anthropology is an interpretive theory of culture. It arises in direct opposition to the program of cultural analysis defined by a set of theoretical models known as structuralism or, more specifically, ethnoscience or cognitive anthropology. The structuralist program is firmly rooted in the logical empiricists' bid to find the "real" meaning of myth, ceremony, and other cultural artifacts. For the structuralist, the categories and structures of culture provide powerful explanatory devices accounting for the behaviors of members of a group or society. Structural-functional research frameworks are reductionist in that they claim to discover the one true interpretation lying behind or beneath the complexity of appearances. Geertz (1973) objects to this understanding of the goal of anthropology, preferring to define the analysis of human action as an "interpretive science in search of meaning, not an experimental science in search of laws" (p. 5).

He rejects the philosophical anthropology assumed by ethnoscientific models. He objects to a methodology that aims to reify the world of lived experience in a specialized language of science. For example, his assessment of the literary features of the works of the structuralist Lévi-Strauss reveal more than a critique of that author's prose:

> The marking characteristic of all of Levi-Strauss's work, one upon which almost everyone who deals with it sooner or later remarks [is] its extraordinary air of abstracted self-containment. "Aloof," "closed," "cold," "airless," "cerebral"—all the epithets that collect around any sort of literary absolutism collect around it. Neither picturing lives nor evoking them, neither interpreting them nor explaining them, but rather arranging and rearranging the materials the lives have somehow left behind into formal systems of correspondences—his books seem to exist behind glass, self-sealing disclosures into which jaguars, semen, and rotting meat are admitted to become oppositions, inversions, isomorphisms. (Geertz, 1988, p. 48)

Culture, for Geertz, is a more complicated, less bloodless, more ideational, and, fundamentally, an irreducibly interactive, hermeneutical phenomenon that begs for interpretation, not causal explanation. *Pace* the

230

structuralists, Geertz (1973) argues: "As interworked systems of construable signs (what, ignoring provincial usages, I would call symbols), culture is not a power, something to which social events, behaviors, institutions, or processes can be causally attributed; it is a context, something within which they can be intelligibly—that is *thickly*—described" (p. 14).

A distinguishing feature of Geertz's understanding of both the object of the anthropologist's gaze and the method of his or her gazing is that both are semiotic and hermeneutical phenomena. The language and other symbols in a culture do not simply refer to objects but are constitutive of them, hence, Geertz (1973) claims, "man is an animal suspended in webs of significance he himself has spun" (p. 5). The actions of members of a culture (and the actions and writing of the anthropologist qua ethnographer) both construct and signify meaning. Following Ricoeur (1971), Geertz argues that the ways in which meanings are constituted in a culture must be read or interpreted by the ethnographer in much the same manner as one would read or interpret a complicated text.

Geertz further explains *what* it is that the ethnographer reads and *how* this activity of reading should be construed. For Geertz (1973), there is no world of social facts "out there" waiting to be observed, recorded, described, and analyzed by the inquirer. Rather, the inquirer constructs a reading of the meaning-making process of the people he or she studies. What the ethnographer does is "trace the curve of social discourse; fixing it into respectable form" (p. 19). What the activity of writing "fixes" is the "said" of an event the ethnographer observes—the meaning, the gist, the thought of a speech event—not the event itself. In so doing, the inquirer rescues the activity of participants' meaning making, changing it "from a passing event, which exists only in its own moment of occurrence, into an account, which exists in its inscriptions and can be consulted" (p. 19).

Access to the meaning of an event is not to be had through some process of empathic identification with an informant or respondent, getting inside the person's head, so to speak. Geertz (1983) rejects this neopositivist interpretation of *Verstehen,* arguing that ethnographers cannot claim "some unique form of psychological closeness, a sort of transcultural identification, with our subjects" (p. 56). Rather, the activity of understanding (*Verstehen*) unfolds as one looks over one's respondents' shoulders at what they are doing: "The trick is not to get yourself into some inner correspondence of spirit with your informants. Preferring, like the rest of us, to call their souls their own, they are not going to be altogether keen about such an effort anyhow. The trick is to figure out what the devil they think they are up to" (p. 58).

For example, Geertz (1983) explains that in his study of selfhood in Javanese, Moroccan, and Balinese societies, "I have tried to get at this most intimate of notions not by imagining myself someone else, a rice peasant or a tribal sheikh, and then seeing what I thought, but by searching out and analyzing the symbolic forms—words, images, institutions, behaviors—in terms of which, in each place, people actually represented themselves to themselves and to one another" (p. 58). The task of ethnography is not observation and description, but the inscription or thick description of these meanings of human action.

Because the activity of ethnographic analysis is not a matter of discovering the "Continent of Meaning and mapping out its bodiless landscape" (Geertz, 1973, p. 20) but rather one of "inscribing," writing, fashioning meaning, Geertz blurs the distinction between science and literature in anthropology. Echoing Schutz's understanding of *Verstehen,* Geertz argues that the anthropologist inscribes a text that is itself a second- or third-order interpretation of respondents' interpretations.

This text is built upon the delicate interplay of experience-near and experience-distant concepts: "Confinement to experience-near concepts leaves an ethnographer awash in immediacies, as well as entangled in vernacular. Confinement to experience-distant ones leaves him stranded in abstractions and smothered in jargon" (Geertz, 1983, p. 57).[14] Finally, this text offers a theoretical formulation or interpretation, a statement of what the "meaning particular social actions have for the actors whose actions they are . . . demonstrates about the society in which it is found and, beyond that, about social life as such" (Geertz, 1973, p. 27). Yet, Geertz understands theory (interpretation) to be always grounded and local, not speculative and abstract. He explains that "theoretical formulations hover so low over the interpretations they govern that they don't make much sense or hold much interest apart from them" (1973, p. 25).

Symbolic Interactionism

Another interpretive science in search of portraying and understanding the process of meaning making is the social psychological theory of symbolic interactionism. This approach to the study of human action is difficult to summarize briefly because of the many theoretical and methodological variants of the position (for summaries, see Denzin, 1992;

Hammersley, 1989; Meltzer, Petras, & Reynolds, 1975; Plummer, 1991). I offer a characterization of the Blumer-Mead model of symbolic interactionism, followed by an outline of a postmodern version of the approach, namely, Norman Denzin's interpretive interactionism.

Drawing on the work of G. H. Mead, Herbert Blumer (1969, p. 2) claims that symbolic interactionism rests on three premises: First, human beings act toward the physical objects and other beings in their environment on the basis of the meanings that these things have for them. Second, these meanings derive from the social interaction (communication, broadly understood) between and among individuals. Communication is symbolic because we communicate via languages and other symbols; further, in communicating we create or produce significant symbols. Third, these meanings are established and modified through an interpretive process: "The actor selects, checks, suspends, regroups, and transforms the meanings in light of the situation in which he is placed and the direction of his action. . . . meanings are used and revised as instruments for the guidance and formation of action" (p. 5).

The Blumer-Mead version of symbolic interactionism regards human beings as purposive agents. They engage in "minded," self-reflexive behavior (Blumer, 1969, p. 81); they confront a world that they must interpret in order to act rather than a set of environmental stimuli to which they are forced to respond. Despite disavowing a substantive or philosophical behaviorism, symbolic interactionism does endorse a kind of methodological behaviorism (Denzin, 1971, p. 173).[15] In other words, the symbolic interactionist holds that a necessary (although not sufficient) condition for the study of social interaction is careful attention to the overt behaviors and behavior settings of actors and their interaction (i.e., "behavior specimens"; see Denzin, 1989c, pp. 79ff.). Thus symbolic interactionists evince a profound respect for the empirical world. Whether they overestimate the obduracy of that world or imagine that it can be directly apprehended is a matter of some dispute (Blumer, 1980; Denzin, 1989c; Hammersley, 1989).

In much the same way that Geertz rejects a structural-functional approach to the study of human action, Blumer (1969) objects to methodologies in which "participants in . . . a societal organization are logically merely media for the play and expression of the forces or mechanisms of the system itself; [in which] one turns to such forces or mechanisms to account for what takes place" (pp. 57-58). On the contrary, symbolic interactionism requires that the inquirer actively enter the worlds of people being studied in order to "see the situation as it is seen by the actor, observing what the actor takes into account, observing how he interprets what is taken into account" (p. 56). The process of actors' interpretation is rendered intelligible not merely through the description of word and deed, but by taking that rich description as a point of departure for formulating an interpretation of what actors are up to.

As Denzin (1971) explains, symbolic interactionists begin with a "sensitizing image of the interaction process" (p. 168) built around such concepts as self, language, social setting, social object, and joint act. The inquirer then "moves from sensitizing concepts to the immediate world of social experience and permits that world to shape and modify his conceptual framework [and, in this way, the inquirer] moves continually between the realm of the more general social theory and the worlds of native people" (p. 168). Symbolic interactionists seek explanations of that world, although, like Geertz, they view explanatory theories as interpretive, grounded, and hovering low over the data (Denzin, 1989c).

Pragmatism informs the philosophical anthropology, epistemology, and social philosophy of the Blumer-Mead version of symbolic interactionism. Like Dewey, Mead and Blumer criticize associationist theories of cognition that reduce action to environmentally determined conduct. They view human beings as acting (not responding) organisms who construct social action (Blumer, 1969). Consequently, such epistemological terms as *truth* and *meaning* are not expressions of relationships of correspondence to reality, but refer to the consequences of a purposeful action. Mead's political pragmatism also shaped the symbolic interactionist persuasion. Denzin (1992), for one, claims that Mead's political philosophy was more culturally conservative and less critical than Dewey's and often issued in a "conservative cultural romanticism which turned the modern self and its interactional experiences into a moral hero" (p. 6).[16]

Interpretive Interactionism

Denzin finds several faults with the Blumer-Mead version of symbolic interactionism: a naive empirical realism, a romantic conception of the "other," and a conservative social philosophy.[17] He thinks it important that Blumer's respect for the empirical world—his call for "close and reasonably full familiarity with area[s] of life under study" (Blumer, 1969, p. 37)— remain at the heart of symbolic interactionism. However, he is keen on developing a postmodern politics of "interpretive interactionism" (Denzin,

1989a, 1989b) that does not offer inscription in the place of description; present a romantic realist picture of human actors; or obscure, decontextualize, or overtheorize the presentation of the voices, emotions, and actions—that is, the lived experience—of respondents.[18]

To become more self-consciously "interpretive," symbolic interactionism must, in Denzin's view, shed its pretensions to ethnographic realism and adopt insights from poststructural philosophy, principally work in cultural and feminist studies. The former facilitates connecting the study of meaning making in social interaction to the communication process and the communication industry "that produce and shape the meanings that circulate in everyday life" (Denzin, 1992, p. 96). Cultural studies directs the interpretive interactionist toward a critical appraisal of "how interacting individuals connect their lived experiences to the cultural representations of those experiences" (p. 74). From feminist studies, the interactionist learns that the language and activity of both inquirer and respondent must be read in gendered, existential, biographical, and classed ways. As a result, a "phenomenologically, existentially driven view of humans and society positions self, emotionality, power, ideology, violence, and sexuality at the center of the interactionist's interpretive problems [and] [t]hese are the topics that an interactionist cultural studies aims to address" (p. 161).

Finally, in Denzin's (1992) reformulation, interpretive interactionism must explicitly engage in cultural criticism. He argues that this can be accomplished through the development of an "oppositional cultural aesthetic" (p. 151) crafted through a rereading of the pragmatic tradition and an appropriation of insights from critical theory. In true deconstructionist fashion, this approach (a) "aims to always subvert the meaning of a text, to show how its dominant and negotiated meanings can be opposed"; (b) "expose[s] the ideological and political meanings that circulate within the text, particularly those which hide or displace racial, class, ethnic and gender biases"; and (c) "analyze[s] how texts address the problems of presence, lived experience, the real and its representations, and the issues of subjects, authors, and their intentionalities" (p. 151).

◆ Constructivist Thinking

Constructivism, at least in the social sciences, is of more recent vintage than interpretivist thinking, although its roots reach back to the earliest philo-

sophical arguments over a rational foundation for knowledge. Constructivists are preoccupied with related but somewhat different concerns from
those of their interpretivist counterparts. As described earlier, interpretivism was conceived in reaction to the effort to develop a natural science of
the social. Its foil was largely logical empiricist methodology and the bid
to apply that framework to human inquiry.

Constructivists share this concern, and they resonate with the interpretivists' emphasis on the world of experience as it is lived, felt, undergone
by social actors. Yet, their particular foils are the notions of objectivism,
empirical realism, objective truth, and essentialism. Karin Knorr-Cetina
(1981) explains that "to the objectivist, the world is composed of facts and
the goal of knowledge is to provide a literal account of what the world is
like" (p. 1). And Kenneth Gergen (1991) adds: "Modernism was deeply
committed to the view that the facts of the world are essentially *there* for
study. They exist independently of us as observers, and if we are rational
we will come to know the facts as they are" (p. 91).

Constructivists are deeply committed to the contrary view that what we
take to be objective knowledge and truth is the result of perspective.
Knowledge and truth are created, not discovered by mind. They emphasize
the pluralistic and plastic character of reality—pluralistic in the sense that
reality is expressible in a variety of symbol and language systems; plastic
in the sense that reality is stretched and shaped to fit purposeful acts of
intentional human agents. They endorse the claim that, "contrary to
common-sense, there is no unique 'real world' that preexists and is
independent of human mental activity and human symbolic language"
(Bruner, 1986, p. 95). In place of a realist view of theories and knowledge,
constructivists emphasize the instrumental and practical function of theory
construction and knowing.

Constructivists are antiessentialists. They assume that what we take to
be self-evident kinds (e.g., man, woman, truth, self) are actually the product
of complicated discursive practices. Accordingly, as Diana Fuss (1989)
explains,

> what is at stake for the constructionist are systems of representations, social
> and material practices, laws of discourses, and ideological effects. In short,
> constructionists are concerned above all with the *production* and *organiza-*
> *tion* of differences, and they therefore reject the idea that any essential or
> natural givens precede the process of social determination. (p. 3)

Everyday Constructivist Thinking

In a fairly unremarkable sense, we are all constructivists if we believe that the mind is active in the construction of knowledge. Most of us would agree that knowing is not passive—a simple imprinting of sense data on the mind—but active; mind does something with these impressions, at the very least forms abstractions or concepts. In this sense, constructivism means that human beings do not find or discover knowledge so much as construct or make it. We invent concepts, models, and schemes to make sense of experience and, further, we continually test and modify these constructions in the light of new experience.

However, as Kenneth Strike (1987) points out, "the claim that people are active in learning or knowledge construction is rather uninteresting. It is uninteresting because no one, beyond a few aberrant behaviorists, denies it" (p. 483). Even the logical positivists, the favorite target of many who currently claim the label "constructivist," were themselves constructivists in the sense sketched above. They held that theoretical terms were in fact abstractions, human inventions that were simply convenient devices for managing and expressing the relations among observables.

Further, one need not be an antirealist to be a constructivist. One can reasonably hold that concepts and ideas are invented (rather than discovered) yet maintain that these inventions correspond to something in the real world. The logical empiricist picture of theory described by Herbert Feigl—a set of human constructs that have meaning by virtue of their relation to the "soil of experience"—is just such a view.[19] Likewise, the notion that knowledge is invented and error-prone (epistemological fallibilism) cohabits quite comfortably with a belief in a real world independent of human knowledge of same (ontological realism) in the evolutionary epistemology of Donald Campbell and in the Popperian philosophy of social science characteristic of D. C. Phillips.

Given that, by their own admission, the constructivists discussed below would indeed make odd bedfellows with the likes of Feigl, Campbell, Phillips, and the ghosts of the logical empiricists, the former group must be staking a claim to something more than this trivial sense of constructivism. Yet the terrain of constructivist approaches is marked by multiple uses of the term. The sketch of constructivist persuasions that follows can at least alert the reader to the kind of intellectual spadework necessary to come to terms with this concept.

Defining the Contours of Constructivist Philosophy

The philosopher most responsible for defining the contours of a constructivist theory of reality and cognition is Nelson Goodman (1984).[20] He characterizes his view as "irrealism," a kind of rigorously constrained radical relativism that "does not hold that everything or even anything is irreal, but sees the world melting into versions and versions making worlds, finds ontology evanescent, and inquires into what makes a version right and a world well-built" (p. 29). Irrealism is not a doctrine that seeks to takes its place alongside realist and idealist accounts of the world, but rather "an attitude of unconcern with most issues between such doctrines" (p. 43). Goodman (1978) quotes the worldly philosopher Woody Allen to make this point:

> Can we actually "know" the universe? My God, it's hard enough finding your way around Chinatown. The point, however, is: Is there anything out there? And why? And must they be so noisy? Finally, there can be no doubt that the one characteristic of "reality" is that it lacks essence. That is not to say it has no essence, but merely lacks it. (The reality I speak of here is the same one Hobbes described, but a little smaller.) (p. 97)

Or, in Goodman's words, the point is "never mind mind, essence is not essential, and matter doesn't matter" (p. 97). Goodman seeks to transcend the debates of realism versus idealism by reconceptualizing philosophy.

Goodman's constructivist philosophy is pluralistic and pragmatic.[21] Through our nonverbal and verbal symbol systems we create many versions of the world in the sciences, the arts, and the humanities. Our process of inquiry is not a matter of somehow getting in touch with the ready-made world; rather, "worldmaking as we know it always starts from worlds already on hand; the making is a remaking" (Goodman, 1978, p. 6). These "remakings" are not simply different interpretations of the same world, but literally different world versions. Stated somewhat differently, our frames of interpretation (versions) belong both to what is interpreted (worlds) and to a system of interpretation. How we go about the business of making and judging world versions is Goodman's principal concern.

We are inclined to judge claims, interpretations, statements, and world versions for their "truth" (usually understood as correspondence between a claim and some ready-made world) and "certainty." But, in Goodman's view, these are excessively restricted concepts beset with trouble (see Goodman & Elgin, 1988). He proposes that we adopt the more pragmatic notion of "rightness," a term with "greater reach" than truth. *Rightness* is defined as an act of fitting and working but "not a fitting *onto*—a correspondence or matching or mirroring of independent Reality—but a fitting *into* a context or discourse or standing complex of other symbols" (p. 158). He claims that the notion of certainty—"a pretentious muddle of the psychological and the pseudological—is unsalvageable" and proposes instead that we use the term *adoption*: "We can adopt habits, strategies, vocabularies, styles, as well as statements" (p. 159).

Accordingly, the cognitive endeavor is not to be taken as the pursuit of knowledge that seeks "to arrive at an accurate and comprehensive description of 'the real' readymade world" (p. 163). Rather, cognition is reconceptualized as the advancement of understanding wherein we begin "from what happens to be currently adopted and proceed to integrate and organize, weed out and supplement, not in order to arrive at truth about something already made but in order to make something right—to construct something that works cognitively, that fits together and handles new cases, that may implement further inquiry and invention" (p. 163).

Radical Constructivism

The contrast between a view of mind as the vessel for the acquisition, storage, and retrieval of information and an instrumentalist notion of mind as an active creator and manipulator of symbols is taken up in a version of constructivist thinking called "radical constructivism" as defined by the psychologist Ernst von Glasersfeld,[22] who is concerned with the nature of knowledge and what it means to know. He argues that radical constructivism signals a particular relationship between mind and world. Following the arguments advanced by the skeptics, von Glasersfeld claims that we cannot know such a thing as an independent, objective world that stands apart from our experience of it. Hence we cannot speak of knowledge as somehow corresponding to, mirroring, or representing that world.

Radical constructivism rejects the notion that "knowledge ought to be a veridical 'representation' of a world as it 'exists' prior to being experienced" (von Glasersfeld, 1991, p. 16). In von Glasersfeld's view, knowledge is not a particular kind of product (i.e., a representation) that exists independent of the knower, but an activity or process. He believes that this process is best understood in Piagetian terms of adaptation and equilibration (von Glasersfeld, 1989, 1991). Correspondingly, criteria for evaluating knowledge claims are revised: The validity of a knowledge claim is not to be found in the relationship of reference or correspondence to an independently existing world; rather, a claim is thought to be valid if it is viable or if it provides functional fit, that is, if it works to achieve a goal. The relationship between knowledge and reality is instrumental, not verificative: To know is "to possess ways and means of acting and thinking that allow one to attain the goals one happens to have chosen" (von Glasersfeld, 1991, p. 16).[23]

Social Constructionism

Kenneth and Mary Gergen also challenge the idea of some objective basis for knowledge claims and examine the process of knowledge construction. But, instead of focusing on the matter of individual minds and cognitive processes, they turn their attention outward to the world of intersubjectively shared, social constructions of meaning and knowledge. Acknowledging a debt to the phenomenology of Peter Berger and Alfred Schutz, Kenneth Gergen (1985) labels his approach "social constructionism" because it more adequately reflects the notion that the world that people create in the process of social exchange is a reality *sui generis*.

The social constructionist approach is predicated on the assumption that "the terms by which the world is understood are social artifacts, products of historically situated interchanges among people" (Gergen, 1985, p. 267). Knowledge is one of the many coordinated activities of individuals and as such is subject to the same processes that characterize any human interaction (e.g., communication, negotiation, conflict, rhetoric). As Gergen and Gergen (1991) explain: "Accounts of the world . . . take place within shared systems of intelligibility—usually a spoken or written language. These accounts are not viewed as the external expression of the speaker's internal processes (such as cognition, intention), but as an expression of relationships among persons" (p. 78). Contrary to the emphasis in radical constructivism, the focus here is not on the meaning-making activity of the individual mind but on the collective generation of meaning as shaped by conventions of language and other social processes.

Although both von Glasersfeld and Gergen emphasize that their versions of constructivist philosophy are concerned with epistemology (knowing) not ontology (being), each also takes a stand on the latter. Von Glasersfeld (1991) does not deny that there is an ontological reality, but claims that we

240

cannot in any sense know a "real" world. He sounds very much like an ontological idealist when he says, "I claim that we cannot even imagine what the word 'to exist' might mean in an ontological context, because we cannot conceive of 'being' without the notions of space and time, and these two notions are among the first of our conceptual constructs" (p. 17).

Gergen's theory of reality is both idealist and relative. He claims that "there are no independently identifiable, real-world referents to which the language of social description [or explanation, for that matter] are cemented" (1986, p. 143). Further, he at least implies that language is the only reality we can know, hence his view borders on the radical linguistic relativism or contextualist theory of reality characteristic of Stanley Fish (1989).[24] According to Fish, reality *is* the result of the social processes accepted as normal in a specific context, and knowledge claims are intelligible and debatable only within a particular context or community.

Feminist Standpoint Epistemologies

These constructivist persuasions blend the phenomenological interpretive perspective with critical hermeneutics.[25] They are concerned with portraying the lived reality of women's lives. As Riger (1992) explains, "Giving voice to women's perspectives means identifying ways women create meaning and experience life from their particular position in the social hierarchy" (p. 734). Feminist standpoint persuasions argue that women's life experiences are not captured in existing conceptual schemes (e.g., Belenky, Clinchy, Goldberger, & Tarule, 1986; Gilligan, 1982; D. Smith, 1987), and thus they focus in particular on the ways in which gender is socially constructed, treating it as an analytic category in its own right.[26]

In her review of perspectives in feminist anthropology, Micaela di Leonardo (1991) explains that social constructionists regard language seriously as more than a transparent representational medium. Studies by Susan Gal (1991) on women's speech and silence, Emily Martin (1987) on women's discourse about their own reproductive processes compared with the dominant discourse of medical science, and Jane Radway (1984) on the social event of reading popular romance novels are examples of sociolinguistic analyses of how verbal practices in social interaction construct gender. However, discourse analysis does not replace social analysis. Reflecting the influence of critical theorists of the Frankfurt school, feminist social constructionists evince profound concern for the material conditions of women's lives. Analysis of discourse is thus often combined with political economic research.[27]

Another feature of these persuasions that they share, in part, with recent developments in postmodern ethnography is the careful, public scrutiny of the inquirer's history, values, and assumptions. Although there is a vast fieldwork literature on researcher-respondent relations, feminist standpoint epistemologies are particularly keen on exploring the social construction of the research encounter (e.g., Mies, 1983; Oakley, 1981; Reinharz, 1992; Stacey, 1988).

The social, dialogic nature of inquiry is central to the constructivist thinking of Gergen and Gergen (1991) and Guba and Lincoln (1989) (discussed below) as well. For them, inquiry methodology requires attending both to the inquirer's own self-reflective awareness of his or her own constructions and to the *social* construction of individual constructions (including that of the inquirer). For example, Gergen and Gergen (1991) sketch an interactive approach to inquiry called the "reflexive elaboration of the event," in which the researcher and participants open a sociopsychological phenomenon to inspection and through dialogue generate a process of continuous reflexivity, thereby "enabling new forms of linguistic reality to emerge" (p. 88). The overall aim of this approach is "to expand and enrich the vocabulary of understanding."

Guba and Lincoln (1989) echo a similar view. They believe that the best means of developing joint constructions is the "hermeneutic-dialectic" process, so called because it is interpretive and fosters comparing and contrasting divergent constructions in an effort to achieve a synthesis of same. They strongly emphasize that the goal of constructivist inquiry is to achieve a consensus (or, failing that, an agenda for negotiation) on issues and concerns that define the nature of the inquiry.

A "Constructivist Paradigm"

Egon Guba and Yvonna Lincoln's "constructivist paradigm" is a wide-ranging eclectic framework. They originally discussed their approach under the heading of "naturalistic inquiry" (Lincoln & Guba, 1985). However, recently they have begun using the term *constructivism* to characterize their methodology (Guba & Lincoln, 1989, p. 19), although they acknowledge that constructivist, interpretive, naturalistic, and hermeneutical are all similar notions. They propose their constructivist paradigm as a replacement for what they label the conventional, scientific, or

242

positivist paradigm of inquiry, and they have spelled out in detail the epistemological and ontological assumptions, aims, procedures, and criteria of their approach.

Their constructivist philosophy is idealist; that is, they assume that what is real is a construction in the minds of individuals (Lincoln & Guba, 1985, p. 83).[28] It is also pluralist and relativist: There are multiple, often conflicting, constructions, and all (at least potentially) are meaningful. For Guba and Lincoln, the question of which or whether constructions are true is sociohistorically relative. Truth is a matter of the best-informed and most sophisticated construction on which there is consensus at a given time.

Like those who espouse the feminist standpoint epistemologies noted above, Guba and Lincoln assume that the observer cannot (should not) be neatly disentangled from the observed in the activity of inquiring into constructions. Hence the findings or outcomes of an inquiry are themselves a literal creation or construction of the inquiry process. Constructions, in turn, are resident in the minds of individuals: "They do not exist outside of the persons who create and hold them; they are not part of some 'objective' world that exists apart from their constructors" (Guba & Lincoln, 1989, p. 143).

The act of inquiry begins with issues and/or concerns of participants and unfolds through a "dialectic" of iteration, analysis, critique, reiteration, reanalysis, and so on that leads eventually to a joint (among inquirer and respondents) construction of a case (i.e., findings or outcomes). The joint constructions that issue from the activity of inquiry can be evaluated for their "fit" with the data and information they encompass; the extent to which they "work," that is, provide a credible level of understanding; and the extent to which they have "relevance" and are "modifiable" (Guba & Lincoln, 1989, p. 179).

The properties of constructions can be further elaborated as follows (Guba & Lincoln, 1989):

1. Constructions are attempts to make sense of or to interpret experience, and most are self-sustaining and self-renewing.
2. The nature or quality of a construction that can be held depends upon "the range or scope of information available to a constructor, and the constructor's sophistication in dealing with that information" (p. 71).
3. Constructions are extensively shared, and some of those shared are "disciplined constructions," that is, collective and systematic attempts to come to common agreements about a state of affairs, for example, science (p. 71).

4. Although all constructions must be considered meaningful, some are rightly labeled "malconstruction" because they are "incomplete, simplistic, uninformed, internally inconsistent, or derived by an inadequate methodology" (p. 143).

5. The judgment of whether a given construction is malformed can be made only with reference to the "paradigm out of which the constructor operates" (p. 143); in other words, criteria or standards are framework specific, "so for instance a religious construction can only be judged adequate or inadequate utilizing the particular theological paradigm from which it is derived" (p. 143).

6. One's constructions are challenged when one becomes aware that new information conflicts with the held construction or when one senses a lack of intellectual sophistication needed to make sense of new information.

Educational Connoisseurship and Criticism

Elliot Eisner's version of constructivism is grounded in the work of Suzanne Langer and Michael Polanyi, and in John Dewey's aesthetic theory. It is proposed as an alternative to qualitative approaches to educational studies stemming from ethnographic traditions in social science. Acknowledging a partial debt to Goodman's philosophy of cognition and his philosophy of art, Eisner assumes that perception is framework or theory dependent and that knowledge is a constructed (versus discovered) form of experience. His methodology is concerned with how inquirers develop an enhanced capacity to perceive the qualities that comprise the educational experience and, further, how they can develop the skills to render those perceptions in representational forms that portray, interpret, and appraise educational phenomena. The selection of representational forms is critical because, in Eisner's (1991) view, "the selection of a form through which the world is to be represented not only influences what we can say, it also influences what we are likely to experience" (p. 8).

Connoisseurship is the art of apperception. It is grounded in the "consummatory function" of aesthetic knowing—"the developed ability to experience the subtleties of form" (Eisner, 1985, p. 28). What the connoisseur perceives or experiences are qualities—the sensory features of a phenomenon. Yet perception of qualities is not mere impression of sense data on the mind; rather, the act of perception is a framework- or schema-dependent cognitive act. For the connoisseur, perceiving or experiencing is a kind of heightened awareness or educated perception—a

244

particular kind of attention to nuance and detail, to multiple dimensions or aspects—that comes from intimate familiarity with the phenomenon being examined. The connoisseur's eye (as metaphor for all the senses) is in a state of enlightenment.

What the connoisseur "sees" he or she must eventually "say," and the act of rendering apperception in some publicly available form is the task of criticism. Here, Eisner (1985, p. 28) draws on what he calls the "referential function" of aesthetic knowing—its function of pointing to some aspect of the world beyond our immediate ken, thereby allowing us to experience some phenomenon via vicarious participation. The inquirer as connoisseur-turned-critic reconstructs or transforms his or her perceptions into some representational form that "illuminates, interprets, and appraises the qualities that have been experienced" (Eisner, 1991, p. 86). This form is most typically some kind of narrative that is presentational rather than representational. In other words, the narrative is not an iconic image or mirror of reality but a poetic, expressive form that is a reconstrual or reconstitution of the experience from which it originates. The critic describes, interprets, and appraises the phenomenon and thereby aids in the reeducation of the reader's perception. This narrative, storied mode of re-presenting the connoisseur's experience is particularly significant because it points to the importance of an aesthetic (versus scientific or propositional) form of knowing in human inquiry. These narrative accounts can themselves be evaluated or appraised for their "rightness" through the judgment of their coherence, referential adequacy, and instrumental utility (Eisner, 1991, pp. 53ff.).

◆ On Common Criticisms and Future Directions

Interpretivist and constructivist persuasions have been somewhat artificially disentangled here to afford a closer look at salient aspects of each. Yet it should be apparent that current work in these methodologies reflects the synthetic impulse of the postmodern zeitgeist. Decades from its origins in challenges to scientism and efforts to restore to human inquiry a principal focus on the everyday world of lived experience, the phenomenological-interpretive perspective is now being blended with insights from constructivist epistemology, feminist methodologies, poststructuralism, postmodernism, and critical hermeneutics.[29] This bid to redescribe and reconceptualize makes for an often bewildering array of conflicting

245

considerations, yet it also signals that in-house controversies are now far more intellectually vital and exciting than the simplistic debates between so-called quantitative and qualitative methodologies that continue to be waged in some quarters of the academy. These challenges from within that demand our attention are principally centered on four issues in interpretive work—the perdurable problems of criteria and objectivity, the lack of a critical purchase, the problem of inquirer authority and privilege, and the confusion of psychological and epistemological claims.

The Problem of Criteria

The issue is deceptively simple: What is an adequate warrant for a subjectively mediated account of intersubjective meaning?[30] In the absence of some set of criteria, such accounts are subject to the charges of solipsism (they are only *my* accounts) and relativism (all accounts are equally good or bad, worthy or unworthy, true or false, and so on). Contemporary interpretivists and constructivists are not likely to hold that there are unquestioned *foundations* for any interpretation. They are nonfoundationalists who have given up the quest for objectivism (Bernstein, 1976), hence a solution to the problem of criteria is not likely to be found in this venue.

Nonfoundational resolutions to the problem have arisen in the following ways. One is to claim the middle ground of methodology, as noted at the beginning of this chapter. The notion of an appeal to procedural criteria as grounds for judging the goodness of interpretations is strong. It is evident in the painstaking attention to goodness criteria in the otherwise constructivist frame of reference of Guba and Lincoln.

A second effort issues from arguments for subtle realism. This resolution stems from a bid to rescue an important realist intuition from otherwise incoherent correspondence theories of truth (Matthews, 1992). The intuition is that the truth, worth, or value of a claim, theory, interpretation, construction, and so forth is ultimately determined by something *beyond* the claim, theory, interpretation, construction. Hammersley (1992b), for example, argues that interpretivists investigate independent, knowable, actor-constructed phenomena, but denies that we have an unmediated grasp of or access to those phenomena. He maintains that there can be "multiple, non-contradictory descriptive and explanatory claims about any phenomenon" (Hammersley, 1989, p. 135), "without denying that if those interpretations are accurate they must correspond in relevant aspects to the phenomena described" (p. 194).

A third resolution is to give up the worry about a separation of mind and world and focus instead on intentional, meaningful behavior that is by definition historically, socially, and culturally relative. It acknowledges that a human inquirer is permanently engaged in a discourse with his or her own object, "a discourse in which the object and subject of study employ essentially the same resources" (Bauman, 1978, p. 234; see also Giddens, 1976). Interpretive accounts (efforts to make clear what seems to be confused, unclear) are to be judged on the pragmatic grounds of whether they are useful, fitting, generative of further inquiry, and so forth.

The Lack of a Critical Purchase

This problem is variously identified as one of descriptivism, of the lack of a critical purchase, and of privileging the views of actors. The principal objection here is that interpretive accounts lack any critical interest or the ability to critique the very accounts they produce. Burrell and Morgan (1979), for example, note that interpretive theoretical frameworks reflect a politics that they call the "sociology of regulation" as opposed to a "sociology of radical change" (p. 254). In their view, these frameworks "present a perspective in which individual actors negotiate, regulate, and live their lives within the context of the *status quo*" (p. 254). A similar kind of concern underlies Denzin's critique of the Blumer-Mead version of symbolic interactionism. Also, as noted above, some feminist social constructionists address this challenge by drawing on the critical theory tradition.

This criticism is, in part, traceable to the origins of the image of the social inquirer as disinterested theorist—one whose practice is defined by the careful separation of empirical from normative concerns, descriptive theory from prescriptive theory (see Berger & Kellner, 1981; Bernstein, 1976; Clifford, 1983). Weber's insistence on the separation of facts and values (the ethics of responsibility versus the ethics of conviction) in interpretive sociology, and Schutz's distinction between the fundamental interests of the individual as ordinary citizen and the individual as scientist are central sources of this idea.

For example, Schutz (1967) held that the world of social scientific investigation constituted a particular finite province of meaning (one of many such finite provinces or multiple realities) that demanded a particular relevance structure, cognitive style, and attitude.[31] The individual-as-social-scientist operates with the attitude of the disinterested observer and abides by the rules for evidence and objectivity within the scientific community. Whereas the individual-as-citizen legitimately has a practical (in a classic sense), pragmatic, interested attitude, the individual-turned-social-scientist brackets out that attitude and adopts the posture of objective, disinterested, empirical theorist. This disinterested attitude is readily evident, for example, in traditional ethnography, where the inquirer is warned not to become more than a marginal native and to discipline his or her subjectivity. Critics hold that it is precisely because of this distancing of oneself as inquirer that interpretivists cannot engage in an explicitly critical evaluation of the social reality they seek to portray.

The Problem of Authority

A third set of criticisms is directed at what might be called the "dangers of high interpretive science" and the "overly sovereign" authoritative stance of the interpreter as inscriber (Rabinow, 1986, p. 258).[32] Postmodern ethnographers (e.g., Clifford, 1983, 1990; Clifford & Marcus, 1986; Rabinow, 1977) argue that defining interpretation as act of inscription vests authority and control in the anthropologist as inscriber and suppresses the dialogic dimension of constructing interpretations of human action. A related worry expressed by some critics of this linguistic, textualist turn, particularly in anthropology (e.g., Jackson, 1989), is that quarrels over whether anthropology is best viewed as an analytic or interpretive science are making for both a bad science and a bad art of anthropological investigation.

The Making of Epistemological Claims

A special set of criticisms is directed at the constructivists' bid to argue from a psychological claim to an epistemological conclusion (Matthews, 1992; Strike, 1987). Recall that the constructivist makes the claim, in Eisner's (1991) words, that there is no "pristine, unmediated grasp of the world as it is" (p. 46) and, further, that no sharp distinction can be drawn between knower and known, between accounts of the world and those doing the accounting. Taken as a *psychological* claim, this is not particularly problematic, even for those who call themselves empiricists. It is a belief that knowledge is not simply the impression of sense data on the mind, but instead is actively constructed.

248

Yet many constructivists are not making simply a psychological claim, they are making an *epistemological* claim as well. That is, they argue that knowledge does not discover a preexisting, independent, real world outside the mind of the knower, that the process of making or constructing meaning cannot be connected to an "independent world 'out there,' but [only] to our own constructing processes" (Steier, 1991, p. 2).

The difficulty here is how to account for the fact of knowledge as a form of theoretical production, the fact that knowledge is somehow available to individuals, and the fact that knowledge is shared and transmitted. To borrow some language from Guba and Lincoln (1989), if constructions "are resident in the minds of individuals" (p. 143)—that is, they cannot be said to exist outside the self-reflective capacity of an individual mind— then how is it possible that they can be "extensively shared" (p. 71), and that "a range [and] scope of information [knowledge] is available to a constructor" (p. 71) such that constructions can be modified, changed, or abandoned?

One way in which this problem has been addressed, as we have seen, is to emphasize the *social* construction of knowledge. Yet the tension between claiming that knowledge is the property of individual minds and the view that knowledge can be publicly shared is evident.[33]

Future Directions

Having surveyed the contemporary scene and appraised the arguments for nonfoundationalist, antiessentialist thinking, Richard Rorty (1982) concludes that we stand at the head of two paths. One is the path of Dewey, with his liberal social hope; the other is the path of Foucault, with his despair over the prison house of language. I for one can find little comfort in a form of interpretivism that degenerates into nihilism, where we do nothing but engage in endless parasitical deconstruction and deny the existence of social order and our very selves.

To be sure, the future of interpretivist and constructivist persuasions rests on the acceptance of the implications of dissolving long-standing dichotomies such as subject/object, knower/known, fact/value. It rests on individuals being comfortable with the blurring of lines between the science and art of interpretation, the social scientific and the literary account (Geertz, 1980). Yet, in rejecting these rigid distinctions, we need not, as Michael Jackson (1989) argues, dissolve the lived *experience* of inquirer or respondents into the anonymous field of discourse.

We can reject dichotomous thinking on pragmatic grounds: Such distinctions simply are not very useful anymore. We can continue to respect the bid to make sense of the conditions of our lives without claiming that either inquirer or actor is the final arbiter of understanding. The interpretive undertaking thus becomes, in Jackson's (1989) words, the practice of "*actively* debating and exchanging points of view with our informants. It means placing our ideas on a par with theirs, testing them not against predetermined standards of rationality but against the immediate exigencies of life" (p. 14).

I read this union of the interpretive turn and the tradition of practical philosophy, with its defense of the Socratic virtues and its emphasis on our fundamental character as dialogic, conversational, questioning beings, to be a most promising and hopeful development. The interpretivists' profound respect for and interest in socially constructed meaning and practice is consonant with the turn toward the moral-practical (*phronesis*) and away from *theoria* (as explored, although in very different ways, by Bernstein, 1986, 1992; Rorty, 1982; Sullivan, 1986).[34]

The thesis of this chapter is that what marks constructivist or interpretivist work as a unique form of human inquiry is a set of theoretical commitments and philosophical assumptions about the way the world must be in order that we can know it. In reviewing the philosophical roots of this work and in summarizing the kinds of epistemological problems it raises, my intent has not been to make all those who claim the title "constructivist" or "interpretivist" inquirer into philosophers. Rather, my goal has been to enhance the level of awareness of the kind of philosophical investigation that is entailed in proposing alternatives to an empiricist social science. My purpose has been at least partially accomplished if the reader has been drawn to further investigation of the issues raised here.

Notes

1. Following a distinction developed by Stake (1991), I prefer the term *persuasions* or *approaches* to *models*. *Models* overpromises because it suggests that the student of interpretive inquiry would find guidance in the discussions of these methodologies for answering the question of what a completed inquiry should look like. It suggests that these statements are blueprints that should be followed. Yet models are not found in discussions of methodology but in the published accounts of various forms of interpretive inquiry. The term *persuasions,* on the contrary, connotes that what we are dealing with here are statements of particular commitments, purviews, and concerns.

2. A comparison with feminist methodologies is instructive here. In some cases, differences in method *do* help explain what is different about feminist approaches to human inquiry; however, this claim is contested (see, for example, Harding, 1987; Reinharz, 1992; Riger, 1992).

3. This caveat drawing attention to the distinction between methodological commitments and methods is warranted in view of the persistent mistaken belief that making the interpretive turn in the social sciences is principally a matter of employing different means of collecting and analyzing data. Understanding constructivist or interpretivist approaches to the study of human action (or any of the other approaches examined in this volume) is not simply a matter of mastering technique, copying a method, or following a model. Rather, understanding is to be had through an examination of the epistemological assumptions and claims of a methodology, through study of its conceptualization of what we are about when we inquire. This is a philosophical inquiry.

4. Other interpretive and constructivist persuasions are explained elsewhere in this series: Holstein and Gubrium discuss ethnomethodology in Volume 2, Chapter 6; Greene explores constructivist thinking in evaluation in Volume 3, Chapter 13; Stake, in Volume 2, Chapter 4, notes the influence of interpretivist and constructivist thinking in shaping notions of case study strategies; and Atkinson and Hammersley, in Volume 2, Chapter 5, discuss how the interpretivist's goal for human inquiry is manifest in ethnography.

5. For different accounts of these roots, see Bauman (1978), Bernstein (1976), and Bleicher (1980).

6. See Richard J. Bernstein's (1976) discussion of the definition of scientific explanation in mainstream social science.

7. See Taylor (1989, pp. 159ff.) for a thorough discussion of the tensions between Romanticist and Cartesian notions of the self. Although his work is an exercise in moral philosophy, much of his argument is relevant to understanding the tension referred to here. See also Gergen (1991, chap. 2).

8. According to Smith (1989), advocates of this solution hold that "although the ideas of objectivity, detachment, and methodological constraints as defined by empiricists are a fiction, interpretive inquiry must be made more systematic and rigorous. The claim here is that methods cannot eliminate researcher subjectivity but that they can certainly minimize it; they are thereby the criteria against which to judge that some results are more objective than others" (p. 157).

9. See Taylor (1964) for an account of both kinds of explanations. Interpretivists typically use the term *human action* (as opposed to *behavior*) to signal not only that intentions of the actor are relevant but that these intentions and the behavior itself are socially, temporally, and culturally situated and constituted. See also Bruner (1990, p. 19) and Erickson (1990, p. 98).

10. The bid to explicate the nature of interpretation is directed, in part, at the naturalists' claim that the aim (and form) of causal explanation in the natural sciences applies equally well to the social sciences. To argue that we "understand" human action *by means of interpretation* is to argue for an altogether different aim of the social sciences. Erickson (1990) explains this shift as follows: "If people take action on the grounds of their interpretations of the actions of others, then meaning-interpretations themselves are causal for humans. This is not true in nature. . . . The billiard ball does not make sense of its environment. But the human actor in society does, and different humans make sense

differently. They impute symbolic meaning to other's actions and take their own actions in accord with the meaning interpretations they have made" (p. 98).

11. For an example of the difference this interpretation of *Verstehen* makes in humanistic and hermeneutical psychology, see Sass (1988).

12. Critical hermeneutics (e.g., Abel and Habermas) challenges the idealist assumptions of this commitment to interpretation as ontological hermeneutics and points to its failure to consider the extralinguistic considerations that constitute the world of thought and action. In the discussion of feminist standpoint epistemologies that appears later in this chapter these concerns are revisited. See also Chapter 9, by Olesen, and Chapter 10, by Stanfield, in this volume.

13. This reconceptualization of criteria for appraisal is evident in constructionist thinking. See below and Eisner (1991, pp. 53ff.), Goodman and Elgin (1988, pp. 153ff.), and Gergen (1991, pp. 226ff.)

14. Experience-near and experience-distant concepts are roughly analogous to emic and etic perspectives, respectively.

15. For a brief discussion of the difference between philosophical and methodological behaviorism, see Nagel (1961, p. 480).

16. Joas (1987) argues that the Chicago school of symbolic interactionism only partially realized the full promise of a social philosophy of pragmatism.

17. Denzin's (1989a, 1989b, 1992) recent work is in the main a deconstruction of the texts that form the tradition of symbolic interactionism. It is a highly synthetic, complex reformulation of the interactionist project that draws on insights from postmodern ethnography, feminist critiques of positivism, hermeneutical and existential phenomenology, cultural studies, and poststructuralist thought of Foucault and Derrida, as well as a recovery of a critically engaged social pragmatism.

18. For an examination of the ways in which realism is inscribed in a fieldwork text, see Clifford (1983), Clifford and Marcus (1986), Van Maanen (1988).

19. Furthermore, as Stephen Toulmin (1982) has argued, natural scientists are also in the business of construing reality, and the regulative ideals of objectivity and rationality are not necessarily at odds with a constructivist point of view.

20. Goodman is not principally concerned with applying his insights to social science, and furthermore, understanding Goodman is not easy going; by his own admission he disdains writing "flatfooted philosophy." Hence few who label their methodologies constructivist (with the notable exception of Eisner and Bruner) make any reference to Goodman's work. Eisner is discussed below. Bruner (1986, 1990) acknowledges Goodman's influence on his own account of cultural psychology, which takes seriously the activity of meaning making and the intentional states of social agents. Bruner's recent work is a redescription of the cognitive enterprise grounded in the examination of how meaning is constructed. It stands as a corrective to accounts of cognitive science shaped by the metaphors of computation and information processing.

21. See Cornel West (1989) for a brief discussion of Goodman's contribution to the philosophy of American pragmatism.

22. Radical constructivist thinking informs much current work in curriculum inquiry in mathematics and science education (e.g., Bodner, 1986; Cobb & Steffe, 1983; Cobb, Yackel, & Wood, 1992; Davis, Maher, & Noddings, 1990; Driver & Oldham, 1986; Novak, 1987). It is becoming something of a rallying cry for reformulating theories of teaching and

learning among instructional technologists and educational psychologists (e.g., Duffy & Jonassen, 1991). As Matthews (1992) has noted, the emphasis here is not on knowledge as something that tells us about the world, but knowledge as something that tells us about our experiences and the best ways to organize them. Learning is redefined as a process of experiencing and developing the knowledge construction process, and teaching becomes less a matter of communicating content (i.e., a transmission model) and more a matter of facilitating a process.

23. Of course, an instrumentalist view of theory and knowledge was also characteristic of the logical empiricists' view. They would no doubt have taken great delight in von Glasersfeld's (1991) choice of the title "Knowing Without Metaphysics."

24. Gergen (1991) claims that "words are not maps of reality. Rather, words gain their meaning through their use in social interchange, within the 'language games' of the culture. We don't use words like *perception, thought,* and *memory* because they accurately map a world we call mental. Rather, such terms gain their meaning from the way they are used in social life" (p. 102).

25. See Harding (1986) and Riger (1992) for an overview of different feminist epistemologies.

26. See also the chapters in this volume by Olesen (Chapter 9), Stanfield (Chapter 10), and Fiske (Chapter 11).

27. Di Leonardo (1991) argues that social constructionism need not degenerate into the nihilist stance of poststructuralism that denies the existence of social order, declares the death of the subject, and levels the distinctions between truth and falsehood.

28. It should be noted that Lincoln and Guba (1985, pp. 83-87) are somewhat equivocal on this issue. They claim to be drawn to the position that all reality is created by mind, yet are willing to settle for a less radical view of "constructed realities." They hold that constructions are invented or created, yet those constructions are related to "tangible entities"—events, persons, objects. If these tangible entities are not solely creations of mind, then they must be ontically "real." The distinction they draw here seems to be one of a difference between experiential reality (constructions) and ontological reality (tangible entities).

29. See di Leonardo (1991) and Rosenau (1992) for discussions of the difference between postmodernism and poststructuralism.

30. See also J. K. Smith (1989, chap. 7) for an extended discussion of this issue.

31. Schutz's (1967) idea of multiple realities is often wrongly interpreted. He describes the world of science, the world of mythology, the world of religion, the world of dreams, and so forth as multiple realities, or more specifically as "finite provinces of meaning" (p. 230). Yet he does not claim that these are literally different realities: "We speak of provinces of *meaning* . . . because it is the meaning of our experiences and not the ontological structure of the objects [in a given province] which constitutes reality." He views these multiple realities as "merely names for different tensions in one and the same life, unbroken from birth to death, which is attended to in different modifications" (p. 258).

32. See, for example, Crapanzano's (1986) unmasking of Geertz's authority as ethnographer in the study of the Balinese cockfight.

33. Following Matthews (1992), we might hazard the explanation that this tension arises from the fact that constructivism rightly criticizes empiricist assumptions yet clings to an empiricist epistemological paradigm. One alternative is a nonempiricist, objectivist

epistemology of Matthews (1992) and Chalmers (1982). Another is the analysis of practices wherein the epistemology of hermeneutics is not detached from the sociology of communication (see, e.g., Giddens, 1976, 1984; Habermas, 1972).

34. This development is also supported by the growing interest in narrative and storytelling as a means of shaping, organizing, and understanding human experience (see MacIntyre, 1977, 1981; Sarbin, 1986).

◆ References

Abel, T. (1948). The operation called *Verstehen*. *American Journal of Sociology, 54*, 211-218.

Bauman, Z. (1978). *Hermeneutics and social science*. London: Hutchinson.

Belenky, M. F., Clinchy, B. M., Goldberger, N. R., & Tarule, J. M. (1986). *Women's ways of knowing: The development of self, voice and mind*. New York: Basic Books.

Berger, P. L., & Kellner, H. (1981). *Sociology reinterpreted: An essay on method and vocation*. Garden City, NY: Anchor.

Bernstein, R. J. (1976). *The restructuring of social and political theory*. Philadelphia: University of Pennsylvania Press.

Bernstein, R. J. (1986). What is the difference that makes a difference? Gadamer, Habermas, and Rorty. In B. R. Wachterhauser (Ed.), *Hermeneutics and modern philosophy* (pp. 343-376). Albany: State University of New York Press.

Bernstein, R. J. (1992). *The new constellation*. Cambridge: MIT Press.

Bleicher, J. (1980). *Contemporary hermeneutics: Hermeneutics as method, philosophy and critique*. London: Routledge & Kegan Paul.

Blumer, H. (1954). What is wrong with social theory? *American Sociological Review, 19*, 3-10.

Blumer, H. (1969). *Symbolic interactionism: Perspective and method*. Englewood Cliffs, NJ: Prentice Hall.

Blumer, H. (1980). Mead and Blumer: The convergent methodological perspectives of social behaviorism and symbolic interactionism. *American Sociological Review, 45*, 409-419.

Bodner, G. M. (1986). Constructivism: A theory of knowledge. *Journal of Chemical Education, 63*, 873-878.

Bruner, J. (1986). *Actual minds, possible worlds*. Cambridge, MA: Harvard University Press.

Bruner, J. (1990). *Acts of meaning*. Cambridge, MA: Harvard University Press.

Burrell, G., & Morgan, G. (1979). *Sociological paradigms and organizational analysis*. London: Heinemann.

Chalmers, A. F. (1982). *What is this thing called science?* St. Lucia: University of Queensland Press.

Clifford, J. (1983). On ethnographic authority. *Representations, 1*, 118-146.

Clifford, J. (1990). Notes on (field)notes. In R. Sanjek (Ed.), *Fieldnotes: The makings of anthropology* (pp. 47-70). Albany: State University of New York Press.

Clifford, J., & Marcus, G. E. (Eds.). (1986). *Writing culture: The poetics and politics of ethnography*. Berkeley: University of California Press.

254

Cobb, P., & Steffe, L. (1983). The constructivist researcher as teacher and model builder. *Journal for Research in Mathematics Education, 14*(2), 83-94.

Cobb, P., Yackel, E., & Wood, T. (1992). A constructivist alternative to the representational view of mind in mathematics education. *Journal for Research in Mathematics Education, 23*(1), 2-34.

Crapanzano, V. (1986). Hermes' dilemma: The masking of subversion in ethnographic description. In J. Clifford & G. E. Marcus (Eds.), *Writing culture: The poetics and politics of ethnography* (pp. 51-76). Berkeley: University of California Press.

Davis, R. B., Maher, C. A., & Noddings, N. (Eds.). (1990). *Constructivist views on the teaching and learning of mathematics.* Reston, VA: National Council of Teachers of Mathematics.

Denzin, N. K. (1971). The logic of naturalistic inquiry. *Social Forces, 50,* 166-182.

Denzin, N. K. (1989a). *Interpretive biography.* Newbury Park, CA: Sage.

Denzin, N. K. (1989b). *Interpretive interactionism.* Newbury Park, CA: Sage.

Denzin, N. K. (1989c). *The research act: A theoretical introduction to sociological methods* (3rd ed.). Englewood Cliffs, NJ: Prentice Hall.

Denzin, N. K. (1992). *Symbolic interactionism and cultural studies.* Oxford: Basil Blackwell.

di Leonardo, M. (1991). Introduction: Gender, culture and political economy: Feminist anthropology in historical perspective. In M. di Leonardo (Ed.), *Gender at the crossroads of knowledge: Feminist anthropology in the postmodern era* (pp. 1-48). Berkeley: University of California Press.

Driver, R., & Oldham, V. (1986). A constructivist approach to curriculum development in science. *Studies in Science Education, 13,* 105-122.

Duffy, T. A., & Jonassen, D. H. (Eds.). (1991). Continuing the dialogue on the implications of constructivism for educational technology [Special issue]. *Educational Technology, 31*(9), 9-48.

Eisner, E. (1985). Aesthetic modes of knowing. In E. Eisner (Ed.), *Learning and teaching the ways of knowing: Eighty-fourth yearbook of the National Society for the Study of Education* (Part 2, pp. 23-36). Chicago: National Society for the Study of Education.

Eisner, E. (1991). *The enlightened eye: Qualitative inquiry and the enhancement of educational practices.* New York: Macmillan.

Erickson, F. (1986). Qualitative methods. In M. C. Wittrock (Ed.), *Handbook of research on teaching* (3rd ed., pp. 119-161). New York: Macmillan.

Erickson, F. (1990). Qualitative methods. In *Research in teaching and learning* (Vol. 2, pp. 77-194). New York: Macmillan.

Fish, S. (1989). *Doing what comes naturally: Change, rhetoric, and the practice of theory in literary and legal studies.* Durham, NC: Duke University Press.

Fuss, D. (1989). *Essentially speaking: Feminism, nature, and difference.* London: Routledge.

Gadamer, H. G. (1989). *Truth and method* (2nd rev. ed.) (J. Weinsheimer & D. G. Marshall, Trans.). New York: Crossroads.

Gal, S. (1991). Between speech and silence: The problematics of research on language and gender. In M. di Leonardo (Ed.), *Gender at the crossroads of knowledge: Feminist anthropology in the postmodern era* (pp. 175-203). Berkeley: University of California Press.

Geertz, C. (1973). *The interpretation of cultures: Selected essays.* New York: Basic Books.

Geertz, C. (1980). Blurred genres: The refiguration of social thought. *American Scholar,* *49,* 165-179.

Geertz, C. (1983). *Local knowledge: Further essays in interpretive anthropology.* New York: Basic Books.

Geertz, C. (1988). *Works and lives: The anthropologist as author.* Stanford, CA: Stanford University Press.

Gergen, K. J. (1985). The social constructionist movement in modern psychology. *American Psychologist, 40,* 266-275.

Gergen, K. J. (1986). Correspondence versus autonomy in the language of understanding human action. In D. W. Fiske & R. A. Shweder (Eds.), *Metatheory in social science.* Chicago: University of Chicago Press.

Gergen, K. J. (1991). *The saturated self: Dilemmas of identity in contemporary life.* New York: Basic Books.

Gergen, K. J., & Gergen, M. M. (1991). Toward reflexive methodologies. In F. Steier (Ed.), *Research and reflexivity* (pp. 76-95). Newbury Park, CA: Sage.

Giddens, A. (1976). *New rules of sociological method: A positive critique of interpretative sociologies.* New York: Basic Books.

Giddens, A. (1984). *The constitution of society.* Berkeley: University of California Press.

Gilligan, C. (1982). *In a different voice: Psychological theory and women's development.* Cambridge: Harvard University Press.

Goodman, N. (1978). *Ways of worldmaking.* Indianapolis: Hackett.

Goodman, N. (1984). *Of mind and other matters.* Cambridge, MA: Harvard University Press.

Goodman, N., & Elgin, C. (1988). *Reconceptions in philosophy and other arts and sciences.* Indianapolis: Hackett.

Guba, E. G., & Lincoln, Y. S. (1989). *Fourth generation evaluation.* Newbury Park, CA: Sage.

Habermas, J. (1972). *Knowledge and human interests* (T. McCarthy, Trans.). Boston: Beacon.

Hammersley, M. (1989). *The dilemma of qualitative method: Herbert Blumer and the Chicago tradition.* London: Routledge.

Hammersley, M. (1992a). Some reflections on ethnography and validity. *International Journal of Qualitative Studies in Education, 5,* 195-203.

Hammersley, M. (1992b). *What's wrong with ethnography? Methodological explorations.* London: Routledge.

Harding, S. (1986). *The science question in feminism.* Ithaca, NY: Cornell University Press.

Harding, S. (1987). Is there a feminist method? In S. Harding (Ed.), *Feminism and methodology: Social science issues* (pp. 1-14). Bloomington: Indiana University Press.

Jackson, M. (1989). *Paths toward a clearing: Radical empiricism and ethnographic inquiry.* Bloomington: Indiana University Press.

Joas, H. (1987). Symbolic interactionism. In A. Giddens & J. Turner (Eds.), *Social theory today* (pp. 82-115). Stanford, CA: Stanford University Press.

Jonsen, A. R., & Toulmin, S. (1988). *The abuse of casuistry: A history of moral reasoning.* Berkeley: University of California Press.

Kirk, J., & Miller, M. L. (1986). *Reliability and validity in qualitative research.* Newbury Park, CA: Sage.

Knorr-Cetina, K. D. (1981). *The manufacture of knowledge: An essay on the constructivist and contextual nature of science.* New York: Pergamon.

LeCompte, M. D., & Preissle, J., with Tesch, R. (1993). *Ethnography and qualitative design in educational research* (2nd ed.). New York: Academic Press.

Lincoln, Y. S., & Guba, E. G. (1985). *Naturalistic inquiry.* Beverly Hills, CA: Sage.

MacIntyre, A. (1977). Epistemological crises, dramatic narrative and the philosophy of science. *Monist, 60,* 453-472.

MacIntyre, A. (1981). *After virtue.* Notre Dame, IN: University of Notre Dame Press.

Madison, G. B. (1988). *The hermeneutics of postmodernity.* Bloomington: Indiana University Press.

Magoon, A. J. (1977). Constructivist approaches in educational research. *Review of Educational Research, 47,* 651-693.

Martin, E. (1987). *The woman in the body.* Boston: Beacon.

Matthews, M. R. (1992, March). *Old wine in new bottles: A problem with constructivist epistemology.* Paper presented at the annual meeting of the Philosophy of Education Society, Denver, CO.

Meltzer, B. N., Petras, J. W., & Reynolds, L. T. (1975). *Symbolic interactionism: Genesis, varieties and criticism.* London: Routledge & Kegan Paul.

Mies, M. (1983). Towards a methodology for feminist research. In G. Bowles & R. Duelli-Klein (Eds.), *Theories of women's studies* (pp. 117-139). London: Routledge & Kegan Paul.

Nagel, E. (1961). *The structure of science.* New York: Harcourt Brace.

Novak, J. D. (Ed.). (1987). *Proceedings of the second international seminar: Misconceptions and educational strategies in science and mathematics* (Vols. 1-3). Ithaca, NY: Cornell University Press.

Oakley, A. (1981). Interviewing women: A contradiction in terms. In H. Roberts (Ed.), *Doing feminist research* (pp. 30-61). London: Routledge.

Plummer, K. (Ed.). (1991). *Symbolic interactionism: Vols. 1 and 2. Classic and contemporary issues.* Hauts, England: Edward Elgar.

Rabinow, P. (1977). *Reflections on fieldwork in Morocco.* Berkeley: University of California Press.

Rabinow, P. (1986). Representations are social facts: Modernity and post-modernity in anthropology. In J. Clifford & G. E. Marcus (Eds.), *Writing culture: The poetics and politics of ethnography* (pp. 234-261). Berkeley: University of California Press.

Rabinow, P., & Sullivan, W. M. (1987). The interpretive turn: A second look. In P. Rabinow & W. M. Sullivan (Eds.), *Interpretive social science: A second look* (pp. 1-30). Berkeley: University of California Press.

Radway, J. (1984). *Reading the romance: Feminism and the representation of women in popular culture.* Chapel Hill: University of North Carolina Press.

Reinharz, S. (1992). *Feminist methods in social research.* New York: Oxford University Press.

Ricoeur, P. (1971). The model of the text: Meaningful action considered as a text. *Social Research, 38,* 529-562.

Riger, S. (1992). Epistemological debates, feminist voices: Science, social values, and the study of women. *American Psychologist, 47,* 730-740.

Rorty, R. (1982). *Consequences of pragmatism.* Minneapolis: University of Minnesota Press.

Rosenau, P. M. (1992). *Post-modernism and the social sciences: Insights, inroads, and intrusion.* Princeton, NJ: Princeton University Press.

Rudner, R. (1966). *Philosophy of social science.* Englewood Cliffs, NJ: Prentice Hall.

Sarbin, T. (Ed.). (1986). *Narrative psychology: The storied nature of human conduct.* New York: Praeger.

Sass, L. A. (1988). Humanism, hermeneutics, and the concept of the human subject. In S. B. Messer, L. A. Sass, & R. L. Woolfolk (Eds.), *Hermeneutics and psychological theory* (pp. 222-271). New Brunswick, NJ: Rutgers University Press.

Schutz, A. (1967). *Collected papers* (Vol. 1, M. Natanson, Ed. and Trans.). The Hague: Martinus Nijhoff.

Shapiro, M. J. (1981). *Language and political understanding: The politics of discursive practices.* New Haven, CT: Yale University Press.

Smith, D. (1987). *The everyday world as problematic.* Boston: Northeastern University Press.

Smith, J. K. (1989). *The nature of social and educational inquiry: Empiricism versus interpretation.* Norwood, NJ: Ablex.

Stacey, J. (1988). Can there be a feminist ethnography? *Women's Studies International Forum, 11,* 21-27.

Stake, R. E. (1991). Retrospective on "The countenance of educational evaluation." In M. W. McLaughlin & D. C. Phillips (Eds.), *Evaluation and education at the quarter century: Ninetieth yearbook of the National Society for the Study of Education* (Part 2, pp. 67-88). Chicago: University of Chicago Press.

Steier, F. (1991). Introduction: Research as self-reflexivity, self-reflexivity as social process. In F. Steier (Ed.), *Research and reflexivity* (pp. 1-11). Newbury Park, CA: Sage.

Strike, K. A. (1987). Toward a coherent constructivism, In J. D. Novak (Ed.), *Proceedings of the second international seminar: Misconceptions and educational strategies in science and mathematics* (Vol. 1, pp. 481-489). Ithaca, NY: Cornell University Press.

Sullivan, W. (1986). *Reconstructing public philosophy.* Berkeley: University of California Press.

Taylor, C. (1964). *The explanation of behaviour.* London: Routledge & Kegan Paul.

Taylor, C. (1987). Interpretation and the sciences of man. In P. Rabinow & W. M. Sullivan (Eds.), *Interpretive social science: A second look* (pp. 33-81). Berkeley: University of California Press. (Reprinted from *Review of Metaphysics,* 1971, *25,* 3-51)

Taylor, C. (1989). *Sources of the self.* Cambridge, MA: Harvard University Press.

Toulmin, S. (1982). The construal of reality: Criticism in modern and postmodern science. In W. J. T. Mitchell (Ed.), *The politics of interpretation* (pp. 99-117). Chicago: University of Chicago Press.

Van Maanen, J. (1988). *Tales of the field: On writing ethnography.* Chicago: University of Chicago Press.

von Glasersfeld, E. (1989). Cognition, construction of knowledge, and teaching. *Synthese, 80,* 121-140.

von Glasersfeld, E. (1991). Knowing without metaphysics: Aspects of the radical constructivist position. In F. Steier (Ed.), *Research and reflexivity* (pp. 12-29). Newbury Park, CA: Sage.

Wachterhauser, B. R. (1986). Introduction: History and language in understanding. In B. R. Wachterhauser (Ed.), *Hermeneutics and modern philosophy* (pp. 5-61). Albany: State University of New York Press.

West, C. (1989). *The American evasion of philosophy: A genealogy of pragmatism.* Madison: University of Wisconsin Press.

Wolcott, H. F. (1988). Ethnographic research in education. In R. M. Jaeger (Ed.), *Complementary methods for research in education* (pp. 187-249). Washington, DC: American Educational Research Association.

Wolcott, H. F. (1992). Posturing in qualitative inquiry. In M. D. LeCompte, W. L. Millroy, & J. Preissle (Eds.), *The handbook of qualitative research in education* (pp. 3-52). New York: Academic Press.

8

Rethinking Critical Theory and Qualitative Research

Joe L. Kincheloe & Peter L. McLaren

◆ The Roots of Critical Research

Some 70 years after its development in Frankfurt, Germany, critical theory retains its ability to disrupt and challenge the status quo. In the process, it elicits highly charged emotions of all types—fierce loyalty from its proponents, vehement hostility from its detractors. Such vibrantly polar reactions indicate at the very least that critical theory still matters. We can be against critical theory or for it, but, especially at the present historical juncture, we cannot be without it. Indeed, qualitative research that frames its purpose in the context of critical theoretical concerns still produces, in our view, undeniably dangerous knowledge, the kind of information and insight that upsets institutions and threatens to overturn sovereign regimes of truth.

Critical theory is a term that is often evoked and frequently misunderstood. It usually refers to the theoretical tradition developed by the Frankfurt school, a group of writers connected to the Institute of Social Research at the University of Frankfurt. However, none of the Frankfurt

AUTHORS' NOTE: Thanks to Yvonna Lincoln and Norman Denzin for their helpful suggestions on an earlier draft of this chapter.

school theorists ever claimed to have developed a unified approach to cultural criticism. In its beginnings, Max Horkheimer, Theodor Adorno, and Herbert Marcuse initiated a conversation with the German tradition of philosophical and social thought, especially Marx, Kant, Hegel, and Weber. From the vantage point of these critical theorists, whose political sensibilities were influenced by the devastations of World War I, postwar Germany with its economic depression marked by inflation and unemployment, and the failed strikes and protests in Germany and Central Europe in this same period, the world was in urgent need of reinterpretation. From this perspective, they defied Marxist orthodoxy while deepening their belief that injustice and subjugation shaped the lived world (Bottomore, 1984; Gibson, 1986; Held, 1980; Jay, 1973). Focusing their attention on the changing nature of capitalism, the early critical theorists analyzed the mutating forms of domination that accompanied this change (Giroux, 1983; McLaren, 1989).

Only a decade after the Frankfurt school was established, the Nazis controlled Germany. The danger posed by the exclusive Jewish membership of the Frankfurt school, and its association with Marxism, convinced Horkheimer, Adorno, and Marcuse to leave Germany. Eventually locating themselves in California, these critical theorists were shocked by American culture. Offended by the taken-for-granted empirical practices of American social science researchers, Horkheimer, Adorno, and Marcuse were challenged to respond to the social science establishment's belief that their research could describe and accurately measure any dimension of human behavior. Piqued by the contradictions between progressive American rhetoric of egalitarianism and the reality of racial and class discrimination, these theorists produced their major work while residing in the United States. In 1953, Horkheimer and Adorno returned to Germany and reestablished the Institute of Social Research. Significantly, Herbert Marcuse stayed in the United States, where he would find a new audience for his work in social theory. Much to his own surprise, Marcuse skyrocketed to fame as the philosopher of the student movements of the 1960s. Critical theory, especially the emotionally and sexually liberating work of Marcuse, provided the philosophical voice of the New Left. Concerned with the politics of psychological and cultural revolution, the New Left preached a Marcusian sermon of political emancipation (Gibson, 1986; Wexler, 1991).

Many academicians who had come of age in the politically charged atmosphere of the 1960s focused their scholarly attention on critical theory. Frustrated by forms of domination emerging from a post-Enlightenment culture nurtured by capitalism, these scholars saw in critical theory a method of temporarily freeing academic work from these forms of power. Impressed by critical theory's dialectical concern with the social construction of experience, they came to view their disciplines as manifestations of the discourses and power relations of the social and historical contexts that produced them. The "discourse of possibility" implicit within the constructed nature of social experience suggested to these scholars that a reconstruction of the social sciences could eventually lead to a more egalitarian and democratic social order. New poststructuralist conceptualizations of human agency and their promise that men and women can at least partly determine their own existence offered new hope for emancipatory forms of social research when compared with orthodox Marxism's assertion of the iron laws of history, the irrevocable evil of capitalism, and the proletariat as the privileged subject and anticipated agent of social transformation. For example, when Henry Giroux and other critical educators criticized the argument made by Marxist scholars Samuel Bowles and Herbert Gintis—that schools were capitalist agencies of social, economic, cultural, and bureaucratic reproduction—they contrasted the deterministic perspectives of Bowles and Gintis with the idea that schools, as venues of hope, could become sites of resistance and democratic possibility through concerted efforts among teachers and students to work within a liberatory pedagogical framework. Giroux (1988), in particular, maintained that schools can become institutions where forms of knowledge, values, and social relations are taught for the purpose of educating young people for critical empowerment rather than subjugation.

◆ Partisan Research in a "Neutral" Academic Culture

In the space available here it is impossible to do justice to all of the critical traditions that have drawn inspiration from Marx, Kant, Hegel, Weber, the Frankfurt school theorists, continental social theorists such as Foucault, Habermas, and Derrida, Latin American thinkers such as Paulo Freire, French feminists such as Irigaray, Kristeva, or Cixous, or Russian sociolinguists such as Bakhtin and Vygotsky—most of whom regularly find their way into the reference lists of contemporary critical researchers. Today there are criticalist schools in many fields, and even a superficial discussion of the most prominent of these schools would demand much more space than we have available.

The fact that numerous books have been written about the often-virulent disagreements among members of the Frankfurt school only heightens our concern with "packaging" the different criticalist schools. Critical theory should not be treated as a universal grammar of revolutionary thought objectified and reduced to discrete formulaic pronouncements or strategies. We have chosen to define the critical tradition very broadly and heuristically, and this will undoubtedly trouble many researchers who identify themselves as criticalists. We have decided to place our stress on the underlying commonality among these schools of thought, at the expense of focusing on their differences. This, of course, is always risky business in terms of suggesting a false unity or consensus where none exists, but such concerns are unavoidable in a survey chapter such as this. We are defining a criticalist as a researcher or theorist who attempts to use her or his work as a form of social or cultural criticism and who accepts certain basic assumptions: that all thought is fundamentally mediated by power relations that are social and historically constituted; that facts can never be isolated from the domain of values or removed from some form of ideological inscription; that the relationship between concept and object and between signifier and signified is never stable or fixed and is often mediated by the social relations of capitalist production and consumption; that language is central to the formation of subjectivity (conscious and unconscious awareness); that certain groups in any society are privileged over others and, although the reasons for this privileging may vary widely, the oppression that characterizes contemporary societies is most forcefully reproduced when subordinates accept their social status as natural, necessary, or inevitable; that oppression has many faces and that focusing on only one at the expense of others (e.g., class oppression versus racism) often elides the interconnections among them; and, finally, that mainstream research practices are generally, although most often unwittingly, implicated in the reproduction of systems of class, race, and gender oppression.

In today's climate of blurred disciplinary genres, it is not uncommon to find literary theorists doing anthropology and anthropologists writing about literary theory, or political scientists trying their hand at ethnomethodological analysis, or philosophers doing Lacanian film criticism. We offer this observation not as an excuse to be wantonly eclectic in our treatment of the critical tradition but to make the point that any attempts to delineate critical theory as discrete schools of analysis will fail to capture the hybridity endemic to contemporary criticalist analysis.

Readers familiar with the criticalist traditions will recognize essentially four different "emergent" schools of social inquiry in this chapter: the neo-Marxist tradition of critical theory associated most closely with the work of Horkheimer, Adorno, and Marcuse; the genealogical writings of Michel Foucault; the practices of poststructuralist deconstruction associated with Derrida; and postmodernist currents associated with Derrida, Foucault, Lyotard, Ebert, and others. In our view, critical ethnography has been influenced by all of these perspectives in different ways and to different degrees. From critical theory, researchers inherit a forceful criticism of the positivist conception of science and instrumental rationality, especially in Adorno's idea of *negative dialectics,* which posits an unstable relationship of contradiction between concepts and objects; from Derrida, researchers are given a means for deconstructing objective truth or what is referred to as "the metaphysics of presence." For Derrida, the meaning of a word is constantly deferred because it can have meaning only in relation to its difference from other words within a given system of language; Foucault invites researchers to explore the ways in which discourses are implicated in relations of power and how power and knowledge serve as dialectically reinitiating practices that regulate what is considered reasonable and true. We have characterized much of the work influenced by these writers as the "ludic" and "resistance" postmodernist theoretical perspectives.

Critical research can be best understood in the context of the empowerment of individuals. Inquiry that aspires to the name *critical* must be connected to an attempt to confront the injustice of a particular society or sphere within the society. Research thus becomes a transformative endeavor unembarrassed by the label "political" and unafraid to consummate a relationship with an emancipatory consciousness. Whereas traditional researchers cling to the guard rail of neutrality, critical researchers frequently announce their partisanship in the struggle for a better world. Traditional researchers see their task as the description, interpretation, or reanimation of a slice of reality, whereas critical researchers often regard their work as a first step toward forms of political action that can redress the injustices found in the field site or constructed in the very act of research itself. Horkheimer (1972) put it succinctly when he argued that critical theory and research are never satisfied with merely increasing knowledge (see also Giroux, 1983, 1988; Quantz, 1992).

Research in the critical tradition takes the form of self-conscious criticism—self-conscious in the sense that researchers try to become aware of the ideological imperatives and epistemological presuppositions that inform their research as well as their own subjective, intersubjective, and normative reference claims. Thus critical researchers enter into an investigation with their assumptions on the table, so no one is confused concerning the epistemological and political baggage they bring with them to the research site. Upon detailed analysis these assumptions may change. Stimulus for change may come from the critical researchers' recognition that such assumptions are not leading to emancipatory actions. The source of this emancipatory action involves the researcher's ability to expose the contradictions of world of appearances accepted by the dominant culture as natural and inviolable (Giroux, 1983; McLaren, 1989, 1992a, 1997a, 1997b). Such appearances may, critical researchers contend, conceal social relationships of inequality and injustice. For instance, if we view the violence we find in classrooms not as random or isolated incidents created by aberrant individuals willfully stepping out of line in accordance with a particular form of social pathology, but as narratives of transgression and resistance, then this could indicate that the "political unconscious" lurking beneath the surface of everyday classroom life is not unrelated to issues of race, class, and gender oppression.

There exists among critical researchers a firm recognition that ideologies are not simply deceptive and imaginary mental relations that individuals and groups live out relative to their material conditions of existence, but are also very much inscribed in the materiality of social and institutional practices (Kincheloe, 1993; McLaren, 1989, 1997a). For instance, people act *as if* certain social and cultural relations were true even when they know them not to be true. They choose, in other words, essentially to misrecognize these relations of power (e.g., state power exists only because we obey its rules). Generally speaking, people do not necessarily want to give up this misrecognition (Zizek, 1990) because of the power it affords them as dominant groups or, in the case of subordinate groups, because "the ruled accept their subordinate position for the sake of a degree of freedom that indulges certain libidinal drives, sutures fissured egos, fulfills fantasies, and so forth" (San Juan, 1992, p. 114). This willful misrecognition on the part of both dominant and subordinate groups creates a quarantined site where the political dimensions of everyday life can be shrouded by commonsense knowledge and, in effect, rhetorically disengaged. This also explains how the ascendancy of a historic bloc of forces is able to reproduce its economies of power and privilege hegemonically (Gramsci, 1971). Hegemony is secured when the virulence of oppression, in its many guises (e.g., race, gender, class, sexual orientation), is accepted as consensus.

◆ Critical Ethnography: Reclaiming the Marxist Legacy in an Age of Socialist Decline

Still in its infancy as a research approach that has developed within the qualitative tradition over the past 20 years, and lacking that obviousness of meaning that would secure its disciplinary status, critical ethnography continues to redefine itself through its alliances with recent theoretical currents. As a nascent transdisciplinary project, it is more readily identified with its celebrated exponents and coprotagonists (e.g., Paul Willis, George Marcus, Christine Griffin, James Clifford, and Michael Taussig) than with the way it has spawned innumerable alliances with leftist political agendas in general and neo-Marxian ones in particular in both Britain and the United States. It is hardly surprising, then, that its distinctive mode of entry into mainstream anthropological and sociological discourses has been stalled because of the quickening predicament generated by the recent demise of Marxism following the collapse of Soviet communism.

The loss of favor accorded to Marxist theory is certainly a partial explanation for critical ethnography's current—and sometimes narcissistic—infatuation with certain inflections and mutative combinations of postmodern social theory that have found their way into the writings of critical ethnographers. We are not suggesting that the turn to high-vogue postmodernism and the fashionable apostasy of deconstruction among some critical ethnographers is simply a substitute for the flagging credibility of Marxism. Rather, we are in basic agreement with Cornel West (1991), who notes that the "fashionable trashing of Marxist thought in the liberal academy" is primarily the result of the misunderstanding that vulgar Marxist thought (monocausal accounts of history, essentialist concepts of society, or reductionist accounts of history) somehow exhausts the entire Marxist tradition. West argues that the epistemic skepticism found in some strands of faddish deconstructive criticism and the explanatory agnosticism, or nihilism, associated with the work of descriptivist anthropologists and historians have made the "category mistake" of collapsing epistemological concerns of justification in philosophy into methodological concerns of explanation in social theory. This has caused ironic skeptics to avoid any theory that promotes purposeful social action for social and economic transformation. This category mistake has also caused the aesthetic historicists to illuminate the contingency and indeterminacy of social life "with little concern with how and why change and conflict take place" (p. xxii).

We follow West in arguing that, although nationalism, racism, gender oppression, homophobia, and ecological devastation have not been adequately understood by many Marxist theorists, Marxist theory nevertheless "proceeds within the boundaries of warranted assertable claims and rationally acceptable conclusions" and that it has helped to explain how "the dynamic processes of capital accumulation and the commodification of labor condition social, and cultural practices in an *inescapable* manner" (p. xxiii).

Douglas Kellner (1993) has recently argued that blaming the failure of Soviet communism on the work of Marx is highly unwarranted, dishonest, misleading, and, ultimately, philosophically indefensible. This is especially the case when one recognizes that Marx's writings support the claim that he was a consistent democrat, argued for workers' self-activity as the locus of popular sovereignty, and refused to advocate a party state or communist bureaucracy. Instead, Marx argued passionately and lucidly for a free society and democratically empowered citizenry. In fact, Kellner maintains, rather convincingly in our view, that the ideas of Rousseau and those of the Right Hegelians actually go much further in legitimating forms of societal oppression and the modern totalitarian state than Marx's theoretical work. Further, Kellner maintains that it is precisely the case that Marxian theorists have themselves produced some of the most trenchant and powerful criticisms of the repressive incarnations of socialism in the Soviet Union, such as the work of the Frankfurt school theorists. Admittedly, however, one of the serious flaws of Marxist discourse is that it regularly fails to incorporate the work of bourgeois revolutionary traditions (i.e., bourgeois traditions of rights and individual liberty) and the Marxian revolutionary socialist heritage into its system.

We suggest that there is nothing inconsistent in the critical and historical impulses of Marxian thought that would preclude the formation of a theoretical alliance with some of the more political strands of postmodern social theory. In fact, postmodern social theory could help to deepen and extend current incarnations of Marxian criticalist thinking significantly by helping to problematize what Stuart Hall (1990) refers to as "the disappearance of unified agency, like the 'ruling class' or 'the state,' as the

267

instrumentality of oppression" (p. 31). In our view, postmodern criticism does not so much weaken the Marxian tradition as help to expand the Marxian critique of capitalist social relations by addressing the ambiguity currently surrounding the reconstituted nature of classes and class consciousness and by interrogating "the cultural logic of late capitalism" (to cite the now-famous phrase coined by Frederic Jameson to describe the postmodern condition). According to Jameson (1990), arguably the most important Marxian literary critic in the United States, "Democracy must involve more than political consultation. There must be forms of economic democracy and popular control in other ways, some of them are very problematic, like workers' management" (p. 31). The popular sovereignty practiced by the Paris Commune and celebrated by Marx and Engels as a democratic mode of worker self-management is a good example of what Jameson means by "economic democracy."

We agree with Jameson that the Marxian tradition still has an indispensable role to play in the reconstitution and reformation of capitalist democracy. We further share Kellner's (1993) sentiment that "only with genuine democracy can socialism provide a real alternative to the democratic capitalist societies of the West and East" (p. 34). The current crisis of Marxism suggests to us not that Marxist discourse is dead and should be displayed, like Lenin, in a glass case as an embalmed reminder of our debt to the founding fathers of the communist state. Nor in a more postmodern sense do we feel it to be destined to lie frozen like the corpse of Walt Disney, hidden away in a theme park vault, waiting to be reanimated at some future moment during the technological triumph of late capitalism. Rather, we believe that a Marxian-inspired critical ethnography deepened by a critical engagement with new currents of postmodern social theory has an important if not crucial role to play in the project of constructing new forms of socialist democracy.

◆ Babes in Toyland: Critical Theory in Hyperreality

Postmodern Culture

In a contemporary era marked by the delegitimation of the grand narratives of Western civilization, a loss of faith in the power of reason, and a shattering of traditional religious orthodoxies, scholars continue to debate what the term *postmodernism* means, generally positing it as a periodizing concept following modernism. Indeed, scholars have not agreed if this epochal break with the "modern" era even constitutes a discrete period. In the midst of such confusion it seems somehow appropriate that scholars are fighting over the application of the term *postmodernism* to the contemporary condition. Accepting postmodernism as an apt moniker for the end of the twentieth century, a major feature of critical academic work has involved the exploration of what happens when critical theory encounters the postmodern condition, or hyperreality. *Hyperreality* is a term used to describe an information society socially saturated with ever-increasing forms of representation: filmic, photographic, electronic, and so on. These have had a profound effect on constructing the cultural narratives that shape our identities. The drama of living has been portrayed so often on television that individuals, for the most part, are increasingly able to predict the outcomes and consider such outcomes to be the "natural" and "normal" course of social life (Gergen, 1991).

As many postmodern analysts have put it, we become pastiches, imitative conglomerations of one another. In such a condition we approach life with low affect, with a sense of postmodern ennui and irremissible anxiety. Our emotional bonds are diffused as television, computers, VCRs, and stereo headphones assault us with representations that have shaped our cognitive and affective facilities in ways that still remain insufficiently understood. In the political arena, traditionalists circle their cultural wagons and fight off imagined bogeymen such as secular humanists, "extreme liberals," and utopianists, not realizing the impact that postmodern hyperreality exerts on their hallowed institutions. The nuclear family, for example, has declined in importance not because of the assault of "radical feminists" but because the home has been redefined through the familiar presence of electronic communication systems. Particular modes of information put individual family members in constant contact with specific subcultures. While they are physically in the home, they exist emotionally outside of it through the mediating effects of various forms of communication (Gergen, 1991; McLaren, 1997a; Poster, 1989). We increasingly make sense of the social world and judge other cultures through conventional and culture-bound television genres. Hyperreality has presented us with new forms of literacy that do not simply refer to discrete skills but rather constitute social skills and relations of symbolic power. These new technologies cannot be seen apart from the social and institutional contexts in which they are used and the roles they play in the family, the community, and the workplace. They also need to be seen in terms of how "viewing competencies" are socially distributed and the diverse social and discursive practices in which these new media literacies are produced (Buckingham, 1989).

Electronic transmissions generate new formations of cultural space and restructure experiences of time. We often are motivated to trade community membership for a sense of psuedobelonging to the mediascape. Residents of hyperreality are temporarily comforted by proclamations of community offered by "media personalities" on the 6 o'clock *Eyewitness News.* "Bringing news of your neighbors in the Tri-State community home to you," media marketers attempt to soften the edges of hyperreality, to soften the emotional effects of the social vertigo. The world is not brought into our homes by television as much as television brings its viewers to a quasi-fictional place—hyperreality (Luke, 1991).

Postmodern Social Theory

We believe that it is misleading to identify postmodernism with poststructuralism. Although there are certainly similarities involved, they cannot be considered discrete homologies. We also believe that it is a mistake to equate *postmodernism* with *postmodernity* or that these terms can be contrasted in some simple equivalent way with *modernism* and *modernity.* As Michael Peters (1993) notes, "To do so is to frame up the debate in strictly (and naively) modernist terminology which employs exhaustive binary oppositions privileging one set of terms against the other" (p. 14). We are using the term *postmodernity* to refer to the postmodern condition that we have described as *hyperreality* and the term *postmodern theory* as an umbrella term that includes antifoundationalist writing in philosophy and the social sciences. Again, we are using the term in a very general sense that includes poststructuralist currents.

Postmodern theoretical trajectories take as their entry point a rejection of the deeply ingrained assumptions of Enlightenment rationality, traditional Western epistemology, or any supposedly "secure" representation of reality that exists outside of discourse itself. Doubt is cast on the myth of the autonomous, transcendental subject, and the concept of praxis is marginalized in favor of rhetorical undecidability and textual analysis of social practices. As a species of criticism, intended, in part, as a central requestioning of the humanism and anthropologism of the early 1970s, postmodernist social theory rejects Hegel's ahistorical state of absolute knowledge and resigns itself to the impossibility of an ahistorical, transcendental, or self-authenticating version of truth. The reigning conviction that knowledge is knowledge only if it reflects the world as it "really" exists has been annihilated in favor of a view in which reality is socially constructed or semiotically posited. Furthermore, normative agreement on what should constitute and guide scientific practice and argumentative consistency has become an intellectual target for epistemological uncertainty.

Postmodern criticism takes as its starting point the notion that meaning is constituted by the continual playfulness of the signifier, and the thrust of its critique is aimed at deconstructing Western metanarratives of truth and the ethnocentrism implicit in the European view of history as the unilinear progress of universal reason. Postmodern theory is a site of both hope and fear, where there exists a strange convergence between critical theorists and political conservatives, a cynical complicity with status quo social and institutional relations and a fierce criticism of ideological manipulation and the reigning practices of subjectivity in which knowledge takes place.

◆ Ludic and Resistance Postmodernism

Postmodernist criticism is not monolithic, and for the purposes of this essay we would like to distinguish between two theoretical strands. The first has been astutely described by Teresa Ebert (1991) as "ludic postmodernism" (p. 115)—an approach to social theory that is decidedly limited in its ability to transform oppressive social and political regimes of power. Ludic postmodernism generally occupies itself with a reality that is constituted by the continual playfulness of the signifier and the heterogeneity of differences. As such, ludic postmodernism (see, e.g., Lyotard, Derrida, Baudrillard) constitutes a moment of self-reflexivity in deconstructing Western metanarratives, asserting that "meaning itself is self-divided and undecidable" (Ebert, in press).

We want to argue that critical researchers should assume a cautionary stance toward ludic postmodernism critique because, as Ebert (1991, p. 115) notes, it tends to reinscribe the status quo and reduce history to the supplementarity of signification or the free-floating trace of textuality. As a mode of critique, it rests its case on interrogating specific and local enunciations of oppression, but often fails to analyze such enunciations in relation to larger dominating structures of oppression (Aronowitz & Giroux, 1991; McLaren, 1997a).

The kind of postmodern social theory we want to pose as a counterweight to skeptical and spectral postmodernism has been referred to as "oppositional postmodernism" (Foster, 1983), "radical critique-al theory" (Zavarzadeh & Morton, 1991), "postmodern education" (Aronowitz & Giroux, 1991), "resistance postmodernism" (Ebert, 1991, in press), and "critical postmodernism" (Giroux, 1992; McLaren, 1992b, 1997a; McLaren & Hammer, 1989). These forms of critique are not alternatives to ludic postmodernism but appropriations and extensions of this critique. Resistance postmodernism brings to ludic critique a form of materialist intervention, because it is not solely based on a textual theory of difference but rather on one that is also social and historical. In this way, postmodern critique can serve as an interventionist and transformative critique of Western culture. Following Ebert (1991), resistance postmodernism attempts to show that "textualities (significations) are material practices, forms of conflicting social relations" (p. 115). The sign is always an arena of material conflict and competing social relations as well as ideas. From this perspective we can "rewrite the sign as an ideological process formed out of a signifier standing in relation to a matrix of historically possible or suspended signifieds" (Ebert, in press). In other words, difference is politicized by being situated in real social and historical conflicts.

Resistance postmodernism does not abandon the undecidability or contingency of the social altogether; rather, the undecidability of history is understood as related to class struggle, the institutionalization of asymmetrical relations of power and privilege, and the way historical accounts are contested by different groups (Giroux, 1992; McLaren & Hammer, 1989; Zavarzadeh & Morton, 1991). On this matter Ebert (1991) remarks, "We need to articulate a theory of difference in which the differing, deferring slippage of signifiers is not taken as the result of the immanent logic of language but as the effect of the social conflicts traversing signification" (p. 118).

The synergism of the conversation between resistance postmodern and critical theory involves an interplay between the praxis of the critical and the radical uncertainty of the postmodern. As it invokes its strategies for the emancipation of meaning, critical theory provides the postmodern critique with a normative foundation (i.e., a basis for distinguishing between oppressive and liberatory social relations). Without such a foundation the postmodern critique is ever vulnerable to nihilism and inaction. Indeed, the normatively ungrounded postmodern critique is incapable of providing an ethically challenging and politically transformative program of action. Aronowitz, Giroux, and McLaren argue that if the postmodern critique is to make a valuable contribution to the notion of schooling as an emancipatory form of cultural politics, it must make connections to those egalitarian impulses of modernism that contribute to an emancipatory democracy. In doing this, the project of an emancipatory democracy and the schooling that supports it can be extended by new understandings of how power operates and by incorporating groups who had been excluded by their race, gender, or class (Aronowitz & Giroux, 1991; Codd, 1984; Godzich, 1992; Lash, 1990; McLaren, 1986, 1997a; Morrow, 1991; Rosenau, 1992; Welch, 1991; Yates, 1990).

◆ A Step Beyond the Empirical: Critical Research

Critical research has never been reluctant to point out the limitations of empirical research, calling attention to the inability of traditional models of inquiry to escape the boundaries of a narrative realism. The rigorous methodological approaches of empirical inquiry often preclude larger interpretations of the forces that shape both the researcher and the researched. Empirical observation cannot supplant theoretical analysis and critical reflection. The project of critical research is not simply the empirical re-presentation of the world but the transgressive task of posing the research itself as a set of ideological practices. Empirical analysis needs to be interrogated in order to uncover the contradictions and negations embodied in any objective description. Critical researchers maintain that the meaning of an experience or an observation is not self-evident. The meaning of any experience will depend on the struggle over the interpretation and definition of that experience (Giroux, 1983; McLaren, 1986; Weiler, 1988).

Kincheloe (1991) argues that the way we analyze and interpret empirical data is conditioned by the way it is theoretically framed. It is also dependent upon the researcher's own ideological assumptions. The empirical data derived from any study cannot be treated as simple irrefutable facts. They represent hidden assumptions—assumptions the critical researcher must dig out and expose. As Einstein and Heisenberg pointed out long ago, what we see is not what we see but what we perceive. The knowledge that the world yields has to be interpreted by men and women who are a part of that world. What we call information always involves an act of human judgment. From a critical perspective this act of judgment is an interpretive act. The interpretation of theory, critical analysts contend, involves understanding the relationship between the particular and the whole and between the subject and the object of analysis. Such a position contradicts the traditional empiricist contention that theory is basically a matter of classifying objective data.

One of the most important sites of theoretical production in the history of critical research has been the Centre for Contemporary Cultural Studies (CCCS) at the University of Birmingham. Attempting to connect critical theory with the particularity of everyday experience, the CCCS researchers have argued that all experience is vulnerable to ideological inscription. At the same time, they have maintained that theorizing outside of everyday experience results in formal and deterministic theory. An excellent representative of the CCCS's perspectives is Paul Willis, who published *Learning to Labour: How Working Class Kids Get Working Class Jobs* in 1977, seven years after Colin Lacey's *Hightown Grammar* (1970). Redefining the nature of ethnographic research in a critical manner, *Learning to Labour* inspired a spate of critical studies: David Robins and Philip Cohen's *Knuckle Sandwich: Growing Up in the Working-Class City* in 1978, Paul Corrigan's *Schooling the Smash Street Kids* in 1979, and Dick Hebdige's *Subculture: The Meaning of Style* in 1979.

Also following Willis's work were critical feminist studies, including an anthology titled *Women Take Issue* (Centre for Contemporary Culture Studies, 1978). In 1985 Christine Griffin published *Typical Girls?*, the first extended feminist study produced by the CCCS. Conceived as a response to Willis's *Learning to Labour, Typical Girls?* analyzes adolescent female consciousness as it is constructed in a world of patriarchy. Through their recognition of patriarchy as a major disciplinary technology in the production of subjectivity, Griffin and the members of the CCCS gender study group move critical research in a multicultural direction. In addition to the examination of class, gender and racial analyses are beginning to gain in importance (Quantz, 1992). Poststructuralism frames power not simply as one aspect of a society, but as the basis of society. Thus patriarchy is not simply one isolated force among many with which women must contend; patriarchy informs all aspects of the social and effectively shapes women's lives.

274

Cornel West pushes critical research even further into the multicultural domain as he focuses critical attention on women, the Third World, and race. Adopting theoretical advances in neo-Marxist postcolonialism criticism and cultural studies, he is able to shed greater light on the workings of power in everyday life.

In *Schooling as a Ritual Performance,* Peter McLaren (1986) integrates poststructuralist and postcolonial criticism theory with the project of critical ethnography. He grounds his theoretical analysis in the poststructuralist claim that the connection of signifier and signified is arbitrary yet shaped by historical, cultural, and economic forces. The primary cultural narrative that defines school life is the resistance by students to the school's attempts to marginalize their street culture and street knowledge. McLaren analyzes the school as a cultural site where symbolic capital is struggled over in the form of ritual dramas. *Schooling as a Ritual Performance* adopts the position that researchers are unable to grasp themselves or others introspectively without social mediation through their positionalities with respect to race, class, gender, and other configurations. The visceral, bodily forms of knowledge, and the rhythms and gestures of the street culture of the students, are distinguished from the formal abstract knowledge of classroom instruction. Knowledge as it is constructed informally outside of the culture of school instruction is regarded by the teachers as threatening to the universalist and decidedly Eurocentric ideal of high culture that forms the basis of the school curriculum.

As critical researchers pursue this synergism between critical theory and postmodernism, they are confronted with postmodernism's redefinition of critical notions of democracy in terms of the concepts of multiplicity and difference. Traditional notions of community often privilege unity over diversity in the name of Enlightenment values. Poststructuralists in general and poststructuralist feminists in particular see this communitarian dream as politically disabling because of the suppression of race, class, and gender differences and the exclusion of subaltern voices and marginalized groups whom community members are loath to engage. What begins to emerge in this instance is the movement of feminist theoretical concerns to the center of critical theory. Indeed, after the feminist critique critical theory can never return to a paradigm of inquiry in which the concept of social class is antiseptically privileged and exalted as the master concept in the Holy Trinity of Race, Class, and Gender. A critical theory reconceptualized by poststructuralism and feminism promotes a politics of difference that refuses to pathologize or exoticize the Other. In this context, communities are more prone to revitalization; peripheralized groups in the thrall of a condescending Eurocentric gaze are able to edge closer to the borders of respect, and "classified" objects of research potentially acquire the characteristics of subjecthood. Kathleen Weiler's *Women Teaching for Change: Gender, Class, and Power* (1988) serves as a good example of critical research framed by feminist theory. Weiler shows not only how feminist theory can extend critical research, but how the concept of emancipation can be reconceptualized in light of a feminist epistemology (Aronowitz & Giroux, 1991; Lugones, 1987; Morrow, 1991; Weiler, 1988; Young, 1990).

As a "postmodernized" critical theory comes to grasp the particularity of oppression more adequately, it realizes that such particularity cannot be explained away by abstract theories of political and cultural systems that exalt the fixed virtues of cultural rootedness over the instability and uncertainty of cultural struggle. At the same time, the concept of totality, which locates the particularity of experience in wider totalities such as patriarchy and capitalism, must not be forsaken (Giroux, 1993; McLaren, 1993a). Feminists such as Britzman (1991), Fine (1988), Benhabib and Cornell (1987), Flax (1990), Pagano (1990), Hutcheon (1989), Kipnis (1988), and Morris (1988), and analysts of gender and race such as hooks (1989), Fox-Genovese (1988), Jordan (1985), and Walker (1983), have taught critical theorists that whereas larger social forces clearly exert a profound impact on society at large, their impact on individuals and localities is ambiguous and idiosyncratic. In this same context Joe Kincheloe and William Pinar's theory of place in *Curriculum as Social Psychoanalysis: Essays on the Significance of Place* (1991a) expands the notion of particularity and its relationship to wider, discursive regimes in the context of critical social theory and the politics of curriculum theory.

In light of this work in gender, race, and place, the traditional critical concept of emancipation cannot remain unaffected. The narrative of emancipation is not forsaken, but it no longer becomes a determining master narrative. Rather, it takes the form of a contingent foundation out of which further dialogue can develop that is attentive to the contextual specificity of the local and the overdetermining characteristics of larger institutional and social structures (Butler, 1990). Further, critical researchers understand that individual identity and human agency form such a chaotic knot of intertwined articulations that no social theorist can ever completely disentangle them. Without such a cautionary stance, any critical theory is vulnerable to the rationalistic tendency to develop a road map to a "logical future," a direct turnpike to the Emerald City of emancipation. Foucault, of course, placed the final postmodern obstacle in the road to emancipation in his prescient exegesis on the relationship between power and discourse. By arguing that power is innate to the structure of discourse, Foucault shed important light on the naive utopian thinking that would annul power relations (Luke, 1991; Morrow, 1991). If history is traveling to some emancipated and unitary community, then subjectivity must become unified and coherent. Postmodernist critical perspectives deny such a simplistic view of identity (postidentity). Thus modernist conceptions of critical emancipation are defrocked as the "blessed redeemer" of sociopolitical life. After this poststructuralist confrontation, the modernist deployment of the term *emancipation* can never escape questioning; it can never "hide out" in the form of a grand (usually phallocentric) narrative guarding the vital ingredients of the Western Enlightenment and supplanting and transcending the postmodern emphasis on social and cultural particularity—a particularity always in dialogue with the totality of social relations.

◆ An Example:
Workers as Critical Researchers

An example of how qualitative research grounded in postmodern critical theory might be employed involves a discussion of workers as critical researchers. Here in this traditionally class-driven category, how might postmodern theory help researchers reconceptualize critical inquiry? Many of us have been conditioned to believe that work is improving in terms of both job satisfaction and worker involvement in the administration of the workplace. Management-dominated media assure the public that the field of management has become more self-reflective about the ideologies that inform its own procedural norms, that is, top-down authoritarian management styles and low-skill labor policy. The service and information-based economy, we are told, with its high-tech innovations and computerization, is producing empowered white-collar workers. Such claims do not hold up under examination. First of all, service and information jobs are primarily low-skill, low-paying positions. Contrary to the media message, even goods-producing jobs demand higher pay than service and information jobs. Second, women hold more than half the jobs in the service and information economy, and females have traditionally received less money and decision-making power in the workplace than have males. This feminization of service and information jobs does not bode well for the long-term prospects for democratizing work (Harris, 1981; Wirth, 1983).

Embracing critical postmodern goals of empowerment, workers can use qualitative research to uncover the way power operates to construct their everyday commonsense knowledge and undermine their autonomy as professionals. As they explore the market-driven objectives that shape the ways their jobs are defined, workers can begin to see themselves in relation to the world around them, and to perceive the workplace as a site within larger economies of power and privilege. Such explorations can serve as invitations to workers to understand both the way the workplace is "governed" by a top-down series of directives and the way power is utilized on a day-to-day basis. They come to see the language of the marketplace as a tradition of mediation that defines whose knowledge is most legitimate and whose voices count the most. In the workplace of the late industrial era, workers as critical qualitative researchers are encouraged to challenge their positionality as reified objects of administration defined by prevailing discourses of what counts as "work" and "being a worker." As critical workers uncover the regimes of discourse that construct the meaning of work within the context of a post-Fordist global economy and workplace and the organizational hierarchy that supports them, they can begin to realize that the systems of discourse that interpellate them as workers operate within a milieu driven by the logic of capital. Further, questions of production and profit take precedence over questions of justice and humanity. Workers as researchers discover that concerns with the intellectual or moral development of the workforce often cannot be granted serious consideration in the "no-nonsense" ambience of business discourse. The democratic vision of critical workers who are capable of evaluating a job in terms of its social significance or its moral effects becomes, from the perspective of management, the talk of an impractical and quixotic group of workers too removed from the demands of economic survival in a global marketplace (Feinberg & Horowitz, 1990; Ferguson, 1984).

Confronted by the antidemocratic features of the postmodern condition, workers as critical qualitative researchers become translators of democracy in a hegemonically expanding landscape. In their struggle to translate and interpret the conditions that define their own labor, critical workers recognize capital's growing control over information flow. They come to understand that fewer and fewer corporations control more and more of the production of information. They discover that the postmodern corporation frequently regards the advertising of products to be secondary to the promotion of a positive corporate image. Controlling information in this way enhances the corporation's power, as it engages the public in relating positively to the goals and the "mission" of the corporation. In this way corporations can better shape government policy, control public images of labor-management relations, and portray workers in a way that enhances the self-interest of management. As a result, corporate taxes are minimized, wages are lowered, mergers are deregulated, corporate leaders are lionized, and managerial motives are unquestioned (Harvey, 1989).

So powerful is this corporate control over information flow that other social institutions often defer to its authority. Because of the fear of corporate reprisals, television news often covers only the consequences, and not the causes, of news events. In its coverage of unemployment, for example, TV news has typically avoided analysis of miscalculated corporate policies or managerial attempts to discipline employees. Fearful of corporate charges of bias, broadcasters frame explanations of unemployment within a "times are tough" motif. The current situation victimizes workers, but, reporters assure us, bad times will pass. Unemployment is thus causeless, the capricious result of a natural sequence of events. There is nothing we can do about it. This is the point of intervention for worker researchers; critical workers attempt to uncover the causes of unemployment unaddressed by the media. As these researchers demand access to the airwaves, the public comes to understand that unemployment is not as natural a process as it has been portrayed. A democratic debate about national economic policy is initiated (Apple, 1992).

Bringing a number of postmodern discourses to the negotiating table, critical worker researchers question the productivist biases of a post-Fordist industrial capitalism. In place of a model of unlimited growth and ever-increasing productivity, critical worker researchers propose an ecological model grounded in attempts to limit growth in order to improve the quality of life. Thus workers as critical researchers begin to push on the walls of modernity with their concerns for autonomy and self-reflection in opposition to the instrumental rationality of scientific management (Kellner, 1989).

This notion of self-reflection is central to the understanding of the nature of critically grounded qualitative research. As critical researchers attempt to restructure social relations of domination, they search for insights into an ever-evolving notion of social theory and the understanding it brings to their struggle for self-location in the net of larger and overlapping social, cultural, and economic contexts. As worker researchers analyze their location in the hierarchy of the workplace, they uncover ways in which they are controlled by the diagnostic and prescriptive discourse of managerial experts in their quest for the perfectly controlled workplace. Workers as critical researchers draw upon critical social theory to help them employ their understanding of their location in the corporate hierarchy in an effort to restructure the workplace. Social theory in this case becomes a vehicle for resistance, a means of social transformation through collective participation. In line with the project of critical research, worker researchers attempt not simply to describe the reality of work but to change it (Brosio, 1985; Ferguson, 1984; Zavarzadeh, 1989).

Not only do workers as critical researchers attempt to change the demeaning reality of work, but they also endeavor to change themselves. Critical worker researchers view their own roles as historical agents as a significant focus of their research. Analyzing the various discourses that shape their subjective formation, critical workers attend to the effects of the disjunctures in the social fabric. These disjunctures reveal themselves in routine actions, unconscious knowledge, and cultural memories. Workers trace the genealogies of their subjectivities and the origins of their personal concerns. At this point in their self-analysis, critical workers acquaint themselves with the postmodern condition and its powerful mobilization of affect. Workers study the postmodern condition's consumer-driven production of desire, its culture of manipulation, and its electronic surveillances by large organizations. Fighting against the social amnesia of a media-driven hyperreality, critical worker researchers assess the damage inflicted on them as well as the possibilities presented by the postmodern condition (Collins, 1989; Giroux, 1992; Hammersley & Atkinson, 1983).

Indeed, the postmodern workplace co-opts the language of democracy, as workers are positioned within by TQM (total quality management) programs and other "inclusive," "worker-friendly," and "power-sharing" plans. Workers as critical researchers are forced to develop new forms of demystification that expose the power relations of the "democratic" plans. Upon critical interrogation, workers find that often "the elimination of we/they perceptions" means, as it did in the Staley corn processing plant in Decatur, Illinois, increased worker firings as disciplinary action, required "state of the plant" meetings marked by managerial lectures to workers about the needs of the plant, the development of new contracts outlining "management rights," the introduction of 12-hour shifts without overtime pay, and the formation of work teams that destroy seniority. Whereas the managerial appeal to efficiency is a guise in the modernist workplace to hide worker control strategies, worker researchers find that in the post-modern workplace *cooperation* becomes the word *du jour.* Add to this illusion of cooperation the appearance of upward mobility of a few workers into the ranks of management, and attention is deflected from insidious forms of managerial supervision and hoarding of knowledge about the work process (Cockburn, 1993; Ferguson, 1984; Giroux, 1993).

The only way to address this degradation of worker dignity is to make sure that worker researchers are empowered to explore alternative work-place arrangements and to share in decision making concerning production and distribution of products. Workers distribute their research findings so that the general public understands how the present organization of work has served to concentrate wealth and power in the hands of industrial leaders. Worker researchers explore alternatives to present forms of bu-reaucratic control.

One of the best sources for such alternatives involves recent feminist research (Brosio, 1985; Cook & Fonow, 1990; Eiger, 1982; Wirth, 1983). Feminist research illustrates how traditional grand narratives that rely on class analysis of the workplace are insufficient. Modernist radical literature frequently used class as a unitary conceptual frame, and as a consequence the androcentric and patriarchal structures of the worker worldview were left uninterrogated. Postmodern forms of critical analysis drawing upon feminist reconceptualizations of research alert critical researchers to the multiple subject positions they hold in relation to the class, race, and gender dimensions of their lives. Critical worker researchers, for example, come to understand that the speaking subject in the discourse of the workplace is most often male, whereas the silent and passive object is female. Only recently has the analysis of workplace oppression foregrounded the special forms of oppression constructed around gender and race. Issues of promo-tion and equal pay for women and nonwhites and sexual harassment are relatively new elements in the public conversation about work (Fraser & Nicholson, 1990).

One of the most traumatic experience workers have to face involves the closing of a plant. Taking advantage of postmodern technology, factory managers have engaged in "outsourcing" and moved plants to "more attractive" locales with lower business taxes and open shops (often in Third World countries, where it becomes easier to exploit workers). Because more attractive locales exist only for management, workers have few options and typically have to scramble for new lower-paying jobs in the old venue. Worker researchers caught in such situations analyze alternatives to closings or relocations. Worker researchers in plants marked for closing from Detroit to the British Midlands have researched the causes of shutdowns as well as the feasibility of the production of alternate product lines, employee ownership, or government intervention to save their jobs. In relation to the causes of shutdowns, worker researchers employ what feminist researchers call "situation-at-hand" inquiry. Such research takes an already given situation as a focus for critical sociological inquiry. Researchers who find themselves in an already given situation possess little or no ability to control events because they have already happened or have happened for reasons that have nothing to do with the research study. Plant managers would probably be far more guarded about offhand comments made about plant closings if they were taking part in traditional interviews or completing questionnaires. Finding themselves in sensitive and controversial situations in which millions of dollars may be involved, critical worker researchers can make good use of situation-at-hand inquiry as a germane and creative way of uncovering data (Cook & Fonow, 1990; Eiger, 1982).

Critical postmodern research refuses to accept worker experience as unproblematic and beyond interrogation. Critical worker researchers respect their participation in the production of their craft as they collect and document their experiences; at the same time, however, they aver that a significant aspect of the critical research process involves challenging the ideological assumptions that inform the interpretation of their experiences. Simon and Dippo (1987) argue that critical workers must challenge the notion that experience is the best teacher. In this context, critical theoretical research must never be allowed to confirm simply what we already know. As Joan Scott (1992) says: "Experience is a subject's history. Language is the site of history's enactment" (p. 34). Foucault echoes this sentiment in arguing that the experience gained in everyday struggle can, upon examination, yield critical insights into the ways in which power works and the process by which knowledge is certified. In this process, conditions of everyday life mean first of all uncovering the assumptions that privilege particular interpretations of everyday experience (Foucault, 1980; Simon & Dippo, 1987; Simon, Dippo, & Schenke, 1991).

Experience, McLaren (1992b) has written elsewhere, never speaks for itself. Experience is an understanding derived from a specific interpretation of a certain "engagement with the world of symbols, social practices, and cultural forms" (p. 332). Particular experiences, critical researchers maintain, must be respected but always made theoretically problematic. Kincheloe and Pinar (1991b) address this concept in their theory of place, which brings particular experience into focus, but in a way that grounds it contextually through a consideration of the larger political, economic, social, and linguistic forces that shape it. Kincheloe and Steinberg (1993) extend this notion in their critically grounded theory of postformal cognition. Here, theoretical interpretations of experience are contextualized by the particularity of visceral experience. Such experience grounded in lust, fear, joy, love, and hate creates a synergistic interaction between theoretical understanding and the intimacy of the researchers' own autobiography. Critical workers acting on these insights gain the ability to place themselves theoretically within the often messy web of power relations without losing touch with the emotion of their everyday lives.

Drawing upon some ideas promoted by European labor organizations, critical workers can form research and study circles to explore important labor issues. In Sweden, for instance, workers have created 150,000 study circles involving 1.4 million participants. Buoyed by the possibilities held out by the Swedish example, critical workers imagine cooperatives that organize interpretations of everyday events in the economy and the workplace (Eiger, 1982). Motivated by the preponderance of management perspectives on television news programs, critical worker researchers offer alternative views of how workers are positioned in larger material, symbolic, and economic relations and how critical theory can serve to restructure such relations. As workers connect their individual stories of oppression to the larger historical framework, social as well as institutional memory is created (Harrison, 1985). This social memory can be shared with other study circles and with teachers, artists, intellectuals, social workers, and other cultural workers. At a time when few progressive labor voices are heard, worker research and study circles can make an important contribution to the creation of a prodemocracy movement.

Critical theory-based research can be exceedingly practical and can contribute to progressive change on a variety of levels. Below we summarize some of the progressive and empowering outcomes offered by critical theory-based worker research.

Production of more useful and relevant research on work. Worker research provides an account of the world from the marginal perspective of the workers, taking into consideration perspectives of both business and labor (Hartsock, 1989). Research from the margins is more relevant to those who have been marginalized by the hierarchical discourse of mainstream science, with its cult of the expert. Worker researchers ask questions about labor conditions that are relevant to other workers (Garrison, 1989).

Legitimation of worker knowledge. The discourse of traditional modernist science regulates what can be said under the flag of scientific authority and who can say it. Needless to say, workers and the practical knowledge they have accumulated about their work are excluded from this discourse (Collins, 1989). Worker research grounded in critical postmodern theory helps legitimate worker knowledge by pointing out the positionality and limitations of "expert research." James Garrison (1989) contends that practitioner research tends to distort reality less often than expert research because the practitioner is closer to the purposes, cares, everyday concerns, and interests of work. For this reason, critical worker research benefits from the multiplicity of ethnographic approaches available, such as worker sociodramas, life histories/autobiographies, journaling, personal narratives, writing-as-method, and critical narratology (McLaren, 1993b). With the growth of worker research in Scandinavia, analysts report that the gap between scientists and workers is being diminished. Such reports point to the progressive impact of worker research and the value of such inquiry in the movement toward a more egalitarian community (Eiger, 1982).

Empowerment of workers. Critical worker research operates under the assumption that the validation of workers' knowledge can lead to their empowerment (Garrison, 1989). But worker researchers must not be satisfied simply with producing a catalog of incidents of worker exploitation. Worker researchers must produce a provisional vision of empowerment as part of a larger critical project. This provisional vision must decide which concepts from the present study are essential for worker empowerment (Cook & Fonow, 1990) and which can be extended and elaborated for larger consideration such as the development of a socialist democracy.

Forced reorganization of the workplace. Western science has produced a set of fixed hierarchical binarisms, including the knower and the known, the researcher and the researched, the scientific expert and the practitioner. Critical worker research subverts the existing hierarchical arrangement of the workplace as it challenges the assumptions upon which the cult of the expert and scientific management are based. Without a Cartesian epistemological structure to justify them, the hierarchical binarisms of modernist science are significantly weakened (Butler, 1990; Garrison, 1989; McLaren, 1992a).

Inspiration of the democratization of science. As John Dewey maintained decades ago, science narrowly conceived as a technique puts the power of inquiry in the hands of those at the top of the hierarchy who, by way of their education or status, are pronounced most qualified. These elites engage in research, turning over the data (the product), not the methods (the process), of their inquiries to low-status practitioners who follow their directions. When workers take part in research and legitimate their own knowledge, then scientific research will be better able to serve progressive democratic goals (Garrison, 1989).

Undermining of technical rationality. Technical rationality is an epistemology of worker practice derived from modernist Cartesian science. Technical rationality maintains that workers are rationalistic problem solvers who apply scientifically tested procedures to workplace situations. Well-trained workers solve well-formed problems by applying techniques derived from expert-produced knowledge. Worker researchers have learned, however, that the problems encountered in the workplace are not reducible to simple propositions or assertions. For instance, workers in a garbage recycling plant must decide to balance environmental concerns with business survival demands. They must not only know what waste materials cause environmental damage but what materials bring high market prices. When extraction costs are calculated into this problem, it becomes apparent that no simple technical procedure exists that can lead workers to the solution of problems that confront such a workplace. The relationship between worker competence and expert knowledge needs to be flip-flopped. In the modernist workplace hierarchy, managers start with research provided by "experts" and train workers in accordance with such findings. A critical workplace would start instead with research by the workers themselves on the conditions of their labor. For instance, worker researchers could document the forms of intelligence competent workers exhibit. An important aspect of the worker's job would be to help create nonexploitive conditions that promote such competence (Feinberg & Horowitz, 1990; Raizen, 1989; Schön, 1987).

Promotion of an awareness of worker cognition. Critical worker research encourages a relationship to worker production that is expressed in

285

aesthetic appreciation for the process and product of one's labor, awareness of the relationship between work and world, and solidarity with other workers. In addition, this critical productive orientation highlights an awareness of reality by way of both logic and emotion. Critical research holds many cognitive benefits that transcend Piagetian forms of formal analytic reasoning. As workers as researchers transcend procedural logic, they move to a critical realm of knowledge production. In this realm, researchers organize and interpret information, no longer caught in the hierarchy as passive receivers of "expert" knowledge. As critical researchers, workers learn to teach themselves. In this context, learning in the work-place becomes a way of life, a part of the job. Workers as researchers come to see events in a deconstructive manner, in ways that uncover privileged binary oppositions within logocentric discourses not necessarily apparent before critical reflection (Feinberg & Horowitz, 1990; Kincheloe, 1993; Wirth, 1983).

◆ Critical Postmodern Research: Further Considerations

As much as critical researchers may claim to see meanings that others miss, critical postmodern research respects the complexity of the social world. Humility in this context should not be self-deprecating, nor should it involve the silencing of the researcher's voice; research humility implies a sense of the unpredictability of the sociopolitical microcosm and the capriciousness of the consequences of inquiry. This critical humility is an inescapable feature of a postmodern condition marked by a loss of faith in an unreconceptualized narrative emancipation and the possibility of a privileged frame of reference. A postmodernized critical theory accepts the presence of its own fallibility as well as its contingent relation to progressive social change (Aronowitz, 1983; McLaren, 1997a; Morrow, 1991; Ruddick, 1980).

In light of this reflective humility, critical researchers do not search for some magic method of inquiry that will guarantee the validity of their findings. As Henry Giroux (1983) maintains, "methodological correctness" will never guarantee valid data, nor does it reveal power interests within a body of information (p. 17). Traditional research argues that the only way to produce valid information is through the application of a rigorous research methodology, that is, one that follows a strict set of objective procedures that separate researchers from those researched. To be meaningful, the argument goes, social inquiry must be rigorous. The pursuit of rigor thus becomes the shortest path to validity. Rigor is a commitment to the established rules for conducting inquiry. Traditional modernist research has focused on rigor to the neglect of the dynamics of the lived world—not to mention the pursuit of justice in the lived world. Habermas and Marcuse maintain that post-Enlightenment science has focused research on the how and the form of inquiry, to the neglect of the what and the substance of inquiry. Thus social research has largely become a technology that has focused on reducing human beings to taken-for-granted social outcomes. These outcomes typically maintain existing power relationships, Habermas (1971, 1973) and Marcuse (1964) argue, as they disregard the ways in which current sociopolitical relationships affect human life. We do not want to suggest that an absolute dialogism is possible, but we support attempts to create conditions of rational social discourse and the establishment of normative claims, noncoerced discussion, and debate.

Because of critical research's agenda of social critique, special problems of validity are raised. How do you determine the validity of information if you reject the notion of methodological correctness and your purpose is to free men and women from sources of oppression and domination? Where traditional verifiability rests on a rational proof built upon literal intended meaning, a critical qualitative perspective always involves a less certain approach characterized by participant reaction and emotional involvement. Some analysts argue that *validity* may be an inappropriate term in a critical research context, as it simply reflects a concern for acceptance within a positivist concept of research rigor. To a critical researcher, validity means much more than the traditional definitions of internal and external validity usually associated with the concept. Traditional research has defined *internal validity* as the extent to which a researcher's observations and measurements are true descriptions of a particular reality; *external validity* has been defined as the degree to which such descriptions can be accurately compared with other groups. *Trustworthiness,* many have argued, is a more appropriate word to use in the context of critical research. It is helpful because it signifies a different set of assumptions about research purposes than does *validity*. What criteria might be used to assess the trustworthiness of critical research (Anderson, 1989; Lincoln & Guba, 1985; Reinharz, 1979)?

One criterion for critical trustworthiness involves the credibility of portrayals of constructed realities. Critical researchers reject the notion of internal validity that is based on the assumption that a tangible, knowable, cause-and-effect reality exists and that research descriptions are able to portray that reality accurately. Critical researchers award credibility only when the constructions are plausible to those who constructed them, and even then there may be disagreement, for the researcher may see the effects of oppression in the constructs of those researched—effects that those researched may not see. Thus it becomes extremely difficult to measure the trustworthiness of critical research; no TQ (trustworthiness quotient) can be developed.

A second criterion for critical trustworthiness can be referred to as *anticipatory accommodation.* Here critical researchers reject the traditional notion of external validity. The ability to make pristine generalizations from one research study to another accepts a one-dimensional, cause-effect universe. Kincheloe (1991) points out that in traditional research all that is needed to ensure transferability is to understand with a high degree of internal validity something about, say, a particular school classroom and to know that the makeup of this classroom is representative of another classroom to which the generalization is being applied. Many critical researchers have argued that this traditionalist concept of external validity is far too simplistic and assert that if generalizations are to be made—that is, if researchers are to be able to apply findings in context A to context B—then we must make sure that the contexts being compared are similar. The Piagetian notion of cognitive processing is instructive because it suggests that in everyday situations men and women do not make generalizations in the ways implied by external validity. Piaget's notion of accommodation seems appropriate in this context, as it asserts that humans reshape cognitive structures to accommodate unique aspects of what they perceive in new contexts. In other words, through their knowledge of a variety of comparable contexts, researchers begin to learn their similarities and differences—they learn from their comparisons of different contexts (Donmoyer, 1990; Kincheloe, 1991).

As critical researchers transcend regressive and counterintuitive notions of validating the knowledge uncovered by research, they remind themselves of their critical project—the attempt to move beyond assimilated experience, the struggle to expose the way ideology constrains the desire for self-direction, and the effort to confront the way power reproduces itself in the construction of human consciousness. Given such purposes,

Patti Lather (1991) extends our position with her notion of catalytic validity. Catalytic validity points to the degree to which research moves those it studies to understand the world and the way it is shaped in order for them to transform it. Noncritical researchers who operate within an empiricist framework will perhaps find catalytic validity to be a strange concept. Research that possesses catalytic validity will not only display the reality-altering impact of the inquiry process, it will also direct this impact so that those under study will gain self-understanding and self-direction (Lather, 1991).

Recent attempts by critical researchers to move beyond the objectifying and imperialist gaze associated with the Western anthropological tradition (which fixes the image of the so-called informant from the colonizing perspective of the knowing subject), although laudatory and well-intentioned, are not without their shortcomings (Bourdieu & Wacquaat, 1992). As Fuchs (1993) has so presciently observed, serious limitations plague recent efforts to develop a more reflective approach to ethnographic writing. The challenge here can be summarized in the following questions: How does the knowing subject come to know the Other? How can researchers respect the perspective of the Other and invite the Other to speak?

Although recent confessional modes of ethnographic writing attempt to treat so-called informants as "participants" in an attempt to avoid the objectification of the Other (usually referring to the relationship between Western anthropologists and non-Western culture), there is a risk that uncovering colonial and postcolonial structures of domination may, in fact, unintentionally validate and consolidate such structures as well as reassert liberal values through a type of covert ethnocentrism. Fuchs (1993) warns that the attempt to subject researchers to the same approach to which other societies are subjected could lead to an " 'othering' of one's own world" (p. 108). Such an attempt often fails to question existing ethnographic methodologies and therefore unwittingly extends their validity and applicability while further objectifying the world of the researcher.

Michel Foucault's approach to this dilemma is to "detach" social theory from the epistemology of his own culture by criticizing the traditional philosophy of reflection. However, Foucault falls into the trap of ontologizing his own methodological argumentation and erasing the notion of prior understanding that is linked to the idea of an "inside" view (Fuchs, 1993). Louis Dumont fares somewhat better by arguing that cultural texts need to be viewed simultaneously from the inside and from the outside

(Fuchs, 1993, p. 112). However, in trying to affirm a "reciprocal interpretation of various societies among themselves" (Fuchs, 1993, p. 113)
through identifying both transindividual structures of consciousness and
transsubjective social structures, Dumont aspires to a universal framework
for the comparative analysis of societies. Whereas Foucault and Dumont
attempt to "transcend the categorical foundations of their own world"
(Fuchs, 1993, p. 118) by refusing to include themselves in the process of
objectification, Pierre Bourdieu integrates himself as a social actor into
the social field under analysis. Bourdieu achieves such integration by
"epistemologizing the ethnological content of his own presuppositions"
(Fuchs, 1993, p. 121). But the self-objectification of the observer (anthropologist) is not unproblematic. Fuchs (1993) notes, after Bourdieu, that
the chief difficulty is "forgetting the difference between the theoretical and
the practical relationship with the world and of imposing on the object the
theoretical relationship one maintains with it" (p. 120). Bourdieu's approach to research does not fully escape becoming, to a certain extent, a
"confirmation of objectivism," but at least there is an earnest attempt by
the researcher to reflect on the preconditions of his own self-understanding—an attempt to engage in an "ethnography of ethnographers"
(p. 122).

Postmodern ethnography—and we are thinking here of works such as
Paul Rabinow's *Reflections on Fieldwork in Morocco* (1977), James Boon's
Other Tribes, Other Scribes (1982), and Michael Taussig's *Shamanism,
Colonialism, and the Wild Man* (1987)—shares the conviction articulated
by Marc Manganaro (1990) that "no anthropology is apolitical, removed
from ideology and hence from the capacity to be affected by or, as crucially,
to effect social formations. The question ought not to be if an anthropological text is political, but rather, what kind of sociopolitical affiliations
are tied to particular anthropological texts" (p. 35).

Judith Newton and Judith Stacey (1992-1993) note that the current
postmodern textual experimentation of ethnography credits the "postcolonial predicament of culture as the opportunity for anthropology to reinvent
itself" (p. 56). Modernist ethnography, according to these authors, "constructed authoritative cultural accounts that served, however inadvertently,
not only to establish the authority of the Western ethnographer over native
'others,' but also to sustain Western authority over colonial cultures." They
argue (following James Clifford) that ethnographers can and should try to
escape

the recurrent allegorical genre of colonial ethnography—the pastoral, a nostalgic, redemptive text that preserves a primitive culture on the brink of extinction for the historical record of its Western conquerors. The narrative structure of this "salvage text" portrays the native culture as a coherent, authentic, and lamentably "evading past," while its complex, inauthentic, Western successors represent the future. (p. 56)

Postmodern ethnographic writing faces the challenge of moving beyond simply the reanimation of local experience, an uncritical celebration of cultural difference (including figural differentiations within the ethnographer's own culture), and the employment of a framework that espouses universal values and a global role for interpretivist anthropology (Silverman, 1990). What we have described as resistance postmodernism can help qualitative researchers challenge dominant Western research practices that are underwritten by a foundational epistemology and a claim to universally valid knowledge at the expense of local, subjugated knowledges (Peters, 1993). The choice is not one between modernism and postmodernism, but one of whether or not to challenge the presuppositions that inform the normalizing judgments one makes as a researcher. Vincent Crapanzano (1990) warns that "the anthropologist can assume neither the Orphic lyre nor the crown of thorns, although I confess to hear salvationist echoes in his desire to protect his people" (p. 301).

The work of James Clifford, which shares an affinity with ethnographic work associated with Georges Bataille, Michel Lerris, and the College de Sociologie, is described by Connor (1992) as not simply the "writing of culture" but rather "the interior disruption of categories of art and culture correspond[ing] to a radically dialogic form of ethnographic writing, which takes place across and between cultures" (p. 251). Clifford (1992) describes his own work as an attempt "to multiply the hands and discourses involved in 'writing culture' . . . not to assert a naive democracy of plural authorship, but to loosen at least somewhat the monological control of the executive writer/anthropologist and to open for discussion ethnography's hierarchy and negotiation of discourses in power-charged, unequal situations" (p. 100). Citing the work of Marcus and Fisher (1986), Clifford warns against modernist ethnographic practices of "representational essentializing" and "metonymic freezing" in which one aspect of a group's life is taken to represent them as a whole; instead, Clifford urges forms of multilocale ethnography to reflect the "transnational political, economic and cultural forces that traverse and constitute local or regional worlds" (p. 102). Rather than fixing culture into reified textual portraits, culture needs to be better understood as displacement, transplantation, disruption, positionality, and difference.

Although critical ethnography allows, in a way conventional ethnography does not, for the relationship of liberation and history, and although its hermeneutical task is to call into question the social and cultural conditioning of human activity and the prevailing sociopolitical structures, we do not claim that this is enough to restructure the social system. But it is certainly, in our view, a necessary beginning. We follow Patricia Ticineto Clough (1992) in arguing that "realist narrativity has allowed empirical social science to be the platform and horizon of social criticism" (p. 135). Ethnography needs to be analyzed critically not only in terms of its field methods but also as reading and writing practices. Data collection must give way to "rereadings of representations in every form" (p. 137). In the narrative construction of its authority as empirical science, ethnography needs to face the unconscious processes upon which it justifies its canonical formulations, processes that often involve the disavowal of oedipal or authorial desire and the reduction of differences to binary oppositions. Within these processes of binary reduction, the male ethnographer is most often privileged as the guardian of "the factual representation of empirical positivities" (p. 9).

Critical research traditions have arrived at the point where they recognize that claims to truth are always discursively situated and implicated in relations of power. Yet, unlike some claims made within "ludic" strands of postmodernist research, we do not suggest that because we cannot know truth absolutely that truth can simply be equated with an effect of power. We say this because truth involves regulative rules that must be met for some statements to be more meaningful than others. Otherwise, truth becomes meaningless and, if this is the case, liberatory praxis has no purpose other than to win for the sake of winning (Carspecken, 1993). As Phil Carspecken (1993) remarks, every time we act, in every instance of our behavior, we presuppose some normative or universal relation to truth. Truth is internally related to meaning in a pragmatic way through normative referenced claims, intersubjective referenced claims, subjective referenced claims, and the way we deictically ground or anchor meaning in our daily lives.

Carspecken explains that researchers are able to articulate the normative evaluative claims of others when they begin to see them in the same way as their participants by living inside the cultural and discursive positionalities that inform such claims. Claims to universality must be recognized in each particular normative claim and questions must be raised about whether such norms represent the entire group. When the limited claim of universality is seen to be contradictory to the practices under observation, power relations become visible. What is crucial here, according to Carspecken, is that researchers recognize where they are ideologically located in the normative and identity claims of others and at the same time be honest about their own subjective referenced claims and not let normative evaluative claims interfere with what is observed. Critical research continues to problematize normative and universal claims in a way that does not permit them to be analyzed outside of a politics of representation, divorced from the material conditions in which they are produced, or outside of a concern with the constitution of the subject in the very acts of reading and writing.

A critical postmodern research requires researchers to construct their perception of the world anew, not just in random ways but in a manner that undermines what appears natural, that opens to question what appears obvious (Slaughter, 1989). Oppositional and insurgent researchers as maieutic agents must not confuse their research efforts with the textual suavities of an avant-garde academic posturing in which they are awarded the sinecure of representation for the oppressed without actually having to return to those working-class communities where their studies took place. Rather, they need to locate their work in a transformative praxis that leads to the alleviation of suffering and the overcoming of oppression. Rejecting the arrogant reading of metropolitan critics and their imperial mandates governing research, insurgent researchers ask questions about how what is has come to be, whose interests are served by particular institutional arrangements, and where our own frames of reference come from. Facts are no longer simply "what is"; the truth of beliefs is not simply testable by their correspondence to these facts. To engage in critical postmodern research is to take part in a process of critical world making, guided by the shadowed outline of a dream of a world less conditioned by misery, suffering, and the politics of deceit. It is, in short, a pragmatics of hope in an age of cynical reason.

◆ References

Anderson, G. (1989). Critical ethnography in education: Origins, current status, and new directions. *Review of Educational Research, 59*, 249-270.

Apple, M. (1992). *Constructing the captive audience: Channel one and the political economy of the text.* Unpublished manuscript.

Aronowitz, S. (1983, December 27). The relativity of theory. *Village Voice*, p. 60.

Aronowitz, S., & Giroux, H. (1991). *Postmodern education: Politics, culture, and social criticism.* Minneapolis: University of Minnesota Press.

Benhabib, S., & Cornell, D. (1987). *Feminism as critique.* Minneapolis: University of Minnesota Press.

Boon, J. (1982). *Other tribes, other scribes: Symbolic anthropology in the comparative study of cultures, histories, religions, and texts.* Cambridge: Cambridge University Press.

Bottomore, T. (1984). *The Frankfurt school.* London: Tavistock.

Bourdieu, P., & Wacquaat, L. (1992). *An invitation to reflexive sociology.* Chicago: University of Chicago Press.

Britzman, D. (1991). *Practice makes practice: A critical study of learning to teach.* Albany: State University of New York Press.

Brosio, R. (1985). *A bibliographic essay on the world of work.* Paper presented at the annual meeting of the American Educational Studies Association, Chicago.

Buckingham, D. (1989). Television literacy: A critique. *Radical Philosophy, 51*, 12-25.

Butler, J. (1990). *Gender trouble: Feminism and the subversion of identity.* New York: Routledge.

Carspecken, P. (1993). *Power, truth, and method: Outline for a critical methodology.* Unpublished manuscript.

Centre for Contemporary Culture Studies. (1978). *Women take issue: Aspects of women's subordination.* Birmingham, England: University of Birmingham, Women's Studies Group.

Clifford, J. (1992). Traveling cultures. In L. Grossberg, C. Nelson, & P. A. Treichler (Eds.), *Cultural studies* (pp. 96-116). New York: Routledge.

Clough, P. T. (1992). *The end(s) of ethnography: From realism to social criticism.* Newbury Park, CA: Sage.

Cockburn, A. (1993). Clinton and labor: Reform equals rollback. *The Nation, 256*, 654-655.

Codd, J. (1984). Introduction. In J. Codd (Ed.), *Philosophy, common sense, and action in educational administration* (pp. 8-28). Victoria, Australia: Deakin University Press.

Collins, J. (1989). *Uncommon cultures: Popular culture and postmodernism.* New York: Routledge.

Connor, S. (1992). *Theory and cultural value.* Cambridge: Basil Blackwell.

Cook, J. A., & Fonow, M. M. (1990). Knowledge and women's interests: Issues of epistemology and methodology in feminist sociological research. In J. Nielsen (Ed.), *Feminist research methods: Exemplary reading in the social sciences* (pp. 69-93). Boulder, CO: Westview.

Corrigan, P. (1979). *Schooling the Smash Street kids.* London: Macmillan.

Crapanzano, V. (1990). Afterword. In M. Manganaro (Ed.), *Modernist anthropology: From fieldwork to text* (pp. 300-308). Princeton, NJ: Princeton University Press.

Donmoyer, R. (1990). Generalizability and the single-case study. In E. Eisner & A. Peshkin (Eds.), *Qualitative inquiry in education: The continuing debate* (pp. 175-200). New York: Teachers College Press.

Ebert, T. (1991). Political semiosis in/or American cultural studies. *American Journal of Semiotics, 8*, 113-135.

Ebert, T. (in press). Writing in the political: Resistance (post) modernism. *Critical Theory.*

Eiger, N. (1982). The workplace as classroom for democracy: The Swedish experience. *New York University Education Quarterly, 17*, 16-23.

Feinberg, W., & Horowitz, B. (1990). Vocational education and the equality of opportunity. *Journal of Curriculum Studies, 22*, 188-192.

Ferguson, K. (1984). *The feminist case against bureaucracy.* Philadelphia: Temple University Press.

Fine, M. (1988). Sexuality, schooling, and adolescent females: The missing discourse of desire. *Harvard Educational Review, 58*, 29-53.

Flax, J. (1990). Postmodernism and gender relations in feminist theory. In L. Nicholson (Ed.), *Feminism/postmodernism* (pp. 39-62). New York: Routledge.

Foster, H. (Ed.). (1983). *The anti-aesthetic: Essays on postmodern culture.* Port Townsend, WA: Bay.

Foucault, M. (1980). *Power/knowledge: Selected interviews and other writings* (C. Gordon, Ed.). New York: Pantheon.

Fox-Genovese, E. (1988). *Within the plantation household: Black and white women of the Old South.* Chapel Hill: University of North Carolina Press.

Fraser, N., & Nicholson, L. (1990). Social criticism without philosophy: An encounter between feminism and postmodernism. In L. Nicholson (Ed.), *Feminism/postmodernism* (pp. 19-38). New York: Routledge.

Fuchs, M. (1993). The reversal of the ethnological perspective: Attempts at objectifying one's own cultural horizon. Dumont, Foucault, Bourdieu? *Thesis Eleven, 34*, 104-125.

Garrison, J. (1989). The role of postpositivistic philosophy of science in the renewal of vocational education research. *Journal of Vocational Education Research, 14*(3), 39-51.

Gergen, K. J. (1991). *The saturated self: Dilemmas of identity in contemporary life.* New York: Basic Books.

Gibson, R. (1986). *Critical theory and education.* London: Hodder & Stroughton.

Giroux, H. (1983). *Theory and resistance in education: A pedagogy for the opposition.* South Hadley, MA: Bergin & Garvey.

Giroux, H. (1988). Critical theory and the politics of culture and voice: Rethinking the discourse of educational research. In R. Sherman & R. Webb (Eds.), *Qualitative research in education: Focus and methods* (pp. 190-210). New York: Falmer.

Giroux, H. (1992). *Border crossings: Cultural workers and the politics of education.* New York: Routledge.

Giroux, H. (1993). *Living dangerously: Multiculturalism and the politics of difference.* New York: Peter Lang.

Godzich, W. (1992). Afterword: Reading against literacy. In J. F. Lyotard, *The postmodern explained.* Minneapolis: University of Minnesota Press.

Gramsci, A. (1971). *Selections from the prison notebooks* (Q. Hoare & G. Nowell Smith, Eds. & Trans.). New York: International.

Griffin, C. (1985). *Typical girls? Young women from school to the job market.* London: Routledge & Kegan Paul.

Habermas, J. (1971). *Knowledge and human interests* (J. Shapiro, Trans.). Boston: Beacon.

Habermas, J. (1973). *Theory and practice* (J. Viertel, Trans.). Boston: Beacon.

Hall, S. (1990, September). A conversation with F. Jameson: Clinging to the wreckage. *Marxism Today*, pp. 28-31.

Hammersley, M., & Atkinson, P. (1983). *Ethnography: Principles in practice.* London: Tavistock.

Harris, M. (1981). *America now.* New York: Simon & Schuster.

Harrison, B. (1985). *Making the connections: Essays in feminist social ethics.* Boston: Beacon.

Hartsock, N. (1989). Foucault on power: A theory for women? In L. Nicholson (Ed.), *Feminism/postmodernism* (pp. 83-106). New York: Routledge.

Harvey, D. (1989). *The condition of postmodernity.* Cambridge: Basil Blackwell.

Hebdige, D. (1979). *Subculture: The meaning of style.* London: Methuen.

Held, D. (1980). *Introduction to critical theory: Horkheimer to Habermas.* Berkeley: University of California Press.

hooks, b. (1989). *Talking back: Thinking feminist, thinking black.* Boston: South End.

Horkheimer, M. (1972). *Critical theory.* New York: Seabury.

Hutcheon, L. (1989). *The politics of postmodernism.* New York: Routledge.

Jameson, F. (1990, September). A conversation with S. Hall: Clinging to the wreckage. *Marxism Today*, pp. 28-31.

Jay, M. (1973). *The dialectical imagination: A history of the Frankfurt school and the Institute of Social Research 1923-1950.* Boston: Little, Brown.

Jordan, J. (1985). *On call: Political essays.* Boston: South End.

Kellner, D. (1989). *Critical theory, Marxism, and modernity.* Baltimore: Johns Hopkins University Press.

Kellner, D. (1993). *The obsolescence of Marxism?* Unpublished manuscript.

Kincheloe, J. (1991). *Teachers as researchers: Qualitative paths to empowerment.* London: Falmer.

Kincheloe, J. (1993). *Toward a critical politics of teacher thinking: Mapping the postmodern.* Granby, MA: Bergin & Garvey.

Kincheloe, J., & Pinar, W. (1991a). *Curriculum as social psychoanalysis: Essays on the significance of place.* Albany: State University of New York Press.

Kincheloe, J., & Pinar, W. (1991b). Introduction. In J. Kincheloe & W. Pinar, *Curriculum as social psychoanalysis: Essays on the significance of place* (pp. 1-23). Albany: State University of New York Press.

Kincheloe, J., & Steinberg, S. (1993). A tentative description of post-formal thinking: The critical confrontation with cognitive theory. *Harvard Educational Review, 63,* 296-320.

Kipnis, L. (1988). Feminism: The political conscience of postmodernism. In A. Ross (Ed.), *Universal abandon? The politics of postmodernism* (pp. 149-166). Minneapolis: University of Minnesota Press.

Lacey, C. (1970). *Hightown Grammar: The school as a social system.* London: Routledge & Kegan Paul.

Lash, S. (1990). Learning from Leipzig . . . or politics in the semiotic society. *Theory, Culture & Society, 7*(4), 145-158.

Lather, P. (1991). *Getting smart: Feminist research and pedagogy with/in the postmodern.* New York: Routledge.

Lincoln, Y. S., & Guba, E. G. (1985). *Naturalistic inquiry.* Beverly Hills, CA: Sage.

Lugones, M. (1987). Playfulness, "world"-traveling, and loving perception. *Hypatia, 2*(2), 3-19.

Luke, T. (1991). Touring hyperreality: Critical theory confronts informational society. In P. Wexler (Ed.), *Critical theory now* (pp. 1-26). New York: Falmer.

Manganaro, M. (1990). Textual play, power, and cultural critique: An orientation to modernist anthropology. In M. Manganaro (Ed.), *Modernist anthropology: From fieldwork to text* (pp. 3-47). Princeton, NJ: Princeton University Press.

Marcus, G., & Fischer, M. (1986). *Anthropology as cultural critique: An experimental moment in the human sciences.* Chicago: University of Chicago Press.

Marcuse, H. (1964). *One dimensional man.* Boston: South End.

McLaren, P. (1986). *Schooling as a ritual performance: Toward a political economy of educational symbols and gestures.* London: Routledge & Kegan Paul.

McLaren, P. (1989). *Life in schools.* New York: Longman.

McLaren, P. (1992a). Collisions with otherness: "Traveling" theory, post-colonial criticism, and the politics of ethnographic practice—the mission of the wounded ethnographer. *Qualitative Studies in Education, 5*(1), 77-92.

McLaren, P. (1992b). Literacy research and the postmodern turn: Cautions from the margins. In R. Beach, J. Green, M. Kamil, & T. Shanahan (Eds.), *Multidisciplinary perspectives on research.* Urbana, IL: National Council of Teachers of English.

McLaren, P. (1993a). Border disputes: Multicultural narrative, identity formation, and critical pedagogy in postmodern America. In D. McLaughlin & W. G. Tierney (Eds.), *Naming silenced lives: Personal narratives and the process of educational change.* New York: Routledge.

McLaren, P. (1993b). Multiculturalism and the postmodern critique: Towards a pedagogy of resistance and transformation. *Cultural Critique, 7,* 118-146.

McLaren, P. (Ed.). (1997a). *Postmodernism, postcolonialism and pedagogy.* Albert Park, Australia: James Nicholas.

McLaren, P. (1997b). *Revolutionary multiculturalism: Pedagogies of dissent for the new millennium.* Boulder, CO: Westview.

McLaren, P., & Hammer, R. (1989). Critical pedagogy and the postmodern challenge. *Educational Foundations, 3*(3), 29-69.

Morris, M. (1988). Tooth and claw: Tales of survival and Crocodile Dundee. In A. Ross (Ed.), *Universal abandon? The politics of postmodernism* (pp. 105-127). Minneapolis: University of Minnesota Press.

Morrow, R. (1991). Critical theory, Gramsci and cultural studies: From structuralism to post-structuralism. In P. Wexler (Ed.), *Critical theory now* (pp. 27-69). New York: Falmer.

Newton, J., & Stacey, J. (1992-1993). Learning not to curse, or, feminist predicaments in cultural criticism by men: Our movie date with James Clifford and Stephen Greenblatt. *Cultural Critique, 23,* 51-82.

Pagano, J. (1990). *Exiles and communities.* Albany: State University of New York Press.

Peters, M. (1993). *Against Finkielkraut's la defaite de la pensee: Culture, postmodernism and education.* Unpublished manuscript.

Poster, M. (1989). *Critical theory and poststructuralism: In search of a context.* Ithaca, NY: Cornell University Press.

Quantz, R. A. (1992). On critical ethnography (with some postmodern considerations). In M. D. LeCompte, W. L. Millroy, & J. Preissle (Eds.), *The handbook of qualitative research in education* (pp. 447-505). New York: Academic Press.

Rabinow, P. (1977). *Reflections on fieldwork in Morocco.* Berkeley: University of California Press.

Raizen, S. (1989). *Reforming education for work: A cognitive science perspective.* Berkeley, CA: National Center for Research in Vocational Education.

Reinharz, S. (1979). *On becoming a social scientist.* San Francisco: Jossey-Bass.

Robins, D., & Cohen, P. (1978). *Knuckle sandwich: Growing up in the working-class city.* Harmondsworth: Penguin.

Rosenau, P. M. (1992). *Post-modernism and the social sciences: Insights, inroads, and intrusion.* Princeton, NJ: Princeton University Press.

Ruddick, S. (1980). Material thinking. *Feminist Studies, 6,* 342-367.

San Juan, E., Jr. (1992). *Articulations of power in ethnic and racial studies in the United States.* Atlantic Highlands, NJ: Humanities Press.

Schön, D. (1987). *Educating the reflective practitioner: Toward a new design for teaching and learning in the professions.* San Francisco: Jossey-Bass.

Scott, J. W. (1992). Experience. In J. Butler & J. W. Scott (Eds.), *Feminists theorize the political* (pp. 22-40). New York: Routledge.

Silverman, E. K. (1990). Clifford Geertz: Towards a more "thick" understanding? In C. Tilley (Ed.), *Reading material culture* (pp. 121-159). Cambridge: Basil Blackwell.

Simon, R., & Dippo, D. (1987). What schools can do: Designing programs for work education that challenge the wisdom of experience. *Journal of Education, 169*(3), 101-116.

Simon, R., Dippo, D., & Schenke, A. (1991). *Learning work: A critical pedagogy of work education.* South Hadley, MA: Bergin & Garvey.

Slaughter, R. (1989). Cultural reconstruction in the post-modern world. *Journal of Curriculum Studies, 3,* 255-270.

Taussig, M. (1987). *Shamanism, colonialism, and the wild man: A study in terror and healing.* Chicago: University of Chicago Press.

Walker, A. (1983). *In search of our mothers' gardens: Womanist prose.* San Diego, CA: Harcourt Brace Jovanovich.

Weiler, K. (1988). *Women teaching for change: Gender, class, and power.* South Hadley, MA: Bergin & Garvey.

Welch, S. (1991). An ethic of solidarity and difference. In H. Giroux (Ed.), *Postmodernism, feminism, and cultural politics: Redrawing educational boundaries* (pp. 83-99). Albany: State University of New York Press.

West, C. (1991). *The ethical dimensions of Marxist thought.* New York: Monthly Review Press.

Wexler, P. (1991). Preface. In P. Wexler (Ed.), *Critical theory now.* New York: Falmer.

Willis, P. (1977). *Learning to labour: How working class kids get working class jobs.* Farnborough, England: Saxon House.

298

Wirth, A. (1983). *Productive work—in industry and schools.* Lanham, MD: University Press of America.

Yates, T. (1990). Jacques Derrida: "There is nothing outside of the text." In C. Tilley (Ed.), *Reading material culture* (pp. 206-280). Cambridge: Basil Blackwell.

Young, I. (1990). The ideal of community and the politics of difference. In L. Nicholson (Ed.), *Feminism/postmodernism* (pp. 300-323). New York: Routledge.

Zavarzadeh, M. (1989). Theory as resistance. *Rethinking Marxism, 2,* 50-70.

Zavarzadeh, M., & Morton, D. (1991). *Theory, (post) modernity, opposition.* Washington, DC: Maison-neuve.

Zizek, S. (1990). *The sublime object of ideology.* London: Verso.

9

Feminisms and Models of Qualitative Research

Virginia Olesen

◆ At this highly labile moment in the history of feminist thought this
chapter attempts to outline feminist qualitative research even as the
context and contours of both feminism and qualitative research are shifting. To accomplish this I will review briefly how current complexities
emerged, indicate the scope of work, detail some models of research, and
discuss issues feminist researchers face.[1]

I emphasize here that there are many feminisms, hence many views,
some conflicting (DeVault, 1993; Reinharz, 1992; Stanley & Wise, 1990,
p. 47; Tong, 1989). Whatever the qualitative research style, and whether
or not self-consciously defined as feminist, these many voices share the
outlook that it is important to center and make problematic women's
diverse situations and the institutions and frames that influence those
situations, and then to refer the examination of that problematic to
theoretical, policy, or action frameworks in the interest of realizing social
justice for women (Eichler, 1986, p. 68). Feminists use a variety of qualitative styles, but share the assumptions held generally by qualitative or
interpretive researchers that interpretive human actions, whether found in

AUTHOR'S NOTE: The editors of this volume, Norman Denzin and Yvonna Lincoln, as well
as Michelle Fine and Meaghan Morris provided very helpful criticisms.

TABLE 9.1 Elements in the Growing Complexity of Feminist Research and Representative Texts

1. Absent and invisible
   Finch and Groves(1982), Lorber (1975), Nakano Glenn (1990)
2. Who can know?
   Cook and Fonow (1986), Jordan (1977), MacKinnon (1982), Ruzek (1978)
3. Frameworks and unframed
   a. frames and their critics
      male oriented: Gilligan (1982), Lewin and Olesen (1981), Smith (1974)
      white feminist oriented: Collins (1986), Davis (1978), Dill (1979), Garcia (1989), Green (1990), Hurtado (1989), Zavella (1987), Zinn (1982)
      Western feminist oriented: Mohanty (1988), Spivak (1988)
      able-bodied female: Fine (1992)
      heterosexual: Hall and Stevens (1991), Lewin (1993), Stanley and Wise (1990)
   b. intellectual style
      postmodernism: Clough (1992), Flax (1987), Haraway (1991), Hekman (1990), Nicholson (1990)

women's reports of experience or in the cultural products of reports of experience (film and so on), can be the focus of research.

◆ Emergent Complexities in Feminists' Research

Early in the second phase of the women's movement in the United States (1960s onward), one could roughly categorize qualitative feminist researchers in terms of their political views—liberal, radical or Marxist (Fee, 1983)—their academic disciplines (for those few who had made it into the male-dominated academy), or their preferred research styles. These distinctions have blurred: Political orientations are no longer as clear and are characterized by internal divisions within feminist thought; scholars in the social sciences borrow freely from other fields, particularly literary criticism, cultural studies, and history; many researchers mix qualitative methods or attempt to create new styles (see Table 9.1 for a summary of the elements that make up the growing complexity in feminist research). Concomitantly, views of women's lives and the assumptions about their subjectivity, once seen by some as universally homogeneous, have been sharpened and differentiated dramatically (DeVault, 1990; Ferguson, 1993).

This has led to a highly reflexive stance among many about the conduct of the research, the feminist's place in it, the researcher's relationship to participants, the philosophical location and nature of knowledge and the handling of the report, and the impact of feminist research on the researcher's discipline, issues to be discussed shortly.

Women: Absent and Invisible

In the 1970s and for some time, research concerns were quite straightforward, though nevertheless politically charged. These focused on the absence of women in certain contexts and the invisibility of women in other contexts where they are in fact ubiquitous. Concerned about inequities derived from male dominance rooted in the gender and economic spheres, investigators critically examined contexts such as medicine (Lorber, 1975) and law (Epstein, 1981), where there were few or no women. (These studies led to the later recognition that in female-free contexts "add women and stir" would not redress issues of access or inequity, which lay in deeper interactional and structural problems, a point vividly made in Darlene Clarke Hine's 1989 analysis of African American women and the nursing profession.)

Somewhat later, research from Britain and the United States made visible the widespread caring for children, the ill, and the elderly and exposed the taken-for-grantedness of such work, its oppressiveness, and also its value to women and their societies (Abel & Nelson, 1990; Finch & Groves, 1982; Graham, 1985; Nelson, 1990). Such work highlighted this aspect of women's lives as worthy of analysis and prompted a prominent British feminist sociologist to question the male-framed sociological division of labor (M. Stacey, 1981). Hochschild and Machung (1989) further differentiate the working wife's labor at home with the finding that such labor is embedded in the political economy of domestic emotion.

Later studies on women's preparation of food by Anne Murcott (1983) on Welsh households and Marjorie DeVault (1991) on U.S. homes added to the complexity with revelations of the oppression and satisfactions as well as gender-creating activities in the act of women's cooking. With the exception of Phyllis Palmer's (1989) historical analysis of domestic service, the expansion of feminist research to the critical and previously invisible topic of women who do paid domestic work was accomplished by women of color: Evelyn Nakano Glenn's (1990) analysis of Japanese American women who did domestic service between 1905 and 1940, based on interviews and historical labor market data, spells out how the women transcended contradictions in the various forms of oppression they experienced. Judith Rollins's (1985) participant observation research on black women working for white women (she herself did such work) revealed racial dominance within the female sphere, as did Mary Romero's (1992) interview study of Latina domestic workers. These studies are notable for their analysis of class as well as racial issues, an analytic approach feminist researchers stress (Sacks, 1989) but often find difficult to implement (Cannon, Higginbotham, & Leung, 1991; Ferguson, 1993).

Who Can Know?

Simultaneously, the fundamental question of who can be a knower (Code, 1991, p. xi), a query referential both to women as participants and women as researchers, motivated feminist inquiries, thanks to the influences of "consciousness-raising" described by legal scholar Catherine MacKinnon (1982, p. 535; 1983), among others, as *the* basis of feminist methodology (see also Cook & Fonow, 1986). Sheryl Ruzek's (1978) analysis of the rise of the women's health movement took the feminist concern for women as knowers and illustrated how *feminist* research on a social movement differs from standard sociological inquiry. She carefully attended to a familiar sociological issue, professionalization in medicine, but grounded her work and analysis in women's experience and knowledge of medical practice, particularly gynecology, to show how relationships emergent from collective discontent eventuated in social organization, the gynecological self-help clinic. In a phenomenological vein, Brigitte Jordan (1977) showed how women's knowledge of their own bodies enabled them to be competent judges of being pregnant, even in the face of medical refusal to acknowledge this state without scientific tests.

Frameworks Unframed

If topic and knower were becoming problematized, so too were interpretive frameworks, particularly those embedded in studies of men's lives. Carol Gilligan's (1982) well-known study of moral development showed that young girls were not flawed or stunted in their development, as frameworks based on the lives of young boys would suggest, but displayed a pattern appropriate for them. Ellen Lewin and I demonstrated the inadequacy of male-based concepts of success as an endless vertical rise. In our study, nurses viewed lateral career patterns that were characterized by autonomy and satisfaction as success (Lewin & Olesen, 1981).

Male-oriented and -influenced frameworks were not the only perspectives crumbling. Steadily rising incisive criticisms from women of color, Third World feminists, disabled women, and lesbian women decentered and fractured white feminists' formulations of women's place in the world. White feminists' unexamined use of a woman or women who stood for all women came under fire early from African American scholars Angela Davis (1978) and Bonnie Thornton Dill (1979). They argued that the impact of slavery in the United States created a sharply different past and present for black women, with more complex gender relationships than had been seen or understood by white feminists. Twenty years after these critiques, legal scholar Kimberly Crenshaw (1992), commenting on the 1991 Clarence Thomas hearings, found it necessary to reiterate and update this criticism.

This body of criticism, expressed by Maxine Baca Zinn (1982), Aida Hurtado (1989), and Esther Garcia (1989) concerning Latina women, Esther Chow (1987) about Chinese American women, and Rayna Green (1990) about Native American women, decried the tendency to construct, speak for, and, in bell hooks's (1990) incisive words, "to know us better than we know ourselves" (p. 22). Citing research by African American sociologists and literary critics, Patricia Hill Collins (1986) further refines these views when she reminds sociologists in general and feminists in particular how "Black women's family experiences represent a clear case of the workings of race, gender and class oppression in shaping family life" (p. 529). Patricia Zavella's (1987) study of Mexican American women who do cannery work affirmed this.

Powerful critiques by Third World feminists further dissolved the conceptualization of "woman." Their criticisms, along with those of women of color and feminists attuned to postcolonial deconstructionism, anticipated much of the critique of "defining the Other" (invidious, oppressive, and unthinking definition of persons with whom research is done), which was to become influential in the hands of critics of postcolonial anthropology (Clifford, 1986; Marcus & Fisher, 1986), who initially seemed quite unaware of this body of feminist writing. It also became clear that Western feminist frameworks would not work in many Third World contexts because "differences could not simply be absorbed into dominant frameworks" (Kirby, 1991, p. 398). Along with questions of research authority, the very question of asking research questions became problematic, with

Gayatri Chakravorty Spivak (1988) posing the hard question of whether the subordinated can speak at all, a point also made by Chandra Mohanty (1988).

Other, more refined, conceptualizations of women's lives emerged from women, who by virtue of deeply rooted American stigma around physical disability and nonheterosexuality, had been rendered invisible by male-dominated frames, and by feminists blinded by these cultural norms. Michelle Fine (1992, p. 142), reviewing the emergence of disabled women as a problematic issue, insightfully noted that even sympathetic research on disabilities tended to overlook disabled women's multiple statuses and instead viewed them only in terms of their specific disabilities. Stanley and Wise's (1990, pp. 29-34) parallel criticism regarding lack of attention to or understanding of lesbians heralded lesbian feminist research, which has refined views of lesbians, for instance Patricia Stevens and Joanne Hall's (1991) historical analysis of how medicine has invidiously framed lesbian-ism and Ellen Lewin's (1993) interview study of lesbian mothers in America and the surpassing importance to them of the maternal role.

The potentially unsettling and fundamental question of the meaning and construction of gender, largely the concern of feminist anthropologists (Ortner & Whitehead, 1981) and more recently philosophers (J. Butler, 1990) and sociologists (West & Zimmerman, 1987), has emerged to provide some fundamental challenges, as yet not fully explored, to feminist research assumptions. Parallel to and often intersecting with these disrup-tive criticisms is the steadily growing influence of deconstructive and postmodern studies, which often unsettles not only taken-for-granted male-originated frames but the feminist frames as well.[2] As Jane Flax (1987) succinctly states, "Postmodern discourses are all 'deconstructive' in that they seek to distance us from and make us skeptical about beliefs concerning truth, knowledge, power, the self and language that are often taken for granted within and serve as legitimation for Western culture" (p. 624). Among the provocative consequences of these modes of thinking is a proliferation of conceptualizations of women's subjectivity that attempt to grapple with the potential for multiple sources of women's identity as women without sliding into essentialism (Ferguson, 1993, p. 154).

As this too-brief review suggests, the topic of women's lives has become increasingly differentiated. Before I present a discussion of models and issues that have arisen from that differentiation, it will be useful to outline the scope of research in terms of level of inquiry (phenomenological, relational, structural, policy).

◆ The Scope of Qualitative Feminist Work

Subjectivity

Though one may think that qualitative feminist research would focus on subjectivity and interpersonal relationship, an assumption that reflects the flaws and inaccurate criticism that qualitative work cannot deal with structure or larger issues, the by now substantial body of feminist research ranges over all these levels and utilizes the full span of qualitative methods (for a densely rich compendium that details many of these, see Reinharz, 1992).

Some of the most skillful work on women's subjectivity and experiences has been done in the area of women's health, in ways that unsettle the frames just mentioned and lead to theoretical or pragmatic consequences. Using interviews with women patients who did not follow doctor's orders, Linda Hunt, Brigitte Jordan, and Carole Browner (1989) found that the women were not difficult, noncompliant cranks, but acted for reasons that made sense in their own lives. Robin Saltonstall's (1993) analysis of in-depth interviews with men and women shows important gender differences in embodiment and the construction of health. Using narratives from women who had been battered but were able to seek and find help, Lora Bex Lempert (1992) depicts the women's difficulties in interpreting this experience to themselves and, critically, to others who did not always believe their stories. Susan Bell's (1988) narrative analysis of DES daughters shows the connection between personal problems and collective action.

Relationships and Interaction

Feminists have also looked at women's relationships and interactions with others to reveal aspects of male control lodged in linguistic and conversational structures. Utilizing discourse analysis, Alexandra Dundes Todd (1989) and Sue Fisher (1988) outline the extent to which maleness dominates interaction between female patients and male doctors and significantly influences diagnosis and care. With conversational analysis, Candace West (1988) demonstrates how gender supersedes professional status where the patient is male and the physician female, a finding that reveals the replication of gender dominance.

Women's interactions and relationships have also been examined in a variety of work settings. Maria Patricia Fernandez-Kelly's (1983) participation and observation in border factories unveiled lives of Mexican-American women working there. Anne Game (1991) details the patriarchal nature of secretarial work in Australia. Frances Katsuranis and I have shown how temporary clerical workers, thought by some feminists to be powerless and without agency, exert control of their work assignments and link their work to their private lives (Olesen & Katsuranis, 1978). Arlene Daniels's (1988) interview study of upper-class female volunteers and their work discloses how these women's interactions sustain and create class position.

Social Movements, Organizations, Structures

Analysis of interaction is also central in feminist research on larger units, such as social movements and social organizations, but these rely on historical analysis of structures as well. Dorothy Broom's (1991) account of the emergence of state-sponsored women's health clinics in Australia explicates contradictions faced by feminists interested in reform and transformation of the health care system while working within the system. In a historical analysis of states' laws on informed consent for breast cancer patients undergoing treatment and interviews with key leaders, Theresa Montini (1991) found that medical interests partially co-opted the women's goals. Of interest and perhaps concern to feminists interested in feminist movements, she also found that the activists themselves, although willing to borrow feminist principles, would not define themselves or their work as "feminist." Brandy Britton's (1993) examination of the political economy of the battered women's movement also utilizes historical analysis and interviews that reveal state or federal funding's sometimes pernicious effects on members of movement organizations in terms of race, class, and sexual orientation. All three of these studies attempted to bridge the so-called gap between microinteractional studies and inquiries that look at macro or larger sociological units.

This work borders on an emerging style of analysis within symbolic interactionism that Clarke (1990) calls "meso analysis." This refers to analysis of the "mesostructure" or "how societal and institutional forces mesh with human activity" (Maines, 1982, p. 10). Adele Clarke's (1990; Clarke & Montini, 1993) historical research shows how these processes play out in the arena of women's reproductive health around such issues as production of contraceptives. Where meso analysts have looked at gender and science in the case of technologies, these studies elevate the question of research for women to an important critique of contemporary and historical male-dominated science and its control not only of women but also of the policy process.

Policy

In her review of qualitative analysis and policy in Britain, Janet Finch (1986, p. 127) optimistically argues that feminist qualitative research can make an important contribution to the understanding and making of policy. Though issue- or topic-oriented feminist qualitative research has had small impact on U.S. policy makers, probably because of their preference for quantitative research, it has productively exposed aspects and consequences of the policy-making process. Using aging as their topic, Carroll Estes and Beverly Edmonds (1981) articulate a symbolic interactionist model for understanding how emergent policy issues become framed. They recognize that ambiguousness characterizes much policy activity and that the "transformation of intentions" (their definition of policy) turns on who frames and controls the definitions emergent from the ambiguities.

Joyce Gelb and Marian Lief Palley (1987) detail histories of feminist organizations in such policy issues as credit discrimination, Title IX, and reproductive choice. How deeply divided viewpoints about policy issues can be is shown by Patricia Kaufert and Sonja McKinlay (1985), who used content analysis of scientific and lay publications to display divergent views of clinicians and medical researchers. Shelley Romalis's (1988) ethnographic/interview study of Canadian physicians and women who wanted to have home births outlines the dynamics of policy conflict in the context of home and hospital. Feminist studies from Britain on health (McIntyre, 1985), education (Stanworth, 1985), and housing (Austerberry & Watson, 1985) also excel in showing constructions of and contentions within policy issues, as does Rosalind Petchesky's (1985) analysis of how women's health is framed by feminists and others in the abortion debate and Amanda Rittenhouse's (1991) examination of why premenstrual syndrome emerged as a social problem.

However, feminist researchers have yet to explore other critical areas, for example, policy making (exceptions include Margaret Stacey's 1992 observational research on the British Medical Council and Susan Chase's 1992 narrative studies with female school administrators), how feminist-inspired policies are implemented (Craddock & Reid's 1993 participatory work with a well-woman clinic is an example), or the state's definition and control of women, such as political scientist Wendy Brown (1992) has done in questioning Barbara Ehrenreich and Frances Fox Piven's (1983) positive feminist view of the state for women. These papers, like Nancy Fraser's (1989) examination of women's needs, are a type of theoretical-analytic research importantly oriented as critiques of the state and state systems.

◆ Models of Feminists' Research

The lability noted at the outset of this chapter deeply characterizes more than scope. It is definitely the hallmark of reflections on the nature of feminist research. In 1987 Sandra Harding, a philosopher, described certain social science models as reflecting transitional epistemologies, a characterization that would still apply to feminists both in the social or behavioral sciences and in history and literary studies. Here I will discuss these models, feminist standpoint research, feminist empiricism, and postmodernism, including the rapidly developing area of feminist cultural studies. My discussion may make these viewpoints seem more discrete than they are, but I wish to sharpen core attributes in order to highlight certain criticisms of the approaches and to lead to issues that feminist qualitative researchers face. The labile moment noted previously calls for rethinking these categories, a task not possible in the confines of this chapter.

Feminist Standpoint Research

Reflecting long-standing feminist criticisms of the absence of women from or marginalized reports of women in research accounts, research done from the perspective of standpoint theories stresses a particular view that builds on and from women's experiences (Harding, 1987, p. 184). The work of sociologist Dorothy Smith (1974, 1989, p. 34), who conceptualized women's "perspective," and Marxist political scientist Nancy Hartsock (1983, 1985) exemplifies research starting from women's actual experience in everyday life within the material division of labor (Stanley & Wise, 1990, p. 34). Because Smith's agenda springs from a serious critique of traditional sociology, I will detail her views more fully; this is not intended to slight Hartsock's important contributions to the genre of standpoint theory and research. Much of the feminist work cited earlier could be defined as standpoint work, though not all proceeds from a Marxist orientation and not all self-consciously examines the researcher's place "in the relations of ruling," as Dorothy Smith urges. A body of work by feminist legal scholars (Ashe, 1988; Bartlett, 1990; Fry, 1992; MacKinnon 1982, 1983; Matsuda 1992) that utilizes content analysis also falls within this genre.

Blending Marxist, phenomenological, and ethnomethodological per-spectives, Dorothy Smith (1987) moves well beyond widely accepted understandings of the importance of intersubjectivity in qualitative work such as ethnography, participant observation, and interview. Aware of women's exclusions and silencing in many realms, not the least of which are academic disciplines, she conceptualizes the everyday world as a problematic, that is, continually created, shaped, and known by women within it and its organization, which is shaped by external material factors or textually mediated relations (p. 91). To understand that everyday world of women as it is known by the women who continually create and shape it within the materialist context, the researcher herself must not create it as an object for study as would be done traditionally in sociology, which would divide subject and object. She must, instead, "be able to work very differently than she is able to with established sociological strategies of thinking and inquiry" (Smith, 1992, p. 96) that are not outside the relations of ruling. This clearly demands a high degree of reflexivity from the feminist qualitative researcher and a recognition of how feminist sociolo-gists "participate as subjects in the orders of ruling" (p. 96), an example of which is her own work with Alison Griffith on mothers' work on children's schooling (Griffith & Smith, 1987), which discloses how she and her colleague found in their own discussions the effects of the North American discourse on mothering of the 1920s and 1930s (Smith, 1992, p. 97).

For feminist researchers the standpoint position, particularly as power-fully set forth by Nancy Hartsock and subtly argued by Dorothy Smith, stimulates thought, work in this style (for other examples, see Smith, 1992, p. 97), and, importantly, doubts and questions: Is there an essential tone, for example, an overarching inference, as to the nature of woman (Lemert, 1992, p. 69)? Does relativism rear its head (Harding, 1987, p. 187)? Is the model of knowledge generated from women's position simplistic (Hawkes-worth, 1989, p. 347)? Does it neglect alternative traditions of knowledge, such as those of women of color (Collins, 1992, p. 77)? Does it raise anew the problem of "validity" (Ramazanoglu, 1989)? Assuming that women's lives are fragmented, can the standpoint researcher understand these fragmented identities (Lemert, 1992, p. 68)? Is "experience" an untenable focus for feminist investigation when it, too, is continually mediated and constructed from unconscious desire (Clough, 1993a)? In these questions lie debates about the nature of disciplines, especially sociology, the vexed issues of experience and text, passion, and rationality, which I will discuss more fully in the section on issues, below.

Feminist Empiricism

These researchers work with thoughtful adherence to the standards of the current norms of qualitative inquiry, whatever the discipline. Their work proceeds on the assumptions of intersubjectivity and commonly created meanings and "realities" between researcher and participants (Olesen, 1992a). Much of the research noted in the discussion of complexities and scope is of this type (Harding, 1987, p. 182). However, some, instead of applying the research standards in their field—which, being male based, produce androcentric findings—self-consciously try to create new, but rigorous, research practices to give their findings credibility.

Just as with standpoint research, questions arise about feminist empiricism: In spite of concern and respect for women's lived experiences, do these studies nevertheless replicate old disciplinary practices and women's subordinated status? How is it possible to achieve the "neutrality/objectivity demanded in standard qualitative procedures whilst recognizing subjectivity, and, more importantly, intersubjectivity between researcher and participants" (Hawkesworth, 1989, p. 329)? Is it even possible to attempt to find a "truth about reality" (Hawkesworth, 1989, p. 330)? Can validity or its shadow cousins in qualitative work, credibility and adequacy, ever be realized? (We will return to this question in the section on issues.) Does the emphasis on subjectivity come "too close . . . to a total elimination of intersubjective validation of description and explanation" (Komarovsky, 1988, p. 592; 1991)?

Postmodernism

Concerned with the difficulties of ever producing more than a partial story of women's lives in oppressive contexts, postmodernist feminist researchers regard "truth" as a destructive illusion. The endless play of signs, the shifting sands of interpretation, language that obscures—all prompt these feminists to view the world as endless stories or texts, many of which sustain the integration of power and oppression and actually "constitute us as subjects in a determinant order" (Hawkesworth, 1989, p. 349). Their focus is therefore narrative and "the nebulous distinction between text and reality" (Hawkesworth, 1989, p. 348). In such a view gender is no longer privileged.

Nowhere has the postmodern debate among feminist qualitative researchers in the social sciences occurred with more vigor and sophistication than in anthropology and political science. Mary Hawkesworth (1989), a political scientist, argues that neither feminist empiricism (commitment to traditional research methods) nor feminist standpoint research (taking women's view as particular and privileged) can deal with what she calls "the politics of knowledge" (p. 346), by which she means the utilization of "the mode of analysis appropriate to a specific problem" (p. 346). Similarly, she criticizes postmodern thought as too relativistic and overlooking life's real problems, which get lost in the emphasis on textuality. Her solution: a critical feminist analysis to demonstrate rationally "deficiencies of alternative explanations" about women's situation. Her fear, like that of others, concerning postmodernism is that "in a world of radical inequality, relativist resignation enforces the status quo" (p. 351). (For replies to Hawkesworth, see Hawkesworth, 1990a, 1990b; Hekman, 1990a; Shogan, 1990.)

Expressing similar worries, anthropologists Frances E. Mascia-Lees, Patricia Sharpe, and Colleen Ballerino Cohen (1989) point out that the postmodern or "new" ethnography, because of its lack of centeredness, "directs attention away from the fact that ethnography is more than 'writing it up' " (p. 33); it can obscure power relationships. (For a reply, see Kirby, 1991; see also Mascia-Lees, Sharpe, & Cohen, 1991.) Agneta M. Johannsen (1992) further characterizes postmodern anthropological ethnographers with her claim that they let "the people" speak for themselves, which neither addresses problems nor represents a cultural system.

Carrying the imprint of feminist forebears from deconstructionism and postmodernism (French feminists such as Cixous and Irigaray, and Foucault, Lyotard, Baudrillard), feminist research in the rapidly developing area of cultural studies stresses representation and text. This area is intellectually particularly complex, for scholars working within it utilize Marxist theorizing from Althusser, French feminist theory (Irigaray, Cixous, and so on), psychoanalytic views (Lacan—though by no means do all feminists agree on Lacan's utility for feminism; see Ferguson, 1993, p. 212, n. 3), literary criticism, and historical analysis.

Three types of inquiry are of interest. First is "the production, distribution, consumption and exchange of cultural objects and their meanings" (Denzin 1992, p. 80), such as video, film, music, and the body itself

312

(Balsamo, 1993; deLauretis, 1987; Morris, 1992). Second is "the textual analysis of these cultural objects, their meanings, and the practices that surround them" (Denzin, 1992, p. 81), including various discourses (Game, 1991) and the work of other feminists or sociologists (Clough, 1992). Third is "the study of lived cultures and experiences, which are shaped by the cultural meanings that circulate in everyday life" (Denzin, 1992, p. 81). Here will be found the by now voluminous (and growing) work in gender and science, where science, the sacred cow of the Enlightenment, modernity, and the contemporary moment, is dismembered as a culture to reveal its practices, discourses, and implications for control of women's lives (Haraway, 1991; Jacobus, Keller, & Shuttleworth, 1990). Research about women's reproductive health, an issue central to feminist research from the start and productive of sociological and historical works regarded as classics in feminist inquiry (Gordon, 1976; Luker, 1984), is moving into the gender and science arena.

Within cultural studies some feminists, following Foucault and Lacan, emphasize text and the point that "desire" is produced and replicated through various discourses. More precisely, as Patricia Clough (1993a) has argued, "The textuality never refers to a text, but to the processes of desire elicited and repressed, projected and introjected in the activity of reading and writing" (p. 175). The term *desire* seems to include (a) passion, (b) the mischievous and mysterious contributions of the unconscious, (c) libidinal resources not squeezed out of us by childhood and adult socialization, and (d) the sexuality and sexual politics of cultural life and its reproduction and representation (e.g., films, video, magazines).

This type of work is not easily classified, for multidisciplinary borrowing, both of content and method, is widespread, legitimate, and, indeed, encouraged as new forms and understandings are sought (Grossberg, Nelson, & Treichler, 1992). Compared with customary qualitative feminist work, these studies are apt to appear as hybrids, radical (in terms of form, content, and substance) and, for some, threatening and subversive, not merely of male dominance but of feminism itself.

Even as standpoint and empiricist perspectives have excited and worried feminist researchers, so has the work of feminists doing cultural studies: Is the world nothing more than text (Hawkesworth, 1989, p. 349)? Are there only stories, no action, no "progress" (Harding, 1987, p. 188)? Does focus on the text obscure enduring oppressive institutions and practices (Hawkesworth, 1989, p. 350)? Which academic disciplines are prepared to accept such "unusual" work and recognize it?

Emergence of these three models and the growing complexity of qualitative feminist research has prompted highly self-conscious examination (O. Butler, 1986; Collins, 1986; Fine, 1992; Fonow & Cook, 1991; Lather, 1991; Mies, 1982; Moore, 1988; Nielsen, 1990; Reinharz, 1992; Roberts, 1981; Stanley, 1990; Stanley & Wise, 1983; Tom, 1989). This has led to the realization that embedded in all three models are troublesome issues for feminist researchers, though researchers in the three traditions, if they can be called that at this point, do not necessarily confront all of these. These issues derive from criticisms of empirical qualitative work, such as bias, questions about adequacy or credibility, relationships with persons in the research, and ethical implications. Others emerge from the impact of postcolonial deconstructive thought and postmodernism, such as whose voices are heard and how, and whether text or experience should be created, and by whom. Discussion of these issues takes us to the question of how and whether qualitative feminist research addresses boundaries and content of current disciplines, and to some concluding observations.

◆ Issues Derived From Criticisms of Qualitative Research

Bias

Concern with bias, a concept from logicopositivist work, has been a long-standing criticism of qualitative research (Huber, 1973; Denzin, 1992, pp. 49-52). To the charges that the researcher brings her own biases, qualitative feminist researchers would reply that bias is a misplaced term. To the contrary, these are resources and, if the researcher is sufficiently reflexive about her project, she can evoke these as resources to guide data gathering or creating and for understanding her own interpretations and behavior in the research, as Arlene Daniels's (1983) candid account of her fieldwork mistakes in her studies of military psychiatrists and upper-class volunteers shows.

What is required, they would argue, is sufficient reflexivity to uncover what may be deep-seated but poorly recognized views on issues central to the research and a full account of the researcher's views, thinking, and conduct. Commenting on the self in fieldwork, Nancy Scheper-Hughes (1992) writes, "We cannot rid ourselves of the cultural self we bring with us into the field any more than we can disown the eyes, ears and skin through which we take in our intuitive perceptions about the new and strange world we have entered" (p. 28). However, the researcher still needs to be reflexive about her views: Sherry Gorelick (1991) specifically identifies potential problems when inductivist feminist researchers who espouse a Marxist framework "fail to take account of the hidden structure of oppression (the research participant is not omniscient) and the hidden relations of oppression (the participant may be ignorant of her relative privilege over and difference from other women)" (p. 461). Scheper-Hughes (1983) asks whether feminist researchers in anthropology may unwittingly replicate androcentric perspectives.

Speaking directly to questions of bias around race and class that might be introduced by researchers' failure to recognize or incorporate diversity, and anticipating Kathy Ferguson's (1993, p. 168) later criticisms of the underthematizing of class in feminist theory and research, Cannon et al. (1991) draw attention to the problems faced by qualitative studies, which are typically smaller than quantitative projects and hence face greater difficulties in recruiting women of color and of different classes.

Bias is related to the central issue of subjectivity in feminist research and the concomitant problem of objectivity in empirical research. Jennifer Ring (1987) proposes dialectics (following Hegel) as a solution to the problems of subjectivity and objectivity: "Dialectical thought contains the possibility for a radical departure from an empiricist conception of objectivity when it refuses to allow the border between objectivity and subjectivity to rest long enough to take a static form" (p. 771).

Adequacy and Credibility

Perhaps no issue is as challenging to feminist empiricist researchers as that of adequacy or credibility, the parallel to validity in quantitative work (Hall & Stevens, 1991). Because they often problematize taken-for-granted situations, raise difficult and uncomfortable questions about women's contexts, and stress the importance of subjectivity, feminist empiricists working in the qualitative mode are particularly vulnerable to positivists' criticisms about credibility.

Feminist empiricists have struggled with this in a number of ways. Janet Finch and Jennifer Mason (1990) meticulously detail their use of theoretical sampling to find "negative cases" with which to refute or amend their interpretations, a strategy from grounded theory (Strauss & Corbin, 1990). Catherine Kohler Riessman (1990) explicates her analysis and her worries

315

about the sociologist's interpretive voice and the integration of respondents' voices, as many methodologists urge (Burgess, 1984, pp. 209-219). Many of the accounts noted earlier (e.g., DeVault, 1991; Ruzek, 1978) detail how the research problem emerged and how different data sources were "triangulated" or how the researcher conducted herself (Rollins, 1985; Warren, 1988). Although "taking the account back to respondents" has been widely discussed, along with cautions about its use (Bloor, 1983; Emerson & Pollner, 1988; Hammersley & Atkinson, 1983), it has not been used as often as perhaps one might expect in feminist research, where concern for respondents is emphasized.

One attempt to achieve this, however, that recognizes the dual task of seeking "objectivity" while dealing with the relations between the researcher and the researched, a task not always easily realized, was made by Joan Acker, Kate Barry, and Johanna Esseveld (1991, pp. 142-150). They tried to create new criteria for adequacy, such as being sure the subjects' voices are heard, accounting for the investigators as well as those participating, and revealing conditions that result in the daily lives being studied, but they also recognize that "it is impossible to create a research process that erases the contradictions (in power and consciousness) between researcher and researched" (p. 150). These struggles with the tension between intersubjective understanding and the goal of objective reporting in feminist qualitative research foreground ethical issues.

Ethical Concerns

Feminists have sharpened the numerous discussions in anthropology and sociology on ethical issues. They draw on the theme that at once characterizes feminist qualitative research and leads to ethical dilemmas, namely, concern for and even involvement with the participating persons. Janet Finch (1984) delineates a part of this problem in her insightful comments on interviewing lonely or isolated women hungry for contact with other people who may be unwittingly manipulated by the researcher. Judith Stacey's (1988) widely cited paper on the fundamental contradictions in feminist ethnography reminds feminist qualitative researchers that their methods can be as worrisome as those of quantitative researchers. More specifically, she calls attention to the uncomfortable question of getting data from respondents as a means to an end and the difficult compromises that may be involved in promising respondents control over the report. Feminist nurse researchers have pointed out that additional ethical dilemmas arise when doing research in one's own professional culture, where the researcher and professional roles may conflict (Field, 1991). These issues emerge with even more urgency in studies where participants are also researchers.

Degree of Participants' Involvement in the Research

All feminist qualitative research shares with interpretive work in general the assumption of intersubjectivity between researcher and participant and the mutual creation of data. In a certain sense, participants are always "doing" research, for they, along with the researchers, construct the meanings that become "data" for later interpretation by the researcher (Olesen, 1992a). Qualitative researchers in general have differed in the extent to which participants are involved as researchers in the inquiry and the nature of the involvement when they are.

Some feminists, however, have undertaken projects in which participants whose lives and situations are the focus of the work become coresearchers, in the interests of not exploiting women as research "subjects" and of empowering women to do research for themselves on issues of interest to them. Participants as researchers are generally found in action-oriented research projects, where the nature of participation ranges from researcher consultation with participants regarding topics and research instruments such as questionnaires, through training women to do research under the direction of a feminist researcher (Lather, 1986, 1988), to participants and researchers working together on all phases of the project (Cancian, 1992; Craddock & Reid, 1993).

Nancy Kleiber and Linda Light's (1978; Light & Kleiber, 1981) early study of a Vancouver women's health collective is an instance of the last of these styles, termed interactive or participatory research. Kleiber and Light describe their conversion from traditional field-workers to coresearchers with the members of the women's health collective and the difficulties of closing the distance between researchers and participants when both engage in the research. Their text, a traditional, not experimental, account written by themselves and their participants, reflects many voices, for the data gathering, analysis, and writing are collective.

Working out modes of participant research in consultation with participants, rather than as an afterthought, challenges feminist researchers on many levels: assumptions about women's knowledge; representations of women; modes of data gathering, analysis, interpretation, and writing the

317

account; relationships between researcher and participants and, critically, diversity among women's views about women, particularly where views are not similar to feminist outlooks (Hess, 1990); and the risk of appropriating participant-generated data to or along the lines of the researcher's interests (Opie, 1992).

◆ Issues Posed by Deconstructionism and Postmodernism

Voice and the Account

Deeply implicated in the very foundations of feminist research lies the question of voice and, by implication, the account. Forcefully stated by women of color and Third World feminists (see earlier sections of the chapter) and reiterated in critical comments on postcolonial research practices, this question concerns how voices of participants are to be heard, with what authority, and in what form. This concern has moved far beyond postmodernism and deconstructionism and has become lodged in the worries of feminist qualitative researchers in general. They are highly conscious of the absence of women's voices, distortions, and the charge that preparing the account in the usual social science modes only replicates hierarchical conditions found in the parent discipline, where women are outside the account (Smith, 1989, p. 34).

Working with the intertwined problem of realizing as fully as possible women's voices in data gathering and preparing an account that transmits those voices poses some difficult questions, though a number of creative attempts have been made. Regarding difficulties, Ellen Lewin (1991) has pointed out that merely letting the tape recorder run to achieve full representation overlooks the fact that respondents' accounts are already mediated when they come into the interview. Michelle Fine (1992) delineates some worrisome issues about use of voices (use of pieces of narrative, taking individual voices to reflect group behavior, assuming that voices are free of power relations, failure to make clear the researcher's own position in relationship to the voices) and forcefully urges feminist researchers to "articulate how, how not, and within what limits" voices are used (pp. 217-219). Borrowing literary devices to express voices may also contain hidden problems of control (Mascia-Lees et al., 1989, p. 30).

Some feminists have developed some innovative ways to reflect and present voice, though not all would be free of the problems Fine discusses (for an extensive roster of new ethnographic accounts, see Mascia-Lees et al., 1989, pp. 7-8, n. 1). Two contrasting examples: Marjorie Shostak (1981) gives a verbatim dialogic account of her voice and that of Nisa, a !Kung woman. In Susan Krieger's (1983) fieldwork report of a lesbian community in the Midwest, members' voices are heard as a polyphonic chorus on various issues, but Susan Krieger's voice as narrator is absent, though she clearly selected the materials for the account.

Margery Wolf (1992) presents three different versions of an event in her fieldwork in Taiwan: a piece of fiction, her anthropological field notes, and a social science article. Ruth Behar (1993) explodes the traditional anthropological form of life history to intertwine the voice of her cocreator with her own in an extended double-voiced text. Her apt title, *Translated Woman,* reflects Behar as researcher and narrator as much as it does her cocreator, "Esperanza."

Calling for new textual and presentational practices, Laurel Richardson (1991, 1992) has utilized poetry; Michael McCall and Howard Becker (1990) have given dramatic readings, a technique also suggested by the late Marianne Paget (1990). Carolyn Ellis and Art Bochner (1992) have used the technique of telling personal stories. (For greater detail on textual practice, see Richardson, Chapter 12, Volume 3, this series.) Though sessions at meetings of academic disciplines where unusual presentations are given are lively and well attended, and many feminist journals publish creative presentations, the worrisome question remains, given the style and framing of mainstream academic journals, how feminist qualitative researchers can alter present publication practices to realize greater receptivity to these new forms. Is the solvent of feminist scholarship sufficient to break through the ossified academic structures?

Experience and Analysis

Although much research in the empiricist and standpoint styles takes women's experience as the core concern, largely on the basis of women's having been excluded from male-dominated versions of "reality" (Gregg, 1987), some critics have highlighted the unstable nature of a concept of "experience" and have advocated as well analysis of conditions that produce "experience." Feminists in both history (e.g., Scott, 1991) and psychology (e.g., Morawski, 1990) argue that merely taking experience into account does not reflect on how that experience came to be. In short, oppressive systems are replicated rather then criticized in the unquestioning reliance on "experience." As Joan Scott (1991) comments, "Experience is at once always already an interpretation *and* in need of interpretation" (p. 779). Several feminist research accounts both report experience and interpret economic or class influences on the framing of experience. Examples include Arlie Hochschild's (1983) analysis of the experience of flight attendants' management of emotion in the context of the workings of the airline industry, Nona Glazer's (1991) examination of racism and classism in professional nursing, and Nancy Scheper-Hughes's (1992) exploration of motherhood and poverty in northeastern Brazil.

Other feminist researchers, such as Patricia Clough (1993a, p. 179), who look to deconstruction or psychoanalytic feminist semiotics disavow any attention to actual experience on the grounds that, irrespective of how close the researcher, experience is always created in discourse and textuality. Text takes primacy here, constituting the bases for incisive analyses of text production as a fundamental mode of social criticism (Clough, 1992).

◆ Consequences:
Disciplines Bounded and Unbounded

How comfortable are feminist qualitative researchers with their own disciplines, and do they see transformation of the discipline as a part of the agenda that urges research for women? Whether the types of qualitative feminist research noted here and the theoretical and epistemological assumptions supporting it can alter, much less transform, the disciplines in which these researchers work cannot be easily answered: Sectors of different disciplines, such as sociology and psychology, hold tenaciously to positivistic outlooks, and there are diverse theoretical views within disciplines that blunt or facilitate feminist transformation (Stacey & Thorne, 1985). Moreover, it is simplistic to think of a single feminist research impact, for as I have tried to show in this chapter, qualitative feminist research is not homogeneous but highly differentiated and complex, with different potentials for influence on the disciplines.

Within anthropology, Lila Abu-Lughod (1990) and Ruth Behar (1993) argue that dissolving the self/other, subject/object distinctions fundamental to traditional ethnography holds the promise of "unsettling boundaries" (Abu-Lughod, 1990, p. 26) and liberating the discipline from "the colonizing domination" of its colonial past (Behar, 1993, p. 302). Writing about the "awkward relationship between anthropology and feminism," Marilyn Strathern (1987, p. 292), however, has contended that feminist and anthropological views are not paradigms that can be shifted, but are so fundamental to the practice of each that they are not open to conscious challenge and in fact "mock" rather than challenge one another.

Calls from feminists for overhaul of their disciplines reflect the diverse views on research noted in this chapter as well as the intellectual inertia and embedded resistance in various fields (Stacey & Thorne, 1985). Dorothy Smith's (1987, 1989, 1990a, 1990b) radical critique of sociology (radical in the sense of "going to the roots" and an orientation to the left politically), initially put forth in 1974 and enriched in subsequent rethinking, formulated a way, unutilized in sociology, to discover women's experience and to link it to the "politics and practice of progressive struggle" (Smith, 1992, p. 88).

In a long-overdue review of Smith's work, several theorists highlight the potential of her thinking for the alteration of sociology, the concept of subjectivity pushed to its limit (Lemert, 1992, p. 71), the integral part of knowledge in "the relations of ruling for contemporary capitalism" (Collins, 1992, p. 73), and the "problematizing of [sociology's] practical underpinnings" (Connell, 1992, p. 81). (Some of their criticisms are noted in the earlier section on standpoint research.) For some, however, Smith has not gone far enough in deconstructing sociology as a dominant discourse of experience (Clough, 1993a, p. 169), a view Smith (1993) herself rejects as overly oriented to text and neglecting experience (see Clough, 1993b, for a reply to Smith).

Other feminist researchers' work strains at the boundaries and hammers at foundations of sociology in particular and the social sciences in general. Patricia Hill Collins's (1986, 1990) analysis of black feminists in sociology raises questions about the impact of dualistic thought in the discipline and its pernicious contribution to the continuance of racism and argues that sociologists should attend more carefully to the anomalies introduced into their discipline by their own biographies. Two feminists, writing in a deconstructive vein, have offered different criticisms. Patricia Clough (1992), through the lens of psychoanalytic semiotics, urges the task of social criticism and asks that feminists and sociologists strip privilege away

321

from observation and "factual" description, hallmarks of traditional ethnography, and turn to "rereadings of representations in every form of information processing," be it literature or empirical science (p. 137). In a similar deconstructive mode, Australian Ann Game (1991, p. 47) rejects the sacred concept of the "social" in favor of discourses as the sociological focus.

In spite of, or perhaps because of, their gloomy assessment of the extent to which feminist psychologists have made or can make an impact on their discipline, Fine and Gordon (1992, p. 25) ask that feminist psychologists work in the space between the personal and the political to reconstitute psychology and urge activist research in feminist psychology.[3]

Whether the subversive potential of feminist cultural studies will influence disciplinary boundaries (Denzin, 1992, p. 75) may well be answered in a trade-off between the rapid growth of this area, including the intellectually exciting gender and science arena, and the constraints of the 1990's fiscal crisis in American universities, a crisis that will also influence the impact of other qualitative feminist research on disciplinary focus and boundaries.

◆ Future Questions for Qualitative Feminist Research

The diversity of approaches, methods, topics and epistemologies noted here suggests that a major future question for qualitative feminist research will be the degree to which these various approaches speak effectively to a sociology for rather than about women. This question is crucial, quite aside from its centrality in the qualitative feminist research agenda, for it raises the issue of audiences and contexts. From the 1970s through the 1990s there has been an unslaked thirst for feminist publications, both theoretical and empirical, but that audience has been largely academic. The extent to which the new participatory forms, discussed here, and the traditional styles or the experimental work reach beyond the academy, and in what mode, will influence feminist qualitative research. It is unlikely, given the range of feminisms, that any orthodoxy, traditional or postmodern, will prevail—nor indeed, in my view, should it. The complexities and problems of women's lives, whatever the context, are sufficiently great that multiple approaches via qualitative research are required.

Notes

1. What you, the reader, will see here is constructed by and filtered through my research experience as a socialist feminist sociologist interested in women's health and women in health and healing systems. I have worked primarily within the emergent or Blumerian wing of the interactionist-social constructionist tradition (Denzin, 1992, pp. 1-21), though I also start with keen interest in the study of cultural products by virtue of a long-ago career in journalism and early graduate study in mass media of communication (Olesen, 1956). I am sympathetic to postmodern currents in both interactionism and feminism, which encourage provocative and productive unpacking of taken-for-grantedness about women in specific historical and material contexts, and I deeply appreciate all attempts to respect women in the research process and to give voice to the voiceless. However, I still believe that research for rather than merely about women is possible through qualitative modes and theoretical writings, imperfect and transitory though they may be and irrespective of researcher's locale. Both experiential and text-oriented styles in combination ought to be utilized. I see that feminist work sets the stage for other research, other actions (I here refer to community, policy, and so on) that transcend and transform (Olesen, 1993). For me, feminist inquiry is dialectical, with different standpoints fusing to produce new syntheses that in turn become the grounds for further work (Nielsen, 1990, p. 29; Westkott, 1979, p. 430). Most of all, feminist qualitative researchers, in making women's lives problematic, should not turn away from rendering their own practices problematic in the interests of more fully realized research for women. If one's own work is overturned or altered by another researcher with a different, more effective approach, then one should rejoice and move forward.

2. The literature on deconstructionism, postmodernism, and feminism is voluminous. For readers starting to explore this area, the following works are helpful: the entire spring 1988 issue of *Feminist Studies*, Nicholson (1990), Hekman (1990b), Flax (1990), and Rosenau (1992).

3. Feminist activist researchers not only work on issues of concern to women, but themselves engage various arenas on women's behalf, participating as lay members of the Food and Drug Administration or its advisory boards (Sheryl Ruzek and Jane Zones) or testifying on behalf of battering women (Julie Blackman; see Blackman, 1989).

◆ References

Abel, E. K., & Nelson, M. K. (1990). *Circles of care: Work and identity in women's lives*. Albany: State University of New York Press.

Abu-Lughod, L. (1990). Can there be a feminist ethnography? *Women and Performance, 5*, 7-27.

Acker, J., Barry, K., & Esseveld, J. (1991). Objectivity and truth: Problems in doing feminist research. In M. M. Fonow & J. A. Cook (Eds.), *Beyond methodology: Feminist scholarship as lived research* (pp. 133-153). Bloomington: Indiana University Press.

Ashe, M. (1988). Law-language of maternity: Discourse holding nature in contempt. *New England Law Review, 521*, 44-70.

Austerberry, H., & Watson, S. (1985). A woman's place: A feminist approach to housing in Britain. In C. Ungerson (Ed.), *Women and social policy* (pp. 91-108). London: Macmillan.

Balsamo, A. (1993). On the cutting edge: Cosmetic surgery and the technological production of the gendered body. *Camera Obscura, 28,* 207-237.

Bartlett, K. (1990). Feminist legal methods. *Harvard Law Review, 103,* 45-50.

Behar, R. (1993). *Translated woman: Crossing the border with Esperanza's story.* Boston: Beacon.

Bell, S. (1988). Becoming a political woman: The reconstruction and interpretation of experience through stories. In A. D. Todd & S. Fisher (Eds.), *Gender and discourse: The power of talk* (pp. 97-123). Norwood, NJ: Ablex.

Blackman, J. (1989). *Intimate violence: A study of injustice.* New York: Columbia University Press.

Bloor, M. J. (1983). Notes on member validation. R. M. Emerson (Ed.), *Contemporary field research* (pp. 156-172). Boston: Little, Brown.

Britton, B. M. (1993). *The battered women's movement in the U.S. c1973-1993: A micro-macro analysis.* Unpublished doctoral dissertation, University of California, San Francisco, School of Nursing, Department of Social and Behavioral Sciences.

Broom, D. (1991). *Damned if we do: Contradictions in women's health care.* Sydney: Allen & Unwin.

Brown, W. (1992). Finding the man in the state. *Feminist Studies, 18,* 7-34.

Burgess, R. (1984). *In the field: An introduction to field research.* Boston: Unwin Hyman.

Butler, O. (1986). *Feminist experiences in feminist research.* Manchester, UK: University of Manchester Press.

Butler, J. (1990). *Gender trouble: Feminism and the subversion of identity.* London: Routledge.

Cancian, F. M. (1992). Participatory research. In E. F. Borgatta & M. Borgatta (Eds.), *Encyclopedia of sociology* (pp. 1427-1432). New York: Macmillan.

Cannon, L. W., Higginbotham, E., & Leung, M. L. A. (1991). Race and class bias in qualitative research on women. In M. M. Fonow & J. A. Cook (Eds.), *Beyond methodology: Feminist scholarship as lived research* (pp. 107-118). Bloomington: Indiana University Press.

Chase, S. E. (1992). *Narrative practices: Understanding power and subjection and women's work narratives.* Paper presented at the Qualitative Analysis Conference, Carleton University, Ottawa.

Chow, E. N. (1987). The development of feminist consciousness among Asian American women. *Gender & Society, 1,* 284-299.

Clarke, A. (1990). A social worlds research adventure: The case of reproductive science. In S. E. Cozzens & T. F. Gieryn (Eds.), *Theories of science in society* (pp. 15-43). Bloomington: Indiana University Press.

Clarke, A., & Montini, T. (1993). The many faces of RU486: Tales of situated knowledges and technological considerations. *Science, Technology and Human Values, 18,* 42-78.

Clifford, J., & Marcus, G. E. (Eds.). (1986). *Writing culture: The poetics and politics of ethnography.* Berkeley: University of California Press.

Clough, P. T. (1992). *The end(s) of ethnography: From realism to social criticism.* Newbury Park, CA: Sage.

Clough, P. T. (1993a). On the brink of deconstructing sociology: A critical reading of Dorothy Smith's standpoint epistemology. *Sociological Quarterly, 34,* 169-182.

Clough, P. T. (1993b). Response to Smith. *Sociological Quarterly, 34,* 193-194.

Code, L. (1991). *What can she know? Feminist theory and the construction of knowledge.* Ithaca, NY: Cornell University Press.

Collins, P. H. (1986). Learning from the outsider within: The sociological significance of black feminist thought. *Social Problems, 33,* 514-532.

Collins, P. H. (1990). *Black feminist thought: Knowledge, consciousness and the politics of empowerment.* New York: Routledge.

Collins, P. H. (1992). Transforming the inner circle: Dorothy Smith's challenge to sociological theory. *Sociological Theory, 10,* 73-80.

Connell, R. W. (1992). A sober anarchism. *Sociological Theory, 10,* 81-87.

Cook, J. A., & Fonow, M. M. (1986). Knowledge and women's interests: Issues of epistemology and methodology in feminist sociological research. *Sociological Inquiry, 56,* 22-29.

Craddock, E., & Reid, M. (1993). Structure and struggle: Implementing a social model of a well woman clinic in Glasgow. *Social Science and Medicine, 19,* 35-45.

Crenshaw, K. (1992). Whose story is it, anyway? Feminist and antiracist appropriations of Anita Hill. In T. Morrison (Ed.), *Race-ing justice, en-gendering power* (pp. 402-440). New York: Pantheon.

Daniels, A. K. (1983). Self-deception and self-discovery in field work. *Qualitative Sociology, 6,* 195-214.

Daniels, A. K. (1988). *Invisible careers: Civic leaders from the volunteer world.* Chicago: University of Chicago Press.

Davis, A. Y. (1978). Rape, racism and the capitalist setting. *Black Scholar, 9,* 24-30.

deLauretis, T. (1987). *Technologies of gender: Essays on theory, film, and fiction.* Bloomington: Indiana University Press.

Denzin, N. K. (1992). *Symbolic interactionism and cultural studies.* Oxford: Basil Blackwell.

DeVault, M. L. (1990). Talking and listening from women's standpoint: Feminist strategies for interviewing and analysis. *Social Problems, 37,* 96-116.

DeVault, M. L. (1991). *Feeding the family: The social organization of caring as gendered work.* Chicago: University of Chicago Press.

DeVault, M. L. (1993). Different voices: Feminists' methods of social research. *Qualitative Sociology, 16,* 77-83.

Dill, B. T. (1979). The dialectics of black womanhood. *Signs, 4,* 543-555.

Ehrenreich, B., & Piven, F. F. (1983). Women and the welfare state. In I. Howe (Ed.), *Alternatives: Proposals for America from the democratic left* (pp. 30-45). New York: Pantheon.

Eichler, M. (1986). The relationship between sexist, nonsexist, woman-centered and feminist research. *Studies in Communication, 3,* 37-74.

Ellis, C., & Bochner, A. P. (1992). Telling and performing personal stories. In C. Ellis & M. G. Flaherty (Eds.), *Investigating subjectivity: Research on lived experience* (pp. 79-101). Newbury Park, CA: Sage.

Emerson, R., & Pollner, M. (1988). On the use of members' responses to researchers' accounts. *Human Organization, 47,* 189-198.

Epstein, C. F. (1981). *Women in law.* New York: Basic Books.

Estes, C. L., & Edmonds, B. C. (1981). Symbolic interaction and social policy analysis. *Symbolic Interaction, 4,* 75-86.

Fee, E. (1983). Women and health care: A comparison of theories. In E. Fee (Ed.), *Women and health: The politics of sex in medicine* (pp. 17-34). Englewood Cliffs, NJ: Baywood.

Ferguson, K. (1993). *The man question: Visions of subjectivity in feminist theory.* Berkeley: University of California Press.

Fernandez-Kelly, M. P. (1983). *For we are sold: I and my people.* Albany: State University of New York Press.

Field, P. A. (1991). Doing fieldwork in your own culture. In J. M. Morse (Ed.), *Qualitative nursing research: A contemporary dialogue* (rev. ed., pp. 91-104). Newbury Park, CA: Sage.

Finch, J. (1984). "It's great to have someone to talk to": The ethics and politics of interviewing women. In C. Bell & H. Roberts (Eds.), *Social researching: Politics, problems, practice* (pp. 70-87). London: Routledge & Kegan Paul.

Finch, J. (1986). *Research and policy: The uses of qualitative research in social and educational research.* London: Falmer.

Finch, J., & Groves, D. (1982). *A labour of love: Women, work and caring.* London: Routledge & Kegan Paul.

Finch, J., & Mason, J. (1990). Decision taking in the fieldwork process: Theoretical sampling and collaborative working. In R. G. Burgess (Ed.), *Studies in qualitative methodology: Vol. 2. Reflections on field experience* (pp. 25-50). Greenwich, CT: JAI.

Fine, M. (1992). Passions, politics and power: Feminist research possibilities. In M. Fine (Ed.), *Disruptive voices* (pp. 205-232). Ann Arbor: University of Michigan Press.

Fine, M., & Gordon, S. M. (1992). Feminist transformations of/despite psychology. In M. Fine (Ed.), *Disruptive voices* (pp. 1-25). Ann Arbor: University of Michigan Press.

Fisher, S. (1988). *In the patient's best interest: Women and the politics of medical decisions.* New Brunswick, NJ: Rutgers University Press.

Flax, J. (1987). Postmodernism and gender relations in feminist theory. *Signs, 14,* 621-643.

Flax, J. (1990). *Thinking fragments: Psychoanalysis, feminism and postmodernism in the contemporary West.* Berkeley: University of California Press.

Fonow, M. M., & Cook, J. A. (Eds.). (1991). *Beyond methodology: Feminist scholarship as lived research.* Bloomington: Indiana University Press.

Fraser, N. (1989). Struggle over needs: Outline of a socialist-feminist critical theory of late capitalist political culture. In N. Fraser, *Unruly practices: Power, discourse and gender in contemporary social theory* (pp. 161-187). Minneapolis: University of Minnesota Press.

Fry, M. J. (1992). *Postmodern legal feminism.* London: Routledge.

Game, A. (1991). *Undoing the social: Towards a deconstructive sociology.* Milton Keynes, UK: Open University Press.

Garcia, A. M. (1989). The development of Chicana feminist discourse 1970-1980. *Gender & Society, 3,* 217-238.

Gelb, J., & Palley, M. L. (1987). *Women and public policies* (rev. ed.). Princeton, NJ: Princeton University Press.

Gilligan, C. (1982). *In a different voice: Psychological theory and women's development.* Cambridge: Harvard University Press.

Glazer, N. Y. (1991). "Between a rock and a hard place": Women's professional organizations in nursing and class, racial, and ethnic inequalities. *Gender & Society, 5,* 351-372.

Gordon, L. (1976). *Women's body, women's right.* New York: Grossman.

Gorelick, S. (1991). Contradictions of feminist methodology. *Gender & Society, 5,* 459-477.

Graham, H. (1985). Providers, negotiators and mediators: Women as the hidden carers. In E. Lewin & V. Olesen (Eds.), *Women, health and healing: Toward a new perspective* (pp. 25-52). London: Tavistock.

Green, R. (1990). The Pocahontas perplex: The image of Indian Women in American culture. In E. C. DuBois & V. L. Ruiz (Eds.), *Unequal sisters: A multi-cultural reader in U.S. women's history* (pp. 15-21). London: Routledge.

Gregg, N. (1987). Reflections on the feminist critique of objectivity. *Journal of Communication Inquiry, 11,* 8-18.

Griffith, A., & Smith, D. E. (1987). Constructing knowledge: Mothering as discourse. In J. Gaskell & A. McLaren (Eds.), *Women and education* (pp. 87-103). Calgary: Detselig.

Grossberg, L., Nelson, C., & Treichler, P. A. (Eds.). (1992). *Cultural studies.* New York: Routledge.

Hall, J. M., & Stevens, P. E. (1991). Rigor in feminist research. *Advances in Nursing Science, 13,* 16-29.

Hammersley, M., & Atkinson, P. (1983). *Ethnography: Principles in practice.* London: Tavistock.

Haraway, D. J. (1991). *Simians, cyborgs and women: The reinvention of nature.* London: Routledge.

Harding, S. (1987). Conclusion: Epistemological questions. In S. Harding (Ed.), *Feminism and methodology: Social science issues* (pp. 181-190). Bloomington: Indiana University Press.

Hartsock, N. (1983). The feminist standpoint: Developing the ground for a specifically feminist historical materialism. In S. Harding & M. B. Hintikka (Eds.), *Discovering reality* (pp. 283-310). Amsterdam: D. Reidel.

Hartsock, N. (1985). *Money, sex and power: Towards a feminist historical materialism.* Boston: Northeastern University Press.

Hawkesworth, M. E. (1989). Knowers, knowing, known: Feminist theory and claims of truth. In M. R. Malson, J. F. O'Barr, S. Westphal Wihl, & M. Wyer (Eds.), *Feminist theory in practice and process* (pp. 327-351). Chicago: University of Chicago Press. (Reprinted from *Signs,* 1989, *14,* 533-557)

Hawkesworth, M. E. (1990a). Reply to Hekman. *Signs, 15,* 420-423.

Hawkesworth, M. E. (1990b). Reply to Shogan. *Signs, 15,* 426-428.

Hekman, S. (1990a). Comment on Hawkesworth's "Knowers, knowing, known: Feminist theory and claims of truth." *Signs, 15,* 417-419.

Hekman, S. (1990b). *Gender and knowledge: Elements of a postmodern feminism.* Boston: Northeastern University Press.

Hess, B. (1990). Beyond dichotomy: Drawing distinctions and embracing differences. *Sociological Forum, 5,* 75-94.

Hine, D. C. (1989). *Black women in white: Racial conflict and cooperation in the nursing profession, 1890-1950.* Bloomington: Indiana University Press.

Hochschild, A. R. (1983). *The managed heart: Commercialization of human feeling.* Berkeley: University of California Press.

Hochschild, A. R., & Machung, A. (1989). *The second shift: Inside the two-job marriage.* New York: Avon.

hooks, b. (1990). The politics of radical black subjectivity. In b. hooks, *Yearning: Race, gender, and cultural politics* (pp. 15-22). Boston: South End.

Huber, J. (1973). Symbolic interaction as a pragmatic perspective: The bias of emergent theory. *American Sociological Review, 38,* 274-284.

Hunt, L. M., Jordan, B., & Browner, C. H. (1989). Compliance and the patient's perspective. *Culture, Medicine and Psychiatry, 13,* 315-334.

Hurtado, A. (1989). Relating to privilege: Seduction and rejection in the subordination of white women and women of color. *Signs, 14,* 833-855.

Jacobus, M., Keller, E. F., & Shuttleworth, S. (1990). *Body/politics: Women and the discourses of science.* New York: Routledge.

Johannsen, A. M. (1992). Applied anthropology and post-modernist ethnography. *Human Organization, 51,* 71-81.

Jordan, B. (1977). The self-diagnosis of early pregnancy: An investigation of lay competence. *Medical Anthropology, 2,* 20-35.

Kaufert, P. A., & McKinlay, S. M. (1985). Estrogen-replacement therapy: The production of medical knowledge and the emergence of policy. In E. Lewin & V. Olesen (Eds.), *Women, health and healing: Toward a new perspective* (pp. 113-138). London: Tavistock.

Kirby, V. (1991). Comment on Mascia-Lees, Sharpe and Cohen's "The postmodernist turn in anthropology: Cautions from a feminist perspective." *Signs, 16,* 394-400.

Kleiber, N., & Light, L. (1978). *Caring for ourselves: An alternative structure for health care.* Vancouver: University of British Columbia, School of Nursing.

Komarovsky, M. (1988). The new feminist scholarship: Some precursors and polemics. *Journal of Marriage and the Family, 50,* 585-593.

Komarovsky, M. (1991). Some reflections on the feminist scholarship in sociology. *Annual Review of Sociology, 17,* 1-25.

Krieger, S. (1983). *The mirror dance: Identity in a woman's community.* Philadelphia: Temple University Press.

Lather, P. (1986). Research as praxis. *Harvard Educational Review, 56,* 257-277.

Lather, P. (1988). Feminist perspectives on empowering research methodologies. *Women's Studies International Forum, 11,* 569-581.

Lather, P. (1991). *Getting smart: Feminist research and pedagogy with/in the postmodern.* New York: Routledge.

Lemert C. (1992). Subjectivity's limit: The unsolved riddle of the standpoint. *Sociological Theory, 10,* 63-72.

Lempert, L. B. (1992). *The crucible: Battered women's experiences in help seeking.* Unpublished doctoral dissertation, University of California, San Francisco, School of Nursing, Department of Social and Behavioral Sciences.

Lewin, E. (1991). Writing gay and lesbian culture: What the natives have to say for themselves. *American Ethnologist, 18,* 786-792.

Lewin, E. (1993). *Lesbian mothers.* Ithaca, NY: Cornell University Press.

Lewin, E., & Olesen, V. (1981). Lateralness in women's work: New views on success. *Sex Roles, 6, 619-629.*

Light, L., & Kleiber, N. (1981). Interactive research in a feminist setting. In D. A. Messerschmidt (Ed.), *Anthropologists at home in North America: Methods and issues in the study of one's own society* (pp. 167-184). Cambridge: Cambridge University Press.

Lorber, J. (1975). Women and medical sociology: Invisible professionals and ubiquitous patients. In M. M. Millman & R. M. Kanter (Eds.), *Another voice: Feminist perspectives on social life and social science* (pp. 75-105). Garden City, NY: Anchor.

Luker, K. (1984). *Abortion and the politics of motherhood.* Berkeley: University of California Press.

MacKinnon, C. (1982). Feminism, Marxism, method and the state: An agenda for theory. *Signs, 7, 515-544.*

MacKinnon, C. (1983). Feminism, Marxism and the state: Toward feminist jurisprudence. *Signs, 8, 635-658.*

Maines, D. (1982). In search of the mesostructure: Studies in the negotiated order. *Urban Life, 11, 267-279.*

Marcus, G., & Fischer, M. (1986). *Anthropology as cultural critique: An experimental moment in the human sciences.* Chicago: University of Chicago Press.

Mascia-Lees, F. E., Sharpe, P., & Cohen, C. B. (1989). The postmodernist turn in anthropology: Cautions from a feminist perspective. *Signs, 15, 7-33.*

Mascia-Lees, F. E., Sharpe, P., & Cohen, C. B. (1991). Reply to Kirby. *Signs, 16, 401-408.*

Matsuda, M. (1992). *Called from within: Early women lawyers of Hawaii.* Honolulu: University of Hawaii Press.

McCall, M., & Becker, H. (1990). Performance science. *Social Problems, 37, 117-132.*

McIntyre, S. (1985). Gynaecologist/woman interaction. In C. Ungerson (Ed.), *Women and social policy* (pp. 175-184). London: Macmillan.

Mies, M. (1982). *Fighting on two fronts.* The Hague: Institute of Social Studies.

Mohanty, C. (1988). Under Western eyes: Feminist scholarship and colonial discourses. *Feminist Review, 30, 60-88.*

Montini, T. (1991). *The informed consent for breast cancer patients' movement.* Unpublished doctoral dissertation, University of California, San Francisco, School of Nursing, Department of Social and Behavioral Sciences.

Moore, H. (1988). *Feminism and anthropology.* London: Polity.

Morawski, J. (1990). Toward the unimagined: Feminism and epistemology in psychology. In R. Hare-Mustin & J. Marecek (Eds.), *Making a difference: Psychology and the construction of gender* (pp. 159-183). New Haven, CT: Yale University Press.

Morris, M. (1992). On the beach. In L. Grossberg, C. Nelson, & P. A. Treichler (Eds.), *Cultural studies* (pp. 450-472). New York: Routledge.

Murcott, A. (1983). "It's a pleasure to cook for him . . . ": Food mealtimes and gender in South Wales households. In E. Garmarnikov, J. Purvis, D. Taylorson, & D. Morgan (Eds.), *The public and the private* (pp. 1-19). London: Heinemann.

Nakano Glenn, E. (1990). The dialectics of wage work: Japanese-American women and domestic service, 1905-1940. In E. C. DuBois & V. L. Ruiz (Eds.), *Unequal sisters: A multi-cultural reader in U.S. women's history* (pp. 345-372). London: Routledge.

Nelson, M. K. (1990). *Negotiated care: The experience of family day care givers*. Philadelphia: Temple University Press.

Nicholson, L. (Ed.). (1990). *Feminism/postmodernism*. London: Routledge.

Nielsen, J. M. (Ed.). (1990). *Feminist research methods: Exemplary readings in the social sciences*. Boulder, CO: Westview.

Olesen, V. (1956). *Pre-school children's television viewing*. Unpublished master's thesis, University of Chicago, Committee on Communication.

Olesen, V., & Katsuranis, F. (1978). Urban nomads: Temporary clerical service workers. In A. Stromberg & S. Harkess (Eds.), *Women working* (pp. 20-32). Palo Alto, CA: Mayfield.

Olesen, V. (1992). *Re-writing ethnography, re-writing ourselves: Whose text is it?* Paper presented at the Qualitative Analysis Conference, Carleton University, Ottawa.

Olesen, V. (1993). Unfinished business: The problematics of women, health and healing. *The Science of Caring, 5,* 3-6.

Opie, A. (1992). Qualitative research, appropriation of the "other" and empowerment. *Feminist Review, 40,* 52-69.

Ortner, S. B., & Whitehead, H. (1981). *Sexual meanings: The cultural construction of gender and sexuality*. London: Cambridge University Press.

Paget, M. (1990). Performing the text. *Journal of Contemporary Ethnography, 19,* 136-155.

Palmer, P. (1989). *Domesticity and dirt: Housewives and domestic servants in the U.S. 1920-1945*. Philadelphia: Temple University Press.

Petchesky, R. P. (1985). Abortion in the 1980's: Feminist morality and women's health. In E. Lewin & V. Olesen (Eds.), *Women, health and healing: Toward a new perspective* (pp. 139-173). London: Tavistock.

Ramazanoglu, C. (1989). Improving on sociology: The problems of taking a feminist standpoint. *Sociology, 23,* 427-442.

Reinharz, S. (1992). *Feminist methods in social research*. New York: Oxford University Press.

Richardson, L. (1991). Postmodern social theory: Representational practices. *Sociological Theory, 9,* 173-179.

Richardson, L. (1992). The consequences of poetic representation: Writing the other, rewriting the self. In C. Ellis & M. G. Flaherty (Eds.), *Investigating subjectivity: Research on lived experience* (pp. 125-140). Newbury Park, CA: Sage.

Riessman, C. K. (1990). *Divorce talk: Women and men make sense of personal relationships*. New Brunswick, NJ: Rutgers University Press.

Ring, J. (1987). Toward a feminist epistemology. *American Journal of Political Science, 31,* 753-772.

Rittenhouse, C. A. (1991). The emergence of pre-menstrual syndrome as a social problem. *Social Problems, 38,* 15-25.

Roberts, H. (Ed.). (1981). *Doing feminist research*. London: Routledge.

Rollins, J. (1985). *Between women: Domestics and their employers*. Philadelphia: Temple University Press.

Romalis, S. (1985). Struggle between providers and recipients: The case of birth practices. In E. Lewin & V. Olesen (Eds.), *Women, health and healing: Toward a new perspective* (pp. 174-208). London: Tavistock.

Romero, M. (1992). *Maid in the U.S.A.* London: Routledge.

Rosenau, P. M. (1992). *Post-modernism and the social sciences: Insights, inroads and intrusions.* Princeton, NJ: Princeton University Press.

Ruzek, S. R. (1978). *The women's health movement: Feminist alternatives to medical care.* New York: Praeger.

Sacks, K. (1989). Toward a unified theory of class, race and gender. *American Ethnologist, 16,* 534-550.

Saltonstall, R. (1993). Healthy bodies: Gendered constructions of health and illness. *Social Science and Medicine, 19,* 45-52.

Scheper-Hughes, N. (1983). Introduction: The problem of bias in androcentric and feminist anthropology. *Women's Studies, 19,* 109-116.

Scheper-Hughes, N. (1992). *Death without weeping: The violence of everyday life in Brazil.* Berkeley: University of California Press.

Scott, J. (1991). The evidence of experience. *Critical Inquiry, 17,* 773-779.

Shogan, D. (1990). Comment on Hawkesworth's "Knowers, knowing, known: Feminist theory and claims of truth." *Signs, 15,* 424-425.

Shostak, M. (1981). *Nisa: The life and words of a !Kung woman.* Cambridge, MA: Harvard University Press.

Smith, D. E. (1974). Women's perspective as a radical critique of sociology. *Sociological Inquiry, 4,* 1-13.

Smith, D. E. (1987). *The everyday world as problematic.* Boston: Northeastern University Press.

Smith, D. E. (1989). Sociological theory: Methods of writing patriarchy. In R. A. Wallace (Ed.), *Feminism and sociological theory* (pp. 34-64). Newbury Park, CA: Sage.

Smith, D. E. (1990a). *The conceptual practices of power: A feminist sociology of knowledge.* Boston: Northeastern University Press.

Smith, D. E. (1990b). *Texts, facts and femininity: Exploring the relations of ruling.* London: Routledge.

Smith, D. E. (1992). Sociology from women's experience: A reaffirmation. *Sociological Theory, 10,* 88-98.

Smith, D. E. (1993). High noon in Textland: A critique of Clough. *Sociological Quarterly, 34,* 183-192.

Spivak, G. C. (1988). Subaltern studies: Deconstructing historiography. In G. C. Spivak, *In other worlds: Essays in cultural politics* (pp. 197-221). London: Routledge.

Stacey, J. (1988). Can there be a feminist ethnography? *Women's Studies International, 11,* 21-27.

Stacey, J., & Thorne, B. (1985). The missing feminist revolution in sociology. *Social Problems, 32,* 301-316.

Stacey, M. (1981). The division of labor revisited or overcoming the two Adams: The special problems of people work. In P. Abrams, R. Deem, J. Finch, & P. Rock (Eds.), *Practice and progress: British sociology 1950-1980* (pp. 172-204). London: George Allen & Unwin.

Stacey, M. (1992). *Regulating British medicine: The General Medical Council.* New York: John Wiley.

Stanley, L., & Wise, S. (1983). *Breaking out: Feminist consciousness and feminist research.* London: Routledge & Kegan Paul.

331

Stanley, L., & Wise, S. (1990). Method, methodology and epistemology in feminist research processes. In L. Stanley (Ed.), *Feminist praxis: Research, theory and epistemology in feminist sociology* (pp. 20-60). London: Routledge.

Stanley, L. (Ed.). (1990). *Feminist praxis: Research, theory and epistemology in feminist sociology.* London: Routledge.

Stanworth, M. (1985). "Just three quiet girls." In C. Ungerson (Ed.), *Women and social policy* (pp. 137-148). London: Macmillan.

Stevens, P. E., & Hall, J. H. (1991). A critical historical analysis of the medical construction of lesbianism. *International Journal of Health Services, 21,* 271-307.

Strathern, M. (1987). An awkward relationship: The case of feminism and anthropology. *Signs, 12,* 276-292.

Strauss, A. L., & Corbin, J. (1990). *Basics of qualitative research: Grounded theory procedures and techniques.* Newbury Park, CA: Sage.

Todd, A. D. (1989). *Intimate adversaries: Cultural conflict between doctors and patients.* Bloomington: Indiana University Press.

Tom, W. (1989). *Effects of feminist research on research methods.* Toronto: Wilfred Laurier.

Tong, R. (1989). *Feminist thought: A comprehensive introduction.* Boulder, CO: Westview.

Warren, C. A. B. (1988). *Gender issues in field research.* Newbury Park, CA: Sage.

West, C. (1988). *Routine complications: Troubles with talk between doctors and patients.* Bloomington: Indiana University Press.

West, C., & Zimmerman, D. (1987). Doing gender. *Gender & Society, 1,* 125-151.

Westkott, M. (1979). Feminist criticism of the social sciences. *Harvard Educational Review, 4,* 422-430.

Wolf, M. (1992). *A thrice-told tale: Feminism, postmodernism and ethnographic responsibility.* Stanford, CA: Stanford University Press.

Zavella, P. (1987). *Women's work and Chicano families: Cannery workers of the Santa Clara Valley.* Ithaca, NY: Cornell University Press.

Zinn, M. B. (1982). Mexican-American women in the social sciences. *Signs, 8,* 259-272.

10
Ethnic Modeling in Qualitative Research

John H. Stanfield II

◆ In this essay, *ethnicity* denotes the synthesis of biological and fictive ancestry and cultural elements. As a social phenomenon, ethnicity should not be confused with tribalism and race, even though it is intrinsically related to the formation of both culturally and politically constructed categories. That is, although tribes are localized forms of social organization with an emphasis on ancestry rights and "the camp" or "the village," there is also, obviously, the presence of a localized culture reproduced and at times transformed intergenerationally. Races are constructed categories of populations that gain social and cultural relevance when random human qualities such as intellectual abilities, moral fiber, personalities, aesthetic tastes, and physical abilities become fixed and systematized through their association with phenotypical attributes. Ethnicity is a critical attribute of race in that it is a basis of diversity within and between racial categories. For instance, although "Hispanic American" constitutes a "racial category" in the United States, there is great ethnic diversity among those of Cuban, Puerto Rican, Mexican, and Central American descent, as well as within even those more specific anthropological formations.

AUTHOR'S NOTE: I wish to thank the editors of this volume as well as Mitch Allen and Rutledge Dennis for their comments on earlier versions of this chapter.

Whereas race and tribe are special forms of social organization and stratification associated with certain historical and political economic conditions, ethnicity is a more universal human attribute. In short, we all have ethnicity, even though it may be entangled with status and social organizational attributes such as class, gender, age, ethnoregionalism, and religion.

There are certain corners of Western life, such as the modern social sciences and sciences in general, in which the fundamental influences of ethnicity in shaping interpretations of reality are ignored or given only minimal attention. Thus, more clearly, it is difficult for many to understand or to see that even the most "rational" modes of scientific thought are fundamentally ethnic products (Stanfield, 1993a, 1993b).

In this essay, I will discuss several ways in which the conventional concerns regarding racialized ethnicity and related status categories in qualitative research can be understood better when contextualized in critical analytic frameworks. I will then present suggestions as to how we can best create qualitative research methods indigenous to the experiences of Afro-Americans and other people of color in the United States and elsewhere.

◆ Some Conventional Considerations

Usually, when we think about the roles of ascribed status—such as race, ethnicity, and tribe—in research methods, several issues come to mind, depending upon the aspect of the research process we choose as a focus. When it comes to qualitative research methods, whether we focus on the researcher, the examined human beings, data analysis, or knowledge dissemination, the point is that ascribed status influences the meanings of subjective experiences. Scholars who have written about the impacts of the ascribed status of qualitative researchers such as ethnographers, oral historians, and archival experts have commented on the insider and outsider dilemmas investigators experience in the research process. What is at least implicit in the insider/outsider researcher debate is that the autobiographies, cultures, and historical contexts of researchers matter; these determine what researchers see and do not see, as well as their ability to analyze data and disseminate knowledge adequately. Although the rule has been that it is possible for researchers of traditional dominant status (meaning white, usually male) to develop value-free methodological procedures to study outsider persons, recently such traditional outsiders with professional credentials have begun to challenge that sacred presumption.

People of color, women, and others traditionally outside the domain of research authority have argued that only those researchers emerging from the life worlds of their "subjects" can be adequate interpreters of such experiences. Dominant researchers (whites and traditional outsiders who embrace mainstream perspectives) have argued fervently against the claims of those outsider scholars claiming to have an insider monopoly on the production of knowledge regarding the life worlds from which they hail. This response on the part of dominant researchers to outsider claims has been especially apparent in the negative treatment of Afrocentric scholarship in the mainstreams of sociology and other social sciences (Asante, 1987; Basu et al., 1980; Hamnett, Porter, Singh, & Kumar, 1984; Hymes, 1972; Kuper, 1983; Ladner, 1973; Magubane & Faris, 1985; Merton, 1972).

It should be noted that, ironically, scholars have yet to debate the outsider/insider knowledge controversy from the standpoint of traditional outsiders, such as people of color, conducting research on traditionally dominant subjects, that is, whites. This issue will become increasing important as a growing number of traditional outsiders begin to break out of the molds of studying "their own," because of choice or career tracking, and begin to gain the access and professional authority necessary to study whites.

When the focus shifts from the researcher to the examined human beings in racialized ethnic concerns in qualitative research, we find studies that mention at least in passing the impact of the skin color and nationality of the researcher on the behavior of those under investigation. Some researchers, for instance, have noticed how the white skin of dominant researchers adds to the authoritative posture of European-descent ethnographers. Others, writing from the perspective of people of color, note the ways in which phenotypical and cultural similarity between ethnographer and subjects in non-Western settings create interesting interaction roles and subject perceptions of the researcher (Sudarkasa, 1986; Whitehead, 1986; R. Williams, 1990). Scholars have also noted the profound human rights problems that continue to haunt qualitative research on people of color, especially those in low socioeconomic status populations. The growing participatory research movement is a partial solution to the historical tendency for people of color to be abused and otherwise exploited as "subjects" in research processes. I consider the participatory research movement only a partial solution because, although participatory research attempts to empower examined human beings and their social organizations, rarely do researchers share career rewards with "subjects" of color, such as coauthorships and access to authoritative credentializing processes.

Conventional concerns about data interpretation and knowledge dissemination have focused on the ethnocentrism tradition that drives so much American and other Western social research on people of color, including those perspectives that claim to be radical and liberating. The tendency for Western researchers to impose even their most enlightened cultural constructs on Others rather than creating indigenized theories and methods to grasp the ontological essences of people of color is, of course, legendary. Another growing concern is the politics of knowledge distribution, that is, the maldistribution of processed knowledge products (specialized information) and knowledge technologies in the world society. It is more than apparent, in other words, that many if not most people of color in Western nation-states and in the so-called Third World reside in oppressed communities and institutions that do not receive the same quality or quantity of specialized information as do (affluent) Eurocentric communities and institutions.

The basic problem with the extensive conventional literature on racialized ethnicity and related status categories in qualitative research is that nowhere is there a conceptual framework for understanding the structures that organize and even marginalize and exclude knowledge production regarding Afro-Americans and other people of color. In the next section I attempt to introduce and apply such a framework before moving on to some suggestions concerning ways to create indigenous paradigms rooted in the experiences of people of color.

◆ Some Radical Musings

I have been asked by the editors of this volume to give some advice about how to do "ethnic" qualitative research. As I am an Afro-American sociologist who has extensive qualitative research experience in Afro-American and African institutions and communities, my remarks are drawn from such African-descent studies. But before embarking on the discussion in question, I must attempt to clarify the matter of the political problematics of truly culturally diversified qualitative research strategies with people of color in the mainstream of qualitative research in the social sciences. Below

I shall emphasize, with some detail, using Afro-American experiences as the major case in point, that the ethnic hegemonic character of American and other Eurocentric traditions in the social sciences has made quite problematic the legitimation of competitive, empowering research questions and strategies in work with people of color. I will elaborate a bit and then give examples of how, historically, even though Afro-American intellectuals have developed their own unique qualitative research methods and research results, the more empowering and normality-revealing aspects of their work have been ignored, marginalized, or reinterpreted to fit into the more orthodox norms of social scientific communities (Stanfield, 1985, 1993a, 1993b). I will end with suggestions regarding the development of indigenous qualitative methods that draw from the cosmos of people of color, such as African-descent populations.

In multiracial/multiethnic nation-states such as the United States, Canada, Brazil, Great Britain, Australia, South Africa, and the Netherlands, correlating perceived intellectual abilities, behavior, personality, and moral fiber with real or imagined phenotypical attributes is fundamental to human developmental issues such as self-concept, concepts of others, organizing daily life, and making routine and critical life decisions (such as mate selection, residence, church affiliation, friendship selection, and legitimating authority in politics and employment) (Stanfield, 1991). Thus, whether residents in a multiracial/multiethnic nation are aware of it or not, and despite their personal preferences and political beliefs, they are socialized in their homes and schools and by the mass media and popular and material culture to assume that ethnicity defined in racial terms is normal. Social scientists reared in such societies are not exempt from what Herbert Blumer once called "group feeling." Multiethnic/multiracial nation-states are segmented societies held together through rigid forms of sociocultural and political hegemony.

At least in this essay, *sociocultural and political hegemony* denotes an oligarchical status that the dominant ethnic population enjoys through maintaining virtually exclusive control over political, cultural, social, and technological resources and institutions. The sociocultural and political hegemony of the dominant is legitimated and reproduced through the imposition, if not the diffusion, of particular ethnic cultural attributes throughout the nation-state. What makes hegemony such a powerful source of social and political control is that the imposition and diffusion of the ethnic cultural particulars of the dominant create and institutionalize impressions in public culture and life that there is a societal consensus that the culture of the dominant is universalistic rather than particularistic. Hegemonic racialized ethnic expressions include civil religious practices, conventional historical interpretations of the nation-state, and, related to the point at hand (Stanfield, 1992), the formation of sciences and humanities as institutions and as knowledge producers and disseminators (Stanfield, 1993a, 1993b).

We cannot divorce the history of American social sciences, let alone of course the individual life histories of social scientists, from the origins and transformation of a normative multiethnic/ multiracial society. Although there have long been class critiques of the social sciences as middle-class knowledge institutions and producers (Furner, 1975; Haskell, 1977; Hinkle, 1954), only recently have we begun to understand the racialized ethnic character of social sciences as institutions and practices. The social sciences in the United States and in comparable nations are hegemonic racialized ethnic social organizations and forms of knowing and interpreting life worlds.

The hegemonic character of the social sciences in the United States is apparent in many ways. It is apparent in the historical Euro-American dominance in defining and constructing the organizational configurations of social science knowledge production and disciplinary public culture. *Organizational configurations* refers to credentializing settings, such as graduate school programs, professional associations, and invisible colleges. *Disciplinary public culture* is what Merton long ago called the ethos of science: rules of evidence, community norms and values, criticism privileges, and so on.

When it comes to qualitative research as an academic enterprise cutting across disciplines, the sociocultural and politic hegemony of Eurocentric interests and ontology is quite obvious. Qualitative research methods textbooks and handbooks rarely touch upon racialized ethnic diversity issues (Ashworth, Giorgi, & de Koning, 1986; Atkinson, 1992; Burgess, 1985; Crabtree & Miller, 1992; Filstead, 1970; Gilgren, Daly, & Handel, 1992; Goetz & LeCompte, 1984; LeCompte, Millroy, & Preissle, 1992; Merriam, 1988; Seidman, 1991; Shaffir & Stebbins, 1991; Strauss, 1987; Tesch, 1990; Walker, 1985). When racialized ethnic diversity issues are discussed, it is usually within the confines of orthodox (conventional or radical) Eurocentric perspectives, such as symbolic interactionism, phenomenology, or Marxism, rather than as attempts to develop ethnic diversity in logics of inquiry grounded in the indigenous experiences of people of color. This neglect or marginalization of racialized cultural

338

diversity as logic of inquiry issues has continued to be the case in the post-1980s, as qualitative research has increasingly become the dominion of education scholars (Goetz & LeCompte, 1984; LeCompte et al., 1992). Considering the central presence of racialized ethnic diversity in education, the absence of an emerging body of methodological literature that attempts to de-Europeanize approaches to issues concerning people of color through the introduction of more indigenous approaches is, to say the least, curious.

When we grasp the political history of the ethnic hegemony of American and comparable social science communities, it becomes apparent why there continues to be an absence of diverse racialized ethnic approaches in qualitative and quantitative research perspectives in the mainstreams of such disciplines. This is especially the case when it comes to research strategies designed and applied by nonwhite scholars that approach people of color as normal human beings or in power and privilege terms.

To the extent that ethnic models of research have filtered through the mainstreams of social sciences, they have mirrored pathological and culture-of-poverty interpretations of people of color and of the poor in conformity with historically specific folk beliefs in the dominant societal culture. The work of Clyde Kluckhohn (1944) on Native Americans, Oscar Lewis (1966) on Mexicans and Chicanos, and qualitative studies of Afro-American experiences by E. Franklin Frazier (1967, 1968), Kenneth Clark (1965), Lee Rainwater (1970a, 1970b), Elliot Liebow (1967), William J. Wilson (1974), Elijah Anderson (1978, 1990), Joyce Ladner (1971), and Carol Stack (1974) have all contributed to the forging of mainstream ethnic models. Also, historically, professional and mass-media review organs have contributed greatly to conservative ethnic models in mainstream social sciences through the selection and interpretation of bits and pieces of the works of more critical-minded scholars of color that seem to reconfirm dominant pathological assumptions about people of color.

Besides this mainstream conservative ethnic modeling tradition in American social sciences, more radical traditions of qualitative research have been ignored or misinterpreted, and these should be discussed. This can be done by recovering texts in two senses of the word: first, discovering the works of scholars of color who have been excluded from discipline historical memories because of their critical perspectives on social structure and processes; and second, rereading the texts of scholars of color who have enjoyed some degree of historical immortality but have had the more conservative aspects of their work applauded and remembered even as their more radical statements have been ignored or distorted.

There are two historical traditions in Afro-American scholarship that stand out as critical examples of the use of qualitative research to collect and interpret data in anti-status quo fashions. First, among generations of Afro-American intellectuals such as Carter G. Woodson, William E. B. Du Bois, Charles S. Johnson, and Ida B. Wells, there has been the use of historical documents to critique the origins and dynamics of social domination and social and political economic conflict. Second, Afro-American scholars such as Du Bois, Johnson, St. Clair Drake, Horace Cayton, E. Franklin Frazier, Zora Neale Hurston, Joyce Ladner, Judith Rollins, and Karen Fields used participant observation and oral history techniques to explore the normality of Afro-Americans and their daily struggles to survive in oppressed environments. In both historical traditions there are excluded Afro-American scholars and those who are more mainstream but who have had the more critical edges of their works ignored or distorted in dominant discipline discourse.

There have also been a number of epistemological critiques of conventional approaches to the study of Afro-Americans and other people of color. These approaches are qualitative only in the sense that they offer attempts to demonstrate the flaws in conventional theories and methods and argue for the utilization of perspectives stressing subjective interpretations of human experiences. What is most fascinating about these approaches is that many of their proponents are theologians and literary figures rather than credentialed social scientists. Their importance lies more in their offering a critical critique of logical positivism than in their developing models of research. This is crucial to point out, because my goal in discussing the following individuals is not to offer examples of models of research, but to demonstrate the importance of understanding radical opposition to the conventions of how social research on Afro-Americans and other people of color is usually done.

First, we have the theological critiques of social scientific research done on Afro-Americans advanced by scholars such as Cornel West (1982, 1988). These critiques offer a brilliant synthesis of moral theories of social justice and Marxism as the means to advocate liberation strategies for Afro-Americans. In the process of making their case, West and other theologians of like cloth inevitably get involved in the epistemological and ideological flaws that limit the value of orthodox social sciences in understanding the plight of the racially oppressed or, more important, in participating in efforts to liberate the oppressed from their bondage.

Ralph Ellison's *Shadow and Act* (1964), which offered a commentary on Gunnar Myrdal's *An American Dilemma* (1944), was probably the first comprehensive effort by a literary figure to critique conventional quantitative approaches to Afro-American experiences. In a most eloquent fashion, Ellison argued that Afro-Americans and their experiences, as rich as they are, cannot be reduced to statistical tables, which seemed to be the fad in race relations research during the 1940s and 1950s (although it should be pointed out that earlier journalists, such as Ida B. Wells, Walter White, and Carl Sandburg, along with such literary figures as James Weldon Johnson, Langston Hughes, and Richard Wright, offered humanistic "qualitative" approaches to sociological interpretations of Afro-American experiences well before the quantitative movement in the social sciences began to institutionalize in the 1940s and 1950s—see, e.g., Johnson, 1945, 1979).

The literary critique of orthodox social scientific perspectives on Afro-American experiences would reappear in powerful force in the 1980s and 1990s as part of the rise of the feminist movement among women of color. Intentionally or unintentionally, bell hooks, Gloria Hull, Toni Morrison, Alice Walker, Paule Marshall, and Paula Giddings all have offered radical alternatives to viewing the lives of women of color as studied in the social sciences and interpreted in literature. Although bell hooks is closest to Cornel West's Marxist critique of social scientific constructions of Afro-Americans, Gloria Hull offers insights in doing literary oral histories through using the diaries and personal correspondence of prominent Afro-American women writers to reconstruct and interpret black female life worlds. Toni Morrison's urban sociological imagination serves as a context of Afro-American women's development in ways that parallel the rural sociological contexts of Alice Walker (and of her literary anthropological "mentor," Zora Neale Hurston). Paule Marshall's brilliant comparative historical sociological sense of Afro-American womanhood in America and in the West Indies and Paula Giddings's sociological history of Afro-American women are additional examples of Afro-American feminist literary approaches that at least remind us of the limitations of both orthodox social scientific and literary analyses. More needs to be said about the rise of feminist thought in relation to ethnic modeling in critical qualitative research, this time in reference to feminism in social sciences.

On the other hand, in the social sciences, feminist critics of Western social sciences from anthropology through sociology (to be alphabetical) have brilliantly exposed the sociological and political bare wires of what used to be viewed as universal forms of objective knowledge and objective methods of inquiry (Abramowitz, 1982; Bernick, 1991; Christman, 1988; Currie, 1988; DeVault, 1990; Ergas, 1978-1979; Grant & Ward, 1987; Lather, 1986; Marburg, 1981; Mascia-Lees, Sharpe, & Cohen, 1989; McKeganey & Bloor, 1991; Peplau & Conrad, 1989; Rapp, 1988; Sprague & Zimmerman, 1989; Warren, 1988; A. Williams, 1987, 1990). They have demonstrated in thought-provoking ways how cultural and social elements of male-centric cosmologies silently and more explicitly shape the epistemologies, theories, methods, and other paradigmatic attributes of modern social scientific disciplines and their classical antecedents. We learn through their work how the predominance of patriarchal and hierarchical presumptions and assumptions of male-centric norms and values influence not only the contents of research but, perhaps more important, the conduct of research as a structured power relationship and as an intricate process of creating, interpreting, and disseminating knowledge.

When it comes to qualitative research methods such as ethnography, participant observation, and oral history, feminists have been quick to point out and document how much the hierarchical power relations between researcher and subject or respondent is a cultural product of a male-centric cosmos. This has lead to the revision of classical ethnographic texts steeped in male-centric conceptions of the world and in hierarchical research processes (di Leonardo, 1991). Such feminist critiques have also encouraged power-sharing approaches to ethnographic research that have converged quite well with growing concerns about the human rights of subjects and the growing resistance and awareness on the part of heavily researched populations.

Perhaps the major Achilles' heel of feminist interpretations of how to conduct qualitative research is the absence of a central racialized ethnic component. Once again, we all have ethnicity, just as we all have gender. Indeed, ethnicity, in its subtle and explicit ways, compounded by other synchronic status variables, gives biological sex categories their historical, cultural, social, and political economic meanings. When we speak of ethnic hegemony in the history of qualitative research as well as in the social sciences in general, we must remember that we must consider the female as well as the male dimensions of this unique social inequality problem. As underprivileged as white females have been in comparison with white males in social science historiography, we cannot forget that their gendered interpretations of the world are derived from European-descent experiences (Cannon, 1988; Collins, 1990; Facio, 1993; Hurston, 1969a, 1969b,

1971a, 1971b, 1990; Marks, 1993; Rollins, 1985; Sudarkasa, 1986; Terrell, 1980). Although white women were discriminated against and still continue to be in the structures and processes of knowledge production, they have always enjoyed more political weight and access privileges than have women of color and people of color in general. Only recently have feminist social scientists, especially anthropologists and, to a lesser extent, sociologists, begun to acknowledge their places of white privilege, especially in relation to women of color.

The problem here is how to untangle the gender and ethnic attributes of the historical formation of dominant patterns of research in the social sciences. One way to do this is to argue that, most fundamentally, attributes of orthodox research designs, such as hierarchical relations between researchers and their subjects, are gender issues embedded within a particular ethnic sphere. The development of twentieth-century orthodox social scientific thought, in other words, has been drawn largely from the cosmos of upper-middle-class WASP (white Anglo-Saxon Protestant) and WIE (white immigrant ethnic) males. They created and institutionalized their authority as preeminent reality interpreters by controlling access to credentializing processes and dominating the academic and professional agencies, media, and reward systems that define the "nature of knowing and knowledge." Issues such as deviance and social control in sociology, life-cycle development in psychology, voting behavior and political philosophy in political science, kinship in anthropology, and market behavior in economics all are rooted in the ethnic experiences of privileged whites. The extent to which people of color, no matter their national context, have been absorbed into the confines of orthodox social sciences has been well within the norms and values of the dominant ethnic ways of interpreting and constructing realities (Stanfield, 1993a). Only recently have people of color in some disciplines, the humanities in particular, been allowed to speak in different legitimated voices (Baker, 1980, 1984, 1989, 1991; Carby, 1987; hooks, 1981, 1984, 1989, 1990, 1991, 1992). For the most part, however, post-1970s Western and Westernized academic disciplines, particularly in most social sciences, continue to marginalize and exclude ethnically diverse interpretations of reality and styles of knowing in relation to mainstream normative knowledge creation and reproduction. To the extent to which feminists have engaged in oppositional discourses regarding orthodox social sciences, their struggles have usually been "in the ethnic family" debates. Most of their preoccupations have been with matters related to white maleness, which in many cases are not applicable to nonwhite maleness. For instance, the entire issue of patriarchal hierarchies is a matter of historical and political dominance enjoyed by white men wherever they conquered and settled; this is not so easily attributed to men of color. Aggressiveness, assertiveness, societal and political control, and economic productivity are additional attributes of white male masculinity that have been penalized or discouraged when found among men of color. This is obvious in scholarly studies and in the popular press in multiracial nation-states such as the United States, Great Britain, South Africa, and Australia, which document the negative imagery of men of color who act too much like white men.

Although literary figures are way ahead of us, social scientists sensitive to the issues of women of color are finally beginning to study the sociological and political aggravations that women of color experience (Collins, 1990; Rollins, 1985; Sudarkasa, 1986; Warren, 1988). The more we do so, the more apparent it becomes that even the most revisionist feminist studies of women of color in the social sciences have been conducted within the context of Eurocentric as well as male-centric reasoning. The use of phenomenological concepts and methods of inquiry in understanding how women of color construct their worldviews and identities (Collins, 1990) ignores how much the voluntaristic presumptions of social constructions of reality are very much notions of social privilege. Although the powerful—be they men, whites, or adults—have had the luxury of constructing their realities, a characteristic of the oppressed—women, Afro-Americans and other people of color, and children—has been the sociopolitical controls that have limited the reality construction choices they can choose from and enjoy. This is what makes the work of interpretive social scientists such as Schutz, Geertz, Goffman, and Berger and Luckmann so problematic when applied to the experiences of the oppressed. The problem becomes particularly cumbersome when it comes to populations experiencing two or more subordinate statuses, such as women of color in the United States and in other multiracial nation-states.

The racialized ethnic differences between white women and women of color in multiracial nation-states must be taken into consideration if one is to understand the erroneous ways in which concepts drawn from the experiences of white women are imposed on the experiences of nonwhite women. It has been a common mistake, for instance, to assume that power relations and distributions in (middle-class) white gender relations can be readily applied to Afro-American experiences. Cultural concepts such as masculinity and femininity are often articulated as universals and applied without critical revision to Afro-American male and female gender role development. This misappropriated generalization pattern has been stretched to Western impositions of notions of femininity and masculinity on non-Western, ex-colonial societies and regions. Thus what is missed or not understood properly are the socialization processes in Afro-American and other populations of color, which do not so neatly package and dichoto-mize femininity and masculinity as social and cultural qualities attributed to females and males.

The external political and economic factors that blur the dichotomy between masculinity and femininity in Afro-American socialization pro-cesses, such as the racialization of labor markets and the gender biases of welfare policies, also contribute to the racialized ethnic and social differ-ences between white males and females and Afro-American males and females. Concretely, historically, Afro-American men have experienced employment patterns in which they perform jobs that traditionally have been viewed as female-dominated service work. The extensive underem-ployment and unemployment many Afro-American men experience creates a cultural scenario in Afro-American communities that actually feminizes Afro-American males as seen in gendered stereotypes in indigenous and broader public cultures.

On the other hand, dire economic conditions and imbalanced sex ratios have prevented many Afro-American women from developing the helpless, passive personal characteristics usually attributed to femininity. As an economic imperative, Afro-American women across classes have histori-cally participated in labor markets and have frequently served as breadwin-ners and as community leaders.

In white middle-class terms, not a few Afro-American women have masculine cultural attributes, whereas African American men tend to be feminized. But, actually, Afro-American gender socialization processes are much more complicated and paradoxical than the reversal of traditional male/female roles idealized in white contexts. There is a need to study such human experiences within their unique cultural contexts rather than employing alien cognitive maps (i.e., paradigms) for research design and data interpretation.

To sum up, it is no accident that the most powerful historical and contemporary attacks on orthodox reasoning in the social sciences in respect to racial and ethnic studies have been carried out by intellectuals outside the social sciences. Although within their own disciplines and intellectual spheres such outsiders may be greatly celebrated, within the

345

hegemonic walls of the social sciences their work tends to be ignored or marginalized. As is the case for critical epistemological and theoretical perspectives in general in American academic life (especially in the most distinguished circles), conventional reasoning rather than reflective analysis holds center stage when it comes to the study of the souls of black folks and other people of color.

Thus, if the marginal career of Oliver C. Cox is any clue (Hare, 1965; Hunter & Abraham, 1987), those who dare to critique racial orthodoxy from within the lion's den find their work ridiculed as militant, unscientific, and otherwise unworthy of significant attention. The case of Afro-American feminists is a contemporary example of how radical work from within and outside the social sciences may have the attention of other marginals in the academy, such as culturally enlightened women's studies academics, but not the needed professional acknowledgment of those who guard the highest gates of the professional discipline.

As much as it is important to point to and document normality-revealing and empowering studies of people of color within and outside the borders of discussions on qualitative research in the social sciences, such analyses tend to remain within the pale of conventional assumptions and arguments. In the next section I discuss why and how this is the case even when it comes to the most radical thinking going on today about people of color in research processes. More important, I outline some ways to step beyond even the most radical edges of orthodox thinking regarding issues concerning people of color in qualitative research. My thoughts in the next section were influenced mostly by Bernal (1987), Boahen (1987), Chinweizu (1975), Daniel and Renfrew (1988), Das (1935), Du Bois (1965, 1968), Hodgkin (1960), Khaldun (1981), Kuhn (1962), Mbiti (1970), Mudimbe (1988), Nandy (1988), Nkrumah (1973), Nsamenang (1992), O'Connor (1986), Polkinghorne (1988), Said (1978), Suret-Canale (1988), Vansina (1988), and Zaslavsky (1973).

◆ Creating Indigenous Qualitative Methods

A paradigm is a cognitive road map (Kuhn, 1962). In the case of sciences and humanities, paradigms are taken-for-granted assumptions, norms, values, and traditions that create and institutionalize the ontological roots of knowledge definitions and productions. The experiences that construct paradigms in sciences and humanities are derivatives of cultural baggage imported into intellectual enterprises by privileged residents of historically specific societies and world systems. This is important to point out, because it is common for scholars to lapse into internal analyses while discussing paradigms and thus to ignore the rather commonsense fact that sciences and humanities are products of specific cultural and historical contexts that shape the character of intellectual work.

Paradigms, in the sense being articulated here, are actually the cultural foundations of sciences and humanities, because they are really the experiential places in which the realities of the intellectual enterprise are created and given legitimated expression, such as language, conceptions of human nature and the universe, and beliefs about what can and cannot be known. As cultural foundations, paradigms are the guides to more explicit intellectual activities, most fundamentally, theory construction, methodological strategizing, data interpretation, and knowledge dissemination.

When it comes to criticizing the knowledge contents of science and humanities disciplines, there are two levels of analysis. The first of these is the paradigmatic critique, which is the attempt to critique and perhaps revise the cognitive map of a particular discipline or cluster of disciplines. The second level of analysis is the knowledge production critique, which involves examination and perhaps revision of formal epistemologies, theories, methods, data interpretation styles, and patterns of knowledge dissemination.

When we review the critical literature related to ethnicity, race, and tribe in qualitative research, we cannot help but notice that most of them are knowledge production critiques with little or no in-depth concern for paradigmatic critiques. So we have, for instance, Afrocentric scholars (Asante, 1987) who may call for more culturally relevant approaches to Afro-American experiences in the social sciences and humanities but who do so while embracing and even advocating the most sacred norms of logical positivistic reasoning. This results in Afrocentrists' contradicting themselves by claiming to be producing knowledge sensitive to the experiences of African-descent peoples as a unique cultural population even as they insist on using Eurocentric logics of inquiry that reduce the knowable to the measurable or to evolutionary or linear variables.

This peculiar contradictory thinking in Afrocentric scholarship is most prevalent among Afrocentric psychologists (e.g., Hale-Benson and Hilliard) who promote their cultural views by advocating the refining of standardized testing instruments and applying evolutionary concepts of human development to Afro-American experiences, such as Afrocentric childhood studies. In sociology there is the additional problem of Afrocentric scholars attempting to apply phenomenological and symbolic interaction theoretical and methodological principles to Afro-American experiences without realizing the cultural limitations of the conception of voluntary action (i.e., reality construction) when applied to oppressed populations. More specifically, oppressed peoples, whether they be Americanized people of color, women, the differently abled, or the poor, have had little opportunity to construct realities meaningful and empowering in their lives. At worst, the socially constructed realities of the oppressed as official status categories and definitions are the intrusively imposed views of the dominant and at least partially internalized by not a few of the oppressed (Fanon, 1967; Memmi, 1965). At best, the oppressed can construct their own worlds as modes of action in private spheres only, hidden from the eyes and ears of the dominant, such as in racially oppressed communities and institutions. But such private reality constructions of the oppressed are restricted by the parameters of "objective realities" constructed and entrenched by the dominant.

Thus, no matter how people of color define themselves, there are still the more powerful stereotypes embedded in public culture that define their status and identities within the cosmos of the dominant. This is the racialized ethnic dimension of what Frankfurt school theorists refer to as the chronic discrepancies between an intrusive capitalistic (multiethnic/racial) state bent on defining its (racialized ethnically diverse) citizenry in "objective terms" and the growing repression of subjective meanings of individual and collective identities created by its citizenry. It has been the political and cultural interpretation of the persistent discrepancy between the objective and subjective realities on the part of the racially oppressed and of (in terms of temporal sequence) women, the differently abled, and lesbians and gays during the past 40 years that has fueled the emergence of the civil rights and other liberation movements redefining the United States.

Cultural studies proponents also tend to engage in knowledge production critiques with little or no consideration of paradigmatic or societal contexts. In Afro-American and African studies, cultural studies scholars have spent most of their time and energy offering Marxist and postmodern critiques of African-descent experiences via textual analyses. Although cultural studies scholars attempt to draw experiential comparisons between Americanized Africans and indigenous Africans, most cultural studies scholars concentrate on African-descent experiences in the Western Hemisphere, with the focus on the United States and, to a lesser extent, the Caribbean.

Besides a reified fixation on textual discourse analysis, a serious flaw in cultural studies logic of inquiry is the dependence on European theorists. In this regard, cultural studies scholars are well within the American intellectual tradition of receiving most of their inspiration from distinguished European thinkers such as Karl Marx, Foucault, Stuart Hall, and the Frankfurt school. This love affair with European-derived theorizing about the nature of human beings and their collective inventions—institutions, communities, societies, socialization, and so on—has resulted in the failure of even the most astute cultural studies theorists to realize how culturally limiting the work of otherwise brilliant thinkers, such as Alfred Schutz, Karl Marx, and Michel Foucault, is when applied to the United States and, most important, to the experiences of populations such as Americanized people of color who deviate from what we used to call mainstream (i.e., white middle-class) America.

The same criticism can be applied to cultural studies theorists who uncritically embrace American theorists and unintentionally extend folk wisdoms into their work. Perhaps the major example here is the tendency for cultural studies scholars to adopt a highly routinized functional view of American society. Unwittingly, even those who insist that they value and understand cultural diversity as an integral aspect of American society do not differ from most others socialized in the United States in their assumptions that there is, basically, one American society. At most, multiculturalism as a topic of discussion and debate is treated as a growing phenomenon sitting uncomfortably on top of a "singular social system." Needless to say, this causes a number of dilemmas and contradictions in cultural studies scholarship, such as the celebration, on one hand, of racialized ethnic diversity through the recovery and interpretation of the texts of the racially oppressed and, on the other, the attempt to explain the texts as extensions of mainstream canons instead of as culturally unique canons reflective of the normal plural character of the United States. To give a concrete example, cultural studies scholars specializing in Harlem Renaissance literary figures more often than not attempt to use the works of these seminal intellectuals to demonstrate cultural deviations from accepted paradigms of American literature (canons), rather than as examples of paradigms reflecting the normal ethnic pluralism of the United States.

What I wish to suggest here is that ethnic modeling in qualitative research must involve calling into serious question the vast warehouse of knowledge that researchers of European descent have been accumulating and legitimating as ways of knowing and seeing. Until we engage in radical efforts to criticize and revise the paradigms underlying qualitative research strategies and, more important, to create and legitimate new ones, the more secondary traditions of critiquing racialized ethnic theories, methods, styles of data interpretation, and patterns of knowledge dissemination will remain grossly incomplete.

In recent decades, the pendulum in qualitative social science research on people of color in Western nation-states and in the so-called Third World has been swinging gradually toward a greater sensitivity to social and cultural differences in research processes. A growing number of researchers are redefining their relationships with "subjects" and their communities, stressing less hierarchal approaches. Scholarship on "how to" develop participatory bridges between researchers and "subjects" has been increasing dramatically over the past decade.

But with all this said, there is still little comprehensive work being published on how to develop indigenous "ethnic" models of qualitative research. At most we have a developing literature for dominant researchers on how to be more sensitive in doing qualitative research in settings involving people of color. That is not, of course, the same thing as creating novel indigenous paradigms grounded distinctly in the experiences of people of color.

The purpose of establishing such qualitative research paradigms is twofold. First, and most apparent, research paradigms grounded in the experiences of people of color will isomorphize rather than impose cognitive map criteria that structure theory development, methodological strategies, data interpretations, and knowledge dissemination. This would eliminate the dilemmas, contradictions, and distortions generated when researchers involved in work with people of color operate on Eurocentric cognitive map criteria, no matter how progressive and liberating.

Second, although much has been written about the use of Eurocentric cognitive map criteria in examining people of color, to date no one has published a comprehensive text discussing what happens when the tables are turned—when the life worlds of the dominant are investigated and interpreted through the paradigmatic lenses of people of color. In other words, what would, say, anthropology or sociology "look like" as intellectual enterprises if they were invented by native West Africans and applied to Western contexts? Suppose classical qualitative texts on American issues by Lloyd Warner, Hortense Powdermaker, W. I. Thomas, Robert E. Park,

350

Elliot Liebow, E. Franklin Frazier, Joyce Ladner, and Robert Lynd had been written by West Africans unexposed to Western norms of professional education. What would have been different in the cognitive map ingredients the African intellectuals would have drawn upon to develop outsider perspectives on American social issues? This question is not so far-fetched; in fact, the concept can even be studied through examination of the diaries, autobiographies, and travelers' accounts of West Africans who have spent time observing American life since the colonial period and even before. There are also ample qualitative documents about views of British society left by Africans who have resided in the United Kingdom for centuries. The most striking classical African intellectual who created an indigenous qualitative research paradigm to study his world and that of Europeans was the fourteenth-century Arab scholar Ibn Khaldun. In later times, up through the early 1900s, there were West Africans writing indigenous sociological analyses, such as Ghanian Casey Haywood's comparative legal institutions and double-consciousness scholarship, and Liberian Edward Blyden's and Sierra Leonean James Horton's theories of cultural nationalism. These intellectuals preceded and influenced mid-twentieth-century African new nation leaders such as Kwame Nkrumah, who wrote in a distinct indigenous vein about the United States and the general West (much of Nkrumah's thinking about the United States was influenced by his years in America during the 1930s, when he was a student at Lincoln University).

Much more recently, a number of African intellectuals with social scientific imaginations if not credentials have begun not only to criticize Western paradigms but to go beyond them, introducing indigenous cognitive maps to interpret African worldviews and the West. Much of this critique and indigenizing work has involved African intellectuals pointing out not only how Western documentation of African experiences (such as missionary and professional anthropological ethnographies) has often been part of an effort to rationalize and reinforce Eurocentric domination on the continent but, more important, how Western production of knowledge about Africa has more often than not deceived African researchers depending upon such records to interpret their own cultures and societies.

In weaving an indigenous paradigm, it becomes apparent that phenomena such as time, space, spirituality, and human relationships with nature are culture bound. So are the most fundamental configurations and contents of human communication and interaction in a culture. In the Western cosmos, time is linear and is viewed as a commodity—something to be used up for a profit. Time is also viewed as a horizontal sequence of events, such as the life cycle and the aging process. Space tends to have a privatized, individualistic definition and function in Western worldviews. Up until very recently, American and other Western intellectuals tended to define spirituality in institutional terms (i.e., religion) and to view it suspiciously as something inherently separate from human affairs. Thus issues such as relationships with dead ancestors have been viewed in mainstream Western social science as not relevant for serious research. Until the environmental consciousness movement of the post-1970s, Western social scientists, steeped in Judeo-Christian presumptions, viewed human beings as separate from and "naturally" dominant over their environments.

We do not want to make the common mistake of Afrocentrists, of approaching Africa as a simplistic geographic place with no cultural and social diversity. But it has been noticed and documented that there are major differences between the ways in which Africans, with their various historical and cultural backgrounds, and Westerners, with their various historical and cultural backgrounds, socially construct interpretations of realities about themselves and others. Culturally indigenous Africans do not tell time or count the same way Westerners or perhaps Westernized Africans do, nor do they embrace individualized conceptions of space and property. Time in many, if not most, indigenous African cultures is qualitative rather than quantitative and is not viewed as "money spent." Ancestors are viewed as central to family life in many African cultures, including in the kinship systems of Africans who have been converted to Christianity or Islam. In general, spirituality is central rather than marginal or absent in the way Africans explain human development, as opposed to in the West, where up until recently social scientists have tended to shy away from studying spirituality as an integral part of social and emotional well-being and as an explanation for human fortunes and misfortunes.

It used to be claimed that cultures depending upon oral rather than written communication were primitive or underdeveloped. Although this ethnocentric perspective may still be held by some, it is becoming apparent in the most sophisticated circles of intellectuals searching for human understanding that oral communication-based cultures are *different from* rather than *inferior to* written word-based cultures. The oral basis of most African cultures and among aboriginal peoples around the world offers a major challenge, because adequate study of such cultures requires a different portfolio of skills from what researchers reared in written word-based cultures acquire easily. For one thing, in oral-based cultures the records from which data are to be collected come in the form of poems, songs, testimonies, stories, performing arts, and proverbs, rather than diaries, newspapers, census reports, and surveys (Johnson, 1987).

Oral-based cultures, I should add, can also be found in otherwise written-word nation-states. In societal contexts such as that in the United States, oral-based cultures are derived from (a) surviving historical aboriginal social organizations; (b) the marginalization and exclusion of populations from centers of capitalistic modes of production, such as inner-city residents and Appalachians; (c) the imported cultural baggage of voluntary and involuntary non-Western immigrants; and (d) the convergence of b and c. Oral communication research strategies are often more valuable for understanding the nature of people within these four oral culture categories than are methodologies dependent upon written responses. Folklorists of Afro-American life, for instance, have long understood the value of examining sociological and anthropological aspects of inner-city Afro-Americans through the study of the oral traditions and games of "ghetto dwellers." It is also possible to use data from oral traditions to track the quality of life experiences of those living in poor white or Afro-American communities. Testimony in Afro-American churches that serve the inner-city poor can be valuable sources of data about health care, labor market activities, and child rearing.

Given that so many non-Western cultures within and outside industrial nation-states are oral communication based, it would make sense to suggest a generalizable qualitative methods epistemology for people of color structured around verbal communication. As so many non-Westerners view the social, the emotional, and the spiritual as integral parts of a whole person linked to a physical environment, it would also be crucial for such a qualitative methods epistemology to be grounded in holistic rather than fragmented and dichotomized notions of human beings. Operationally, this would be done through the collection of oral histories that allow the examined people of color to articulate holistic explanations about how they construct their realities. This means, among other things, that American researchers would have to discard their usual dislike of religious topics and realize that many Afro-Americans and other people of color (especially aboriginal populations) cannot be understood fully unless the central place of spirituality in their lives is given serious consideration. Other cultural constructs, such as time and space, as paradigmatic principles, which I do not have latitude to discuss here, also have profound implications for developing qualitative research methods derived from paradigms for people of color.

The purpose of creating the new baby is not to bury the old one, but instead to create a family of qualitative research paradigms and derived theories, methodologies, and styles of data interpretation that more adequately reflects the plural character of American society and the global community. Thus, as much as researchers concerned with meaning and realities as social and cultural constructions should continue the noble task of confessing their human biases up front, we need to be about the more complex task of creating paradigms grounded in the experiences of people of color that offer more adequate knowledge production about non-Europeans and that offer fascinating turns of the table in which those of European descent are viewed from the standpoints of "the usually studied."

◆ References

Abramowitz, S. I. (1982). The sexual politics of sex bias in psychotherapy research. *Micropolitics, 2*(1), 21-34.

Anderson, E. (1978). *A place on the corner.* Chicago: University of Chicago Press.

Anderson, E. (1990). *Streetwise: Race, class, and change in an urban community.* Chicago: University of Chicago Press.

Asante, M. K. (1987). *The Afrocentric idea.* Philadelphia: Temple University Press.

Ashworth, P. D., Giorgi, A., & de Koning, A. J. J. (1986). *Qualitative research in psychology.* Pittsburgh, PA: Duquesne University Press.

Atkinson, P. A. (1992). *Understanding ethnographic texts.* Newbury Park, CA: Sage.

Baker, H. A. (1980). *The journey back: Issues in black literature and criticism.* Chicago: University of Chicago Press.

Baker, H. A. (1984). *Blues, ideology, and Afro-American literature: A vernacular theory.* Chicago: University of Chicago Press.

Baker, H. A. (1989). *Afro-American literary study in the 1990s.* Chicago: University of Chicago Press.

Baker, H. A. (1991). *Workings of the spirit: The poetics of Afro-American women's writing.* Chicago: University of Chicago Press.

Basu, A., Biswas, S. K., Balakrishnan, V., Chattopadhyay, H., Pollitzer, W. S., & Tripathi, T. P. (1980). Is Indian anthropology dead/dying? *Journal of the Indian Anthropological Society, 15,* 4-14

Bernal, M. (1987). *Black Athena.* New Brunswick, NJ: Rutgers University Press.

Bernick, S. E. (1991). Toward a value-laden theory: Feminism and social science. *Hypatia, 6,* 118-136.

Boahen, A. A. (1987). *African perspectives on colonialism.* Baltimore: Johns Hopkins University Press.

Burgess, R. G. (1985). *Strategies of educational research.* Philadelphia: Falmer.

Cannon, L. W. (1988). Race and class bias in qualitative research on women. *Gender & Society, 2,* 449-462.

Carby, H. V. (1987). *Reconstructing womanhood: The emergence of the Afro-American woman novelist.* Wellesley, MA: Wellesley College, Center for Research on Women.

Chinweizu. (1975). *The West and the rest of us: White predators, black slavers, and the African elite.* New York: Vintage.

Christman, J. B. (1988). Working in the field as the female friend. *Anthropology and Education Quarterly, 19*(2), 70-85.

Clark, K. B. (1965). *Dark ghetto: Dilemmas of social power.* New York: Harper & Row.

Collins, P. H. (1990). *Black feminist thought: Knowledge, consciousness and the politics of empowerment.* New York: Routledge.

Crabtree, B. F., & Miller, W. L. (Eds.). (1992). *Doing qualitative research.* Newbury Park, CA: Sage.

Currie, D. (1988). Re-thinking what we do and how we do it: A study of reproductive decisions. *Canadian Review of Sociology and Anthropology, 25,* 231-253.

Daniel, G., & Renfrew, C. (1988). *The idea of prehistory.* Edinburgh: Edinburgh University Press.

Das, B. (1935). *The laws of Manu.* Adyar, Madras, India: Theosophical Publishing House.

DeVault, M. L. (1990). Talking and listening from women's standpoint: Feminist strategies for interviewing and analysis. *Social Problems, 37,* 96-116.

di Leonardo, M. (1991). *Gender at the crossroads of knowledge: Feminist anthropology in the postmodern era.* Berkeley: University of California Press.

Du Bois, W. E. B. (1965). *The world and Africa: An inquiry into the part which Africa has played in world history.* New York: International.

Du Bois, W. E. B. (1968). *Atlanta University publications* (No. 7-11—1902-1906). New York: Octagon.

Ellison, R. (1964). *Shadow and act.* New York: Random House.

Ergas, Y. (1978-1979). Feminism and sociology: Cultivating the garden of women's studies or constructing a cultural perspective? *Critica Sociologica, 48,* 29-39.

Facio, E. (1993). Ethnography as personal experience. In J. H. Stanfield II & R. M. Dennis (Eds.), *Race and ethnicity in research methods* (pp. 75-91). Newbury Park, CA: Sage.

Fanon, F. (1967). *Black skin, white masks.* New York: Grove.

Filstead, W. J. (Ed.). (1970). *Qualitative methodology: Firsthand involvement with the social world.* Chicago: Markham.

Frazier, E. F. (1967). *Negro youth at the crossways: Their personality development in the middle states.* New York: Schocken.

Frazier, E. F. (1968). *E. Franklin Frazier on race relations: Selected writings.* Chicago: University of Chicago Press.

Furner, M. O. (1975). *Advocacy and objectivity: A crisis in the professionalization of American social science, 1865-1905.* Lexington: University Press of Kentucky.

Gilgren, J., Daly, K., & Handel, G. (Eds.). (1992). *Qualitative methods in family research.* Newbury Park, CA: Sage.

Goetz, J. P., & LeCompte, M. D. (1984). *Ethnography and qualitative design in educational research.* New York: Academic Press.

Grant, L., & Ward, K. (1987). Is there an association between gender and methods in sociological research? *American Sociological Review, 52,* 856-862.

Hamnett, M., Porter, D. J., Singh, A., & Kumar, K. (1984). *Ethics, politics, and international social science research.* Honolulu: University of Hawaii Press.

Hare, N. (1965). *The black Anglo-Saxons*. New York: Marzani & Munsell.

Haskell, T. L. (1977). *The emergence of professional social science: The American Social Science Association and the nineteenth-century crisis of authority*. Urbana: University of Illinois Press.

Hinkle, R. C. (1954). *The development of modern sociology: Its nature and growth in the United States*. Garden City, NY: Doubleday.

Hodgkin, T. (1960). *Nigerian perspectives: An historical anthology*. London: Oxford University Press.

hooks, b. (1981). *Ain't I a woman: Black women and feminism*. Boston: South End.

hooks, b. (1984). *Feminist theory from margin to center*. Boston: South End.

hooks, b. (1989). *Talking back: Thinking feminist, thinking black*. Boston: South End.

hooks, b. (1990). *Yearning: Race, gender, and cultural politics*. Boston: South End.

hooks, b. (1991). *Breaking bread: Insurgent black intellectual life*. Boston: South End.

hooks, b. (1992). *Black looks: Race and representation*. Boston: South End.

Hunter, H. M., & Abraham, S. Y. (Eds.). (1987). *Race, class, and the world system: The sociology of Oliver C. Cox*. New York: Monthly Review Press.

Hurston, Z. N. (1969a). *Mules and men*. New York: Negro Universities Press.

Hurston, Z. N. (1969b). *Their eyes were watching God*. New York: Negro Universities Press.

Hurston, Z. N. (1971a). *Dust tracks on a road: An autobiography*. Philadelphia: J. B. Lippincott.

Hurston, Z. N. (1971b). *Jonah's gourd vine*. Philadelphia: J. B. Lippincott.

Hurston, Z. N. (1990). *Tell my horse: Voodoo and life in Haiti and Jamaica*. New York: Perennial Library.

Johnson, C. F. (1987). *Bitter Canaan* (John Stanfield, Ed.). New Brunswick, NJ: Transaction.

Johnson, J. W. (1945). *Along this way: The autobiography of James Weldon Johnson*. New York: Viking.

Johnson, J. W. (1979). *The autobiography of an ex- coloured man*. New York: A. A. Knopf.

Khaldun, I. (1981). *The Muqaddimah* (N. J. Dawood, Ed.; F. Rosenthal, Trans.). Princeton, NJ: Princeton University Press.

Kluckhohn, C. (1944). *Navajo witchcraft*. Boston: Beacon.

Kuper, A. (1983). *Anthropology and anthropologists: The modern British school*. London: Routledge & Kegan Paul.

Ladner, J. A. (1971). *Tomorrow's tomorrow: The black woman*. Garden City, NY: Anchor.

Ladner, J. A. (1973). *The death of white sociology*. New York: Random House.

Lather, P. (1986). Issues of validity in openly ideological research: Between a rock and a soft place. *Interchange, 17*(4), 63-84.

LeCompte, M. D., Millroy, W. L., & Preissle, J. (Eds.). (1992). *The handbook of qualitative research in education*. New York: Academic Press.

Lewis, O. (1966). *La vida*. New York: Random House.

Liebow, E. (1967). *Tally's corner: A study of Negro street corner men*. Boston: Little, Brown.

Magubane, B., & Faris, J. C. (1985). On the political relevance of anthropology. *Dialectical Anthropology, 9*, 91-104.

Marburg, S. L. (1981, April 19-22). *Paradigms of production: Theoretical basis for bias? A history of the idea "man's role, woman's place: in geography."* Paper presented at the annual meeting of the Association of American Geographers, Los Angeles.

Marks, C. C. (1993). Demography and race. In J. H. Stanfield II & R. M. Dennis (Eds.), *Race and ethnicity in research methods* (pp. 159-171). Newbury Park, CA: Sage.

Mascia-Lees, F. E., Sharpe, P., & Cohen, C. B. (1989). The postmodernist turn in anthropology: Cautions from a feminist perspective. *Signs, 15,* 7-33.

Mbiti, J. S. (1970). *African religions and philosophy.* Garden City, NY: Anchor.

McKeganey, N., & Bloor, M. (1991). Spotting the invisible man: The influence of male gender on fieldwork relations. *British Journal of Sociology, 42,* 195-210.

Memmi, A. (1965). *The Colonizer and the colonized.* Boston: Beacon.

Merriam, S. B. (1988). *Case study research in education.* San Francisco: Jossey-Bass.

Merton, R. K. (1972). Insiders and outsiders: A chapter in the sociology of knowledge. *American Journal of Sociology, 78,* 44-47.

Mudimbe, V. Y. (1988). *The invention of Africa: Gnosis, philosophy, and the order of knowledge.* Bloomington: Indiana University Press.

Myrdal, G., with Sterner, R., & Rose, A. (1944). *An American dilemma: The Negro problem and modern democracy.* New York: Harper & Row.

Nandy, A. (Ed.). (1988). *Science, hegemony and violence.* Tokyo: United Nations University.

Nkrumah, K. (1973). *Autobiography of Kwame Nkrumah.* London: Panaf.

Nsamenang, A. B. (1992). *Human development in cultural context: A Third World perspective.* Newbury Park, CA: Sage.

O'Connor, A. (1986). *The African city.* London: Hutchinson University Library for Africa.

Peplau, L. A., & Conrad, E. (1989). Beyond nonsexist research: The perils of feminist methods in psychology. *Psychology of Women Quarterly, 13,* 379-400.

Polkinghorne, D. E. (1988). *Narrative knowing and the human sciences.* Albany: State University of New York Press.

Rainwater, L. (1970a). *Behind ghetto walls: Black families in a federal slum.* Chicago: Aldine.

Rainwater, L. (1970b). *Soul.* Chicago: Aldine.

Rapp, R. (1988). Is the legacy of second wave feminism postfeminism? *Socialist Review, 18,* 31-37.

Rollins, J. (1985). *Between women: Domestics and their employers.* Philadelphia: Temple University Press.

Said, E. W. (1978). *Orientalism.* London: Penguin.

Seidman, I. E. (1991). *Interviewing as qualitative research.* New York: Teachers College Press.

Shaffir, W. B., & Stebbins, R. A. (Eds.). (1991). *Experiencing fieldwork.* Newbury Park, CA: Sage.

Sprague, J., & Zimmerman, M. K. (1989). Quality and quantity: Reconstructing feminist methodology. *American Sociologist, 20,* 71-86.

Stack, C. B. (1974). *All our kin: Strategies for survival in a black community.* New York: Harper Colophon.

Stanfield, J. H., II. (1985). *Philanthropy and Jim Crow in American social science.* Westport, CT: Greenwood.

Stanfield, J. H., II. (1991). Racism in America and in other race-centered nation-states: Synchronic considerations. *International Journal of Comparative Sociology, 32,* 243-260.

Stanfield, J. H., II. (1992). Ethnic pluralism and civic responsibility in post-Cold War America. *Journal of Negro Education, 61*(3).

Stanfield, J. H., II. (1993a). Epistemological considerations. In J. H. Stanfield II & R. M. Dennis (Eds.), *Race and ethnicity in research methods* (pp. 16-36). Newbury Park, CA: Sage.

Stanfield, J. H., II. (1993b). Methodological reflections: An introduction. In J. H. Stanfield II & R. M. Dennis (Eds.), *Race and ethnicity in research methods* (pp. 3-15). Newbury Park, CA: Sage.

Strauss, A. L. (1987). *Qualitative analysis for social scientists.* New York: Cambridge University Press.

Sudarkasa, N. (1986). In a world of women: Field work in a Toruba community. In P. Golde (Ed.), *Women in the field: Anthropological experiences* (pp. 47-64). Berkeley: University of California Press.

Suret-Canale, J. (1988). *Essays on African history: From the slave trade to neocolonialism.* Trenton, NJ: Africa World Press.

Terrell, M. C. (1980). *A colored woman in a white world: Mary Church Terrell.* New York: Arno.

Tesch, R. (1990). *Qualitative research.* New York: Falmer.

Vansina, J. (1988). *Oral tradition as history.* London: James Currey.

Walker, R. (Ed.). (1985). *Applied qualitative research.* Hants, England: Gower.

Warren, C. A. B. (1988). *Gender issues in field research.* Newbury Park, CA: Sage.

West, C. (1982). *Prophesy deliverance! An Afro-American revolutionary Christianity.* Philadelphia: Westminster.

West, C. (1988). *Prophetic fragments.* Grand Rapids, MI/Trenton, NJ: Eerdmans/Africa World Press.

Whitehead, T. L. (1986). Breakdown, resolution and coherence: The fieldwork experiences of a big, brown pretty-talking man in a West Indian community. In T. L. Whitehead & M. E. Conaway (Eds.), *Self, sex and gender in cross-cultural fieldwork* (pp. 213-239). Urbana: University of Illinois Press.

Williams, A. (1987). Reading feminism in fieldnotes. *Studies in Sexual Politics, 16,* 100-109.

Williams, A. (1990). Reflections on the making of an ethnographic text. *Studies in Sexual Politics, 29,* 1-63.

Williams, R. (1990). *Culture and society.* London: Hogarth.

Wilson, W. J. (1974). The new black sociology: Reflections on the "insiders and outsiders" controversy. In W. J. Wilson, *Black sociologist* (pp. 322-338). Chicago: University of Chicago Press.

Zaslavsky, C. (1973). *Africa counts: Number and pattern in African culture.* Boston: Prindle, Weber & Schmidt.

11

Audiencing

Cultural Practice and
Cultural Studies

John Fiske

◆ *Cultural studies* is such a contested and currently trendy term that I must disclaim any attempt to either define or speak for it. There have been a number of recent studies of television's audiences and ways of watching that have contributed to the field, and I list some of them in the appendix to this chapter. What I wish to do here is to give an example of one way of understanding television watching that falls within "cultural studies," and through that example to highlight some theoretical and methodological issues by which this sort of cultural studies differs from other critical modes of analysis, and from positivist or scientific approaches.

I propose to tell a story about a particular program and a particular group of young people who watched it. I choose such a specific example because the attempt to understand the particularity of experience is one of the priorities of the approach I am illustrating. The program is *Married . . . With Children*; the audience, a group of teenage students who gathered together regularly to watch it.

Married . . . With Children is a situation comedy that premiered in the United States in April 1987 on the new Fox network. By January 1989 it was Fox's top-rated show, with an estimated 21 million viewers, and, as 1989 is the year of the show's major cultural impact, it forms the focus of my study. This, incidentally, signals another difference from many scientific studies, which, because they typically aim for human universals, do not find their dates of particular significance. The date is, however, significant for cultural studies, and it is for this chapter.

By the late 1980s the dominance of the three major networks was cracking. New technologies, particularly cable, but also VCRs, video games, and home computers, had weakened the networks' grip on domestic leisure activities. Statistics here are very suspect, because they are supplied by a commercial organization, the Nielsen Group, to the networks primarily to determine the advertising rates for each time slot and to sell each slot to advertisers. It is therefore in the interests of the networks to use a counting system that keeps the ratings as high as possible and that overlooks defections. And it is in Nielsen's interests to serve the networks' interests. But arguments over stray percentage points could not disguise the steady erosion of the network audience.

New technologies do not in themselves produce social change, however, though they can and do facilitate it. These new technologies met the marketing strategies of late capitalist industries, which can be summarized briefly as ones of market segmentation rather than mass marketing. Advertisers now increasingly target their products to specified social groups or market segments, and do not wish to pay for their messages to reach nontarget groups. The networks, however, grew and prospered by attracting the largest possible audiences whose internal differentiations were kept to the broadest social categories with the weakest categorical boundaries. So although cop/adventure shows might have appealed primarily to men, women were important too, so female characters and "feminine" appeal were featured as strongly as the producers thought was possible without alienating the men. The consequence was that advertisers for razors paid to reach a nonshaving audience. But on a cable channel devoted to sports, they would pay much less and target their advertising dollars more accurately.

But, however dominant the market economy is, our society is not determined by it entirely. Market segmentation is an economic transformation of changes in the social order at large. Throughout the 1970s and 1980s, people's sense of social differences began to challenge the homogenization of consensus more and more openly. The women's movement was one key player, as it asserted women's rights to control not only their

360

economic and domestic relations, but also the sense of the feminine and thus the meaning of feminine identity. Very similar demands were made by the black power movement, and gays and lesbians began to assert their difference from the mainstream. As Reaganism widened the gaps between rich and poor, men and women, whites and those of color, the sense of social differences sharpened and became conflictual. Race, gender, and class were far from the only players in the scene; regional differences became marked, as did those between the urban and the rural, the religious and the secular, the traditionally married and the rest. In this essay the key axis of social difference is one not yet mentioned—that of age.

New information technologies were developed by marketing companies to track the intersections of all these axes of social difference and thus to target market segments more accurately than ever before. Market research found, for instance, that a product aimed at reproducing the old-fashioned satisfaction of baking from scratch would have its strongest appeal among married women with more than two children who lived in the rural South, attended church regularly, did not have full-time jobs outside the home, and watched *Cops* and *Rescue 911* because these programs melodramatized the everyday dangers of the outside world.

This conjuncture of forces, technological, economic, and sociocultural, left the three networks looking like dinosaurs wondering what to do with a changing world. Rupert Murdoch, Fox's owner, thought he knew. He wanted to develop a fourth network that combined the big three's traditional wide geographic reach with a new ability to deliver accurately segmented audiences, particularly ones that lay outside the massed middle America that the other networks vied for. So Fox launched its new network on weekends with a schedule aimed at the teenage and young adult nonfamily audience. (Of course, many teenagers lived in families while wishing, for some of the time at least, that they did not.) With programs such as *The Tracey Ullman Show* and *It's Garry Shandling's Show*, Fox gained a core audience in its targeted segment, but *Married . . . With Children* and *The Simpsons*, which followed soon after, were its first shows to achieve general ratings that challenged those of the big three. It was the high visibility of these shows, as much as their content or audiences, that made them controversial.

Since its origin in the 1950s, the category of "the teenager" has been a site of trouble and anxiety for adult America. As this was the social formation that Fox wished to turn into an audience that it could sell to advertisers, the programs designed for this strategy were predictably controversial. T-shirts showing Bart Simpson and his slogan, "Under-achiever—and proud of it" have been banned from schools, and Bart has been identified as one of the causes of the poor record of U.S. schools. *Married . . . With Children* has been similarly controversial, and it is upon this controversy that I wish to focus (Fiske, 1994).

The program was widely seen by adult America as offensive and as sending a "wrong" message to teenagers; by publicly inverting the norms of the "good" family, it offended those whose social interests were inscribed in the family and appealed to those who identified themselves as outside-the-family. The carnivalesque offense of the show runs along a continuum in which offensive bodies extend into offensive family relationships and thence into offensive social relations.

Bodies and bodily functions are its main vehicles for representing the identities and relationships of the Bundy family. Al, the father/husband, has a body that smells and an ugly face that is given to grotesque expressions; he inverts the social norms of masculine power by being economically and sexually inadequate and by being incapable of controlling his children or his wife. Peg, the wife/mother, is oversexed, overcoiffed, over-made-up, and overdressed. Her body movements, gestures, and expressions mock by exaggeration the conventions of feminine attractiveness normally used in patriarchy to discipline the bodies of its women. As she teeters across the room, her high heels thrust her bosom and buttocks into prominence while restricting her movements to those that are sexually attractive but ineffective practically. She exposes to mocking laughter the patriarchal control over feminine bodies and behavior that is applied in the design of high-heeled shoes. Her overblown lips and overblown hair serve a similar parodic function. Her mocking of the feminine body in patriarchy is also accompanied by an inversion of normal social relations. She never provides for the family and neither buys nor prepares food, and in every way is the opposite of the nurturing wife/mother figure. Kelly and Bud, the two teenage children, are similarly defined by their bodily appearances and appetites. They are constantly hungry for both food and sex; in their search for sexual pleasure, Kelly is an excessive success, Bud an excessive failure. She parodies the body and behavior of the "dumb blonde," whereas he is constantly trying to convince himself and others that his inadequate teenage body is that of a macho stud.

The relationships among the family members conflict across gender and age differences. The language in which they are conducted is scatological and often emphasizes their bodily and sexual attributes as markers of identity and of social relationships. The normative family in which gender and age differences are contained within a consensual harmony is simultaneously mocked and inverted by the show.

The show attracted a large and devoted audience of teenagers and young adults to the new Fox network when it was first aired. Many of my students called it the most "realistic" show on television, and they used its carnivalesque elements as ways of expressing the difference between their experience of family life and that proposed for them by the dominant social norms.

One of my graduate students, David Brean, spent a season watching the show with a typical audience of young people. They were undergraduates, mainly freshmen and sophomores, of both sexes who attended a Catholic university and met after evening Mass, which many attended, each Sunday in one or another of their apartments. Some of the group had known each other through high school, others were more recent members, but the group's communitas was organized around the shared taste for *Married . . . With Children.*

The seven members who attended one particular Sunday met in Mick and John's apartment, the main room of which had once been the living room of the single-family house that was now converted into student apartments. The furniture was an eclectic mix of whatever they had been able to scrounge from their families. The couch, for instance, carried the scars of its history, during which it had moved from living room to family room to kids' basement, to student apartment. Its stains and tears spoke against the domestic order still faintly discernible in the traces of what it used to be. During the show, beer was spilled on it and nobody cared, a half-eaten hamburger on a thin piece of paper was set down on it with no thought of grease or ketchup stains seeping through, and, later on, John and Sarah lay on it in a body-hugging embrace that would have sent their parents into conniptions had the couch still been in the family living room.

The walls were decorated with posters of pop and film stars that may have been tolerated at home, though not in the living room, and with signs advertising beer, which almost certainly would have been prohibited, particularly as they had clearly been stolen from a bar, not purchased from a store. Nobody in the apartment had reached the legal drinking age, so the signs were doubly illicit.

The theme music of the show, "Love and Marriage," a Frank Sinatra number from their parents' generation, provoked the group into singing along in vacuous parody of both its "older" style and "older" sentiments.

A similar parody of their parents' taste (as they saw it) hung on the wall—a somewhat moth-eaten painting of Elvis on black velvet. The "bad taste" of the picture was different from the "bad taste" of the program, for it was their view of teenage culture then as opposed to now. The picture was a site for experiencing the differences between their parents-as-teenagers and themselves, just as the program enabled them to mock the differences between their parents now and themselves. These differences were not shown on the screen, but were constructed in the process of audiencing and only there: The Bundys did not represent the teenagers' parents, but the teenagers' view of the Bundys and the comedy lay in the difference between parents-as-seen-by-teenagers (represented on the screen) and parents-as-seen-by-themselves (known by the audience, and brought to the screen by them, but never shown on it).

Watching the program involved a series of interactive comments that took every opportunity the show offered to draw disrespectful parallels between it and the families the teenagers had so recently left. These comments ranged from delight in representations of a counterknowledge ("My Dad does that"—said of an action that a father would disown as typically his but that a teenager would know differently) to more engaged family politics ("I wish Mom had seen that").

The show enabled the teenagers to engage in and reconfigure the age politics of their relations with their absent parents: equally, they used it to engage in gender politics with their present partners. The gender conflicts between the parents and the children consisted of verbal punches and counterpunches in which, generally, the females outpointed the males. This caused few problems for the men in this particular audience, and though both sexes would cheer the punches thrown by their own sides, they also gained great pleasure from any well-aimed riposte. When a girl nudged her boyfriend at a remark on the TV, she brought their own interpersonal history to the program just as significantly as the Fox network brought the program to them.

This particular audience, or rather group of people who came together to "audience" the show, is best understood not as a social category, though its members clearly belonged to one (that of white middle-class youth), but as a social formation. As a social unit they were formed around a TV program and a set of social interests. The members of this formation did not experience all their social relations in this antifamily mode, nor even did they necessarily spend much time together as a social formation with other interests in common. Indeed, it is quite possible that some of them were members of other formations that entered more conservative and complicit relations with the social order (some did, after all, attend Mass immediately before watching the show). They did not appear to align themselves with the class identities of the blue-collar Bundys, but confined their observable alignments to ones of gender and age. The fact that no class alignments were observable does not necessarily mean that none were made, but it probably indicates that, if made, they were either secondary or displacements by which class disempowerment was made to stand for age disempowerment. Indeed, it is quite possible that some members of the group were class snobs, but that their social competencies developed to cope with such elaborately transected societies as ours enabled them to experience a comfortable fit between what an objective analysis would describe as contradictory political positions. Audiencing the show as this group did involved a tactical alliance of age interests and little more. Those who formed this alliance may well have been typical of the social category that was the core of Fox's target audience, but the alliance was not coterminous with the category (many of whose members would have shared neither the alliance's tastes nor its interests). A social category holds its members constantly within its conceptual grip; a social formation is formed and dissolved more fluidly, according to its contextual conditions. It is identified by what its members do rather than by what they are, and as such is better able to account nonreductively for the complexities and contradictions of everyday life in a highly elaborated society.

The show's carnivalesque inversions of official family values and its emphasis on the bodily pleasures of eating, drinking, and sexuality reproduced and were reproduced in the practices of this audience formation. Out of them, they produced a cultural experience within which the show, the behavior of watching it, and the place where it was watched were all mobilized to produce social identities and social relations that were within their control as opposed to, and in emancipation from, those institutionalized for them in the officially approved family. The carnivalesque offensiveness of these practices differentiated them from what was officially approved, but it did not in itself do anything positive. It opened up a gap in top-down power that this particular social formation was able to fill with the social identities/relations it produced for itself. The carnivalesque can do no more than open up spaces; it is upon what fills them that we should base our analysis and evaluation.

But the creation of gaps is enough to provoke the power bloc to rush to repair its system. The show provoked wide-ranging and vehement criticism from official, profamily voices. None of them was concerned about what might be used to fill these gaps; rather, it was the attack on family values, that is, the gaps themselves, that concerned them. Terry Rakolta, for example, a wealthy housewife, gained much publicity for her campaign to persuade advertisers to withdraw from the show on the grounds that it resembled soft-core pornography and contained "blatant exploitation of women and sex, and anti-family attitudes" (Dell, 1990). According to a front-page story in the *New York Times* (March 2, 1989), Procter & Gamble, McDonald's, Tambrands, and Kimberly-Clark all withdrew advertising support or promised to monitor the show's values more carefully in the future. Procter & Gamble cited the show's "negative portrayal of American family life"; the chairman of Coca-Cola in a letter to Rakolta wrote that he was "corporately, professionally and privately embarrassed" that ads for Coke had appeared on the show; and Gary Lieberman, chairman of Columbia Pictures Television, which produced the show, offered Rakolta "our sincere apology" (*Los Angeles Times,* March 4, 1989). Rakolta's husband was president of a family-owned construction firm worth $400 million (which gives a particular inflection to the term *family values*), so the social positions of those forming this set of allegiances within the power bloc were particularly close. Rakolta attempted to broaden the allegiance, but not its intent, by enlisting the support of lobbying groups within conservative "middle America," specifically, Concerned Women of America and the American Family Association (which had started life as the National Federation for Decency, an organization founded by a fundamentalist minister, the Reverend Donald Wildmon). Rakolta's rallying cry, around which this allegiance was forged, was "Free TV is the last bastion for the American family, or anybody who wants decent programming."

Initially, the press reaction to her campaign was favorable. The *Detroit News* (her local newspaper) was typical in applauding "Mrs. Rakolta's stand for decency" (March 3, 1989). (It is noteworthy how frequently the concept of "decency" is used to disguise class taste and power under the mask of universally agreed-upon standards.) But the press support for the alliance weakened as its narrow social base and repressive strategy became clearer: In the months that followed, the typical line became "If the show offends you, switch it off, don't try and censor it" (*Denver Post,* March 8, 1989; *Detroit News,* July 24, 1989; and *Wall Street Journal,* July 31, 1989; all cited in Dell, 1990). Ironically, the longer-term result of Rakolta's campaign was to increase the show's ratings and expose an alliance of the power bloc to popular rejection.

Rakolta's campaign against the program did not originate in her own living room only; it was part of a sociocultural context in which "family values" had become a crucial political battlefield. Throughout the 1980s, the gap between the ideological norm of "the family" and the material conditions in which people actually lived widened to the extent that less than one-third of U.S. children were growing up in families that would be considered "normal." When the abnormal outnumbers the normal by more than two to one, the ideological power to produce the normal is put under immense pressure, and conflicts become sharpened and multifrontal.

So the conflict over "family values" has been central in every political campaign for the past decade. The high divorce rate, the increasing number of single-parent families, the growth of same-sex parenting—all are taken as evidence of the collapse of the normal family and therefore of danger to the social order in general. Vice President Dan Quayle provided a perfect example of this when he linked the 1992 Los Angeles riots with the collapse of family values and the decision of sitcom character Murphy Brown to become a single mother. When the media reported that Quayle thought Murphy Brown was the cause of the riots, they (typically) oversimplified his argument but did not categorically distort it: He did say that the program's legitimation of single motherhood was one of the causes of the collapse of family values that underlay the riots.

Family values are continuous with social values, for the family is seen as both a miniaturization of society and the building block with which the social order is constructed. The family is not only the foundation of today's social order, it is also the seed ground of tomorrow's. Parental discipline is the politics of the future, and any form of youth culture that appears to oppose or disrupt it is consequently viewed as socially threatening.

Culture is the social circulation of meanings, pleasures, and values, and the cultural order that results is inextricably connected with the social order within which it circulates. Culture may secure the social order and help to hold it in place, or it may destabilize it and work toward changing it, but it is never either neutral or detached. The social circulation of meanings is always a maelstrom, full of conflicting currents, whirlpools, and eddies. The mainstream attempts to keep its current as smooth and inexorable as possible, but around its edges there are always rough, intransigent rocks and promontories that disrupt or divert it.

The cultural analyst cannot possibly chart all of this maelstrom—not only is it so complex as to defy total description, but much of it occurs far beneath the surface and beyond analytic access. The analyst, then, has to select sites of analysis when this circulation of meanings becomes accessible and use them as points from which to theorize the inaccessible undercurrents. Audiences and texts are two of those sites, but neither is sufficient in itself, nor are they together. The social meanings of *Married . . . With Children* will have been circulated as much by those who never saw the show but who read or talked about the controversy it provoked as by those who watched it. The meaning of *Married . . . With Children* is produced at a variety of intersections, with the general "crisis of the family" at the macro social level as well as at the huge number of encounters with it at the micro level of particular viewings, one of which was Terry Rakolta's viewing of one episode in the company of her daughters (which was the origin of her campaign) and another of which was this group of students on this Sunday night. The conflict of interests between socioethical alliances within the power bloc that wish to maintain the nuclear family (itself a product of the capitalism they endorse) and economic alliances that wish to profit from oppositional or subordinate interests reproduces within the power bloc the dinner-table arguments between parents and teenagers—and neither could take the form that it does without the other.

We have been looking at three ways of understanding the audience: Fox's economic category of a market segment defined by its consumer preferences and buying power; Rakolta's sense of it as a site of the inculcation of values; and the students' audiencing as the process of producing, through lived experience, their own sense of their social identities and social relations, and of the pleasures that this process gave them. There are both overlaps and contradictions among these ways of constructing "the audience," but the most significant theoretically are the contradictory relations. Fox and Rakolta struggle over the construction of "the teenager." For Fox, the teenager is a market segment to be differentiated from the adult; for Rakolta, the teenager is a child to be kept under adult control within the family. Between Rakolta and this one student audience there is a struggle over the meanings of the family, over the age and gender politics within it, and thus over the social identities of those who occupy different roles within its structure of relationships. And between Fox and the teenage audience there is the struggle between incorporation and excorporation, in which the industry constantly seeks to incorporate the tastes and practices of subordinate social formations whose members, in their turn, scan the products of the culture industries looking for elements that they can excorporate and use to promote their own sociocultural interests.

The definition of "the audience" depends upon the way it is positioned in the social order. Located within the economic system, the audience is a market segment to be reached and, simultaneously, a commodity to be traded; located within the socioethical system, the audience is a site of acculturation or socialization; and located in the materiality of everyday life, the audience stops being a social category and becomes a process, a constituent element in a way of living. John and Sarah were members of all three "audiences" (and of others, not yet analyzed), but each audience is distinguished from the others only in the process of analysis: In lived culture there are no boundaries between categories, but only a complex of continuities. These different "audiences" merge into each other at the micro level of John and Sarah as social beings, and at the macro level of the social order of late capitalism at a particular point and place in its history.

The cultural analyst faces the inevitable paradox that categories and the distinctions between them are necessary tools in the process of analysis, but they distort the object of analysis, for culture works not in categorically distinct ways but as "a whole way of life" (to use one of Raymond Williams's definitions). What makes a way of life whole is the production of continuities across domains of experience that the analyst may choose to categorize as different. "Specimens" taken out of these continuities for microscopic analysis (a text, an audience, a marketing strategy) are distorted by the extraction, for any extraction disqualifies certain elements and relations in the cultural process while privileging others. And although the analyst is careful to return the specimen to the organic process from which it was taken, extraction and return are productive, not objective, practices.

As an analyst, I extract a specimen—let us say John's laying down a half-eaten hamburger on a sofa that was once in a family living room as he watches Peg Bundy "failing" to produce a family meal. I can never describe fully the relations that make that moment culturally significant. On most Sundays the hamburger will have been bought from a nearby McDonald's, but if John feels particularly self-indulgent and wishes to reward himself he will have gone further afield to buy a "better" burger at a small one-off burger joint. Which burger he bought will be connected to whether or not he finished a class paper he had to write, or whether or not he and Sarah had had a minor tiff, or whatever. The continuities among hamburgers, beer, *Married . . . With Children,* and Sarah in John's Sunday night stretch through into their relationships of not-school, not-church, not-family.

369

Whether the hamburger was one-off or mass produced by McDonald's connects not only with John's sense of the week or day that has passed, but also with the fact that McDonald's advertises on the show, that the local burger joint does not, and that the McDonald's advertising campaign promotes the restaurants as places for the family, particularly for parents and children, and thus with Rakolta's letter-writing campaign and McDonald's (temporary) withdrawal of advertising from the program. McDonald's advertising image of itself as a "family place" is, of course, designed to counter the perception that fast food is opposed to the family dinner table, and that it is itself a sign of and an agent in the breakdown of family values, particularly of the maternal responsibilities within them. The hamburger is much more than ground beef. This complex of continuities, still inadequately traced, will not exist in total in John's consciousness, but the continuities do exist in the culture, and in audiencing the program John activates them (and others not yet described) in a particular configuration more or less consciously, more or less emphatically.

My analysis of the hamburger on the sofa could go further, but my point here is that in extracting it as a specimen I have deformed it. I have set it into cultural relations (with a multinational corporation and a letter-writing upper-middle-class housewife) that are highly significant to me-as-analyst but that may have signified little in John's mouthful in front of the TV set. So in returning that specimen for his second bite, I have changed it, if not for him, then certainly for the reader of this analysis. The analyst's experience of that mouthful is quite different from that of the young man who took the bite in the first place. These differences do not invalidate the analysis, nor do they define John's experience of his own culture as inadequate, nor do they privilege the superiority of theory. They indicate the incompleteness of any understanding (experiential or theoretical) and the need for an academic modesty that acknowledges that the aim of analysis is not to reveal the truth but to contribute to a process of understanding, and to provoke other, probably contradictory, contributions.

A cultural analysis of audiences or audiencing is not, then, "scientific," and for the final section of this essay, I would like to indicate some of the differences between the two paradigms (obviously privileging the cultural, I make no claim to being unbiased) (Fiske, 1991).

The model underlying cultural analysis is one drawn from discourse analysis, and is systemic, not representative, in its model of validation. Its data are empirical but not empiricist. So, the hamburger is not representative of the audience-as-a-whole of *Married . . . With Children*; it is significant regardless of whether or not John is the only audience member in the universe who eats hamburgers while watching, just as the significance of a sentence does not depend on how many people speak it. It is significant because it is a practice of a system, not because it reproduces other practices. In discourse analysis, no utterance is representative of other utterances, though of course it shares structural features with them; a discourse analyst studies utterances in order to understand how the potential of the linguistic system can be activated when it intersects at its moments of use with a social system. The utterance is an actualization in a historical social relationship of the linguistic potential. So the cultural analyst studies instances of culture in order to understand both the system that structures "the whole way of life" and the ways of living that people devise within it.

This study of this audience, or rather example of audiencing, was not an ethnography in the anthropological or social scientific sense of the term; it did not aim to attain a full or objective understanding of the teenagers' whole way of life, for that would be impossible. Rather, it was an attempt to get glimpses of culture in practice that could be set in systemic relationship to other glimpses such as those afforded by Terry Rakolta or by Fox's economic strategy. Insofar as these glimpses, or sites of analysis, come from widely different points in the social order, the systematicity that links them and makes them part of a whole way of life is a generalized one. What links the empirical detail to the general and thus establishes its theoretical significance is a systemic relationship and not a representative one. The data then are empirical in that they derive from a material experience, but not empiricist in that there is no claim that the material plane has an objective existence that provides the terms of its own significance. Their significance is produced only at their intersection with another ontological plane—that of the system, or the structuring principle.

The term *structure,* or *structural,* is common to both positivist and systemic models, but there are crucial differences in the ways in which each uses it. For positivism (e.g., content analysis), a structure is a coherent patterning of empirical data that is part of the larger social reality theoretically derived from the data. Such a structure may be related to more abstract, less empirically derived structures in that social reality (particularly value structures, as in Gerbner's cultivation theory). So a content analysis of gender portrayal on television revealing that women are portrayed less frequently than men and in a narrower range of occupations and settings may be convincingly related to the more abstract values of patriarchy. The tracing of such interstructural relationships is common to

371

both systemic models and positivist ones, but the similarity ends there. Systemic theories of structure go further than do positivist ones, for systemic structures, such as language, are generative, whereas positivist structures are descriptive. Systemic structures generate the practices by which they are used and are, in their turn, modified by those practices. Positivist structures, however, have effects, not practices, and the relationship between structure and effect is one-way. In positivism, structures have no practice.

The structure of language, on the other hand, has a mutually informing relationship with the utterances that are its practices. The system is produced in part, at least, by its practices, as the practices are produced in part, at least, by the system. Systems and practices both structure each other and are structured by each other; structuration is a two-way process, though not an equal one. Because positivism does not theorize structures in relationship to practice, it does not have a theory of either how they change or how they can act as agents of change. Bourdieu (1984) makes the point that theoretical methods are better able to account for social change than those of quantitative positivism, for these produce snapshots of a social system as a particular moment, and positivism therefore tends to model social differences as social stratification. Theory, however (and for Bourdieu the word seems to be a code for Marxist critical theory), is better able to trace social struggle, for that occurs over time as part of the dialectic of history; consequently, this type of theory models social differences not as stratification but as struggle.

When positivism models the differences in the social order as relatively stable and/or harmonious, its policies tend toward liberal pluralism; when it evacuates that social order from the research agenda altogether (as in much TV effects research), its politics shift toward the reactionary. Some of the differences between liberal pluralist positivism and cultural studies emerge in the debate around "the active audience." The "active audience" of uses and gratifications (a positivist theory) differs significantly from that of cultural theory, particularly in its claim that active uses of the media actually gratify needs. This is not the case in cultural studies. Here the needs (for more material or symbolic resources, for more power and control) can be met only by social action; the activity of the media user is that of articulating those needs within the social relations that both produce and frustrate them and of establishing and validating a social identity that is a bottom-up product rather than a top-down one. Audience activity is an engagement in social relations across social inequality; the satisfaction in the process lies in control over the terms of that engagement, but there is no satisfaction of the needs generated by the inequality.

Equally, the psychological brand of positivism assumes that the audience is not just where the effects of television occur but is itself an effect of television. There is no sense that the audience precedes or outlasts the effects of watching. But John and Sarah were social beings and members of social formations long before they watched *Married . . . With Children,* and their experiences of family life affected the ways they watched the program just as much as the program affected their sense of "family values," if not more. In this sense, the meanings of the program are an effect of their social behavior, rather than their social behavior being an effect of the program. Programs, the industry that makes them, and the people who watch them are all active agents in the circulation of meanings, and the relationships among them are not ones of cause and effect, in which one precedes another, but of systematicity.

The word *audience* suggests a priority that is misleading, for an audience can exist only when hearing something. This sense of precedence lies not only in the model of the process (in which the imagined procedure is from message to audience) but also in the history of the chosen word, which originally referred to subjects being summoned to an audience with the monarch or pope. This discursive construction of the audience as the disempowered empty receptacle waiting for the message underlies both Rakolta's fear of *Married . . . With Children* and the whole tradition of effects research.

In a systemic model, in one set of relations "the audience" can be seen to precede the message. The social category of "the teenager" preceded Fox's attempts to turn it into a market segment. Within it there were already tastes and practices, social relations and social identities, ways of living within a social order that entered relations of opposition to some of its structuring forces and of complicity with others. All this not only preceded the first episode of *Married . . . With Children,* but it constituted the social goal at which the text was aimed. The text is an effect of this audience, and the skill of its producers lies in their ability to respond to the ways of living within the category of "the teenager."

In calling the text an effect of the audience, I am attempting to score a point in a debate, not to provide an essential definition, for a text is no more nor less an effect of the audience than is the audience of the text. The relationships between them are not ones of cause and effect, in which one spatially, temporally, or epistemologically takes precedence over the other;

the relations are systemic ones of a complex of reciprocities in which contradictions and complicities struggle to gain ground over one another.

In media studies, positivism has tended to produce a normative episte-mology; cultural studies, however, does not. It does not assume that what is statistically most normal is therefore most significant. Instead, discourse analysts (like poets) often find that marginal and abnormal uses of language are highly significant because they reveal, in a way that more normal linguistic usages do not, the extremes of which a system is capable. Systems are often more susceptible to change or modification at their margins than at their centers; social change typically originates in marginalized or subordinated minorities and, as cultural studies has a political stake in social change, it requires a model that allows the marginal, the deviant, and the abnormal to be always granted significance and at times major significance. History may show that the 29% of women who were not represented on television as housewives, stewardesses, or models may be more significant than the 71% who were (Dominick & Rauch, 1972).

Let us return to our hamburger for a moment, for we have now refigured it into a statement, not a commodity. This identifies another point of difference between cultural studies and other forms of critical (Marxist) theory, of which I wish to refer to two main schools, broadly known as political economy and ideology theory. The hamburger, as a theoretical construct, is a different cultural object in each theory.

Political economy sees the hamburger as a commodity, and thus in consuming it (in both senses of the word) John is inserted into one set of social relations that override all others—the economic relations of pro-ducer and consumer that are specific to capitalism (*mass* production and consumption): The functions of John's dollar bill are first to produce capital for McDonald's and thus to underwrite corporate capitalism, and second to fix him as a consumer and therefore reproducer of capitalism. The more he eats at McDonald's, the more his needs are commodified, and the more his needs that cannot be met by a commodity are extinguished. As a commodity, the hamburger is economic (it transfers money from the subordinate to capital) and it is political—it represses human and social needs that the capitalist social order cannot turn to a profit and thus produces those who eat it into consumers. McDonald's advertisements work in exactly the same way; they promote those family values that can be met in its restaurants and repress the rest. Fox's television programs are equally commodities: *Married . . . With Children* promotes only those identities and behaviors within the category of "teenager" that it can commodify; it recognizes that teenagers do have some say in who they are and what they do, but it always seeks to produce a commodity by which they can say it. In this view, consumption is a reproduction of capitalism, and the function of the media is to ensure that the whole of social life, particularly in the realm of leisure, is turned into an enormous site of consumption. Through its ubiquity, the commodity extinguishes noncapitalist ways of thinking, behaving, relating, and identifying.

Cultural studies accuses political economy of mistaking the strategy for its effectiveness. Political economy does a fine job in analyzing a central (it would claim *the* central) strategic force in capitalism, and it properly identifies the comprehensiveness, the energy, and the enormous resources with which that strategy is applied. It is limited because it limits its terrain of analysis to the macro level; it cannot recognize social difference because social differences are brought into play beneath its level of analysis.

One of the earliest breaks between cultural studies and political economy centered on the text: Cultural studies wished to understand what sort of texts and what semiotic work within texts were characteristic of capitalism, and to devise ways of critically evaluating texts, that is, of distinguishing between them, not as aesthetic objects but as sociopolitical agents. In defining the text as a cultural commodity, political economy left little room for criticism, evaluation, and differentiation. But cultural studies and political economy do agree that texts are political.

Ideology theory joins in this agreement, but again cultural studies differs. Like political economy, ideology theory, particularly in its Althusserian mode, emphasizes one social force over all others. In ideology theory, subjectivity plays the role that the commodity does in political economy. Capitalism reproduces itself, in this account, in the way that its dominant ideology makes all who live under it into "subjects-in-ideology." This concept implies that the overridingly effective part of our consciousness, of our ways of understanding our identities, social relations, and social experiences, is a totally pervasive ideology. This ideology and its ways of working is *institutionalized* into the "ideological state apparatuses"— the law, education, the media, the political system, and so on—and in the ways they go about their daily operations; it is *internalized* into the consciousness, or rather subconsciousness, of the individuals who live within that society and its institutions. The socially colonized consciousness that results is called *subjectivity*. Subjectivity works in the domain of ideology (that is, of meanings, identities, and social relations) in the same way as does the commodity in that of political economy, and similarly, the totality of its pervasiveness is all too easily elided into the totality of its effectiveness.

Althusser brought psychoanalysis into the ideological picture, and this proved particularly fruitful for a powerful school of feminism. Ideology theory had class domination at its center, but central to psychoanalytic theory was sexuality. The combination of the two enabled feminism to develop a theory and mode of analysis that revealed the pervasiveness of patriarchy through all social domains from the institutional to the subconscious. It also showed how capitalism and patriarchy were inextricably intertwined and interdependent.

Cultural studies found both to be helpful, for both provided incisive methodologies for analyzing texts and social behavior, and both provided convincing theoretical paradigms by which to link texts and behavior with individual subjectivity on the one hand and the social system on the other.

But their totalizing tendency still caused problems for cultural studies: In both ideology and psychoanalytic theories, texts became agents of domination. Cultural studies attempts to be multilevel in its methodology and in particular to explore the interface between the structuring conditions that determine our social experience and the ways of living that people devise within them. What has been called "the turn to Gramsci" identifies the crucial difference between cultural studies and the macro-level, determinist, and reductionist tendencies of some other critical theories.

Stuart Hall is largely responsible for drawing our attention to Gramsci and Volosinov. Both these theorists emphasized struggle—Gramsci in the realm of politics and social life, Volosinov in that of language and meaning. Hegemony theory (Gramsci's contribution) argues that ideology has to work by means of negotiation and struggle to win the consent of the subordinates to the system that subordinates them. It does not impose itself on them, but has to take some account (as little as possible) of subordinate social interests in order to secure temporary consent. Such points of consent are never fixed, but can be shifted in one direction or another according to historical conditions and the conjuncture of forces within them. Hegemony is thus a constant process of unequal struggle between unequal social forces. The social struggle is continued in language and texts as the struggle for meaning. Here texts are neither commodities nor agents of the dominant ideology, but sites of struggle where the subordinate can engage in contested relations with the social interests that attempt to subordinate them. Texts always carry the interests of the dominant classes, for those interests have developed the conditions of production, and the conditions of production are necessarily inscribed in the product. Commodification, capitalist ideology, and patriarchy are powerful forces at work within texts, but describing those forces does not describe the totality of ways in which texts can be put to work.

Although cultural studies differs from other critical theories, it shares with them the most important characteristic of all—the critical. The basic assumption of all critical theories is that the inequalities of capitalism need to be changed and that the world would be a better place if we could change them. There are three interrelated reasons for studying capitalism—to expose its mechanisms of inequality, to motivate people to change them, and to reveal sites and methods by which change might be promoted. The differences among forms of critical theory are ones of tactics, not of strategy. Between critical theory and positivism, however, the differences are strategic.

Audiencing is a concept that can exist only in critical theory aimed exclusively at exposing the structural working of capitalism. Audiencing understands consumption, whether of the text or the hamburger, to be an act of micro-level clandestine production, not of reproduction. This clandestine production is a practice: It produces meanings, not objects (whether a commodity or a text); it exists as process rather than product, and can thus escape our notice. Its low visibility, however, should not be translated into low significance. Indeed, the interests of subordinated social formations may well be served by keeping much of their practice unseen and out of the reach of incorporating tentacles.

Dominant interests are most effectively promoted in social domains on the macro level, that is, that of structure, which is why macro-level social theories are best at analyzing the structural strategies of domination; equally, it is why macro social theories often cannot see beyond them to the level of practice. Subordinate culture is one where practice at the micro level engages with these macro-level forces in particular social conditions. Indeed, one of the key locations where social and semiotic struggles are entered, where the weak engage with the strong, is this interface between practice and structure. This is also where social differences of identity and social relations can be struggled over, where the top-down or bottom-up control over such difference can be contested. It is a crucial site of the hegemonic process, and it can be analyzed only by a theory that grants particularities a greater significance than do macro-level critical theories.

The system by which meanings are circulated in a society resembles a maelstrom rather than an engineering diagram. It is a system of conflicting currents in which the slope of the ground always favors one set, but whose flow can be disrupted and even diverted if the terrain is rocky enough. Audiencing is part of this flow and eddy—sometimes part of the mainstream flow, sometimes part of an upstream eddy. The audience that positivism tries to extract and hold still in the calm of its laboratory or in the fixity of its statistical relations is not an audience that cultural studies recognizes. Equally, cultural studies does not recognize the audience pacified and massified, one whose identities and differences have been homogenized through either commodification or ideology: Audiencing is a variety of practices, an activity, not a social category or a site of a victory.

◆ Appendix: Selected Further Reading

Ang, I. (1985). *Watching Dallas.* London: Routledge.

Ang, I. (1991). *Desperately seeking the audience.* London: Routledge.

Lewis, J. (1991). *The ideological octopus: An exploration of television and its audience.* New York: Routledge.

Lull, J. (1990). *Inside family viewing.* New York: Routledge.

Morley, D. (1988). *Family television.* New York: Routledge.

Morley, D. (1993). *Television, audiences and cultural studies.* London: Routledge.

Press, A. (1991). *Women watching television.* Philadelphia: University of Pennsylvania Press.

Seiter, E., Kreutzner, G., Warth, E. M., & Borchers, H. (Eds.). (1989). *Remote control: Television, audiences and cultural power.* London: Routledge.

◆ References

Bourdieu, P. (1984). *Distinction: A social critique of the judgment of taste.* Cambridge, MA: Harvard University Press.

Dell, C. (1990). Married . . . with children *and the press: Sex, lies and reading strategies.* Paper presented at the annual meeting of the Popular Culture Association, Toronto.

Dominick, J. R., & Rauch, G. E. (1972). The image of women in network TV commercials. *Journal of Broadcasting, 16,* 259-265.

Fiske, J. (1991). For cultural interpretation: A study of the culture of homelessness. *Critical Studies in Mass Communication, 8,* 455-474.

Fiske, J. (1994). *Media matters.* Minneapolis: University of Minnesota Press.

PART III

◆ The Future of Qualitative Research

And so we come to the end, which is only the starting point for a new beginning. We opened this volume with the argument that the field of qualitative research is defined by a series of tensions and contradictions. These tensions have been felt in every chapter in this volume. Here we list many of them, for purposes of summary only. They take the form of questions:

1. Whose history and which applied and theoretical traditions do we follow into the future?

2. How do we study the "Other" without studying ourselves?

3. What ethical codes must be formulated to fit the contemporary period?

4. Will a new interpretive paradigm emerge out of the conflicts that exist between the many paradigms and perspectives we have presented in this volume?

5. How will ethnic and feminist paradigms be fitted to this new synthesis, if it comes?

6. What will the cultural studies paradigm bring to qualitative research?

7. What new methods and strategies of inquiry will emerge?

8. How will the next generation of qualitative researchers react to data management methods and computer-assisted models of analysis?

9. Will the postmodern sensibility begin to form its own foundational criteria for evaluating the written text?

10. What place does positivism and its successor, postpositivism, have in a research endeavor that devalues universals to local interpretation, questions the existence of a guiding "truth," and emphasizes subjectivity in the research process?

11. What part can "fifth moment" qualitative research, including program evaluation and analysis, play in the understanding and improvement of programs and policy?

12. When all universals are gone, including the postmodern worldview, in favor of local interpretations, how can we continue to talk and learn from one another?

There are no definitive answers to any of these questions. Here we can only suggest, in the barest of detail, our responses to them. In our concluding chapter we elaborate these responses, grouping them around six basic themes, or issues: positivism and postpositivism, the crises of representation and legitimation, the treatment of the Other and the Other's voice, conflicts between science and religion, and the implications of new technologies for qualitative research. Examined from another angle, the questions listed above focus on the social text, history, politics, ethics, the Other, and interpretive paradigms.

◆ The Social Text

George Marcus, in Chapter 12, tells us that we are in a new historical moment, where simplistic, ethnographic cultural translations will cease to be accepted. The age of final authoritative readings of any cultural situation seems to be over. Reflexive, experimental texts that are messy, subjective, open-ended, conflictual, and feminist influenced will become the norm.

We agree with Marcus, and predict that three dominant forms of textuality will emerge in the sixth moment. The first form will be the classic, realist ethnographic text, redefined in postpositivist terms. The second form will be Marcus's messy, experimental text. The third textual form will mold the classic realist text with experimental variations, defined by poststructural considerations. (A fourth form, a legacy from the modernist moment, will be the qualitative text defined by traditional, positivist criteria.)

These four forms correspond, of course, to the four basic positions on evaluating the qualitative text that we outlined in our introduction to Part V. In the sixth moment these forms will inform and interact with one another. At the same time, there will be a merging of evaluative criteria that cross-cut these four forms. Positivist and postpositivist texts will be criticized from the poststructural and postmodern perspectives, especially in their treatment and representation of the Other. In turn, postmodern and poststructural texts will be held accountable to the kinds of issues raised by Altheide and Johnson in Chapter 10, Volume 3 of this series, including features from an ethnographic ethic that are sensitive to the situated, relational, and textual aspects of the research process.

Computer-assisted methods for managing empirical materials will shape each of these textual forms. Writers-as-field-workers will learn new ways of conversing with themselves as they represent their field experiences textually.

◆ History, Paradigms, Politics, Ethics, and the Other

Many things are changing as we write our way out of writing culture and move into the sixth moment of qualitative research. Multiple histories and theoretical frameworks, where before there were just a few, now circulate in this field. Today positivism and postpositivism are challenged and supplemented by constructivist, critical theory, feminist, ethnic, and cultural studies paradigms and perspectives. Many different applied action and participatory research agendas inform program evaluation and analysis.

We now understand that we study the other to learn about ourselves, and many of the lessons we have learned have not been pleasant. We seek a new body of ethical directives fitted to postmodernism. The old ethical codes failed to examine research as a morally engaged project. They never seriously located the researcher within the ruling apparatuses of society. A contextual-consequentialist ethical system will continue to evolve, informed at every point by the feminist, ethnic, and cultural studies sensibilities. Blatant voyeurism will continue to be challenged.

The cultural studies and critical theory perspectives, with their emphases on moral criticism, will shape the traditional empiricist foundations of qualitative research. The dividing line between science and morality will continue to be erased. A postmodern, poststructural science will move closer to a sacred science of the moral universe.

As we draw near to the end of the twentieth century, we see more clearly the iron cage, to use Weber's phrase, that has trapped us. Like a bird in a cage, for too long we have been unable to see the pattern that we have been caught up in. Coparticipants in a secular science of the social world, we became part of the problem. Entangled in the ruling apparatuses we wished to undo, we perpetuated systems of knowledge and power that we found, underneath, to be all too oppressive. It is not too late to get out of the cage. Like birds set free, we are now able to move about, to fly into the sixth moment.

And so we enter, or leave, the fifth moment. In our concluding chapter, we elaborate our thoughts about the next generation of qualitative research.

12

What Comes (Just) After "Post"?

The Case of Ethnography

George E. Marcus

◆ In an important sense, we are already in a post-"post" period—post-poststructuralism, post-postmodernism, and so on. At a recent conference, Clifford Geertz observed, in response to a question about the impact of postmodern influences upon the interpretive mode of qualitative social science, that the storm seems to have blown over, but its effects will be enduring and far-reaching. Indeed, as a half-serious ethnographer of the many academic conferences I have attended over the past several years, but particularly over the past year or so, I have noted a widespread "reaction formation" to the years of postmodern debate that might best be characterized as ambivalent rejection. Most, who have undoubtedly been influenced by it in their own thinking, ironically now hold postmodernism apart as an object or referent, applying to some unspecified others—definitely not to themselves—and view the term with ambivalence and suspicion, but as a fatal attraction nonetheless.

Discussions of the contemporary world of immense social and cultural changes in terms of postmodernism may thus be showing distinct signs of exhaustion. Indeed, at conferences and seminars I have noted several scholars carefully avoiding reference to the term in their own work; it has become the unmentionable "P word," often referred to as such. Yet, the substantive influences of whatever it was that was discussed in these seminal debates, apparently in the process of being exorcized as a fashion that has gone on for too long, have had profound, transformative effects on how all varieties of qualitative social science are now conducted. Thus, absent or receding as a riveting controversy of academic discussion, postmodernism is still very much present in its specific effects on particular disciplinary traditions and interdisciplinary efforts such as "cultural studies." (*Cultural studies* seems to be a successor identity for the space occupied by earlier postmodern debates, but with the aim of giving these debates both institutional presence and a political, ethical relevance to academic work concerning contemporary global social movements and events; see Grossberg, Nelson, & Treichler, 1992.)

We now have the opportunity—perhaps for the first time—to examine what this controversy has meant for the practices and debates of academic and disciplinary projects it has touched (some would say infected). The remainder of this chapter is intended as a contribution to this opportunistic re-vision of disciplines in the immediate wake of the "post" debates as fashionable moments of controversy—in this case, of ethnography in anthropology and cultural studies generally, which has become, along with "reading texts," one of the most favored and prestigious forms of conceiving the style in which scholars do qualitative research.

In anthropology, the intervention of postmodernism has centered on the critique of ethnography, as both mode of inquiry and writing. The emerging presence of various styles of reflexivity in ethnographic writing has stood, accurately or not, for the influence of (or, for some, infection by) postmodernism. In much of this chapter I will consider the kinds of interests at stake in positions taken on reflexivity in the writing of ethnography.

In the United States, discussions of postmodernism have grown over the past decade and a half from their specific references to aesthetic styles in art, architecture, and literature to a general sign of radical critique concerning styles of discourse and research in all the disciplines of the humanities and social sciences. Postmodernism has been given theoretical substance by the works of the French poststructuralists (who themselves had little use for the term, save, momentarily, Lyotard), which only became available through frequent translation in the early 1980s. Existentially, it has been powered by the widespread feeling that the conditions of social life (especially in the West, and especially in the frame of American postwar hegemony) were in fundamental transformation, a breakup of a world order, systemically conceived, into fragments that have not yet taken new configurations that can be easily identified. This world of established, but unstable, institutions rapidly generating emergent forms of diversity has defined the social conditions of a *postmodernity* for which the ethos, at least, of *postmodernism* as a style of knowledge production is particularly appropriate. Both in *revealing* conditions of postmodernity as well as in *enacting* them, postmodernist writing has been seductively attractive in defining the radical form of contemporary cultural criticism.

Yet it is important to understand that the critiques of disciplinary traditions (especially the traditions' post-World War II penchant for privileging and desiring to reproduce the perceived achievements of the natural sciences) were already well under way before the specter of postmodernism arose in general awareness in the early 1980s. Postmodernism merely intersected with the developing internal critiques of fields such as literature, history, sociology, law, philosophy, and anthropology, and both radicalized and consolidated them. As suggested, postmodernism has been sustained as an "alien other" by the internal critics of disciplinary traditions who assimilated its powerful and radical aspects for their own purposes while holding postmodernism itself at arm's length as an object of suspicion and ambivalence. All the while, its seductive example of extremity has radicalized, consolidated, and pushed forward alternatives for practice in the ongoing internal critiques of disciplinary traditions.

In anthropology, the ethos of postmodernism has intersected specifically with the strong critique of ethnographic rhetoric and writing that powerfully brought together and rearticulated three separate strands of critique that had been developing in Anglo-American anthropology since the 1960s and even before. The first strand was the exposure of the "messiness" of fieldwork as a method of social science through an outpouring of "trial-and-tribulation," "confessional" accounts (for a partial review of this literature, see Marcus & Fischer, 1986; Van Maanen, 1988). The second strand involved the contextualization of anthropology in the history of colonialism, particularly during the period of decolonization for the British and of the Vietnam War for the Americans (see Asad, 1973; Hymes, 1969). The final strand encompasses the not-yet-pointed critique from hermeneutics of anthropological styles of interpreting language, culture, and symbols (see Geertz, 1973a, 1973b). Influenced by literary theory (in turn influenced by poststructuralists), by the kind of rhetorical critique developed of history by Hayden White (e.g., 1973, 1978), and by a renewed interest in the history of anthropology itself, a group of anthropologists, historians,

385

and theorists of literature and language, with whom I and members of my department have been associated, produced work from the mid-1980s on (including most prominently *Writing Culture* [Clifford & Marcus, 1986], but also *Anthropology as Cultural Critique* [Marcus & Fischer, 1986]; *The Predicament of Culture* [Clifford, 1988]; and *The Unspeakable* [Tyler, 1987], among others) that brought to the surface in an articulate way profound discontents with the state of anthropology. The power of this intervention was in critique rather than in defining a new paradigm or setting a new agenda.[1] The critique has legitimated new objects, new styles of research and writing, and a shift in the historic purpose of anthropological research toward its long-standing, but underdeveloped, project of cultural critique. It has also tended to reorient the relevant interdisciplinary interests of anthropologists toward the humanities, especially as it became obvious that the most energetic thinking about culture, especially in cross-cultural and transcultural frameworks, had been coming from among literary scholars such as Edward Said, Gayatri Spivak, and Homi Bhabha.

The frame of postmodernism, by this time an interdisciplinary focus or sign of radical critique, has merely enhanced and consolidated the radical critical tendencies within anthropology, which were once again powerfully brought to the surface in the mid-1980s through attention to the language, conventions, and rhetoric by which anthropological knowledge through ethnography has been produced. The specter of postmodernism has held anthropology accountable, then, for its own radical critical possibility, which it had submerged in its legitimation as an academic field. How, and to what degree, alternative possibilities of work within the ethnographic tradition might emerge from the specific practices and responses that the critique of the mid-1980s, now labeled (justly or not) postmodern, are questions I want to take up. But before doing so, I want to make certain observations, in the form of a set of listed points, about how postmodernism has posed predicaments for the writing practices of anthropologists, what new tendencies it has encouraged, and what old ones it has radicalized.

1. Regardless of stated commitments to interdisciplinary work through the devaluing of disciplinary traditions, or to postmodern nonconformity in the way research is conceived, I have not seen any works by anthropologists that have not validated the practice of ethnography (this is *not* the same thing as validating ethnographic authority; rather, ethnography is

validated as the central identity of the discipline in its new interdisciplinary, postmodern milieu). Thus, although old forms of ethnography may have been called into question, ethnography itself, in its possibilities beyond its disciplinary uses so far, has not been. In fact, different conceptions of ethnography (and the fieldwork it entails) define the limits within which postmodern reimaginings in anthropology occur. Outside anthropology, the practice of ethnography (especially among exotic others) continues to define its mystique, appeal, and identity for its interdisciplinary partners in history, feminism, film studies, comparative literature, and the like (see the prestigious place that ethnography occupies in the recent collection *Cultural Studies* [Grossberg et al., 1992]).

2. What postmodernism has meant specifically for anthropology is a license to create an interesting traffic between the cognitive techniques of now classic aesthetic, avant-garde modernisms (such as early twentieth-century literary modernism, or Russian formalism, or, especially, the later avant-gardes of the 1920s and 1930s such as the surrealists; for a thorough review of these movements, see Bradbury & McFarlane, 1976). There are no innovative moves in so-called experimental ethnography so far that do not have previous histories in modernism. What *is* new (and perhaps shocking) is the open use of modernist sensibilities and techniques having to do with reflexivity, collage, montage, and dialogism within an empiricist genre with a strong, scientific claim to construct reliable knowledge about other forms of life. The struggle in contemporary works of so-called postmodern anthropology is between the currently liberating techniques and cognitions of a modernist sensibility and the continuing desire to report objectively on a reality other than the anthropologist's own. Maybe it is the conditions of postmodernity in the cultural situations that anthropologists encounter that make this belated migration from the sphere of art to the sphere of aspirant science, at least, feasible. In this heady enterprise, there is a responsibility on the part of experimental ethnographers (or theorists of ethnography) to understand the fate of certain techniques of radical critical aestheticism (such as montage, negative dialectics, and Brechtian theater; again see Bradbury & McFarlane, 1976) in their earlier appearances, and to ensure that their application now does not represent a nostalgia for aesthetics against a villainized positivism.

3. Again, I want to raise here the question of the anthropologist's explicit relation to a postmodernist identity. As I have noted, in discussions about postmodernism that I have read, it is rare that anyone will claim for

him- or herself a postmodernist personal intellectual style—will indeed say, "I am a postmodernist." Rather, for those who have written most cogently about postmodernism (e.g., David Harvey, in *The Condition of Postmodernity,* 1989; or John Rajchman, in his excellent short essay, "Postmodernism in a Nominalist Frame: The Emergence and Diffusion of a Cultural Category," 1987, in which he writes with ironic amazement that such a "motley and elastic range of things" could become such an object of fascination), the term has a phantom, indefinite referent, but certainly not oneself. One takes a critical attitude toward others' practice of it, but rarely in fact do the features attributed to this intellectual style not rub off on the critic (e.g., by the end of his book, Harvey has assimilated the sensible dimensions of postmodernism, while isolating its extremism; through such critical engagement, he ends up infected by it, assuming postmodernist characteristics in spite of himself). So in anthropology, the label "postmodern anthropology" attributed usually hostilely to the critics of ethnography fails to find any (save Tyler, see below) who will own up to it, and one finds that those making the attribution end by claiming postmodernist innovations for themselves, save for its excesses. In effect, by the logic of academic fashions, everyone seems to want to be "with it," more than ever, but at the least cost to the orientations in which they have previously vested themselves. Postmodernism—like anthropology itself—being a *bricoleur*'s art, can, of course, tolerate this ambivalence in individual scholars' ways of absorbing it.

4. The very few cases in which individuals identify themselves as postmodernist or enact postmodernism in their writing are instructive. Stephen Tyler is the only one among the group associated with articulating the critique of ethnography who explicitly champions postmodernism and enacts it in his writing. This entails a radical and endlessly parodic mode of writing. With brilliant consistency and resolution, Tyler creates a thoroughly parodic discourse about parody. Although full of powerful insights about language, writing, orality, and especially ethnographic representation, his bold experiment seems, finally, limiting. He develops some nearly unbearable truths that would make it difficult to lend special importance or justification to any practice of ethnography.

Yet, short of Tyler's bold attempt at endless self-parody, championing postmodernism while making the claim that one is practicing it runs into serious contradictions. One can see this, for instance, in a recent paper by Rosemary Coombe (1991), where she states, "As a postmodernist, I believe that form has implications for the issues that we address and that conventional forms of discourse limit and shape the realities we recognize" (p. 1857). Indeed, in what follows, Coombe's paper looks and reads pretty much like a law journal paper, and submits to most of its conventions (careful citations, long footnotes, and so on) perhaps in spite of Coombe herself. Subverting standard conventions of discourse does seem to be a sign of experiments in ethnographic writing, as we will see in the discussion of "messy" texts below. But subversion is more an indication of tensions in the "messiness" of a text in which a new kind of study is struggling to be born within an older framework, rather than a self-conscious claim or conceit of being postmodernist by doing "it" in one's writing, as fails in the case of Coombe and succeeds in the case of Tyler—neither one being likely replacements for dealing with postmodernism as an infectious object held at arm's length.

5. The following paragraphs address three of the most important effects on current anthropological practices that key features associated with postmodernism would have.

Cultural translation, which is what ethnography is, never fully assimilates difference (see Talal Asad's [1986] keenly critical discussion of this in *Writing Culture*). In any attempt to interpret or explain another cultural subject, a surplus of difference always remains, partly created by the process of ethnographic communication itself. Thus radical, intractable difference, as in Lyotard's (1988) notion of the differend, confronts the idea of difference in the liberal concept of culture that has dominated in Anglo-American anthropology, and that historically triumphed (in parallel with the pervasiveness of consumer culture of late capitalism) over the concept of culture within an earlier evolutionary frame of social thought. Culture as the object of ethnography is predicated on the notion that the difference of others can be fully *consumed,* assimilated to theory and description by cracking codes of structure, through better translation, and so on. The postmodern idea of radical or surplus difference counters the liberal concept with the idea that difference can never be fully consumed, conquered, or experienced, and thus any interpretive framework must remain partly unresolved in a more serious sense than is usually stipulated as a matter of "good manners" in doing interpretive work. Radical, surplus difference is a fundamental challenge and stimulus to remake the language and forms of ethnographic writing.

Associated with the above, the postmodern premise that there is no possibility of fixed, final, or monologically authoritative meaning has radicalized the critique within anthropology of its own forms of representation by challenging the authority on which they have been based. This impossibility also undermines the practice of a kind of interpretation from which authoritative meanings can be derived (the kind of interpretive practice that Geertz earlier promoted in anthropology that constituted cultures through the metaphor of text, and the practice of interpretation through the metaphor of reading; for example, see his seminal essay on the Balinese cockfight included in his 1973 collection).

The postmodern notion of juxtapositions (that is, blocking together incommensurables, as advocated by Lyotard; see Readings, 1991) serves to renew the practice of comparison in anthropology, long neglected, but in altered ways. Juxtapositions do not have the obvious metalogic of older styles of comparisons in anthropology (e.g., controlled comparison within a culture area or "natural" geographic region), but emerge from putting questions to an emergent object of study, whose contours, sites, and relationships are not known beforehand, but that themselves are a contribution of making an account that has different, complexly connected real-world sites of investigation. The postmodern object of study is ultimately mobile and multiply situated, so that any ethnography of such an object has a comparative dimension integral to it, in the form of juxtapositions of seeming incommensurables or phenomena that might conventionally have appeared "worlds apart." Comparison reenters the very act of ethnographic specificity. It does so through a postmodern vision of seemingly improbable juxtapositions, the global collapsed into and made an integral part of parallel, related local situations, rather than being something monolithic and external to them. This move toward comparison as juxtaposition firmly deterritorializes culture in ethnographic writing. It also stimulates accounts of cultures composed in a landscape for which there is as yet no developed theoretical conception.

These three challenges to the conventional ways and premises by which ethnography has been conceived lead to the "messy text" as manifestly the most complex and interesting form of experimentation with ethnographic writing now being produced.

◆ Messy Texts, or Worlds Apart Cultural Criticism

While many in anthropology have at least acknowledged the therapeutic value of the 1980s' critique of ethnographic writing, there has also been a widespread nervousness that this has gone on too long, and as such is leading in unproductive directions, that innovations in the form of ethnography cannot possibly carry the burden that abstract theoretical discourse and clear distinctions between arguments and supporting data once did. Contrary to those who want to move quickly beyond the notion of experimentalism, I remain convinced that the form that ethnographies might take remains a key concern in generating theoretical and research design discussions that especially confront issues of postmodernist styles of knowledge production and of real social conditions of postmodernity among our subjects.

To me, the most interesting experiments, sometimes in spite of themselves, confront the problem that ethnography, which is centrally interested in the creativity of social action through imagination, narrativity, and performance, has usually been produced through an analytic imagination that in contrast is impoverished, and is far too restrictive especially under contemporary conditions of postmodernity. For example, once we know, or analytically fix by naming, that we are writing about violence, migration, the body, memory, or whatever, we have already circumscribed the space and dimensions of the object of study—we know what we are talking about prematurely. But you can be sure that the object of study always exceeds its analytic circumscription, and especially under conditions of postmodernity. That is, there remains the surplus of difference beyond, and perhaps because of, our circumscription.

The mark of experimental, critical work is its resistance to this too-easy assimilation of the phenomenon of interest by given analytic, ready-made concepts. Such resistance is manifested in a work's messy, many-"sited"ness, its contingent openness as to the boundaries of the object of study (which emerge in the space of the work, whose connections by juxtaposition are themselves *the* argument), its concern with position, and its derivation/ negotiation of its analytic framework from indigenous discourse, from mappings within the sites in which the object of study is defined and among which it circulates. Contemporary works I have in mind, by no means all of them within the ethnographic tradition, but all of which have worked well for me in teaching, are *Primate Visions: Gender, Race, and Nature in the World of Modern Science,* by Donna Haraway (1989); *Debating Muslims: Cultural Dialogues in Postmodernity and Tradition,* by Michael M. J. Fischer and Mehdi Abedi (1990); *Shamanism, Colonialism, and the Wild Man: A Study of Terror and Healing,* by Michael Taussig (1987); and *Lives in Trust: The Fortunes of Dynastic Families in Late Twentieth Century America,* by myself with Peter Dobkin Hall (1992).

Although the authors of these texts are often conscious of themselves as engaged in experimental work, there is much more to these texts, struggling with conventional form to provide new cognitive mappings, than special pleading, self-indulgence, avant-gardism, or a genius act. They refuse to assimilate too easily or by foreclosure the object of study, thus committing a kind of academic colonialism whereby the deep assumption seeps into a work that the interests of the ethnographer and those of his or her subjects are somehow aligned.

There are several other reasons for constructing messy texts. I have identified three additional rationales, and mention them only briefly here. First, they arise simply from confronting the remarkable space/time compression that defines the conditions of peoples and culture globally (this is of course the defining empirical feature of the condition of postmodernity for theorists such as David Harvey and Anthony Giddens). This raises the problem of how an account is to be given of everyday life in which what was formerly incommensurable is brought into relationship or at least contact; the global, or aspects of global process, is now encompassed by the local, and purely local meanings are no longer a sufficient object of study.

Second, they wrestle with the loss of a credible holism, so important in previous ethnographic writing, and especially functionalist accounts (see Thornton, 1988). In messy texts there is a sense of a whole, without evoking totality, that emerges from the research process itself. The territory that defines the object of study is mapped by the ethnographer who is within its landscape, moving and acting within it, rather than drawn from a transcendent, detached point.

Third, messy texts are messy because they insist on an open-endedness, an incompleteness, and an uncertainty about how to draw a text/analysis to a close. Such open-endedness often marks a concern with an ethics of dialogue and partial knowledge that a work is incomplete without critical, and differently positioned, responses to it by its (one hopes) varied readers.

Thus the important questions to pose about messy texts concern how they end (openly, with utopian hope, pragmatic resolution, and so on), what space they lay out, and how the conceptual apparatus (and the *naming* of its object) emerges as a function of the hesitation to establish conceptual or analytic authority by fiat. However, it should be clear that messy texts, aside from the features that I have listed, are by no means uniform in their sensibilities or theoretical influences, nor are they models for a new genre of critical work. I find them interesting as *symptoms* of struggle within

392

given formats and practices of analytic writing to produce unexpected connections and thus new descriptions of old realities. In so doing they critically displace sets of representations that seem no longer to account for worlds that we thought we knew, or could at least name.

Indeed, most ethnographers are not writing messy texts, but the specter of postmodernism (and postmodernity) with which the appearance of such unusual writing is associated has been a subject of widespread discussion, and at the level of what most anthropologists might or might not do differently than before, postmodernism comes down to the "sign" of reflexivity—how much of it (if any) and in what form it should appear in one's ethnographic work.[2]

◆ Ideological Strategies of Reflexivity

It is now time to back up and consider what sorts of discussions of postmodernism in contemporary anthropology and other fields that share a strong identification with and valorization of the practice of ethnography lead to the opening of possibility of "messy text" experimentation. The crucial turn, it seems to me, has been the position taken toward self-critical reflexivity in ethnographic writing. The sometimes heated discussions about the desirability of reflexivity mark the opening of the ethnographic tradition to new possibility; a departure from the ideology of objectivity, distance, and the transparency of reality to concepts; and the need to explore the ethical, political, and epistemological dimensions of ethnographic research as an integral part of producing knowledge about others. Rather than being interested here in the theory and philosophy of reflexive practice itself, I am concerned with the complex politics of theory (the different positions taken, interests implied, and stakes defined) that the discussion of postmodernism in the specific terms of reflexivity in ethnography has engendered.

I do not choose reflexivity arbitrarily as the loaded sign of these politics, but from the point of view of an (amateur) ethnographer of these politics. I have noted that reflexivity is the label in common currency used to stand for as-yet unrealized alternative possibility in the production of ethnography. For me, then, reflexivity is not so much a methodological matter as an ideological one that in turn masks anxiety about a broader, but less conceivable, postmodernism. In this regard, Graham Watson, in his paper "Make Me Reflexive—But Not Yet: Strategies for Managing Essential

Reflexivity in Ethnographic Discourse" (1987), makes an important distinction between *essential* reflexivity and a *derived* or, as I call it, ideological reflexivity. Essential reflexivity is an integral feature of all discourse (as in the indexical function of speech acts); one cannot choose to be reflexive or not in an essential sense—it is always a part of language use. What remains is how to deal with the fact of reflexivity, how to strategize about it for certain theoretical and intellectual interests. And this is the ideological dimension of reflexivity in which I am interested here. In the current polemics about the use of reflexivity, one encounters, for example, a frequent bad-faith, flippant dismissal of reflexivity, or, among those who favor it, one often encounters competitive, "more reflexive than thou" positions (see, e.g., in Clifford & Marcus, 1986, Paul Rabinow's critique of the arch critic of ethnography, James Clifford, for not being sufficiently self-critical, and the charge of insufficient critical reflexivity that has been a main line of attack by feminists on the mostly male critics of ethnography, for being *mostly* male).

Finally, it might be noted that perhaps the most intense polemics about reflexivity nowadays occurs in academic departments among dissertation committees over graduate student projects—is reflexivity a self-indulgence or an aspect of method? Graduate students most of all want to know pragmatically how to deal with reflexivity in the writing that will give them a credential within a disciplinary tradition. How much reflexivity? Where in a text and what forms can it take? Finally, why?

◆ Four Styles of Reflexivity

Reflexivity is an immense area of comment and interest. Thus the following discussion needs a controlling frame, the most appropriate of which involves the fields for which ethnography as a practice has had a special value, has been regenerative over the past decade of revitalization in the humanities and related fields in the United States, often powered by a fascination with defining postmodern(ism/ity), but also institutionalized in interdisciplinary centers across American academia (most often known as humanities or "cultural studies" centers). These fields include the following:

◆ sociology of the sort theorized by Pierre Bourdieu and Anthony Giddens (but also the sociology practiced in British cultural studies, and now in American cultural studies, for which ethnography has had a special appeal; see Grossberg et al., 1992)

♦ anthropology, for which ethnography has been a signature practice

♦ feminism, for which ethnography has been one among related genres through which theory and research have been produced

Before examining the stake in reflexivity in each of these fields, I want to discuss a baseline form of reflexivity with which the term is usually associated.

1. The baseline form of reflexivity is associated with the self-critique and personal quest, playing on the subjective, the experiential, and the idea of empathy. It is this sort of reflexivity that most leads to nervous response and dismissals as dead-end self-indulgence, narcissism, and solipsism. Typical is Marshall Sahlins's report of an apocryphal exchange, quoted by Judy Stacey (1990): "But as the Fijian said to the New Ethnographer, 'that's enough talking about you; let's talk about me' " (p. 232). But feminists have shown us why we must be prepared to take this kind of reflexivity much more seriously (see especially Clough, 1992).

In anthropology, elaborate subjectivist accounts of fieldwork experience became the prime means of unfixing the notion that fieldwork could be a method on a par with, say, surveys. Such reflexivity, previously limited to confessional framings of functionalist ethnography, exposed the epistemological and ethical grounds of anthropological knowledge to full critical discussion and opened the way for a critical hermeneutics (as in the debate between Gadamer and Habermas, as lucidly summarized in Holub, 1991), to become a major influence on anthropological theory and research practice. But this is where the main contribution of this kind of reflexivity has rested, and once its critical function has been well absorbed, it loses its power and falls prey to those who would nervously dismiss reflexivity altogether. At most, such reflexivity opens the possibility for the so-called polyphonous text or the completely collaborative project, but often as not, it ends by reinforcing the perspective and voice of the lone, introspective field-worker without challenging the paradigm of ethnographic research at all—to the contrary.

In feminism, this very subjectivist kind of reflexivity has had much more weight. It is indeed the signature of a distinctively feminist cognition that runs through many genres of feminist writing. As such, reflexivity is a performed politics, and the means of overcoming the gendered character of supposedly value-free objectivist discourse. In feminism, this kind of reflexivity was pioneered in the form of autobiography, and its appearance as a style of ethnography is simply a carryover. As such, ethnography is fully integrated into an arena of discourse in which subjectivist reflexivity is not only fully legitimated, but has a special power, function, and politics.

The situation in anthropology is of course quite different. There, subjectivist reflexivity challenged the sacred boundaries of identity, differentiating scientific ethnography from travel accounts, memoirs, missionary reports, and so on. It had nothing like the preexisting legitimacy or purpose in anthropology that it had in feminism. Whereas subjectivist reflexivity in anthropological ethnography dead-ends, as I have suggested, in feminist writing, and ethnography, it leads to the practice of positioning that manifests itself either as a doctrinal kind of identity politics or as an ambitious and comprehensive means of reenvisioning the frameworks and practices of ethnographic research and writing (for a superb example, see Stacey, 1990).

2. Beyond the baseline forms of subjectivist reflexivity is the position on reflexivity in Pierre Bourdieu's sociology, which can also stand here in a general way for the kind of reflexivity in ethnography that has had appeal for British (and, by derivation, American) cultural studies. For instance, the use of reflexivity in Paul Willis's *Learning to Labour* (1977/1981) is tied to the commitment to sustain objectivity, the distance and abstraction of theoretical discourse, and empiricism as distinctive historical contributions of sociology (and a related social theory) as a discipline. With such a commitment, ethnography retains its identity as a method, and reflexivity is valuable only in methodological terms as a research tool. As we have seen, Bourdieu is hostile to reflexivity as touching on the subjective. The following quotations from the preface to *The Logic of Practice* (Bourdieu, 1990a) are revealing:

> In opposition to intuitionism, which fictitiously denies the distance between the observer and the observed, I kept on the side of the objectivism that is concerned to understand the logic of practices, at the cost of a methodical break with primary experience; but I never ceased to think that it was also necessary to understand the specific logic of that form of "understanding" without experience that comes from mastery of the principles of experience— that what had to be done was not to sweep away the distance magically through spurious primitivist participation, but *to objectify the objectifying distance and the social conditions that make it possible, such as the exter-*

nality of the observer, the objectifying techniques that he uses etc. Perhaps because I had a less abstract idea than some people of what it is to be a mountain peasant, I was also, and precisely to that extent, more aware that the distance is insurmountable, irremovable, except through self-deception. Because theory—the word itself says so—is a spectacle, which can only be understood from a viewpoint away from the stage on which the action is played out, the distance lies perhaps not so much where it is usually looked for, in the gap between cultural traditions, as in the gulf between two relations to the world, one theoretical, the other practical. (p. 14; emphasis added)

Distance is not abolished by bringing the outsider fictitiously closer to an imaginary native, as is generally attempted; it is by distancing, through objectification, the native who is in every outside observer, that the native is brought closer to the outsider. . . . In contrast to the personalist denial which refuses scientific objectification and can only construct a fantasized person, sociological analysis, particularly when it places itself in the anthropological tradition of exploration of forms of classification, makes a self-reappropriation possible, by objectifying the objectivity that runs through the supposed site of subjectivity, such as the social categories of thought, perception, and appreciation which are the unthought principles of all representation of the "objective" world. By forcing one to discover externality at the heart of internality, banality in the illusion of rarity, the common in the pursuit of the unique, sociology does more than denounce all the impostures of egoistic narcissism; it offers perhaps the only means of contributing, if only through awareness of determinations, to the construction, otherwise abandoned to the forces of the world, of something like a subject. (pp. 20-21)

In absolutely opposing any sort of identity between the worlds of the observer (the academic social scientist) and the observed (the peasant, for instance), while at the same time privileging, perhaps as the manifestation of reason, the domain of distanced "theory," Bourdieu is outside postmodern sensibilities that find value in various strategies (e.g., through dialogism) for collapsing high and low culture, the theoretical and the practical, and the identities of the narrator and those narrated. As such, reflexivity, which Bourdieu *does* valorize, has a very restrictive function. Self-critical reflexivity is for Bourdieu a renewed and more powerful form of the old project of the sociology of knowledge, but this time, fully integrated as a dimension of sociological method.

In his fervent desire to assert the absolute priority of objectivity/ objectivizing in the sociologist's work, even in being reflexive, Bourdieu presents an account that is tone deaf to the inevitable moments of *subjective* self-criticism that have always been a part of even the most scientific ethnography. In denying or ignoring this integral dimension of the most objectifying methods, Bourdieu misses the sort of tensions that propel the ethnographer toward reflexivity in the first place, whatever eventual ideological form it may take in writing (subjective, an aspect of method, and so on). Personal reflexivity is present in several of his own works (he even appeals to it ironically in the above quotes), but in the conventional way, it is pushed to the margins.

Indeed, the great virtue of Bourdieu's cultural critique is in the personal motivations that led him out of ethnography, which he eventually came to see in a politicized context of decolonizing Algeria, back toward the major educational and class institutions of France that shape "the scholastic point of view" (Bourdieu, 1990b). This move from apolitical structural anthropology in Algeria during the revolution to the critical sociology of his home institutions, especially those that engendered him intellectually as an ethnologist/sociologist, is the process of producing an objectified form of reflexivity, making an object of that which shapes your own knowledge, never giving into a romantic subjectivist fantasy. The objective, critical treatment of the contexts that produce objectifying modes of thought (reason) is indeed a valuable form of reflexivity with many possibilities regarding how to expand/reconstruct the ethnographic research project. But more's the pity, then, to constrain this possibility severely by assimilating this kind of critique as a method that does not seriously alter the forms that past sociological (and ethnographic) practice within it have taken.

3. The most interesting form of self-critical reflexivity in anthropology, beyond its null form discussed above, is one that emphasizes the intertextual or diverse field of representation that any contemporary project of ethnography enters and crosses in order to establish its own subject and define its own voice. This is reflexivity as a politics of location, as Fred Myers (1988) has termed it.

This revision of ethnography changes the understanding of the general character of what ethnography is about. In the past, ethnography has been associated with discovery, that is, with describing specific groups of people who had not been treated before. Restudies have been oddities in anthropology, and the full matrix of existing representations (missionaries, travelers, journalists, the people's own, for instance) in which an ethnographer produces his or her own text has always been downplayed. "One tribe, one ethnographer" is the persisting romantic ethic of the way research is organized long after the European age of exploration and discovery has ended. And there is a careful and sensitive etiquette in force about not working on another anthropologist's people or, at least, group. Against this, modernist (or postmodernist) ethnography is supremely aware that it operates in a complex matrix of already existing alternative representations, and indeed derives its critical power and insight from this awareness (or form of reflexivity). Of a deconstructive bent, modernist ethnography counts on not being first, on not discovering. It remakes, re-presents, other representations.

Experimental ethnography thus depends on preexisting, more conventional narrative treatments and is parasitic on them. Such ethnography is a comment, a remaking of a more standard realist account. Therefore, the best subjects of contemporary ethnography are those that have been heavily represented, narrated, and made mythic by the conventions of previous discourse. Marcus and Hall (1992), for example, show how knowledge of the structure of great American fortunes and the cultural influence they have exercised depends on the displacement of the perennial, pervasive, and mythic "family dynasty" genre in terms of which Americans have written about and comprehended these otherwise overshadowed, or even buried, stories of money "with a cultural face."

Part of the experimentation is in revealing the intertextual nature of any contemporary ethnography; it works through already constituted representations by both the observed and previous observers. There is no sense of discovery in the classic sense in contemporary ethnography. It forgoes the nostalgic idea that there are literally completely unknown worlds to be discovered. Rather, in full, reflexive awareness of the historical connections that already link it to its subject matter, contemporary ethnography makes historically sensitive revisions of the ethnographic archive with eyes fully open to the complex ways that diverse representations have constituted its subject matter. Such representations become an integral part of one's fieldwork.

The field of representations is by no means a mere supplement to fieldwork. Representations are social facts, and define not only the discourse of the ethnographer, but his or her literal position in relation to subjects. Fred Myers shows this well in his paper, "Locating Ethnographic

Practice: Romance, Reality, and Politics in the Outback" (1988). Called to mediate the appearance of a "lost tribe" of aborigines (from a group with whom Myers had worked for years) who had made contact with the domain of white Australian society, Myers found himself involved in a complex set of interests and characterizations of the event (the government's, the media's, the people's own) for which existing anthropological modes of representing aborigines did not prepare him. He had to think his way through various interests and associated representations in order to locate himself and his discipline's discourse in relation to them. As Myers observes:

> For many practicing anthropologists, the literariness of rhetorical self-awareness gives it a rather self-absorbed, intellectualist, elitist, or apolitical quality removed from the nitty-gritty of social life. It can be, on the contrary, quite sensitive to relations of power, conflict, and implicit judgments. The question raised may be appropriate to an anthropology that is less centralized, that has many masters—or many different sorts of audience. . . . so-called postmodern anthropology is . . . asking questions similar to those generated increasingly by work under local auspices, that is, of a decentered and less Eurocentric anthropology. (p. 611)

> The value of rhetorical self-awareness is in drawing our attention to the constructions through which, as professionals, we have learned partly to read but which still mask many difficult and misleading assumptions about the purpose and politics of our work. (p. 622)

Myers in this episode of advocacy fieldwork literally had to renegotiate the meaning of "aborigines" in Australian anthropological discourse through critical self-awareness of the overlapping alternative representations with different valences of social power and influence behind them. In his work, the primary focus is upon a group of aborigines, and as an actor, his commitment remains with them also. Although his concern was not with furthering anthropology through experimental ethnography (which might have led him to a "messy" text), at least he draws attention to the key importance of a kind of reflexivity that locates the ethnographer through a keen sensitivity to the complex overlay of related, but different, accounts of almost any object of ethnographic interest.

4. The feminist version of the highly valued, powerfully evoked baseline form of subjectivist, experiential reflexivity has more recently been

discussed and theorized as the practice of *positioning,* which is not that different from the politics of location that gives shape to reflexivity in critical ethnography within anthropology as described above. Positioning (of standpoint epistemologies) as a practice in feminism is most committed to the situatedness and partiality of all claims to knowledge, and hence contests the sort of essentialist rhetoric and binarism (male/female, culture/ nature) as a cognitive mode that has so biased toward rigidity and inflexibility questions of gender or "otherness" in language use. The *ethic* and practice of positioning defeats these rigidities of language and opens possibilities for different sorts of identities and concepts of race, culture, and gender to emerge.

On the one hand, the practice of positioning envisions a satisfying ethics of research practice (one that is a major motivation in the production of messy texts): any positioned or situated argument is an invitation to critical response to its partiality. Positioning assumes all work is incomplete, and requires response (and thus engagement) from others positioned differently. This ethical concern of positioning carries with it the antiessentialism so central to feminist thought.

On the other hand, the limitation of positioning is that it is often focused as a deeply reflexive meditation upon a relationship that produces ethnography (e.g., see Judy Stacey's "Can There Be a Feminist Ethnography?" 1988). As such, it yields the map, the totality, the social whole in which it is embedded, or it uses a "canned" monolithic construction to stand for this whole beyond the intimacy of ethnography, such as "patriarchal, corporate, and/or late consumer capitalism." To yield the larger landscape in which it operates out of concern for not "totalizing" only lets this landscape be constructed in reception—by readers who will give the framework of the ethnography a larger context, and not of course necessarily in the way that the feminist ethnographer might want. As noted, one goal of "messy" texts is to reclaim this larger framing "whole" of ethnography without being totalizing.

As we will see in a moment, it is Donna Haraway's specific formulation of the positioning practice out of feminism that most pushes it in the direction of ambitious, messy experimentation. Yet the practice of positioning can easily get stuck in a sterile form of identity politics, in which it is reduced to a formulaic incantation at the beginning of ethnographic papers in which one boldly "comes clean" and pronounces a positioned identity (e.g., "I am a white, Jewish, middle-class, heterosexual female"). This kind of reflexive location of oneself, while potentially a practice of key importance, all too often becomes a gesture that is enforced by politically correct convention. (The locating of one's position by parsing it into components of identity is most powerful, in my readings, when it is done as a critique of a writer's monologic authority; e.g., see the brilliant conclusion of Aijaz Ahmad's 1987 critique of a paper by Fredric Jameson, "Third-World Literature in the Era of Multinational Capital," published in *Social Text,* in which he deconstructs Jameson's identity into its unacknowledged gendered, racial, and cultural components.)

In her 1988 paper "Situated Knowledges: The Science Question in Feminism and the Privilege of Partial Perspective," Donna Haraway builds the feminist version of reflexivity as positioning into a reimagining of the dimensions of fine-grained, interpretive research (in her case coming out of the feminist study of science, but also fully congenial to anthropology's ethnographic study of forms of life as cultures). The following manifestolike quotations give a sense of her scheme:

So, I think my problem, and "our" problem, is how to have *simultaneously* an account of radical historical contingency for all knowledge claims and knowing subjects, a critical practice for which recognizing our own "semiotic technologies" for making meanings, *and* a no-nonsense commitment to faithful accounts of a "real" world, one that can be partially shared and that is friendly to earthwide projects of finite freedom, adequate material abundance, modest meaning in suffering, and limited happiness. (p. 579)

Not so perversely, objectivity turns out to be about particular and specific embodiment and definitely not about the false vision promising transcendence of all limits and responsibility. The moral is simple: only partial perspective promises objective vision. All Western cultural narratives about objectivity are allegories of the ideologies governing the relations of what we call mind and body, distance and responsibility. Feminist objectivity is about limited location and situated knowledge, not about transcendence and splitting of subject and object. It allows us to become answerable for what we learn how to see. (pp. 582-583)

Situated knowledges are about communities, not about isolated individuals. The only way to find a larger vision is to be somewhere in particular. The science question in feminism is about objectivity as positioned rationality. Its images are not the products of escape and transcendence of limits (the view from above) but the joining of partial views and halting voices into a collective subject position that promises a vision of the means of ongoing

402

finite embodiment, of living within limits and contradictions—of views from somewhere. (p. 590)

As with Bourdieu, in Haraway's essay we have a committed return to objective knowledge, but what a difference in how Haraway's notion of objectivity is constituted, and what a difference in the practice of reflexivity she defines in order to constitute it! Haraway's visionary program defines a space of juxtapositions and unexpected associations formed by a nomadic, embedded analytic vision constantly monitoring its location and partiality of perspective in relation to others. Whether or not one appreciates fully Haraway's "gonzo" idiom and rhetoric, she has taken the locational and positioning conception of reflexivity (shared by both feminism and anthropology) and expanded it into a field of experimentation of both open possibility and an open-ended ethics. As such, we have come full circle to my identification of "messy" texts as the most interesting current form that postmodernism specifically takes in ethnographic writing, and the way that certain strategies for practicing reflexivity might lead to such experimentation. In so doing, Haraway's program within the frame of feminism parallels and expresses more completely the implication of the sort of study encouraged by the locational politics of reflexivity in anthropology.

◆ A Closing Note

I believe the major fear in the general reception to the now decade-long radicalization of tendencies (and possibilities) that have been present from the very inception of qualitative social science is that of transgression, of excessive skepticism, and of a paralyzing relativism—of a crossing of limits beyond which "anything goes" (the form in which one often hears such a fear voiced) and where even the possibility of communitas—of a shared discourse—among scholars has become imperiled. By having taken advantage of what seems to be a current exhaustion with the explicit rhetoric of the postmodern debates themselves in order to assess what they have specifically meant for at least one important domain of qualitative social science—that of ethnography in its appeal across various disciplinary and protodisciplinary boundaries—I hope I have provided in this chapter a contribution to undercutting this fear and its repressive implication. After all, though there may be differing opinions on the ultimate value of the postmodern debates for research traditions, there is little disagreement about the widespread sense of the need for a distinctive set of changes in the ways contemporary societies and cultures are studied.

Messy texts are neither models to follow nor the much-awaited products of a new paradigm, nor empty conformity with radicalizing fashion. Rather, they represent the substantive, deep effects of postmodern debates on personal styles of thought and work in established disciplines. They are the testing ground—always a mix of strong engagement by authors with "what goes on" among particular subjects of study and of an equally strong reflexive engagement with their own self-making as scholars— in which qualitative social science is being remade in the absence of authoritative models, paradigms, or methods. The concerns of such texts, far from being predictable and narrow, are as broad and diverse as the concerns that have shaped traditions of qualitative social science itself. In this immediate post-"post" moment, the only long-range forecast that one could make is that there is no sign of an end to change.

Notes

1. The critical, rather than paradigmatic, character of recent debates cannot be emphasized enough, as well as the difference that full recognition of this should make in the way such debates are received. Most social scientists are in the habit of expecting innovation to come in the form of systematic paradigms from which emerge distinctive models of research practice and product to be tested and shared. No less powerful in its effects, innovation by critique requires a different set of expectations in reception. I have employed the label *experimentation,* for better or worse, to refer to the output from critique (Marcus & Fischer, 1986). A key concern for many social scientists, both pro and con recent trends, is how long critique/experimentation can go on before the return of paradigmatic styles of work. Usually, moments of critique/experimentation tend to be unstable ruptures that fall relatively quickly to the pejorative charge of fashion, however important their residues may be. To the pleasure of some and the despair of others, the postmodern debates have had a remarkable capacity for mutation and development, making the current trend of research and thought in a variety of disciplines unusually enduring.

2. As a sort of ethnohistorian of present trends, I am especially fascinated by those messy texts that register within themselves the larger ongoing transformations of older traditions of qualitative social science on the personal styles of their authors' research and writing. My favorite examples are Renato Rosaldo's influential *Ilongot Headhunting, 1883-1974* (1980) and Dorinne Kondo's more recent, and equally influential, *Crafting Selves* (1990). Rosaldo's work includes a creative analysis of feuding in Ilongot society, very much within the tradition of the ethnographic analysis of these peoples and perhaps his homage to the tradition in which he was raised academically. However, his work is framed and eventually

dominated by questions concerning the nature of indigenous history that set a new agenda entirely for work on peoples such as the Ilongot. Significantly, this new agenda is established by writing in the reflexive mode—by no means self-indulgent—in which Rosaldo precisely defines through personal experience the points at which he was motivated to change his thinking about the Ilongot. Though ten years later, and with a different set of concerns and positioning in relation to her object of study, Kondo develops similar transformations in her ethnography. Once a structural analyst of Japanese society, now an interpreter of Japanese selfhood, with a critical edge established by her opening inquiry into her complex personal relationship to the Japanese in the framework of ethnographic research, Kondo delivers the goods, so to speak, in her analysis of labor-management relations in the sort of small firms on which large corporations in Japan strategically depend. The volume ends poignantly with a statement about the stakes of this kind of anthropology for issues of feminism and ethnic identity that gained stronger definition in Kondo's thinking following her dissertation research.

◆ References

Ahmad, A. (1987). Jameson's rhetoric of otherness and the "national allegory." *Social Text,* 6(2), 3-25.

Asad, T. (Ed.). (1973). *Anthropology and the colonial encounter.* New York: Humanities Press.

Asad, T. (1986). The concept of cultural translation in British social anthropology. In J. Clifford & G. E. Marcus (Eds.), *Writing culture: The poetics and politics of ethnography* (pp. 141-164). Berkeley: University of California Press.

Bourdieu, P. (1990a). *The logic of practice.* Stanford, CA: Stanford University Press.

Bourdieu, P. (1990b). The scholastic point of view. *Cultural Anthropology, 5,* 380-391.

Bradbury, M., & McFarlane, J. (Eds.). (1976). *Modernism, 1890-1930.* New York: Penguin.

Clifford, J. (1988). *The predicament of culture: Twentieth-century ethnography, literature, and art.* Cambridge, MA: Harvard University Press.

Clifford, J., & Marcus, G. E. (Eds.). (1986). *Writing culture: The poetics and politics of ethnography.* Berkeley: University of California Press.

Clough, P. T. (1992). *The end(s) of ethnography: From realism to social criticism.* Newbury Park, CA: Sage.

Coombe, R. J. (1991). Objects of property and subjects of politics: Intellectual property laws and democratic dialogue. *Texas Law Review, 69,* 1853-1880.

Fischer, M. M. J., & Abedi, M. (1990). *Debating Muslims: Cultural dialogues in postmodernity and tradition.* Madison: University of Wisconsin Press.

Geertz, C. (1973a). *The interpretation of cultures: Selected essays.* New York: Basic Books.

Geertz, C. (1973b). Deep play: Notes on the Balinese cockfight. In C. Geertz, *The Interpretation of cultures: Selected essays.* New York: Basic Books.

Grossberg, L., Nelson, C., & Treichler, P. A. (Eds.). (1992). *Cultural studies.* New York: Routledge.

Haraway, D. J. (1988). Situated knowledges: The science question in feminism and the privilege of partial perspective. *Feminist Studies, 14,* 575-599.

Haraway, D. J. (1989). *Primate visions: Gender, race, and nature in the world of modern science.* New York: Routledge.

Harvey, D. (1989). *The condition of postmodernity: An enquiry into the origins of cultural change.* Oxford: Basil Blackwell.

Holub, R. C. (1991). *Jürgen Habermas: Critic in the public sphere.* New York: Routledge.

Hymes, D. (Ed.). (1969). *Reinventing anthropology.* New York: Pantheon.

Kondo, D. (1990). *Crafting selves: Power, gender, and discourses of identity in a Japanese workplace.* Chicago: University of Chicago Press.

Lyotard, J.-F. (1988). *The differend: Phrases in dispute* (2nd ed.). Minneapolis: University of Minnesota Press.

Marcus, G. E., with Hall, P. D. (1992). *Lives in trust: The fortunes of dynastic families in late twentieth century America.* Boulder, CO: Westview.

Marcus, G. E., & Fischer, M. J. M. (1986). *Anthropology as cultural critique: An experimental moment in the human sciences.* Chicago: University of Chicago Press.

Myers, F. (1988). Locating ethnographic practice: Romance, reality, and politics in the outback. *American Ethnologist, 15,* 609-624.

Rajchman, J. (1987). Postmodernism in a nominalist frame: The emergence and diffusion of a cultural category. *Flash Art, 137,* 49-51.

Readings, B. (1991). *Introducing Lyotard: Art and politics.* New York: Routledge.

Rosaldo, R. (1980). *Ilongot headhunting, 1883-1974: A study in society and history.* Stanford, CA: Stanford University Press.

Stacey, J. (1988). Can there be a feminist ethnography? *Women's Studies International Forum, 11*(1), 21-27.

Stacey, J. (1990). *Brave new families: Stories of domestic upheaval in late twentieth century America.* New York: Basic Books.

Taussig, M. (1987). *Shamanism, colonialism, and the wild man: A study in terror and healing.* Chicago: University of Chicago Press.

Thornton, R. (1988). The rhetoric of ethnographic holism. *Cultural Anthropology, 3,* 285-303.

Tyler, S. A. (1987). *The unspeakable: Discourse, dialogue, and rhetoric in the postmodern world.* Madison: University of Wisconsin Press.

Van Maanen, J. (1988). *Tales of the field: On writing ethnography.* Chicago: University of Chicago Press.

Watson, G. (1987). Make me reflexive—but not yet: Strategies for managing essential reflexivity in ethnographic discourse. *Journal of Anthropological Research, 43,* 29-41.

White, H. (1973). *Metahistory.* Baltimore: Johns Hopkins University Press.

White, H. (1978). *Tropics of discourse.* Baltimore: Johns Hopkins University Press.

Willis, P. (1981). *Learning to labour: How working class kids get working class jobs.* New York: Columbia University Press. (Original work published 1977)

13

The Fifth Moment

Yvonna S. Lincoln & Norman K. Denzin

◆   Writing the present is always dangerous, a biased project conditioned by distorted readings of the past and utopian hopes for the future. In what follows we sketch our utopian vision of the future of qualitative research. This vision is based on our reading of the fifth moment. We begin by delineating the central characteristics of this moment and the problems that define it. We then discuss how researchers are coping with these problems. We conclude with predictions about the sixth moment, based on our readings of the present.

Two theses organize our discussion. First, the history of qualitative research is defined more by breaks and ruptures than by a clear evolutionary, progressive movement from one stage to the next. These breaks and ruptures move in cycles and phases, so that what is passé today may be in vogue a decade from now. Just as the postmodern, for example, reacts to the modern, some day there may well be a neomodern phase that extols Malinowski and the Chicago school and finds the current poststructural, postmodern moment abhorrent.

Our second assumption builds on the tensions that now define qualitative research. There is an elusive center to this contradictory, tension-riddled enterprise that seems to be moving further and further away from grand narratives and single, overarching ontological, epistemological, and methodological paradigms. This center lies in the humanistic commitment of the qualitative researcher to study the world always from the perspective of the interacting individual. From this simple commitment flow the liberal and radical politics of qualitative research. Action, feminist, clinical, constructivist, ethnic, critical, and cultural studies researchers are all united on this point. They all share the belief that a politics of liberation must always begin with the perspectives, desires, and dreams of those individuals and groups who have been oppressed by the larger ideological, economic, and political forces of a society, or a historical moment.

This commitment defines an ever-present but always shifting center in the discourses of qualitative research. The center shifts and moves as new, previously oppressed or silenced voices enter the discourse. Thus, for example, feminists and ethnic researchers have articulated their own relationship to the postpositivist and critical paradigms. These new articulations then refocus and redefine previous ontologies, epistemologies, and methodologies, including positivism and postpositivism. These two theses suggest that only the broad outlines of the future, the sixth moment, can be predicted.

◆ Defining the Present

Recall our definition of this sprawling field. Slightly rephrased, it reads as follows:

> Qualitative research is an interdisciplinary, transdisciplinary, and sometimes counterdisciplinary field. It cross-cuts the humanities, the social sciences, and the physical sciences. Qualitative research is many things at the same time. It is multiparadigmatic in focus. Its practitioners are sensitive to the value of the multimethod approach. They are committed to the naturalistic perspective and to the interpretive understanding of human experience. At the same time, the field is inherently political and shaped by multiple ethical and political positions.
>
> Qualitative research embraces two tensions at the same time. On the one hand, it is drawn to a broad, interpretive, postmodern, feminist, and critical sensibility. On the other hand, it can also be drawn to more narrowly defined positivist, postpositivist, humanistic, and naturalistic conceptions of human experience and its analysis.

In the fifth moment all of these tensions will continue to operate as the field confronts and continues to define itself in the face of six fundamental issues embedded in these tensions. The first issue involves positivism and postpositivism. The present moment is characterized, in part, by a continuing critique of positivism and postpositivism that is coupled with ongoing self-critique and self-appraisal. Every contributor to this volume has reflectively wrestled with the location of his or her topic in the present moment, discussing its relationship to previous positivist and postpositivist formulations.

The second and third issues are what we have called the *crises of representation and legitimation.* These two crises speak, respectively, to the Other and its representation in our texts and to the authority we claim for our texts. The fourth issue is the continued emergence of a cacophony of voices speaking with varying agendas from specific gender, race, class, ethnic, and Third World perspectives.

Fifth, throughout its history, qualitative research has been defined in terms of shifting scientific, moral, sacred, and religious discourses. Vidich and Lyman clearly establish this fact in their history of colonial ethnography in Chapter 2 of this volume. Since the Enlightenment, science and religion have been separated, but only at the ideological level, for in practice religion has constantly informed science and the scientific project (Rosaldo, 1989, p. 74). The borders between these two systems of meaning are becoming more and more blurred. Critics increasing see science from within a magical, shamanistic framework (Rosaldo, 1989, p. 219). Others are moving science away from its empiricist foundations and closer to a critical, interpretive project that stresses morals and moral standards of evaluation (Clough, 1992, pp. 136-137).

The sixth issue crucial to qualitative research in the fifth moment is that of the influence of technology. As we shall argue below, technology will continue to mediate, define, and shape qualitative research practices.

The tensions that surround the six issues described here and the strategies developed to address them will continue to define the center and the margins of qualitative research.

◆ Coping With the Present

Our challenge here is not to produce yet another critique of qualitative research. The salient features of that critique are well-known, and have been discussed throughout the various chapters and section introductions of this volume. They mark the central controversies that define this field of discourse. Postmodernists take these issues for granted, whereas they are sites of contention for postpositivists:

- ◆ The qualitative researcher is not an objective, authoritative, politically neutral observer standing outside and above the text (Bruner, 1993, p. 1).
- ◆ The qualitative researcher is "historically positioned and locally situated [as] an all-too-human [observer] of the human condition" (Bruner, 1993, p. 1).
- ◆ Meaning is "radically plural, always open, and . . . there is politics in every account" (Bruner, 1993, p. 1).

These controversies shape the questions we listed in our introduction to Part III. Clearly, the problems in the fifth moment are multiple.

Correcting Excesses and Revisiting the Past

The fifth moment addresses these problems in three ways. First, it continues to sharpen the above critique while, second, attempting to correct its excesses. Qualitative research, like other scholarly domains, displays a tendency to move from one intellectual fashion to another, from positivism to postpositivism, semiotics and structuralism, poststructuralism and postmodernism, and so on (see Bruner, 1993, p. 24; Ortner, 1984). In such moves there is often a tendency to reject wholesale an entire theoretical perspective, or paradigm, as if postpositivism were passé, for example. It should not work this way. There is a real need to return, as Bruner (1993) argues, to "the originals of out-of-fashion texts" (p. 24). Such a return is necessary for two reasons: First, we need to relearn these texts, to see if standard criticisms still hold today; second, we need to study the best works from these traditions, so as to understand how the masters in a given "passé" perspective in fact did their work.

It must be noted that revisiting works from earlier historical moments operates at different levels of abstraction. Although colonialist, positivist ethnography may be passé, the basic strategies and techniques of case studies, ethnographies, observation, interviewing, and textual analysis still form the basis for research in the fifth and sixth moments. In a parallel vein, although certain of the postpositivist assumptions of the grounded theory approach may be criticized, the generic method of building interpretations up out of observations and interactions with the world will not change.

Third, it is time to get on with the multidisciplinary project called qualitative research. Too much critique will stifle this project. This critique, it must be noted, assumes two forms, and both can be counterproductive. Endless self-referential criticisms by poststructuralists can produce mountains of texts with few referents to concrete human experience. Such are not needed. The same conclusion holds for positivist and postpositivist criticisms of poststructuralism (and the responses to these criticisms). These criticisms and exchanges can operate at a level of abstraction that does little to help the people who just go out and do research.

The basic issue is simple: how best to describe and interpret the experiences of other peoples and cultures. The problems of representation and legitimation flow from this commitment.

The Crisis of Representation

As indicated above, this crisis asks the questions, Who is the Other? Can we ever hope to speak authentically of the experience of the Other, or an Other? And if not, how do we create a social science that includes the Other? The short answer to these questions is that we move to including the Other in the larger research processes that we have developed. For some, this means participatory, or collaborative, research and evaluation efforts. These activities can occur in a variety of institutional sites, including clinical, educational, and social welfare settings.

For still others, it means a form of liberatory investigation wherein Others are trained to engage in their own social and historical interrogative efforts, and then are assisted in devising answers to questions of historical and contemporary oppression that are rooted in the values and cultural artifacts that characterize their communities.

For yet other social scientists, including the Other means becoming coauthors in narrative adventures. And for still others, it means constructing what are called "experimental," or "messy," texts, where multiple voices speak (see, in this volume, Marcus, Chapter 12; see also Richardson, Volume 3, Chapter 12), often in conflict, and where the reader is left to sort out which experiences speak to his or her personal life. For still others, it means presenting to the inquiry and policy community a series of autohistories, personal narratives, lived experiences, poetic representations, and sometimes fictive and/or fictional texts (see, in Volume 3, Clandinin & Connelly, Chapter 6, and Richardson, Chapter 12) that allow the Other to speak for him- or herself. The inquirer or evaluator becomes merely the connection between the field text, the research text, and the consuming community in making certain that such voices are heard. Sometimes, increasingly, it is the institutionalized Other who speaks, especially as the Other gains access to the knowledge-producing corridors of power and achieves entrée into the particular group of elites known as intellectuals and academics or faculty. John Stanfield, in Chapter 10 of this volume, elaborates the issues that are involved when this happens.

The point is that both the Other and more mainstream social scientists recognize that there is no such thing as unadulterated truth, that speaking from a faculty, an institution of higher education, or a corporate perspective automatically means that one speaks from a privileged and powerful vantage point—and that this vantage point is one to which many do not have access, whether because of social station or level of education.

Judith Stacey (1988) speaks of the difficulties involved in representing the experiences of the Other about whom texts are written. Writing from a feminist perspective, she argues that a major contradiction exists in this project, despite the desire to engage in egalitarian research characterized by authenticity, reciprocity, and trust. This is so because actual differences of power, knowledge, and structural mobility still exist in the researcher-subject relationship. The subject is always at grave risk of manipulation and betrayal by the ethnographer. In addition, there is the crucial fact that the final product is too often that of the researcher, no matter how much it has been modified or influenced by the subject.

Thus, even when research is written from the perspective of the Other—for example, women writing about women—the women doing the writing may "unwittingly preserve the dominant power relations that they explicitly aim to overcome" (Bruner, 1993, p. 23; see also Mascia-Lees, Sharpe, & Cohen, 1993, p. 245). The feminist solution requires a merger of scholarship "with a clear politics to work against the forces of oppression" (Mascia-Lees et al., 1993, p. 246).

The recent libel trial of Janet Malcolm and *New Yorker* magazine is instructive on these points (Gross, 1993). Malcolm was accused by Jeffrey N. Masson of fabricating five quotations in her two-part 48,500-word *New Yorker* profile of him. The federal jury ruled for Masson, concluding that Malcolm had fabricated the five quotations, and that two of them met all of the criteria for libel, as defined by the Supreme Court: They were made up, or materially altered, Malcolm knew they were defamatory and acted with "reckless disregard" for their accuracy, and Masson had been damaged by them (Gross, 1993).

This case is important for several reasons. As ethnographers move more deeply into the production of fictional texts, they must take steps to ensure that the words they put in subjects' mouths were in fact spoken by those subjects. The ethics of textual production argue for the meticulous checking of verifiable facts; that is, one must be certain that statements depicted as quotes were in fact made. But more important, the ethnographer must take care when changing contexts and reordering events for dramatic purposes. No one wants to libel another individual. The ethnographer must walk a fine line in those situations where he or she wishes to uncover wrongdoing, illegal acts, or morally offensive conduct.

The Author's Place in the Text

The feminist solution clarifies the issue of the author's place in the interpretations that are written. This problem is directly connected to the problem of representation. It is often phrased in terms of a false dichotomy, that is, "the extent to which the personal self should have a place in the scientific scholarly text" (Bruner, 1993, p. 2). This false division between the personal and the ethnographic self rests on the assumption that it is possible to write a text that does not bear the traces of its author. Of course, this is not possible. All texts are personal statements.

The correct phrasing of this issue turns on the amount of the personal, subjective, poetic self that is in fact openly given in the text. Bruner (1993) phrases the problem this way: "The danger is putting the personal self so deeply back into the text that it completely dominates, so that the work becomes narcissistic and egotistical. No one is advocating ethnographic self-indulgence" (p. 6). The goal is to return the author to the text openly, in a way that does "not squeeze out the object of study" (p. 6).

There are many ways to return the author openly to the qualitative research text. Authors may write fictional narratives of the self, or produce performance texts. Authors can give dramatic readings, or transform their field interviews into poetic texts, or poetry, or short stories and plays (Rose, 1993). Authors can engage in dialogue with those studied. Authors may write through narrators, "directly as a character . . . or through multiple characters, or one character may speak in many voices, or the writer may come in and then go out of the [text]" (Bruner, 1993, p. 6; see also Ellis, 1991, 1994; Ellis & Bochner, 1992).

The Crisis of Legitimation

It is clear that postmodern and poststructural arguments are moving further and further away from postpositivist models of validity and textual authority. This is the *crisis of legitimation*. This so-called crisis arose when anthropologists and other social scientists addressed the authority of the text. By *the authority of the text* we reference the claim any text makes to being accurate, true, and complete. Is a text, that is, faithful to the context and the individuals it is supposed to represent? Does the text have the right to assert that it is a report to the larger world that addresses not only the researcher's interests, but also the interests of those studied?

This is not an illegitimate set of questions, and it affects all of us and the work that we do. And although different social scientists might approach the questions from different angles, these twin crises are confronted by everyone.

A poststructural interpretive social science challenges postpositivist arguments concerning the text and its validity. It interprets validity as a text's call to authority and truth, and calls this version of validity *epistemological*. That is, a text's authority is established through recourse to a set of rules concerning knowledge, its production, and representation. These rules, as Scheurich (1992, p. 1) notes, if properly followed, establish validity. Without validity there is no truth, and without truth there can be no trust in a text's claims to validity. With validity comes power (Cherryholmes, 1988), and validity becomes a boundary line that "divides good research from bad, separates acceptable (to a particular research community) research from unacceptable research . . . it is the name for inclusion and exclusion" (Scheurich, 1992, p. 5).

Poststructuralism reads the discussions of logical, construct, internal, ethnographic, and external validity, text-based data, triangulation, trustworthiness, credibility, grounding, naturalistic indicators, fit, coherence, comprehensiveness (see Eisenhart & Howe, 1992, pp. 657-669), plausibility, truth, and relevance (Atkinson, 1990, pp. 68-72) as attempts to reauthorize a text's authority in the postpositivist moment. Altheide and Johnson (Chapter 10, Volume 3, this series) review extensively the assumptions that organize this project.

These words, and the methodological strategies that lie behind them, represent attempts to thicken and contextualize a work's grounding in the external, empirical world. They represent efforts to develop a set of transcendent rules and procedures that lie outside any specific research project. These rules, if successfully followed, allow a text to bear witness to its own validity. Hence a text is valid if it is sufficiently grounded, triangulated, based on naturalistic indicators, carefully fitted to a theory (and its concepts), comprehensive in scope, credible in terms of member checks, logical, and truthful in terms of its reflection of the phenomenon in question. The text's author then announces these validity claims to the reader. Such claims now become the text's warrant to its own authoritative re-presentation of the experience and social world under inspection.

Epistemological validity can now be interpreted as a text's desire to assert its own power over the reader. Validity represents the always just out of reach, but answerable, claim a text makes for its own authority. (After all, the research could have always been better grounded, the subjects more representative, the researcher more knowledgeable, the research instruments better formulated, and so on.) A fertile obsession, validity is the researcher's mask of authority (Lather, 1993), which allows a particular regime of truth within a particular text (and community of scholars) to work its way on the world and the reader.

It is now necessary to ask, What do we do with validity once we have met poststructuralism? Several answers are suggested. They all turn back on the crisis of representation, and involve, in one form or another, the problem of how the Other's perspective and experience are expressed in a text.

The first answer is political. If there is a center to poststructural thought it lies in the recurring attempt to strip a text, any text, of its external claims to authority. Every text must be taken on its own terms. Furthermore, the desire to produce an authoritative (valid) text is renounced, for any text can be undone in terms of its internal structural logic.

The unmasking of validity-as-authority now exposes the heart of the argument. If validity is gone, values and politics, not objective epistemology, govern science. This is familiar territory, and the answer is equally familiar. It is given in Foucault's concept of a subversive genealogy, a strategy that refuses to accept those "systems of discourse (economic, political, scientific, narrative)" (Denzin, 1991, p. 32) that "ignore who we are collectively and individually" (Racevskis, 1983, p. 20).

A poststructural social science project seeks its external grounding not in science, in any of its revisionist forms, but rather in a commitment to a post-Marxism and a feminism with hope, but no guarantees (Hall, 1986, p. 58). It seeks to understand how power and ideology operate through systems of discourse, asking always how words and texts and their meanings play a pivotal part in "those decisive performances of race, class, gender . . . [that] shape the emergent political conditions . . . we refer to as the postmodern world" (Downing, 1987, p. 80). A good text is one that invokes these commitments. A good text exposes how race, class, and gender work their ways in the concrete lives of interacting individuals.

Lather (1986, p. 67) calls this catalytic validity, the degree to which a given research project empowers and emancipates a research community.

Verisimilitude

The second solution dispenses with the quest for validity and seeks to examine critically, instead, a text's verisimilitude, or ability to reproduce (simulate) and map the real. There are two essential levels of verisimilitude— as a set of laws set by convention, and as a mask that presents these laws as a text's submission to the rules of a particular genre (Todorov, 1977, p. 84). In its most naive form, verisimilitude describes a text's relationship to reality. It asks, Are the representations in a text consistent with the real? Is the text telling the truth? Certain actions, for example, are said to lack verisimilitude "when they seem unable to occur in reality" (Todorov, 1977, p. 82). A second meaning of verisimilitude refers to the relationship of a particular text to some agreed-upon opinion, for example, epistemological validity, or what Mishler (1990, p. 417) calls valid exemplars accepted by a relevant community of scientists. Here it is understood that separate interpretive communities (Fish, 1980) have distinctively unique standards or versions of verisimilitude as proof, truth, or validity.

As Todorov (1977, p. 83) notes, there are as many verisimilitudes as there are genres (comedy, detective fiction, tragedy, and so on). In the social sciences there are multiple genres, or writing forms: book reviews, presidential addresses to scholarly societies, research notes, critical essays, grant proposals, research reports, committee reports, and so on (see Agger, 1989; see also Richardson, Chapter 12, Volume 3, this series). Each form has its own laws of genre. The validity of a statistical table is different from the so-called validity of thick description in an ethnographer's report (Geertz, 1973). Two separate verisimilitudes are operating in these two contexts.

Verisimilitude can be described as the mask a text assumes as it convinces the reader it has conformed to the laws of its genre; in so doing, it has reproduced reality in accordance with those rules. Every text enters into a relationship with verisimilitude and its laws, including taking verisimilitude, or validity, as its theme, in which case the text must establish an *antiverisimilitude,* that is, a text that appears to lack truth, validity, or verisimilitude. Such moves allow a text to make a separation between truth and verisimilitude, for what appears to be true is false, and what appears to be false is true.

Two questions now emerge. The first doubles back on itself: Can a text have verisimilitude and not be true, and, conversely, can a text be true, but lack verisimilitude? The recent controversy surrounding William Foote Whyte's classic work *Street Corner Society* (1943, 1955, 1981), as discussed in a special issue of the *Journal of Contemporary Ethnography* (April 1992), illuminates this question, which turns on the status of a text's grounding in the real world. Whyte's work, historically accepted as a truthful text with high verisimilitude, is challenged by Boelen (1992, p. 49), another researcher, who claims Whyte's study, while having some degree of verisimilitude, lacks truth. Whyte, Boelen argues, misrepresented the real structure of Italian street-corner life, and perpetuated false truths about that life. Whyte (1992) replies that his study was based on member checks and hence had both verisimilitude and truth. His critic, he asserts, has misunderstood his original text and has not penetrated the real fabrics of street-corner life in the Italian community.

The implications of this exchange are clear.[1] The truth of a text cannot be established by its verisimilitude. Verisimilitude can always be challenged. Hence a text can be believed to be true even as it lacks verisimilitude. (The opposite case holds as well.) Challenges to verisimilitude in qualitative research rest on the simple observation that a text is always a site of political struggle over the real and its meanings. Truth is political, and verisimilitude is textual.

The second question following from this discussion of verisimilitude becomes, Whose verisimilitude? It is the researcher's goal to contest multiple verisimilitudes, multiple versions of reality, and the perceived truths that structure these realities. A text's verisimilitude is given in its ability to reproduce and deconstruct the reproductions and simulations that structure the real. This is *deconstructive verisimilitude.*[2]

◆ The Crisis of Vocality: New and Old Voices Coping With the Present

A variety of new and old voices—such as critical theory, feminist, and ethnic scholars—have also entered the present situation, offering solutions to the crises and problems that have been identified above. The move is toward pluralism, and many social scientists now recognize that no picture is ever complete, that what is needed is many perspectives, many voices, before we can achieve deep understandings of social phenomena, and before we can assert that a narrative is complete.

The modernist dream of a grand or master narrative is now a dead project; the recognition of the futility and oppression of such a project is the postmodern condition. The postmodern project challenges the modernist belief (and desire) that it is possible to develop a progressive program for incorporating all the cultures of the world under a single umbrella. The postmodern era is defined, in part, by the belief that there is no single umbrella in the history of the world that might incorporate and represent fairly the dreams, aspirations, and experiences of all peoples.

Critical Theorists

The critical theorists, from the Frankfurt, to the Annales, world-system, and participatory action research schools, continue to be a major presence in qualitative research, as Kincheloe and McLaren observe in Chapter 8 of this volume. The critique and concern of the critical theorists has been an effort to design a pedagogy of resistance. The pedagogy of resistance, of taking back "voice," of reclaiming narrative for one's own rather than adapting to the narratives of a dominant majority, has been most explicitly laid out by one working with adults, Paolo Freire in Brazil. Freire's work is echoed most faithfully by a group of activist priests and scholars who are exploring what is called "liberation theology"—the joining of the Catholic church to egalitarian ends for the purposes of overturning oppression and achieving social justice through empowerment of the marginalized, the poor, the nameless, the voiceless. Their project is nothing less than the radical restructuring of society toward the ends of reclaiming historic cultural legacies, social justice, the redistribution of power, and the achievement of truly democratic societies.

Feminist Researchers

The feminists have argued that there is a missing voice, and a missing picture, in the history of the sciences, religion, and the arts. Three different groups—feminist philosophers, scientists, and theologians—are represented in this discourse. Each has had an unsettling—if not unnerving—effect on arguments about how we "do" qualitative research.

The first two groups—the philosophers and the scientists—have mounted two separate, but related, arguments. The first is that traditional science has acted to maintain the Enlightenment dualism, with its major premise that there is a separate and distinct "social reality" "out there" somewhere, separated from those who experience it, and that it is the scientists' job to uncover this separate reality, and report on it, for that is the essence of "Truth."

Poststructural feminists urge the abandonment of any distinction between empirical science and social criticism. That is, they seek a morally informed social criticism that is not committed to the traditional concerns of empirical science. This traditional science, they argue, rests a considerable amount of its authority on the ability to make public what has traditionally been understood to be private (Clough, 1992, p. 137). Feminists dispute this distinction. They urge a social criticism that takes back from science the traditional authority to inscribe and create subjects within the boundaries and frameworks of an objective social science. This social criticism "gives up on data collection and instead offers rereadings of representations in every form of information processing, empirical science, literature, film, television, and computer simulation" (Clough, 1992, p. 137).

A second set of feminist philosophers notes distinct problems with several of the scientific method's most basic premises: the idea that scientific objectivity is possible, the effect that the mandate for objectivity has on the subjects of research, and the possibility of conducting an unbiased science at all. Olesen reviews these arguments in Chapter 9 of this volume, explicating the disastrous consequences of objectifying the targets, subjects, and participants of our research.

Liberation and feminist theologians are central to this new discourse. They ask hard questions, such as, Where and what are the places of women, persons of color, the poor, the homeless, and the hungry in the church, in science, in art, and in literature?

Ethnic Scholars

There is yet another group of concerned scholars determining the course of qualitative research: the ethnic/racial/cultural studies experts who examine the question of whether history has deliberately omitted some cultures from speaking. This new generation of scholars, many of them persons of color, challenges both historical and contemporary social scientists on the accuracy, veracity, and authenticity of the latter's work, contending that no picture can be considered final when the perspectives and narratives of so many are missing, distorted, or subordinated to self-serving dominant majority interests. The result of such challenges has been two-fold; they have brought about a reconsideration of the Western canon, and they have contributed to an increase in the number of historical and scientific works that recognize and reconstruct the perspectives of those whose perspectives and constructions have been missing for so long. In Chapter 10 of this volume John Stanfield outlines this literature and its major moments, figures, and arguments.

Thus have we written the present. A messy moment, multiple voices, experimental texts, breaks, ruptures, crises of legitimation and representation, self-critique, new moral discourses, and technologies. We venture now into the future, attempting to describe the possibilities of the sixth moment. Several themes emerge, or will not go away: the voice and presence of the Other, historically called *the native*; the social text; and the sacred, the humanistic, and the technological.

◆ Back to the Future

We cannot predict the future, but we can speculate about it, because the future never represents a clean break with the past.

The Other's Voice

Throughout its twentieth-century history, up to a scant quarter century ago, qualitative researchers were still talking seriously about the problems of "going native," using the word that previously inscribed the Other in qualitative discourse. Who today can even use the word! After-hours tales, over drinks, mostly white, male, middle-class North American ethnographic researchers whispered of those of their colleagues who had engaged that final perdition, overidentification with those he (seldom she) had studied. Today, no one takes seriously talk of "going native." In fact, its disappearance as a category of concern among sociologists and anthropologists is scarcely remarked, but, like the silences between lovers, it is all the more significant for its absence. In its place looms the Other, whose voice researchers now struggle to hear.

The disappearance of the word *native* is significant; its silence, deafening. In the postmodern world we are executing as our own heirs, in the legacy we have left ourselves and the students who come after us, "going native" is a category that speaks volumes to both our distorted senses of scientific objectivity and our colonial past. We struggle to find ways to make our texts meaningful beyond the artificial structures of conventional objectivity. We try to come to terms with our own "critical subjectivities." All the while, we have also admitted our guilt and complicity in the colonizing aspects of our work, pointedly subsumed by the term *native* itself. Even using the term is offensive.

But worse than politically incorrect, it stands as witness to our conceits as field-workers. How could we have considered ourselves civilized and objective alongside another class of individuals clearly not "civilized," or well below us on a presumed continuum of becoming civilized? Vidich and Lyman, in Chapter 2 of this volume, trace the history of those ideas that undergirded and supported the very concepts that gave rise to the professional tragedy of "going native." Key to this was the Enlightenment legacy that led us to believe we could, indeed, prepare texts that purported to be whole and truthful accounts, objective accounts, of those "natives"/Others.

So we are not likely to hear much about "going native" again. That world has passed. Few mourn its passing—in fact, quite the opposite. Today we are trying to live ever closer to the lives about which we write. Many examples are available. Others are forthcoming that try to show not that we can live those lives, but that we have lived close enough to them to begin to understand how their worlds have been constructed (see, for instance, the May 5, 1993, issue of the *Chronicle of Higher Education,* pp. A6-A7, A12).

The Social Text: Telling Stories From the Field

We are becoming extremely conscious of how our "tales of the field" can be categorized. We now understand at least the flaws that accompany "realist" and "confessional" tales, if not other kinds (Van Maanen, 1988). And many are trying to move toward extended understandings, extended vicariousness, in their texts. Many now are experimenting with form, format, voice, shape, style. Laurel Richardson, in her excellent and moving chapter in Volume 2 of this series, shares with us some of the more powerful literary narrative styles that are being utilized.

This experimentation with text grows from several sources: our concern with representation of the Other; our willingness to all but abandon, or at least drastically modify, the realist text; and our growing sophistication surrounding the problems of situatedness in texts. We know that our texts have specific locations. We know that they represent—whether in some hidden way or openly—our baggage as individual social scientists. We care less about our "objectivity" as scientists than we do about providing our readers with some powerful propositional, tacit, intuitive, emotional, historical, poetic, and empathic experience of the Other via the texts we write.

The problem of representation will not go away. Indeed, at its heart lies an inner tension, an ongoing dialectic, a contradiction, that will never be resolved. On the one hand there is the concern for validity, or certainty in the text as a form of isomorphism and authenticity. On the other hand there is the sure and certain knowledge that all texts are socially, historically, politically, and culturally located. We, like the texts we write, can never be transcendent.

So the experiments will continue, proliferate, grow both more "ironic" (see, e.g., Marcus, Chapter 12, this volume) and simultaneously less self-mocking. There will also be an expansion of the genres of literature from which they borrow. The tension of this dialectic will continue to be felt throughout the ethnographic community, but resolved publicly and privately in many more ways than we have yet seen.

The Sacred, the Humanistic, and the Technological

The West has become increasingly aware of the ecological disasters that massive industrialization and consumption have wrought. We have slowly begun to reconnect with the sense of conjoint destiny with Planet Earth. As these understandings increase, we are likely to see a reconsideration of whether science and religion are truly separate entities.

The modernist idea of separation of religion and science overturned centuries of marriage between the two. The modernist project ignored the deeply spiritual search for meaning and prophecy thought to be hidden in the whole of the universe. It read through the stars (astrology), or the search for the "philosopher's stone," an element thought to have the power to bring spiritual wisdom and riches to the alchemist who discovered it. No one would argue that we need to return to the days of astrologers or alchemists. But it is true that many, including scientists, are searching to find some spiritual core in themselves, a way of reconnecting to meaning,

422

purpose, and the sense of wholeness and holiness that once, in another age, permeated the everyday lives of ordinary men and women.

Peter Reason (1993) writes about the return of spirituality to science. He talks about "sacred experience and sacred science." He—and perhaps others—is beginning to think deeply about how we use science, and what kinds of science we might have. Can there be a sacred science? Such a science would link all its practitioners and participants in bonds that are respectful of our humanity. A sacred science would be supportive of our struggle for dignity. It would lead us to understand how we can throw off oppression and help others to do likewise.

Since the turn of the century, the human disciplines have been moving on a spiritual journey that would join science and the sacred. This can be seen in the writings of many, from Durkheim, Weber, James, Freud, Jung, Fromm, Horney, and Gregory Bateson through Carlos Castañeda, Mary Daly, Renato Rosaldo, Bennetta Jules-Rosette, Mary Douglas, and many others. Indeed, anthropological writers from Rosalie Wax onward have spoken, in their "confessional" tales, of the changes in themselves that resulted from their engaging particular questions to study.

Peter Reason (1993) would have us consider the more elemental spiritualities of these inquiry processes. The connections among spirituality, shamanism, magic, the world of the spirit (for instance, in studies of Santeria), the world of the sorcerer (as in Castañeda's or Lévi-Strauss's work)—all relate in some way to the larger questions of how we use science not only to "know," to "understand," but also to grow spiritually (see also Taussig, 1987).

And so we will likely see a reemergence of deliberation about how science and the sacred fit together. There will be a gradual denial of the Enlightenment wrench that separated the soul from secular concerns. This process is already in motion. It can be seen everywhere: the interest in vision quests in North America, the curiosity about magical rituals from around the world, the search for objects that have spiritual and healing powers that even the most secular of us collects (the crystal that sits on the computer of one of us; the earthy Indian artifacts that line the study of the other), the dance rituals of some researchers that allow them to "center" with their participants, the growing concern with global ecological issues, the dinner-table conversation around appropriate technology and ideas of how small is beautiful.

All of these happenings and rituals point to the tingling, edgy mindfulness that science and technology have not provided the answers we expected or hoped for. And they suggest that concerns of the spirit are already returning to the human disciplines, and will be more important in the future. A sacred science is certain to make its effects felt within the emerging discourses of qualitative research.

Mediating Technologies

At the everyday, practical level, technology, as it has always done, will continue to mediate the fieldwork and analysis phases of qualitative research. However, in the fifth and sixth moments electronic and video technologies, including interactive computers and interactive video, will radically transform every phase and form of qualitative research. Laptop computers will be taken into the field. Modems will connect researchers to their offices and laser printers. Electronically transmitted texts will replace the printed page. New methods for processing text-based materials, as Richards and Richards argue in Chapter 8, Volume 3 of this series, will be developed. New research topics (e.g., self and identity in cyberspace) grounded in the new media technologies (e.g., digitized video data) are also likely to emerge.

Electronic mail systems have already created new communities of qualitative researchers, and these communities will continue to grow. These new electronic social worlds change the concept of community. They shift its locus away from face-to-face interaction to text-mediated communication contexts. New writing selves interact in this cyberspace, selves lodged and created in the virtual reality of the electronic text. These faceless, electronic selves find themselves located in simulated communities. These communities have their own interactional norms concerning the public, the private, the sacred, the secular, and the rational.

New forms of the text, building on hypertext, will also appear. This will change the traditional relationship between the reader and the writer. In the electronic spaces of hypertext, readers become writers, *bricoleurs* who construct the text out of the bits and pieces and chunks of materials left for them by the writer. The writer now disappears, receding into the background, his or her traces found only in the new hypertext that has been created by the reader (see Foden, 1993, p. 5).

And so we are at, or in, the brink of a moment. Because we cannot see clearly where we are, we have no idea of how far we have come, or when we will get to wherever it is we are going.

◆ Coda

In Chapter 12 of this volume, George Marcus argues that we are already in the post-"post" period—post-poststructuralism, post-postmodernism. What this means for interpretive ethnographic practices is still not clear, but it is certain that things will never again be the same. We are in a new age where messy, uncertain multivoiced texts, cultural criticism, and new experimental works will become more common, as will more reflexive forms of fieldwork, analysis, and intertextual representation.

Another way, then, of describing this moment in time and space is to paraphrase Thomas Berry, who has noted that we are between stories. The Old Story will no longer do, and we know that it is inadequate. But the New Story is not yet in place. And so we look for the pieces of the Story, the ways of telling it, and the elements that will make it whole, but it hasn't come to us yet. So we are now the ultimate *bricoleurs,* trying to cobble together a story that we are beginning to suspect will never enjoy the unity, the smoothness, the wholeness that the Old Story had. As we assemble different pieces of the Story, our *bricolage* begins to take not one, but many shapes.

Slowly it dawns on us that there may not be one future, one "moment," but rather many; not one "voice," but polyvocality; not one story, but many tales, dramas, pieces of fiction, fables, memories, histories, autobiographies, poems, and other texts to inform our sense of lifeways, to extend our understandings of the Other, to provide us with the material for what Marcus and Fischer (1986) label "cultural critique." The modernist project has bent and is breaking under the weight of postmodern resistance to its narratives, to what Berry calls "the Old Story."

The answer to the question, Where have we come to? is unclear, as is the answer to the question, What are the many futures that lie ahead for qualitative research? We are not wandering, for that implies that we have no direction. But likewise, as is plain from the several ontologies and many epistemologies that inform and contradict each other, we are not marching in a column toward a common future. Instead, we seem to be charting different terrain, the geography of which is not clear to us. Like the *bricoleurs* of Lévi-Strauss, we are creating solutions to our problems with makeshift equipment, spare parts, and assemblage. But like Mad Max the Road Warrior, a postnuclear survivor, we have something that runs, and we can indeed weave meaning from even a stark emotional and social landscape.

But *bricoleurs* are more than simply jacks-of-all-trades; they are also inventors, in the best sense of the word. *Bricoleurs* know that they have few tools, and little by way of appropriate parts, and so become inventors. They invent ways of repairing; they recycle used fabric into beautiful quilts; they, like Pirsig's hero in *Zen and the Art of Motorcycle Maintenance,* know that for a particular repair, nothing is better than a strip of a Coors beer aluminum can; having no art lessons, they become Grandma Moses. In the *bricoleur's* world, invention is not only the child of necessity, it is the demand of a restless art.

The methods of qualitative research thereby become the "invention," and the telling of the tales—the representation—become the art, even though, as *bricoleurs,* we all know we are not working with standard-issue parts, and we have come to suspect that there are no longer any such parts made (if ever there were). And so we cobble. We cobble together stories that we may tell each other, some to share our profoundest links with those whom we studied; some to help us see how we can right a wrong or relieve oppression; some to help us and others to understand how and why we did what we did, and how it all went very wrong; and some simply to sing of difference.

And perhaps it is the case that these volumes themselves are the fifth moment. Perhaps it is the particular time in our history to take stock of where we are, to think about where we are going, to try to imagine a new future. Perhaps what we have asked our authors to do is to define this fifth moment, and speculate about what the sixth moment might be like— whether it will be a time when the Story is once again in place, or whether it will continue to be a time when fields and disciplines appear to be in disarray. This book, this effort, might well become, to historians who come long after us, a moment unto itself, a chapter in an evolution that we ourselves are not able to bound, to frame, or to capture for its essence.

Whatever the moment is, we hope that these volumes will be a prompt for new tales, for improvisations, for experiments, for interpolations and additional interpretations. The Story is by no means in place yet, although we await the visit of yet another blind Homer to piece together not only what we know of this fabulous land, but a new set of chapters for us. And as we wait, we remember that our most powerful effects as storytellers come when we expose the cultural plots and practices that guide our writing hands. These practices and plots lead us to see coherence where there is none, or to create meaning without an understanding of the broader structures that tell us to tell things in a particular way. Erasing the boundaries of self, Other, and history, we seek to learn how to tell new stories, stories no longer contained within or confined to the tales of the past. And so we embark together on a new project, a project with its own as yet not fully understood cultural plots and cultural practices.

And what remains, throughout, will be the steady, but always changing, commitment of all qualitative researchers—the commitment to study human experience from the ground up, from the point of interacting individuals who, together and alone, make and live histories that have been handed down from the ghosts of the past.

Notes

1. There have been other exchanges of this order in the history of anthropology, including the one between M. Mead and D. Freeman over Mead's early research.

2. A third answer entertains alternative forms of validity, poststructurally conceived. Lather (1993) suggests five new forms of validity (reflexive, ironic, neopragmatic, rhizomatic, situated), which can be noted only briefly here. *Reflexive validity* describes a text's attempt to challenge its own validity claims. *Ironic validity,* like deconstructive verisimilitude, proliferates multiple representations and simulations of the real, showing the strengths and limitations of each, arguing that no single representation is superior to another. *Neopragmatic validity* foregrounds dissensus, heterogeneity, and multiple discourses that destabilize the researcher's position as the master of truth and knowledge. *Rhizomatic validity* represents attempts to present nonlinear texts with multiple centers where multiple voices speak and articulate their definitions of the situation. *Situated validity* imagines a feminist validity opposed to the dominant male voice, which excludes women in their multiplicities—their bodies, their emotions, the maternal world (see Lather, 1993).

◆ References

Agger, B. (1989). *Reading science: A literary, political and sociological analysis.* Dix Hills, NY: General Hall.

Atkinson, P. A. (1990). *The ethnographic imagination: Textual constructions of reality.* London: Routledge.

Boelen, W. A. M. (1992). *Street corner society*: Cornerville revisited. *Journal of Contemporary Ethnography, 21,* 11-51.

Bruner, E. M. (1993). Introduction: The ethnographic self and the personal self. In P. Benson (Ed.), *Anthropology and literature* (pp. 1-26). Urbana: University of Illinois Press.

Cherryholmes, C. H. (1988). *Power and criticism: Poststructural investigations in education.* New York: Teacher's College Press.

Clough, P. T. (1992). *The end(s) of ethnography: From realism to social criticism.* Newbury Park, CA: Sage.

Denzin, N. K. (1991). Empiricist cultural studies in America: A deconstructive reading. *Current Perspectives in Social Theory, 2,* 17-39.

Downing, D. B. (1987). Deconstruction's scruples: The politics of enlightened critique. *Diacritics, 17,* 66-81.

Eisenhart, M. A., & Howe, K. R. (1992). Validity in educational research. In M. D. LeCompte, W. L. Millroy, & J. Preissle (Eds.), *The handbook of qualitative research in education* (pp. 643-680). New York: Academic Press.

Ellis, C. (1991). Emotional sociology. *Studies in Symbolic Interaction, 12,* 123-145.

Ellis, C. (1994). Telling a story of sudden death. *Sociological Quarterly, 35.*

Ellis, C., & Bochner, A. P. (1992). Telling and performing personal stories: The constraints of choice in abortion. In C. Ellis & M. G. Flaherty (Eds.), *Investigating subjectivity: Research on lived experience* (pp. 79-101). Newbury Park, CA: Sage.

Ellis, C., & Flaherty, M. G. (Eds.). (1992). *Investigating subjectivity: Research on lived experience.* Newbury Park, CA: Sage.

Fish, S. (1980). *Is there a text in this class? The authority of interpretive communities.* Cambridge, MA: Harvard University Press.

Geertz, C. (1973). *The interpretation of cultures: Selected essays.* New York: Basic Books.

Gross, J. (1993, June 4). Impasse over damages in New Yorker libel case. *New York Times,* p. A1.

Hall, S. (1986). On postmodernism and articulation: An interview with Stuart Hall (edited by Lawrence Grossberg). *Journal of Communication Inquiry, 10,* 45-60.

Lather, P. (1986). Issues of validity in openly ideological research: Between a rock and a soft place. *Interchange, 17,* 63-84.

Lather, P. (1993). Fertile obsession: Validity after poststructuralism. *Sociological Quarterly, 35.*

Marcus, G. E., & Fischer, M. J. M. (1986). *Anthropology as cultural critique: An experimental moment in the human sciences.* Chicago: University of Chicago Press.

Mascia-Lees, F. E., Sharpe, P., & Cohen, C. B. (1993). The postmodernist turn in anthropology: Cautions from a feminist perspective. In P. Benson (Ed.), *Anthropology and literature* (pp. 225-248). Urbana: University of Illinois Press.

Mishler, E. G. (1990). Validation in inquiry-guided research: The role of exemplars in narrative studies. *Harvard Educational Review, 60,* 415-441.

Ortner, S. B. (1984). Theory in anthropology since the sixties. *Society for Comparative Study of Society and History, 26,* 126-166.

Reason, P. (1993). Sacred experience and sacred science. *Journal of Management Inquiry, 2,* 10-27.

Racevskis, K. (1983). *Michel Foucault and the subversion of intellect.* Ithaca, NY: Cornell University Press.

Rosaldo, R. (1989). *Culture and truth: The remaking of social analysis.* Boston: Beacon.

Rose, D. (1993). Ethnography as a form of life: The written word and the work of the world. In P. Benson (Ed.), *Anthropology and literature* (pp. 192-224). Urbana: University of Illinois Press.

Scheurich, J. J. (1992). *The paradigmatic transgressions of validity.* Unpublished manuscript.

Stacey, J. (1988). Can there be a feminist ethnography? *Women's Studies International Forum, 11,* 21-27.

Taussig, M. (1987). *Shamanism, colonialism, and the wild man: A study in terror and healing.* Chicago: University of Chicago Press.

Todorov, T. (1977). *The poetics of prose.* Ithaca, NY: Cornell University Press.

Van Maanen, J. (1988). *Tales of the field: On writing ethnography.* Chicago: University of Chicago Press.

Whyte, W. F. (1943). *Street corner society: The social structure of an Italian slum.* Chicago: University of Chicago Press.

Whyte, W. F. (1955). *Street corner society: The social structure of an Italian slum* (2nd ed.). Chicago: University of Chicago Press.

Whyte, W. F. (1981). *Street corner society: The social structure of an Italian slum* (3rd ed.). Chicago: University of Chicago Press.

Whyte, W. F. (1992). In defense of *Street corner society. Journal of Contemporary Ethnography, 21,* 52-68.

Suggested Readings

◆ CHAPTER 1

Behar, R. (1996). *The vulnerable observer: Anthropology that breaks your heart*. Boston: Beacon.

Behar, R., & Gordon, D. A. (Eds.). (1996). *Women writing culture*. Berkeley: University of California Press.

Olson, G. A., & and Olson, E. (Eds.). (1995). *Women writing culture* (foreword by Donna Haraway; afterword by Henry A. Giroux). Albany: State University of New York Press.

◆ CHAPTER 2

Appiah, K. A., & Gutman, A. (1996). *Color conscious: The political morality of race*. Princeton, NJ: Princeton University Press.

Bensman, J., & Lilienfeld, R. (1991). *Craft and consciousness: Occupational technique and the development of world images* (2nd ed.). New York: Aldine de Gruyter.

Clifford, J., & Marcus, G. E. (Eds.). (1986). *Writing culture: The poetics and politics of ethnography*. Berkeley: University of California Press.

Denzin, N. K. (1997). *Interpretive ethnography: Ethnographic practices for the 21st century*. Thousand Oaks, CA: Sage.

Fine, M., Weis, L., Powell, L. C., & Wong, L. M. (Eds.). (1997). *Off white: Readings on race, power, and society*. New York: Routledge.

Goldberg, D. T. (1997). *Racial subjects: Writing on race in America*. New York: Routledge.

Habermas, J. (1996). *Between facts and norms: Contributions to a discourse theory of law and democracy* (W. Rehg, Trans.). Cambridge: MIT Press.

Haraway, D. J. (1991). *Simians, cyborgs, and women: The reinvention of nature*. New York: Routledge.

Hutchinson, J., & Smith, A. D. (Eds.). (1996). *Ethnicity*. New York: Oxford University Press.

Lopez, I. F. H. (1996). *White by law: The legal construction of race*. New York: New York University Press.

Min, P. G. (1996). *Caught in the middle: Korean communities in New York and Los Angeles*. Berkeley: University of California Press.

Radin, P. (1987). *The method and theory of ethnology*. South Hadley, MA: Bergin & Garvey. (Original work published 1933)

Salomon, A. (1963). Symbols and images in the constitution of society. In A. Salomon, *In praise of enlightenment* (pp. 237-260). Cleveland: World.

Schutz, A. (1967). On multiple realities. In A. Schutz, *Collected papers* (M. Natanson, Ed. and Trans.) (pp. 207-259). The Hague: Martinus Nijhoff.

Soja, E. W. (1990). *Postmodern geographies: The reassertion of space in critical social theory*. London: Verso.

Vidich, A. J. (1955). Participant observation and the collection and interpretation of data. *American Journal of Sociology, 60,* 335-360.

Vidich, A. J., Bensman, J., & Stein, M. R. (Eds.). (1964). *Reflections on community studies*. New York: John Wiley.

Waldinger, R. (1996). *Still the promised city? African-Americans and new immigrants in postindustrial New York*. Cambridge, MA: Harvard University Press.

Weber, M. (1949). *The methodology of the social sciences* (E. Shils & H. Finch, Ed. and Trans.). Glencoe, IL: Free Press. (See especially "The Meaning of Ethical Neutrality in Sociology and Economics," pp. 1-49; and "Objectivity in Social Science and Social Policy," pp. 50-112.)

◆ CHAPTER 3

Bernstein, R. J. (1991). *The new constellation: The ethical-political horizons of modernity and post-modernity*. Cambridge: Polity.

Freire, P. (1996). *Letters to Cristina: Reflections on my life and work*. New York: Routledge.

Hammersley, M. (1995). *The politics of social research*. Thousand Oaks, CA: Sage.

Latour, B. (1987). *Science in action: How to follow scientists and engineers through society*. Cambridge, MA: Harvard University Press.

McLaren, P., & Lankshear, C. (Eds.). (1994). *Politics of liberation: Paths from Freire*. New York: Routledge.

Ravetz, J. R. (1971). *Scientific knowledge and its social problems*. Oxford: Oxford University Press.

Rickman, H. P. (1979). *Wilhelm Dilthey: Pioneer of the human sciences*. Berkeley: University of California Press.

Silverman, D. (Ed.). (1997). *Qualitative research: Theory, method, and practice*. Thousand Oaks, CA: Sage.

◆ CHAPTER 4

Anzaldúa, G. (1987). *Borderlands/la frontera: The new mestiza*. San Francisco: Aunt Lute.

Behar, R. (1996). *The vulnerable observer: Anthropology that breaks your heart.* Boston: Beacon.

Early, G. (Ed.). (1993). *Lure and loathing: Essays on race, identity, and the ambivalence of assimilation.* New York: Penguin.

Fine, M., Weis, L., Powell, L. C., & Wong, L. M. (Eds.). (1997). *Off white: Readings on race, power and society.* New York: Routledge.

hooks, b. (1989). *Talking back: Thinking feminist, thinking black.* Boston: South End.

hooks, b. (1994). *Teaching to transgress: Education as the practice of freedom.* New York: Routledge.

hooks, b. (1995). *Killing rage: Ending racism.* New York: Routledge.

Lather, P. (1991). *Getting smart: Feminist research and pedagogy within the postmodern.* New York: Routledge.

Lorde, A. (1980). *The cancer journals.* San Francisco: Aunt Lute.

Silin, J. G. (1995). *Sex, death, and the education of children: Our passion for ignorance in the age of AIDS.* New York: Teachers College Press.

Williams, P. J. (1991). *The alchemy of race and rights.* Cambridge, MA: Harvard University Press.

◆ CHAPTER 5

Denzin, N. K. (1992). *Symbolic interactionism and cultural studies.* Cambridge: Basil Blackwell.

Hobbs, D. (1989). *Doing the business: Entrepreneurship, the working class, and detectives in the East End of London.* Oxford: Oxford University Press.

Miller, G., & Dingwall, R. (Eds.). (1997). *Context and method in qualitative research.* Thousand Oaks, CA: Sage.

Silverman, D. (Ed.). (1997). *Qualitative research: Theory, method, and practice.* Thousand Oaks, CA: Sage.

Van Maanen, J. (Ed.). (1995). *Representation in ethnography.* Thousand Oaks, CA: Sage.

Watson, T. J. (1994). *In search of management: Culture, chaos and control in managerial work.* London: Routledge.

Wolf, D. L. (Ed.). (1996). *Feminist dilemmas in fieldwork.* Boulder, CO: Westview.

◆ CHAPTER 6

Atkinson, P. A. (1990). *The ethnographic imagination: Textual constructions of reality.* London: Routledge.

Denzin, N. K. (1997). *Interpretive ethnography: Ethnographic practices for the 21st century.* Thousand Oaks, CA: Sage.

Ellis, C., & Bochner, A. P. (Eds.). (1997). *Composing ethnography: Alternative forms of qualitative writing.* Walnut Creek, CA: AltaMira.

Golden-Biddle, K., & Locke, K. D. (1997). *Composing qualitative research.* Thousand Oaks, CA: Sage.

Heron, J. (1996). *Co-operative inquiry: Research into the human condition.* London: Sage.

Smith, J. K. (1989). *The nature of social and educational inquiry: Empiricism versus interpretation.* Norwood, NJ: Ablex.

Smith, J. K. (1993). *After the demise of empiricism: The problem of judging social and educational inquiry.* Norwood, NJ: Ablex.

◆ CHAPTER 7

Berger, P. L., & Luckmann, T. (1967). *The social construction of reality: A treatise in the sociology of knowledge.* Garden City, NY: Doubleday.

Geertz, C. (1973). *The interpretation of cultures: Selected essays.* New York: Basic Books.

Gergen, K. J. (1994). *Toward transformation of social knowledge* (2nd ed.). Thousand Oaks, CA: Sage.

Goodman, N. (1978). *Ways of worldmaking.* Indianapolis: Hackett.

Latour, B., & Wollgar, S. (1986). *Laboratory life: The social construction of scientific facts* (rev. ed.). Princeton, NJ: Princeton University Press.

Outhwaite, W. (1975). *Understanding social life: The method called verstehen.* Sydney: Allen & Unwin.

Prus, R. (1996). *Symbolic interaction and ethnographic research: Intersubjectivity and the study of human lived experience.* Albany: State University of New York Press.

Rabinow, P., & Sullivan, W. M. (Eds.). (1979). *Interpretive social science: A reader.* Berkeley: University of California Press.

Sarbin, T. R., & Kitsuse, J. I. (Eds.). (1993). *Constructing the social.* London: Sage.

Schutz, A. (1967). *Collected papers* (Vol. 1) (M. Natanson, Ed. and Trans.). The Hague: Martinus Nijhoff.

Searle, J. R. (1995). *The construction of social reality.* New York: Free Press.

Taylor, C. (1985). *Philosophical papers, 2: Philosophy and the human sciences.* Cambridge: Cambridge University Press.

◆ CHAPTER 9

Behar, R., & Gordon, D. A. (Eds.). (1996). *Women writing culture.* Berkeley: University of California Press.

Bell, D., & Karim, W. J. (1993). *Gendered fields: Women, men and ethnography.* London: Routledge.

Cancian, F. M. (1992). Feminist science: Methodologies that challenge inequality. *Gender & Society, 6,* 623-642.

Ellis, C. (1995). *Final negotiations: A story of love, loss, and chronic illness.* Philadelphia: Temple University Press.

Hawkesworth, M. (1997). Confounding gender. *Signs, 22,* 649-686. (See also the comments following this article by McKenna & Kessler, Smith, Scott, and Connell, and the reply by Hawkesworth.)

Hochschild, A. R. (1997). *The time bind: When work becomes home and home becomes work.* New York: Henry Holt.

Kleinman, S. L. (1996). *Opposing ambitions: Gender and identity in an alternative organization.* Chicago: University of Chicago Press.

Lather, P. (1995). The validity of angels: Interpretive and textual strategies in researching the lives of women. *Qualitative Inquiry, 1,* 41-68.

Maguire, P. (1996). Considering more participatory feminist research: What's congruency got to do with it? *Qualitative Inquiry, 2,* 106-118.

Pierce, J. L. (1995). *Gender trials: Emotional lives in contemporary law firms.* Berkeley: University of California Press.

Reay, D. (1996). Insider perspectives, or stealing the words out of women's mouths. In Speaking out: Researching and representing women [Special issue]. *Feminist Review, 53*(Summer), 57-73.

Smith, D. (1996). Telling the truth after postmodernism. *Symbolic Interaction, 19,* 171-202.

Stacey, J. (1990). *Brave new families: Stories of upheaval in late twentieth century America.* Berkeley: University of California Press.

Visweswaran, K. (1996). *Fictions of feminist ethnography.* Minneapolis: University of Minnesota Press.

Wolf, D. L. (Ed.). (1996). *Feminist dilemmas in fieldwork.* Boulder, CO: Westview.

◆ CHAPTER 10

Bogle, D. (1994). *Toms, coons, mulattoes, mammies, and bucks: An interpretive history of blacks in American films* (3rd ed.). New York: Continuum.

Crenshaw, K., Gotanda, N., Peller, G., & Thomas, K. (1995). Introduction. In K. Crenshaw, N. Gotanda, G. Peller, & K. Thomas (Eds.), *Critical race theory: The key writings that formed the movement* (pp. xii-xxxii). New York: New Press.

Gray, H. (1995). *Watching race: Television and the struggle for "blackness."* Minneapolis: University of Minnesota Press.

Hall, S. (1996). Gramsci's relevance for the study of race and ethnicity. In S. Hall, *Critical dialogues in cultural studies* (D. Morley & K.-H. Chen, Eds.) (pp. 411-440). London: Routledge.

Hall, S. (1996). New ethnicities. In S. Hall, *Critical dialogues in cultural studies* (D. Morley & K.-H. Chen, Eds.) (pp. 441-449). London: Routledge.

Hall, S. (1996). What is this "black" in black popular culture? In S. Hall, *Critical dialogues in cultural studies* (D. Morley & K.-H. Chen, Eds.) (pp. 465-475). London: Routledge.

Trinh T. M.-H. (1989). *Woman, native, other: Writing postcoloniality and feminism.* Bloomington: Indiana University Press.

◆ CHAPTER 11

Chow, R. (1993). *Writing diaspora: Tactics of intervention in contemporary cultural studies.* Bloomington: Indiana University Press.

Du Gay, P., Hall, S., Janes, L., Mackay, H., & Negus, K. (1997). *Doing cultural studies: The story of the Sony Walkman.* London: Sage.

◆ CHAPTER 12

Behar, R. (1996). *The vulnerable observer: Anthropology that breaks your heart.* Boston: Beacon.

Bourgois, P. (1995). *In search of respect: Selling crack in el barrio.* New York: Cambridge University Press.

Boyarin, J. (1996). *Thinking in Jewish.* Chicago: University of Chicago Press.

Fox, R. G. (Ed.). (1991). *Recapturing anthropology: Working in the present.* Sante Fe, NM: School of American Research Press.

Gupta, A., & Ferguson, J. (Eds.). (1997). *The concept of fieldwork in anthropology.* Berkeley: University of California Press.

Jackson, M. (1985). *Paths toward a clearing: Radical empiricism and ethnographic inquiry.* Bloomington: Indiana University Press.

Kondo, D. (1997). *About face: Performing race in fashion and theater.* New York: Routledge.

Marcus, G. E. (Ed.). (1993). *Perilous states: Conversations on culture, politics, and nation* (Vol. 1). Chicago: University of Chicago Press.

Marcus, G. E. (1995). Ethnography in/of the world system: The emergence of multi-sited ethnography. *Annual Review of Anthropology, 24,* 95-117.

Marcus, G. E. (1997). The uses of complicity in the changing mise-en-scene of anthropological fieldwork. *Representations, 59*(Summer), 1-24.

Marcus, G. E. (Ed.). (1998). *Critical anthropology now: Unexpected contexts, shifting constituencies, new agendas.* Santa Fe, NM: School of American Research Press.

Martin, E. (1994). *Flexible bodies: The role of immunity in American culture from the days of polio to the age of AIDS.* Boston: Beacon.

Panourgia, N. (1995). *Fragments of death, fables of identity: An Athenian anthropography.* Madison: University of Wisconsin Press.

Tsing, A. (1994). *In the realm of the Diamond Queen: Marginality in an out-of-the-way place.* Princeton, NJ: Princeton University Press.

◆ CHAPTER 13

Ellis, C., & Bochner, A. P. (Eds.). (1997). *Composing ethnography: Alternative forms of qualitative writing.* Walnut Creek, CA: AltaMira.

Gubrium, J. F., & Holstein, J. A. (1997). *The new language of qualitative methods.* New York: Oxford University Press.

Lewin, E., & Leap, W. L. (Eds.). (1996). *Out in the field: Reflections of lesbian and gay anthropologists.* Urbana: University of Illinois Press.

Richardson, L. (1997). *Fields of play: Constructing an academic life.* New Brunswick, NJ: Rutgers University Press.

Name Index

Abedi, M., 391
Abel, E. K., 302
Abel, T., 226
Abeyesekere, G., 48
Abraham, S. Y., 346
Abrahams, R. D., 70
Abrahamson, H. J., 71
Abramowitz, S. I., 342
Abu-Lughod, L., 320, 321
Acker, J., 316
Adler, P., 42
Adorno, T., 123, 261
Agar, M. H., 77
Agger, B., 416
Ahmad, A., 402
Alba, R., 68
Aldrich, R., 49
Allen, W., 238
Anderson, E., 70
Anderson, K. J., 71
Anderson, N., 62
Anderson, R., 163
Anderson, T. I., 71
Angell, R. C., 74
Apple, M., 188, 279
Argyris, C., 163
Aronowitz, S., 142, 272, 273, 276, 286
Asad, T., 385, 389
Asante, M. K., 335, 347
Ashe, M., 310

Ashworth, P. D., 338
Atkinson, P. A., 5, 44, 113, 157, 158, 280, 316, 338, 414
Austerberry, H., 308
Austin, R., 141, 143, 144, 149

Bacon, F., 112
Bahr, H. M., 60
Bailey, B. L., 62
Baker, H. A., 343
Baker, J. R., 47
Ball, D. W., 62
Balsamo, A., 313
Barber, B., 167
Barkan, E., 47
Barnes, J. A., 168
Barry, K., 316
Bartlett, K., 310
Basu, A., 335
Bataille, G., 291
Bateson, G., 1, 15, 26, 423
Baudrillard, J., 76, 78
Bauman, Z., 227, 247
Becker, H. S., 3, 8, 9, 16, 17, 65, 124, 157, 168, 319
Beegle, J. A., 66
Behar, R., 320, 321
Belenky, M. F., 241
Bell, C., 159, 164

Bender, T., 62
Bendix, R., 78
Benhabib, S., 276
Benja, O., 56
Bensman, J., 12, 65, 66, 160, 166, 167
Berger, B., 78
Berger, P., 123, 240, 247
Berlin, I., 223
Berlo, J. C., 70
Bernal, M., 346
Bernick, S. E., 342
Bernstein, R. J., 199, 247, 250
Berry, B., 70
Berry, T., 425
Berverly, J., 77
Bhabha, H. K., 76, 77, 138
Bhavnani, K., 131, 149
Bieder, R. E., 55
Bigham, D. E., 70
Biklen, S. K., 124
Blackman, J., 151
Blackwell, B. R., 70
Blake, C. N., 62
Blanck, D., 68
Blassingame, J. W., 70
Bleicher, J., 228
Bloom, H., 73
Bloor, D., 125
Bloor, M., 342
Bloor, M. J., 316
Blumer, H., 56, 221, 223, 233, 234, 337
Blyden, E., 351
Boahen, A. A., 346
Boas, F., 123
Bochner, A., 319, 413
Bock, K. E., 53
Boeke, J. H., 49
Boelen, W. A. M., 176, 417
Bogardus, E. S., 69
Bogdan, R., 16, 124
Bogue, D. J., 61, 62
Bok, S., 214
Bond, H. M., 190
Bookman, A., 149
Boon, J., 290
Booth, C., 121
Borgmann, A., 78
Boruch, R. F., 168
Bottomore, T., 261
Bourdieu, P., 289, 290, 372, 396, 398

Bowen, E. S., 171
Bowles, S., 262
Boxer, C. R., 49
Bradbury, M., 387
Bradford, P. V., 56
Brand, A., 126
Brandt, A. M., 167
Brewer, J., 4
Britton, B., 307
Britzman, D., 276
Brookhiser, R., 68
Broom, D., 307
Brosio, R., 280, 281
Brown, R., 51
Brown, W., 308
Brown, W. O., 69
Browner, C., 306
Bruner, E. M., 410, 412, 413
Bruner, J., 225, 236
Buchdahl, G., 117
Buchmann, M., 113
Buckingham, D., 270
Bulmer, M., 158, 168, 174-176
Burawoy, M., 80, 131, 141
Burgess, E. W., 59, 61, 62
Burgess, R. G., 156, 158, 316, 338
Burns, J., 206
Burns, T., 160, 166
Burton, A., 131, 141
Butler, J., 276, 285, 305
Butler, O., 314
Button, J. W., 70

Callaway, H., 162
Calloway, C. G., 54
Campbell, D., 16, 125, 205, 237
Cancian, F. M., 317
Cannon, L. W., 303, 315, 342
Caplow, T., 60
Caraway, N., 152
Carby, H. V., 343
Carey, J. W., 6
Carr, W., 126, 211
Carspecken, P., 188, 292
Castañeda, C., 423
Caudill, W., 172
Cavan, R. S., 62
Cayton, H., 62, 340
Cecil, J. S., 168

Chadwick, B. A., 60
Chambers, C. A., 58
Chambers, I., 78
Chan, S., 71
Chase, S., 308
Cherryholmes, C. H., 414
Chow, E., 304
Christman, J. B., 342
Christopher, R. C., 68
Cicourel, A. V., 16
Clark, K., 339
Clarke, A., 307
Clarke, M., 156, 160, 165
Clifford, J., 19, 44, 70, 75, 137, 140, 162,
    247, 248, 266, 290, 291, 304, 386,
    394
Clinchy, B. M., 241
Clough, P. T., 15, 20, 21, 188, 189, 292,
    310, 313, 320, 321, 395, 409, 419
Cockburn, A., 281
Codd, J., 273
Code, L., 303
Cohen, C. B., 312, 318, 319, 342, 412
Cohen, P., 274
Cohen, S. R., 58
Coleman, M. C., 54
Collins, J., 280, 284
Collins, P. H., 146, 189, 304, 310, 314,
    321, 342, 344
Columbus, S., 46, 111-112
Comte, A., 50-54, 119
Connell, R. W., 321
Connor, S., 291
Conrad, E., 342
Contosta, D. R., 58
Cook, D., 150
Cook, J. A., 22, 157, 161, 178, 281, 282,
    284, 303, 314
Cook, T., 205
Coombe, R., 388, 389
Corbin, J., 9, 198, 205, 315
Cornell, D., 276
Cornell, S., 70
Cornwell, R., 76
Corrigan, P., 274
Covello, L., 68
Cox, O. C., 346
Crabtree, B. F., 338
Craddock, E., 308, 317
Crandall, R., 168, 214

Crenshaw, K., 138, 141, 142, 304
Cressey, D., 74
Cronbach, L. J., 125
Culin, S., 57
Currie, D., 342
Cushing, F. H., 56-57

Dai, B., 62
Dale, E. E., 56
Dalton, M., 171, 172
Daly, K., 338
Daly, M., 423
Daniel, G., 346
Daniels, A., 307, 314
Dansereau, H. K., 62
Degerando, J. M., 48
de Koning, A. J. J., 338
Delamont, S., 113
de las Casas, B., 47
deLauretis, T., 147, 313
Dell, C., 366
Denzin, N. K., 4, 16, 78, 80, 148, 221,
    223, 232-235, 312, 313, 322, 338,
    415
Derrida, J., 78
Descartes, R., 116
de Sola Poole, I., 62
DeVault, M. L., 300-302, 316, 342
Dewey, J., 244, 285
Diamond, S., 49, 75, 165
Dickens, C., 119
Diener, E., 168, 214
di Leonardo, M., 241, 342
Dill, B. T., 304
Dilthey, W., 24, 120-121, 224
Diner, S. J., 65
Dingwall, R., 163
Dippo, D., 282
Dirlik, A., 77
Ditton, J., 180
Dockstader, F. J., 56
Dominick, J. R., 374
Donmoyer, R., 288
Douglas, J. D., 45, 168, 179
Douglas, M., 79, 423
Downing, D. B., 415
Drake, S. C., 62
Du Bois, W. E. B., 58-59, 190, 340, 346
Duffy, J., 49

Dumont, L., 289
Duncan, O. D., 66
Duneier, M., 70
Dunham, H. W., 62

Early, G., 76
Ebert, T., 271, 272
Edmonds, B., 308
Ehrenreich, B., 309
Eichler, M., 300
Eiger, N., 281-284
Eisenhart, M. A., 414
Eisner, E., 19, 223, 244, 245, 248
Elgin, C., 239
Ellis, C., 319, 413
Ellison, R., 341
Emerson, R., 316
Engels, F., 49, 119
Epstein, C. F., 302
Ergas, Y., 342
Erickson, F., 118, 124, 222
Erikson, K., 174
Ermath, M., 117, 120, 121
Espiritu, Y. L., 71
Esseveld, J., 316
Estes, C., 308
Etzioni, A., 67
Evans, A. S., 70

Facio, E., 342
Fals-Borda, O., 126
Fanon, F., 141, 348
Faris, J. C., 335
Faris, R. E. L., 62
Feagin, J. R., 80
Featherstone, M., 76
Fee, E., 301
Feher, M., 76
Feinberg, W., 278, 285, 286
Ferguson, A. A., 131, 141
Ferguson, K., 278, 280, 281, 301, 303,
    305, 312, 315
Fernandez-Kelly, M. P., 306
Festinger, L., 167
Field, P. A., 317
Fielding, N., 4, 80
Fields, K., 340
Filstead, W. J., 16

Finch, J., 302, 308, 315, 316
Fine, M., 131, 141, 148, 150, 276, 305,
    314, 319, 322
Firey, W., 66
Fischer, M., 19, 198, 291, 304, 385, 391,
    425
Fish, S., 241
Fisher, S., 306
Fiske, J., 362, 370
Flax, J., 276, 305
Flick, U., 4
Floden, R. E., 113
Florez, C. P., 160, 164
Fonow, M. M, 161, 178, 281, 282, 284,
    303, 314
Fonow, M. M., 22, 157
Fontana, A., 42, 44, 76
Forbes, J. D., 71
Foster, H., 272
Foucault, M., 112, 282, 349
Fox, K. J., 131, 141
Fox, R. G., 75
Fox-Genovese, E., 276
Franklin, S., 189
Fraser, N., 281, 309
Frazier, E. F., 12, 63, 69, 339, 340, 351
Freire, P., 262
Friedman, L., x
Frisby, D., 77
Fry, M. J., 310
Fuchs, M., 289, 290
Fukuyama, F., 54
Furner, M. O., 338
Furnivall, J. S., 49
Fuss, D., 236

Gadamer, H.-G., 224, 227
Gage, N., 218
Gal, S., 241
Game, A., 307, 313, 322
Gamson, J., 131, 141
Gans, H. J., 12, 68, 137, 156, 172
Garbaccia, D. R., 68
Garcia, E., 304
Garrison, J., 284, 285
Gartrell, N., 131, 141
Geer, B., 9, 17, 124
Geertz, C., 14, 18, 19, 78, 79, 223,
    230-232, 249, 385, 416

Gelb, J., 308
Gellner, E., 44
Georges, R. A., 77
Gergen, K., 223, 236, 240, 242, 269
Gergen, M., 240, 242
Geschwender, J. A., 69
Gibson, R., 261
Giddens, A., 392
Giddings, P., 341
Gilgren, J., 338
Gilligan, C., 241, 303
Gilman, S. L., 76
Ginsburg, C., 48
Gintis, H., 262
Giorgi, A., 338
Giroux, H., 136, 142, 188, 191, 206, 215,
    261, 262, 264, 265, 272-273, 276,
    280, 281, 286
Gist, N. P., 62
Glaser, B. G., 16, 17, 198, 205
Glazer, N., 68, 320
Gleason, P., 71
Glenn, E. K., 302
Glick, C. E., 69
Godzich, W., 273
Goetz, J. P., 338, 339
Goffman, E., 43, 75
Goldberger, N. R., 241
Goldfarb, J. C., 75
Goodman, N., 223, 238-239
Gordon, L., 313
Gordon, S. M., 322
Gorelick, S., 315
Gouldner, A., 168
Graham, H., 302
Gramsci, A., 266
Grant, L., 342
Gray, J., 49
Greek, C. E., 58
Green, R., 304
Gregg, N., 319
Griffin, C., 266, 274
Griffith, A., 310
Gross, J., 412
Grossberg, L., 3, 5, 6, 8, 157, 187, 190,
    313, 384, 387
Groves, D., 302
Guba, E. G., x, 9, 19, 22, 26, 159, 170,
    185, 192, 195, 199, 200, 202, 213,
    215, 223, 242-243, 249, 287

Gubrium, J. F., 159
Gullick, J. M., 49
Gusfield, J. R., 62
Gutierrez, R. A., 71
Gwertzman, B., 54

Habermas, J., 123, 126, 287
Hacking, I., 118
Hahn, H., 141, 147
Halbert, L. A., 62
Hall, J., 55, 305, 315
Hall, P. D., 391, 399
Hall, S., 133-134, 152, 190, 267, 349,
    376, 415
Hamilton, D., 24
Hammer, R., 272
Hammersley, M., 22, 42, 113, 158, 161,
    223, 224, 233, 246, 280, 316
Hammond, P., 159
Hamnett, M., 335
Handel, G., 338
Hansen, M. L., 68
Haraway, D. J., 140, 313, 391, 401, 402
Harding, S., 140, 309-311, 313
Hare, N., 346
Harré, R., 47
Harris, M., 278
Harrison, B., 283
Hartland, E. S., 49
Hartmann, E. G., 58
Hartsock, N., 283, 309, 310
Harvey, D., 279, 388, 392
Haskell, T. L., 338
Havel, V., 140
Hawkesworth, M. E., 310-313
Heidegger, M., 224
Heilbroner, R., 53
Heizer, R. F., 56
Hekman, S., 312
Held, D., 261
Henry, J., 124
Hepworth, M., 76
Herkovitz, M., 50
Hess, B., 318
Hesse, E., 199, 204, 211
Higginbotham, E., 303, 315
Hill, R., 60
Hill-Lubin, M. A., 51
Hine, C., 302

Hinsley, C. M. Jr., 55
Hobsbawm, E., 113
Hochschild, A. R., 302, 320
Hodgen, M. T., 46, 50, 53
Hodgkin, T., 346
Hofman, R., 168
Holdaway, S., 173, 176
Holden, A. C., 58
Hollingshead, A., 12, 63
Holub, R. C., 395
hooks, b., 130, 132, 141, 304, 343
Horkheimer, M., 261, 264
Horowitz, B., 278, 285, 286
Horowitz, I. L., 75, 167
Horton, J., 351
Hosle, V., 47
House, E., 202
Howe, K. R., 414
Huberman, A. M., 17
Hughes, E., 9, 17, 62, 124, 156
Hughes, L., 341
Hull, G., 341
Humphreys, L., 167-168
Hune, S., 71
Hunt, J., 159, 165
Hunt, L., 306
Hunter, A., 4
Hunter, H. M., 346
Hurst, L., 131, 141
Hurston, Z. N., 190, 340-342
Hurtado, A., 304
Hutcheon, L., 276
Hymes, D., 5, 385

Ignacio, L. F., 71
Ishi, 56

Jackson, J. S., 70
Jackson, M., 248-250
Jackson, P., 124
Jacob, E., 112-114, 123
Jacobus, M., 313
Jaimes, M. E., 71
Jalali, R., 72
Jameson, F., 268, 402
Jay, M., 261
Jayaratne, T. E., 161
Johannsen, M., 312

Johnson, C. F., 353
Johnson, C. S., 340
Johnson, E. W., 124
Johnson, J. M., 42
Johnson, J. W., 341
Jones, M. O., 77
Jonsen, A. R., 229
Jordan, B., 303, 306
Jordan, J., 276
Joyner, C., 70
Jules-Rosette, B., 423

Kaldun, I., 351
Kant, I., 116-118
Katsuranis, F., 307
Katz, J., 167
Katz, M., 137
Kaufert, P., 308
Kaufman, M. T., 54
Keegan, W. F., 46
Keller, E. F., 313
Keller, R. W., Jr., 54
Kelling, G. L., 160, 164
Kellner, D., 267, 268, 279
Kellner, H., 247
Kemmis, S., 126, 211
Kennedy, A. J., 58
Khaldun, I., 346
Kierkegaard, S. A., 118
Kimmel, A. J., 170, 176
Kincheloe, J., 187, 265, 273, 283, 286,
    288
Kinloch, G. C., 69
Kipnis, L., 276
Kirk, J., 224
Kitzinger, C., 141, 150
Kivisto, P., 68
Klein, L., 163
Klockars, C. B., 168, 173, 174
Kluckhohn, C., 339
Knoll, T., 71
Knorr-Cetina, K., 236
Komarovsky, M., 311
Kotarba, J. A., 76
Kramer, J. R., 68
Kreiger, L., 124
Krieger, S., 76, 319
Kroeber, A., 56
Kuhn, T., 114

Kumar, K., 335
Kundera, M., 45, 73
Kuper, A., 49, 53, 335
Kurzman, C., 131, 141
Kwan, K. M., 69

Lacey, C., 274
Ladner, J., 136, 340, 351
Ladner, J. A., 335
Landesco, J., 68
LaPierre, R. T., 167
Larson, C., 221
Lash, S., 273
Lather, P., 289, 314, 317, 342, 415
LeCompte, M. D., 5, 28, 224, 338-339
Lee, D., 70
Lee, R. H., 62, 67, 69
Lejeune, R. A., 167
Lemert, C., 76, 310, 321
Lentricchia, F., 5
Lenzer, G., 50
Leonard, K. I., 71
Lerris, M., 291
Leung, M. L. A., 303, 315
Leventman, S., 68
Lévi-Strauss, C., 3, 79
Lewin, E., 303, 305
Lewis, O., 339
Lieberman, G., 366
Lieberson, S., 69
Liebow, E., 70, 339, 351
Lincoln, Y. S., 19, 22, 26, 113, 159, 170,
    195, 199, 200, 202, 211, 213-215,
    221, 223, 242-243, 249, 287
Lindesmith, A., 74
Lingeman, R., 62
Linton, R., 149
Lipset, S. M., 53, 68, 72
Lofland, J. F., 16, 167
Lofland, L. H., 16, 17
Loomis, C. P., 66
Lopata, H. Z., 62
Lopreato, J., 68
Lorber, J., 302
Louch, A. R., 223
Lovejoy, A. O., 50
Luckmann, T., 123
Lugard, L., 49
Lugones, M., 276

Luhmann, N., 45
Luke, T., 270, 277
Luker, K., 313
Lury, C., 189
Lykes, B., 141, 149
Lyman, S. M., 12, 53, 57, 58, 61, 67-70,
    75, 80
Lynd, H., 59
Lynd, R., 59, 351
Lyotard, J. F., 78, 389

Machiavelli, N., 111-112
Machung, A., 302
MacIntyre, A., 115
MacKinnon, C., 303, 310
Madison, G. B., 227, 228
Magoon, A. G., 225
Magubane, B., 335
Malcolm, J., 412
Malinowski, B., 1, 13, 14, 148, 171
Mandeville, J., 137
Manganaro, M., 75, 290
Mangiafico, L., 71
Manicas, P. T., 122, 123
Manning, P. K., 73, 76, 156
Marburg, S. L., 342
Marcus, G. E., 19, 66, 75, 137, 140, 198,
    248, 266, 291, 304, 385, 386, 394,
    399, 425
Marcuse, H., 123, 261, 287
Marks, C. C., 343
Marshall, J., 55
Marshall, P., 341
Martin, B., 134
Martin, C., 70
Martin, E., 241
Martin, S. E., 165
Marty, M. E., 47
Marx, G., 173, 180
Marx, K., 349
Mascia-Lees, F. E., 312, 318-319, 342,
    412
Mason, J., 315
Masson, J. N., 412
Masuoka, J., 69
Matsuda, M., 144
Matthews, M. R., 246, 248
Maunier, R., 48
Mbiti, J. S., 346

McCall, G. J., 158
McCall, M., 319
McCluer, F. L., 62
McClymer, J. F., 58
McFarlane, J., 387
McKeganey, N., 342
McKenney, T. L., 55
McKenzie, R. D., 62
McKinlay, S., 308
McLaren, P., 187, 261, 265, 269, 272,
    273, 275, 282, 284-286
McLaughlin, T., 5
Mead, G. H., 74, 223, 233
Mead, M., 15, 50, 124, 175
Mehan, H., 124
Meltzer, B. N., 233
Memmi, A., 348
Merriam, S. B., 338
Merton, R. K., 335
Messenger, P. M., 71
Mies, M., 161, 242, 314
Miles, M. B., 17
Milgram, S., 167
Mill, J. S., 119-120, 196
Miller, J. B., 146
Miller, M. L., 224
Miller, W. L., 338
Millroy, W. L., 338, 339
Milner, C. A., II, 54
Milson, K., 71
Miner, H., 66
Mishler, E. G., 416
Mohanty, C., 134, 305
Montagu, A., 52
Montini, T., 307
Moore, H., 314
Morawski, J., 319
Morgan, L. H., 49
Morgan, S., 149
Morris, M., 188, 313
Morrison, T., 341
Morrow, R., 273, 276, 277, 286
Morton, D., 272
Mouffe, C., 142
Mudimbe, V. Y., 346
Murcott, A., 302
Murdoch, R., 361
Murdock, G. P., 51
Myers, F., 398, 399-400
Myrdal, G., 341

Nader, L., 52
Nandy, A., 346
Nelli, H. S., 62
Nelson, C., 3, 5, 6, 8, 157, 187, 313, 384,
    387
Nelson, M. K., 302
Newby, H., 159
Newton, J., 290
Nichols, B., 5
Nicholson, L., 281
Nielsen, J. M., 314
Nietzsche, F. W., 118
Nisbet, R. A., 43, 51
Nkrumah, K., 346, 351
Nomura, G. M., 71
Norris, C., 76
Novak, M., 71
Nsamenang, A. B., 346
Numbers, R., 46

Oakes, K. B., 47
Oakley, A., 242
O'Connor, A., 346
O'Connor, F. W., 168, 175
Okely, J., 162
Okihiro, G. Y., 71
Olesen, V., 307, 311, 317
Olivier, S., 48
Olkes, C., 19, 20
O'Neil, F. A., 54
Opie, A., 318
Ortner, S. B., 410
Orum, A., 80

Pagano, J., 276
Paget, M., 319
Palley, L., 308
Palmer, P., 302
Park, R. E., 12, 61-62, 67, 77, 350
Parsons, T., 53, 66
Patrick, R. C., 172
Payne, G., 163
Payne, J., 163
Peacock, J. L., 46
Peplau, L. A., 342
Petchesky, R., 308
Peters, M., 270
Petras, J. W., 233

Phillips, D., 156, 237
Pike, K., 47
Pinar, W., 276, 283
Piven, F. F., 309
Plath, D., 29
Platt, J., 163
Plummer, K., 233
Polanyi, M., 244
Polkinghorne, D. E., 346
Pollner, M., 316
Popper, K., 199
Porter, D. J., 335
Poster, M., 269
Powdermaker, H., 170, 171, 350
Pratt, M. L., 42, 137, 139
Preissle, J., 5, 28, 224, 338, 339
Punch, M., 157, 158, 160, 163, 166, 178
Purdy, J., 15

Quantz, R. A., 264, 274
Quayle, D., 367
Queen, S. A., 172

Rabinow, P., 229, 248, 290, 394
Racevskis, K., 415
Radin, P., 57
Radway, J., 241
Rae, J. B., 62
Rahman, M. A., 126
Rainbow, P., 224
Rainwater, L., 339
Raizen, S., 285
Rakolta, T., 366-368, 371
Ranger, T., 113
Ranke, L., 124
Rapp, R., 342
Ratzel, F., 67
Rauch, G. E., 374
Readings, B., 390
Reason, P., 423
Redfield, R., 12, 61, 62, 65
Reese, W., 207
Reid, M., 308, 317
Reinharz, S., 157, 161, 165, 188, 242,
    287, 300, 306, 314
Reiss, A. J., Jr., 164, 169, 171, 176
Renfrew, C., 346
Reuter, E. B., 69, 70

Reynolds, L. T., 233
Richardson, L., 2, 319, 421
Ricoeur, P., 231
Riecken, H. W., 167
Riessman, C. K., 315
Riger, S., 241
Ring, J., 315
Rittenhouse, A., 308
Roberts, H., 160, 314
Roberts, J., 117, 118
Robins, D., 274
Rock, P., 175
Roffman, P., 15
Rojas, A. V., 65
Rollins, J., 141, 145, 303, 316, 340, 343,
    344
Romalis, S., 308
Roman, L. G., 188
Romero, M., 303
Roper, M. W., 62
Rorty, R., 75, 78, 249, 250
Rosaldo, R., 1, 14, 15, 19, 65, 140, 409,
    423
Rose, D., 77
Rosenau, P. M., 78, 273
Ross, R. H., 69
Ruddick, S., 286
Rudner, R., 226
Ruzek, S., 303, 316
Ryan, K., x
Rynkiewich, M. A., 168

Sachs, W., 49
Sacks, K., 303
Sahlins, M., 395
Said, E., 150, 346, 386
Salmond, A., 48
Saltonstall, R., 306
Salzinger, L., 131, 141
Sanday, P., 124, 141, 146
Sandburg, C., 341
Sanderson, S. K., 51
Sando, J. S., 70
Sanjek, R., 29, 160
San Juan, E., Jr., 265
Sarana, G., 51
Schachter, S., 167
Schatzman, L., 42
Schenke, A., 282

Scheper-Hughes, N., 314, 315
Scheurich, J. J., 414
Schietinger, E. F., 62
Schiffman, J., 131, 141
Schlesinger, A. M., Jr., 68
Schön, D., 126, 285
Schrag, P., 68
Schutz, A., 226, 240, 247, 349
Schwandt, T., 187
Schwartz, M., 160
Scott, J., 151, 319, 320
Scott, M. B., 80
Sechrest, L., 196
Seidman, I. E., 338
Selhorst, J., x
Sepulveda, J. G., 47
Seruton, R., 117
Shaffir, W. B., 158, 338
Shapiro, M. J., 229
Sharpe, P., 312, 318, 319, 342, 412
Sharrock, W., 163
Sheets-Johnstone, M., 76
Shibutani, T., 69
Shils, E., 163
Shipman, P., 47
Shostak, M., 319
Shuttleworth, S., 313
Sieber, J. E., 167, 170, 180
Silverman, D., 159
Silverman, E. K., 291
Simey, T. S., 121
Simmel, G., 73
Simmons, J. L., 158
Simon, R., 282
Singer, M. B., 62
Singh, A., 335
Siu, P. C. P., 62
Sjoberg, G., 80, 168
Slaughter, M., 112
Slaughter, R., 293
Small, A. W., 60-61
Smith, A. D., 46
Smith, D. E., 22, 146, 188, 241, 309, 310, 318, 321
Smith, J. K., 221
Smith, K., 224
Smith, M. G., 49
Smith, M. P., 62
Smith, V., 132
Solzhenitsyn, A., 73

Sorokin, P., 75
Spencer, G., 163
Spindler, G., 9, 17, 124
Spindler, L., 9, 17, 124
Spivak, G. C., 137, 141, 142, 305, 386
Spradley, J., 168
Sprague, J., 342
Spretnak, C., 77
Stacey, J., 189, 242, 290, 316, 320, 321, 395, 396, 401, 412
Stacey, M., 302, 308
Stack, S., 339
Stake, R., 19
Stanfield, J. H., II, 334, 337, 338, 343
Stanley, J., 16, 125
Stanley, L., 300, 305, 309, 314
Stanworth, M., 308
Starr, F. A., 64
Statler, O., 65
Stebbins, R. A., 158, 338
Steier, F., 249
Stein, M., 66
Steinberg, S., 283
Stenhouse, L., 126
Stevens, P., 305, 315
Stewart, A. J., 161
Stoller, P., 19, 20
Stonequist, E. V., 77
Strathern, M., 76, 321
Strauss, A. L., 9, 16, 17, 42, 124, 198, 205, 315, 338
Strauss, G., 112
Strike, K., 237, 248
Sudarkasa, N., 335, 343, 344
Sullivan, M. A., 172
Sullivan, W., 224, 229, 250
Suret-Canale, J., 49, 346

Tarule, J. M., 241
Taussig, M., 266, 290, 391, 423
Taylor, C., 78, 224, 225, 227, 228
Taylor, S. J., 16
Teggart, F. J., 53
Terrell, M. C., 343
Tesch, R., 338
Thernstrom, S., 71
Thomas, C., 304
Thomas, W. I., 61, 62, 74, 350
Thompson, H., 160

Thorne, B., 320, 321
Thornton, R., 392
Thrasher, F. M., 62
Tinder, G., 63
Tischler, H., 70
Tobias, H. J., 71
Todd, A. D., 306
Todorov, T., 48, 416
Toland, J. D., 66
Tom, W., 314
Torgovnick, M., 76
Toulmin, S., 229
Treichler, P. A., 3, 5, 6, 8, 157, 313, 384, 387
Tricarico, D., 68
Trinh, T., 76
Trinkhaus, E., 47
Turner, B. S., 76
Turner, V., 77, 79
Tyler, S., 386, 388

Ui, S., 131, 141

Vanderslice, V., 131, 141
Van Maanen, J., 22, 30, 81, 156, 158, 160, 173, 385, 421
Vansina, J., 346
Vaughan, A. T., 54
Vaughan, T. R., 80
Veblen, T., 64
Verner, S. P., 56
Vidich, A. J., 12, 44, 57, 58, 61, 65, 66, 75, 77, 160, 166, 167
Vigil, J. D., 71
Virding, A., x
von Gierke, O., 67
von Glaserfeld, E., 223, 239, 240
von Wright, G., 211

Wachterhauser, B. R., 224
Wacquaat, L., 289
Walker, A., 276, 341
Walker, R., 338
Wallis, R., 160, 176
Wallraff, G., 172
Walzer, M., 71
Ward, K., 342

Ware, C., 62
Warner, L., 350
Warren, C. A. B., 316, 342, 344
Warren, R. L., 66
Watson, G., 393
Watson, S., 308
Wax, R. H., 160, 171
Webb, B., 121
Weber, A. F., 62
Weber, M., 224
Weiler, K., 273, 276
Weinstein, D., 3, 5, 6, 8, 76, 81
Weinstein, M. A., 3, 5, 6, 8, 76, 81
Weis, L., 134, 141, 147
Welch, S., 157, 273
Wells, I. B., 340, 341
Weppner, R. S., 170, 175
West, C., 17, 77, 138, 187, 189, 190, 266, 275, 305, 306, 340
Wexler, P., 261
Wharton, S. B., 58-59
White, H., 385
White, W., 341
Whitehead, T. L., 335
Whitman, M., 149
Whyte, W. F., 12, 64, 68, 126, 163, 171, 176, 417
Wildmon, D., 366
Wilkins, L. T., 168
Williams, A., 342
Williams, R., 55, 335, 369
Williams, V. J., 70
Williamson, M. H., 60
Willis, P., 266, 274
Willis, W. S., Jr., 52
Wilson, W. J., 339
Winch, P., 223
Wirth, A., 278, 281, 286
Wirth, L., 61, 62, 69
Wise, S., 300, 305, 309, 314
Wissler, C., 59
Wolcott, H. F., 16, 19, 113, 124, 221, 222
Wolf, M., 189, 319
Wolfe, T., 124
Wood, M. M., 77
Woods, F. J., 67
Woods, R. A., 58
Woodson, C. G., 190, 340
Wright, R., 341

Wu, C. C., 62
Wycoff, M. A., 164

Yablonsky, L., 160
Yates, T., 273
Young, I., 276

Zaner, R. M., 76

Zaslavsky, C., 346
Zavarzadeh, M., 272, 280
Zavella, P., 304
Zimmerman, D., 305
Zimmerman, M. K., 342
Zinn, M. B., 304
Zizek, S., 265
Znaniecki, F., 62, 74
Zola, E., 119
Zorbaugh, H. W., 62

Subject Index

Accommodation, anticipatory, 288
*Action and Knowledge: Breaking the
Monopoly With Participatory Action
Research* (Fals-Borda & Rahman),
126
Action research, 161, 169-170
Active audience, 372-373
Activism, 211
Adequacy, 315-316
Adoption, 239
Advocacy, 211, 400
Africa as a complex geographic place, 352
African American(s):
experiences of, 348
gender socialization process, 345
scholarship, Afrocentric, 190, 335, 337,
339-340, 345-348, 351
studies, 7
women, 142-146
See also Audiencing; Cultural studies;
Racial/ethnic issues
Age:
fieldwork, 165-166
social differences, 361-365
Algeria, 398
Amerasian peoples, 71
American Family Association, 366
American Indians, 54-57, 70-71
American Sociologist, 168

American tradition of qualitative research,
7
American *vs.* German ideas, 122-125
Analytic induction, 73-77
Ancient Society (Morgan), 49
Anglo-Saxon social Darwinism, 122
Anthropology:
decolonization movements, 53
Eurocentric bias, 78
feminist studies, 320-321
flaws, inherent, 72
full circle, coming, 52
interpretive, 229-232
philosophical, 224-225
poststructuralists and postmodernists,
385-390
reflexivity, 395
sociology, understanding, 42, 124
See also Sociology/anthropology and
qualitative methods
Anthropology as Cultural Critique (Marcus
& Fischer), 19, 386
Anthropology of Experience, The (Turner &
Bruner), 19
Anticipatory accommodation, 288
Anticolonial assault on Western
ethnocentrism, 52
Antiessentialist thought, 236
Anti-status quo fashions, data
collected/interpreted in, 340

Antiverisimilitude, 416

Apperception, act of rendering, 245

Apprenticeship model of graduate education, 158

Argonauts of the Western Pacific (Malinowski), 148

Art of the Novel, The (Kundera), 45

Assimilation, 67-72

"Assimilation and Pluralism" (Abrahamson), 71

Audiencing:
  commodified needs, 374-375
  critical theory, 377-378
  definition of the audience, 369
  discourse analysis, 370-371
  disempowered empty receptacle, audience as a, 373
  distorting the object of analysis, 369-370
  glimpses of culture, relationships between, 371
  ideology theory, 375-376
  Married . . . With Children, 362-363
  network dominance, crack in, 360-361
  positivist and postpositivist paradigms, 371-374
  social identities/relations produced through lived experiences, 363-365
  social relations across social inequality, 372-373
  structure, 371-372
  three ways of understanding, 368
  values, inculcation of, 365-367

Australia, 337, 344

Authenticity criteria, 213

Authority, Education and Emancipation (Stenhouse), 126

Author's place in the text, 413

Becoming Critical: Education Knowledge and Action (Carr & Kemmis), 126

Being-in-the-world, 227-228

Belief systems and paradigms, 200-204

Betrayal and trust, 177-178

Bias, concern with, 314-315

Bible, the, 46, 55

Biomedical research, 167

"Black Community, Its Lawbreakers and a Politics of Identification" (Austin), 144

Blacks, resistance to the incorporation of, 63-64
  See also Cultural studies; Racial/ethnic issues

Blumer-Mead version of symbolic interactionism, 233, 234, 247

Blurred disciplinary genres, 2, 18-19, 263

Bourdieu's sociology, 396-398

Boys in White: Student Culture in Medical School (Becker, Geer, Hughes, & Strauss), 16, 17, 124

Brazil, 337

Bricoleur, researcher as, 3-5, 191-192, 424, 425-426

Bureau of Indian Affairs (BIA), 55-56

Calvinist-Puritan imagery, 12, 53

Cambridge-Somerville Youth Study, 176

Canada, 337

"Can There Be a Feminist Ethnography?" (Stacey), 401

Capitalism, 375-377

Cartesian/Newtonian paradigm, 124

Case method, 74

Catalytic validity, 289

Census taking, 122

Central Intelligence Agency (CIA), 167

Centre for Contemporary Cultural Studies (CCCS), 274

Certainty, practical, 74

Change, social, 148-153, 360-361

Cherokee Nation vs. Georgia in 1831, 55

Chicago Irregulars, 17

Chinese Americans, 67, 69

Christianity, 47

Chronicle of Higher Education, 421

Church survey methods, 58-59

Cities, 61-62, 65

Civic other, ethnography of the, 57-67

Class domination, 376

Coca-Cola, 366

Code of ethics, 170-171

Cognition and constructivism, 239

Cognitive processing, 117

Cold War and Comteanism, 52-54

Collecting/analyzing empirical materials, 29

Collective homophobia, 147

Collective identity, 134

Colonial ethnography, 12, 48-50, 79, 321, 385
Color, people of, 348
  See also African American(s);
    Audiencing; Cultural studies;
    Racial/ethnic issues
Columbia Pictures Television, 366
Coming of Age in Samoa (Mead), 124
Commodified needs, 374-375, 377
Common culture discourses, 139
Common meanings, intersubjective, 225
Communication:
  -based cultures, 352-353
  democratic forms of, 126-127
  ethnography of, 123
Communism, collapse of, 54, 266
Community studies, 57-67
Comparative method, 50-51, 72
Computer-assisted methods for managing
    empirical materials, 381
Comte, Auguste, 50-54, 119
Concerned Women of America, 366
Condition of Postmodernity, The (Harvey),
    388
*Condition of the Working Class in England,
    The* (Engels), 119
Confidentiality for research subjects,
    175-176
Conflict methodology, 174
Connoisseurship and criticism,
    educational, 244-245
Consciousness-raising and feminist studies,
    161-162, 303
Consensus, homogenization of, 360-361
Consent, concept of, 168, 170-171
Constructivism, 27, 186-187, 235
  antiessentialist thought, 236
  beliefs, basic, 203
  criticisms, 245-249
  cross-paradigm analyses, 208-209
  educational connoisseurship and
    criticism, 244-245
  ethics in inquiry, place of, 215
  everyday constructivist thinking, 237
  feminist standpoint epistemologies,
    241-242
  future directions, 249-250
  Goodman, Nelson, 238-239
  goodness or quality of an inquiry,
    213-214

Guba and Lincoln, 242-244
  hegemony of one paradigm over
    another, 217-218
  intraparadigm analyses, 206-207
  knowledge, accumulation of, 213
  knowledge, what is the nature of, 212
  novice inquirers, training, 216
  paradigms, conflicts between, 216-217
  purpose of inquiry, 211
  radical, 239-240
  social, 240-241
  values in inquiry, role of, 214
  voice, inquirer's, 215
  See also Interpretivist approaches
Context stripping, 197
Contradictions of world of appearances,
    265
Contradictions/tensions defining
    qualitative research, 140, 379-380,
    407-408
Cooking, act of women's, 302
Cornell University, 166
Corporate control over information,
    58-59, 278-279
Cours de Philosophie Positiviste (Comte),
    119
Covering law model of explanation, 225
Covert insider/outsider, 174
Credibility, 315-316
Criteria, problem of, 246-247
Critical multiplism, 205
Critical purchase, lack of a, 247-248
Critical theory, 187-188
  audiencing, 377-378
  beliefs, basic, 202-203
  cross-paradigm analyses, 208
  disagreements between proponents of,
    263
  empirical, a step beyond the, 273-277
  empowerment of individuals, 264
  ethics in inquiry, place of, 215
  experiences, interpreting, 282-283
  goodness or quality of an inquiry, 213
  hegemony of one paradigm over
    another, 217-218
  intraparadigm analyses, 205-206
  knowledge, accumulation of, 212-213
  knowledge, what is the nature of, 212
  Marxism, 266-268
  novice inquirers, training, 216

paradigms, conflicts between, 216
poststructuralists and postmodernists,
    268-273, 286-293
power relations, misrecognizing,
    265-266
purpose of inquiry, 211
roots of, 260-262
self-conscious criticism, 265
traditions drawing inspiration from, 262
values in inquiry, role of, 214
vocality, crisis of, 418
voice, inquirer's, 215
workers as critical researchers, 277-286
Critique of Pure Reason (Kant), 117
Cross-paradigm analyses, 207-209
Cultural inventory, 59-60
Cultural objects,
    production/distribution/exchange of,
    312-313
Cultural sciences, 223
Cultural studies, 27-28, 188-191, 235
    contested and trendy term, 359
    knowledge production critiques, 348
    liberal pluralist positivism, 372-373
    political economy, 375
    reflexivity, 395
    routinized functional view of American
        society, 349-350
    totalizing tendency, 376
    vocality, crisis of, 419-420
    women, 312-313
    See also Audiencing; Interpretive
        perspectives; Racial/ethnic issues
Cultural Studies (Grossberg, Nelson, &
    Treichler), 387
Culture Against Man (Henry), 124
*Curriculum as Social Psychoanalysis:
    Essays on the Significance of Place*
    (Kincheloe & Pinar), 276

Darwinists, social, 122
Data banks and anthropology, 52-53
Data collection and rereadings of
    representations, 292
*Debating Muslims: Cultural Dialogues in
    Postmodernity and Tradition* (Fischer
    & Abedi), 391
Deceit, mutual, 178

Deception/disguise and ethics, 167-168,
    171-175
Decolonization movements, 53
Deconstructionism, 77, 78, 318-320, 417
Decontextualization, 149
Deductive model of the scientific endeavor,
    75
Definitional issues:
    bricoleur, researcher as, 3-5
    historical moments, five, 2-3
    multiple methodologies/research
        practices, 5-7
    qualitative *vs.* quantitative research, 8-11
    resistances to qualitative studies, 7-8
Democratic forms of communication,
    126-127
Denver Post, 366
Descriptive data, 118, 247-248
Detroit News, 366
Deviants, studying, 173-174
Dialecticians, 118, 206, 207
Diasporic view of tradition:
    America or Germany, 122-125
    explanation or understanding, 118-121
    observer-observed dyad, 125-127
    quantity or quality, 116-118
Dichotomous thinking, 250
Differences, production and organization
    of, 236
Disability, works of nondisabled
    researchers on, 147
Disciplinary public culture, 338
Discourse analysis, 348-349, 370-371
Discourse on Method (Descartes), 116
Discovery dimension in inquiry, 198
Discovery of Grounded Theory, The
    (Glaser & Strauss), 17
Disguise/deception and ethics, 167-168,
    171-175
Disinterested scientist, 215
Distorting the object of analysis, 369-370
Domestic service, 302-303
Dominant Other, 146-148
Double crisis of representation and
    legitimation, 21-22
Doubled splitting, 148
Dualist/objectivist acts and intraparadigm
    analyses, 204, 205

Ecological psychology, 123

Economy, information/service-based, 277

Education, broad view of, 124

Educational connoisseurship and criticism, 244-245

Electronic communication systems, 269-270, 424

Emancipatory actions, 73, 265, 276-277

Emic/etic dilemma, 186, 198, 221

Emotions and feminist studies, 161

Empirical analyses contrasted with critical theory, 273-277

Empiricist feminisms, 188, 311

Empowerment of individuals, 264, 284

Enlightenment, the, 115

Enlightenment dualism, 419

Environmental consciousness movement, 352

Epistemology, 185, 201, 248-249, 414-415
    See also Paradigms in qualitative research

Erlebnis, concept of, 120-121, 124

Essay as an art form, 19

Ethics:
    code of ethics, 170-171
    conclusions, 179-180
    deception/disguise, 167-168, 171-175
    feminist studies, 316-317
    generality of codes, 168
    inquiry and role of, 214-215
    neutrality myth, 166-167
    positioning, 401
    privacy/identification/confidentiality, 175-176
    situational and transsituational, 24
    three developments affecting, 169-170
    trust and betrayal, 177-178

Ethnicity and ethnic models of inquiry, 189-191, 333, 342
    See also Audiencing; Cultural studies; Racial/ethnic issues

Ethnocentrism, 336

Ethnography, 12, 46-48, 124, 386-387, 391
    See also Poststructuralists and postmodernists; *various subject headings*

Ethnography Unbound (Burawoy), 149

Etic/emic dilemma, 186, 198, 221

Etymological perspective, 116

Eurocentric perspectives, 12, 77, 78, 275-276, 336-339, 350
    See also Audiencing; Cultural studies; Racial/ethnic issues

Europeans and origins of multiplicity of races, 47

Evolutionary view of tradition, 113-114

Experience(s):
    critical theory and interpreting, 282-283
    feminist studies, 319-320
    -near/distance concepts, 232
    social identities/relations produced through lived, 363-365

"Experimental and Quasi-Experimental Designs for Research on Teaching" (Campbell & Stanley), 125

Experimental ethnography, 204-205, 399

Explanations, interpretation of meaning and casual, 224

Extended case method, 80, 188

External validity, 186, 287, 288

Extraparadigm critiques, 198-200

Facts and theories/values, interdependence of, 199, 224

Falsification, theory, 199

Family, parody on the, 359-368

Family values, 367

Femininity/masculinity and Afro-American socialization process, 345

Feminist studies, 27, 28, 300
    Centre for Contemporary Cultural Studies, 274
    class domination and sexuality, 376
    complexities, emergent, 301-305
    critical purchase, lack of a, 247
    critical theory, 275-276
    criticisms of, 305
    criticisms of qualitative research, 314-318, 341-344
    deconstructionism and postmodernism, 318-320
    disciplines affected by, 320-322
    empiricist feminisms, 188
    future questions for, 322
    insiderness, epistemology of, 160-161
    models, 309-314
    Other, the, 143-146

poststructuralists and postmodernists, 188-189, 242
publishing field experiences, 178
racial/ethnic issues, 342-344
reflexivity, 395, 400-403
representation, crisis of, 412
scope of qualitative, 306-309
situation-at-hand inquiry, 282
standpoint epistemology, 169, 188, 241-242
symbolic interactionism, 235
vocality, crisis of, 418-419
workers as critical researchers, 281
See also Interpretive perspectives
Fieldwork:
advocacy, 400
age of researcher, 165-166
future, speculations on the, 421-422
gatekeepers, 163
gender and race, 165
geographic proximity, 162
institutional background, researchers, 163
messiness of, 385, 390-393
nature of the research object, 163
personality of the researcher, 162
politics of, 159-162
pros and cons, 156-159
publishing, 166
status of field-workers, 164
team research, 164
Fifth moment, the, 22
correcting excesses and revising the past, 410-411
defining and coping with the present, 408-410
future, speculations on the, 420-427
legitimation, crisis of, 413-416
representation, crisis of, 411-413
tensions defining qualitative research, 407-408
verisimilitude, 416-417
vocality, crisis of, 417-420
Fivefold division of qualitative research traditions, 112-113
Five moments of qualitative research:
blurred genres, moment of, 18-19
fifth moment, 22
modernist phase, 16-18
representation, crisis of, 19-22

traditional period, 13-16
Formulaic precision, 196
Fourth Epoch, 80
Fox television networks, 361, 364, 365, 371
See also Audiencing
Framing Dropouts (Fine), 148
Frankfurt school, 241-242, 260-261, 348, 349
Freedom, human, 120-121
French poststructuralists, 384
French tradition of qualitative research, 7
Future, speculations on the, 427
bricoleurs, 425-426
constructivism, 249-250
feminist studies, 322
fieldwork, 421-422
multiple histories, 381
Other's voice, the, 420-421
religion, 422-424
science and morality, dividing line between, 382
social text, the, 380-381
technologies, mediating, 424
tensions and contradictions, 379-380
uncertainty, 425

Gatekeepers, 163
Gay men, 7, 134
Gender:
fieldwork, 165
health issues, 306
interpretations of the world, 342-343
socialization process, Afro-American, 345
See also Women
Generalizations, 198, 212-213, 288
Genre dispersion, 2, 18-19, 263
Geographic proximity and fieldwork, 162
Germany, 7, 122-125
Get out and do it perspective, 157, 180
Ghettos, 61-62
God trick, 138
Golden age, 2, 16-18
Goodness or quality of an inquiry, 213
Great Ascent, The (Heilbroner), 53
Great Britain, 7, 337, 344

Greeks, ancient, 46
Grounded theory approach to qualitative research, 9
Group feeling, 337

Handbook of Qualitative Research, vii-ix
Harvard Encyclopedia of American Ethnic Groups, 71
Health, gender differences and the construction of, 306
Hegel's ahistorical state of absolute knowledge, 271
Hegemony, sociocultural and political, 337-339, 350, 376-377
Hegemony of one paradigm over another, 217-218
Hermeneutical methods/interpretations, 207, 227-228, 242
Higher Learning in America: A Memorandum on the Conduct of Universities by Businessmen (Veblen), 64
Hightown Grammar (Lacey), 274
Hispanic Americans, 333
Historicality, 224
History of qualitative research, 11-13
    conclusions, 22
    correcting excesses and revising the past, 410-411
    definitional issues, 2-3
    fifth moment, the, 407
    interpretivist approaches, 223
    realism, 205
    traditions, 113-114
    values, worldwide disintegration of, 45
Holism, loss of a credible, 392
Holistic ethnography, 123
Home as a site for constituting Self, 134
Homogenization of consensus, 360-361
Homosexuality, 7, 134, 147, 167-168
Human constructions, paradigms as, 201-202
Humanism, 112
Human rights problems and researching people of color, 335
Hyperreality, 269-270

Ideal-typical ethnographers-in-spite-of-themselves, 77
Identity and privacy of research subjects, 175-176
Ideological reflexivity, 393-394
Ideology theory, 375-376
Immigrants and Protestantism, 57-58
Imperial translation, 136-137, 151-152
Indians, American, 54-57, 70-71
Indigenous and aboriginal cultures:
    colonial ethnography, 12, 48-50, 79, 321, 385
    cultural studies, 7-8
    Letoyant Creoles of Louisiana, 67
    Native Americans, 54-57, 70-71
    qualitative methods, creating, 346-354
    Yahi tribe, 56
Individual's point of view, capturing the, 10
Industrial civilization, 65
Infiltration as key to fieldwork, 158
Information-based economy, 277
Information technologies, new, 361
Informed consent, 168, 170-171
Inquiry, 200-201
    discovery dimension in, 198
    ethics, 214-215
    goodness or quality of an, 213-214
    inquirer-inquired into dyad, 200
    interpretive paradigms, 28-29
    social/dialogic nature of, 242
    See also various subject headings
Inscribing the Other, 135-140, 150
Insider view of studied individuals, 160-161, 198, 335
Institute of Social Research, 261-262
Institutional background, researchers, 163
Institutional memory, 283
Instrumentation, 9
Interactionism, 242
    inquirer-inquired into dyad, 200
    interpretive, 229, 234-235
    symbolic, 229, 232-235, 307
Internal validity, 186, 287, 288
Interpretation of Cultures, The (Geertz), 18
Interpretivist approaches, 26-29, 188-191
    anthropology, 230-232
    art of interpretation, 29-30
    criticisms, 245-249
    future directions, 249-250

goal of, 221-222
hermeneutical interpretation of
  Verstehen, 227-228
interactionism, 229, 234-235
method redefined, 228-229
overview, 223-224
phenomenological interpretation of
  Verstehen, 225-227
philosophical anthropology, 224-225
symbolic interactionism, 232-234
See also Constructivism; Critical theory;
  Cultural studies; Feminist studies
Intersectionality, 142-143
Intraparadigm critiques, 197-198, 204-207
Irrealism, 238
Italian Americans, 64

Japanese Americans, 69
Journal of Contemporary Ethnography, 19,
  417

Kimberly-Clark, 366
Knowledge:
  accumulation of, 212-213
  constructivism, 239-240
  corporate control over information,
    278-279
  critical theory, 288
  Hegel's ahistorical state of absolute, 271
  nature of, what is the, 212
  outsider/insider controversy, 335
  psychological claims to epistemological
    conclusions, 248-249
  schools, 262, 275
  substance/form/application of, 112
  worker, legitimation of, 284
Knowledge and Human Interests
  (Habermas), 123, 126
Knowledge and Social Imagery (Bloor), 125
Knowledge production critiques, 347, 348
Knuckle Sandwich: Growing Up in the
  Working Class City (Cohen), 274

Labor, aesthetic appreciation for
  process/product of one's, 285-286
Labor policy, low-skill, 277
Language, the structure of, 372

Language of democracy, 280-281
Latino studies, 7
Learning Lessons (Mehan), 124
Learning to Labour: How Working Class
  Kids Get Working Class Jobs (Willis),
  274, 396
Left and critical theory, the new, 261
Legitimation, crisis of, 21-22, 409, 413-416
Lesbians, 7, 134
Letoyant Creoles of Louisiana, 67
Liberal pluralist positivism, 372-373
Liberation movements, 348
Life in Classrooms (Jackson), 124
Life world, 226
Linguistics, 52-53, 224
Lives in Trust: The Fortunes of Dynastic
  Families in Late Twentieth Century
  America (Marcus & Hall), 391
Local contexts, disjunction of grand
  theories with, 186, 198, 221
Local Knowledge (Geertz), 18
"Locating Ethnographic Practice:
  Romance, Reality, and Politics in the
  Outback" (Myers), 400
Logic of Practice, The (Bourdieu), 396
Lone ethnographer, myth of the, 14-15
Los Angeles Times, 366
LSD (lysergic acid diethylamide), 167
Ludic postmodernism, 271-272

"Make Me Reflexive-But Not Yet:
  Strategies for Managing Essential
  Reflexivity in Ethnographic
  Discourse" (Watson), 393-394
Male-oriented/influenced frameworks,
  303-304, 319, 342, 344
Management styles, top-down
  authoritarian, 277
Manhattan Project, 167
Man in the Principal's Office (Wolcott), 124
Manipulative/experimental acts and
  intraparadigm analyses, 204-205
Marketplace of ideas, 113
Market segmentation, 360
Married . . . With Children (t.v. show),
  359-368
Marxism, 7
  bias, concern with, 315

counter perspective to anthropological
  orientation, 60
extended case study, 188
feminist studies, 312
socialist decline, reclaiming Marxism in
  age of, 266-268
tenets and narration type, 27
Masculinity, black and white, 344, 345
McDonald's, 366, 370
Meaning(s):
  casual explanations, interpretation of,
    224
  purpose, exclusion of, 197-198
  social circulation of, 367
Media studies, 374
Medical research and ethics, 167
Memory, social and institutional, 283
Mental sciences, 223
Men Who Manage (Dalton), 172
Meso analysis, 307
Mesostructure, 307
Messiness of fieldwork, 385, 390-393, 401
Metanarratives, 77
Metaphysics of presence, 264
Methodology, 185, 201, 224, 228-229
  See also Paradigms in qualitative
    research; Sociology/anthropology
    and qualitative methods
Metonymic freezing, 291
Mexican Americans, 71
Middle-class revolution, 66
Middle ground of methodology, 224
*Middletown in Transition: A Study in
  Cultural Conflicts* (Lynd & Lynd),
  59-60
Middletown (Lynd & Lynd), 59
Misdemeanors while in the field,
  professional, 171
Misrecognizing power relations, 265-266
Modernist or golden age, 2, 16-18
Moral obligations. *See* Ethics
Multiple methodologies/research practices,
  5-7
Multiplism, critical, 205
Multiracial/multiethnic nation-states, 337,
  344, 349

Narrative forms, contradictions littering,
  140

Narratives, master, 136
Nation-centered discourses on common
  culture, 139
Native Americans, 54-57, 70-71
Natural areas, 61
Naturalistic methodologies, 27-28
Natural sciences, 223
Negative dialectics, 264
Neoformalism, 76
Neo-Kantianism, 120-122
Neopositivists, 226
Netherlands, 337
Networks, television, 360-361
Neutrality myth, 166-167
New Guinea, 13-14
News, television, 279, 283
New Yorker magazine, 412
New York Times, 366
Nielsen Group, 360
Nomothetic/idiographic disjunction, 198
Nonfoundationalists, 246
Novice inquirers, training, 216
Novum Organum (Bacon), 112
Nuclear family, 269
Nuremberg trials, 166-167

Objectivist/dualist acts and intraparadigm
  analyses, 204, 205
Objectivity, 186, 224, 419
Observation(s):
  communicating the analysis of, 42-43
  observer-observed dyad, 125-127
  pros and cons of fieldwork, 156-159
  socially situated, 24
Ontology, 185, 201, 224, 228-229
  See also Paradigms in qualitative
    research; Reality
Open-endedness and messy texts, 392
Operationism, 225
Oppositional postmodernism, 272
Organizational configurations, 338
*Origins of the Family, Private Property and
  the State, The* (Engels), 49
Other, the, 130
  civic other, ethnography of the, 57-67
  collecting/analyzing empirical materials,
    29
  colonial mentalities and persistence of,
    48-50

Dominant Others, 146-148
feminist studies, 304
future, speculations on, 420-421
inscribing, 135-140
interpretation, the art of, 29-30
against othering, writing, 140-141
as research subject, 23-30
selves-others; co-constructions at the
    hyphen, 131-135
social research for social change,
    148-153
strategies of inquiry, 28-29
truth, 412
uppity voices and writing against,
    141-146
Other Tribes, Other Scribes (Boon), 290
Outsider view of studied individuals, 335
Overt insider, 174
Oxford English Dictionary, 115

Paradigms in qualitative research, 195
beliefs of received/alternative inquiry,
    202-204
Cartesian/Newtonian, 124
conclusions, 191-192, 218
constructivism, 27, 186-188, 242-244
cross-paradigm analyses, 207-209
defining, 185
indigenous qualitative methods,
    creating, 346-354
interpretive perspectives, 26-28,
    188-191
intraparadigm analyses, 204-207
nature of, 200-202
positivist and postpositivist paradigms,
    186
quantitative/qualitative distinction,
    196-197
received view, critiques of the, 197-200
sciences operating with, 114
selected issues, 209-217
strategies of inquiry and interpretive,
    28-29
See also individual paradigms
Participatory Action Research (Whyte), 126
Participatory research, 317-318, 335-336
Passionate participant, 215
Patriarchal nature of academic life, 161
Patriarchy, 274, 344, 376, 377

Perception, human, 117
Personality of the researcher, 162
Personal reflexivity, 398
Phenomenological interpretation of
    Verstehen, 225-227
Philosophical anthropology, 224-225
Piagetian notion of cognitive processing,
    288
Plan for the Study of Tepoztlan, Mexico
    (Redfield), 65
Plant closings, 281-282
Pluralism, 71-72
Poetry, 319
Policymaking and women, 308-309
Politics, 7-8
culturally diversified research, political
    problematics of, 336-337
fieldwork, 159-162
of location, 132-133, 398-400
political economy, 374-375
unconscious, political, 265
women and policymaking, 308-309
Positioning, 401-402
Positivist and postpositivist paradigms, 7,
    8-9
audiencing, 371-374
beliefs, basic, 202-203
cross-paradigm analyses, 207-208
epistemology/ontology/methodology,
    186
ethics in inquiry, place of, 214
goodness or quality of an inquiry, 213
hegemony of one paradigm over
    another, 217
intraparadigm analyses, 204-205
knowledge, accumulation of, 212
knowledge, what is the nature of, 212
media studies, 374
novice inquirers, training, 216
paradigms, conflicts between, 216
psychological brand, 373
purpose of inquiry, 211
structure, 372
values in inquiry, role of, 214
voice, inquirer's, 215
Possibility, discourse of, 262
"Postmodernism in a Nominalist Frame:
    The Emergence and Diffusion of a
    Cultural Category" (Rajchman), 388
Postmodern/present moments, 2, 9-10

See also Poststructuralists and
  postmodernists
Poststructuralists and postmodernists:
  anthropology, 385-390
  avoiding references to, scholars,
    383-384
  conclusions, 403-404
  critical theory, 268-273, 286-293
  cultural studies, 188-191
  feminist studies, 242, 305, 318-320
  messy texts, 390-393
  reflexivity, 393-403
  representation, crisis of, 414, 415
  socially situated observations, 24
  sociology/anthropology and qualitative
    methods, 72-81
  women, 311-314
Posturing, 113
"Posturing in Qualitative Inquiry"
  (Wolcott), 113
Power relations, misrecognizing, 265-266
Practical certainty, 74
Practical knowledge/reason, 117
Pragmatism, 234, 293
Predicament of Culture, The (Clifford), 19,
  386
Prediction and control of phenomena, 211
Preferences, 113
  See also Diasporic view of tradition
Present, defining and coping with the,
  408-410
  See also Fifth moment, the
*Primate Visions: Gender, Race, and Nature
  in the World of Modern Science*
  (Haraway), 391
Primitive *vs.* underdeveloped, 52
Prince, The (Machiavelli), 111
Privacy and identity of research subjects,
  175-176
"Problems of Inference and Proof in
  Participant Observation" (Becker), 16
Process, qualitative research as, 23, 25
Procter & Gamble, 366
Program evaluation, 30
Progressivism, 122-123
Protestantism, immigrants and, 57-58
Psychoanalytic views, 312
Psychology, 248-249, 320, 373
Publishing fieldwork, 166, 178
Purpose and meaning, 197-198, 211

Qualitative research:
  definitional issues, 2-11
  history of, 11-13
  Other as research subject, 23-30
  phases of, five, 13-22
  as process, 23, 25
  quantitative *vs.*, 8-11, 116-118, 125,
    196-197
  revolution in, vii
  See also Fifth moment, the; *various
    subject headings*
*Qualitative Sociology, Symbolic
  Interaction,* 19
Quantitative *vs.* qualitative research, 8-11,
  116-118, 125, 196-197

Racial/ethnic issues:
  African American women, 142-146
  anti-status quo fashions, data
    collected/interpreted in, 340
  assaults on Others, 134
  assimilation, 67-72
  blacks, resistance to the incorporation
    of, 63-64
  community studies, 57-67
  conventional considerations, 334-336,
    340-342
  critical theory, 275
  cultural studies, 27, 189-191
  femininity/masculinity and
    Afro-American socialization process,
    345
  feminist studies, 342-344
  fieldwork, 165
  hegemony, sociocultural and political,
    337-339
  indigenous qualitative methods, 346-354
  intellectuals outside the social sciences,
    345-346
  masculinity, black and white, 344
  political problematics of culturally
    diversified research strategies,
    336-337
  races, origins of multiplicity of, 47-48
  racialized ethnic differences and
    black/white women, 344-345
  racism, 133, 136
  scholarship, 150-151, 190, 335, 337,
    339-340, 345-348, 351

white feminists' formulations of
women's place in the world, 304
white privilege, 342-343
white-working class adolescent males,
147
Radical constructivism, 239-240
Radical critique-al theory, 272
Rationality, Kant's model of human, 117
Readings, dramatic, 319
Readings, suggested, 431-436
Reality:
Afro-American experiences, 348
competing realities, 44-45
historical realism, 205
hyperreality, 269-270
irrealism, 238
male-oriented/influenced frameworks,
319
positivism, 204
postpositivism, 205
social constructivism, 241
subtle realism, 246
voluntaristic presumptions of social
constructions of, 344
Reason, scientific and practical, 117
Received view of science, 196-200
Reflections on Fieldwork in Morocco
(Rabinow), 290
Reflective Practitioner, The (Schön), 126
Reflexivity:
baseline form of, 395-396
Bourdieu's sociology, 396-398
critical theory, 289-290
elaboration of the event, 242
feminist studies, 400-403
ideological strategies of, 393-394
representation, diverse field of, 398-400
textuality, 189
Reganism, 361
Relativist ideas and constructivism,
206-207
Reliability, 186
Religion:
church survey methods, 58-59
communism, collapse of, 54
early ethnography, 46
future, speculations on the, 422-424
Native Americans, 55
people of color and Western views on,
352, 353

Protestantism, immigrants and, 57-58
races, origins of multiplicity of, 47
University of Chicago, 60-61
values, worldwide disintegration of, 45
Western Christian values, 48
Renaissance, the, 111-112
Representation:
crisis of, 2, 19-22, 398-400, 409,
411-413
data collection and rereadings of, 292
representational essentializing, 291
thematization of, 76
Reproductive health, women's, 307
Researchers:
age of, 165-166
author's place in the text, 413
as bricoleur, 3-5, 191-192
dangerous situations faced by, 160
diminished capacity of, 141-142
disabled individuals, work on, 147
ideal-typical
ethnographers-in-spite-of-themselves,
77
institutional background, 163
misdemeanors while in the field,
professional, 171
oppositional and insurgent, 293
Other as research object, 24
personality characteristics, 162
voice, inquirer's, 215
workers as critical, 277-286
Research styles, 8-11
Resistances to qualitative studies, 7-8,
272-273, 291
Rich, studying the, 136-137
Rich descriptions, securing, 11
Romanticizing of narratives, 17, 152

Sapphire Bound! (Austin), 143
Schooling as a Ritual Performance
(McLaren), 275
Schooling the Smash Street Kids (Corrigan),
274
Schooling through anthropology, 124
Schools, 262, 275
Science, 114
cultural/mental/natural, 223
feminist studies, 313
Geistewissenschaft, 120

inspiration of the democratization of, 285

modernist idea of separation of religion and, 422-423

morality and, dividing line between, 382

Naturwissenschaft, 120

reason, scientific, 117

received view of, 196-200

Segregated Sisterhood (Caraway), 152

Self-conscious criticism, 265

Self-Other hyphen, 131-135

See also Other, the

Self-reflection, 279-280

Sensitizing image of the interaction process, 234

Service-based economy, 277

Sexuality, 376

Shadow and Act (Ellison), 341

Shamanism, Colonialism, and the Wild Man: A Study of Terror and Healing (Taussig), 290, 391

Simpsons, The (t.v. show), 361, 362

"Situated Knowledges: The Science Question in Feminism and the Privilege of Partial Perspective" (Haraway), 402

Situational ethics, 24

Situation-at-hand inquiry, 282

Small towns, 63, 65-66

Smithsonian Institution, 55-56

Social categories and audiencing, 365

Social change and technology, 360-361

Social Construction of Reality, The (Berger & Luckmann), 123

Social constructivism, 240-241

Social Darwinism, 122

Social/dialogic nature of inquiry, 242

Social identities/relations produced through lived experiences, 363-365

Socialist decline, reclaiming Marxism in age of, 266-268

Social memory, 283

Social Problems, 168

Social relations across social inequality, 372-373

Social research for social change, 148-153

Social Text, 402

Sociology/anthropology and qualitative methods:

Afrocentric scholarship, 348

anthropology cross-fertilized with sociology, 124

assimilation, 67-72

Cold War and Comteanism, 52-54

colonial mentalities and persistence of the Other, 48-50

comparative method, Comte and the, 50-51

feminist studies, 321-322

Native Americans, 54-57

Other, discovery of the, 46-48

positivist and postpositivist paradigms, 320

postmodern challenge, 72-81

realities, competing, 44-45

reflexivity, 394-398

sociologist's abilities, 41-42

South Africa, 337, 344

Soviet Union, deconstruction of the former, 54

Space/time compression, 392

Spirituality, 352-353, 422-424

Split affinities, 132

Splitting, doubled, 148

"Springdale" (Vidich & Bensman), 65-66, 166

Stages of Economic Growth, The (Rostow), 53

Stages of Political Development, The (Organski), 53

Standards, breaches of professional, 171

Standpoint epistemology, 169, 188, 189, 241-242, 309-311

Statistical inquiry, 118

Stereotypes of people of color, 348

Street Corner Society (Whyte), 64, 163, 176, 417

Structuralist method, 79

Structure, 371-372

Structure of Scientific Revolutions, The (Kuhn), 114

Studies in Symbolic Interaction, 19

Subculture: The Meaning of Style (Hebdige), 274

Subjectivity, 27-28, 206-207, 224, 306, 375-376

Subordinate-dominant relations, 146

Subtle realism, 246

Survey methods, church and corporate sponsored, 58-59

Symbolic interactionism, 229, 232-235, 307
System of Logic, A (Mill), 119

Tambrands, 366
Team research, 164
Technical rationality, undermining of, 285
Technologies of Othering, 147
Technology, 360-361, 424
Teenagers, 361-362
Television watching, 279, 283, 359
    See also Audiencing
Tensions/contradictions defining qualitative research, 140, 379-380, 407-408
Textual analysis of cultural objects, 313
Textual discourse analysis, 348-349
Textuality, reflexive, 189
Theoretical knowledge, 117
Theory:
    fact and, interdependence of, 199
    feminist studies, disciplines affected by, 320-322
    as interpretation, 189
    -neutral data language, 225
    social change, 372
    undertermination of, 199
    See also Paradigms in qualitative research; *specific theories*
Third World, 52, 304
"Third World Literature in the Era of Multinational Capital" (Jameson), 402
Time, 351-352, 392
Totality, concept of, 276
Totalizing tendency and cultural studies, 376
Toward a New Psychology of Women (Miller), 146
Towns, small, 63, 65
Traditional period, 2, 13-16
Traditions, qualitative research, 112-116
    See also Diasporic view of tradition; Paradigms in qualitative research
Tradition (Shils), 115
Transactional/subjectivist acts and intraparadigm analyses, 206, 207
Transcendental perspective, 117
Transformational inquirers, 206
Transformative intellectual, 215

Translated Woman (Behar), 319
Transnational political/economic/cultural forces, 291-292
Transsituational ethics, 24
Travels (Mandeville), 137
Trobriand Islands, 13-14
Trustworthiness, 177-178, 213, 287-288
Truth, 292, 412
Tuskegee Syphilis Study, 167
Typical Girls? (Griffin), 274

Underdeveloped *vs.* primitive, 52
United States, 122-125, 337, 344
Universality, claims to, 293
Universality of the causal generalizations, 74
University of Birmingham, 274
University of Chicago, 60-61, 64-65
University of Frankfurt, 241-242, 260-261
Unspeakable, The (Tyler), 386
Uppity voices and writing against Othering, 141-146
Urban areas, 61-62, 65
Urban Life, 19

Validity:
    catalytic, 289
    epistemological, 414-415
    internal/external, 186, 287, 288
Values:
    audiencing, 365-367
    electronic communication systems, 269-270
    facts and, interdependence of, 199, 224
    family, 367
    -free inquiry for the human disciplines, 24, 334-335
    inquiry and the role of, 214
    races and conflict of, multiplicity of, 47-48
    spatiotemporal hierarchy of, 50
    worldwide disintegration of, 44-45
Verification, theory, 199
Verisimilitude, 416-417
Verstehen,
    phenomenological/hermeneutical interpretation of, 221, 223, 225-228

Vocality, crisis of, 417-420
Voice, inquirer's, 215
Voices of participants, 318-319 ·
Voluntaristic presumptions of social
  constructions of reality, 344

Wall Street Journal, 366
Webb, Beatrice, 121
Western Christian values, 47-48
Western ethnocentrism, anticolonial assault
  on, 52
White:
  feminists' formulations of women's
    place in the world, 304
  privilege, 342-343
  whiteness, studying, 136-137
  -working class adolescent males, 147
  See also Racial/ethnic issues
Wichita Jury Study, 167
Winnebago Indians, 57
Women:
  absence/invisibility in certain contexts,
    302-303
  African American, 142-146
  of color, 344-345
  disabled, 305
  empiricism, feminist, 311
  gendered interpretations of the world,
    342-343
  health, gender differences and the
    construction of, 306
  male-oriented/influenced frameworks,
    303-304
  policymaking, 308-309

poststructuralists and postmodernists,
  311-314
racialized ethnic differences and
  black/white, 344-345
relationships and interaction, 306-307
reproductive health, 307
social
  movements/organizations/structures,
    307-308
standpoint epistemology, 309-311
voices of participants, 318-319
women's movement, 169, 360-361
in the workplace, 277-278, 306-307
  See also Feminist studies
Women and the Politics of Empowerment
  (Bookman & Morgan), 149
Women Take Issue, 274
*Women Teaching for Change: Gender,
  Class, and Power* (Weiler), 276
Workers as critical researchers, 277-286
Workplace, forced reorganization of the,
  284-285
Workplace, women in the, 277-278,
  306-307
Works and Lives (Geertz), 19
Writing Culture (Clifford & Marcus), 19,
  137, 386
Written word-based cultures, 352-353

Yahi tribe, 56

*Zen and the Art of Motorcycle
  Maintenance,* 426
Zuni culture, 57

About the Authors

Norman K. Denzin is Distinguished Professor of Communications, College of Communications scholar, and Professor of Sociology and Humanities at the University of Illinois, Urbana-Champaign. He is the author of numerous books, including *The Cinematic Society, Images of Postmodern Society, The Research Act, Interpretive Interactionism, Hollywood Shot by Shot, Symbolic Interactionism and Cultural Studies, The Recovering Alcoholic,* and *The Alcoholic Self,* which won the Cooley Award from the Society for the Study of Symbolic Interaction in 1988. He is editor of *Studies in Symbolic Interaction: A Research Annual, Cultural Studies,* and *Sociological Quarterly.* He is coeditor of the *Handbook of Qualitative Research* and of *Qualitative Inquiry.* In 1997, he won the George Herbert Mead Award from the Society for the Study of Symbolic Interaction. This award recognizes lifetime contributions to the study of human behavior.

Michelle Fine is Professor of Psychology at the City University of New York Graduate Center. Her recent books include *Becoming Gentlemen* (with Lani Guinier and Jane Balin; 1997), *Off-White: Readings on Society, Race, and Culture* (with Linda Powell, Lois Weis, and Mun Wong; 1996), *Chartering Urban School Reform: Reflections on Public High Schools in the Midst of Change* (1994), *Beyond Silenced Voices: Class, Race and Gender in American Schools* (1992), *Disruptive Voices: The Transgressive Possibilities of Feminist Research* (1992), and *Framing Dropouts: Notes on the Politics of an Urban High School* (1991). She has provided courtroom expert testimony in several cases, including *Anthony T. Lee et al. and the United States of America and the National Education Association, Inc. v. Macon County Board of Education*; *Shannon Richey Faulkner and the United States of America v. James E. Jones et al. for The Citadel, The Military College of South Carolina*; *Ulcena v. Babylon School District, High School and Babylon School Board*; and *Board of Education of the Borough of Englewood Cliffs v. Board of Education of the City of Englewood v. Board of Education of the Borough of Tenafly*. In addition, she works nationally as a consultant to parents' rights groups, community groups, and teacher unions on issues of school reform. In 1994, she received the Janet Helms Distinguished Scholar Award.

John Fiske is Professor of Communication Arts at the University of Wisconsin–Madison, before which he taught in Australia and the United Kingdom. His books on television and popular culture include *Reading Television* (with John Hartley; 1978), *Television Culture* (1987), *Understanding Popular Culture* (1989), *Reading the Popular* (1989), and *Power Plays Power Works* (1993).

Egon G. Guba is Professor Emeritus of Education, Indiana University. He received his Ph.D. from the University of Chicago in quantitative inquiry (education) in 1952, and thereafter served on the faculties of the University of Chicago, the University of Kansas City, the Ohio State University, and Indiana University. For the past 15 years, he has studied paradigms alternative to the received view and has formed a personal commitment to one of these: constructivism. He is coauthor of *Effective Evaluation* (1981), *Naturalistic Inquiry* (1985), and *Fourth Generation Evaluation* (1989), all with Yvonna S. Lincoln, and editor of *The Paradigm Dialog* (1990), which explores the implications of alternative paradigms for social inquiry.

David Hamilton is Professor of Education at Ume University, Sweden. Previously, he was the Sydney Jones Professor of Education at the University of Liverpool. Since completing postgraduate studies at the University of Edinburgh, he has held positions at the Scottish Council for Educational Research and at the Universities of East Anglia, Illinois, and Glasgow. His recent publications include *Towards a Theory of Schooling* (1989) and *Learning About Education: An Unfinished Curriculum* (1990). His long-standing interest in the conduct and rationality of educational research has often taken a historical and international slant. As head of an education department that has a strong interest in teacher education, he is also interested in teaching as a practical science and in the relationship of practical training to the current fortunes of higher education.

Joe L. Kincheloe is Professor of Education at Florida International University, Miami, Florida. He is the author of *Teachers as Researchers: Qualitative Paths to Empowerment, Toward a Critical Politics of Teacher Thinking: Mapping the Postmodern,* and *Toil and Trouble: Good Work, Smart Workers, and the Integration of Academic and Vocational Education.* He is also coauthor of *The Stigma of Genius: Einstein and Beyond Modern Education* (with Shirley Steinberg and Deborah Tippins). He has published 100 articles on social foundations of education, social theory, and education and qualitative research.

Yvonna S. Lincoln is Professor of Higher Education and in the Department of Educational Administration at Texas A&M University. She has an Ed.D. from Indiana University and previously taught at the University of Kansas and Vanderbilt University. She is a specialist in higher education research, organizational analysis, program evaluation, and alternative paradigm research. Her work has been published in such well-received books as *Fourth Generation Evaluation, Naturalistic Inquiry, Effective Evaluation* (all coauthored with Egon Guba), and *Organizational Theory and Inquiry,* as well as in a host of papers and conference presentations. She has been honored with awards for her research from the American Evaluation Association, Division J (Postsecondary and Higher Education) of the American Educational Research Association, and the Association for Institutional Research. She has served as President of the American Evaluation Association and the Association for the Study of Higher Education, and as Vice President of Division J of the American Educational Research Association, and has been keynote speaker at more than a dozen conferences.

Stanford M. Lyman is Robert J. Morrow Eminent Scholar and Professor of Social Science, Florida Atlantic University. In addition to holding posts at major universities in the United States, he has served as Fulbright Lecturer in Japan (1981); Visiting Foreign Expert at Beijing Foreign Studies University, China (1986); and U.S. Information Agency Lecturer in Singapore, Taiwan, Hong Kong, Ghana, Liberia, Nigeria, and former Yugoslavia. In 1976, he was elected to a lifetime honorary appointment as Senior Lecturer, Linacre College, Oxford. He is author or coauthor of 21 books, including *Civilization: Contents, Discontents, Malcontents, and Other Essays in Social Theory* (1990), *The Seven Deadly Sins: Society and Evil* (revised and expanded edition, 1989), *A Sociology of the Absurd* (with Marvin B. Scott; second edition, 1989), *Social Order and the Public Philosophy: An Analysis and Interpretation of the Work of Herbert Blumer* (with Arthur J. Vidich; 1988), *Color, Culture, Civilization: Race and Minority Issues in American Society* (1994), and *Postmodernism and a Sociology of the Absurd* (1997).

George E. Marcus is Chair of the Department of Anthropology at Rice University. He is coeditor, with James Clifford, of *Writing Culture: The Poetics and Politics of Ethnography* (1986) and coauthor, with Michael M. J. Fischer, of *Anthropology as Cultural Critique: An Experimental Moment in the Human Sciences* (1986). He was inaugural editor of the journal *Cultural Anthropology* and currently produces a series of annuals for the University of Chicago Press called *Late Editions: Cultural Studies for the End of the Century.*

Peter L. McLaren is formerly Renowned Scholar-in-Residence and Director of the Center for Education and Cultural Studies, Miami University of Ohio. He is currently a Professor in the Graduate School of Education, University of California, Los Angeles. He is the author of numerous publications, including *Paulo Freire: A Critical Encounter* (coedited with Peter Leonard), *Politics of Liberation* and *Critical Literacy* (both coedited with Colin Lankshear), *Between Borders* (coedited with Henry A. Giroux), *Critical Pedagogy and Predatory Culture: Oppositional Politics in a Postmodern Era* (1995), and *Revolutionary Multiculturalism: Pedagogies of Dissent for the New Millennium* (1997). He is also the author of *Life in Schools* and the recently reissued *Schooling as a Ritual Performance.*

Virginia Olesen, Professor Emerita of Sociology at the University of California, San Francisco, teaches seminars on feminisms and qualitative research and on the sociology of the body and emotions. She is coeditor, with Sheryl Ruzek and Adele Clarke, of *Women's Health: Complexities and Diversities* (1997). With Adele Clarke she is currently editing a collection of papers that bring the perspectives of feminist theory, cultural studies, and techno science studies to the task of re/visioning women's health.

Maurice Punch studied at the universities of Exeter, London, Cambridge, and Essex (M.A., 1966; Ph.D., 1972). He has taught at Essex University; University of Utrecht; State University of New York, Albany; and Nijenrode, the Netherlands Business School. Fellowships from Nuffield and Leverhulme enabled him to visit the University of Amsterdam in 1973 and 1974, and he was Visiting Professor at the SUNY, Albany, School of Criminal Justice, for fall semester 1981. In England he specialized in the sociology of education, and in the Netherlands (where he has lived since 1975) he has researched the management of the police organization (including corruption). He is now concerned with corporate crime, deviant behavior, and regulation and control in business, as well as management of change in the police organization. He has published in English, Dutch, and American journals and has written several books. His latest publication is *Dirty Business: Exploring Corporate Misconduct* (1996). In 1977 he became Professor of Sociology at Nijenrode, where he held many academic and administrative positions; in the period 1985-1989 he launched and developed that institution's international MBA program. Since 1989 he has taught regularly at the Helsinki School of Economics and Business Administration and has also contributed to programs at IESE (Barcelona), INSEAD (Fontainebleau), University of Oregon (Eugene), University of Pennsylvania, and the Free University of Amsterdam. In January 1994 he left Nijenrode to become an independent scholar and freelance consultant. Recently, he completed a study of the Dutch police and justice system and has also been involved in courses on disaster management for the emergency services. In 1997 he was made an Associate of the Centre for Police Studies, Free University, Amsterdam.

Thomas A. Schwandt is Associate Professor and Coordinator of the Inquiry Methodology Program in the School of Education at Indiana University. He is also a member of the faculties in Policy Studies and Foundations of Education and a fellow of the Poynter Center for the Study of Ethics and American Institutions. His work over the past several years has explored the relationships among social inquiry, practical philosophy, and philosophical hermeneutics.

John H. Stanfield II was the Frances and Edwin Cummings Professor of American Studies and Sociology, Scholar in Residence for the Commonwealth Center for the Study of American Culture at the College of William and Mary from 1988 to 1993. He is currently Professor of African

American and African Studies and Professor of Sociology at the University of California at Davis. His research interests and publications include studies in the sociology of knowledge, especially pertaining to race in sciences issues.

Arthur J. Vidich has conducted field research in Virogua, Wisconsin, Palau, the Western Carolines of Micronesia, Springdale, New York, Trujillo Alto, Puerto Rico, the Llanos region of Colombia, Kropa, Slovenia, and other sites in the United States, including in-depth studies of the Universities of Wisconsin, Michigan, Harvard, Cornell, and Connecticut, and the New School for Social Research. Employing an anthropological perspective and attitude, he has examined the functioning of American class and status systems and political, religious, and economic institutions. He continues his research on the American university and is writing a postscript for Thorstein Veblen's *Higher Learning in America.*

CONFIRMATION